1 MONTH OF
FREE
READING

at

www.ForgottenBooks.com

By purchasing this book you are eligible for one month membership to ForgottenBooks.com, giving you unlimited access to our entire collection of over 1,000,000 titles via our web site and mobile apps.

To claim your free month visit:

www.forgottenbooks.com/free912102

ISBN 978-0-266-93464-6
PIBN 10912102

No. 4269

United States
Circuit Court of Appeals
For the Ninth Circuit.

Transcript of Record.
(IN TWO VOLUMES.)

PAUL E. DENIVELLE,

Appellant,

vs.

acGRUER & SIMPSON, a Copartnership, and GEORGE SMITH MacGRUER and ROBERT MORTON SIMPSON, Individually, and Sometimes Doing Business as Mac-GRUER & CO.,

Appellees.

VOLUME I.
(Pages 1 to 352, Inclusive.)

Upon Appeal from the Southern Division of the United States District Court for the Northern District of California, Third Division.

INDEX TO THE PRINTED TRANSCRIPT OF RECORD.

[Clerk's Note: When deemed likely to be of an important nature, errors or doubtful matters appearing in the original certified record are printed literally in italic; and, likewise, cancelled matter appearing in the original certified record is printed and cancelled herein accordingly. When possible, an omission from the text is indicated by printing in italic the two words between which the omission seems to occur.]

Index. Page

Index. Page

Index. Page

Index.   Page

NAMES AND ADDRESSES OF ATTORNEYS OF RECORD.

CHARLES E. TOWNSEND, Esq., Crocker Building, San Francisco, California,
Attorney for Appellant.

Messrs. MUNN, ANDERSON & MUNN, 233 Broadway, New York, N. Y., and T. HART ANDERSON, Esq., Hobart Building, San Francisco, Calif.,
Attorneys for Appellees.

In the District Court of the United States for the Northern · District of California, Southern Division.

IN EQUITY—No. 1078.

PAUL E. DENIVELLE,

Plaintiff,

vs.

MacGRUER & SIMPSON (a Copartnership) and GEORGE SMITH MacGRUER and ROBERT MORTON SIMPSON, Individually and Sometimes Doing Business as Mac-GRUER & CO.,

Defendants.

BILL OF COMPLAINT.

For Infringement of United States Letters Patent
No. 1,212,331.

Now comes PAUL E. DENIVELLE, plaintiff
above named, and complains of MacGRUER &
SIMPSON, a copartnership, and GEORGE
SMITH MacGRUER and ROBERT MORTON
SIMPSON, individually and sometimes doing business as MacGRUER & CO., above-named defendants, and for cause of action alleges:

I.

That the plaintiff, Paul E. Denivelle, during all
the times hereinafter mentioned was and is a citizen of the United States and a resident of the City
and County of San Francisco, State of California.

II.

That the defendant, MacGruer & Simpson, is a
copartnership composed of George Smith Mac-
Gruer and Robert Morton Simpson as copartners,
and residing in the Northern District of California,
Southern Division, and having a place of business in
the City and County of San Francisco, State of California, and that said George Smith MacGruer and
Morton Simpson are and [1*] each of them is
and for a long time hitherto each of them has been
a resident of the City and County of San Francisco,
State of California, and doing business therein, and
sometimes doing business under the firm name and
style of MacGruer & Co. in said City and County.

*Page-number appearing at foot of page of original Certified Tran-
script of Record.

III.

That the ground upon which the Court's jurisdiction depends in this case is that it is a suit in equity arising under the Patent Laws of the United States.

IV.

That heretofore, to wit, prior to the 20th day of October, 1915, said Paul E. Denivelle was the original, first and sole inventor of a certain new and useful invention entitled "The Manufacture of Artificial Stone Structures"; and on said last-named date duly filed in the Patent Office of the United States an application for letters patent for said invention.

V.

That thereafter, to wit, on January 16th, 1917, said letters patent for said invention No. 1,212,331, were granted, issued and delivered unto the said Paul E. Denivelle, in due form of law in the name of the United States of America, under the seal of the Patent Office of the United States and signed by the Commissioner of Patents of the United States, whereby there was granted to the said Paul E. Denivelle, his heirs or assigns, the sole and exclusive right to make, use and vend the said invention throughout the United States and the Territories thereof for the period of seventeen (17) years from January 16th, 1917; and that prior to the issuance thereof all proceedings were had and [2] taken which were required by law to be had and taken prior to the issuance of letters patent for new and useful inventions; that a more particular de-

scription of the said invention patented in and by
said letters patent will more fully appear from the
said letters patent themselves, which are ready in
court to be produced by the plaintiffs and profert
is hereby made thereof.

VI.

That ever since the issuance of said letters patent
the said Paul E. Denivelle has been and still is the
sole owner and holder thereof, and of all the rights
and liberties thereby granted, save and except that
he has granted nonexclusive licenses to various
and sundry persons, to use said invention upon the
payment of a specified royalty.

VII.

That since the issuance of said letters patent
plaintiff has practiced the invention and has given
notice to the public that the same was patented, together with the date of said letters patent by affix-
ing the word "Patented," together with the day
and year in which the said letters patent were
granted, to or in connection with the fabricated
articles.

VIII.

That plaintiff, but for the infringement hereinafter complained of, would still be in the undis-
turbed possession, use and enjoyment of the exclusive rights, powers and privileges granted by
said patent; that the said plaintiff has been to
great trouble and expense in adjudicating and sustaining said patent and in introducing said patented invention to the public, and in advertising and building up a market for the said

patented invention; that the superior utility and novelty of the [3] said patented invention has become generally recognized, and through the efforts of the said plaintiff and the extensive advertising and publicity given said invention plaintiff has been able to build up a market for the said 'patented invention and has created a large demand for the same; that the said patented invention is of great benefit and advantage and the public has acquiesced in the validity of plaintiff's said patent.

IX.

Plaintiff further shows that on the 11th day of December, 1918, he, jointly with his licensee, Los Angeles Lime Company (a corporation), filed two suits in equity in the District Court of the United States for the Southern District of California, Southern Division, against C. L. Nye and against E. Ceriat, individually and doing business under the firm name and style of R. Ceriat & Co., defendants respectively, for the infringement of the said letters patent here in suit, being suits in Equity Nos. D–118 and D–119, and that said causes were consolidated for trial; that the pleadings in the said causes were in the usual form; that the said letters patent were assailed for want of invention and novelty and that the said Paul E. Denivelle was not the original and first inventor and discoverer of the subject matter of the said letters patent or of any material or substantial part thereof, and that the same or material or substantial parts thereof had been in public use and on sale in this country prior to said invention and

for more than two years prior to the application
for said letters patent, and that the same had been
described and illustrated in printed publications
prior to the date of said invention of said Paul E.
Denivelle; that after a trial before said Court   [4]
and the examination of witnesses and the introduction of documentary evidence by the respective parties and the evidence being closed and argued by the
respective parties the cause was submitted to the
Court for consideration and decision, and said
Court thereupon dismissed said bills of complaint
in both causes; whereupon upon due proceedings
had appeal was taken from said decision to the
United States Circuit Court of Appeals for the
Ninth Circuit; and said causes were argued in said
Court and briefs submitted; whereupon after due
deliberation thereon the said Circuit Court of Appeals reversed the Decree of the said District Court
and sustained said patent and adjudged the same to
be valid in all respects, holding that said patent
represented a new, useful and patentable invention
and that the same was infringed; the opinion of
said Court of Appeals by Ross, Judge, being dated
January 17th, 1921, and appearing at 270 Fed. Rep.
155.

X.

That the defendants, and each of them, well knowing the premises and the rights secured to plaintiff,
but contriving to injure plaintiff and deprive him of
the benefits and advantages which might and otherwise would accrue to him from said invention, by
virtue of said patent and the adjudication aforesaid,

did, individually and jointly and as a copartnership, after the issuing of the letters patent, as aforesaid, and before the commencement of this suit, as plaintiff is informed and believes, and without the license or allowance of plaintiff, and in violation of his rights, and in infringement of the aforesaid letters patent, within the Southern District of California and within six (6) years last past, unlawfully and wrongfully, and in defiance of the rights of plaintiff, manufacture, use and sell the said patented invention, [5] and is threatening to continue to manufacture, use and sell the aforesaid patented invention, which manufacture, use, and sale constitute an infringement of all the claims of said letters patent; and that by reason of the said infringement the defendants and each of them have realized profits and plaintiff has suffered damages, but the amounts of such profits and damages are unknown to plaintiff and can be ascertained only by an accounting.

XI.

That plaintiff has requested the defendants to cease and desist from the infringement of said letters patent and account to plaintiff for the profits and damages aforesaid, but defendants have failed and refused to comply with said request or any part thereof.

XII.

That defendants and each of them threaten to continue their said infringement indefinitely, and unless restrained therefrom by this Court will continue the same, whereby plaintiff will suffer great and irreparable damage for which he has no plain, speedy or adequate remedy at law.

WHEREFORE, plaintiff prays a decree of this Court against the defendants, and each of them, as follows:

First. That upon the filing of this bill of complaint a preliminary injunction be granted enjoining and restraining the defendants, and each of them, their agents, servants, attorneys and employees, *pendente lite*, from making, using or selling any apparatus which infringes upon said letters patent or from practicing the patented process in violation of plaintiff's rights aforesaid. [6]

Second. That upon the final hearing defendants herein, and each of them, their servants, agents, attorneys and employees be permanently and finally enjoined and restrained from making, using or selling any device, machine or apparatus which infringes upon said letters patent No. 1,212,331, or from practicing the patented process in violation of plaintiff's rights as aforesaid, and that a writ of injunction be issued out of and under the seal of this Court enjoining the said defendants, and each of them, their agents, servants, attorneys and employees as aforesaid.

Third. That plaintiff have and recover from the defendants, and each of them, the profits realized by the defendants, and each of them, and the damages sustained by the plaintiff from and by reason of the infringement aforesaid, together with costs of suit, and that the said damages be trebled by reason of the willful nature of the infringement by defendants herein, and that plaintiff have such other and further relief as to the Court may seem proper and in accordance with equity and good conscience.

PAUL E. DENIVELLE.

By CHAS. E. TOWNSEND,

His Attorney.

CHAS. E. TOWNSEND,

WM. A. LOFTUS,

Solicitors and Counsel for Plaintiff. [7]

United States of America,

Northern District of California,

City and County of San Francisco,—ss.

Paul E. Denivelle, being duly sworn, deposes and says that he is the plaintiff in the within entitled action; that he has read the foregoing bill of complaint and knows the contents thereof; that the same is true of his own knowledge, except as to the matters which are therein stated on his information or belief, and as to those matters, that he believes them to be true.

PAUL E. DENIVELLE.

Subscribed and sworn to before me this 14th day of July, 1923.

[Seal]   W. W. HEALEY,

Notary Public in and for the City and County of San Francisco, State of California.

[Endorsed]: Filed Jul. 16, 1923. [8]

[Title of Court and Cause.]

AMENDED ANSWER.

The foregoing defendants, and each of them, for answer to the bill of complaint, answering saith:

1. The defendants deny each and every averment set forth in paragraphs "IV" and "V" of the bill of complaint, excepting that they admit that some form of application for patent was made and filed by the said Paul E. Denivelle in the United States Patent Office on the date mentioned, and that letters patent of the United States were issued to the said Paul E. Denivelle on the date and bearing the number set forth in paragraph "V" of the complaint.

2. The defendants deny on information and belief, each and every averment contained in paragraph "VI" of the bill of complaint.

3. The defendants deny on information and belief, each and every averment contained in paragraph "VII" of the bill of complaint.

4. The defendants deny on information and belief, each and every averment contained in paragraph "VIII" of the bill of complaint.

5. The defendants admit the prior adjudication of patent No. 1,212,331 referred to in paragraph "IX" of the complaint, but upon information and belief assert that the defense introduced in that case was incomplete, and that material evidence affecting the validity of the aforesaid patent was not known to the defendants therein at the time said case was tried, or if known was omitted there-

from, and that notwithstanding the decision of the
Circuit Court of Appeals for the Ninth Circuit,
referred to, these defendants deny the validity of
the aforesaid letters patent for the [9] reasons
hereinafter more fully set forth, and upon new
evidence which has been discovered by these defendants and not before the Circuit Court of Appeals in the prior cause, which, when taken in connection with the evidence which was before the
Circuit Court of Appeals in the prior cause, referred to in paragraph "IX" of the complaint,
will show beyond a reasonable doubt that the said
letters patent are, and always have been, invalid
and of no force and effect.

6. Further answering, the defendants deny that
they have individually or jointly, or as a copartnership, after the issuing of said letters patent and
before the commencement of this suit, or at any
time, without the license or allowance of the plaintiff, or in violation of any of his rights, and within
the Southern District of California or elsewhere,
within six years last past or at any time, unlawfully and wrongfully manufactured or used or sold
the alleged invention patented in the aforesaid letters patent, or that they threaten to continue the
said manufacture or use or sale, or that what the
defendants have done in the manufacture of artificial stone and artificial travertine constitutes an infringement of all, or any, of the claims of said
letters patent, or that by reason thereof they, or
either of them, have realized any profits to which
plaintiff can make any lawful claim, or that thereby

the plaintiff has suffered any damage which he can lawfully attribute to any act or deed of those defendants, or either or any of them, and deny that the plaintiff is entitled to any accounting from these defendants.

7. Further answering, the defendants, in answer to paragraphs "XI" and "XII" of the complaint, admit that the plaintiff has requested them not to infringe the aforesaid [10] letters patent, and to account to plaintiff for the alleged infringement thereof, but they deny that they have ever infringed said letters patent, and accordingly refused to cease employing the process used by them, as upon the advice of counsel learned in the law, they are assured that what they have been doing in and about the manufacture of artificial travertine, in nowise constitutes an infringement of any valid claim of the said patent, and in fact that, notwithstanding the decision of the Court of Appeals referred to in paragraph "IX" of the bill of complaint, the said letters patent are invalid for reasons known to the plaintiff; and they deny that if they are permitted to continue what they are doing, the plaintiff will suffer great and irreparable, or any, damage of which he can lawfully complain.

8. Further answering, the defendants aver that said letters patent are void, invalid and of no force and effect for the reason that more than two years before the application therefor was filed, the plaintiff, Paul E. Denivelle, put into public use and on sale in the United States, the alleged new process therein shown, described and claimed, and

constructed and installed imitation travertine made in accordance with that process.

9. Further answering, the defendants aver that Paul E. Denivelle, when he swore to the application upon which the said patent was issued, he falsely ·swore that the subject matter of the said application had not been in public use and on sale in the United States for more than two years before the filing of the said application, knowing the same to be false and thereby intending to deceive, and in fact deceiving, the Commissioner of Patents, whereby said letters patent were fraudulently procured and are not only invàlid but void. [11]

10. Further answering, the defendants say that the said Paul E. Denivelle, if he was ever the first and original inventor of the alleged process and product shown, described and claimed in the aforesaid letters patent, which these defendants deny, he abandoned the same to the public before he filed the application for the said letters patent, by making an extensive public use thereof in the United States, and permitting others to extensively use the same in the United States for more than two years before he filed his said application, without asserting any claim that the same constituted an invention or any exclusive rights in and about the same.

11. Further answering, these defendants aver that at the time of filing the application for the aforesaid letters patent it contained no claims for a cementitious structure or the product of the alleged new process, and that claims 9 and 10, nor

any similar claims, were not contained in the said application when first filed, but such claims were introduced by amendment after the case was filed, without a supplemental oath, and are not covered by the original oath, wherefore said claims constitute new matter and are invalid, void and of no force and effect.

12.   Further answering, the defendants aver that the said letters patent are invalid for the reason that the said Paul E. Denivelle was not the first, original and sole inventor of the alleged invention therein patented, and that the subject matter of the said patent contains no invention in view of the common practices known to the plasterer's art and known to this plaintiff to have been long in use before the claimed date of invention of this plaintiff, in the manufacture of artificial stone [12]   structures, and that the alleged process and product therein set forth and claimed, constitutes nothing more than the exercise of the skill and knowledge of the ordinary plasterer and was in common and notorious use for years before the date of the alleged invention by plaintiff.

13.   Further answering, the defendants aver that the aforesaid letters patent and the subject matter thereof contained no patentable invention or novelty at the date of the alleged invention thereof by the said Paul E. Denivelle, by reason of the disclosures contained in the following letters patent of the United States:

No. 1,125,112 granted April 2, 1872, to George
    Davey:

No. 134,300 granted December 24, 1872, to George H. Mellen;

No. 247,262 granted September 20, 1881, to John W. McKnight;

No. 262,603 granted August 15, 1882, to John W. McKnight;

No. 290,417 granted December 18, 1883, to Richard Guelton;

No. 451,799 granted May 5, 1891, to William Bleiss;

No. 452,254 granted May 12, 1891, to Byron Booth;

No. 527,969 granted October 23, 1894, to Feuillen Grand Montague;

No. 651,657 granted June 12, 1900, to John Esbe;

No. 708,248 granted September 2, 1902, to Frank Orlikowski;

No. 723,281 granted March 24, 1903, to William E. Jaques;

No. 766,893 granted August 9, 1904, to Frank Oliva;

No. 800,931 granted October 3, 1905, to William P. Meeker;

No. 829,249 granted August 21, 1908, to George H. Bartlett;

No. 886,124 granted April 28, 1908, to John C. Henderson;

No. 932,092 granted April 24, 1909, to George H. Bartlett;

No. 978,616 granted December 13, 1910, to Jacinto Mitats;

No. 978,617 granted December 13, 1910, to Jacinto Mitats;

No. 982,029 granted January 17, 1911, to Charles
H. Ballamy;

No. 1,012,016 granted December 19, 1911, to August
Riesch; [13]

No. 1,137,595 granted April 27, 1915, to Emil C.
Eyl;

No. 1,170,791 granted February 8, 1916, to Frank
Zagelmeyer;

No. 1,087,098 granted February 17, 1914, to Jonas
W. Aylsworth.

14. Further answering, the defendants aver that
the said letters patent contain no invention or
patentable novelty for the reason that prior to the
date of the alleged invention thereof by the said
Paul E. Denivelle, and more than two years prior
to the filing of the application on which the said
patent was issued, the subject matter thereof, and
the method of making artificial stone set forth,
described and claimed therein, was described in a
publication entitled, "Limestones and Marbles,"
by S. M. Burnham, Boston, Mass., published in
1883, a copy of which may be inspected at the office
of defendant's counsel in the Hobart Building,
San Francisco, California.

15. Further answering, the defendants aver that
the said letters patent are invalid and of no force
and effect for the reason that the subject matter
thereof was known and publicly used in the United
States more than two years before the filing of the
application on which said patent was granted, at
the places and by the parties set forth in the following list:

John A. Fincke, 319 East 40th Street, New York City.

Frank Whipple, 11 Fulton Ave., Roosevelt or Rosedale, L. I.

William Cooke, 608 Chestnut Street, Roselle Park, N. J.

Carrere & Hastings, 52 Vanderbilt Avenue, New York City.

Louis Massimo, 410 Eleventh Avenue, New York City.

Henry W. Miller, 410 Eleventh Avenue, New York City.

C. Henry Meyn, 41 E. 22nd St. (13–45 E. 21 St.), New York City.

A. L. Harmon, 27 East 40th Street, New York City.

Henry A. Cousins, 35 DeWitt Avenue, Belleville, N. J. [14]

Kenneth Murchison, 101 Park Avenue, New York City.

McKim, Mead & White, 101 Park Avenue, New York City.

George Fuller Co., Fuller Bldg., New York City.

Warren & Wetmore, 16 East 47th Street, New York City.

Julian Holland (with Warren & Wetmore), 16 E. 47th St., New York.

P. J. Durkin, 440 East 140th Street, New York City.

Davis Brown, 306 East 40th Street, New York City.

P. G. Moore, Jr., 549 West 52nd Street, New York City.

Mr. Price (c/o Durastone Co.), 1105 Metropolitan Ave., Bklyn., N. Y.

Klee–Thompson Co., 327 East 40th Street, New
    York City.
Louis Bloom, 516 West 25th Street, New York City.
Jacobson Company, 241 East 44th Street, New York
    City.
John J. Roberts, 207 East 27th Street, New York
    City.
J. K. Krafft, 710–14th Street N. W., Washington,
    D. C.
J. E. Good, 390 Frelinghuysen Avenue, Newark
    N. J.

16. Further answering, the defendants aver that
they have been engaged in the manufacture of artificial travertine in the manner which the plaintiff
charges to be an infringement of the patent here
in suit, long prior to the issuing of said patent and
long prior to the date of the application on which
said patent issued, and of this fact the plaintiff
has always been fully advised, and has also been
fully advised of the defendant's notorious use and
practice of the said process and the manufacture of
artificial travertine before and after the issuing of
the patent to the plaintiff, and yet has refrained
from instituting suit against these defendants,
wherefore plaintiff is guilty of such laches in and
about the premises, as to constitute an abandonment of his said patent, or sufficient to deprive the
plaintiff of any standing in a court of equity as
against these defendants. [15]

WHEREFORE, the defendants, having fully
answered the bill of complaint, deny that the plaintiff is entitled to any part of the relief demanded,

and pray to be hence dismissed with their costs and charges in this behalf most wrongfully sustained, and that the court in dismissing this complaint will refer the same to a Master to ascertain and report to this Court the amount of damage which has accrued to these defendants by reason of the grant of the preliminary injunction herein, and the defendants will ever pray.

R. M. J. ARMSTRONG,
Attorney for Defendants.

MUNN, ANDERSON & MUNN,
T. HART ANDERSON,
Of Counsel for Defendants.

State of California,
County of Los Angeles,—ss.

George Smith MacGruer and Robert Morton Simpson, being first duly sworn, depose and say that they are copartners doing business under the name of MacGruer & Simpson, and are the defendants named in the foregoing amended answer; that they have each of them read the same and the same is true of their own knowledge, excepting as to matters therein stated on information and belief, and as to such matters they believe it to be true.

ROBERT MORTON SIMPSON.
GEORGE SMITH MacGRUER.

Sworn to before me this 29th day of January, 1924.

[Seal]
E. LAWRENCE,
Notary Public, L. A. County.

Receipt of a copy of the within is hereby admitted.

San Francisco, Jan. 26, 1924.

> CHAS. E. TOWNSEND,
>
> Attorney for Plaintiff. [16]

[Endorsed]: Filed Feb. 4, 1924. [17]

[Title of Court and Cause.]

ORDER TO SHOW CAUSE.

Upon reading the affidavits of Paul E. Denivelle and P. V. Keyse, on behalf of plaintiff above named, and good cause appearing therefor,—

IT IS ORDERED that the 23d day of July, 1923, at the hour of 10 o'clock A. M. of said day, or as soon thereafter as counsel may be heard, in the courtroom of said court in the Post-Office Building of the City and County of San Francisco, State of California, be, and it is hereby fixed as the time and place when and where the defendants and each of them shall show cause, if any they have, why a temporary injunction should not issue, restraining and enjoining the said defendants, and each of them, their clerks, agents, workmen and attorneys, from infringing directly or indirectly, upon the patent here in suit.

Dated: July 16th, 1923.

> JOHN S. PARTRIDGE,
>
> Judge.

[Endorsed]: Filed Jul. 16, 1923. [18]

[Title of Court and Cause.]

NOTICE OF MOTION AND MOTION FOR PRELIMINARY INJUNCTION.

To the Above-named Defendants, MacGruer & Simpson (a Copartnership) and George Smith Mac-Gruer and Robert Morton Simpson, Individually and Sometimes Doing Business as MacGruer & Co.:

You are hereby notified that on Thursday, the 2d day of August, 1923, at the hour of 10 o'clock A. M., or as soon thereafter as counsel can be heard, at the courtroom of the above-entitled court, in the United States Post-Office and Court House Building at the corner of Seventh and Mission Sts., in the City and County of San Francisco, State of California, plaintiff will move the above-entitled court for an order granting an injunction, *pendente lite,* in accordance with the prayer in the bill of complaint here and the Order to Show Cause issued by said Court under date of July 16th, 1923, and for such other and further relief as the facts may warrant.

The grounds of this motion are that the plaintiff is the sole and exclusive owner of United States letters patent [19] No. 1,212,331, sued on herein; that said letters patent have heretofore been adjudged good and valid in law; that the defendants have heretofore infringed and now are infringing upon said letters patent by practicing for profit without license the process claimed in and patented by said letters patent, and using or selling the product claimed therein, and, unless restrained by this court, defendants will continue to infringe upon said letters patent; and that defendants' continued infringement on said letters patent during the pendency of this suit will cause irreparable injury and damage to plaintiff; that the validity of the aforesaid letters patent was contested on full proofs in the prior adjudication referred to in the bill of complaint and was held to be valid, title was found to be in the plaintiff and processes and products substantially identical with those of the defendants herein were found to infringe.

In support of said motion and at the hearing thereof, plaintiff will rely upon and use the verified bill of complaint herein, the affidavits of Paul E. Denivelle and P. V. Keyse, together with the exhibits thereto annexed.

Dated: July 30th, 1923.

Yours, etc.,

CHAS. E. TOWNSEND,

WM. A. LOFTUS,

Solicitors and Counsel for Plaintiff.

Service of copy of the within notice of motion and motion for preliminary injunction admitted this ――― day of ―――, A. D. 1923.

R. M. J. ARMSTRONG,

For Defendants.

[Endorsed]: Filed Jul. 31, 1923.   [20]

[Title of Court and Cause.]

AFFIDAVIT OF PAUL E. DENIVELLE ON MOTION FOR PRELIMINARY INJUNCTION.

State of California,
City and County of San Francisco,—ss.

Paul E. Denivelle, being first duly sworn, deposes and says that he is a resident of the City and County of San Francisco, State of California, and is by occupation a contractor and specialist in decorative plastering, having been so engaged since about 1897; that he is patentee of the patent involved in the above-entitled suit and is familiar with the ornamental plastering art; that the patent in suit has been litigated in the cases of Los Angeles Lime Company and Paul E. Denivelle vs. C. L. Nye, and Los Angeles Lime Company and Paul E. Denivelle vs. E. Ceriat, instituted in the Southern District of California, and which resulted in the United States Circuit Court of Appeals for the Ninth Circuit holding said patent valid and infringed (270 Fed. 155). [21]

The patent in suit is for the manufacture of artificial stone in simulation of Roman travertin.

Concerning the method affiant (the patentee) says that it embraces "the application of colored plastic material or ingredients, such as Portland cement, plaster of Paris, Keenes cement, magnesite and water or other liquid substance with or without aggregates to an upturned negative form, or mold of existing type, of wood, plaster, cement, etc., wherein these colored materials are so applied before the final set or crystallization of the mass, in a variety of progressive steps consecutively, as to produce in the case of positive taken from said mold, form, etc., automatically as a result of the progressive steps and special application, a certain striated form of texture and porousness in simulation of a stone known as 'Travertin' or 'Roman Travertin.' This process has to do mainly with producing or obtaining a surface especially desirable for reproducing in architectural and decorative effect; this method of use and effect being an innovation.''

The Century Dictionary gives the following definition of travertin :

> "*travertin,* travertine (trav er-tin), n. (F. travertin (It. travertino, an altered form (due to some interference) of tiburtino (L. tiburtinus, sc. lapis, travertin, lit. 'stone of Tibur'), so called as being formed by the waters of the Anio at Tibur (Tibur, an ancient town of Latium, now Tivoli). The calcareous deposit from springs which occurs in many localities in Italy, and is extensively quarried for use in building. It is a soft, porous, straw-colored rock, easily wrought when freshly quarried, and afterward hardening, and seeming, under the climate of Italy, to be very durable. The exterior walls [22] of the Colosseum and of St. Peter's are built of this material.

> "Blackening in the daily candle-smoke,
> They molder on the damp wall's travertine.
> —"Browning, Pictor Ignotus.''

The patented process like most processes resides in a series or succession of steps taken in a certain order of arrangement and applied to certain materials to produce a desired result. The result of the process is a building slab having much the surface texture of natural travertin, but, of course, the patent is not to be judged by how close it approaches natural travertin. It is primarily an artificial stone of distinctive characteristics which the trade, through affiant's efforts and success, has come to recognize as a new product.

The patented process comprises, briefly, the production of striated or veined artificial stone structures by depositing upon a prepared surface, as for instance a mold which has been suitably greased or lubricated, a series of narrow lines of colored plastic material in simulation of veins; depositing upon said lines or veins and upon the exposed surfaces of the mold between the veins a suitable material of such texture and consistency as will leave numerous small voids or portions of said exposed surfaces out of contact with the material, and then binding together the veining material and the void-forming material with a moist plastic, and allowing the mass to set.   ?

Usually the veining material is of a slightly different color tone from the rest of the mass, thereby enhancing the simulation of artificial travertin. The void-forming material is of a more or less loose, lumpy or cloddy character, but having the quality of cohesion to and with the veining and the backing [23]   material.

The process is well defined in claims 1, 2 and 5 of the patent and these claims were adjudicated, along with claims 9 and 10 covering the product produced by the practice of the process; these claims 9 and 10 being as follows:

"9·—A cementitious structure suitable for decorative purposes, comprising a mass of cementitious material at least one surface of which is shaped and striated and formed with small irregularly spaced depressions, the striae constituting the exposed portions of shallow inlays of uniformly colored cement.

"10·—A cementitious combination for decorative use, such as a finish for exterior or interior building walls and ceilings, which combination is formed of differently toned thin layers or strata, the said layers only partly connected one to the other in such manner as to leave serrated voids in stratified formation between said layers, said layers and voids existing only adjacent to the surface but giving an appearance, when erected, of extending through the depth of the mass, the resulting decorative surface simulating that of a natural stone structure of sedimentary origin."

The tools or apparatus for performing the different steps and producing the patented product are of any suitable sort and are very simple, consisting simply of a greased or prepared mold, upon the surface of which the veining is first run or let out by suitable means as either a can with a pouring spout or spouts, or, as affiant frequently practices the work, with a divided brush which is adapted to be dipped into a suitable material and then drawn in lines over the surface of the mold.

The grease prevents the slab from sticking to the mold. As above stated, over this greased surface and after the veining has been run a suitable cloddy or lumpy material, very much of the consistency of very stiff mortar, is sprinkled over the entire surface of the mold and veins to form the pockets. [24] This pocket-forming material being, as stated in the patent, "a suitable material of such texture and consistency as will leave numerous portions of said exposed surfaces out of contact with said material." The backing material which is then laid into the molds and upon the cloddy material may be of the same consistency and color as the cloddy material itself, so that when the mass is allowed to set the veins and pocket-forming material and backing will be knit into a solid, unitary, durable mass forming an artificial stone slab which can be set up in position as a wall surface or covering.

In practice, sometimes these steps are interchanged; that is the pocket-forming material may be sprinkled on first and then the veins, which are always of more or less fluid consistency and colored slightly by way of contrast, may be run over this crumby or cloddy material, thus giving variety and at the same time similarity between the slabs, which similarity, as has been described as the likeness and yet the unlikeness between two or more human faces.

In the Los Angeles suits above referred to at 270 Fed. 155, the defendants unsuccessfully sought to evade the patent by doing the work in a careless, sloppy manner by seemingly combining steps two (2) and three (3); that is, placing the cloddy material in a mold and then a plastic material on top of them by using the same consistency of material to form the voids and to provide the backing and give the necessary thickness to the slab.

The Circuit Court of Appeals, however, held that that variation did not escape the patent and that the defendants' work there was an infringement of claims 1, 2, 5, 9 and 10.

The intrinsic merit of the invention has found [25] expression in a large practical way in its extensive use by affiant in the monumental structure of the Pennsylvania Railroad Station in New York City and the wall surfacing of the buildings of the Panama-Pacific International Exposition in San Francisco; this work in each instance being under the personal supervision of affiant, the patentee.

Affiant has also applied his process and product of the patent in suit to many other monumental buildings, including the San Francisco Public Library in the Civic Center, the Federal Reserve Bank and the Anglo California Bank Building, all in San Francisco; the Union Station, Ottawa, Canada; and in various other places. The contract for the Pennsylvania Station work alone involved an expensive scheme of interior decoration never before attempted; while the Panama-Pacific International Exposition work involved exterior treatment subject to weather conditions.

Referring to the novelty of the patented invention and the effects produced thereby, Mr. A. H. Markwart, Assistant Director of Works and Chief of Construction of the Exposition, says, at the beginning of his article on the "Wall Surfaces of the Exposition":

"Able critics have judged the exterior appearance of the entire Exposition from a color and texture standpoint to be one of great beauty. In adopting for the wall surfaces a treatment to give the effect of the famous Roman Travertine, that peculiarly beautiful stone found near the River Tiber, there was, as far as expositions are concerned, a unique and original departure from the usual dazzling white plaster effects.

"Consequently the entire exterior of the Exposition, instead of suggesting plaster and stucco, conveyed an impression of rare marble, soft in tone and color, and the stratified texture [26] of its surface produced repose for the eye by day and by night. It had no distinct, sharp color, but may be described as having several warm tones of gray and pink blended together, all an integral part of the mixture.

"While the architecture of the Exposition has many admirable features and has been the subject of favorable comment by all, it undoubtedly would not have created the impression which it did had it not been a 'color Exposition.' It must be conceded that the Exposition was inter-

evad

slopp

(2)

teria

of th

to f

give

T

that

the

clai

T

[25

ext

of

Cit

Pa

Fr

the

of

bu

br

an

Sa

an

P

pe

at

E

to

...McNulty Bros., Inc., of C...
...H. W. Miller, Inc., of New York C...
...Inc., of New York City; Mase...
...of New York City; John J. Robert...
...of New York City; Davis, Brown, In...
...York City; Kline, Thompson Co., of New...
...and L. A. Comiss, Inc., of New York Ci...
...testified as an expert concerning such...
...and products at the trial of the sui...
...to date and the Circuit Court of Appe...
...Ninth Circuit, after considering the te...
...lating to these alleged prior uses, found...
..."That both the process and the...
...the appellant were patentable we...
...doubt. While the record shows...
...rials of artificial stone had bee...

acture any artificial travertin had been
;fully made.'' [27]

urther states that h(is well acquainted
efendants, George S1ith MacGruer and
orton Simpson, and 1ach of them; that
dants acting under th(directions of affiant
oroughly familiar wih affiant's patented
d product aforesaid during the building
'anama-Pacific Interational Exposition,
·ly during the years 913 and 1914 when
defendants, under the direction of affiant,
ffiant's patented procss and product as an
covering for the wak of the Machinery
the Panama-Pacific hternational Exposi-
.t said artificial travetin so used on said
ry Hall was applied y the workmen em-
1y the said George Smith MacGruer and
Morton Simpson and was done under the
ion and instruction of affiant and assistants.
t further states that ne infringement now
ned of is in connectio with the unauthor-
· of affiant's patented 1rocess in the decora-
the Los Angeles **Biltmore** Hotel, in the city
An which **work** i now **in** progress, and
ri mplained of thre to con-
1nle⸱. hy th⸱ c·

nt furt⸱ ᶦa·

ᶦted by

᷀f Lo⸱

esting not only from the architectural view-
point, but also from the texture and color of
the exterior plaster.''

Affiant is familiar with the various types of artificial stone and processes for making the same which
were publicly known or used prior to the invention
of the product and process of the patent in suit,
many of which were referred to in the prior litigation above referred to, and knows that such prior
processes and products are fundamentally different
from the process and product involved herein, both
in construction and appearance. Among the many
instances of prior use and knowledge relied upon by
defendants in the prior suits above referred to were
the following: McNulty Bros., Inc., of Chicago, Illinois; H. W. Miller, Inc., of New York City; P. J.
Durean, Inc., of New York City; Massemoe Hutter
Co., of New York City; John J. Roberts Company,
of New York City; Davis, Brown, Inc., of New
York City; Klee, Thompson Co., of New York City;
and H. A. Cousins, Inc., of New York City. Affiant
testified as an expert concerning such prior processes and products at the trial of the suits referred
to *ante* and the Circuit Court of Appeals for the
Ninth Circuit, after considering the testimony relating to these alleged prior uses, found:

"That both the process and the product of
the appellant were patentable we entertain no
doubt. While the record shows that various
kinds of artificial stone had been theretofore
made, it is not pretended that before De⋯elle's

manufacture any artificial travertin had been
successfully made." [27]

Affiant further states that he is well acquainted
with the defendants, George Smith MacGruer and
Robert Morton Simpson, and each of them; that
said defendants acting under the directions of affiant
became thoroughly familiar with affiant's patented
process and product aforesaid during the building
of the Panama-Pacific International Exposition,
particularly during the years 1913 and 1914 when
the said defendants, under the direction of affiant,
applied affiant's patented process and product as an
exterior covering for the walls of the Machinery
Hall at the Panama-Pacific International Exposition; that said artificial travertin so used on said
Machinery Hall was applied by the workmen employed by the said George Smith MacGruer and
Robert Morton Simpson and was done under the
supervision and instruction of affiant and assistants.

Affiant further states that the infringement now
complained of is in connection with the unauthorized use of affiant's patented process in the decoration of the Los Angeles Biltmore Hotel, in the city
of Los Angeles, which work is now in progress, and
the infringement complained of threatens to continue unless restrained by this court.

Affiant further states that about May 1st, 1922,
he was invited by the Scofield Engineering & Construction Co., of Los Angeles, California, General
Contractors for the said Los Angeles Biltmore
Hotel, to submit a bid for the construction and
e.   n of artificial travertin of certain walls and

parts of said Los Angeles Biltmore Hotel; the architect's plan requiring that such walls be covered or decorated with such artificial travertin.

Affiant further shows that there is no known method of commercially producing artificial travertin except by [28] plaintiff's patented method, and on information and belief affiant states that the said Scofield Engineering & Construction Co. and these defendants and the architect for the said Los Angeles Biltmore Hotel knew such to be the fact.

That affiant, on the invitation of the said Scofield Engineering & Construction Co., in good faith, submitted a bid for the work requiring the production and erection of this artificial or imitation travertin, the amount of affiant's said bid being in excess of Sixty Thousand ($60,000.00) Dollars.

That it was apparently understood that affiant was to be awarded the said contract, but affiant was suddenly called to Seattle in connection with another large job of travertin that he was carrying on there and he was unable to go to Los Angeles as promptly as contemplated and the next thing affiant knew the contract had been awarded to the defendants, George Smith MacGruer and |Robert Morton Simpson, and at a price, so affiant is informed, very much below affiant's stated price and much lower than the work can be done properly and at the same time provide a reasonable profit to the contractor.

Affiant's attention was first called to the award of the contract to defendants, George Smith MacGruer and Robert Morton Simpson, by affiant's Los Angeles licensee, the Los Angeles Lime Company, who had been approached, so affiant is informed, by said defendant, George Smith MacGruer, knowing that said Los Angeles Lime Company was familiar with the plaintiff's patented process and authorized to practice it. Affiant informed the said Los Angeles Lime Company of his dealings already had with the said Scofield Engineering & Construction Co. and in accordance with the license agreement existing between affiant and the said Los Angeles Lime Company [29] and requested that the entire matter be referred by the said Los Angeles Lime Company to affiant. Subsequently the defendants approached affiant with a view of either securing a license or getting permission from affiant to conduct the work and enable them to carry out their contract with the Scofield Engineering & Construction Co. for the erection of the artificial travertin in the said Los Angeles Biltmore Hotel.

At the request of defendants a meeting was had between affiant and his attorney on the one hand and the defendant, George Smith MacGruer, and his attorney on the other hand, at which time the proposed use of artificial travertin in the said Los Angeles Biltmore Hotel was discussed. The said George Smith MacGruer asked affiant to state the terms under which defendants might be licensed to use the process and product of the patent in suit on the said Los Angeles Biltmore Hotel job. Affiant explained to the said George Smith MacGruer that affiant's main concern was the maintenance of a certain standard quality and that the compensation was a secondary matter; this maintenance of

ality being emphasized throughout the meeting.
was suggested that said George Smith MacGruer
ould submit his plans to affiant and the two of
em would figure out how much travertin was
lled for by the MacGruer contract and what af-
nt would do it for should affiant elect to take the
bcontract from said MacGruer.

Affiant stated to said MacGruer that he would not
ke the job except under such conditions that he
ffiant) should have full supervision of the job, see
at it was done correctly and affiant's specifica-
ns and directions carried out so as to maintain
e high standard of quality theretofore set by af-
nt in the practice of the process. [30]

This interview took place on June 16th, 1922, at
e office of the late Chas. A. Patton in the Me-
anics Institute Bldg., 57 Post St., San Francisco,
lifornia. At this meeting on June 16th, 1922, the
fendant, George Smith MacGruer, ridiculed af-
nt's patent and expressed his intention that if he
uld get around affiant's patent he was going to do
and avoid paying royalty. Said George Smith
acGruer was informed by both affiant and the
ter's counsel that the defendants were perfectly
thin their rights if they could do it and not in-
inge affiant's patent; but it was pointed out that
e patent covered both a process and a product and
ile they might devise a process different from
ant's process and which might not infringe,
vertheless it would seem that the claims on the
tented product, characterizing the product as
d claims do, would necessarily cover an artificial

stone having the characteristics specified in said claim. The said George Smith MacGruer, however, stated that he was going to try and that he was then trying to see what he could do, and that he was going to get up something that would not infringe if he could, but was nevertheless very desirous of using affiant's method if he could and said he would address a letter to affiant specifying the travertin work called for in his contract.

Accordingly on June 19th, 1922, said McGruer wrote affiant as follows:

"San Francisco, Cal., June 19, 1922.
"Mr. P. E. Denivelle,
280 Golden Gate Ave.,
San Francisco, Calif.
"Dear Sir:
"We have been awarded the contract for all metal furring, lathing, plastering, artificial stone, [31] etc., on the New Biltmore Hotel, Los Angeles, California, per the plans and specifications of Messrs. Schultze and Weaver, Architects, New York City.

"Under the terms of this contract it is proposed to use a cast artificial Travertin Stone in certain portions of the building, namely:

"Basement elevator lobby and stairways adjacent as covered by Addendas 2 and 3.

"Ground Floor, architraeve at Telephone Room.

"Main Hotel Lobby, including the elevator lobbies on ground and first floors.

"First Floor Dining Room.

"The above, at present, covers all of the cast artificial Travertine Stone according to the terms of our contract.

"We are in receipt of a letter from the Scofield Engineering and Construction Company enclosing a copy of letter from your Attorney, notifying them of the existence of a certain patent held by you for this character of work and asking them to take the matter up so as to avoid any unnecessary complications in the event that it is the intention to use your process for the manufacture of this cast artificial Travertine Stone.

"In keeping with the above and also our interview with you and your Attorney, Mr. Townsend, at the office of Mr. C. L. Patton, our Attorney, on the 16th, may we ask under what terms we can have the privilege of using your process as covered by your Patent #1,212,331 and dated January 16, 1917, so that your interests may be protected?

"As there is a possibility of certain portions of the above enumerated work to be changed to artificial stone of another character, other than cast artificial Travertine, may we request, when submitting your proposal or terms, that you segregate same in the following manner: [32]

"1.   A price for the right to use your process under the terms of a license for this particular building for the work now contemplated.

"2.   A lump sum bid including all metal furring necessary for the erection of the cast artificial Travertine Stone as enumerated above.

"3. A separate bid for the furnishing of all cast artificial Travertine Stone as covered by Proposal #2. This bid is not to include the erection or pointing of same.

"4. A separate bid for the Main lobby and Elevator Lobbies as shown on Ground and First Floor plans.

"5. A separate bid on Proposal #4 for the furnishing of this and not including the metal furring, erection and pointing for the Main Hotel Lobby and Elevator Lobbies on Ground and First Floor.

"6. A separate bid for the Dining Room.

"7. A separate bid for the Basement Elevator Lobby and Stairway.

"8. A separate bid for Dining Room in keeping . with Proposal #5.

"9. A separate bid for the Basement Lobby and Stairway similar to Proposal #5.

"Kindly forward us this information at the earliest possible moment and oblige,

"Very truly yours,

"MacGRUER & SIMPSON,

"(Signed) GEORGE MacGRUER."

In reply thereto affiant addressed a letter to said defendants, MacGruer & Simpson, on June 26th, 1922, said letter reading in words and figures as follows, to wit:

"June 26th, 1922.

"MacGruer & Simpson,
    266 Tehama St.,
        San Francisco, Calif.

"Gentlemen: [33]

"Re: New Biltmore Hotel, Los Angeles.

"In accordance with your letter of June 19 defining the portions of above building in which it is proposed to use cast imitation Travertine stone, am submitting herewith my figures for furnishing and erecting the work complete for the following as described in your letter.

"'Basement elevator lobby and stairways adjacent as covered by Addendas 2 and 3.'

"'Ground Floor, architraeve at Telephone Room.'

"'Main Hotel Lobby, including the elevator lobbies on ground and first floors.'

"'First floor Dining Room.'

"As to the enumerated schedule contained in your other communication with several requests numbered 1 to 9, I do not see my way clear to supply all of the information requested. I have given considerable thought to these different requests with the following conclusions:

"*Request No. 1.* 'A price for the right to use your process under the terms of a license for this particular building for the work now contemplated.'

"I cannot see my way clear to quote you acceptable terms for license at this time as this would involve a division of responsibility for the ultimate result in the work.

"*Request No 2.*. .'A lump sum bid including all metal furring necessary for the erection of the cast artificial Travertine Stone as enumerated above.'

"This is complied with in the bid contained herewith.

"*Request No. 3.* 'A separate bid for the furnishing of all cast artificial Travertine Stone as covered by Proposal #2. This bid is not to include the erection or pointing of same.'

"This likewise involves a division of responsibility which for practical reasons cannot be granted as said imitation Travertine Stone is never completed as a fabricated article until it has been erected and finished.

"*Request No. 4.* 'A separate bid for the Main Lobby and Elevator Lobbies as shown on Ground and First Floor plans.'

"A separate figure for this is furnished herewith.

"*Request No. 5.* 'A separate bid on Proposal #4 for the furnishing of this and not including the metal furring, erection and pointing for the Main Hotel Lobby and Elevator Lobbies [34] on Ground and First Floor.'

"Cannot be complied with for same reasons as pertaining to No. 3.

"*Request No. 6.* 'A separate bid for the Dining Room.'

"A separate bid is contained herewith.

"*Request No. 7.* 'A separate bid for the basement Elevator Lobby and Stairway.'

"A separate bid is contained herewith.

"*Request No. 8.* 'A separate bid for Dining Room in keeping with Proposal #5.'

"Cannot be complied with for the reasons pertaining to No. 3.

"*Request No. 9.* 'A separate bid for the Basement Lobby and Stairway similar to Proposal #5.'

"Cannot be complied with for the reasons pertaining to No. 3.

"I submit herewith my proposal to furnish, execute, and erect (including any incidental furring required therefor) my No. 4 Special imitation Travertine stone finished and complete in every respect per the aforesaid schedule and according to your request No. 2 comprising that portion of your contract for the sum of FORTY-ONE THOUSAND FIVE HUNDRED ($41,500.00) DOLLARS.

"Contained in the foregoing are the following amounts, which, if separated would be as follows:

"Request No. 4, Main Lobby and Elevator
    Lobby $25,000.00
"Request No. 6, Dining Room 18,000.00
"Request No. 7, Basement Elevator
    Lobby and Stairway 2,000.00

"The foregoing figures do not include any models of ornament which I understood are to be provided by others under the head of modeling.

"In complying with your request and submitting figures as above, it is, of course, without prejudice to the fact that the Artificial Travertine which I contemplate using is not only covered by patent on the product but the method as well is also protected. Inasmuch as this is a patented article, I cannot concede that it is open to public bidding.

"On the other hand, the fact that the Product and the Method are patented has had no bearing on the [35] figures given you above.

"As previously explained to you, my object in patenting my Artificial Travertine and my Process was primarily to protect the architect and his clients who see fit to use this material, and to guarantee and to maintain the standard of quality as well as to prevent, by legal means, cheap and unworthy imitations. For the same reason I have felt justified in exercising proper precautions and *restraiing* in the issuance of licenses.

"It is understood as a part of this proposal that, in the event of its acceptance, I shall be awarded all imitation Travertine that shall be contained in your contract and as there may be some deductions therefrom, likewise shall I be awarded any such portions as may be added later.

"Trusting that the above may be acceptable to both yourselves and your clients, I remain,

"Very truly yours,
(Signed) "PAUL E. DENIVELLE.
"PED: W."

No answer was ever received of any kind to the foregoing letter. [36]

Nothing further developing, affiant concluded that the plans on the new Los Angeles Biltmore Hotel had been so altered as to omit the requirement for artificial travertin until within the last two or three

weeks affiant has been informed and believes that
the defendants, George Smith MacGruer and Robert
Morton Simpson, are proceeding unlawfully to cast
and erect slabs of artificial stone in attempted
simulation of travertin in large quantities and in
violation of affiant's patent rights and this work is
now progressing on the said Los Angeles Biltmore
Hotel at Los Angeles.

Affiant has attempted to ascertain first hand just
what is going on, but the greatest secrecy is maintained, both by the Contractors having charge of the
said Los Angeles Biltmore Hotel job and the defendants, to maintain and keep secret just the nature of
the travertin work that has been going on and is going on at the present time. However, one P. V.
Keyse, a former employee of affiant, returned to
affiant's employment after an absence of two
months, and the said Keyse informed affiant that he
had, in the meantime, been working for defendants,
MacGruer and Simpson, on the Biltmore Hotel in
Los Angeles, and, while so employed, he saw workmen in the employ of said defendants, MacGruer
and Simpson, casting slabs of artificial travertin
in large quantities. The said Keyse described to
affiant in detail the process with which said Mac-
Gruer and Simpson were making the artificial
travertin on the said Los Angeles Biltmore Hotel,
and, likewise, the appearance of the product.

Affiant states that the method subsequently and
now being followed by the said MacGruer and Simpson consists in the preparation of the mold, running
veins of colored [37] plastic material on this

mold, scattering lumpy material over the surface
of the mold and veins, and then backing up this with
a plastic mass, which, when allowed to set, produces
a cementitious combination formed of differently
toned thin layers of strata, the said layers only
partly connected one to the other in such manner as
to leave serrated voids in stratified formation between said layers, said layers and voids existing only
adjacent to the surface but giving an appearance
when erected, of extending through the depth of the
mass, the resulting decorative surface simulating
that of a natural stone structure of sedimentary
origin.

The defendants in their imitation of plaintiff's
process color the veining material different from
the rest of the mass so as to emphasize the striated
effect. Also defendants use a split stiff brush.to
draw or let out the veins, just as plaintiff does in
practice.

The said Keyse further explained that defendants
use calcium carbide which has a quality of slacking in the presence of the moisture contained in the
backing material; and this slacking, combined with
the voids otherwise produced enhances the appearance of pockets on the surface, although the general
effect, as affiant is informed, is to produce an article
much inferior but nevertheless in imitation of plaintiff's patented product.

From such description affiant was convinced that
said MacGruer and Simpson were infringing the
patent here in suit. Thereupon affiant arranged
to procure two samples of the artificial travertine so

made by defendants, the same being filed herewith
and marked Plaintiff's Exhibit "A" and Plaintiff's Exhibit "B." Affiant has carefully examined
said Exhibits "A" [38] and "B" and believes
that the same are made according to the process
set forth in claims 1, 2 and 5 and in exact similitude
to the product set forth in claims 9 and 10 of the
patent in suit.

Affiant further states that in his opinion the said
Exhibits "A" and "B" are much closer imitations
of affiant's product than was the product of the defendants in the prior litigation referred to herein.
In said prior litigation the Trial Judge, Hon. Oscar
Trippet, on several occasions during the trial, when
affiant was present, referred to the inartistic appearance of defendants' product as compared with
plaintiff's product, saying, with reference to defendants' product, that it was a very poor imitation
both of the natural travertin as well as the artificial travertin made in the patent in suit. The said
Exhibits "A" and "B" filed herewith are, in
affiant's opinion, a better looking product than the
prior infringing product, and, without close inspection, cannot be distinguished from affiant's product,
even by those skilled in the art.

In producing artificial travertin it is important
that a varied effect be obtained, since the natural
travertin varies considerably in texture. Therefore,
affiant, in practicing his patented process, seldom
produces two slabs which have identically the same
appearance although in general they are similar.
Two samples of artificial travertin made by affiant

in accordance with his patented process are filed herewith and are marked for identification Plaintiff's Exhibit "C" and Plaintiff's Exhibit "D."

Affiant has read the affidavit of P. V. Keyse and from the description contained therein of the manner of producing the artificial travertin made by defendants, affiant is of the   [39]   opinion that the various steps are the same or substantially the same as set forth in the process described in the patent in suit and that the effect of the unslacked calcium carbide is in all material respects identical with that of the loose lumpy or cloddy material referred to in the patent.

Affiant further states that in the practice of this process the said calcium carbide is in every sense the full equivalent of any other suitable material having the purpose and function of producing the voids in the finished slab, at the same time having the characteristics of being cementitiously bonded into the mass.

Further affiant saith not.

                    PAUL E. DENIVELLE.

Subscribed and sworn to before me this 14th day of July, 1923.

[Seal]   W. W. HEALEY,

Notary Public in and for the City and County of San Francisco, State of California.

[Endorsed]: Filed Jul. 16, 1923. [40]

[Title of Court and Cause.]

AFFIDAVIT OF P. V. KEYSE ON MOTION FOR PRELIMINARY INJUNCTION.

State of California,
City and County of San Francisco,—ss.

P. V. Keyse, being first duly sworn, deposes and says that he is a resident of the City and County of San Francisco, State of California; that his occupation is that of ornamental plasterer and casting various kinds and forms of artificial stones and plastic material; that at various times he has been employed by Paul E. Denivelle, plaintiff above named, and in such employment has frequently cast artificial travertin using the following process: A series of progressive steps are used. The tools or apparatus for performing the different steps and producing the patented product are very simple, of any suitable sort, consisting simply of a greased or prepared mould, upon the surface of which the veining is first run or let out by suitable means, as either a can with a pouring [41] spout or spouts or, as said plaintiff frequently practices the work, with a divided brush which is adapted to be dipped into a suitable material and then drawn in lines over the surface of the mould in a similar manner as would be used in pouring the material from a spoon or ladle while passing over said mould. The grease prevents the slab from sticking to the mould. Over this greased surface and after the veining has been run a suitable cloddy or lumpv

material, very much of the consistency of very stiff
mortar, is sprinkled over the entire surface of the
mould and veins to form the pockets; the purpose
of said cloddy or lumpy material being to keep
certain portions of the mould surface out of contact with the material forming the cast. The backing material, which is then laid into the moulds and
upon the cloddy material, is usually of a different
consistency though sometimes of the same color as
the cloddy material itself, so that when the mass
is allowed to set the veins and pocket-forming
material and backing will be knit into a solid mass
or an artificial stone slab which can be set up in
position as a wall surface or covering. These steps
sometimes are interchanged, but the resulting
product is a slab or cast whose outer face shows
colored veins between which are numerous voids
which result from keeping the plastic material out
of contact with the surface of the mould through
the use of said lumpy or cloddy material.

Affiant further states that during his employment by said plaintiff, Paul E. Denivelle, he has
cast such artificial travertin for use in various
buildings, including the Federal Reserve Bank of
San Francisco and the Anglo London and Paris
Bank.

Affiant also states that in the month of May,
1923, he resided in the City of Los Angeles, County
of Los Angeles, [42] State of California, and
was employed by said defendants, George Smith
MacGruer and Robert Morton Simpson, on a build-

ing known as the Los Angeles Biltmore Hotel, working thereon for a total period of three weeks.

While so employed by the said defendants, George Smith MacGruer and Robert Morton Simpson, affiant observed on frequent occasions other workmen in the employ of said defendants, MacGruer and Simpson, making artificial travertin, using a series of progressive steps, in the following manner: A prepared mould was first greased. On said mould the veining was first run or let out; in this case the device being a divided or split brush which was dipped into a suitable material and then drawn in lines over the surface of the mould while passing over it. After the veining has been run a suitable cloddy or lumpy material, (in this case being unslacked calcium carbide), was sprinkled over the entire surface of the mould and veins to form the pockets. The backing material which was then let into the moulds and upon the cloddy material or calcium carbide was of similar consistency to that used by said plaintiff, Paul E. Denivelle, and was also applied in a similar manner and the case was then backed with fiber and more cementitious material until the cast was completed.

The resulting product was a slab having colored veins on its exposed surface and formed with small voids between the veins, and in every respect resembling the artificial travertin which affiant, working under the said plaintiff's process, made for use in the Federal Reserve Bank Building and the Anglo, London and Paris Bank Building, at San Francisco, California.

Affiant further states that during his employment with the said defendants, MacGruer and Simpson, affiant was [43] requested by one Mr. Delaney, who, affiant is informed and believes, was foreman or superintendent for said defendants, MacGruer and Simpson, and also by George Smith MacGruer to work on artificial travertin, but affiant refused to do so, believing that in so doing he would be infringing said plaintiff's patent, and, when he (affiant) decided to discontinue his employment, affiant obtained a small specimen of artificial travertin so made by said MacGruer and Simpson and placed it in his grip and left the same in the building for a few hours before quitting time, but, upon arriving home that afternoon, he opened the grip and found that the sample piece had been removed by someone unknown to affiant.

Affiant returned to San Francisco in the early part of June, 1923, and advised said plaintiff, Paul E. Denivelle, of having seen artificial travertin being made by said MacGruer and Simpson at the Biltmore Hotel in Los Angeles and described to the said Paul E. Denivelle the process of manufacture and the appearance of said artificial travertin. At the request of said plaintiff, Paul E. Denivelle, affiant later went to Los Angeles for the purpose of obtaining one or more specimens of said artificial travertin so made by said defendants, MacGruer and Simpson. Upon reaching Los Angeles affiant found that the Biltmore Hotel building was being carefully guarded.

On June 29th, 1923, affiant went to said Biltmore

Hotel building at 6:30 A. M. and entered said building along with several laborers who were working on the said Biltmore Hotel. Upon entering the main lobby of said Biltmore Hotel building, which at that time was brilliantly illuminated, affiant observed artificial travertin in place upon the walls and a number of broken pieces of same lying on a scaffold. Affiant obtained [44] two of such broken pieces and immediately left the building and returned to San Francisco, meantime keeping said pieces in his possession. Upon arriving in San Francisco he placed said pieces of artificial travertin in the hands of a Mr. Graham, who is an attorney employed in the office of Chas. E. Townsend, counsel for plaintiff, and at the same time affiant wrote his initials and the date and place where he obtained them. Said pieces of artificial travertin are filed with this affidavit and are marked Plaintiff's Exhibit "A" and Plaintiff's Exhibit "B."

Affiant further states that he has examined carefully the specimens of artificial travertin marked Plaintiff's Exhibit "A" and Plaintiff's Exhibit "B" and that they are identical with the artificial travertin which he saw being made by said Mac-Gruer and Simpson's workmen at the Los Angeles Biltmore Hotel and in place upon the main lobby of said hotel and affiant believes that the same were made in the same manner as above set forth.

                            P. V. KEYSE.

Subscribed and sworn to before me this 11th day of July, 1923.

[Seal]   W. W. HEALEY,

Notary Public in and for the City and County of San Francisco, State of California.

[Endorsed]: Filed Jul. 16, 1923. [45]

[Title of Court and Cause.]

AFFIDAVIT OF D. R. WAGNER.

State of California,

County of San Francisco,—ss.

D. R. Wagner, being first duly sworn, deposes and says: That he is a resident of the City of San Francisco, County of San Francisco, State of California; that he is a general contractor and was formerly the junior member of the firm of W. W. Anderson & Company; that said W. W. Anderson & Company was awarded a contract for the erection and completion of Machinery Hall at the Panama-Pacific International Exposition held in the City of San Francisco in the year 1915; that he knows that in connection with work performed on the said Machinery Hall that his firm awarded a subcontract to execute all plain and ornamental plastering upon said Machinery Hall under the terms of the contract of said W. W. Anderson & Company; that said plastering work had to do with imitating what is known as Roman Travertin; that this work was awarded in a subcontract to MacGruer & Simpson of [46] San Francisco, with the approval of the officials in charge of said Panama-Pacific Exposition; that the said MacGruer & Simpson, in order to carry out the provisions and specifications of the contract awarded as aforesaid, prepared samples of artificial travertin for the approval of the Director of Works of said Exposition and in conformity with the terms of said contract awarded to said MacGruer & Simpson; that he knows it to be true that in order that this work could be satisfactorily carried out by said MacGruer & Simpson, in accordance with said contract, it was necessary that said MacGruer & Simpson carry on costly and expensive experiments in order to cause said imitation travertin to meet the full approval of the said Director of Works in charge of the Panama-Pacific International Exposition; that said samples were produced by said MacGruer & Simpson and were subsequently approved by said Director of Works and that said MacGruer & Simpson were then authorized to proceed with the plastering and ornamental work in the construction of said Machinery Hall and that in order that the principal contractor should not be penalized for nonperformance of work on said building in the specified time the said MacGruer & Simpson were authorized to carry on said work with dispatch; that this work was duly performed by the said MacGruer & Simpson after costly experiments on their part and that it consisted in imitating Roman travertin in conformity with the specifications provided by said Panama-Pacific International Exposition; that affiant believes the work to have been done and performed by said

MacGruer & Simpson beginning in the latter part of March or April, 1913.

And further affiant saith not.

DANIEL R. WAGNER.

Subscribed and sworn to before me this 31st day of July, 1923.

[Seal]   C. B. SESSIONS,

Notary Public in and for the City and County of San Francisco, State of California. [47]

[Title of Court and Cause.]

AFFIDAVIT OF F. J. TWAITS ON MOTION FOR PRELIMINARY INJUNCTION.

State of California,

City and County of Los Angeles,—ss.

F. J. Twaits, being duly sworn, deposes and says: That he is a resident of the City and County of Los Angeles, State of California, and is by occupation a general contractor and engineer; that he is vice-president of the Scofield Engineering-Construction Company, General Contractors for the erection of the Biltmore Hotel in the City of Los Angeles, County of Los Angeles, State of California; that he has read the bill of complaint in the above-entitled cause, also the affidavit of the plaintiff, Paul T. Denivelle; that as vice-president of the Scofield-Engineering-Construction Company he was conversant with all the bids received and with all other circumstances connected with the letting of the subcontract for the plain and ornamental plastering, artificial travertin, etc., for the above hotel; that up to the time that his company submitted their bid for this work they had been unable to get from the plaintiff a firm bid for the above work; that they did receive several bids [48] from responsible parties covering the entire plain and ornamental plastering, artificial travertin, etc., required for the hotel.

That after due investigation, they decided to award this work to MacGruer and Simpson, not because they were the lowest bidder, but because it was thought they would most certainly finish on time, and because of their reputation for doing good work; that, after this intention was explained to the architect, the architect requested that we make another effort to get from the plaintiff a firm bid for the above work, the architect being acquainted with the plaintiff and not with the defendants; that in pursuance of this request, and as a matter of accommodation to the architect, we did ask the plaintiff again for a firm bid covering the above work; that they never did receive from him a complete bid so as to enable us to consider letting the work to him; that the price he did submit for a portion of the work was out of range with other prices in our possession, and therefore unusable; that at no time was there any possibility of awarding this work to the plaintiff.

And further affiant saith not.

F. J. TWAITS.

Subscribed and sworn to before me this 27th day of July, 1923.

[Seal]   LUCILLE V. WILKING,

Notary Public in and for the County of Los Angeles,
   State of California.

My commission expires March 21, 1926.   [49]

[Title of Court and Cause.]

AFFIDAVIT OF LEONARD SCHULTZE ON MOTION FOR PRELIMINARY INJUNCTION.

State of California,

City and County of Los Angeles,—ss.

Leonard Schultze, being first duly sworn, deposes and says that he is temporarily a resident of the City of Los Angeles, County of Los Angeles, State of California; that he is an architect and has practiced this profession for many years; that he is the architect of the Biltmore Hotel now in process of erection in the said City of Los Angeles, County of Los Angeles, State of California; that prior to the erection of said hotel, he submitted to one F. J. Twaits, certain plans and specifications with reference to artificial marble, artificial Caenstone or limestone and artificial travertin; that the hereto attached specification, marked Exhibit 2 is a true copy of the plans and specifications submitted by affiant to the said F. J. Twaits; that said plans and specifications truly set forth what is known commercially as artificial travertin; that, as an architect, affiant is well skilled in the matter of constructing this so-called artificial travertin, and is otherwise fully [50] acquainted with the characteristics of structures of this character; that he has known of the existence of artificial travertin for many years; that as an architect he can say that plans and specifications in conformity with the herewith attached Exhibit 2 have been submitted to various contractors for many years; and also affiant says that his affiliations with contractors have shown conclusively that a large number of subcontractors, plasterers, and concerns dealing in kindred businesses have known of the existence of artificial travertin and that estimates on bids for this work have in large numbers been submitted to various contractors for many years.

Affiant further says that he is a member of the firm of Schultze and Weaver, whose principal place of business is at No. 17 East 49th Street, New York City, County of New York, and State of New York; that incident thereto he has become familiar with conditions in the east and in and around the proximity of New York in connection with the manufacture, use and sale of artificial travertin and that use of this material has been made, to affiant's knowledge, by many concerns in the east for many years.

Affiant further says that each of the many imitations of travertin with which he is acquainted, comprise a mass of cementitious material, at least one surface of which is shaped and striated and formed with small irregularly spaced depressions, the striae constituting the exposed portions of shallow inlays of uniformly colored cement, and that in many instances, the strata only partly connect one another in a manner as to leave serrated voids; that artificial travertin, constructed in this manner has been long known and used by others; that Exhibit No. 4, forming part of this affidavit, is a piece of imitation travertin made and sold by others with whom affiant is acquainted, and that, to the best of affiant's knowledge and belief, such [51] imitations of travertin have been made, sold and used by others for many years.

And further affiant saith not.

LEONARD SCHULTZE.

Subscribed and sworn to before me this 28th day of July, 1923.

[Seal]   BERNICE DRIVER BARIE,
Notary Public in and for the County of Los Angeles, State of California.

My commission expires Mar. 7, 1926.   [52]

[Title of Court and Cause.]

AFFIDAVIT OF ERIC LANGE ON MOTION FOR PRELIMINARY INJUNCTION.

State of California,
City and County of San Francisco,—ss.

Eric Lange, being first duly sworn, deposes and says that he is a resident of the City and County of San Francisco, State of California; that he is

a member of the firm of Lange & Bergstrom; that
the firm of Lange & Bergstrom were general contractors engaged by the Panama-Pacific International Exposition Company to erect the building
forming a part of the Panama-Pacific International
Exposition held in the City of San Francisco in the
year 1915, known as the Palace of Education.

That in pursuance of the work necessary to the
construction of said building, said firm of Lange
& Bergstrom on the ninth day of April, 1913, entered into a contract with the firm of Eastman &
Company, as subcontractors under said firm of
Lange & Bergstrom, in and by which said firm of
Eastman & Company were to construct and apply
all lath work and plastering and ornamental plastering necessary to be applied under the plans and
specifications of said building; that thereafter said
firm of Eastman & Company proceeded to and did
apply all lath work, plastering and ornamental plastering necessary to complete said work to the satisfaction of the Director of Works of said   [53]   Exposition, as required in said general contract plans
and specifications; that a part of the work of said
Eastman & Company consisted of applying to said
building ornamental plaster work in exact simulation of the stone known as and called Roman travertin.

And further affiant saith not.

ERIC LANGE.

Subscribed and sworn to before me this 31st day of July, 1923.

[Seal]   C. B. SESSIONS,
Notary Public in and for the City and County of
    San Francisco, State of California.   [54]

[Title of Court and Cause.]

AFFIDAVIT OF FREDERICK L. TOVANI ON MOTION FOR PRELIMINARY INJUNCTION.

State of California,
City and County of Los Angeles,—ss.

Frederick L. Tovani, being first duly sworn, deposes and says: That he is a resident of the City and County of San Francisco, State of California.

That his occupation is that of ornamental plasterer, caster, and moldmaker; that he has worked at this trade for many years; that he is well versed in the art of artificial stone and plastic materials of the character employed in building construction; that he is now in the employ of MacGruer and Simpson; that he was formerly in the employ of the plaintiff; that he knows a material commercially called "artificial travertin" and has cast same on many occasions; that he has full knowledge of the method employed by plaintiff in the construction of artificial travertin; that he has personally made artificial travertin, employing plaintiff's method; that well knowing the two methods employed respectively by plaintiff and defendants, affiant says that defendants did not use the plaintiff's method at any time in the course of work performed by [55] defendants at the Los Angeles Biltmore Hotel; that Exhibit No. 1, forming part of this affidavit, is a sample made by affiant of imitation travertin constructed in accordance with plaintiff's method; that Exhibit No. 3, forming a part of this affidavit, is a sample of imitation travertin made by affiant in accordance with the method used by defendants in constructing the Los Angeles Biltmore Hotel; that he has read plaintiff's affidavit and particularly the last paragraph on page 4 thereof through paragraph 1 on page 5, and that the process outlined therein is not the process used by defendants, and that defendants, in the construction of their imitation travertin did not make use of any so-called crumby or cloudy material.

Further affiant saith not.

FREDERICK L. TOVANI.

Subscribed and sworn to before me this 27th day of July, 1923.

[Seal]   LOUISE N. WELTY,

Notary Public in and for the County of Los Angeles, State of California.

My commission expires April 30, 1927.   [56]

[Title of Court and Cause.]

AFFIDAVIT OF THOMAS LAWRENCE ON MOTION FOR PRELIMINARY INJUNCTION.

State of California,

County of Los Angeles,—ss.

Thomas Lawrence, being first duly sworn, deposes and says that he is a resident of Glendale, county of Los Angeles, State of California, and is at present employed by MacGruer & Simpson; that his occupation is that of plasterer; that some time during the latter part of 1909, or early part of 1910, affiant was employed by H. W. Miller, Incorporated, of New York City, and that he was general foreman on the plastering and construction work performed in the construction of the Pennsylvania Railroad Station, located at Seventh Avenue and Thirty-fourth Street, New York City, County of New York, and State of New York; that among other work performed by affiant was the construction of imitation travertin used as an impost molding in the building of the said Pennsylvania Railroad Station, at the place aforesaid; that he is acquainted with the method of constructing imitation travertin as described and claimed in a patent granted to one Paul Denivelle on January 16, 1917, No. 1,212,-331; [57] that the process employed in the erection of the imitation travertin in the Pennsylvania Railroad Station was in exact keeping with the method and product described in the said Denivelle patent; that he is acquainted with the method employed by McGruer & Simpson in the construction of imitation travertin in the Biltmore Hotel in the City of Los Angeles, County of Los Angeles, and State of California; that he knows the system and method employed by the said MacGruer & Simpson to be entirely different from previous methods known to him, and from the method and product described and claimed in the said Denivelle patent.

Affiant further says that during the time of his employment in the work of the said Pennsylvania Railroad Station in the City of New York, numerous contractors submitted for approval, imitation travertin, and that as a skilled plasterer he knows this imitation travertin to be made in accordance with old and well-known methods which embody in their general characteristics the application of plastic substances to the greased surface of a mold; that these substances were then combed or otherwise formed to provide a stratified or veiny arrangement; that thereafter there was applied lumpy materials to constitute voids or cells; that a backing was finally applied to this mass and the whole permitted to dry and harden and to become one homogeneous substance or material, wherein the said lumpy materials constituted a permanent part, and that to the best of affiant's knowledge and belief, it was impossible to construct imitation travertin of a thickness equal to one inch or less.

And further affiant saith not.

THOMAS LAWRENCE.

Subscribed and sworn to before me this 26th day of July, 1923.

[Seal] ANNA B. LEONARD,
Notary Public in and for the County of Los Angeles, State of California. [58]

[Title of Court and Cause.]

AFFIDAVIT OF STEPHEN VIDA.

State of California,
County of San Francisco,—ss.

Stephen Vida, being first duly sworn, deposes and says: That he is a resident of the City of San Francisco, County of San Francisco, State of California; that he is a plasterer and artificial marble and stone worker; that he has practiced this trade for twenty-four years and has continuously so practiced it for the term herein stated; that for many years he has been fully familiar with the subjects of stucco, cement and various artificial stones and marbles and the methods of manufacturing the same; that he has for many years specialized in decorative plaster; that he knows of a natural stone called travertin; that he knows this stone to present an exposed striated or veined external surface having pockets, crevices or surface inequalities; that these crevices, pockets or the like vary in size and shape and are quite frequently undercut below the surface of the stone; [59] that in the course of affiant's time he has prepared artificial stones in simulation or imitation of San Saba, dark Tennessee marble, dark red granite scagliola and other imitations characterized by the stratified or veined surface in which the said surface is interrupted in some manner, shape or form by means employed in the process of closely simulating the marble or stone to be reproduced; that as an experienced plasterer and maker of imitation stones and marbles, he employs innumerable well-known formulas and recipes, according to the character of the work to be imitated; that he knows how to prepare artificial travertin; that in affiant's experience he prepares this imitation travertin in a manner substantially the same as employed by affiant in imitating stones of the above named varieties, and resorts to certain progressive steps in order that the constituents employed may be ultimately brought into a substantially homogeneous mass and which will give to the exposed surface of the finished product a striated or veined appearance interrupted by certain lumpy materials employed in the formula and which act in connection with the striations to very closely imitate the marble or stone to be duplicated; that with the knowledge acquired by affiant he knows imitation travertin to consist of a process wherein differently colored cementitious materials are placed upon the surface of a greased mould, after which there is applied to these materials lumpy particles preferably formed of Keen's cement and an added color so as to give to the exposed surface certain inequalities; that there is then applied to the whole mass a dryer to absorb the excess

seepage, and that finally there is applied to the mass
a plastic backing and the substance is then permitted to harden and dry in the customary manner;
that in all work connected with the manufacture of
artificial marble, affiant has since the very [60] beginning of his experience used a greased mould; that
affiant has particularly experted in the manufacture of scagliola which, according to various formulas may be changed to permit of the imitation
of natural marbles of all descriptions; that in the
manufacture of scagliola affiant first takes a
greased mould or bench and applies thereto a
cementitious material of the desired color in simulation of veins and in keeping with the color of the
marble to be imitated; that sometimes this cementitious material is carefully laid upon the moulds
to constitute a more or less even stratified arrangement; that at other times this material is promis-
cuously placed upon the surface of the mould by
the act of brushing or splashing the same thereon;
that after this has been done affiant then puts
another plastic material in like manner upon the
greased surface of the mould and permits it to run
together with the material first applied as aforesaid; that affiant then takes an old and well-known
form of rubber graining comb or similar instrument or tool and runs same down across the back
surface of the mass and entirely through the surface of the mass and onto the greased face of the
mould, thereby forming serrations or veins and
leaving ʼls or spaces between the colored mass
thus trea. d, and in condition for the next step

of the process to complete the perfect simulation
of the marble to be imitated; affiant then prepares
a semi-dry cloddy or lumpy mass of material and
sprinkles it upon the mass and causes same to
protrude through the mass and onto the working
or greased surface of the mould; that frequently
these operations are performed in inverse order
to that above referred to and the cloddy, lumpy or
granulated materials applied to the mould first,
the result being the same; that as one of the final
steps to the process affiant backs up the mass thus
formed in the usual well-known manner.

STEPHEN VIDA.

Subscribed and sworn to before me this 31st
day of July.

[Seal] C. B. SESSIONS,
Notary Public in and for the City and County of
San Francisco, State of California. [61]

[Title of Court and Cause.]

AFFIDAVIT OF J. HARRY BLOHME.

State of California,
City and County of San Francisco,—ss.

J. Harry Blohme, being duly sworn, deposes and
says: That he is a resident of Oakland, County of
Alameda, State of California; that he is the junior
member of the firm of Ward & Blohme, architects,
with their principal place of business at 454 California Street, San Francisco, California; that they
were engaged to prepare designs for the construction

of Machinery Hall; that these designs were prepared in 1912; That these designs were for the construction of Machinery Hall, forming one of the
buildings of the Panama-Pacific International
Exposition held in the city of San Francisco in 1915;
that these designs were completed in the fall of
1912; that to the best of affiant's knowledge and
belief bids were received for the work to be performed on the said Machinery Hall in December,
1912; that the actual contract for the work was
signed by W. W. Anderson Co. [62] of San
Francisco, California, and that also to the best of
affiant's knowledge and belief this contract was for
the execution of work in connection with the building of the said Machinery Hall; that to the best
of affiant's knowledge and belief said W. W. Anderson Co. awarded a subcontract with the consent and
approval of the Panama-Pacific International Exposition to the defendants, MacGruer and Simpson,
Contracting Plasterers of San Francisco; that the
said subcontract awarded as aforesaid to MacGruer
and Simpson was for the erection of all plain and
ornamental plastering in the said Machinery Hall
and that this plain and ornamental plastering was
specified under the heading "Lathing and Plastering" in connection with the contract entered into
by and between W. W. Anderson Co. and the said
Panama-Pacific International Exposition; that this
plastering work as performed by the said MacGruer
and Simpson was executed in a manner satisfactory
to the architects, and to the best of affiant's knowledge and behalf, to the officials in charge of the

Panama-Pacific International Exposition; and that this plastering was in imitation of Roman travertin; that he is familiar with the designs aforesaid and that the blue-prints forming part of this affidavit and marked Defendants' Exhibit No. 6 are true copies of the designs referred to herein.

That affiant knows of a publication entitled "Wall Surfaces of the Exposition," published by one Markwart and wherein certain plates or photographs are shown in imitation of artificial travertin; that to the best of affiant's knowledge and belief Exhibit No. 7 forming a part of this affidavit is one of the original copies of said publication and is so identified by affiant, and that certain photographs contained in said publication are in full conformity in design and detail with certain [63] imitation travertin completed on the said Machinery Hall; that affiant further knows that the ground at said Exposition and which was selected as a site for said Machinery Hall was broken on January 1, 1913, and that the work performed by said MacGruer and Simpson was started shortly thereafter; that prior to the date on which any plastering work whatever was performed on the major buildings at said Exposition affiant was introduced and made personally acquainted with one Paul E. Denivelle, the plaintiff herein; that affiant was informed that said Denivelle had expert knowledge in regard to the manufacture of imitation travertin and had for a long time performed work in imitation of Roman travertin, using plastic substances to carry out this work and incorporating this work in buildings in the east prior to 1912.

And further affiant saith not.

J. HARRY BLOHME,

Subscribed and sworn to before me this 1st day of August, 1923.

[Seal]   O. A. EGGERS,

Notary Public in and for the City and County of San Francisco, State of California. [64]

[Title of Court and Cause.]

AFFIDAVIT OF JOHN H. DELANEY ON MOTION FOR PRELIMINARY INJUNCTION.

State of California,

City and County of San Francisco,—ss.

John H. Delaney, being first duly sworn, deposes and says that he is a resident of Los Angeles, County of Los Angeles, and State of California, and is by occupation a Superintendent of Plastering in the employ of MacGruer and Simpson; that he has been employed by said MacGruer and Simpson since the early part of 1914; that he has made an expert study of ornamental plastering and is well acquainted with methods and products entitled "travertin"; that he knows natural material of this name to be a soft, porous, straw-colored rock, when quarried; that same is found principally in Italy and that when hardened has been used as an ornamental surface in building construction; that he has been engaged in the plastering business for more

than twenty years; that for many years he has been
fully familiar with the subject of stucco, cement,
and various artificial stones; that he has for many
years specialized in decorative plastering; [65]
that he knows of a natural stone called "travertin";
that same is imported to these United States from
Italy; that "travertin" is a soft, porous straw-
colored rock used to a very great extent in building
construction and particularly in the construction of
ornamental exterior and interior surfaces; that this
natural travertin consists of a striated or veined
stone having numerous pockets, or voids upon its
outer surface; that these voids or pockets vary in
size and shape and from their very nature are undercut below the surface of the stone and that incident thereto many very beautiful shadow effects
are produced upon the exposed surface of the stone
which are restful to the eye; that to the best of his
knowledge many artificial stones have been produced in imitation of natural travertin and have
been and are now being manufactured in exceedingly
large quantities throughout the United States and
particularly throughout the Eastern States; that all
of these imitations have fallen far short of the natural
Italian travertin; that these artificial stones are
heavy and thick when produced and particularly
unsuitable for certain surface ornamentation in
building construction and lack any true replica of
the aforesaid irregularly shaped undercut voids or
pockets as found in the natural travertin; that he
knows of an imitation of travertin as made by the
plaintiff patentee; that plaintiff's stone or artifi-

cial travertin consists of a striated or veined substance made by arranging or forming upon a greased mold, a series of narrow lines of colored plastic material in imitation of veins; depositing upon said lines or veins and upon the exposed surfaces of the mold between the veins a suitable material of such texture and consistency as will leave numerous small voids of exposed surfaces out of contact with the material, and then binding together the veined material and the void-forming material with a moist plaster material, and allowing the mass to set and harden; that the so-called void-forming material is [66] of a loose, lumpy character which becomes a homogeneous part of the finished product; that this void-forming material never separates from the other materials employed in the manner practiced by plaintiff and that same gives to the finished product a thick heavy body with an outer or exposed surface having pockets or pores; that these pockets or pores are not in true simulation of the natural travertin and are not undercut in agreement with the natural travertin, whereby to produce the desired shadow effect as previously mentioned herein; that the weight and thickness of plaintiff's artificial travertin prevents same from being used in certain ornamental work where a light weight minimum thickness material is required; that affiant has labored for several years to bring into existence an imitation travertin that would meet commercial or trade requirements not heretofore overcome in the material of the plaintiff's or other manufacturers of imitation travertin; that

in order to accomplish this, affiant was compelled to
eliminate the steps of the process referred to in
plaintiff's patent No. 1,212,331 of January 16, 1917;
that except for steps of a process that are long since
well known in the art, affiant's imitation is produced in a contrary manner to plaintiff's and that
no void-forming material is employed which ever
becomes a permanent part of the finished product
or homogeneous part thereof that would give or
add to its thickness, bulk and weight; that affiant
knows that for a long time prior to the invention
of the plaintiff, void-forming materials of various
kinds have been employed for the purpose explained
in the specifications and claims of plaintiff's patent
aforesaid; that materials consisting of sawdust have
been employed by others in decorative stucco, cement
and plastic structures and used in connection with
the manufacture of imitation travertin; that this
sawdust is used to form [67] pockets or voids
upon the exposed surface of the finished imitation
travertin; that after the material has been molded
and set, same is subjected to a process whereby the
sawdust will be removed from the finished product;
that processes using sawdust or the like have been
used to the best of affiant's knowledge and belief for
more than two years prior to October 20, 1915; that
affiant, as a skilled craft worker has studied many
works on the subject of decorative art and particularly decorative art of plastic compositions, and in
this connection, affiant refers to a book entitled
"The Art of The Plasterer," by George P. Bankart,
printed at The Darien Press, Bristo Place, Edin-

burgh, and published by B. T. Botsford, 94 High Holborn, London, the same being a reprint of an earlier publication printed and published for more than two years prior to October 20, 1915; that on page 5 of this book there appears this statement:

"The rough stone used by the Greeks *was like the Roman travertin, very porous,* and not capable of taking a fine surface, so they stuccoed it over, polished it, and sometimes decorated it with paintings. Traces of this are to be found in the Dorian monuments in Sicily, at Paestum, etc." The learned author further goes on and says, on page 5: "It should be explained that this 'travertin,' 'travertine' or Tivoli stone (the Italian term for solid concretionary limestone) was extracted from the springs holding carbonate of lime in solution, etc." The author further states, on page 5 of the publication aforesaid, that "The earliest known example of the use of travertin is said to be at a tomb of Cecelia Metella, and there is merely a veneer over a rubble wall of enormous thickness. This date is assigned by some authorities at 103 N. C. and by others at 50 B. C."

That processes dealing with the manufacture of imitation travertin are old and well known for more than two years prior to October 20, 1915; that these old processes make use of all the essential steps of the process described and claimed in plaintiff's patent aforesaid; that the essentials of work of this character constitute nothing more than the well known principles employed in the manufacture of stucco or like surfaces formed of plastic materials; that such surfaces are commonly formed through the assistance of suitable forms or molds which are previously greased and upon which it is poured, placed or otherwise arranged [68] the various constituents of the mass or plastic substance employed; that use of differently colored plastic substance is made where it is desired to give a stratified effect to the exposed surface of the finished product; that well knowing these old processes and with full knowledge of the defects and imperfections attendant the production of imitation material of plaintiff's character, affiant set about to eradicate these imperfections and to produce a material in closer simulation of natural Roman travertin and to provide a plastic substance which is very porous and rough and which will be provided with a surface having undercut cavities or voids in true conformity with the natural voids or cavities of the so-called Roman travertin; that affiant had among other things the creation of a novel and new and useful composition of matter wherein these cavities can be more or less inconsistently formed upon the exposed surface of the finished product and by means of or through the assistance of chemical instrumentalities which function for the purpose aforesaid and which subsequently become entirely obliterated by chemical reaction so as to never constitute any homogeneous part of the completed mass, and thereby ultimately give to the commercial or finished product a condition or quality not heretofore experienced or found in substance of com-

mon knowledge, or in such substance as could be
produced in any manner, shape or form through
knowledge gained from plaintiff's patent; that essentially speaking, applicant makes use of an old
and well known mold characterized by features of
common knowledge; that he greases his mold as is
also well known; that he then places upon the surface thereof plastic substances, which, while in a
moist state, are combed or otherwise treated to
produce veins, so to speak; that he then introduces
to the surface thus treated granules of calcium carbide, and finally spreads upon the aforesaid constituents a plastic mass which gives to the structure
[69] a form of backing; that this backing is applied while in the moist state, and that incident
thereto a chemical action is set up which causes the
chemical carbide to assume a gaseous state and explode and thereby produce upon the surface of the
finished product a plurality of cells, pockets or
voids of an undercut character. Affiant states that
through this process and by the very inherent qualities of the chemicals employed the mass of the material or lumpy matter employed in plaintiff's patent is entirely eliminated with a functional departure from plaintiff's patent as to arise to the dignity
of a new and patentable invention; that through the
changes inaugurated by affiant's principle the ultimate product is in closer keeping with the natural
Roman travertin, and is light, strong and durable,
and is thin so that it may be advantageously used in
a manner not true to the commercial usages of
plaintiff's product. That a specimen of this last-

mentioned product herewith is produced and marked
for identification in Defendant's Exhibit 5. Affiant
further states that his experience as one skilled in
the art of plastering and the manufacture of artificial stones and marbles has extended over a space
of twenty years; that from the very commencement
of his experience in this art, he has had knowledge
of the imitation marbles of various kinds, including
marble known as "San Saba"; that marble of this
class is characterized by a veining or stratified surface and that in the method of constructing same,
use is always made of a greased mold on which a
plastic substance is poured or suitably arranged in
fine film formation; that after this plastic mass is
so arranged, it is combed to separate the normal
surface into subdivided, or separated surfaces,
wherein intervening spaces, or voids, are formed
between said subdivisions; that, as a next step to
the process, these voids or intervening spaces are
filled in with other plastic colored substances according to the surface ornamentation which is desired to be   [70]   obtained; that sometimes respectively different colored particles of semi-dry cement
are sprinkled upon the veins of the mass thus
formed, and finally, there is placed upon the surface or mass treated as aforesaid a plastic backing
of suitable texture and thickness; that the method
described in the production of San Saba is, in affiant's opinion as one skilled in the art, substantially
identical with plaintiff's method of producing artificial travertin, except perhaps that the former has a
greatly augmented arrangement of color in order

that the ultimate result produced will be typical of the natural marble; that in affiant's education as deals with the production of imitation marbles, and particularly imitations of San Saba, he has paid especial attention to a work entitled "Miller's Book on Plastering," a publication antedating for many years the date of filing of the application of plaintiff's patent in suit, and it is with information obtained by affiant from this book that he has been able to adapt the processes referred to therein to many obvious processes of making typical imitations of well-known natural marbles; that for twenty years affiant has made imitation San Saba in accordance with the foregoing and that Exhibit No. 8 is a sample of San Saba made by affiant in accordance with his knowledge aforesaid.

And further affiant saith not.

JOHN H. DELANEY.

Subscribed and sworn to before me this 1st day of August, 1923.

[Seal]   E. B. SESSIONS,

Notary Public in and for the City and County of San Francisco, State of California.

My commission expires May 20, 1925.   [71]

Receipt of copy of the within affidavits admitted this 1st day of August, 1923, at 12:25 P. M.

CHAS. E. TOWNSEND,
WM. A. LOFTUS,
Solicitors and Counsel for Plaintiff.

[Endorsed]:   Filed August 2, 1923.   [72]

[Title of Court and Cause.]

ORDER FOR PRELIMINARY INJUNCTION.

This cause having come on to be heard on motion of plaintiff for preliminary injunction, and on reading and filing notices of motion for an injunction herein and proof of service thereof, and the affidavits on behalf of the plaintiff annexed thereto, and on reading and filing affidavits on behalf of the defendant, and counsel for defendants as well as for the plaintiff having been heard, and the same having been duly considered by the Court, and it appearing that letters patent of the United States No. 1,212,331, dated January 16th, 1917, were issued in due form of law for an improvement in the manufacture of artificial stone structures to Paul E. Denivelle, and that the said defendants have infringed on the rights secured by the aforesaid letters patent by making and selling to others artificial stone structures embodying the invention set forth in said patent and practicing the process thereof.

NOW, THEREFORE, it is hereby ordered, adjudged and decreed that a preliminary injunction be issued pursuant to [73] the prayer herein, strictly commanding and enjoining the defendants, MacGruer & Simpson (a copartnership) and George Smith MacGruer and Robert Morton Simpson, individually and sometimes doing business as MacGruer & Co., and each of them, their and each of their clerks, agents, servants, workmen, and attorneys, under the pains and penalties which may fall upon them, and each of them, in case of disobedience, that they forthwith, and until further order, judgment and decree of this court, desist from making, using and selling any artificial stone structures as described and claimed in said letters patent or practicing the method or process described and claimed therein.

It is further ORDERED that as a condition to the issuance of the aforesaid injunction, the plaintiff shall file an indemnity bond to be approved by the Court in favor of defendants above named in the sum of Five Thousand ($5,000.00) Dollars.

(Sgd.)   WM. C. VAN FLEET,
Judge of the United States District Court for the Northern District of California.

August 3d, 1923.

[Endorsed]:   Filed Aug. 4, 1923.   [74]

[Title of Court and Cause.]

PRELIMINARY INJUNCTION.

The President of the United States to MacGruer & Simpson (a Copartnership) and George Smith MacGruer and Robert Morton Simpson, Individually and Sometimes Doing Business as MacGruer & Co., and Their Clerks, Agents, Attorneys, Servants, and Workmen, GREETING:

WHEREAS, it has been represented to us in the United States District Court for the Northern District of California, Southern Division, that letters patent No. 1,212,331, were issued in due form of law on the 16th day of January, 1917, for an improvement in the manufacture of artificial stone structures to Paul E. Denivelle, and that you and each of you, jointly, severally and as copartners have infringed the rights secured by the aforesaid letters patent by making, using and selling to others artificial stone structures embodying the invention set forth and claimed in said letters patent and practicing the process claimed therein, contrary to the form of the statute in such cases made and provided:

NOW, THEREFORE, you, and each of you, your and each of your clerks, agents, servants, workmen and attorneys are [75] strictly commanded and enjoined under the pains and penalties which may fall upon you and each of you, in case of disobedience, that you forthwith, and until the further order, judgment and decree of this court, desist from making, using or selling artificial stone structures embodying the invention of said letters patent, substantially as described and claimed in said letters patent.

WITNESS, the Honorable WILLIAM C. VAN FLEET, Judge of the United States District Court for the Northern District of California, this 4th day of August, 1923.

[Seal]   WALTER B. MALING,
Clerk of the United States District Court for the
    Northern District of California.

RETURN ON SERVICE OF WRIT.

United States of America,
Northern District of California,—ss. 1078.

I hereby certify and return that I served the annexed preliminary injunction, on the therein named MacGruer & Simpson, a copartnership, by handing to and leaving a true and certified copy thereof with, George Smith MacGruer, a copartner of the firm of MacGruer & Simpson (a copartnership), personally, at the city and county of San Francisco, in said district on the 20th day of August, A. D. 1923.

J. B. HOLOHAN,
U. S. Marshal.
By I. W. Grover,
Deputy. [76]

RETURN ON SERVICE OF WRIT.

United States of America,
Northern District of California,—ss.

I hereby certify and return that I served the annexed preliminary injunction on the therein named George Smith MacGruer, by handing to and leaving a true and certified copy thereof with George Smith MacGruer, personally, at the city and county of San Francisco, in said district on the 20th day of August, A. D. 1923.

J. B. HOLOHAN,
U. S. Marshal.
By I. W. Grover,
Deputy.

[Endorsed]: Filed Aug. 22, 1923.   [77]

[Title of Court and Cause.]

INJUNCTION BOND.

The United States of America,
Northern District of California,
Southern Division,—ss.

KNOW ALL MEN BY THESE PRESENTS
that Fidelity and Deposit Company of Maryland, a
corporation organized and existing under the laws
of the State of Maryland, and duly licensed to
transact a general surety business in the State of
California, is held and firmly bound unto the defendants above named in the sum of Five Thousand
($5,000.00) Dollars, to the payment of which it
binds itself.

The condition of the above obligation is such, that
whereas, Paul E. Denivelle, a citizen of the United
States and a resident of the city and county of San
Francisco, State of California, having filed in the
United States District Court for the Northern District of California, Southern Division, a bill against
the defendants above named and having obtained
an allowance of an injunction, as prayed for in said
bill, [78] from said court. Now, if the said Fidelity and Deposit Company of Maryland shall
abide the decision of said court and pay all moneys
and costs which shall be adjudged against it in case
the said injunction shall be dissolved, then these
présents shall be void; otherwise to remain in full
force.

IN TESTIMONY WHEREOF, the said surety
has caused its corporate name and seal to be hereunto affixed by its duly authorized officers at the
city and county of San Francisco, State of California, on the 2d day of August, A. D. 1923.

FIDELITY AND DEPOSIT COMPANY
OF MARYLAND.

[Seal] By EDGAR H. BENNETT,

Its Attorney-in-Fact.

And S. CHINO,

Its Agent.

The foregoing bond is approved.

WM. C. VAN FLEET,

Judge.

[Endorsed]: Filed Aug. 4, 1923. [79]

[Title of Court and Cause.]

FURTHER PARTICULARS IN REGARD TO PLAINTIFF'S INTERROGATORIES.

Now come the defendants by their counsel,
R. M. J. Armstrong, Esq., with further particulars
in regard to plaintiff's interrogatories requested and
based on answer to bill of complaint first filed and
stipulation between counsel.

(1) Referring to paragraph 14 of the amended
answer, defendants will not rely upon the publication "Limestone and Marble" as same was inadvertently cited instead of another publication which

defendants had intended to use to show the prior state of the art.

(2) Paragraph 12 of the amended answer denies the validity of plaintiff's patent on the ground that there is no invention because of common practice in the plasterer's art, and that in view of such common practice the subject matter of the patent constitutes nothing more than the exercise of the skill and knowledge of the ordinary plasterers. Defendants did not intend under that section of the answer to refer to any particular job, but based on the prior state of the art as will be shown by the testimony of witnesses whose names and addresses have been duly made known to plaintiff. Defendants will additionally rely on the [80] public use and sale on the part of plaintiff not only on the Pennsylvania job, but the Lord and Taylor, 34th and 5th Avenue, New York City, and other jobs as may be made known to defendants on examination of the witnesses.

(3) Referring to paragraph 13 of the amended answer, defendants say that they refer to any and all patents of the prior art for the purpose of showing the state of the art.

R. M. J. ARMSTRONG,
Solicitor for Defendants.

MUNN, ANDERSON & MUNN,
Of Counsel.

Dated: San Francisco, California, February 16, 1924.

[Endorsed]: Filed Feb. 18, 1924. [81]

[Title of Court and Cause.]

STIPULATION AS TO FORM OF RECORD.

IT IS HEREBY STIPULATED that the testimony, including the depositions, be set out in full in the exact words of the witnesses in the form of question and answer.

CHAS. E. TOWNSEND,

Solicitor and Counsel for Plaintiff.

R. M. J. ARMSTRONG,

Solicitor and Counsel for Defendants.

So ordered.

BOURQUIN,

Judge.

[Endorsed]: Filed Jun. 7, 1924. [82]

[Title of Court and Cause.]

DEPOSITIONS.

Depositions taken on behalf of the defendants, pursuant to notice and an order of the court, and under the provisions of the equity rules of the Supreme Court of the United States and the Revised Statutes of the United States in such cases made and provided, beginning this 27th day of February, 1924, at the offices of Munn, Anderson & Munn, Transportation Building, Washington, D. C.; this deposition being taken at this time contrary to the order stated in the notice, at the request of Mr. Loftus, counsel for the plaintiff, and at whose re-

quest also the beginning of the taking of depositions
in New York is continued until Monday, the third
day of March, 1924, at the New York offices of
Munn, Anderson & Munn.

APPEARANCES:

WILLIAM A. LOFTUS, Esq., of Counsel for
    Plaintiff.

T. HART ANDERSON, Esq., of Counsel for De-
    fendants. [83]

It is stipulated and agreed by and between counsel for the respective parties that the deposition to
be here taken may be taken before Lloyd L. Harkins, Esq., a notary public in and for the District
of Columbia, as special examiner, and that either
party may, if he so desires, have an order *nunc pro
tunc* entered herein so appointing the said Lloyd L.
Harkins, as special examiner; and that the said
deposition shall be taken stenographically by Edwin Dice.

DEPOSITION OF JACOB M. KRAFFT, FOR DEFENDANTS.

JACOB M. KRAFFT, a witness called on behalf
of the defendants, having been first duly cautioned
and sworn, in answer to interrogatories propounded
by Mr. Anderson, testified as follows, to wit:
(By Mr. ANDERSON.)

Q. 1. Your full name, Mr. Krafft, is Jacob M.
Krafft?   A. Yes, sir.

Q. 2. How old are you, Mr. Krafft?   A. 47.

Q. 3. Where do you reside?

(Deposition of Jacob M. Krafft.)

A. In Alexandria, Virginia.

Q. 4. What is your business, Mr. Krafft?

A. Plastering contractor.

Q. 5. How long have you been engaged in that business? A. For 22 years.

Q. 6. Are you in business on your own account, or are you associated with some other concern?

A. The style of my concern is Krafft-Murphy Company, Washington, D. C., at the present time.

Q. 7. A corporation? [84] A. A corporation.

Q. 8. How long have you been connected with that corporation? A. Five years.

Q. 9. Located in Washington during that time? A. Yes, sir.

Q. 10. Now, before that where were you located and with whom were you associated?

A. I was associated with McNulty Bros., Inc., for 16 years, between 1902 and 1918.

Q. 11. Where was that concern located, McNulty Bros., Inc.

A. Their principal offices was located in New York City.

Q. 12. And was that where you were stationed while with that concern? A. Yes, sir.

Q. 13. Is that concern still in existence? A. No.

Q. 14. When did it cease its existence?

A. They entered a voluntary petition in bankruptcy in June, 1918.

Q. 15. What was the business of McNulty Bros., Inc., of New York?

(Deposition of Jacob M. Krafft.)

A. Metal furring, lathing, plastering, and imitation stone.

Q. 16. Was there anyone by the name of McNulty connected with that concern?

A. Mr. P. H. McNulty. [85]

Q. 17. Was he the only McNulty connected with that concern?   A. Yes, sir.

Q. 18. Do you know whether or not he is still alive?   A. No; he is not.

Q. 19. He is dead?   A. He died in 1916.

Q. 20. What was the nature of your duties with McNulty Bros., Inc.?

A. I was vice-president of the company and general manager, and my duties covered the supervision over estimating, the diplomatic compact with our clients in general, and the general supervision of the working elements of the shop and the outside working forces.

Q. 21. While you were associated with McNulty Bros., Inc., was there a man connected with that concern by the name of Lewis Massimo?

A. Yes, sir.

Q. 22. While you were with that concern, did that concern do any work in connection with the building of the Pennsylvania Railroad Station in New York City?

A. We erected a sample of imitation travertine.

Mr. LOFTUS.—I object to any questions and testimony relative to any travertine work alleged to have been done in the Pennsylvania Railway Terminal, on account of the lack of proper notice.

(Deposition of Jacob M. Krafft.)

(By Mr. ANDERSON.)

Q. 23. Do you mean that a sample of imitation travertine [86] was installed in the Pennsylvania Station by McNulty Bros., Inc.?

A. Yes, sir.

Q. 24. When was that done?

A. May I look at some of my papers?

Q. 25. Yes.

Mr. LOFTUS.—Let me ask a question before you do that.

(By Mr. LOFTUS.)

Q. Are you able to answer the question without referring to your notes?

A. I can answer it as to the year when the sample was put up, if that is sufficient, I can answer it.

Mr. LOFTUS.—I just want the record to show what the situation is.

(By Mr. ANDERSON.)

Q. 26. That is sufficient. Go ahead and answer it.   A. 1909.

Q. 27. Can you tell us exactly the location of that particular sample of imitation travertine which was installed in the Pennsylvania Station by McNulty Bros, Inc., in 1909?

A. That sample was put up on the southwest corner of the arcade leading from Seventh Avenue to the main waiting-room, and consisted of a section of a cornice directly below the vaulted ceiling.

Q. 28. Can you tell us the name of the employee

(Deposition of Jacob M. Krafft.)
of McNulty Bros., Inc., who supervised and installed that sample?

A. The sample was made by a man named Adolph Giobbe, and the sample was installed by some of our regular building [87] employees.

Q. 29. Can you tell us the circumstances which led to the McNulty Bros., Inc., installing that sample of imitation travertine?

A. As I recall it there were four concerns invited to experiment with the producing of a satisfactory imitation of a stone known as travertine stone, and to erect a sample in place in the Pennsylvania Station, on the condition that a bid for the work had to be submitted simultaneously with the sample, and that the successful bidder would be obliged to pay to each of the other contractors submitting a sample the sum of $200.

Mr. LOFTUS.—I move to strike the answer, for the reasons that the defendants' answer on file herein does not set up the name of this witness as one having any knowledge of any alleged prior use; and, furthermore, in the notice of the taking of this deposition no information has been given as to the place where any alleged prior use coming within the knowledge of this witness may have occurred.

Mr. ANDERSON.—Counsel for the defendants will reserve his argument as to the admissibility of this evidence until the trial.

(By Mr. ANDERSON.)

Q. 30. Do you know from whom these various

(Deposition of Jacob M. Krafft.)
contesting contractors obtained invitation to bid
and erect samples?

A. I could name only three of the four on my
present recollection, and they were H. W. Miller,
Mr. Denivelle, and McNulty Bros. There was a
fourth, and I cannot recall the name. [88]

Q. 31. But that does not answer the question.
I will ask you another question: From whom did
McNulty Bros., Inc., receive an invitation to bid
and erect a sample of imitation travertine in the
Pennsylvania Station?

A. From the George A. Fuller Company.

Q. 32. That is the George A. Fuller Company, a
building corporation of New York?

A. Yes, sir.

Q. 33. Who got the contract for that work, do
you know? A. Mr. Denivelle.

Q. 34. And Mr. Denivelle is here present, is he
not? A. He is.

Q. 35. Were you acquainted with Mr. Denivelle
before you came into this room this morning?

A. We have not met a great many times before
this, but I always knew Mr. Denivelle by sight.

Q. 36. Did Mr. Miller erect a specimen of artificial travertine in the Pennsylvania Station at
the time McNulty Bros., Inc., erected one?

A. He did.

Q. 37. And also Mr. Denivelle? A. Yes, sir.

Q. 38. And one other whose name you cannot
recall? A. Yes, sir.

Q. 39. Were those specimens erected by those

(Deposition of Jacob M. Krafft.)

contesting contractors in close relation to each other? A. You mean in quality?

Q. 40. No; in location. [89]

A. No; they were not.

Q. 41. After they were erected, what happened?

A. Some time later the decision was made on the basis of price submitted, as I was informed, Mr. Denivelle's price being the lowest, and he was awarded the contract.

Mr. LOFTUS.—I move to strike the answer as hearsay.

(By Mr. ANDERSON.)

Q. 42. Did McNulty Bros., Inc., receive from Mr. Denivelle, $200 in accordance with the arrangement which you have stated on this record?

A. Yes, sir.

Q. 43. You say Mr. Denivelle got this contract. Was it Mr. Denivelle in person, or the company with which he was connected?

A. I believe it was a company. When I say Mr. Denivelle I associate whatever company he had formed to do the work with Mr. Denivelle.

Q. 44. Well, when that contract was awarded, what happened to the specimen which had been constructed by McNulty Bros., Inc.?

A. I could not say of my own knowledge. It is possible it was left in place.

Mr. LOFTUS.—I move to strike the latter part of the answer, regarding possibilities.

(Deposition of Jacob M. Krafft.)
(By Mr. ANDERSON.)

Q. 45. What is your best recollection on that point, Mr. Krafft?

A. My recollection is that the sample was left in place, since it was put up there with due regard to the [90] location of the plumb-line and the level-line that the cornice was to occupy.

Q. 46. What is your best recollection as to when the Pennsylvania Station was completed and opened to the public?

Mr. LOFTUS.—That is objected to as irrelevant, immaterial and incompetent. Those matters can be proven.

Mr. ANDERSON.—I will withdraw that question.

(By Mr. ANDERSON.)

Q. 47. When the Pennsylvania Station was completed, did you inspect it?   A. I did.

Q. 48. Did you note the work which had been done by Mr. Denivelle at the time that station was completed?   A. I did.

Q. 49. Did Mr. Miller do some plastering work in the Pennsylvania Station harmonizing in color with the imitation travertine which was installed by Mr. Denivelle's company?

Mr. LOFTUS.—That is objected to as grossly leading and suggestive.

The WITNESS.—A. He did.

(By Mr. ANDERSON.)

Q. 50. At the time you examined the Pennsylvania Station, had Mr. Denivelle completed his work?

(Deposition of Jacob M. Krafft.)

Mr. LOFTUS.—That is objected to as calling for the opinion and conclusion of the witness.

The WITNESS.—A. The building was entirely completed when I saw it next.

(By Mr. ANDERSON.)

Q. 51. When was that? [91]

A. I would say that that must have been the last part of 1909 or the first part of 1910. I have no definite recollection on just the exact date when that took place, but it was directly after it was completed.

Q. 52. Are you familiar with the practice in the building trade of requiring bonds from contractors doing a job of the magnitude of the job done by Mr. Denivelle in the Pennsylvania Station?

A. It is a customary procedure to require bonds on most any subcontract work, big or little, especially when the responsibility and the ability of the bidder may be in question, and when there may be a doubt as to his ability to carry out the contract to be awarded to him.

Q. 53. Would your knowledge of the conditions of such bonds lead you to state whether it was customary to limit the obligation on those bonds to the time when the work was finished and turned over to the owner or architect?

Mr. LOFTUS.—That is objected to as calling for the opinion and conclusion of the witness.

The WITNESS.—A. My experience with all the bonds we have ever been called upon to furnish

(Deposition of Jacob M. Krafft.)
is that they extend for a period of 12 months after completion of the work.

(By Mr. ANDERSON.)

Q. 54. How many such bonds, approximately, were given by McNulty Bros., Inc., while you were connected with that company?

A. We furnished bonds on all the federal work that we performed, the furnishing of a bond being a customary requirement in that kind of work; and on some of the other [92] contracts of a private nature that we took, and I am not able to give you an exact number of bonds furnished, but there were quite a few.

Q. 55. Was it usual in those bonds to continue the obligation of the bond for 12 months after the work was finished?

A. Some bonds carried with them that obligation; others did not. The bonds that carried with them the obligation of maintenance for 12 months after completion are called maintenance bonds. The other bonds are merely performance bonds, so that in the case of a performance bond the bond was null and void when the work was completed.

Q. 56. Now, just what is the obligation under these so-called maintenance bonds which run for 12 months after the work is completed; I mean, as a usual thing in your line of work?

A. The usual terms of such bonds are that all defects arising out of the use of improper materials, and improper workmanship must be cor-

(Deposition of Jacob M. Krafft.)
rected within the 12 months covered in the bond at
the expense of the contractor furnishing the bond.

Q. 57. Now, based upon your experience in this
building trade, does the giving of such maintenance bond indicate that the work has been completed?

Mr. LOFTUS.—That is objected to as calling
for the opinion and conclusion of the witness.

Mr. ANDERSON.—Absolutely an opinion.

The WITNESS.—A. I would say no. [93]
(By Mr. ANDERSON.)

Q. 58. What does it indicate?

Mr. LOFTUS.—The same objection.

The WITNESS.—A. It merely indicates—it
marks the fulfillment of some part of the requirement of the plans and specifications which obli-
gate the subcontractor to furnish such a bond. If
I were to sign a contract to-day I would know now
whether a maintenance bond was required or no.
If none were required by the plans and specifications I would not expect to furnish any.
(By Mr. ANDERSON.)

Q. 59. But do you desire the Court to understand that you testify that the giving of a maintenance bond does not indicate that that particular
job has been completed?

A. Not in a case of that kind; the giving of a
maintenance bond after the same had been provided for in the specifications is merely a part fulfillment of your obligation to the owner or to the
contractor.

(Deposition of Jacob M. Krafft.)

Q. 60. Is it not true, however, that that maintenance bond is to cover defects which may arise in
the work which has been done, during the 12
months following completion of the work?

Mr. LOFTUS.—That is objected to as leading
and argumentative.

The WITNESS.—A. Yes, sir.

(By Mr. ANDERSON.)

Q. 61. Do you recall any imitation travertine
work other than this sample, which was done by
McNulty Bros., Inc., after [94] that specimen
was made?

Mr. LOFTUS.—That is objected to for the reasons heretofore stated, namely, that no notice has
been given either in the defendants' answer, or in
the notice of the taking of this witness' deposition
as to the place where any alleged prior use may
have occurred.

The WITNESS.—A. I have here (producing
papers)—

(By Mr. ANDERSON.)

Q. 62. You have what?

A. I have here a transcript of the records from
the books of McNulty Bros., which—

Q. 63. Now, you propose to read, do you, Mr.
Krafft, from a letter which you have received
from some person giving you this information?

A. In order to answer your question I have to
refer to some information I called for from the
books of the company.

Q. 64. And from whom?

(Deposition of Jacob M. Krafft.)

A. From Mr. P. G. Moore, Jr., who has custody of the books.

Q. 65. And he wrote you in response to your inquiry?

A. Yes; and I have the dates on which a contract was taken for imitation travertine work in another building, not in the Pennsylvania Station, and I propose to answer your question by referring to this letter. I am not offering the letter.

(By Mr. LOFTUS.)

Q. Did you see the books, Mr. Krafft?

A. I was in intimate touch with the work at the time, but I do not expect to answer any questions for court record [95] without referring to the books, or an extract of the books.

(By Mr. ANDERSON.)

Q. 66. Now, I will ask you, Mr. Krafft, having your recollection refreshed by what Mr. Moore has written to you, do you recall the work about which he has informed you in his letter?

A. I do. I recall everything but the exact date I am asked for.

Mr. LOFTUS.—I object to that.

(By Mr. ANDERSON.)

Q. 67. Now, give us your recollection as to the work.

Mr. LOFTUS.—This line of examination is objected to as grossly improper. This witness has already answered that he could not answer the question without consulting a letter which some

(Deposition of Jacob M. Krafft.)

unknown person has written to him which, therefore, makes his answer purely hearsay.

(By Mr. ANDERSON.)

Q. 68. Now, give us your recollection as to the
other jobs of imitation travertine which were done
by McNulty Bros., Inc.?

A. We signed a contract with the George A.
Fuller Company on April 21, 1921, for a certain
amount of imitation travertine work in the Widener Building, in Philadelphia.

Q. 69. Do you remember that work?

A. He said 1921. That should be 1912. And
the work was done during 1914 and 1915.

Q. 70. Do you remember that work?

A. I do. [96]

Q. 71. Who was in charge of that work on behalf of McNulty Bros., Inc.?

A. Mr. Massimo.

Q. 72. Now, was there any other job of imitation travertine done by McNulty Bros., Inc., which
you can recall?

A. We had a subsequent contract on the same
building, the Widener Building, in Philadelphia,
some time later on.

(By Mr. LOFTUS.)

Q. You are still referring to that letter, aren't
you, Mr. Krafft?

A. No; not now. I am not now going to give
you any subsequent dates, because I haven't got
those.

Q. You have still got the letter in front of you.

(Deposition of Jacob M. Krafft.)

A. I have.

(By Mr. ANDERSON.)

Q. 73. For the purpose of the record, to whom did you write for the purpose of getting this information as to the dates?

A. I wrote to Mr. P. G. Moore, Jr., who was the bookkeeper for the McNulty Bros., Inc., while they existed, and later he was retained by the receiver as his assistant, and he is now employed by the estate of P. H. McNulty, in charge of the real estate matters, and also in charge of the books of the defunct company.

Q. 74. And where is Mr. Moore located now?

A. Mr. Moore is located at 549 West 52d Street, New York City, in the McNulty Building.

Q. 75. Did your firm,—McNulty Bros., Inc., submit a bid for the imitation travertine in the Pennsylvania Station [97] at or about the time it completed this specimen that was installed therein?

A. We did.

Q. 76. Now, Mr. Krafft, Mr. Loftus, who is here present, did you receive a visit from him within the last week or ten days in Washington?

A. There was a young man, not Mr. Loftus, called on me, stating that he represented the Denivelle side of this controversy.

Q. 77. When did he call upon you?

A. About a week ago.

Q. 78. And what did he say to you?

A. He asked me if I would not tell him the nature of my testimony to be taken by you; and I replied

(Deposition of Jacob M. Krafft.)

that I would prefer not to tell him, and that you knew all about it, and if it were proper for him to know that you would undoubtedly tell him.

Q. 79. Did he give his name?

A. He gave his name, but I don't recall it.

Q. 80. It was not Mr. Loftus or Mr. Denivelle?

A. No.

Mr. ANDERSON.—That is all. Direct examination closed.

Cross-examination.

(By Mr. LOFTUS.)

XQ. 1. Isn't it a fact this young man that you have just referred to who called on you, asked you whether or not your testimony related to some prior use—that is, to some particular building where imitation travertine had been [98] installed? Is that what he asked you?

A. No.

XQ. 2. And didn't he, in the course of his conversation, ask you whether imitation travertine, to your knowledge, had ever been put in any public buildings in the City of Washington? A. No.

XQ. 3. You are not positive of that, are you?

A. Yes, sir.

XQ. 4. And didn't he mention as one of those buildings the Smithsonian Institute? A. No.

XQ. 5. You have no recollection of that?

A. No such conversation took place.

XQ. 6. And didn't he further tell you that his purpose in coming there was to find out whether you had any knowledge of any prior use of imita-

(Deposition of Jacob M. Krafft.)

tion travertine in any buildings in the City of Washington?

A. That was evidently his purpose, but he didn't express it in that way.

XQ. 7. And didn't he explain to you at the time that under the law that we were entitled to have notice of the places where any of these alleged public uses took place? A. Yes; he said that.

XQ. 8. He didn't say that? A. Yes, sir.

XQ. 9. And you refused to tell him?

A. No. [99]

XQ. 10. You wouldn't even mention the Pennsylvania Terminal, would you? A. No.

XQ. 11. You didn't mention the Widener Building? A. No.

XQ. 12. You told him that Mr. Anderson had cautioned you to say nothing to anybody with regard to the character of testimony you should give? A. No, sir.

XQ. 13. You didn't say that? A. No, sir.

XQ. 14. You are positive of that?

A. Positive.

XQ. 15. You didn't say anything about Mr. Anderson having cautioned you? A. I did not.

XQ. 16. You did not? A. No, sir.

XQ. 17. What else did you say to this young man?

A. I told him if it was his right for him to know anything about the nature of my testimony Mr. Anderson was fully acquainted with the character of my testimony and would give it to him.

(Deposition of Jacob M. Krafft.)

XQ. 18. Did you say anything else to him?

A. No, sir.

XQ. 19. You didn't tell him anything about what the Master Plasterers' Association was going to do? A. Yes, sir. [100]

XQ. 20. What did you tell him about that?

A. I told him they were going to take it up and come into court alongside of MacGruer and Simpson.

XQ. 21. That you were a member of the Plasterers' Association? A. Yes, sir.

XQ. 22. And you were going to retain other counsel? A. Yes, sir.

XQ. 23. And who was that counsel to be?

A. Melville Church.

XQ. 24. Did you give any reason to this young man why this numerous association was going to band together to defeat Mr. Denivell's patent?

A. I may have; I don't recall it.

XQ. 25. You are a member of that association?

A. I am.

XQ. 26. And you are an interested party in this litigation, are you?

A. I might answer that yes and no.

XQ. 27. How do you happen to be here? Why are you here as a witness?

A. I am here at the request of Mr. Anderson.

XQ. 28. And at the request of this association of plasterers? A. No.

XQ. 29. Just tell us for the purpose of the record what this Master Plasterers' Association is; how

(Deposition of Jacob M. Krafft.)
extensive its operations are, and where its headquarters are located?

A. The headquarters are in Chicago. The
Association [101] embraces local associations in
all the principal cities of the United States and
Canada.

XQ. 30. Have they an international or national
organization any place?   A. Yes; international.

XQ. 31. That is in Chicago?

A. The title of the association is the Contracting
Plasterers' International Association.

XQ. 32. Just how do they propose to handle the
expense of this litigation? Is there an assessment
made on you as a member?

A. I decline to say, because that matter has not
been taken up yet.

XQ. 33. Do you pay dues to this organization,
or assessments of any kind?   A. We do.

XQ. 34. Do you make and install imitation travertine in your business here in Washington, D. C.?

A. We do.

XQ. 35. In other words, you infringe the Denivelle patents, do you?

A. We don't think so. We do not believe Mr.
Denivelle has any patent rights in this patent.

XQ. 36. In other words, you take issue with the
Court of Appeals for the Ninth Circuit, do you?

A. If that is what it means, we do.

XQ. 37. But if the patent is good you do infringe
it, do you not? [102]

A. We have to admit it then.

(Deposition of Jacob M. Krafft.)

XQ. 38. You are afraid you may be sued later as an infringer?

A. We might be sued. I don't think so. I think this case will end it.

XQ. 39. Have you any objection to showing me that letter that you have read herein giving your direct testimony?

A. None whatever. (Handing papers to Mr. Loftus.) That reference to the year 1921 is a misprint, as you will notice, since a contract taken in 1921 could not have been performed in 1914 and 1915.

XQ. 40. And it is from this letter written by P. G. Moore, under date of January 9, 1924, that you obtained your data that was set out in your answers that you have given here?

A. On the dates only.

XQ. 41. I notice that this letter refers to a letter written by you on the 31st of December, 1923. What was the occasion of your writing to Mr. P. G. Moore under that date?

A. A request by Mr. MacGruer that we assist him to the best of our possible ability in handling this case, and furnish with our information the exact dates on which work had been taken and performed; and without reference to the books I could not possibly give him them.

XQ. 42. Mr. McGruer, the defendant, was around to see you, was he? [103]

A. He was later on. I think he asked for this information before he called on me.

(Deposition of Jacob M. Krafft.)

XQ. 43. Well, what was the occasion of asking for this information prior to the time that Mr. MacGruer called on you?

A. Some correspondence had passed between Mr. MacGruer and our company.

Mr. LOFTUS.—I ask that this letter be copied into the record.

Mr. ANDERSON.—I have no objection to it if at the same time Mr. Krafft's letter, to which this is a reply, is copied. I have not seen either one of them. You may have them copied.

(By Mr. ANDERSON.)

Q. Is your copy there, Mr. Krafft?   A. Yes, sir.

Mr. ANDERSON.—Have them both copied on the record.

The WITNESS.—A. Here is mine. (Handing a paper to Mr. Loftus.)

Mr. ANDERSON.—Do you want these letters in?

Mr. LOFTUS.—The one I asked for. I don't care whether the other one goes in, or not.

Mr. ANDERSON.—I ask that they both go in.

(By Mr. LOFTUS.)

XQ. 44. You stated in your direct examination that you believed the sample of Imitation Travertine which McNulty Bros., Inc. made for the Pennsylvania Station was left in place there?

A. Yes, sir.   [104]

XQ. 45. What leads you to that belief?

A. There is no reason why it should have been taken down; it was in its proper place and was a good imitation.

(Deposition of Jacob M. Krafft.)

XQ. 46. You don't know whether it was taken down, or not? A. No; I don't.

XQ. 47. It was a guess on your part?

A. Yes; it was probably inspired by the feeling of what we would do if we had the contract and had a sample of that kind left in place there on that particular corner. We would leave it.

XQ. 48. In order to save expense of replacing? A. Yes, sir.

XQ. 49. Don't you remember, as a matter of fact, that that sample was taken back to your shop?

A. No; it wasn't.

XQ. 50. You have no recollection of it?

A. It was not taken back to our shop. I never saw it after it was put up in the building.

XQ. 51. When did you last see it?

A. I saw it up in place a short while before the awarding of the contract was decided.

XQ. 52. Well, did you see it at any time thereafter? A. I did not.

XQ. 53. I believe you stated that you examined this travertine work after the Pennsylvania Station was completed. Did you see the McNulty sample there at that time?

A. Well, I should say that there would not be such a noticeable difference in the work performed under this [105] contract and the sample furnished by McNulty so as to make it apparent from a distance of 25 feet, standing on the floor.

XQ. 54. In other words, you didn't see it then? Is that your answer?

(Deposition of Jacob M. Krafft.)

A. Naturally the work was performed according to plans and specifications and that corner was occupied with a cornice similar to the one we had put up there as a sample.

XQ. 55. Do you have any recollection of the location of that slab which the McNulty Bros. put in the Pennsylvania Station?   A. I have.

XQ. 56. You have no recollection?   A. I have.

XQ. 57. Can you tell us where it was located in the building?   A. I told you before.

XQ. 58. Just repeat that?

A. On the southwest corner of the arcade leading from Seventh Avenue to the main waiting-room.

XQ. 59. Can you tell us more definitely what you mean by the arcade of the station; where it begins and where it ends?

A. I can sketch it out for you.

XQ. 60. Yes; if you will do that, on a blank sheet of paper.

(Thereupon the witness drew a sketch on a piece of paper, exhibiting the same to Mr. Loftus.)

The WITNESS.—A. Here you are. Here is where the sample was (indicating on the sketch). [106]

XQ. 61. You have written there "sample"?

A. Yes, sir.

XQ. 62. At what height from the floor was that sample located?

A. I would say it was about 20 to 25 feet.

XQ. 63. I notice in this sketch that in the corner

(Deposition of Jacob M. Krafft.)
of this room you have shown a square. Please
tell us what that represents?

A. Why, I probably have not shown this architecturally correct, and it is my recollection that
there are columns on each of the four sides so as to
take the different alignment of these false projections that have been set into each corner similarly
here (indicating) and here (indicating) so that
the overhead work would balance on the center
lines here (indicating).

XQ. 64. Now, on what part was the sample
erected?   A. On the corner.
(By Mr. ANDERSON.)

Q. The southwest corner?

A. On the southwest corner.
(By Mr. LOFTUS.)

XQ. 65. On the corner of the part which you
have called an overhanging—well, just mark on
this sketch, Mr. Krafft, with a small cross there
exactly where the sample was?

A. I have marked it. It occupied a space on
this corner (indicating) of the projection; approximately two feet each way.

XQ. 66. It was a miter? [107]

A. It was a miter.

XQ. 67. A miter meaning an external and right-
angled piece?   A. Yes, sir.

Mr. LOFTUS.—I ask that the sketch just made
by the witness be marked Plaintiff's Exhibit 'A'
for Identification and be attached to the witness'
deposition.

(Deposition of Jacob M. Krafft.)

(The sketch referred to was marked Plaintiff's Exhibit 'A' for Identification and is attached at the end of this deposition.)

(By Mr. LOFTUS.)

XQ. 68. In other words, it was a part of a cornice some 20 or 25 feet from the floor in this particular corner of the rotunda?   A. Yes, sir.

XQ. 69. Just what part, if any, did you have to do with the making or erecting of this sample in the Pennsylvania Station?

A. I supervised all attempts in this imitation, practically daily, until the sample was past a point of perfection where I decided it was good enough to put in here as an exhibit.

XQ. 70. But you did not make the sample?

A. No, sir; I did not make it myself.

XQ. 71. How long a period did these tests occupy?

A. I think they occupied a month, or more.

XQ. 72. How many employees did you have working on this particular job?   A. One.   [108]

XQ. 73. Who was that employee?

A. Adolph Giobbe.

XQ. 74. From whom did you receive the $200 that you referred to in your direct testimony?

A. From Mr. Denivelle, through his company.

XQ. 75. What was the purpose of that payment, if you know?

A. That was according to the terms of the contest, if you choose to call it a contest, that the successful bidder on this work was to pay each of the

(Deposition of Jacob M. Krafft.)

other contestants the sum of $200 for the sample—for the expense incurred in making the sample.

XQ. 76. That did not wholly reimburse you, however, did it? A. Sir?

XQ. 77. The $200 did not fully reimburse you for your expenses? A. No; not on our part.

XQ. 78. Your expenses were a great deal more than that? A. Yes, sir.

XQ. 79. In other words, it was sort of a consolation prize; is that correct? A. A booby prize.

XQ. 80. Did you ever examine the imitation travertine work in the Widener Building in Philadelphia? A. Yes, sir.

XQ. 81. When did you see it?

A. Why, I saw it quite often. McNulty Bros., Inc., [109] had an office in the Widener Building after it was completed, and every time I visited our office I had to march past it.

XQ. 82. That would be what year?

A. That would be between the years 1915 and 1918.

XQ. 83. Do you remember at that time that a question arose as to whether you were infringing Mr. Denivelle's patent? A. Yes, sir.

XQ. 84. You recall it?

A. Yes. Mr. Denivelle said we were not.

XQ. 85. Which Mr. Denivelle are you referring to? A. This Mr. Denivelle.

XQ. 86. You heard him make that statement?
A. No; I didn't.

XQ. 87. You are giving hearsay then, are you?

(Deposition of Jacob M. Krafft.)

A. The statement I make here is based upon the fact that Mr. Denivelle later alleged an infringement of his patent and when, in company with Mr. P. H. McNulty and Mr. Massimo he was taken to our shop in Philadelphia and shown the method of producing this imitation travertine he declared that was not in accordance with his patent and was no infringement upon his patent rights, and from that time on we heard nothing more about it.

XQ. 88. You heard Mr. Denivelle make those statements?

A. I did not, but Mr. Massimo did.

XQ. 89. When did Mr. P. H. McNulty die?

A. In June, 1916.

Mr. LOFTUS.—I think that is all. [110]

Redirect Examination.

(By Mr. ANDERSON.)

RDQ. 1. Mr. Krafft, when was this Widener job finished? I mean the Widener Building in Philadelphia, so far as your imitation travertine was concerned?

A. We had two contracts of imitation travertine on that Widener Building.

RDQ. 2. When did you finish the first one?

A. The first one was finished about 1915, and the second was finished about a year later.

RDQ. 3. Do you remember whether it was in connection with the first contract, or the second one, that this question of the infringement of Mr. Denivelle's patent came up?

A. It was on the second one.

(Deposition of Jacob M. Krafft.)·

RDQ. 4. On the second contract?   A. Yes, sir.

RDQ. 5. And that was finished in 1916?

A. About that time.

RDQ. 6. When McNulty Bros., Inc., was asked to submit this specimen of Imitation Travertine, were they given anything to follow in its construction?

A. They were told to get samples of the real stone from Patterson and Isley, marble contractors in New York City, and do the best they could with this.

RDQ. 7. And that was done?   A. Yes, sir.

RDQ. 8. That is, McNulty Bros., Inc., obtained a specimen of the genuine Travertine stone?   [111]

A. Yes, sir.

RDQ. 9. And endeavored to copy it?

A. Yes, sir.

Mr. ANDERSON.—That is all.

Mr. LOFTUS.—I have nothing further.

(The witness was excused.)

Mr. ANDERSON.—Counsel for defendants now ask that the two letters referred to be copied on the record; that is, a letter from P. G. Moore, Jr., to Mr. J. M. Krafft, dated January 9, 1924, which is copied on the record at the request of counsel for plaintiff; and a carbon copy of a letter addressed to Mr. P. G. Moore, dated December 31, 1923, signed "Krafft–Murphy Company, By ——."

(By Mr. ANDERSON.)

RDQ. 10. Mr. Krafft, that carbon copy is a carbon copy of the letter sent by you to Mr. Moore, is it?   A. Yes sir.

(The letters are as follows:)

McNULTY BROS., INC.

Plain & Decorative Plastering

Metal Furring & Lathing

Imitation Caen Stone

Modeling.

549–551 West 52nd Street.

New York, Jan. 9th, 1924.

Mr. J. M. Krafft,

710–14th St. N. W.

Washington, D. C.

Dear Jake: [112]

Regarding the Travertine Stone sample for Pennsylvania Hotel of which you wrote in your letter of the 31st ultimo, would state that the estimates submitted were long ago destroyed, as we had to make room for renting. However, I found that we received a check for the sample of caen stone from

The Denevelle Hydraulic Composite Stone Co. on June 3d, 1909—200.00

Both the Journal, Cash, & Ledger show this transaction, and a photographic copy with other testimony I think would prove the transaction. Massimo tells me that it is his recollection the successful bidder was to pay for the sample. Three bids were requested by the architect. Miller also states that Massimo tells him he consulted with Deneville at the time we did the Widener Building as to what patent rights he had, and was told he had none. Have you any recollection of this transaction? The Widener contract was signed with The Fuller Co. on April 21st, 1921, and the work done during 1914 & 15.

I will leave you to impart this information to MacGruer & Simpson, as the proposition will now probably shape in your mind, and the more condensed the statements the better for the results to all. With best wishes, I am,

Yours truly,

P. G. MOORE, JR.

P.S.—Miller thinks that most of his papers were destroyed in the fire he had two or three years ago.

The stone was manufactured for us by Giobbo. [113]

"Dec. 31, 1923.

Mr. P. G. Moore,
    551 West 52nd Street,
        New York, N. Y.

Dear Peter:

In the matter of the suit against MacGruer & Simpson, by P. E. Denivelle, upon alleged infringement of certain patent rights, covering the manufacture and use of Imitation Travertine, we believe that the circumstances connected with our bid for the Imitation Travertine work at the Pennsylvania station will prove to be of service to the defendant in this case.

There is certain information which I cannot get without access to the books, which I would like you to procure for me, as follows:

(a) Date of the bid submitted by McNulty

Bros., for Imitation Travertine work in the Pennsylvania station (on or about February, 1909).

(b) The amount of bid.

(c) Date of payment for sample erected in place. (In connection with this item I might explain that several contractors were invited to submit samples in place, for which they were to receive $200 each. This payment in all probability was made by the Geo. A. Fuller Company, the contractors, or possibly by the architects (McKim, Head & White) direct.

When you locate a copy of the Pennsylvania station bid, it would be advisable for you to send me a transcript of the same. We understand that Mr. MacGruer has seen you, [114] and that you have offered your services in any matter which would require access to the books and data of McNulty Bros., Inc. We are equally anxious to assist in a successful defense of this case, as it will be for the interest of the trade in general, and we would ask you to forward the information requested above. as promptly as possible.

Yours very truly,

KRAFFT–MURPHY COMPANY,

By ————.''

Deposition closed.

Signature waived.

Adjournment is now taken to the office of Munn, Anderson & Munn, Woolworth Building, New York City, Monday, March 3, 1924, at 10 o'clock A. M. [115]

United States of America,
District of Columbia,—ss

I, Lloyd L. Harkins, a duly commissioned notary public in and for the District of Columbia, do hereby certify that pursuant to the stipulation made and entered into by and between the attorneys for the respective parties in the case of Paul E. Denivelle, plaintiff, vs. MacGruer & Simpson, a copartnership, and George Smith MacGruer and Robert Morton Simpson, individually, and sometimes doing business as MacGruer & Company, defendants, now pending in the District Court of the United States for the Northern District of California, Southern Division, I took the deposition of Jacob M. Krafft, a witness of lawful age, on behalf of the defendants, on the 27th day of February, 1924, at the offices of Munn, Anderson & Munn, Transportation Building, Washington, D. C.

I further certify that there were present at said hearing William A. Loftus, Esq., attorney for the plaintiff; and T. Hart Anderson, Esq., attorney for the defendants.

I further certify that before the taking of the deposition of said Jacob M. Krafft, he was duly sworn by me to tell the truth, the whole truth, and nothing but the truth, concerning the matters in controversy in said case about which he might be interrogated by the attorneys for the respective parties; that said examination was conducted by oral questions and answers; that said oral questions and answers were taken stenographically by Edwin

Dice and later transcribed on the typewriter under my direction and [116] supervision; that the foregoing is a true and correct transcript of the shorthand notes of said Edwin Dice of the questions and answers, and the objections and proceedings had at the time of taking said deposition.

I further certify that I have no interest in any manner whatsoever in the outcome of said proceeding; that I am not related to, in the employ of, or in any way connected with the parties to said proceeding or the attorneys for the respective parties.

I further certify that by stipulation of the attorneys representing the respective parties, the signature of the witness to said deposition was waived.

In witness whereof I have hereunto set my hand and affixed my notarial seal this 28th day of February, 1924.

[Seal]   LLOYD L. HARKINS,
                   Notary Public.

Notaries fees: $23.50 paid by defendant.

[Endorsed]: Filed Mch. 5, 1924. [117]

[Title of Court and Cause.]

Met pursuant to adjournment at the office of Munn, Anderson & Munn, Woolworth Building, New York City, this 3d day of March, 1924.

Present: WILLIAM A. LOFTUS, Esq., of Counsel for Plaintiff,
         T. HART ANDERSON, Esq., of Counsel for Defendants.

Counsel for plaintiff consents that the following

depositions may be taken before a notary public, Mr. Rollhaus, an employee of Munn & Co., and taken and transcribed by Miss Hoffman, an employee of defendants' counsel, and will make no objection thereto on that account. [118]

DEPOSITION OF CARL HENRY MEYN, FOR DEFENDANTS.

CARL HENRY MEYN, called as a witness on behalf of the defendants, having been duly cautioned and sworn, in answer to interrogatories propounded by Mr. Anderson, testified as follows:

Q. 1. Your full name is Carl Henry Meyn?

A. Yes.

Q. 2. How old are you, Mr. Meyn?   A. 50.

Q. 3. Where do you reside?

A. 1345 East 21st Street, Brooklyn.

Q. 4. What is your business, Mr. Meyn?

A. Plastering contractor.

Q. 5. How long have you been engaged in the business as plastering contractor?

A. In my own business 5 years.

Q. 6. That is to say, you have been in that business on your own account for 5 years?

A. Yes, sir.

Q. 7. And before that, what was your business?

A. I was treasurer of J. W. Kissell, Inc., plastering contractors, for 3 years.

Q. 8. And before that, what was your business?

A. Previous to that I was superintendent for H. W. [119] Miller, Inc., plastering contractors.

(Deposition of Carl Henry Meyn.)

Q. 9. Where are these two concerns located?

A. In New York City.

Q. 10. And how long were you with the Miller concern?   A. Twelve years.

Q. 11. And when did you first go with the Miller concern?   A. In 1904.

Q. 12. So that you have been engaged in the plastering contracting business since 1904?

A. Yes, sir.

Q. 13. While you were employed by H. W. Miller, Inc., did that concern do any work in connection with the building of the Pennsylvania Station in this city?   A. Yes, sir.

Q. 14. Please tell us just what work was done by the Miller Company in connection with the Pennsylvania Station?

Mr. LOFTUS.—Objection is made to any questions or testimony relating to any alleged prior uses in connection with the Pennsylvania Station for the reason that the answer on file here does not set forth the place where any alleged prior use took place within the knowledge of this witness except the address 41 East 22d Street.

(By Mr. ANDERSON.)

I reluctantly place upon this record at this time a statement in the nature of an argument which could more [120] conveniently be brought to the attention of the Court at the time of the trial of this cause. In so far as the objection which has been placed on this record by counsel for plaintiff is concerned, I suggest that he has no warrant to

(Deposition of Carl Henry Meyn.)

assume that I am trying to prove by this witness a so-called "prior" use, and even if I were, I propose to show this Court that it is admissible without notice, and that any other evidence which I may offer as showing the prior state of the art, which may involve the proof of a prior existing installation of artificial stone having the characteristics of that of the patent in suit, is admissible as showing the prior state of the art, without notice. I shall not repeat this argument during the taking of these depositions but shall submit the evidence of any prior structure, patent, publication or anything else I may find in the prior art as showing the state of the art, without notice.

Mr. LOFTUS.—Are we to understand by this that the purpose of this witness' testimony is merely to show the state of the prior art?

(By Mr. ANDERSON.)

That is one purpose—not the sole purpose. The main purpose of this witness' deposition is to show that this patentee put his alleged invention into public use in this city and other places, two years before he applied for his patent. [121]

(Question repeated.)

A. H. W. Miller, Inc., had the contract for the metal furring, lathing and plain and ornamental plastering.

Q. 15. Were you in the employ of the Miller Company at the time that work was done?

A. Yes, sir.

(Deposition of Carl Henry Meyn.)

Q. 16. Just what plastering was done by the Miller Company on the Pennsylvania Station?

A. All the plastering.

Q. 17. Do you make any distinction between the term "plastering" and installing so-called "artificial stone?"

Mr. LOFTUS.—Objected to as leading.

By Mr. ANDERSON (Addressing the Witness). You can answer it.

A. The installing of imitation stone is one branch of plastering.

Q. 18. Did the Miller Company install any artificial stone in the Pennsylvania Station?

Mr. LOFTUS.—Objected to as leading.

A. We installed samples of imitation stone.

Q. 19. When did they install samples of imitation stone in the Pennsylvania Station?

A. After we had started the plastering.

Q. 20. What year was that?

A. To the best of my recollection it was 1907. [122]

Q. 21. What was the character of this sample of artificial stone which was installed by the Miller Company in the Pennsylvania Station in 1907?

A. The sample was an imitation of travertin stone.

Q. 22. Did you have anything to do with the installation of that sample of travertin stone?

A. Yes, sir.

Q. 23. Please tell us just what you had to do with it?

(Deposition of Carl Henry Meyn.)

A. I was in charge of the making of those samples in the shop of H. W. Miller, Inc.

Q. 24. Can you tell us where those samples were installed—in what part of the station?

A. They were installed in what was called the rotunda of the arcade.

Q. 25. And where does that rotunda lead to?

A. It leads to the main waiting-room, the dining-room and the lunch-room.

Q. 26. And what entrance of the Station leads to that rotunda?

A. The Seventh Avenue entrance—Seventh Avenue Arcade.

Q. 27. What was the form of those samples of artificial travertin?

A. It was a section of the entablature.

Q. 28. What do you mean by the "entablature?"

A. The entablature is the cornice which was supported [123] by the pilasters of the arcade and rotunda.

Q. 29. How far from the floor would that sample be? A. About 20 feet.

Q. 30. Was it set in place where it was intended to remain?

Mr. LOFTUS.—Objected to as leading.

A. It was set in place alongside of samples of that kind submitted by other firms.

Q. 31. What other firms submitted samples of artificial travertin at that time?

A. McNulty Bros. and the Denivelle Hydraulic Composite Stone Company.

(Deposition of Carl Henry Meyn.)

Q. 32. Where did the Miller Company get its instructions to make and install that sample, if you know?

A. From McKim, Mead & White, Architects.

Q. 33. Did you have anything to follow in making that sample that you installed?

A. Yes, sir, a sample of natural travertin stone which was given us by the architects.

Q. 34. What was the object of the Miller Company making and installing that sample?

Mr. LOFTUS.—Objected to as calling for an opinion and conclusion of the witness.

A. The samples were to be made with a view to getting a very large contract for that type of imitation stone which was to be installed in that building and on which we were to submit estimates with the samples. [124]

Q. 35. Do you know whether the Miller Company submitted a bid or estimate on that contract?

A. Yes, sir.

Q. 36. Did you have anything to do with the preparation of that bid or estimate?

A. I made up that estimate.

Q. 37. Do you know to whom the Miller Company submitted its bid on that artificial travertin work on the Pennsylvania Station?

A. To the George A. Fuller Company.

Q. 38. Did the Miller Company get the contract?

A. They did not.

Q. 39. Who did get it, do you know?

(Deposition of Carl Henry Meyn.)

A. The Denivelle Hydraulic Composite Stone Company.

Q. 40. Did the Miller Company get paid for the sample which it submitted? A. Yes, sir.

Q. 41. Who paid the Miller Company for that sample? A. George A. Fuller Company.

Q. 42. I introduced you this morning to Mr. Denivelle, here present—had you ever met Mr. Denivelle before? A. Yes, sir.

Q. 43. When did you first meet Mr. Denivelle?

A. I have known Mr. Denivelle for 20 years.

Q. 44. Did you have charge of the plastering work which [125] was done by the Miller Company in the Pennsylvania Station? A. Yes, sir.

Q. 45. Now, just what plastering work did the Miller Company do in the Pennsylvania Station?

A. It did all the plastering.

Q. 46. Did the Miller Company furnish any artificial travertin for the Pennsylvania Station?

Mr. LOFTUS.—Objected to as leading.

A. Only the samples.

Q. 47. Were you present while the Denivelle Company was doing its work in furnishing artificial travertin for the Pennsylvania Station?

A. Yes, sir.

Q. 48. Can you state when that work was finished —the Denivelle travertin work in the Pennsylvania Station?

A. To the best of my recollection, about the early part of 1909.

Q. 49. Do you know whether anyone except the

(Deposition of Carl Henry Meyn.)
Miller Company submitted a bid for the imitation travertin work in the Pennsylvania Station?

A. Yes, sir, McNulty Brothers and the Denivelle Company.

Q. 50. Were you present at the opening of those bids?   A. No, sir.

Q. 51. Do you know whether or not the Denivelle Company was the lowest bidder?

A. I do not. [126]

Q. 52. In the preparation of your bid, did you work from any specifications?   A. Yes, sir.

Q. 53. Where did you get those specifications?

A. They were given us with the plans by the George A. Fuller Company.

Q. 54. Was there a man by the name of Webster on that Pennsylvania Station job?

A. Yes, sir; superintendent for the architects, McKim, Mead & White.

Q. 55. What was Webster's full name, do you know?   A. Daniel T. Webster.

Q. 56. Now, Mr. Meyn, will you tell us exactly the samples of artificial travertin which were installed by the Miller Company in the Pennsylvania Station, were made?

Mr. LOFTUS.—Objected to as incompetent, irrelevant and immaterial.

A. We were given a sample of the real stone from which we first made an impression; from this impression we then cast various veins of colored plaster composition. We then tried a method of reproducing the veinings and holes of the natural

(Deposition of Carl Henry Meyn.)

stone in a plaster cast, and we then cast from that. We tried casting the veins on marble slabs, using salt to obtain the holes, which salt we later washed out. We made crumbs of semi-dry material which we spread on the slab, over which we then poured the veins to back it up with the body [127] color of the material.

Q. 57. Which method did you employ in making the specimen which was actually installed by the Miller Company?

A. The latter method.

Q. 58. Were the samples submitted by McNulty Brothers and the Denivelle Company located in the same arcade and in the same entablature as the Miller sample?   A. Yes, sir.

Q. 59. Were these samples all under installation at the same time?   A. Yes, sir.

Q. 60. Do you know whether the sample installed by Miller was left in the place?

A. It was taken down.

Q. 61. Who took it down?   A. I don't recall.

Q. 62. Now, how long did you remain with Miller after the installation of that sample?

A. Until 1915.

Q. 63. To your knowledge, when was the Pennsylvania Station opened to the public?

Mr. LOFTUS.—Objected to as incompetent, irrelevant and immaterial, and not best evidence.

A. In 1909.

Q. 64. Did you see that Station and inspect the plastering [128] work and artificial travertin after it had been opened?   A. Yes, sir.

(Deposition of Carl Henry Meyn.)

Q. 65. How soon after?

A. Why, I saw it most every week going through the Station.

Q. 66. About how much imitation travertin stone was installed in that Station by the Denivelle Company?

A. Just what do you mean by that—how many square feet?

Q. 67. I mean for you to tell us, if you can, just what work was done by the Denivelle Company and as to its location and character, so far as artificial travertin is concerned.

A. The entablature of the arcade and rotunda; the walls of the main waiting-room above the real travertin base course, and including the cornice, the arches at the North and South ends and leading into the concourse—I guess that's all.

Q. 68. Mr. Denivelle, who is here present—do you associate him with that work and with the Denivelle Company?   A. Yes, sir.

Q. 69. And this is Mr. Paul E. Denivelle?

A. Yes, sir.

Q. 70. After that work was done, and in the period while you remained with the Miller Company which I understand was up to 1915, were you invited or your Company invited, to bid [129] on any other installation of artificial travertin?

Mr. LOFTUS.—Objected to for lack of proper notice in the answer.   A. Yes, sir.

Q. 71. Can you tell us the jobs upon which Miller

(Deposition of Carl Henry Meyn.)
was invited to bid for the installation of imitation
travertin up to 1915?

Mr. LOFTUS.—Objected to for lack of proper
notice in the answer.

A. Not very well, without looking it up.

Q. 72. Do you know whether the Denivelle Company or Mr. Denivelle, after the completion of the
Pennsylvania Station and prior to 1915, bid upon
or worked upon the installation of artificial travertin in connection with other jobs?

A. I don't know.

Q. 73. Had you while with the Miller Company
been called upon to make imitations of any other
stone?   A. Yes, sir.

Q. 74· Had you made such imitations?

A. Yes, sir.

Q. 75. What materials have been employed by
you and the Miller Company in making those imitations of stone?

Mr. LOFTUS.—Objected to as incompetent, irrelevant and immaterial.

A. Plaster of Paris, Keene's Cement, Portland
Cement [130]   and ready-made materials made by
manufacturers,   and   materials   imported   from
France and England.

Q. 76. State what other stones were imitated by
Miller and yourself while you were with Miller?

Mr. LOFTUS.—Objected to as incompetent, irrelevant and immaterial.

A. Limestone, Caenstone, Yorkshire Stone.

Q. 77. Are these stones smooth-surfaced stones?

(Deposition of Carl Henry Meyn.)

A. Some are, and some have holes.

Q. 78. The imitation travertin has holes in its surface, has it not?　A. Yes, sir.

Q. 79. What other stone imitated by you and the Miller Company had holes in its surfaces?

A. Laminated limestone.

Q. 80. How did the process employed by you in manufacturing the sample of imitation travertin compare with the process employed by you in manufacturing other imitations of stone?

Mr. LOFTUS.—Objected to as incompetent, irrelevant and immaterial, also as calling for an opinion and conclusion of the witness.

A. There was no difference.

Q. 81. That is, you made the imitation travertin installed in the Pennsylvania Station in the same way that you had theretofore made other imitations of stone? [131]

Mr. LOFTUS.—Objected to as leading.

A. Yes, by casting them on a slab or bench.

Q. 82. How about the materials employed—were they any different in the artificial travertin than in the other imitations of stone which were made by you?

A. Only as to color and coarseness of ingredients.

Q. 83. Which was the imitation made by you having the coarsest material?　A. Limestone.

Q. 84. How did the imitation travertin compare as to material, with the limestone.

Mr. LOFTUS.—Objected to as calling for an opinion and conclusion of the witness, and not the ro er method of proof.

(Deposition of Carl Henry Meyn.)

A. The travertin we used was a finer material than that we used for coarse limestone.

Q. 85. What does the term "isolator" mean as applied to the production of a cast sample of imitation stone?   A. I don't know.

Q. 86. In the manufacture of imitations of stone you employ a mold, do you?   A. Sometimes.

Q. 87. What do you mean by "sometimes?"

A. Sometimes we cast in a mold and sometimes we cast on a slab.

Q. 88. In casting on a slab, did you employ anything to confine the marginal edges of the cast? [132]

Mr. LOFTUS.—Objected to as leading.

A. Yes, sir.

Q. 89. Now, assuming that you are using a mold, please designate what the mold consisted of.

Mr. LOFTUS.—Objected to as hypothetical.

A. It all depends upon the nature of the cast that we want to make. We may have to have a gelatine mold; we may use a plaster mold; we may use a wooden mold; we have used metal molds for some castings.

Q. 90. Well, now, in preparing that mold for making the cast, what was the first step that you employed?   A. The mold had to be greased or oiled.

Q. 91. And did you grease or oil these molds?
A. We did.

Q. 92. In making the specimen of imitation travertin which was installed in the Pennsylvania Station

by the Miller Company, did you provide for the
forming of veins in the surface of that specimen?

Mr. LOFTUS.—Objected to as leading.

A. Yes, sir.

Q. 93. Now, please tell us how those veins were
'formed in that specimen?

A. We used a teapot; in some instances we tried
a metal bowl with a spout; and we tried a brush.

Q. 94. Now, just what did you do with the teapot
and the metal mold and the brush? [133]

A. We mixed some of the material to a consistency so it could be poured, and then poured it on to
the mold or slab.

Q. 95. Well, did you cover the entire surface of
the mold?   A. No, sir.

Q. 96· Just to form the veins?   A. Yes, sir.

Q. 97. That is, you pour it in lines on the surface
of the mold?   A. Yes.

Q. 98· Now, having poured the lines on the surface
of the mold, what else did you do in making that
sample of artificial travertin for the Pennsylvania
Station?

A. We took some of the darker material and
dampened it slightly; then rolled it into crumbs
which we spread on this mold.

Q. 99. Did you cover the surface with that
crumbly material?   A. Only in spots and lines.

Q. 100. Well, now, having performed that operation, what next did you do in the manufacture of
that specimen or sample for the Pennsylvania Station?

(Deposition of Carl Henry Meyn.)

A. We then took the darker shade of the material, mixed it, and poured it over the veins and crumbs already placed on the mold or slab. [134]

Q. 101. How much of that material did you pour into the mold?

A. To the thickness of about ⅜ of an inch.

Q. 102. What else was done in making that sample?

A. We then backed the mass up with plaster and burlap.

Q. 103. And allowed it to set.

A. And allowed it to set.

Q. 104. When it was taken out of the mold, what was the appearance of the cast?

A. The cast showed veins, and showed holes very similar to those in the natural stone.

Q. 105. Were the veins of a different shade from the body?

Mr. LOFTUS.—Objected to as leading.

A. Yes, sir.

Q. 106. Well, now, that process which you have described as having been used in manufacturing the specimen or sample of artificial travertin for the Pennsylvania Station—had you and Miller employed that process before in the manufacture of artificial stone?   A. Not that process.

Q. 107. Do you remember whether Miller was called upon to submit a bid for a house built for Robert Goelet or some member of the Goelet family, in Goshen, New York? [135]

A. I have some recollection of that.

(Deposition of Carl Henry Meyn.)

Q. 108. Do you know whether artificial travertin was employed in the construction of that house?

A. I have heard that it was.

Q. 109. Do you know?   A. I do not.

Q. 110. Did the Miller Company install the ceiling of the main waiting-room or concourse in the Pennsylvania Station?

A. The ceiling of the main waiting-room.

Q. 111. Now, how was that ceiling made?

A. That ceiling was cast of a material colored to match the travertin in gelatine molds.

Q. 112. Did you have anything to do with the construction of that ceiling?   A. Yes, sir.

Q. 113. You say it was cast—just what do you mean by that?

A. It was cast of a colored material—some of it we cast with veins.

Q. 114. Was it cast as one piece?

A. Each coffer was cast as one piece.

Q. 115. And how big a piece would each coffer be?

A. Octagons of about 8 feet, at the largest.

Q. 116. When was that ceiling completed, do you know?

A. Early in 1909, to the best of my recollection. [136]

Q. 117. Now, as I understand you, in the casting of those blocks for the ceiling you imitated the color of artificial travertin and also the lines or striations, but you did not roughen the surface with holes?   A. No, sir.

(Deposition of Carl Henry Meyn.)

Q. 118. What sort of material were those ceiling blocks made of? A. Gibson plaster.

Q. 119. Since the completion of the Pennsylvania Station and before 1915, do you recall any other installation of artificial travertin in and around New York?

A. There was imitation travertin stone work in the Vanderbilt Hotel, 34th Street and Park Avenue.

Q. 120. When was that imitation travertin installed in the Vanderbilt Hotel, do you know?

A. About 1912.

Q. 121. Did you see it at the time it was installed?

A. No, sir.

Mr. LOFTUS.—I move to strike the witness' answers as apparently based on hearsay.

Q. 122. Have you seen that installation of imitation travertin in the Vanderbilt Hotel?

A. I saw it shortly after it was finished, being in the bar-room of the Hotel.

Q. 123. And in those days the bar was open?

A. Exactly. [137]

Q. 124. Do you know who installed that artificial travertin in the Vanderbilt Hotel? A. I do not.

Q. 125. Can you recall any other installations of imitation travertin in and around New York from the time the Pennsylvania Station was opened to the public and up to October, 1915?

A. I can't recall any, just now.

Mr. ANDERSON.—Direct examination closed.

(Deposition of Carl Henry Meyn.)

• Cross-examination.

(By Mr. LOFTUS.)

XQ. 1. You stated that the Pennsylvania Station was opened in 1909?

A. That's to the best of my recollection.

XQ. 2. You haven't made any effort to verify that?

A. I haven't, no sir,—it's a matter of record.

XQ. 3. And all these other dates that you have given here are simply from your recollection?

A. To the best of my knowledge and recollection.

XQ. 4. On what do you base that recollection as to the opening of the Pennsylvania Station in 1909?

A. Why, we worked on that job very nearly 2 years, and we started along in 1907, and I have a picture home that was taken just before the opening, of all the co-workers on that Station—I don't know whether that has a date or not. [138]

XQ. 5. What were you doing in 1910?

A. Just what do you mean by what I was doing?

XQ. 6. Can you name any buildings that you worked on in 1910?

A. I can't name any definitely without looking it up.

XQ. 7. Any in 1911?

A. Yes, in 1911, we were doing the Wick House in Youngstown, Ohio. I think we started the Kansas City Station in that year.

XQ. 8. When did you complete the Kansas City Station? A. About 1913.

(Deposition of Carl Henry Meyn.)

XQ. 9. You stated that you erected this sample of artificial travertin in the Pennsylvania Station in New York in 1907—how do you fix that date?

A. Because it was that year that we got that contract, to the best of my recollection, and after we started we were asked to submit this sample.

XQ. 10. How far along was the Pennsylvania Station at the time that you erected this sample in 1907?. A. As to what part of the Station?

XQ. 11. The building as a whole—what was the condition of the building—the interior?

A. We were plastering then; we had at that time finished the arcade ceiling; we had started the work in the lunch and dining-rooms. [139]

XQ. 12. In 1907? A. Yes.

XQ. 13. How many samples of artificial travertin did you put in the Pennsylvania Station?

A. Two or three.

XQ. 14. Some of those were put in after you saw the Denivelle sample, were they not? A. No, sir.

XQ. 15. Are you certain as to that?

A. Quite certain.

XQ. 16. Can you describe just where the Miller sample, the Denivelle sample, and the McNulty samples were located in the Pennsylvania Station, with respect to each other?

A. They were very close together on the south wall of the rotunda leading to the dining-room.

XQ. 17. Were they all in a line or was one above the other?

A. They were all a section of the same entabla-

(Deposition of Carl Henry Meyn.)
ture and they were placed in the proper position where they were to go.

XQ. 18. Was there any miter in them?

A. They were on the corner of a wall. As I recall it, we had a drawing showing just exactly where the section we were to make was to be.

XQ. 19. What kind of furring material was this sample applied to? [140]

A. We backed it up with wood furring, that is, it was a cast and was set up to the terra cotta wall and tied into it.

XQ. 20. There was a terra-cotta wall there, was there?   A. Yes, sir.

XQ. 21. Are you sure of that?   A. Yes, sir.

XQ. 22. How far above the floor were those samples?   A. About 20 feet.

XQ. 23. The floor was in, was it?

A. The floor was not in—the rough floor was in.

XQ. 24. How long did you experiment on the making of these samples?

A. Two or three months.

XQ. 25. Who assisted you?

A. A man in the shop.

XQ. 26. How many men?   A. One.

XQ. 27. You stated that you put in two or three different samples, is that correct?   A. Yes.

XQ. 28. Were all of them removed before the travertine work was commenced by Mr. Denivelle?

A. As near as I can recall.

XQ. 29. The McNulty sample removed to, was it?

A. I think so. [141]

(Deposition of Carl Henry Meyn.)

XQ. 30. What kind of material was your sample made of?

A. We made one of White Portland Cement; we made another one of gypsum plaster.

XQ. 31. Were these samples made in a Paris Plaster cast, you stated? A. Some were.

XQ. 32. Are you making artificial travertin at the present time in your business?

A. Not just now.

XQ. 33. Have you made any in your business?

A. I have.

XQ. 34. To what extent have you made it and installed it?

A. What do you mean, "to what extent?"

XQ. 35. How many different buildings have you installed it in? A. That is, under my own—?

XQ. 36. In your own business? I think you stated you had been in business yourself for 5 years? A. One.

XQ. 37. Just one building? When was that?

A. Last year.

XQ. 38. And what building was that?

A. Scottish *Right* Building, New York City.

XQ. 39. Where is that located?

A. 34th Street between 8th and 9th Avenues.

XQ. 40. Are you a member of the Contracting Plasterers' [142] International Association?

A. Yes, sir.

XQ. 41. How do you happen to appear in this case as a witness?

A. I was approached by Mr. MacGruer last—I

(Deposition of Carl Henry Meyn.)

think it was some time in November, to ask if I would appear in this case.

XQ. 42. Had you known Mr. MacGruer prior to that time?   A. No, sir.

XQ. 43. What action has this Plasterers' Association taken in the matter of this suit?

A. None that I know of.

XQ. 44. Has it been discussed at any of the meetings of the Association?   A. Yes.

XQ. 45. Did they decide to take a part in the defense of the suit?   A. Not that I know of.

XQ. 46. What method did you use in the manufacture of this travertin that you installed in the Scottish *Right* Building?

A. Used a method of paraffin.

XQ. 47. Can you describe that a little more in detail?

A. Paraffin crumbs that were melted out of the cast; we also made some with semi-dry crumbs.

XQ. 48. Getting back now to the samples which Miller placed in the Pennsylvania Station, which of those was made [143] from White Portland Cement?

A. To the best of my recollection, the entablature piece was made of White Portland Cement—we had several other pieces there—slabs made of plaster?

XQ. 49. What was the size of that piece?

A. Which, the entablature?

XQ. 50. Yes, the one made from White Portland Cement?   A. It was made in 3 pieces.

XQ. 51. What was the size?

(Deposition of Carl Henry Meyn.)

A. The total was about 6 feet by 6 feet.

XQ. 52. Now, was that placed before or after the ones which you made from plaster or gypsum?

A. Before.

XQ. 53. Are you clear on that, are you?

A. Pretty sure.

XQ. 54. What process was used in making this sample which contained the White Portland Cement?

A. Just what do you mean by "what process?"

XQ. 55. What method did you use to form this sample which was made of White Portland Cement?

A. We used the method of putting in the veins necessary with a bowl with a spout on it, spreading crumbs into it, and then filling it in with other material.

XQ. 56. Wasn't that sample made in a plaster paris cast?

A. It was made in a plaster mold; the molded parts were made in a plaster mold and the plain piece on a slab. [144]

XQ. 57. And this plaster mold, was a negative taken from the genuine travertin—was it not?

A. It was not. We had no molded section; it was taken from a plaster model.

XQ. 58. Don't you recall that a controversy arose as to the method which you employed in making this sample that contained White Portland Cement?

A. Controversy, with whom?

XQ. 59. With the architects and engineers?

A. I do not.

(Deposition of Carl Henry Meyn.)

XQ. 60. You don't remember that?   A. No.

XQ. 61. Was one of these samples which you erected in the Pennsylvania Station made by a method which uses what they call "sausages"?

A. What kind of a thing?

XQ. 62. "Sausages"?   A. I don't know.

XQ. 63. You don't remember anything about that?   A. Not about "sausages."

XQ. 64. That is, a string of stiff material that could be laid parallel in the mold—have you used that method?   A. No, sir.

XQ. 65. You don't recall that?   A. No.

XQ. 66. Were all three of these samples that you put [145] in place for Miller in the Pennsylvania Station on the same level?   A. No, sir.

XQ. 67. What was their relative position?

A. We had some other samples—largest slabs—which we had down where our building shanty was in the arcade.

XQ. 68. Well, did you have three in place in the rotunda?

A. No, we had the 6x6 sample I spoke of before which was placed in the rotunda.

XQ. 69. You had but one in place in the rotunda?

A. Yes, sir.

XQ. 70. And that one was made of White Portland Cement?   A. Yes, sir.

XQ. 71. You did not put any in place in the rotunda which was made of plaster or gypsum?

A. No, sir.

XQ. 72. At the time you put your sample in the

(Deposition of Carl Henry Meyn.)

rotunda, were the other samples in place there that were made by Mr. Denivelle and by McNulty?

A. They were all being put up at the same time, as I recall it.

XQ. 73. Do you remember putting one up about two weeks after the Denivelle sample was placed?

A. No, I do not.

XQ. 74. What was the purpose of your casting these sections of the coffered ceiling in the Pennsylvania Station?   [146]

A. We were asked by the—you mean purpose—I don't just get you.

XQ. 75. That is, the purpose of casting rather than running it?

A. Casting was the only practical way to do it.

XQ. 76. Well, couldn't this ceiling have been run —these moldings?

A. Not practically.

XQ. 77. Is there not a Union rule as to the running of moldings longer than certain lengths?

A. If there had been it would have been applied to this case.   There is such a rule but it didn't apply to that case because that was within the restrictions that the Union put on those things.

XQ. 78. You don't remember, then, that by introducing a color into these cast sections that you got around this Union rule and saved some money?

A. That isn't so. I had to appear before the Union Trade Board at the time in the matter. We were paid for putting the color in that. McKim, Mead &

(Deposition of Carl Henry Meyn.)

White asked us if we could color that ceiling to match the travertin and we were paid for doing it.

XQ. 79. You did have a controversy with the Union over that ceiling, did you not? A. Yes, sir. [147]

XQ. 80. If the ceiling had been a white color, would you have been permitted under the Union rules to cast it? A. Yes, sir.

XQ. 81· What was the minimum length of molding which the Union rules permitted to be cast?

A. In feet, you mean?

XQ. 82. Yes.

A. Two feet on the ceiling line from miter to miter.

XQ. 83. And everything longer than 2 feet was required to be run? A. Yes.

XQ. 84. And these mouldings on the ceiling of the Pennsylvania Station, were longer than 2 feet?

A. They were not on the miter line—not on what was called the ceiling line.

By Mr. ANDERSON.—But they were longer than 2 feet?

A. Not on the miter line—over all they were.

(Mr. LOFTUS.)

XQ. 85. So, upon convincing the Union that these mouldings were but 2 feet long they permitted you to cast them, was that the result of the controversy?

A. The matter was settled by the joint Trade Board consisting of Union men and employers, which was in force at that time. [148]

(Deposition of Carl Henry Meyn.)

XQ. 86. Was it settled on the basis of the fact that this molding was but 2 feet long?

A. It was settled on the basis of fact that everything we had done was within the requirements of the agreement.

XQ. 87. The matter of the length of the molding, then, didn't enter into the settlement, is that it?

A. No, sir. What do you mean by the length—do you mean the miter length?

XQ. 88. In other words, you showed the Union that this molding was within the 2-feet limitation?

A. Requirement on the ceiling line, yes, sir.

XQ. 89. Did the fact that you introduced a color into this material have anything to do with your success with the Unions?

A. No, sir; the same rule would have applied.

XQ. 90. That ceiling was completed in 1909, you stated?

A. Late in 1909 or early in 1910—early in 1910—as I recall, we did have a Christmas there.

XQ. 91. Was Mr. Denivelle working there when you were working on the ceiling?   A. Yes, sir.

XQ. 92. As late as 1910?   A. Yes, sir.

XQ. 93. Didn't you state elsewhere that Denivelle had finished his work in the early part of 1909? [149]

A. It was 1909 that I had in mind when I said 1910.

XQ. 94. You're not certain as to any of these dates, are you?   A. Only by going back mentally.

XQ. 95. You don't know why Miller didn't get this travertin job, do you?

(Deposition of Carl Henry Meyn.)

A. I understand he was not the low bidder—I understood at the time we were not the low bidders.

XQ. 96. You were low on the other plastering work though, is that true?

A. So far as I know, or we wouldn't have got it.

XQ. 97. You also stated that the Fuller Construction Company paid you for the expense you were put to in making these samples of imitation travertin?   A. Yes, sir.

XQ. 98. What was the amount of that payment?

A. $200, as near as I recall it.

XQ. 99. Did you cover all your expenses in connection with the travertin installations?

A. No, sir.

XQ. 100. Was that money paid to you by Fuller?

A. Yes.

XQ. 101. Mr. Denivelle didn't give it to you?

A. No, sir.

XQ. 102. You're sure of that?

A. Quite sure of that.   [150]

XQ. 103. Were there any other samples put in there except the three that you have mentioned, namely, Denivelle, McNulty and Miller?

A. Not that I know of.

Mr. ANDERSON.—Is that all?

Mr. LOFTUS.—I think that is all.

Cross-examination closed.

Redirect Examination.

(By Mr. ANDERSON.)

RDQ. 1. This sample that was made of White

(Deposition of Carl Henry Meyn.)

Portland Cement—what color was it when it was installed?

A. A light soft grey about the same color as natural travertin.

RDQ. 2. In making it you tried to imitate the color of the natural travertin, did you?

A. Yes, sir.

RDQ. 3. Now, Mr. Meyn, you stated that you prepared the bids submitted by the Miller Company from specifications furnished to you—do you think you could recognize a copy of those specifications if you saw it to-day? A. I think so.

RDQ. 4. I show you a document and ask you to examine it carefully and state whether you recognize that as a copy of the specifications from which you prepared your bid?

A. Yes, that looks like the specification. [151]

Mr. ANDERSON.—I ask that this be marked for identification, Defendants' Exhibit 1. (Addressing Mr. Loftus.) Are you through?

Mr. LOFTUS.—Just one thing more—

Recross-examination.

RXQ. 1. Do you mean, Mr. Meyn, that that is the one that you worked from, or does it appear to be a copy?

A. It looks to be a copy of the specifications we had.

RXQ. 2. That isn't the identical one?

A. I couldn't tell.

RXQ. 3. Those specifications require that these samples be done in White Portland Cement, didn't

(Deposition of Carl Henry Meyn.)

RXQ. 4. So that in making a sample of gypsum you were ignoring the terms of the specifications?

A. Yes, sir.

RXQ. 5. These specifications appear to be dated March 1909. Would that change your testimony at all regarding any samples that you might have made in 1907?

A. I may be confused on those dates—it's pretty long ago, you know, that this thing happened.

RXQ. 6. In other words, you're not certain of any of these dates that you have given here?

A. Not within possibly a year.

RXQ. 7. Two years?

A. Within a year, I said. [152]

RXQ. 8. When you stated then that you made travertin in 1907, were you only off one year in your date, or were you off two years?

A. I don't know that these specifications were written in 1909.

RXQ. 9. You said that that appears to be a copy?

A. To the best of my recollection we did this in 1907 or 1908.

RXQ. 10. You don't think that's a true copy of the specifications then?

A. I didn't say that—it looks like the specifications.

RXQ. 11. Then is it your impression that that date—March 1909—on those specifications is incorrect?   A. I don't know.

Deposition closed.

Signature waived.

[Title of Court and Cause.]

New York, N. Y., March 3, 1924—3 P. M.

DEPOSITION OF RICHMOND H. SHREVE, FOR DEFENDANTS.

RICHMOND H. SHREVE, a witness produced on behalf of the defendants, having been first duly sworn, deposes and says as follows, to wit:

Direct Examination.

(By Mr. ANDERSON.)

It is agreed by counsel that the deposition of Mr. Shreve may be taken before George H. Emslie, Esq., a notary public, and taken down in shorthand and transcribed by Miss Helen I. Gorman, a stenographer, Mr. Emslie being in the employ of Munn & Co., and Miss Gorman [154] in the employ of counsel for the defendants in this case.

Q. 1. What is your full name, Mr. Shreve?

A. Richmond Harold Shreve.

Q. 2. And your age?   A. Forty-seven.

Q. 3. Where do you reside?

A. Hastings-on-Hudson, N. Y.

Q. 4. And what is your business or profession?

A. Architect.

Q. 5. Are you in business for yourself or are you associated with some firm?

A. I am one of the partners of the firm of Carrere and Hastings, Shreve, Lamb and Blake.

Q. 6. How long has that firm been in existence?

A. The original partnership was formed some-

(Deposition of Richmond H. Shreve.)

thing over thirty years ago. The name of the original partnership was Carrere and Hastings.

Q. 7. When was your new firm organized?

A. As Carrere and Hastings, Shreve, Lamb and Blake, January 1, 1921, I think. Since then, Mr. Blake, while continuing with the office, has withdrawn his name from the partnership.

Q. 8. Were you associated with the firm of Carrere and Hastings at any time? [155]

A. I was employed by them first, and later became a member of the firm.

Q. 9. How long were you in the employ of Carrere and Hastings?

A. From 1903 it was, I think, until the date above, January 1, 1921.

Q. 10. Do you know Mr. Denivelle, who is here present?   A. I know Mr. Denivelle.

Q. 11. How long have you been acquainted with Mr. Denivelle?

A. I am not sure of the date of meeting Mr. Denivelle. It was when he first came to work with our office.

Q. 12. And you recognize him as Mr. Paul Denivelle?

A. I don't remember that name. I thought it was H. C. S. or something. I didn't know him as Paul Denivelle. I knew him as Mr. Denivelle.

Q. 13. Connected with the H. C. S. Company?

A. It was those initials that I remember.

Q. 14. While you were in the employ of Carrere and Hastings did that firm design and superintend

(Deposition of Richmond H. Shreve.)

the construction of a residence for Robert Goelet, at Goshen, N. Y.?

By Mr. LOFTUS.—Objection is made at this time to any alleged prior use occurring in the home of Goelet, for the reason that no mention thereof has been made in the answer on file herein.

A. Yes. [156]

Q. 15. In the construction of that residence was there installed in or about the same any imitation or artificial travertine stone?

Mr. LOFTUS.—Same objection.

A. There was.

Q. 16. Do you know who did that work in connection with the installing of artificial travertine stone?

A. That work was done under the contract with a company with whom we dealt, through Mr. Denivelle as the active party.

Q. 17. And was that company the Denivelle Hydraulic Composite Stone Company?

A. As I remember it; we knew them as the Denivelle Hydraulic Composite Stone Company. I haven't looked that up. I don't know more than that.

Q. 18. I show you what purports to be a letter written by the Denivelle Hydraulic Composite Stone Company, signed by Paul E. Denivelle, President, per "A," dated April 4, 1912, addressed to Carrere and Hastings, Fifth Avenue and 26th Street, New York City. A carbon copy of a letter, in the corner of which appears the word

(Deposition of Richmond H. Shreve.)

"Copy," with the legend "From Carrere and Hastings to" addressed to "Mr. Hammond," dated April 16, 1912. A letter dated April 30, 1912, on the letterhead of Denivelle Hydraulic Composite Stone Company, signed in the name of that company, by Paul Denivelle, President, addressed [157] to Carrere and Hastings. A carbon copy of a letter on a thin sheet of paper, bearing the legend "Copy," from Carrere and Hastings to Mr. Hammond, dated June 17, 1912. A letter on the letterhead of Denivelle Hydraulic Composite Stone Company, dated June 17, 1913, addressed to Carrere and Hastings, 225 Fifth Avenue, signed in the name of Denivelle Hydraulic Composite Stone Company, Paul E. Denivelle, President, per A. G. Z. (or "R," I cannot make out which). Another carbon copy bearing the legend "Copy," from Carrere and Hastings to Mr. Battersby, dated August 4, 1913, addressed to Denivelle Hydraulic Composite Stone Company. A piece of white paper bearing the legend "Letter to Mr. Goelet, re credit attached to final certificate. Papers on pumping system." Another letter on the letterhead of Denivelle Hydraulic Composite Stone Company, dated July 17, 1913, addressed to Carrere & Hastings, signed in the name of the Company, Edward J. Connor, Secretary. A carbon copy bearing the legend in the left-hand corner, "Copy" from Carrere and Hastings to Mr. Battersby, dated July 18, 1913, beginning "Dear Mr. Goelet"; and another carbon copy on

(Deposition of Richmond H. Shreve.)

the same kind of copy sheet, bearing the legend "Copy" from Carrere and Hastings to Mr. Battersby, dated August 4, 1913. Are you familiar with those papers?

A. Yes; I recognize them as papers most of which I think I have handled, and most of which I think bear my initials or signature. [158]

Q. 19. At my request did you send those papers to me? A. I did.

Q. 20. And where did you obtain them?

A. From the contract files of the office.

Q. 21. Do those papers relate to the construction of the Goelet house at Goshen, N. Y.?

A. They do.

Q. 22. Do they relate to the artificial travertine stone work which was installed by Mr. Denivelle or his company in or about the Robert Goelet house?

Mr. LOFTUS.—Objected to as leading, and on the further ground that the documents speak for themselves.

A. They relate to a contract for artificial or composite travertine and to work in connection with stucco on that residence.

Q. 23. Of your own knowledge do you know that Mr. Denivelle or his company did install in or about that Robert Goelet house some so-called imitation or composition travertine stone?

A. I dealt with the contract, gave the orders for the work, knew of the reports of its being executed, and subsequently saw it in place. I did

(Deposition of Richmond H. Shreve.)
not personally see Mr. Denivelle's organization
at work on it.

Q. 24. And that contract was executed by Mr.
Denivelle [159] or his company, was it?

A. He was paid for it.

Q. 25. Can you state, Mr. Shreve, when that
work was done under that contract?

A. I saw the work in place, complete, in the fall
of 1913, on a visit which I made to Mr. Goelet's
house. I do not know more than that as to the
time in which it was executed.

Q. 26. And that is the imitation travertine work
supposed to have been executed by Mr. Denivelle
or his company? A. Yes.

Q. 27. Did the firm of Carrere and Hastings
have a representative on that Goelet house?

A. Yes, we had two men representing us in the
direction or inspection of this work. One was
Mr. J. F. Gaylor and the other was Mr. Vance
Torbert. Mr. Gaylor was the visiting superintendent for the office, and Mr. Vance Torbert was
resident superintendent or clerk of works.

Q. 28. Was Mr. Denivelle's work in the installation of imitation travertine inside of the house or
outside of the house, or terraces surrounding the
house?

A. Some of it was in the patio or open court of
the house, and on the terraces or loggias surrounding that court. I don't remember where there
was any other work. The terraces are covered
terraces. [160]

(Deposition of Richmond H. Shreve.)

Q. 29. Was the Denivelle Company paid for that imitation travertine work?

A. Our office certified payment to them and the payments were made by the owners. I presume in this case they were paid.

Q. 30. Is there anything in those papers which you have identified, which shows when the office certified the payments?

A. No, this is a set of papers relating to the order or contract for the work. The file of payments to contractors is not here.

Q. 31. Who was the contractor?

A. If I recollect, it was the Harriman Industrial Corporation.

Q. 32. Is there anything in those papers to show when Mr. Denivelle completed his work—or the Denivelle Company?

A. No, nothing that I see here.

Q. 33. Have you had occasion within the last two months to look up in your records when that contract with Denivelle was made and when completed?

A. I got that information some time ago through the accountant at the office, at the time that you asked for these contract papers.

Q. 34. At that time that you asked for that information from the accountant did you make a pencil memorandum and hand it to me? [161]

A. I believe I did.

Q. 35. Do you recognize this piece of paper that I hand you?

(Deposition of Richmond H. Shreve.)

A. Yes, this is a memorandum slip from our office, in the handwriting of the accountant.

Q. 36. Is there not some of your handwriting on that slip?   A. No.

Q. 37. What does that slip show as to when the Denivelle contract was executed?

Mr. LOFTUS.—Objected to as incompetent, irrelevant and immaterial, and as hearsay and not calling for the best evidence.

A. This memorandum shows that the Denivelle contract began in April, 1912, and was closed out on our books in August, 1913.

Q. 38. That memorandum was obtained by you from one of your regular employees in Carrere and Hastings?

Mr. LOFTUS.—Same objection.

A. Yes, it was.

Q. 39. How was it procured by you; in the customary way of your seeking information on such particulars?

Mr. LOFTUS.—Same objection.

A. It was.

Q. 40. At the time that memorandum was made did you personally examine the records of your office concerning the [162] same, to verify the information given by your employee?

A. I examined the papers which are here to-day. I did not examine the books from which the notes were taken.

Q. 41. What is your personal recollection at this

(Deposition of Richmond H. Shreve.)

time as to the accuracy of the memorandum given to you by your employee?

A. I am entirely satisfied that it represents the facts.

Q. 42. Now you say that you have dealt with the contract between your office, Carrere and Hastings, and the Denivelle Company, or Mr. Denivelle. Was the Denivelle Company the only bidder for that imitation travertine work?

A. I am unable to answer that question at this time.

Q. 43. At the time that contract was given to Mr. Denivelle or his company did he call your attention to any imitation travertine which he or his company had done, in the way of referring you to an example of his work in making imitation travertine?

A. I did not discuss that matter with Mr. Denivelle personally. I knew from members of the firm that he was engaged on this work for Mr. Goelet because of satisfactory work he had done elsewhere.

Q. 44. Did you know at that time that Mr. Denivelle had done or claimed to have done some imitation travertine work in the Pennsylvania Station, New York City? [163]

Mr. LOFTUS.—Objected to as leading.

A. I knew that from the members of the firm who selected him for this work and advised Mr. Goelet to have it done.

Q. 45. And before that work was given had you

(Deposition of Richmond H. Shreve.)
gone down to the Pennsylvania Station and examined some imitation travertine work which had
been done down there?

Mr. LOFTUS.—Objected to as leading.

A. I had not examined them in connection with
this contract. Other members of the firm had
done so.

Q. 46. Now, your reference to "other members
of the firm" leads me to ask whether there is now
associated with your firm anyone who would have
a more complete knowledge of this contract and
work in connection with the imitation travertine
furnished by Mr. Denivelle or his company, for
the Goelet house, than you have?

A. Mr. Hastings would know personally about
this work, and something about its execution. I
don't know how detailed his information would be.
Mr. Gaylor, who was at that time the superintendent, would know more fully the details of the
work and its execution, and Mr. Torbert would
also know a good deal about it.

Q. 47. Is Mr. Hastings available at this time?

A. Mr. Hastings is in New York. [164]

Q. 48. Now, I will ask you, Mr. Shreve, whether
I have your permission to retain these letters and
copies of letters which you have identified, until
after the trial of this case, or whether you would
prefer that I have copies made and introduce the
copies as evidence in this case?

A. No, you may have those papers as long as
they are of value to you.

(Deposition of Richmond H. Shreve.)

Mr. ANDERSON.—I will return them to you at the end of the trial.

Mr. SHREVE.—At your service.

Q. 49. Do you recognize these carbon copies as being copies of correspondence sent out of the office of Carrere and Hastings, or what they purport to be?

A. Yes, I am personally entirely satisfied that those are carbon copies from our files in the office. Mr. Hammond was at that time the accountant, some of the copies having been given to him for his financial records. Mr. Gaylor was at that time the superintendent in charge of this work, and I know the letters bearing the initials "J. F. G.," also the initial "R," which is that of Miss Roberts, who was and is the stenographer, or of Miss Evertson, "M. A. E." those initials are, also one of the stenographers. Also Mr. Battersby, to whom certain of the carbons are assigned, succeeded Mr. Hammond as our accountant. In the stamped endorsements on the original Denivelle letters I find my own initials, "R. H. S.," [165] in the blank following the name "Carrere and Hastings."

Q. 50. From that stamped endorsement you are able to swear are you, Mr. Shreve, that those letters were received by Carrere and Hastings, from the Denivelle Hydraulic Composite Stone Company at or about the times indicated in the stamped endorsements, or as indicated in the dates of the letters?

A. Yes. In addition to the points of identifica-

(Deposition of Richmond H. Shreve.)

tion which you mention, I recognize other office stamps: The one relating to distribution of copies; the one relating to the papers belonging to the bookkeeper's files; and the personal stamps of Mr. Pryor (initials R. T. P.); and Mr. Gaylor (initials J. F. G.); also those of Mr. Pond (initials W. A. P.), who was at that time my assistant, and the initials of Mr. Battersby (A. C. B.); and of Mr. Meloth (initials H. B. M.), who was the assistant to the accountant.

By Mr. ANDERSON.—Counsel for defendants offers in evidence, as Plaintiff's Exhibit 2, the letter dated April 4, 1912, from Denivelle Hydraulic Composite Stone Company to Carrere and Hastings; the carbon copy of a letter from Carrere and Hastings, dated April 16, 1912, to Denivelle Hydraulic Composite Stone Company, 609 West 53d St., New York City; original letter from Denivelle Hydraulic Composite Stone Company to Carrere and Hastings, dated April 30, 1912; carbon copy of a letter from Carrere and Hastings to Denivelle Hydraulic Composite Stone Company, dated June 17, 1912; original letter from Denivelle Composite Stone Company to Carrere and Hastings, dated June 17, 1913; carbon copy of a letter from Carrere & Hastings, dated Aug. 4, 1913, [166] to Denivelle Hydraulic Composite Stone Company; the memorandum in green pencil as follows: "Letter to Mr. Goelet *re* credit attached to final certificate"; papers on pumping system, and stamped in green ink "H. B. M., Au-

(Deposition of Richmond H. Shreve.)

gust 6, 1913"; original letter from Denivelle Hydraulic Composite Stone Company to Carrere and Hastings, dated July 17, 1913; carbon copy of a letter from Carrere and Hastings to Robert Goelet, Esq., 9 West 17th Street, New York City, dated July 18, 1913; carbon copy of a letter from Carrere and Hastings, dated August 4, 1913, to Denivelle Hydraulic Composite Stone Company.

Counsel for defendants calls upon plaintiff to produce the originals of the carbon copies of the letters from Carrere and Hastings to Denivelle Hydraulic Composite Stone Company, and gives notice that if such originals are not produced the carbon copies will be noticed as the best evidence of such originals.

Mr. LOFTUS.—Objection is made to the offer on the ground that the letters are incompetent, irrelevant and immaterial, and on the further ground that if they are material at all, they relate to special matters or features not set up in the answer.

Mr. ANDERSON.—Counsel for defendants notes that all of the letters and copies which have been referred to in the offer of the exhibit are connected together and will be offered as one exhibit: "Defendants' Exhibit 2, Carrere and Hastings correspondence."

Q. 51. Mr. Shreve, since that work was done on the Goelet house by Mr. Denivelle or his company, has your firm made use of imitation travertine in any other construction work?

(Deposition of Richmond H. Shreve.)

A. Yes, we have. The most recent work that I recall is that for work in the Bank of Niagara, Niagara Falls, N. Y. [167]

Q. 52. And when was that done?

A. That work was done during the year 1923.

Q. 53. Between the construction of the Goelet house, and, we will say, down to October, 1915, can you recall the use of any artificial travertine in any other building designed by your firm?

A. I don't remember enough about the details of our contracts to recall that sort of thing.

Q. 54. Aside from the Mr. Denivelle here present do you know another Mr. Denivelle who was engaged in making imitation stone travertine?

A. I believe that I knew of another Mr. Denivelle. I don't think that I knew him personally or knew much about his business. I had heard of him.

Q. 55. Can you recall his name? A. No.

Q. 56. Did he do any work on the Goelet house?

A. Not that I know of.

Q. 57. How recently have you seen the Goelet house?

A. Not for eight or nine years.

Q. 58. When you last saw it was the work done by Denivelle or his company still standing and in good shape? A. Yes.

Q. 59. And that was eight or nine years ago? [168]

A. I think that was in the fall of 1913 or the

(Deposition of Richmond H. Shreve.)
spring of 1914, on a visit that I made to the place
with Mr. Torbert.

Direct examination closed.

Cross-examination.
(By Mr. LOFTUS.)

XQ. 60. On this visit that you have just referred
to, which you made with Mr. Torbert, either in
the fall of 1913 or the spring of 1914, how near
to completion was the Goelet home? Had it been
furnished as yet? Was it occupied?

A. My recollection is that it was finished and
that some of the property of the owner was in it,
but I do not think that it had been finally or fully
occupied and taken over.

XQ. 61. And how far from a street or thoroughfare were these buildings that contained the Denivelle travertine? Were they close to the street
or some distance back?

A. They were on the large property which Mr.
Goelet owns there, on the top of the hill, facing
the lake, and perhaps two or three hundred yards
from any highway.

XQ. 62. And at the time of this visit just referred to you had not finished your work in connection with the house had you?

A. My recollection is that our work in connection with the house in which Mr. Denivelle's work
was done had been completed, or virtually so, but
that we were then engaged in [169] work for
Mr. Goelet on other parts of the property; a wall,

(Deposition of Richmond H. Shreve.)
or an icehouse, or a pump-house or something of the kind which was a later part of the work.

XQ. 63. And the contractor, namely, the Harriman Industrial Corporation, they had not completed their work as yet, at that time, had they?

A. I think they were finished on the house but were engaged on other work around the property.

XQ. 64. That, you recall, was in the fall of 1913, or the spring of 1914? A. Yes.

XQ. 65. What was the first artificial or composite travertine that you ever heard of or saw; where was it used?

A. I don't think it is possible for me to answer that question accurately at this time. The first I remember was work done at the Pennsylvania Station, which I understand Mr. Denivelle had done, but at that time I had not met him, and I don't recall that situation clearly enough to state anything about it in detail.

Cross-examination closed.

Redirect Examination.

(By Mr. ANDERSON.)

RDQ. 66. Is it your recollection, Mr. Shreve, that Mr. Denivelle's imitation or artificial travertine work on the Goelet house had been completed before this visit that you speak of in the fall of 1913 or the spring of 1914? [170]

A. It is my recollection that the work on the Goelet house was given to Mr. Denivelle by the owner on our advice, because of previous work

(Deposition of Richmond H. Shreve.)

which he had done, which our office thought established him as a competent contractor for the residence under our direction, and it is my recollection that some of the work which they saw was the work on the Pennsylvania Station If I recall that, it is referred to in these notes.

RDQ. 67. Now, I am asking you, Mr. Shreve, as to the completion of Mr. Denivelle's, or his company's artificial travertine work on the Goelet house. When was that finished?

A. It was finished before the visit which I speak of, which I made to the house.

RDQ. 68. And that visit was either in the fall of 1913, or early in 1914?

A. I think, if you wish me I can establish the date, because I have a diary of such matters. It is at the office. It would mean looking page by page to see when I did it.

Adjourned to Tuesday, March 4, 1924, at 10 A. M. [171]

New York, N. Y., March 4, 1924—10 A. M.

Parties present as before.

Deposition of Mr. Shreve continued.

Redirect Examination.

(By Mr. ANDERSON.)

RDQ. 69. Mr. Shreve, did you locate your diary upon which you rely for fixing the date of your visit to the Goelet house, which you say was either in the fall of 1913 or in the spring of 1914? If so, please produce it and state whether the entry

(Deposition of Richmond H. Shreve.)
therein confirms your testimony given yesterday
as to that date.

A. I have here my diary for the year 1914, and
I find an entry as of Saturday, May 9th of that
year, that I was at the Robert Goelet house, and
on Sunday, May 10th, a further entry of the same
visit, with a note that I was with Mr. Torbert.

RDQ. 70. Those entries are in the book?

A. They are.

Mr. ANDERSON.—The diary is submitted to
Mr. Loftus for his inspection.

RDQ. 71. So that now your testimony will be
that on Saturday and Sunday, May 9th and 10th
you visited the Goelet house at Goshen, N. Y., and
that the house at that time was   [172]   completed.

A. Substantially completed.

Mr. LOFTUS.—But not occupied?

A. I said yesterday I thought there were some
of the owner's things in there.

Redirect Examination.

(By Mr. ANDERSON.)

RDQ. 72. You also promised yesterday after_
noon to look up the data in your office to deter_
mine just when the Denivelle Hydraulic Com_
posite Stone Company was paid for the artificial
travertine work which was installed by that com_
pany in the Goelet house. Please tell us whether you
have looked up such date; in what records of your
office you found that data; and what that record
shows?

A. I have an extract here from the contract

(Deposition of Richmond H. Shreve.)
ledger of the office, showing the payments certified
to Mr. Denivelle or the contractor, giving the
dates of the certificates, the numbers of the certificates, and the amounts of the certificates, the
first payment was made in August, 1912. Other
payments through that year and 1913, and the
final payment was certified on June 9, 1914.

RDQ. 73. Would you state the dates of the several payments and the amounts?

A. In answer to this question I submit the
memorandum [173] made from our records this
morning.

By Mr. ANDERSON.—By agreement of counsel the memorandum is copied on the record as
follows:

March 4, 1924.

Certificate issued to Denivelle.

Date		Certificate No.		Amount
Aug.	2, 1912,	No.	9380	$1500.00
Sept.	9, 1912,	"	9450	1200.00
Oct.	14, 1912,	"	9480	1000.00
Nov.	23, 1912,	"	9544	1000.00
Mar.	11, 1913,	"	9659	1500.00
Aug.	19, 1913,	"	9860	500.00
June	9, 1914,	"	10176	349.50

$7049.50

Extract from books of Carrere & Hastings.

R. H. SHREVE.

Redirect examination closed.

Deposition closed.

Signature waived.

Adjourned until 11:30 A. M. [174]

[Title of Court and Cause.]

Tuesday, March 4, 1924—11:30 A. M.

Met pursuant to adjournment for recess.

Parties present as before.

It is agreed that Mr. Fenner's deposition may be taken before George H. Emslie, Esq., notary public, and taken stenographically by Miss Hoffman, a stenographer in the employ of defendants' counsel.

DEPOSITION OF BURT L. FENNER, FOR DEFENDANTS.

BURT L. FENNER, subpoenaed as a witness on behalf of the defendants, having been duly cautioned and sworn, in answer to interrogatories propounded by Mr. Anderson, testified as [175] follows:

Q. 1. Your full name, Mr. Fenner.

A. Burt L. Fenner.

Q. 2. And your age?   A. 54.

Q. 3. Where do you reside, Mr. Fenner?

A. Croton-on-Hudson.

Q. 4. What is your occupation or profession?

A. Architect.

Q. 5. And you are one of the firm of McKim, Mead & White?   A. Yes.

(Deposition of Burt L. Fenner.)

Q. 6. How long have you been engaged in the architectural profession?   A. Since 1891.

Q. 7. And how long have you been associated with McKim, Mead & White?

A. I have been associated with McKim, Mead & White since 1891. I became a partner January 1, 1906.

Q. 8. This present controversy relates to a patent for artificial stone and a process of making it, issued to Paul E. Denivelle—do you know Mr. Denivelle?   A. Yes.

Q. 9. And he is present at this hearing?

A. Yes.

Q. 10. How long have you known Mr. Denivelle? [176]   A. Approximately 20 years.

Q. 11. Are you familiar with the so-called artificial travertin which was installed by Mr. Denivelle or his company, the Denivelle Hydraulic Composite Stone Company, in the Pennsylvania Railroad Station in this city?   A. Yes.

Q. 12. McKim, Mead & White were the architects for that station?   A. Yes.

Q. 13. And the general contractors for that work were?   A. George A. Fuller Company.

Q. 14. I show you a document entitled, "Pennsylvania Tunnel & Terminal Railroad Company, New York City—Terminal Station—Specifications for Artificial Stone Work—McKim, Mead & White, Architects, New York City"—do you recognize that document?   A. Yes.

Q. 15. Is that a copy of the original specifica-

(Deposition of Burt L. Fenner.)
tions prepared in the office of McKim, Mead &
White for the artificial stone work in the Pennsylvania Station?   A. Yes.

Q. 16. Do you recollect whether a copy of those
specifications was furnished to Mr. Denivelle at
the time his bid was solicited for installing the
artificial travertin?

A. That I can't testify from my own personal
knowledge, [177] but it is a fair assumption
that everyone who figured on the artificial travertin figured on this specification. We assumed that
Mr. Denivelle had it.

Q. 17. Now, I call your attention to the fact that
that copy is dated March 1909—is it?   A. Yes.

Q. 18. Was that before or after the work was
done, from your recollection?

A. Why, I have no recollection of the date on
which the work was done but I assume, certainly
this was issued before the work was done; the
specifications are issued before work is done, and
as a basis for contract.

Q. 19. Do you recall the names of other bidders
than Mr. Denivelle, for installing the artificial
travertin in the Pennsylvania Station?

A. Yes, I find in the records the names of Mc-
Nulty Brothers, and H. W. Miller. I don't know
whether there were others or not.

Q. 20. Was that copy of the specifications which
I have just handed you prepared in the office of
McKim, Mead & White?   A. Yes.

Q. 21. Who prepared it?   A. L. R. Holske.

(Deposition of Burt L. Fenner.)

Counsel for defendants offers a copy of the specifications of McKim, Mead & White as "Defendants' Exhibit 3, [178] McKim, Mead & White Specifications," and it is stipulated that the said copy may be received with the same force and effect as the document about which the witness has testified, subject to corrections by either party, from the original document, should such corrections appear to be necessary.

Mr. LOFTUS.—It is stipulated that the copy may be filed in lieu of the original which has been identified by the witness. This stipulation applies to the introduction of a copy in lieu of the original identified by the witness, and is not to be understood as intending to concede any force or effect or weight to the document itself.

(By Mr. ANDERSON.)

Q. 22. Is it conceded that the copy which has been offered in evidence will not be questioned because it is a copy and not the original?

Mr. LOFTUS.—That is the purpose of the stipulation.

Q. 23. Mr. Fenner, do you recognize the document which I now show you?

A. Well, I don't know that I ever saw the document before, but it appears clearly to be a copy of a contract between the Denivelle Hydraulic Composite Stone Company and the George A. Fuller Company, under which the Denivelle Company agreed to provide all labor and materials for furnishing and installing all the imitation travertin

(Deposition of Burt L. Fenner.)
and imitation stone work required in the construction of the new Terminal Station for the Pennsylvania Tunnel & Terminal Railway Company.
[179]

Q. 24. One of those documents appears to be a
bond of the Denivelle Company and the National
Surety Company, and the other document, both
fastened together, is the agreement between the
Denivelle Company and the George A. Fuller Company—is it customary in your business to require
such bonds from building contractors?   A. Yes.

Q. 25. You sent me from your office some files—
just what were those files that you sent me?

A. They were the files of correspondence relating to this particular subject—the artificial stone
work in the Pennsylvania Station. I haven't examined those files; they were prepared by our
file clerk and forwarded to you as I received them
from her.

Q. 26. Did you examine them personally before
sending them to me?   A. No.

Q. 27. Have you examined them since you sent
them to me?   A. No.

Q. 28. Will you look at them and state whether
you can recognize them as files and documents of
McKim, Mead & White?   A. Yes, they are.

Q. 29. This bond and contract to which I called
your attention was in one of those files. Is there
anything on it which will enable you to identify
those documents on the   [180]   part of a witness

(Deposition of Burt L. Fenner.)
of McKim, Mead & White, as taken from the files
which you caused to be sent to me?

A. I don't see any mark on the document itself
which directly identifies it with McKim, Mead &
White's files, but I am quite sure that it came
from those files—it is written and bound in the
way that we customarily write and bind such documents. I have no doubt that it is the document
from our files.

Q. 30. Do you think your file clerk who sent
these files to me, would be able to identify this
document as a portion of the contents of the files
that were sent to me from your office?

A. Possibly, I don't know.

The document is marked for identification, "Defendants' Exhibit 4—Bond and Agreement."

Q. 31. Did you personally have anything to do
with the construction of the Pennsylvania Station?   A. Nothing whatever.

Q. 32. You know Mr. Denivelle here?
A. Yes.

Q. 33. Could you personally identify any of the
papers in these files which you caused to be sent to
me?   A. Well, just what does it mean?

Q. 34. At my request you sent me four files, did
you not?   A. Yes.

Q. 35. And where did you get those, or where
were they obtained, and by whose instructions
were they gotten out of the [181] records of
McKim, Mead & White?

(Deposition of Burt L. Fenner.)

A. They were gotten out by my instructions to a file clerk.

Q. 36. Do you know where she got them?

A. From the files.

Q. 37. Did she submit them to you before you sent them to me?   A. Yes.

Q. 38. Do you recognize these as the four files which were gotten out and sent to me by your instructions?   A. Yes, I do.

Q. 39. And your testimony is that those files contained records of McKim, Mead & White?

A. Yes.

Q. 40. I show you what purports to be a letter from George A. Fuller Company to McKim, Mead & White, dated December 31, 1908; a carbon copy of what purports to be a letter to George A. Fuller Company, dated December 29, 1908; a letter from the George A. Fuller Company to McKim, Mead & White, dated December 28, 1908; a letter from Hammerstein & Denivelle Company to Geo. A. Fuller Co., dated December 28, 1908; a typewritten memorandum addressed, "Dear Mr. Richardson," dated August 6, 1908, with the signature in typewriting, F. L. Ellingwood; a letter from George A. Fuller Company to McKim, Mead & White, dated September 29, 1908; a letter from Hammerstein & Denivelle Company, signed "Paul E. Denivelle," to Geo. A. Fuller Co., [182] dated September 28, 1908; a letter from Hammerstein & Denivelle to George A. Fuller Co., dated August 31, 1908; a letter from Hammerstein &

(Deposition of Burt L. Fenner.)

Denivelle to the George A. Fuller Co., dated July 20, 1908; a carbon copy of a letter addressed to George A. Fuller Company, dated April 23, 1909; and carbon copy of a letter addressed to George A. Fuller Co., dated April 15, 1909—do you recognize those documents as part of the records of your office? A. Yes.

Q. 41. Now, about these letters, Mr. Fenner, may I borrow them until after the termination of this trial, such as I need in this case, on my promise to have them returned?

A. Yes, I have no objections.

The papers referred to in next to the last question, are offered in evidence as "Defendants' Exhibit 5—Letters from McKim, Mead & White File"—there are 11 sheets altogether, held together by a paper clip.

Mr. LOFTUS.—The carbon copies contained in the exhibit are objected to for lack of identification.

Mr. ANDERSON.—Would you mind for the purpose of identification, Mr. Loftus, marking your initials on each one of those sheets?

(Mr. Loftus initials papers.)

(By Mr. ANDERSON.)

Q. 42. Mr. Fenner, did you have in the employ of McKim, [183] Mead & White, a man by the name of Webster—Daniel T. Webster? A. Yes.

Q. 43. Do you recall whether he had anything to do with the construction of the Pennsylvania Station?

he was the eneral su erintendent.

(Deposition of Burt L. Fenner.)

Q. 44. Representing the architects?

A. Representing the architects.

Q. 45. Did you have anything to do with the negotiations leading up to the granting of this contract to the Denivelle Company?   A. No.

Q. 46. Do you know whether the contractors who were bidding on that job furnished samples with their bids?

A. Not of my own personal knowledge, but certain letters which I have read indicate that that was the case.

Q. 47. Are these some of the letters to which you refer?

A. Yes, particularly the carbon copy of the letter from McKim, Mead & White to George A. Fuller Company, November 6, 1908.

Q. 48. Do you recognize that carbon copy as a letter sent from your office?   A. Yes.

Q. 49. The letters to which I call your attention are apparently one from McNulty Bros., Inc., to McKim, Mead & White, dated December 28, 1908; a carbon copy of a letter addressed to George A. Fuller Company, dated November 6, 1908; a carbon [184] copy of a letter to George A Fuller Company dated October 24, 1908; a carbon copy of a letter addressed to George Gibbs, Esq., October 15, 1908; a carbon copy of a letter addressed to George Gibbs, Esq., October 2, 1908; a letter from H. T. Lilliendah, addressed to George A. Fuller Company, dated October 8, 1908; a letter from George A. Fuller Company to McKim, Mead &
19 1907· a letter from Geor e A.

(Deposition of Burt L. Fenner.)

Fuller Company to McKim, Mead & White, dated June 21, 1907; a letter from H. W. Miller addressed to George A. Fuller Company, dated March 8, 1907; a letter from George A. Fuller Company addressed to McKim, Mead & White, dated November 16, 1906; and a copy of a letter addressed to The George A. Fuller Company, dated November 15, 1906—there are 15 sheets in all, held together by a paper clip—do you recognize those papers as a part of the files which you sent to me? A. Yes.

The papers are offered in evidence as "Defendants' Exhibit 6—Letters from McKim, Mead & White Files."

Mr. LOFTUS.—Objection is made to the carbon copies on the ground of lack of identification, and the further ground that the originals have not been properly accounted for.

Mr. ANDERSON.—The papers constituting "Exhibit 6" are submitted to counsel for plaintiff, and he is requested to mark his initials on each sheet thereof, for the purpose of identification in the future.

(Mr. Loftus initials papers.) [185]

Q. 50. I show you a carbon copy of a letter dated April 22, 1910, addressed to Mr. Keekes of Hiss & Weekes, 1123 Broadway, New York City,—do you recognize that as a carbon copy of a letter going out of the office of McKim, Mead & White?

A. It's impossible to identify that. It appears to be such a copy but I can't swear that it is.

Q. 51. I wrote you, I think, Mr. Fenner, recently,

(Deposition of Burt L. Fenner.)
asking you to look up the release from the Denivelle Company in connection with work done in
the Pennsylvania Station—did you bring that with
you?

A. No, I don't recall that letter, did you specifically mention that in the letter?

Q. 52. I think so.

A. The letter that you wrote me I turned over
to our file clerk, and my instructions were to her
to get out everything in the files that related to
this matter, and I assumed it was all here.

Q. 53. This letter was written a couple of days
ago?   A. I didn't see it.

Q. 54. I show you a document and ask you if
you recognize that; if so, state what it is.

A. The document appears to be a copy of a release executed by the Denivelle Hydraulic Composite Stone Company on its contract for imitation travertin and artificial stone for the Pennsylvania Station. [186]

Q. 55. Do you recognize Mr. Denivelle's signature
to that document?   A. Yes.

Q. 56. You are familiar with his signature?

A. Yes, I am familiar with his signature, and I
should say that that was it.

The document is offered in evidence as "Defendants' Exhibit 7—Denivelle Release."

Q. 57. Do you also recognize the signature of Edw.
J. Connor?   A. County?

Q. 58. County. You are familiar with that signature?   A. Yes.

(Deposition of Burt L. Fenner.)

Mr. LOFTUS.—I would like to see that paper.

The WITNESS.—I would also like to see it again.

Mr. LOFTUS.—(Addressing the witness.) You might correct your statement as to that name—it looks like Connor.

The WITNESS.—Yes, it is Connor—I don't know Mr. Connor—I don't know his signature—I was mistaken in reading it as "County."

(By Mr. ANDERSON.)

Q. 59. Now, Mr. Fenner, you were with the architects, McKim, Mead & White, when this Pennsylvania Station was being constructed, were you?

A. Yes. [187]

Q. 60. Of your own knowledge you knew that Mr. Paul E. Denivelle or his company were installing some imitation travertine in that building?

A. Yes.

Q. 61. Of your own knowledge, do you know that Mr. Denivelle or his company was paid for that work?

A. I don't know that of my own knowledge, no.

Q. 62. Would the payments be made on order of the architects?

A. On a certificate of the architects, yes.

Q. 63. To the building contractor—the general contractor?

A. No, normally the general contractor would make his applications for payments which would include payments to subcontractors, and McKim, Mead & White's certificate would be to the Fuller Company.

(Deposition of Burt L. Fenner.)

Q. 64. And that would be the warrant of the Fuller Company to pay the subcontractor?

A. Yes.

Q. 65. Now, what is the policy adopted by McKim, Mead & White in certifying such payments—what would influence them in making a certificate?

A. An examination of the work done, to determine its stage of completion and whether or not the work was in accordance with the agreement.

Q. 66. And as I understand you, such payment would indicate that the work had been done to a certain point and [188] entirely satisfactory and in accordance with the specifications?

Mr. LOFTUS.—Objected to as leading.

A. Yes.

Q. 67. Of your own knowledge, Mr. Fenner, was that imitation travertine work which was done by Denivelle or his company, a complete and satisfactory job?

A. I couldn't say that of my own knowledge.

Q. 68. Who, in your firm, had direct charge of that work?   A. Mr. Richardson.

Q. 69. Is he available at the present time for testimony?

A. No, he is not. He received a very serious injury to his spine something over two years ago, and has been incapacitated ever since, and is now in Europe.

Q. 70. Mr. Denivelle, in a suit in California, has testified that that work he did in the Pennsylvania Station was an experiment. Would McKim, Mead

(Deposition of Burt L. Fenner.)

& White cause to be installed on a building designed and constructed under their direction—permit an experiment to be put in such a building?

Mr. LOFTUS.—Objected to as calling for an opinion and conclusion of the witness.

A. Why, the question is just what "experiment" means. Certainly the preparation of samples was an experiment, for to the best of my knowledge nothing of the sort had ever been attempted before. As a result of the samples, McKim, Mead & White and the officers representing the Railroad Company felt sufficient confidence in the result to warrant McKim, Mead & [189] White in recommending its use to the Railroad Company and the Railroad Company in agreeing to its use and making the contract. It is obvious that both the Railroad Company and McKim, Mead & White felt pretty certain that they were going to get a successful result, and they wouldn't have been justified in trying what I understand as an experiment on so large a scale, and yet until the work was completed and had stood certain tests of time and use, no one could be certain that the results indicated from the samples would actually be brought about in reality.

Q. 71. That's true also of almost every building construction, isn't it?

A. It's true of every new material, I should say, but not of every building construction. We know perfectly well what the result of laying up a brick wall is going to be, or putting in an ordinary plastered ceiling, but here is a new material with

(Deposition of Burt L. Fenner.)

no data, no precedent to enable anybody to determine with any accuracy, certainty or finality what the result would be. The evidence produced by the samples convinced us all that we should get a satisfactory result.

Q. 72. And samples of artificial travertin were furnished by other competitors for that work?

A. Yes.

Q. 73. Assuming that the final payment to Mr. Denivelle had been made, we'll say in 1910, wouldn't that indicate that McKim, Mead & White had satisfied themselves that the job was   [190]   all right and was in accordance with the specifications, and a complete job at that time?

Mr. LOFTUS.—Objected to as leading and argumentative.   A. Yes.

Q. 74. This was the first time that genuine travertin had been used in this country, wasn't it?

A. Yes.

Q. 75. In the Pennsylvania Station?   A. Yes.

Direct examination closed.

Cross-examination.

(By Mr. LOFTUS.)

XQ. 1. It is true, is it not, Mr. Fenner, that at the time of those final payments made to Mr. Denivelle there were certain conditions attached that Denivelle was to continue to make repairs and replacements, and otherwise maintain the job in good condition?

A. That I couldn't testify from my own personal knowledge, but I find it stated, approximately as

(Deposition of Burt L. Fenner.)
you have stated it, in the document introduced here
—the release.

XQ. 2. In a building such as the Pennsylvania
Terminal Station. what peculiar conditions arise
that would be likely to cause cracking or flaking or
warping of a product such as this artificial travertin? [191]

A. Why, the only condition that occurs to me
which would differentiate it from another building
would be the possibility that the vibration caused
by trains underneath might affect it.

XQ. 3. The matter of vibration was a considerable
factor in that building, was it not, Mr. Fenner?

A. It was the thing that had to be guarded
against.

XQ. 4. And considering the fact that this imitation travertin is not of uniform density in cross-
section, that is, the outer surface is more or less
coarse whereas the back wall is denser, wouldn't
it require some time in actual use to determine
whether or not the travertin would stand up and
be satisfactory under the conditions it was used
there in the Station?

A. Well, you are asking for an opinion—my
opinion would be that there would be no more reason to anticipate difficulty due to vibration with
that material than with any other similar applied
material, like slabs of marble or slabs of stone.

XQ. 5. Well, in the case of marble the density
in cross-section is uniform, whereas in artificial
travertin the density is not uniform—would that

(Deposition of Burt L. Fenner.)
be a factor either in the way of causing cracks or warpage, flaking or any other form of deterioration, whether due to vibration or to temperature changes?

A. Well, I suppose that might be, possibly; I am [192] really not sufficiently familiar with the manufacture of the material to express an opinion.

XQ. 6. Were there any peculiar conditions of air currents present in this Station due to the many doors and travel of the public?

A. That I don't know—I don't think of any.

XQ. 7. I notice in one of the letters written by McNulty Bros., namely the letter dated December 28, 1908, it is stated: "We have not followed your request to submit a sample made of white Portland cement, because the short time allowed for the execution of this work precludes its use, aside from the possibility of efflorescence due to certain ingredients contained in this material." Have you any opinion as to how long a time before this condition of efflorescence might show up on this material?   A. No, I have no idea.

XQ. 8. It might be a matter of some years, is that possible?   A. Possibly.

XQ. 9. As I understand it, the material used in that Station was a white Portland cement, was it not?

A. I don't know.

XQ. 10. Have you any knowledge of the extent of use of artificial travertin at the present time—to what extent it is used?

A. Why, I've seen a good deal of it; I think it

(Deposition of Burt L. Fenner.)

is coming into a very general use—an alleged artificial travertin. [193] I have very rarely seen any so-called artificial travertin that looked very much like the original, with the exception of that in the Pennsylvania Station and one or two other jobs which I don't recall now.

XQ. 11. You haven't seen any of Mr. Denivelle's work of late? A. No.

XQ. 12. Referring again to that clause in the release which Mr. Denivelle signed, wherein he agreed to make all repairs and replacements needed during the next year, is that an ordinary custom in the business?

A. Why, it is usually provided in the specifications—in the contract—that a guaranty of a certain period— 1, 2 or 5 years—should be given, but this is somewhat different.

XQ. 13. That is what is termed a "maintenance" bond—but this is unusual?

A. I think this is unusual, yes.

Mr. LOFTUS.—I don't think I have anything further.

Redirect Examination.

(By Mr. ANDERSON.)

RDQ. 1. Mr. Fenner, do you mean that it is unusual for a contractor to agree to repair any fault in the work which appears within one year from the date of its completion?

A. No, not at all. I don't know whether those [194] specifications provide that the contractor shall be responsible for damage due to defective

(Deposition of Burt L. Fenner.)

material or faulty workmanship for any given period; it is our usual custom to insert such a paragraph in all specifications but this form of release including the requirement that the contractor continue to maintain the work for a given period and devote his own time to that, is somewhat unusual— I don't recall any other case in our practice where just that course has been followed.

RDQ. 2. But is it usual to require a contractor to take care of defects that may arise within one year or a certain period after a job is completed?

A. Yes.

RDQ. 3. Of your own knowledge, do you know that the Miller Company installed the plastering work in that Station and the ceiling of the main waiting-room?

A. I know that they had the general plastering contract for the station, but whether that included the ceiling of the main waiting-room, I don't know of my own knowledge.

RDQ. 4. Is it to be assumed that McKim, Mead & White in drawing up the specifications for the Pennsylvania Station, took into consideration the condition which would arise owing to the use of that Station by trains, etc.?   A. Yes.

Redirect examination closed.

Mr. LOFTUS.—I have nothing further.

Deposition closed.

Signature waived.

Recess.   [195]

[Title of Court and Cause.]

        3:00 P. M., Tuesday, March 4, 1924.

Met pursuant to adjournment for recess.

Parties present as before.

It is agreed that Mr. Torbert's deposition may be taken before George H. Emslie, Esq., notary public, and taken stenographically by Miss Hoffman, a stenographer in the employ of defendants' counsel.

DEPOSITION OF VANCE W. TORBERT, FOR DEFENDANTS.

VANCE W. TORBERT, a witness produced on behalf of the defendants, having been duly cautioned and sworn, in answer to interrogatories propounded by Mr. Anderson, testified as follows: [196]

Q. 1. Your full name, Mr. Torbert, is—?

A. Vance W. Torbert.

Q. 2. How old are you?   A. 33.

Q. 3. And where do you reside?

A. Brooklyn, New York.

Q. 4. What is your occupation or profession?

A. Architect.

Q. 5. Are you in business on your own account or associated with some firm?

A. On my own account.

Q. 6. You were formerly associated with Carrere & Hastings, Architects, of New York City?

A. Yes, sir.

Q. 7. When were you associated with Carrere & Hastings?

(Deposition of Vance W. Torbert.)

A. June, 1911, until September, 1918.

Q. 8. While you were with that firm, did they construct for Robert Goelet at Goshen, New York, a house or residence?   A. Yes, sir.

Q. 9. Did you have anything to do with the work in connection with the Robert Goelet house?

A. Yes, sir.

Q. 10. Just what was your connection with that piece of work?

A. Resident superintendent, representing Carrere & Hastings.   [197]

Q. 11. And how long were you representing Carrere & Hastings as resident superintendent, in the construction of that Goelet house?

A. From about the middle of May until the middle of December 1913.

Q. 12. You recognize Mr. Paul E. Denivelle, who is here present?   A. Yes, sir.

Q. 13. Did he or his company do any work in connection with that Robert Goelet house?

A. Yes, sir.

Q. 14. Just what work was done by Mr. Denivelle or the Denivelle Company on the Goelet house?

Mr. LOFTUS.—Objection is made to any testimony intended to show any alleged prior use in connection with the Goelet house, on the ground of lack of proper notice.

A. I suppose I should tell what I know, not what I've heard—tell just what I know?

Mr. LOFTUS.—That's all you can testify to— what you know.

(Deposition of Vance W. Torbert.)

A. Various walls and railings and garden wall.

Q. 15. When did you go on that job as resident superintendent?   A. Middle of May, 1913.

Q. 16. And what was the condition of the job when you went on it? [198]

A. The main house was practically completed except for the interior finish, and the surrounding terraces were just being started in construction.

Q. 17. And the work on the surrounding terraces which was being started, was that being done by Mr. Denivelle or his company?

A. Only the stucco and imitation travertin.

Q. 18. Do you recall just what work Mr. Denivelle did which you might call imitation travertin?

A. Yes, sir.

Q. 19. What was it?

A. Railings of the terraces and the coping of the four-court wall about the driveway entrance.

Q. 20. What were your duties on that particular job?

A. The duties which are generally known as clerk of the works.

Q. 21. And what do they consist of?

A. Superintendence of construction.

Q. 22. Was Mr. Denivelle's imitation travertin work done under your superintendence?

A. I wouldn't say so much under my superintendence as under my observation.

Q. 23. You saw the work being done?

A. Yes, sir.

(Deposition of Vance W. Torbert.)

Q. 24. Do you know what we mean when we speak of imitation travertin? [199]   A. Yes, sir.

Q. 24. Had you seen any imitation travertin before that Goelet house was constructed?

A. I don't recall that I had.

Q. 25. You hadn't seen similar work done by Mr. Denivelle in the Pennsylvania Station?

A. Not before I went up on that job, no, sir.

Q. 26. Have you seen the imitation travertin work done by Mr. Denivelle in the Pennsylvania Station since that job was done?   A. Yes, sir.

Q. 27. How did the work which he did on the Goelet house compare, as to appearance, with the imitation travertin which you saw in the Pennsylvania Station?

A. The general texture and color compares quite —about the same.

Q. 28. Now, you say you left that job on the Goelet house in December, 1913?   A. Yes, sir.

Q. 29. When you left there in December, 1913, had Mr. Denivelle finished his work on that house?

A. So far as I recall; if there was work done subsequent to my time I don't know of it.

Q. 30. Well, do you recall now whether Mr. Denivelle or his company had completed the work which you have specifically mentioned here, and had gone away from the Goelet house before [200] you left there?   A. Yes, sir, they had.

Q. 31. Now, Mr. Gaylor, representing Carrere & Hastings, was also on that job with you, was he not?

(Deposition of Vance W. Torbert.)

A. Yes, sir.

Direct examination closed.

Cross-examination.

(By Mr. LOFTUS.)

XQ. 1. When you left the Goelet job in December, 1913, was the house occupied by the family—completed and occupied?

A. It was completely furnished but not yet occupied.

XQ. 2. Well, then, it was occupied some time after December, 1913, is that right?　　A. Yes, sir.

XQ. 3. How do you fix the date of December, 1913, as the time when you left the job?

A. I don't just understand what you mean—how do I fix it.

XQ. 4. Have you looked that date up recently or—?　　A. I know it from positive recollection.

XQ. 5. Your recollection?

A. Yes, sir; to be exact, it was December 13th when I left there.

XQ. 6. While you were on that job, did you have occasion to observe the process or method which Mr. Denivelle used in [201] constructing the imitation travertin?　　A. Yes, sir.

XQ. 7. Can you describe what that process or method was?

A. I have particular recollection of the manner in which the terrace wall railing was formed, and that is, it was run in a plastic form and the moldings were shaped by means of a template.

(Deposition of Vance W. Torbert.)

XQ. 8. In other words, these moldings were run in place, were they?

A. That's right, and of course after they were run they used a wire brush or some such stiff instrument to pick out little spots and create the imitation of the travertin.

XQ. 9. How far was this house or building from the highway?

A. When you refer to a highway you mean public road?

XQ. 10. The public highway, yes?

A. A thousand feet, I should say.

XQ. 11. This house was situated on a large tract of ground owned by Mr. Goelet, was it?

A. Yes, sir.

XQ. 12. Private grounds?　　A. Yes, sir.

XQ. 13. You don't know if Mr. Denivelle did any work there after you left in December, 1913?

A. I do not.

XQ. 14. Do you recall the names of any of Mr. Denivelle's [202] employees or foremen on that job?

A. There is only one name that comes to my mind at all—I remember their faces and their characters quite well—there was one man named "Jim" as I recall; that's not much of a name to give you—and a short red-headed fellow up there—couldn't recall his name.

Mr. LOFTUS.—I haven't anything further.

Cross-examination closed.

(Deposition of Vance W. Torbert.)

Redirect Examination.

(By Mr. ANDERSON.)

RDQ. 1. When you went on that job, was there some imitation travertin work already completed?

A. Yes, sir.

RDQ. 2. And what part was already completed?

A. The main entrance doorway, all of the window sills and some window trim.

RDQ. 3. Was that all imitation travertin?

A. As I recall it, yes, sir.

RDQ. 4. Did you leave the employ of Carrere & Hastings in December, 1913?   A. No, sir.

RDQ. 5. You went back to the New York office?

A. Yes, sir.

RDQ. 6. Did you have anything to do with the installation [203] of any other imitation travertin during the years 1914 and 1915?   A. No, sir.

Redirect examination closed.

Mr. LOFTUS.—I have nothing further.

Deposition closed.

Signature waived.

Recess.   [204]

[Title of Court and Cause.]

5:00 P. M., Tuesday, March 4, 1924.

Met pursuant to adjournment for recess.

Parties present as before.

It is agreed that the deposition of Mr. Whipple may be taken before George H. Emslie, Esq., notary public, and taken and transcribed by Miss Hoffman, a stenographer in the employ of Munn, Anderson & Munn.

DEPOSITION OF FRANK A. WHIPPLE, FOR DEFENDANTS.

FRANK A. WHIPPLE, a witness subpoenaed on behalf of the defendants, having been duly cautioned and sworn, in answer to interrogatories propounded by Mr. Anderson, testified as follows: [205]

Q. 1. Your full name, Mr. Whipple, is Frank A. Whipple?   A. Frank A. Whipple.

Q. 2. How old are you, Mr. Whipple?   A. 61.

Q. 3. And where do you live?

A. Roosevelt, Long Island.

Q. 4. What business are you in?

A. Plastering.

Q. 5. And how long have you been a plasterer?

A. Well, let's see; I was 18 years old when I started—ever since I was 18 years of age.

Q. 6. You are acquainted with Mr. Paul E. Denivelle, here present?   A. Yes, sir.

Q. 7. How long have you known Mr. Denivelle?

A. Well, I should say over 20 years, probably 23 or 24 years, something like that.

Q. 8. Did you work with Mr. Denivelle or his company on the Pennsylvania Station in this city?

A. Yes, sir.

Q. 9. And that work was the installation of some so-called imitation travertin stone, was it?

A. Yes, sir.

Q. 10. How long were you working on that job?

A. Six or seven months—we started in the spring and it was—as far as my part of it went—   [206]

(Deposition of Frank A. Whipple.)

Q. 11. The spring of what year?

A. 1909 or 1910—I don't just remember the year.

Q. 12. Just what work were you doing on that job?

A. Well, I had the job of erecting the stone— the cast stone.

Q. 13. You were in charge of the installation of the cast blocks of imitation travertin, is that right?

A. Yes, sir.

Q. 14. Were you representing Mr. Denivelle or his company on that job?

A. I was working for him—under his supervision.

Q. 15. You were foreman of the job?

A. Yes.

Q. 16. Were you on that job at the time Mr. Denivelle or his company submitted and installed a sample preparatory to going to work on the job?

A. No.

Q. 17. Do you know whether or not Mr. Denivelle or his company did submit and install a sample?

A. There was a sample put up and my attention was called to it at one time that he had put it there —just one piece of stone.

Q. 18. Did you see at that time samples that had been installed by anyone else?

A. I saw one sample that they told me McNulty had put up—that was before the job was started.

[207]

(Deposition of Frank A. Whipple.)

Q. 19. And do you know where that McNulty sample was?

A. Well, to the best of my recollection, it would be on the west end at the south side of the Seventh Avenue Arcade—just as you go in the rotunda— it has been so long—I only took a glance at it.

Q. 20. Well, now, do you know whether that sample which you were told had been put there by Mc-Nulty, was taken down?   A. Yes.

Q. 21. It was taken down?

A. It was. It wasn't there when I came back to start setting the stone.

Q. 22. You were not there at the time these samples were installed?

A. No, I was on another job.

Q. 23. Now, when you got through with that Pennsylvania job, what did you do?

A. Well, I was sent away from there before it was completed, to go and do some other work for Mr. Denivelle.

Q. 24. And what other work did you do after that?

A. If I remember right, we did some Caenstone hallways up on 81st Street near Central Park West —3 or 4 houses there.

Q. 25. And you had charge of that for Mr. Deni-velle?   A. Yes, sir.

Q. 26. And after that job was finished, what did you do?

A. And from there, if I remember right, I went out to Howard Carroll's house at Tarrytown.

[208]

(Deposition of Frank A. Whipple.)

Q. 27. Did you do any artificial travertin work in that house? A. No.

Q. 28. Did you continue on that Pennsylvania job with Mr. Denivelle until it was completed?

A. No, after that I came back and there was a couple of more rooms—some waiting-rooms were done, but not in travertin.

Q. 29. Not in travertin?

A. No, the walls had been plastered white, and then they changed it into what they called a Uval model for the limestone—or something of that description—2 subwaiting-rooms.

Q. 30. Where was this imitation travertin stone installed that was put in by Mr. Denivelle in the Pennsylvania Station?

A. In the Seventh Avenue vestibule or Arcade; the main waiting-room; the walls; and as you go up the stairs, the hallways like—and each end of the balconies above—just off the main waiting-room.

Q. 31. Was that work finished when you left the job—I mean the installation of imitation travertin?

A. No, there was work there after I left—I never had anything to do with that after I left.

Q. 32. You mean the imitation travertin work?

A. After I touched up the maps I didn't have anything to do with that—I was on other jobs. [209]

Q. 33. How much imitation travertin had been installed at the time you left?

A. Considerable of it—I was back there a num-

(Deposition of Frank A. Whipple.)

ber of times—little things had to be done like the
figures over the arches that we helped set up, and different things like that.   Then there was lots of in-
completed parts around the maps—they didn't get
the design.   Not being there, I couldn't tell you
why it wasn't done, but we had gone as far as we
could and I was sent to other work.

Q. 34. Well, now, had you finished the wall of
the large waiting-room before you went on this
other job?

A. No, not around the maps nor the figures, and
I have seen other work that was done there after
I left, that wasn't completed.

Q. 35. Did you go to Canada on a job for Mr.
Denivelle?   A. Yes, sir.

Q. 36. When did you go there on the job for Mr.
Denivelle?

A. I think that was in the spring of 1911.

Q. 37. What job was that?

A. The Ottawa Station—Union Station, if I remember right.

Q. 38. And did you install imitation travertin
in that station?

Mr. LOFTUS.—The question is objected to on
the ground that any use of this invention in a foreign country is incompetent, irrelevant and immaterial.   Further objection is made   [210]   on the
ground of lack of proper notice.

By Mr. ANDERSON.—Obviously this evidence
is not offered to prove any prior use; it is mainly
offered to show Mr. Denivelle's activities in the in-

(Deposition of Frank A. Whipple.)

stallation of imitation travertin, particularly after the Pennsylvania job had been completed, and in support of the defense that Mr. Denivelle himself had put his alleged invention into public use more than two years before he filed his application for patent.   A. Well, yes.

Q. 39. And was that imitation travertin which you installed in the Ottawa Station like that which you had installed in the Pennsylvania Station for Mr. Denivelle?

A. Pretty near the same—well, I had charge of the applied work there, the same as at the Pennsylvania Station.

Q. 40. Was this work in the Ottawa Station applied work or cast work?   A. Both.

Q. 41. And how did that compare with the work which you had supervised for Mr. Denivelle in the Pennsylvania Station?

A. We got along better there.

Q. 42. Well, was it the same kind of stone?

A. I don't know—it was imitation travertin—as to the material, I couldn't say—I think it was a little different material but it looked like imitation travertin which we had put in the Pennsylvania Station.   [211]

Q. 43. The same?   A. Yes.

Q. 44. Do you remember when this was that you went to Ottawa; I think you said 1911?

A. It was 1911—in April.

Q. 45. When was that work completed?

(Deposition of Frank A. Whipple.)

A. I couldn't tell you—I left there in October—about the 1st of October.

Q. 46. 1911? A. Yes.

Q. 47. Had the imitation travertin work been put in when you left there?

A. I left some men there when I left—

Q. 48. Before you left, had you put some imitation travertin work in that Station? A. Yes.

Q. 49. And you put it in there for Denivelle? You were working for Mr. Denivelle?

A. Yes, sir.

Q. 50. Did you also work on a job which Mr. Denivelle had in Montreal, Canada?

A. Travertin?

Q. 51. Yes?

A. No, I never did any travertin in Montreal—other imitations though, but not travertin. I worked for Mr. Denivelle but not on travertin work. [212]

Q. 52. What job did you have in Montreal for Mr. Denivelle? A. Well, the Windsor Station.

Q. 53. What kind of work was that?

A. That wasn't artificial stone—I think they called it "Yorkshire" or "Limestone." That's one job and then I was on another one just before I went to Ottawa.

Q. 54. What was that job?

A. That was the imitation Botticeno—it was in a private residence.

Q. 55. Did you work on a job for Mr. Denivelle

(Deposition of Frank A. Whipple.)

in a building on 23d Street, just east of Broadway on the South side?   A. Yes, sir.

Q. 56. And was that artificial travertin?

A. Artificial travertin applied.

Q. 57. And when did you work on that job?

A. I think that was done, if I'm not mistaken, in 1912.

Q. 58. Now, you went out to California for Mr. Denivelle, didn't you?   A. Yes, sir.

Q. 59. And when did you go to California for Mr. Denivelle?

A. I left here the 10th day of April, 1913.

Q. 60. And did you go with Mr. Denivelle or was he there and sent for you?

A. No, I went with him.   [213]

Q. 61. And that was in 1913?   A. Yes.

Q. 62. What month?

A. The 10th of April we left here.

Q. 63. And what did you do out in California?

A. When we first went there we did a lot of experimenting.

Q. 64. What were you doing there?

A. My position there was to supervise the applied work, also to supervise the erection of the staff of imitation travertin.

Q. 65. And by "staff" you mean what is called colored stone?

A. Colored stone—imitation travertin.

Q. 66. Did you do any installation of cast imitation travertin in California for Mr. Denivelle?

A. We had charge of the erection of some of the

(Deposition of Frank A. Whipple.)

—there was some of the fountains—alongside—just a supervisory capacity to see that they were put up properly—that is all I had to do with it.

Q. 67. And when did you say you left for California?

A. The 10th day of April, 1913,—left New York.

Q. 68. Was the imitation travertin work which you did in California like that which you had done in the Pennsylvania Station?

A. Similar—it might have been a little coarser [214] in texture.

Q. 69. Did you in that California work, use blocks of imitation travertin slabs?

A. Of cast work?

Q. 70. Yes? A. Yes.

Q. 71. And how did those slabs compare with the work which was done in the Pennsylvania Station?

A. Well, they were about the same—it was more of a—everything seemed to be a little coarser texture than what they would have for interior jobs.

Q. 72. And this was the exterior work on the Exposition Buildings, was it? A. Yes, sir.

Q. 73. Did you work on the Goelet house for Mr. Denivelle?

A. I was sent there for one day when they first started to stipple the work—I was part of two days there.

(Deposition of Frank A. Whipple.)

Q. 74. When you went to California—in October, 1913, was it? A. April.

Q. 75. —April, 1913, was the Pennsylvania Station opene and being used for passengers?

A. Yes, so far as I know; I don't know as I hadn't been there, but what I understand it was.

Q. 76. This was April, 1913? A. Yes. [215]

Q. 77. Did you leave by the Pennsylvania Station or the New York Central? A. By the Erie.

Q. 78. Had you visited the Pennsylvania Station after the time it was completed?

A. Not as I know of—I had been in Montreal for Mr. Denivelle and I came right down from Montreal, and had some of my own business to attend to, and we started for California.

Q. 79. When did you come back from Montreal?

A. In March that same year, 1913.

Q. 80. Well, it was in 1911 that you went to Ottawa, wasn't it?

A. I was up there again in Montreal—I went up there, I think, in January—about the 1st of January, 1913.

Q. 81. Am I correct in my statement that you testified that it was in 1911 that you went to Ottawa and installed some imitation travertin for Mr. Denivelle in the Railroad Station at Ottawa?

A. Yes, sir; I think it's the Union Station—I don't just remember.

Q. 82· Now, in just what part of that Station did you put in the imitation travertin?

A. It would be the entrance hall, virtually a

(Deposition of Frank A. Whipple.)
duplicate of the Pennsylvania—the main waiting-
room—and some in the concourse—and some in
the basement corridor. [216]

Q. 83. I understood you to say that that imitation
travertin that you installed in that Ottawa Station
was in appearance like that which you had put into
the Pennsylvania Station for Mr. Denivelle?

A. Yes, sir.

Direct examination closed.

Cross-examination.

(By Mr. LOFTUS.)

XQ. 1. In this work that was done in the Pennsylvania Station, Mr. Whipple, where were these
slabs or pieces of travertin made? Did you have
a shop of any kind there?

A. Well, in the beginning they were made at Mr.
Denivelle's shop uptown, but later they were made
in—a week or so after we started they were made
in the Pennsylvania Station.

XQ. 2. Was there a part fenced off for a shop
there in the station?

A. Yes, in the Seventh Avenue Arcade.

XQ. 3. And was that shop open to the public?

A. No.

XQ. 4. Outsiders were not permitted to enter
there?   A. No.

XQ. 5. Now your work, as I understand it, was
erecting these cast pieces?   A. Yes, sir.   [217]

XQ. 6. Did you find it necessary to reject many
of these cast pieces in your work there?

(Deposition of Frank A. Whipple.)

A. Lots of them.

XQ. 7. For what reason—were they imperfectly made?

A. Well, imperfectly made—some would be smooth; some would be too rough; some of them part of the face would fall off; and they seemed to be having a divil of a time with it.

XQ. 8. Were there different methods or processes used at that time to get better results?

A. I could answer that only from hearsay. I had nothing to do with the manufacture of it—I would hear the men talking—and what they were trying to do—

XQ. 9. They were having a great deal of difficulty with it? A. Yes.

XQ. 10. Now, what kind of material was used in the work in the Pennsylvania Station?

A. As I understand it, it was a white Portland cement.

XQ. 11. Now, in your work at Ottawa, did you use a white Portland cement? A. No.

XQ. 12. What did you use there?

A. I don't know what it was; it wasn't a Portland [218] cement; it was either Keene's cement or plaster combination, or something like that.

XQ. 13. Anyway, it was different from the Pennsylvania job?

A. It looked the same, but it was different.

XQ. 14. And in the work at the San Francisco Exposition, did you use white Portland cement?

A. On some portions of it.

(Deposition of Frank A. Whipple.)

XQ. 15. Prior to this Pennsylvania job had you ever seen any artificial travertin?   A. No, sir.

XQ. 16. Had you ever handled or worked with any artificial stone structures in which a part of the structure is porous and the rest is more or less solid?

A. Before that time?

XQ. 17. Before that time?   A. No.

XQ. 18. Now, would the fact that this artificial travertin was made partly porous and partly solid be likely to cause trouble in warpage or flaking off?

A. I know that was one of our troubles—it would peel off in places.

XQ. 19. Have you any idea how long a test would be necessary to find out whether a new material like that would be satisfactory and would stand up and be valuable?   [219]

Mr. ANDERSON.—I object to that as calling for a mere opinion.

XQ. 20. Would it be likely to need several years' time and use?

A. Well, I couldn't say to that. I know that if a stone is put up green and dries, it is liable to peel off. · We had a lot of that difficulty—a stone would be set up there and maybe in a few weeks you would come back and a part of the face would be off.

XQ. 21. The only way to find out about these things is to put them up and try them out?

A. Well, that's what we did—it looked all right but you come back and find a part of the face dropped off for some reason or other.

(Deposition of Frank A. Whipple.)

XQ. 22. There were unusual conditions there in that Station on account of vibration—was that one of your troubles?

A. That was the great trouble there—it was the vibration.

XQ. 23. Do you know whether or not Mr. Denivelle or his organization had to make repairs or replacements in the Pennsylvania work after the work was finished?

A. I heard when I came back from Montreal that he had a gang of men there doing repairs.

XQ. 24. That would be what time?

A. That's when we left for San Francisco because [220] I was in his shop in April, 1913, and he told me there he had some men working on the Pennsylvania job doing some repairs, or something there—I didn't go down there to see.

XQ. 25. Now, the work on the Pennsylvania Station was cast work, wasn't it, casting or molding, as they call it?

A. The greater part of it—part of it was applied.

XQ. 26. And when you went to work on the Ottawa job you changed that mode to one of applying it with a trowel?

A. There was very little cast work on the Ottawa job.

XQ. 27. What parts were cast there?

A. There were some molded bases and some fluted columns and Corinthian caps; the cornices were all made in place, and all the plain surfaces, ordinary particles, pilasters, etc., were all made in place.

(Deposition of Frank A. Whipple.)

XQ. 28. You know the defendants in this case, MacGruer and Simpson? A. Yes, sir.

XQ. 29. When did you become acquainted with them?

A. In 1913 when we reached California.

XQ. 30. Did they do any work on the Exposition Buildings? A. Yes.

XQ. 31· What work did they do?

A. They were doing Machinery Hall when we got there.

XQ. 32. Was that artificial travertin?

A. Artificial travertin. [221]

XQ. 33. Under whose instructions and directions were they working on the artificial travertin?

A. When we got there?

XQ. 34. Yes,—in connection with the imitation travertin?

A. When they got started they were under Mr. Denivelle and myself—Mr. Denivelle first gave them instructions.

XQ. 35. In other words, you and Mr. Denivelle taught them how to apply this travertin?

A. And we also had another man who taught them how to cast it.

XQ. 36. In other words, you and Mr. Denivelle taught them? A. Yes.

XQ. 37. Did you have any difficulties in teaching them how to do this work? A. The applied work?

XQ. 38. Yes?

A. Well, everyone seemed to be bucking against it when they went there—every contractor—they

(Deposition of Frank A. Whipple.)

just seemed to see how rotten they could do the thing—they wanted to drive it out if they could—

XQ. 39. In other words, they were opposed to the idea of artificial travertin?

A. They were opposed to it strong.

XQ. 40. Was the work delayed and made more difficult on that account?

A. The only thing—I would have to condemn it [222] and they would have to do it over.

XQ. 41. You found it necessary to condemn a great deal of the work?

A. Condemned quite a little in the start, and when they saw they had to do it over they straightened out and tried to do it passable.

XQ. 42. Mr. MacGruer felt at one time that he would be able to stop the use of this travertin on the Exposition work, did he?

A. Well, not Mr. MacGruer alone,—all the contractors.

XQ. 43. What did they say or do in that connection?

A. Well, they said they wouldn't be dictated to by us and they called a meeting of all the employees in the Service Building to try to have our supervision stopped, saying that we wanted too good a job done.

XQ. 44. How long since you have been in Mr. Denivelle's employ?

A. I haven't been employed by Mr. Denivelle since I got through with the Fair, 1915—about the 1st of May.

(Deposition of Frank A. Whipple.)

X.Q. 45. Now, this job that was done on 23d Street, which you referred to in your direct examination— what kind of material was used there?

A. White Portland cement.

X.Q. 46. Was that a cast job or was it applied?

A. No, that was applied—made in place— [223] everything there.

X.Q. 47. That was a different method from that used in the Pennsylvania?

A. Well, there was some of that applied work in the Pennsylvania.

X.Q. 48. Do you know anything about how extensive this artificial travertin is used at the present time in and around New York?

A. I see a great deal of it every day I go out. I saw a new job to-day—I never heard tell of it before—I went up to get a new automobile license— got into a door and there was a hallway of applied travertin.

X.Q. 49. How does that work compare with the travertin work that was done by Denivelle while you were in his employ?

A. I would call it rotten what I saw to-day—it's a disgrace to call it that—but they try to imitate it.

X.Q. 50. How long have you been in the plastering business, Mr. Whipple?   A. Since I was 18.

X.Q. 51. How much experience have you had in connection with artificial stone structures?

A. Well, I have been working on artificial stone at different times since about 1898.

X.Q. 52. Until this work came up in the Pennsyl-

(Deposition of Frank A. Whipple.)

vania Station, had you ever seen anything that looked like this [224] artificial travertin, or was made in any way like it?

A. No, I never saw anything like it—never heard of it.

XQ. 53. In your answer regarding the 23d Street job you mentioned that that travertin was applied —in what manner was it applied?

A. With a trowel and hawk, stippled with a brush.

Mr. LOFTUS.—I think that's all.

Cross-examination closed.

Redirect Examination.

(By Mr. ANDERSON.)

RDQ. 1. Mr. Whipple, you said that there were some applied imitation travertin in the Pennsylvania Station, and that was done by Mr. Denivelle or his company? A. Yes.

RDQ. 2. And this was also applied imitation travertin in the 23d Street job, was it? A. Yes, sir.

RDQ. 3. And that was done under your supervision by Mr. Denivelle or his company? A. Yes.

RDQ. 4. Was that done in the same way as the Pennsylvania applied travertin? A. Same way.

RDQ. 5. And in this Ottawa job, was the applied imitation [225] travertin in the Ottawa Station done in the same way as that which was done in the Pennsylvania Station?

A. In the same manner. We discovered a different brush when we got up there to give it more of a natural look that we didn't have in the Pennsylvania job.

(Deposition of Frank A. Whipple.)

RDQ. 6. Well, now, in making this applied travertin, you produce the holes by a brush?   A. Yes.

RDQ. 7. A wire brush?

A. A wire brush or a fibre.

RDQ. 8. And drive it into the surface before it is dried and set?

A. While it's in a putty state—before it is set.

RDQ. 9. And in any event, the 23d Street applied imitation travertin, and the applied imitation travertin in the Ottawa Station, and the applied imitation travertin in the Pennsylvania Station, was all done in the same way with the exception of a different brush?

A. A brush that gave it a more natural look.

RDQ. 10. And is your testimony also that the cast imitation travertin which was employed in the Pennsylvania Station, and that which was employed in the Ottawa Station were exactly the same in construction and appearance?

Mr. LOFTUS.—Objected to as leading and suggestive.

A. They had the idea—as to a copy of real travertin they had the same color, but as for the construction [226] I don't know as they were the same, for this reason, that Portland cement would be backed up with Portland cement, and a plaster proposition or gypsum proposition would be backed up with fibre and plaster.

RDQ. 11. But so far as the appearance was concerned—

(Deposition of Frank A. Whipple.)

A. The outside appearance—it looked virtually the same.

RDQ. 12. Do you know what the cast imitation travertin which was installed in the Pennsylvania Station was made of?   A. Portland cement.

RDQ. 13. Do you know that?

A. I could tell that, yes, sir.

RDQ. 14. And what was the cast imitation travertin which was installed in the Ottawa Station made of?

A. I should call it a gypsum product—it wasn't a Portland cement—gypsum or Keene's cement; I couldn't say what the formula was, but it looked to me—it wasn't a Portland cement proposition.

RDQ. 15. Well, now, when did you get out to California?   A. The 15th of April, 1913.

RDQ. 16. Did you do any work for Mr. Denivelle on those Exposition Buildings?   A. Yes.

RDQ. 17. Was it applied or cast imitation travertin which you were doing for Mr. Denivelle? [227]

A. Personally you mean—with my own hands?

RDQ. 18. Yes?   A. Both.

RDQ. 19. Was that applied and imitation travertin which was being installed by Mr. Denivelle on the Exposition Buildings in California of the same character as that which you had done at Ottawa and in the Pennsylvania Station?

A. It was the same character but of a coarser texture.

RDQ. 20. That is to say, you made deeper holes in the surface, is that right?   A. Yes.

(Deposition of Frank A. Whipple.)

RDQ. 21. What was that material made of?

A. That's a pure plaster proposition.

RDQ. 22. It wasn't made of cement at all?

A. But there was some cement there too.

RDQ. 23. When did you first install or supervise the installation of any applied or cast imitation travertin for Mr. Denivelle on one of those Exposition Buildings?

A. I supervised it—I think it would be long about August.

RDQ. 24. August, what year?

A. 1913—that's to the best of my memory.

RDQ. 25. Now, you went there as representing Mr. Denivelle, to instruct MacGruer and Simpson and the other contractors how [228] to make this imitation travertin, is that right?

A. And to get a good material to stand outside.

RDQ. 26. You went there to instruct them how to make imitation travertin, did you?   A. Yes, sir.

RDQ. 27. And did you give them instructions as how to make imitation travertin?   A. Yes, sir.

RDQ. 28. And did you see that they made it according to your instructions?   A. Yes, sir.

RDQ. 29. And did you instruct them according to Mr. Denivelle's instructions to you?

A. Yes, sir.

RDQ. 30. Now, was it your understanding that aside from the difference in the material used, you were following the instructions under which the travertin had been installed in the Pennsylvania Station?   A. No.

(Deposition of Frank A. Whipple.)

RDQ. 31. Was it different in texture?

A. It was coarser. I mean in building it up—

RDQ. 32. Was it done the same way?

A. For the applied work we used a different brush again—when we got there we used a different brush altogether than we had ever used. [229]

RDQ. 33. But aside from the difference in brush, was that applied work done in the same way that you had done it in the Pennsylvania Station?

A. It was the same at the Pennsylvania—with hawk and trowel—but there was a different brush to get a different effect—more exaggerated—altogether different brush there.

RDQ. 34. But you are sure that so far as the applied work is concerned, the job which was done on 23rd Street in this city by you for Mr. Denivelle, was done in the same manner as the applied work in the Pennsylvania Station?

A. No, there was another difference there—in the Fair grounds on the outside work—

RDQ. 35. I have left the Fair grounds; I am talking now about the 23rd Street job?

A. That had 3 colors in it—all those blocks of material had 3 colors in it.

RDQ. 36. Well, aside from the difference in color?

A. Aside from the difference in color it was the same method—only a different brush.

RDQ. 37. Well, now, you supervised the installation of this applied imitation travertin in the Pennsylvania Station? A. Yes.

(Deposition of Frank A. Whipple.)

RDQ. 38. Was that all one color?

A. Part of it—when we started we didn't know [230] anything about putting more than one color into it, but as we got started we found we could apply the base—

RDQ. 39. And how did you put the base in?

A. With a brush—a long narrow brush—and it was mixed up in a thick cream, applied on, and squeezed in while it was soft.

RDQ. 40. And what did you do to the surface before putting in the color lines?

A. We applied one body color first, and that was in a soft, putty state, and then we took this mold and darker part, and put it in—and spread them in with a trowel.

RDQ. 41. Would you lay it on the surface?

A. Right on the surface, and then squeeze it in with a trowel and put the seams to set, and when they were blended in a way they thought they belonged, then it was stippled afterwards—the lines, I mean—and smoothed off.

RDQ. 42. Now, you didn't go back to the Pennsylvania Station and do any repair work, did you?

A. No.

RDQ. 43. When you got through there the work which had been put up under your supervision was in good shape, wasn't it—when you left there?

A. When I left it was all right, naturally.

RDQ. 44. Now, you say you went back there. what for?

(Deposition of Frank A. Whipple.)

A. Well, I went back once to help put up some extension of imitation travertin. [231]

RDQ. 45. And that was before you went to California? A. Yes.

RDQ. 46. Now, you were subpoenaed in this case, weren't you, Mr. Whipple? A. Yes, sir.

RDQ. 47. Since you were subpoenaed, have you seen and talked with Mr. Denivelle?

A. Mr. Denivelle called me up after he came to New York a couple of weeks ago, about the matter.

RDQ. 48. And he talked to you about the testimony which you were going to give in this case?

A. No, he discussed the case a little—not much—I told him I had seen Mr MacGruer and he said they had a suit on—

RDQ. 49. And did you only talk to him over the telephone?

A. No, I saw him at the Pennsylvania Hotel.

RDQ. 50. You saw him at the Pennsylvania Hotel? A. Yes, sir.

RDQ. 51. He asked you to come and see him? A. Yes.

RDQ. 52. Was that within the last two weeks? A. Yes.

RDQ. 53. How long did you talk with him?

A. Probably three-quarters of an hour.

RDQ. 54. And he went over with you the various travertin jobs that you had been connected with? [232] .

A. We talked about some jobs we had done

(Deposition of Frank A. Whipple.)

—mostly conversation about old times in California.

Redirect examination closed.

Recross-examination.

RXQ. 1. As I understand from your testimony, Mr. Whipple, there were changes and improvements being constantly made in this process from the time that you did the Pennsylvania Station until the time of the work in California?

A. Yes, lots of changes—lots of improvements.

RXQ. 2. Now, unless this material would stand up under varying temperature changes, and withstand the vibrations of this railroad station for 4 or 5 years, it wouldn't be of much account?

A. No, it would have to be pretty strong material to stand there.

RXQ. 3. Was there any way of finding out whether it would stand up, except to put it in place?

A. I don't know that there was any other way unless you put it there and see what it would do.

RXQ. 4. No way of testing it in the shop, was there?

A. Don't see how you could because that would be under different conditions.

RXQ. 5. You would have no way of imitating these vibrations, would you?

A. Well, I don't know of any—no more than you [233] could tell whether this house was going to crack or not—

RXQ. 6. But with materials that are old and well-known you know what they will do before you put

(Deposition of Frank A. Whipple.)
them in place, don't you?—when you are dealing
with materials that are well known?

A. Yes, sir.

Mr. LOFTUS.—I haven't anything further.

Re-redirect Examination.

(By Mr. ANDERSON.)

RRDQ. 1. As representing Mr. Denivelle on that
Pennsylvania job, did you inspect and pass each
piece of cast imitation travertin that was put up
on the wall?   A. That was my work.

RRDQ. 2. And you didn't put into that wall
knowingly any defective slab of imitation travertin?   A. No; not knowingly.

RRDQ. 3. When you passed it, according to
your judgment it was fit to go on that wall, wasn't
it?   A. Yes.

Mr. ANDERSON.—That is all.

Deposition closed.

Signature waived.

Adjourned until Wednesday morning at 10:30.
[234]

[Title of Court and Cause.]

New York, N. Y., March 5, 1924—10:30 A. M.

Met pursuant to adjournment.

Present: WILLIAM A. LOFTUS, Esq., Representing the Plaintiff.

T. HART ANDERSON, Esq., Representing the Defendants.

It is agreed by counsel that the deposition of Mr.
Julius F. Gayler may be taken before George H.

(Deposition of Julius F. Gayler.)

Emslie, Esq., a notary public, and taken down in shorthand and transcribed by Miss Helen · I. Gorman, a stenographer Mr. Emslie, being in the employ of Munn & Co., and Miss Gorman in the employ [235] of counsel for the defendants in this case.

DEPOSITION OF JULIUS F. GAYLER, FOR DEFENDANTS.

Direct Examination.

(By Mr. ANDERSON.)

JULIUS F. GAYLER, a witness appearing on behalf of the defendants, having been first duly cautioned and sworn, testifies as follows:

Q. 1. Mr. Gayler, your full name is Julius F. Gayler? A. Yes.

Q. 2. How old are you, Mr. Gayler? A. 51.

Q. 3. Mr. Gayler, where do you reside?

A. White Plains, N. Y.

Q. 4. What is your business or profession?

A. Architect.

Q. 5. How long have you been engaged in that profession?

A. Except when I was in college, since 1891.

Q. 6. Were you formerly associated with the firm of Carrere and Hastings, architects, of New York? A. Yes, sir.

Q. 7. When were you associated with that firm?

A. From 1895 to 1915, I think. I am not sure [236] it was 1915 or later than that.

(Deposition of Julius F. Gayler.)

Q. 8. And since leaving Carrere and Hastings have you been in business on your own account?

A. No, I went two years to Boston and was a partner there with Bellows & Aldrich for about two years; then opened up an office in New York on my own account.

Q. 9. Now, while you were with Carrere and Hastings, did they plan and construct a home for Robert Goelet, near Goshen, N. Y.?

A. Yes, sir.

Q. 10. Did you have anything to do with the building of that home for Robert Goelet?

A. Yes, sir.

Q. 11. Just what did you do in connection with the building of the Goelet home?

A. I had charge of the letting of the contracts, correspondence, interviews of the clients, and the general supervision of the job, both at the building and in the office.

Q. 12. Can you state when that Goelet house was begun and when it was finished?

A. No. I can't state, excepting that I know it was finished, from my recollection, I am reasonably positive of this, it was completed before February, 1914, that date being in my mind because then I went to Europe, and the house was completed before I went. [237]

Q. 13. Did you see the house in course of construction?

A. I went out once or twice a week during the process of its construction.

(Deposition of Julius F. Gayler.)

Q. 14. Do you know Mr. Paul E. Denivelle who is here present at this time? A. I do.

Q. 15. How long have you known Mr. Denivelle?

(Witness asks permission to consult some memoranda which he has brought with him, and does so.)

A. From March, 1912, about.

Q. 16. You spoke about letting the contracts for the Goelet house. Did Mr. Denivelle or any company with which he was associated get a contract in connection with that Goelet house?

A. Yes, sir.

Q. 17. And just what contract was given to Mr. Denivelle or his company?

A. Stuccoing the entire exterior of the house in pink stucco, with certain features in imitation travertin stone. He also had further contracts for various work and approaches, which were ordered later.

Q. 18. Do you recall the name of the company with which Mr. Denivelle was associated at that time? [238]

A. I do not. My impression was it was just Mr. Denivelle. I don't remember it as a company.

Q. 19. With whom did you conduct your negotiations concerning that contract?

A. With Mr. Denivelle here present.

Q. 20. You mentioned imitation travertin stone as being part of Mr. Denivelle's contract. How much of that imitation travertin stone did Mr. Denivelle install in connection with the Goelet house?

(Deposition of Julius F. Gayler.)

A. The features around the front door and certain features around the windows, the exact nature of which I do not recall.

Q. 21. Was that the extent of the imitation travertin stone installed by Mr. Denivelle in connection with the Goelet house?

A. Yes, sir, on the house itself, yes.

Q. 22. Was any other imitation travertin stone furnished on that job, by Mr. Denivelle?

A. Yes, sir.

Q. 23. What other parts were furnished by Mr. Denivelle?

A. Some work on the terrace, handrail and balustrade. He also did the stuccoing around the entrance court, and my impression is that there was an imitation travertine coping on this terrace wall, but I am not sure of it. [239]

Q. 24. I call your attention to a letter from the Denivelle H. C. S. Company, addressed to Carrere and Hastings dated April 4, 1912; a similar letter dated July 17, 1913; and a letter dated April 30, 1912; and a similar letter dated June 17, 1913, such letters being "Defendants' Exhibit 2, Carrere and Hastings' Correspondence," and I ask you whether you ever saw those letters before, and if you recognize them state whether there is anything on the letters which enables you to recognize them?

A. I have seen them before, and the stamp with my initials and the date on the lower right-hand corner indicates that I answered the letters for Carrere and Hastings.

(Deposition of Julius F. Gayler.)

Q. 25. Now, Mr. Gayler, I think that inadvertently you referred to a stamp in the lower right-hand corner of those letters, and I ask you if you meant to indicate a stamped endorsement in red ink which in some of the letters appears at the left-hand corner?

A. I mean in the lower right-hand corner. Our system was that whoever answered a letter in Carrere and Hastings stamped it in the lower right-hand corner.

Q. 26. Then you refer to the endorsement stamp in red "J. F. G." with the date immediately under it?   A. That's it.

Q. 27. Now, I call your attention to the other stamped endorsement, and ask if your initials appear in that. [240]

A. I will look it over. (Witness does so.) That is my initials "J. F. G." in each case.

Q. 28. Now, you state that the first stamped endorsement to which we have referred, "J. F. G.," with the date, indicates that you answered that letter. Now, will you look at the carbon copies forming a part of Exhibit 2, and state whether or not they are copies of letters dictated by you?

A. Yes, the initial "J. F. G." in the lower left-hand corner indicates that they are copies of letters dictated by me.

Q. 29. Now, having examined those carbon copies of letters dictated by you, can you state whether or not those letters were mailed to the company to whom they are apparently addressed?

(Deposition of Julius F. Gayler.)

A. I can only judge they were. I can't say they were. I judge so because Mr. Denivelle executed the work in accordance with them.

Q. 30. Now, the first letter to which I call your attention, letter dated April 4, 1912, is that the Denivelle Company's bid for the work on the Goelet house? A. It is.

Q. 31. Now, what is the letter dated July 17, from the Denivelle Company to Carrere and Hastings?

A. That is for the stucco work on the walls and the entrance court, as indicated by the letter. [241]

Q. 32. And what is the letter dated April 30, 1912, from the Denivelle Company?

Mr. LOFTUS.—Objected to, as the letter, if competent at all, speaks for itself.　　　.

A. It is the estimate for the stucco and travertine work on the terrace.

Q. 33. Now, the letter of April 4, 1912, submits an estimate for the perforated portion of the balcony railings, of the color of composite travertine, and other features in "our composite travertine," and the several loggias of composite travertine. The letter of April 30, 1912, refers to balusters of composite travertine. Did the Denivelle Company install the artificial travertine in the places on that Goelet house to which I have called your attention?

Mr. LOFTUS.—Objected to as leading.

A. Yes, sir.

(Deposition of Julius F. Gayler.)

Q. 34. What is your present recollection as to when the Denivelle contract was completed?

(The witness is referring to a memorandum which he has brought here, in answer to this question.)

A. I have a memorandum of the payments or certificates of payments, reading as follows:

Mr. LOFTUS.—The question, Mr. Gayler, was what was your recollection as to this. Have you any recollection, independent of this memorandum? [242]

A. None, excepting the general recollection that all work was generally done about 1913. I have no recollection of dates.

Q. 35. Now, this memorandum which you have brought here; where did you get the data which is on that memorandum?

A. It was given to me by Carrere and Hastings' bookkeeper, who wrote it.

Q. 36. When?   A. Yesterday.

Q. 37. What was your object in getting that memorandum from Carrere and Hastings' bookkeeper?

A. I thought that you might ask the question.

Q. 38. Now, having refreshed your recollection from that memorandum, will you please state whether that agrees with your recollection?

Mr. LOFTUS.—Objected to on the ground that the witness' memorandum is based on hearsay.

A. The memorandum agrees with my recollection.

(Deposition of Julius F. Gayler.)

Q. 39. Is this memorandum which you have brought here in the handwriting of Carrere and Hastings' bookkeeper? A. Yes, sir.

Q. 40. And what is the bookkeeper's name?

A. I don't know. It is not the same one that was there when I was there.

Mr. ANDERSON.—The memorandum to which the witness has referred contains the following entries. [243]

August 20, 1912,	# 9350	1500.00
Sept. 9, 1912	9450	1200.00
Oct. 14, 1912	9480	1000.00
Nov. 23, 1912	9544	1000.00
Mar. 11, 1913,	9659	1500.00
Aug. 19, 1913	9860	500.00
June 9, 1914	10176	349.50
		$7049.50

Q. 41. Now, what do these entries indicate? That at the respective dates, you, on behalf of Carrere and Hastings certified the payments indicated by numbers, to the Denivelle Company, for the work done on the Goelet house?

Mr. LOFTUS.—Objected to as leading.

A. Yes. And terraces and other work. The whole job.

Q. 42. Now, you say, Mr. Gayler, that you negotiated this contract with the Denivelle Company. Did Mr. Denivelle call your attention to any imitation travertine work which he had theretofore done? [244]

(Deposition of Julius F. Gayler.)

Mr. LOFTUS.—Objected to as leading.

A. He did.

Q. 43. And what was the job to which he called your attention?

A. The interior of the Pennsylvania Station in New York City.

Q. 44. Before letting that contract did you go and inspect that imitation travertine work in the Pennsylvania Station? A. I did.

Q. 45. Did Mr. Dennivelle go with you?

A. No, sir.

Q. 46. At the time you went to inspect that imitation travertine work in the Pennsylvania Station was it a completed job or was it in course of construction. A. Completed.

Q. 47. And was that inspection made by you before giving the contract to Mr. Denivelle or his company, for the Goelet house? A. Yes, sir.

Q. 48. Was there another Mr. Denivelle working on the Goelet house?

A. Not to my knowledge.

Q. 49. Did any other man by the name of Denivelle put in a bid for any work on the Goelet house?
[245]

A. A man who I understood was Mr. Denivelle's brother put in an estimate on the imitation travertine stone work of the stair hall.

Q. 50. Do you recall his first name?

A. I do not.

Q. 51. So far as you know, did he have anything to do with Mr. Paul E. Denivelle?

(Deposition of Julius F. Gayler.)

A. He informed me that he did not.

Q. 52. Did he install any imitation travertine in the stair hall?　　A. No, he did not.

Q. 53. Was any imitation travertine installed in that stair hall?　　A. Yes, sir.

Q. 54. Who did that?

A. The builder, the Harriman Industrial Corporation.

Q. 55. Was that done with your consent, by that builder, and under your supervision?

A. Yes, sir.

Q. 56. How did that imitation travertine work which was installed in the stair hall, compare as to structure, materials and appearances, with the imitation travertine work which Mr. Denivelle had done on that Goelet job?

A. The material was different because it was inside [246] work. The finished appearance of it was practically the same as that on the outside. So Mr. Hastings said and so I said.

Q. 57. What material was employed in that imitation travertine work in the stair hall?

A. The base was plaster of paris with coloring matter.

Q. 58. Did you see that imitation travertine in the stair hall in the course of construction?

A. Yes, sir.

Q. 59. Can you state how it was made?

A. The finished coat was colored plaster. After having been applied it was ruled to make the joints,

(Deposition of Julius F. Gayler.)

to imitate blocks of stone, and then the surface was roughened with various tools and pieces of wire.

Q. 60. Was the surface all one color-tone?

A. No, it was varied by the varying amount of coloring matter in the plaster.

Q. 61. How did the job which Mr. Denivelle and his company executed under the Goelet contract compare with the work which he called your attention to in the Pennsylvania Station, as to color, appearance, and otherwise?

A. It was quite a little different. It was done in a simpler manner. I do not know how the result achieved in the Pennsylvania Station was arrived at, but it must have [247] been a more complicated method than that used in the Goelet house and exterior, where they used, so Mr. Denivelle informed me, cement, with coloring matter, and obtained the texture by means of various tools, in a manner similar to that I described as used in the entrance hall by the Harriman Industrial Corporation.

Q. 62. How did it compare in appearance with the Pennsylvania job?

A. The color was similar, at a distance of say, 30 to 35 feet, the appearance would be practically the same; as you got nearer you could see the difference. The work was not so finely done.

Q. 63. Did you watch Mr. Denivelle's employees, or observe how the imitation travertin work which was done on the Goelet house was made?

A. Oh, yes.

(Deposition of Julius F. Gayler.)

Q. 64. Will you tell us as fully and complete as you can recall, just how Mr. Denivelle and his employees constructed that imitation travertine work on the Goelet house and on the Goelet grounds?

A. The cast work and the run work was done as I have described above. I do not recall the balusters or ornamental features—how they were done.

Q. 65. Do you remember whether the balustrades and the ornamental features to which you have referred were cast [248] or "run"?

A. I would say they were probably cast; that is the only way to do it, but I don't remember how it was done, as I did not see it being done.

Q. 66. What is your knowledge as to the use of artificial or imitation travertine during the period from 1912 to 1915, in the building trade, by these builders?

A. I do not remember offhand any other work done in that time excepting the Goelet house.

Q. 67. Is it customary in the building trade to require contractors during a relatively large job to give a bond for the completion of the work, and also a bond for maintenance?

A. Sometimes done. Sometimes it is not.

Q. 68. What is the general understanding in the architectural and building trade as to the requirements of a contractor under the maintenance bond?

A. That he will make good any defects which develop in the work within the time specified in this maintenance bond.

(Deposition of Julius F. Gayler.)

Q. 69. And is such a maintenance bond customarily required in relatively large contracts?

A. Not often.

Q. 70. Was the Denivelle job on the Goelet house and grounds completed to your satisfaction and to that of Carrere [249] and Hastings?

A. Yes, sir.

Q. 71. And payment was made therefor, in accordance with the contract?   A. Yes, sir.

Q. 72. Now, Mr. Gayler, has Mr. Denivelle been to see you within the last week or ten days?

A. Yesterday.

Q. 73. And what was the substance of the conversation between you and Mr. Denivelle yesterday?

A. We talked mostly of old times. He didn't say much about this case except, that Mr. Denivelle told me that the other party is moved somewhat by *animus*. He spoke of the 'Frisco Fair.

Q. 74. Did he discuss with you the Goelet job?

A. Excepting as mentioned there—and then I told him that I didn't remember exactly when it was done, but I didn't think it was under process in February, 1914, because at that time I went to Europe and I didn't recall turning it over to anybody else. I found out since that the house was practically completed before I went.

Direct examination closed.

Cross-examination.

(By Mr. LOFTUS.)

XQ. 75. Now, Mr. Gayler, these dates relating

(Deposition of Julius F. Gayler.)

to payments show payments as late as June, 1914. What does that indicate [250] with refer- ence to the time of completion of Mr. Denivelle's work?

A. That means that the last payment was made at that time.

XQ. 76. Would that indicate approximately when the work was completed? In other words, how long would the final payment be after the comple- tion of the work? Would it be a matter of a few weeks?

A. It would be in the case of a contractor like Mr. Denivelle, in whom we had confidence, a matter of a few weeks or months.

XQ. 77. When you left for Europe in Febru- ary, 1914, was this Goelet house occupied by any family? A. They moved in shortly after that.

XQ. 78. Where was this Goelet house situated with relation to a public highway?

A. I should say less than a quarter of a mile; about 100 yards less than a quarter of a mile.

XQ. 79. Was this highway very much traveled?

A. Not very much. Principally in the winter- time for the skating at the lake. Summer not so much traveled over.

XQ. 80. Were there any other buildings in the vicinity?

A. No, I think the nearest was the village of Florida, about three miles away. That is, to the best of my [251] recollection.

XQ. 81. Now, this travertin work in the stair

(Deposition of Julius F. Gayler.)
hall that was put in by the Harriman Company,
was that after the Denivelle work was done?

A. No, it was—I can't say exactly. I can't say
whether it was done after the house was completed
or not—or at the time that he had completed the
work on the house.

XQ. 82. How large a job was that stair hall.
How many square feet of travertin?

A. To the best of my recollection it was a hall
about 30 feet square and 25 feet high, with one
window and two doors, including the trim of the
doors and including the cornice.

XQ. 83. Had you ever heard of artificial or imitation travertine prior to seeing it in the Pennsylvania
Station?   A. No.

Cross-examination closed.

Redirect Examination.
(By Mr. ANDERSON.)

RDQ. 84. You have brought with you a memorandum. Please state what it is and where you obtained it?

A. It is a memorandum of the orders issued, and
the card for certain omissions in connection with
Mr. Denivelle's work. I obtained this from Carrere
and Hastings' bookkeeper yesterday.

Mr. LOFTUS.—I move to strike out any and all
[252] testimony relating to this memorandum, on
the ground that it is mere hearsay.

RDQ. 85. And that shows the payments to Mr.
Denivelle or his company?

(Deposition of Julius F. Gayler.)

A. No, it shows the orders.

RDQ. 86. What do you mean by "orders," Mr. Gayler?

A. We obtained an estimate from Mr. Denivelle for certain work, and we wrote him a letter authorizing him to proceed with it.

RDQ. 87. I see. And you obtained this memorandum from the bookkeeper of Carrere and Hastings yesterday?   A. Yes, sir.

Mr. ANDERSON.—Defendants' counsel asks that the memorandum be copied on the record.

Mr. LOFTUS.—Objected to as incompetent, irrelevant and immaterial, and on the further ground that it is hearsay.

April 16, 1912.	Exterior stucco work in pink	$5884.00
June 19, 1912.	Furnishing and erecting plain face of porch terrace of pink stucco with hand-rail balusters of Composite Travertine	961.50
Aug. 4, 1913.	Stuccoing walks around entrance court of residence	300.00
		$7145.50
Aug. 4, 1913.	Omission of certain stucco work in connection with terraces	96.00
		$7049.50

(Deposition of Julius F. Gayler.)

RDQ. 88. You have stated your best recollection to be that Mr. Denivelle's work in connection with the Goelet job was completed before you went away in February, 1914?   A. I said house, not "job."

RDQ. 89.   Please look over Exhibit 2 of the correspondence with Carrere and Hastings, and state whether or not you find anything therein which indicates to your mind when the Denivelle job was completed?

Mr. LOFTUS.—Objected to as leading and suggestive.

A. Nothing indicates it in Exhibit 2.

RDQ. 90. When was Mr. Denivelle's job on the house completed?

A. That I cannot state definitely, because the payments on the house and the other work were carried on together.

RDQ. 91.   When you left in February, 1914, what was the condition of that Denivelle job on the Goelet property?

A. To the best of my recollection the work on the walls around the entrance court was still to be done.

RDQ. 92. Was that imitation travertine, the walls around the entrance court?

A. No, that was pink stucco, but there is a possibility that the coping was imitation travertine; but I don't know positively.

RDQ. 93. Now at the time you visited the Pennsylvania [254] station to look at the imitation travertine work which he had done there, was that

(Deposition of Julius F. Gayler.)

Station open to the public? A. Yes, sir.

RDQ. 94. And have you stated when you made that visit?

A. It was made before the original order to Mr. Denivelle. Before April 16, 1912; how long before I don't remember.

Redirect examination closed.

Deposition closed.

Signature waived.

Recess until 3 P. M. [255]

[Title of Court and Cause.]

3:00 P. M., Wednesday, March 5, 1924.

Met pursuant to adjournment for recess.

Parties present as before.

It is agreed that the deposition of Mr. Webster may be taken before George H. Emslie, Esq., notary public, in the employ of Munn & Co., and that it may be taken stenographically and transcribed by Miss Hoffman, an employee of counsel for defendants.

DEPOSITION OF DANIEL T. WEBSTER, FOR DEFENDANTS.

DANIEL T. WEBSTER, a witness subpoenaed on behalf of the defendants, having been duly cautioned and sworn, in answer to interrogatories propounded by Mr. Anderson, testified as [256] follows:

Q. 1. Your full name, Mr. Webster, is Daniel T. Webster? A. Daniel Thomas Webster.

(Deposition of Daniel T. Webster.)

Q. 2. How old are you, Mr. Webster?   A. 47.

Q. 3. What is your profession or occupation?

A. At present I am connected with the firm of Marc Eidlitz & Son, Builders, being assistant to the President of the Company.

Q. 4. Where do you reside?

A. 344 West 72d Street, New York City.

Q. 5. You were formerly associated with the firm of McKim, Mead & White, Architects, of this city, were you not?   A. Yes, sir.

Q. 6. And when were you with that firm?

A. Well, I was with them for about 18 years.

Q. 7. Covering what period?

A. Let's see, back to 1911—I was a kid then—I was with them from about 1893 until 1911—after I went to Canada, being connected with my own firm of Barrott, Blackader & Webster. I also represented McKim, Mead & White in connection with work carried on in Canada.

Q. 8. McKim, Mead & White were the architects of the Pennsylvania Station in this city, were they not?   A. Yes, sir.

Q. 9. Did you have anything to do with the building of [257] the Pennsylvania Railroad Station in this city?

A. I was delegated by McKim, Mead & White to act as general superintendent for the architects at the site.

Q. 10. And in that capacity, did you supervise the work of the various contractors that was going into that Station?   A. I did.

(Deposition of Daniel T. Webster.)

Q. 11. On behalf of the architects?

A. On behalf of the architects.

Q. 12. Now, you know Mr. Paul E. Denivelle, do you, who is here present?   A. I do.

Q. 13. How long have you known Mr. Denivelle?

A. I first met Mr. Denivelle around 1909.

Q. 14. And what was the occasion of that first meeting?

A. Why, as I recollect, he was requested by McKim, Mead & White to make some samples of imitation stone using a new material, at that time known as white Portland cement, and he was asked to get in touch with me to see the real stone; it was the first time I met him.

Q. 15. Now, just what was the character of this stone, and what was the character of the sample which Mr. Denivelle was asked to make?

A. Why, the stone—or some people call it a marble —is Italian travertin that had been contracted for for the main base and wainscot in the waiting-room, and also in the arcade.   [258]

Q. 16. And the sample?

A. The architects had been in a quandary as to getting the proper kind of material for the finishing out of the balance of the wall surfaces where real travertin had not been contracted for due to its expense.

Q. 17. What was the sample Mr. Denivelle was requested to make?

A. The first sample Mr. Denivelle made, I remember, was a small piece; that had been instigated, I

(Deposition of Daniel T. Webster.)

think, by Mr. Mead, who was senior member of the firm, asking Mr. Denivelle to try and see what he could do using this white Portland cement—that small sample I saw after it had been completed.

Q. 18. As a representative of McKim, Mead & White, just what were your duties in the construction of the Pennsylvania Station?

A. Primarily, my duties were of an executive nature. I had assistants under me as deputies, to whom I assigned various duties. The job was quite a big proposition and I could not cover all the ground myself and attend to all the correspondence and details in connection with my position.

Q. 19. Who were the other assistants you had under you?

A. I had Mr. Clay M. McClure, and Mr. Mapes; Mr. Lamb; Mr. L. C. Curtis.

Q. 20. Can you give me the initials of Mr. Mapes?

A. I have forgotten Mr. Mapes' initials.

Q. 21. There were several others, too? [259]

A. Yes; I will give you the whole list if you want them.

Q. 22. Now, was Mr. McClure an employee of McKim, Mead & White?   A. He was.

Q. 23. And Mr. Mapes?

A. Mr. Mapes was an inspector at the works—an employee of McKim, Mead & White but paid for by the Pennsylvania Railroad as a deputy inspector.

Q. 24. And Mr. Curtis?

A. He was in the same category with Mr. Mapes.

Q. 25. Not an employee of McKim, Mead & White?

(Deposition of Daniel T. Webster.)

A. They were all reporting to me, but their services were paid for by the Pennsylvania Company—more like clerks of the work—but they actually reported to my assistant or myself.

Q. 26. Was the Mr. Mapes you referred to, D. H. Mapes? A. He is a brother of D. H. Mapes.

Q. 27. And D. H. Mapes—do you known him, and do you know who he is?

A. He was at one time—I still believe he has charge of the construction of the Canadian Pacific Railway, Montreal.

Q. 28. Now, is Mr. McClure still an employee of McKim, Mead & White, to your knowledge?

A. No, sir. [260]

Q. 29. Do you know where he is located?

A. He is employed now by John Russell Pope, architect, here in New York City.

Q. 30. Now, Mr. Webster, I show you a document which has been marked for identification as Defendants' Exhibit 1—do you recognize that document?

A. The specifications of the artificial stone work of the Pennsylvania Station, New York City.

Q. 31. You mean by that, that that is a copy of the specifications actually produced by McKim, Mead & White's office and distributed to bidders or others having to do with the artificial stone work at the Pennsylvania Station?

A. Presumably it is; I couldn't say without verifying it.

Q. 32. Well, look at it; see if you can identify it?

(Deposition of Daniel T. Webster.)

A. I presume this is the specification that was issued at the time, yes.

Q. 33. I assumed that you had at some time in your possession, or had access to, a copy of such document and would know whether or not you recognize that as such a document?

A. I do. I recognize this as the specification of imitation stone work.

(The document is offered in evidence as Defendants' Exhibit 1,—McKim, Mead & White Specification for Artificial Stone Work for the Pennsylvania Station, New York City.) [261]

Q. 34. Now, did Mr. Denivelle or his Company do any work in connection with that Pennsylvania Station?

A. They had the contract for the imitation travertin work in the Station.

Q. 35. And did he or his company perform that contract?   A. They did.

Q. 36. To your knowledge, did any other concern, excepting Mr. Denivelle and his company, furnish a sample of artificial travertin and bid on that artificial travertin work for the Pennsylvania Station?

A. Other companies furnished samples in imitation of the travertin stone, and Mr. Denivelle also furnished an additional sample other than the one I first mentioned.

Q. 37. Is it your recollection that these other companies also bid on that work?   A. Yes.

Q. 38. Did McNulty Bros., Inc., bid on that work?
A. They did.

(Deposition of Daniel T. Webster.)

Q. 39. Do you recognize a letter dated December 28, 1908, from McNulty Bros. to McKim, Mead & White, directed to the attention of Mr. Daniel T. Webster, the said letter forming a part of Defendants' Exhibit 6, which I now show you?   A. Yes.

Q. 40. Did that letter pass through your hands as a representative of McKim, Mead & White? [262]
A. Yes.

Q. 41. I show you a yellow carbon copy of a letter dated November 6, with the year 1908 partly filled in in pencil, that is to say, the figures 1–9–0 are pencilled in—do you recognize that as a copy of a letter going from the office of McKim, Mead & White to George A. Fuller Company? (Note: The said carbon copy also forms a part of Defendants' Exhibit 6.)   A. Yes.

Q. 42. That letter was presumably signed by someone designated as "Genl. Supt."?
A. Myself.

Q. 43. That's yourself?   A. Yes.

Q. 44. I show you a carbon copy of a letter dated October 24, 1908, addressed to George A. Fuller Company, forming a part of Defendants' Exhibit 8, and ask you whether you can identify that carbon copy of a letter?

A. I did not write that particular letter; I think that was written from the main office; my letters always bore my title.

Q. 45. So that you cannot identify that positively as going from the office of McKim, Mead & White?

(Deposition of Daniel T. Webster.)

A. I presume I have seen copies of that but I did not write that particular letter.

Q. 46. I call your attention to a carbon copy of a letter addressed to George Gibbs, Esq., Chief Engineer of [263] Electric Traction, P. T. & I. R. R. Co., dated October 15, 1908, and ask you whether or not you can identify that carbon copy (said carbon copy forming a part of Defendants' Exhibit 6)?

A. I remember seeing such a copy before, but that was written at the main office also.

Q. 47. It was not written by you?   A. No, sir.

Q. 48. And would your answer to the last question be the same if it related to the carbon copy of a letter dated October 2, 1908, addressed to George Gibbs, Esq., which I now show you (said copy forming a part of Defendants' Exhibit 6)?

A. That was written from the main office also; I have seen the copy before.

Q. 49. You have seen the copy before?   A. Yes.

Q. 50. I show you a letter purporting to be a letter from H. T. Lilliendahl, dated October 8, 1908, addressed to George A. Fuller Company, and ask you if you ever saw that letter before (said letter forming a part of Defendants' Exhibit 6)?

A. I don't recollect seeing that letter before.

Q. 51. I show you a letter (forming part of Defendants' Exhibit 6), purporting to be from George A. Fuller Company, to McKim, Mead & White, dated July 19, 1907, and ask you if you remember

(Deposition of Daniel T. Webster.)

having seen such a letter while you were with [264]
McKim, Mead & White?

A. I don't recall that letter.

Q. 52. You do not recall it?

A. No, sir, that was sent to the main office, too.

Q. 53. Am I to assume that you are unfamiliar
with the letters which went out and were received
in the main office of McKim, Mead & White?

A. To the extent that letters of that nature were
handled by the main office; we had a staff of men
in the main office under Mr. Ellingwood's direction,
who handled all the details in connection with drawings, specifications and contracts.

Q. 54. I call your attention to a letter from
George A. Fuller Company, dated June 21, 1907,
addressed to McKim, Mead & White, attention of
Mr. Richardson (forming a part of Defendants' Exhibit 6)—do you recall seeing that letter when you
were with McKim, Mead & White?

A. I recollect seeing that letter before, yes.

Q. 55. Was Mr. Richardson one of your assistants
on the Pennsylvania Railroad job?

A. Mr. Richardson was one of the junior members of McKim, Mead & White—of the firm—and
he had direct charge of the Pennsylvania Station
at that time.

Q. 56. Is Mr. Richardson still a member of
McKim, Mead & White?

A. To the best of my knowledge, yes. Mr.
Richardson, [265] by the way, had a very serious

(Deposition of Daniel T. Webster.)
accident several years ago—his back was broken, and he is now abroad.

Q. 57. Now, that letter refers to a sample of imitation travertin stone prepared by McNulty Bros., and also samples which had been furnished theretofore by H. W. Miller and Mycenian Marble Company—Do you recall those samples?

A. These samples, as I recollect, were the first series of samples that the architects were experimenting—with trying to get some duplication of travertin. What's the date of that letter, please, I didn't notice?

Q. 58. June 21, 1907? A. Yes.

Q. 59. I show you a letter (forming a part of defendants' exhibit 6) from H. W. Miller, dated March 8, 1907, addressed to Geo. A Fuller Co., and ask you if you have ever seen that letter before?

A. I recollect that Mr. Miller submitted additional samples after his first sample was erected on the Pennsylvania site—that may refer to those samples. That is addressed to the Fuller Company and therefore I don't think that I have seen it before.

Q. 60. I show you a letter from George A. Fuller Company dated November 16, 1906, addressed "Attention of Mr. Richardson," McKim, Mead & White (said letter forming a part of Defendants' Exhibit 6), and ask you if you recall seeing that letter when you were with McKim, Mead & White?
[266]

A. I don't recall that letter, no, sir.

(Deposition of Daniel T. Webster.)

Q. 61. 1906—you were with McKim, Mead & White at that time?

A. Yes, but I had not been assigned to the Pennsylvania Station job, I don't think, at that time.

Q. 62. I call your attention to a copy of a letter dated November 15, 1906, addressed The George A. Fuller Company (forming a part of Defendants' Exhibit 6), and ask if you remember seeing either that copy or the original of that letter?

A. No, sir, that was before my time.

Q. 63. Now, is it your recollection that bids for that imitation travertin work in the Pennsylvania Station were submitted by Hammerstein & Denivelle, H. W. Miller, McNulty Bros. and H. T. Lilliendahl?   A. Yes, sir.

Q. 64. They all submitted bids on that imitation travertin work?

A. They submitted bids to the George A. Fuller Company which were transmitted to us.

Q. 65. And you remember, as an associate of Mc-Kim, Mead & White, receiving and examining such bids?

A. The bids were not examined by me; these bids were transmitted to the main office and by the main office transmitted to the executive officer of the Pennsylvania Station—Mr. George Gibbs. [267]

Q. 66. Now, you remember the firm of Hammerstein & Denivelle, do you?   A. Yes, sir.

Q. 67. Was Mr. Paul E. Denivelle connected with that concern?

A. In the early stages of the proposition that was

(Deposition of Daniel T. Webster.)
his firm name, Hammerstein & Denivelle, as I recall.

Q. 68. And afterward what was the name of the
company, when Mr. Denivelle got the contract?

A. Well, then he formed a new company, and,
frankly, I have forgotten—what was it—Denivelle
Hydraulic Composite Stone Company?

Q. 69. Please look at the papers constituting Defendants' Exhibit 5, and state whether or not you
ever saw any of those papers before, and noting
those which you can recognize, if you ever saw
them before?

A. I never saw that first letter—do you want me
to name each one as I go along?

Q. 70. You can look the whole thing over and then
tell us whether you recognize any of them, and tell
us which ones; take it all in one answer to save time.

A. I had no knowledge of these letters; they were
handled from the main office by Mr. Ellingwood—
there is a memorandum to that effect in there. Of
course I knew they were taking estimates and going
through all the details in the main office, but that
was all handled from the main office of [268] the
architects.

Q. 71. Will you look at a letter from McNulty
Bros., Inc., dated June 1, 1908, addressed to McKim,
Mead & White, attention Mr. Richardson, and tell
me whether or not you ever saw that letter while
you were with McKim, Mead & White?

A. No, sir.

Q. 72. That letter refers to a sample of travertin

(Deposition of Daniel T. Webster.)
stone—do you remember McNulty Bros. submitting a sample of travertin stone?

A. Well, I think that's—no, he couldn't submit a sample of travertin stone—he might submit an imitation of travertin.

Q. 73. Do you remember that McNulty Bros. submitted a sample of imitation travertin stone?

A. They submitted samples of imitation of travertin.

Q. 74. Can you identify a letter which I show you, dated February 4, 1909, addressed to Mr. William R. Mead of McKim, Mead & White, and signed by George Gibbs, Chief Engineer of the Pennsylvania Tunnel and Terminal Railroad Company?

A. Yes, I have seen this letter before.

Q. 75. Where did you see that letter before?

A. That was shown to me by Mr. Richardson while I was in the main office one day.

Q. 76. You mean in the main office of McKim, Mead & White?   A. Yes.

Q. 77. And do you recognize that as a letter received [269] in the office of McKim, Mead & White?

A. Yes, it is addressed there, isn't it?

(The letter is offered in evidence as Defendants' Exhibit 8—Gibbs' letter of Feb. 4, 1909.)

Q. 78. I show you, Mr. Webster, a letter dated February 8, 1909, from the Denivelle Hydraulic Composite Stone Co., addressed to Mr. Webster, c/o

(Deposition of Daniel T. Webster.)
McKim, Mead & White, signed "Paul E. Denivelle"
—do you recall receiving such a letter?

A. Yes, it was a circular letter addressed to the
trade in general.

(The letter is offered in evidence as Defendants'
Exhibit 9—Denivelle Circular Letter.)

Q. 79. I show you what purports to be a carbon
copy of a letter dated August 10, 1909, addressed
to George Gibbs, Esq., 10 Bridge Street, New York,
and ask whether the original of that letter was
written by you?

A. That letter I assume was written at the main
office; I do not recollect it—I always add my title.

Q. 80. I show you a carbon copy of a letter dated
August 12, 1909, addressed to George A. Fuller Co.,
signed McKim, Mead & White, per ——, Genl. Supt.
Did you write the original of that letter?

A. Yes, I wrote that letter.

(Offered in evidence as Defendants' Exhibit 10—
Webster letter of August 12, 1909.)

Q. 81. I show you a carbon copy of a letter dated
Nov. 11, 1909, addressed to George A. Fuller Co.,
signed [270] McKim, Mead & White, per ——,
Genl. Supt. Is that a carbon copy of one of your
letters?   A. Yes, sir.

(Offered in evidence as Defendants' Exhibit 11—
Webster letter of Nov. 11, 1909.)

Q. 82. I show you a carbon copy of a letter dated
December 6, 1909, addressed to George A. Fuller
Co., signed McKim, Mead & White, per ——, Genl.
Supt. Did you dictate the original of that letter?

(Deposition of Daniel T. Webster.)

A. Yes, sir.

(Offered in evidence as Defendants' Exhibit 12—
Webster letter of December 6, 1909.)

Q. 83. I show you a carbon copy of a letter dated
Jan. 7, 1910, addressed The Geo. A. Fuller Co.,
signed McKim, Mead & White, per ——, Genl. Supt.,
and ask whether or not you dictated or wrote the
original of that letter.

A. I signed that letter; some of these letters were
dictated by my auditor or checkers but I assumed
responsibility for the figures.

Q. 84. But you signed the letters?   A. Yes.

(Offered in evidence as Defendants' Exhibit 13—
Webster letter of Jan. 7, 1910.)

Q. 85. I show you a carbon copy of a letter dated
Feb. 15, 1910, addressed George A. Fuller Co.,
signed McKim, Mead & White, per ——, Genl.
Supt., and ask whether or not you signed the
original of that letter?   [271]

A. After consulting the head office I signed that
letter.

(Offered in evidence as Defendants' Exhibit 14—
Webster letter of Feb. 15, 1910.)

Q. 86. Can you in like manner identify the carbon
copy of a letter dated February 16, 1910, addressed
George A. Fuller Co., Fuller Building, New York,
as a copy of a letter signed by you?

A. Yes, sir, I recollect the letter.

(Offered in evidence as Defendants' Exhibit 15—
Webster letter of February 16, 1910.)

Q. 87. Did you also sign the original of a letter,

(Deposition of Daniel T. Webster.)

of which I show you a carbon copy, dated February 26, 1910, addressed to Mr. Faulkner Hill, c/o The George A. Fuller Co.?

A. Yes, sir; Faulkner Hill is the attorney for the Fuller Company.

(Offered in evidence as Defendants' Exhibit 16— Webster letter of February 26, 1910.)

Q. 88. I show you a carbon copy of a letter dated March 11, 1910, addressed Geo. A. Fuller Co., signed McKim, Mead & White, per ——, Genl. Supt., and ask if you signed the original of that letter.

A. Yes, sir.

(Letter is offered in evidence as Defendants' Exhibit 17—Webster letter of March 11, 1910.)

Q. 89. I show you a carbon copy of a letter dated March 28, 1910, addressed to Mr. George Gibbs, and ask if you [272] signed the original of that letter?

A. That letter was written in the main office—I have seen it before—I was conversant with the facts.

Q. 90. But you did not sign it?

A. I didn't sign that letter, no sir. I might explain, letters of that nature I might dictate and have written, to be sent to the main office, and they transmitted the proposition to the executive office of the Pennsylvania Railroad Company.

Q. 91. Do you recall dictating that letter?

A. I think I dictated the original draft of that letter.

(Deposition of Daniel T. Webster.)

(Offered in evidence as Defendants' Exhibit 18— Letter dictated by Mr. Webster.)

Mr. LOFTUS.—The offer is objected to on the ground of lack of identification.

(By Mr. ANDERSON.)

Q. 92. I show you a carbon copy of a letter dated March 21, 1910, addressed to George Gibbs, Esq., and ask whether or not you dictated and signed the original of that letter?

A. That letter was written at the main office.

Q. 93. You cannot identify it?   A. No.

Q. 94. Do you recall that in March 1910, McKim, Mead & White received a bid from H. W. Miller, Inc., for $4188, and   [273]   also from the Denivelle Hydraulic Composite Stone Co. for $2421, for furring, lathing and plastering of the six map spaces in the general waiting-room of the Pennsylvania Station?

A. I remember estimates were obtained but I do not recollect the figures.

Q. 95. But both the Miller Company and the Denivelle Company bid on that job?   A. Yes, sir.

Q. 96. On that date, March 21, 1910, had the Denivelle Company installed artificial travertin in the general waiting-room of the Pennsylvania Station?

A. They were working there and had installed quite a lot of that material.

Q. 97. I show you a carbon copy of a letter dated March 28, 1910, addressed Geo. A. Fuller Co., and

(Deposition of Daniel T. Webster.)

ask you whether or not you signed the original of that letter?   A. Yes, sir, I signed that letter.

(Offered in evidence as Defendants' Exhibit 19— Webster Letter of March 28, 1910.)

Q. 98. I show you a carbon copy of a letter dated April 22, 1910, addressed to Mr. Weekes of Hiss & Weekes, 1123 Broadway, New York City, and ask whether or not you dictated and signed the original of that letter.

A. I don't recall that letter, no, sir.

Q. 99. I call your attention to a carbon copy of a letter dated May 25, 1910, addressed Geo. A. Fuller Co., and   [274]   ask whether or not you recognize that as a copy of a letter which you signed on behalf of McKim, Mead & White?   A. Yes, sir.

(Offered in evidence as Defendants' Exhibit 20— Webster letter of May 25, 1910.)

Q. 100. I will ask you to read Defendants' Exhibit 20 and state whether or not the statements therein set forth, as to the condition of the work to be performed by the Denivelle Company on that date, is in accordance with your recollection—I mean the work in the Pennsylvania Station, New York City?

A. To the best of my knowledge and belief, it was at that time.

Q. 101. And that is your present recollection?

A. Yes, sir.

Q. 102. I call your attention to a carbon copy of a letter dated May 7, 1910, addressed to George A. Fuller Company, and ask whether or not you signed

(Deposition of Daniel T. Webster.)

the original of that letter on behalf of McKim, Mead & White?   A. Yes, sir.

(Offered in evidence as Defendants' Exhibit 21— Webster letter of May 7, 1910.)

Q. 103. Calling your attention to Defendants' Exhibit 21, I will ask you whether at the date of that letter the Denivelle contract for the installation of artificial travertin in the Pennsylvania Station in New York City, had been completed, and whether that is your present recollection of the matter? [275]   A. As stated in the letter, yes.

Q. 104. Now, that letter refers to procuring from the Denivelle Hydraulic Composite Stone Company a general release—what is your recollection as to whether or not a general release was procured in accordance with the instructions contained in that letter?

A. I knew such a release was procured by the Fuller Company.

Q. 105. Do you remember, as an officer or associate of McKim, Mead & White, ordering such a release?

A. I can't say offhand, sir; I don't want to commit myself. I am quite sure there was a release, but I don't recall all the facts of that now.

Q. 106. I hand you a document which is marked Defendants' Exhibit 7—Denivelle Release—and ask you if you ever saw that document before; if so, when and where?

A. Yes, this is the one, but I confused the word "release" with "guaranty"; that is what we call

(Deposition of Daniel T. Webster.)
a guaranty bond for fulfillment of a contract and
maintenance of same.

Q. 107. You wouldn't call that a release?

A. It is in fact—it is a release—but I was revolving in my mind—I know we insisted on a guaranty.

Q. 108. You identify that as being the release and
guaranty received by McKim, Mead & White from
the Denivelle Company?

A. That is a copy, yes, sir. [276]

Q. 109. Do you recognize the signature on that defendants' Exhibit 7?   A. Yes, sir.

Q. 110. You are familiar with those signatures?

A. I know Mr. Denivelle's signature.

Q. 111. Who is Mr. Connor who signed that release?

A. He was an associate of Mr. Denivelle, secretary of the company.

Q. 112. I show you a carbon copy of a letter dated
May 17, 1910, addressed to George A. Fuller Co.,
signed McKim, Mead & White, per ——, Genl.
Supt., and ask if you signed the original of that
letter?   A. Yes, sir.

(Offered in evidence as Defendants' Exhibit 22—
Webster letter of May 17, 1910.)

Q. 113. I notice that letter—Defendants' Exhibit
22—refers to a form of release which was sent to
George A. Fuller Co.—is that intended to refer to
the form of release which you have identified, and
which is marked Defendants' Exhibit 7?

A. Yes, sir.

Q. 114. I call your attention to the fact that

(Deposition of Daniel T. Webster.)

the release is signed on the 29th day of November, 1910, whereas Defendants' Exhibit 22 is dated May 17, 1910. Have you any explanation to offer as to the time intervening between those two dates—the date when the form of release was sent to the Fuller Company and the date when it was signed? [277]

A. The only thing I can remember about that was that this form of release was prepared by the attorneys for the Pennsylvania Railroad Company in connection with the contract—not as utilized as the final form when contracts are closed.

Q. 115. I call your attention to a carbon copy of a letter dated May 17, 1910, addressed to Geo. A. Fuller Co., and ask whether or not you signed the original of that letter?   A. Yes, sir.

(Offered in evidence as Defendants' Exhibit 23— Webster letter of May 17, 1910.)

Q. 116. I show you a carbon copy of a letter dated June 3, 1910, addressed George A. Fuller Co., and ask whether or not you signed the original of that letter for McKim, Mead & White?   A. Yes, sir.

(Offered in evidence as Defendants' Exhibit 24— Webster letter of May 31, 1910.)

Q. 117. I call your attention to a carbon copy of a letter dated May 31, 1910, addressed to Geo. A. Fuller Co., and ask whether or not you signed the original of that letter for McKim, Mead & White?

A. Yes, sir.

(Offered in evidence as Defendants' Exhibit 25— Webster letter of May 31, 1910.)

Q. 118. I call your attention to a carbon copy of

(Deposition of Daniel T. Webster.)

a letter dated June 8, 1910, addressed to Geo. A. Fuller Co., and ask whether you signed the original of that letter for McKim, [278] Mead & White?

A. Yes, sir.

(Offered in evidence as Defendants' Exhibit 26— Webster letter of June 8, 1910.)

Q. 119. I call your attention to a carbon copy of a letter dated Sept. 12, 1910, addressed to Mr. George Gibbs, and ask whether or not you remember signing the original of that letter?

A. That was sent from the main office.

Q. 120. You do not recognize it?

A. I recognize the letter—I remember seeing it before.

Q. 121. You identify it as a copy of a letter sent out of the office of McKim, Mead & White?

A. Yes, sir.

(Offered in evidence as Defendants' Exhibit 27— Letter of McKim, Mead & White of Sept. 12, 1910.)

Q. 122. Mr. Webster, I show you what purports to be a copy of a letter addressed to you, signed Paul E. Denivelle, September 9, 1910—do you recall receiving the original of that letter?

A. Yes, sir.

Q. 123. I notice a pencil notation on here, "Refer to Mr. Richardson—copy sent to Mr. Gibbs, Sept. 12"—is that in your handwriting?

A. Yes, that's in my handwriting.

Q. 124. That's in your handwriting? [279]

A. Yes.

(Deposition of Daniel T. Webster.)

Q. 125. What was done with the original of that letter, do you know?

A. I don't recall—it must be in the files somewhere.

Q. 126. Was this copy made under your direction?

A. Presumably, yes, sir; it's got my note on it. The original might have been in my personal files.

Q. 127. Did you keep those files?

A. Yes, they are stored away in my trunk.

(Offered in evidence as Defendants' Exhibit 28— Webster copy of Denivelle letter of Sept. 9, 1910.)

Q. 128. I show you a carbon copy of a letter dated September 23, 1910, addressed to George A. Fuller Co., and ask whether you signed the original of that letter?   A. Yes, sir.

(Offered in evidence as Defendants' Exhibit 29— Webster letter of Sept. 23, 1910.)

Q. 129. I call your attention to a carbon copy of a letter dated October 20, 1910, addressed to George Gibbs, Esq., and ask whether or not you remember signing the original of that letter?

A. I don't recall that letter. I have no doubt that is authentic—it was sent from the main office.

Q. 130. You recognize that as a copy of a letter sent from the main office of McKim, Mead & White?

A. Yes, sir. [280]

(Offered in evidence as Defendants' Exhibit 30— Letter of McKim, Mead & White, Oct. 20, 1910.)

Q. 131. I show you a carbon copy of a letter dated Nov. 4, 1910, addressed to George Gibbs, Esq.,

(Deposition of Daniel T. Webster.)
and ask whether or not you recognize that letter as
one from McKim, Mead & White?

A. That letter was sent from the main office; but
I know it to be a fact.

Q. 132. You recognize it as a McKim, Mead &
White letter?   A. Yes, sir.

(Offered in evidence as Defendants' Exhibit 31—
Letter of McKim, Mead & White, Nov. 4, 1910.)

Q. 133. I show you a carbon copy of a letter
dated November 9, 1910, addressed to Geo. A. Fuller
Co., and ask whether or not you recognize that as a
copy of a letter signed by you.   A. Yes, sir.

(Offered in evidence as Defendants' Exhibit 32—
McKim, Mead & White letter of Nov. 9, 1910.)

Q. 134. I show you a carbon copy of a letter dated
November 30, 1910, addressed to Geo. A. Fuller Co.,
and ask whether or not you signed the original of
that letter.   A. Yes, sir.

(Offered in evidence as Defendants' Exhibit 33—
McKim, Mead & White letter of Nov. 30, 1910.) .

Q. 135. I show you a carbon copy of a letter dated
Nov. 30, 1910, addressed Mr. George Gibbs, and ask
whether or not you signed the original of that letter.

A. Yes, sir.

(Offered in evidence as Defendants' Exhibit 34—
McKim, Mead & White letter of Nov. 30, 1910.)
[281]

Q. 136. I show you what purports to be a copy of
a letter dated December 2, 1911, addressed McKim,
Mead & White, signed Denivelle H. C. S. Company,
by Paul E. Denivelle, President, and ask you

(Deposition of Daniel T. Webster.)
whether you recall receiving the letter of which that
purports to be a copy?

A. I don't recall that letter; it was sent to the
main office.

Q. 137. I call your attention to a carbon copy of
a letter dated December 5, 1911, addressed to Mr.
George Gibbs, signed McKim, Mead & White, per
——, Genl. Supt., and ask whether you recognize
that copy?

A. Yes, sir, I do; now this letter was sent to me
from the main office and I in turn transmitted it
to Mr. Gibbs with my letter of December 5th.

Q. 138. As I understand your answer, you now
recognize the copy I first showed you as being a copy
of a letter received by McKim, Mead & White from
the Denivelle Company, and as a copy of a letter
actually so received?

A. After I recalled it by association with my own
letter addressed to Mr. Gibbs, yes.

Q. 139. And the letter referred to in the carbon
copy of McKim, Mead & White's letter dated December 5, 1911, is the original letter of which the
first is a copy—you say, "We enclose herewith original letter—"?

A. The original of that letter, yes, sir, sent to me
from the main office. [282]

(A copy of what purports to be a letter from
Denivelle Co. to McKim, Mead & White, is offered
in evidence as Defendants' Exhibit 35, copy of
Denivelle letter dated Dec. 2, 1911; and the carbon
copy of the letter from McKim, Mead & White,

(Deposition of Daniel T. Webster.)
dated Dec. 5, 1911, addressed to Mr. George Gibbs, is offered in evidence as Defendants' Exhibit 36, McKim, Mead & White letter, Dec. 5, 1911.)

Q. 140. Do you identify, Mr. Webster, a bill from the Denivelle Hydraulic Composite Stone Co. dated Dec. 12, 1911, addressed to Pennsylvania Tunnel & Terminal Railroad Co., and the carbon copy of a letter dated Dec. 11, 1911, addressed to Denivelle Hydraulic Composite Stone Co., signed McKim, Mead & White, per ——, Genl. Supt., which I now show you? A. Yes, sir.

Q. 141. There is some endorsements on the bill to the effect, "Approved Dec. 12, 1911, D. T. W. Genl. Supt., office copy"—did you so endorse that Denivelle bill? A. Yes, those are my initials.

Q. 142. And you signed the original letter of which a carbon copy is attached to that bill?

(Bill and carbon copy of letter are offered as one exhibit—Defendants' Exhibit 36A—Denivelle bill of Dec. 12, 1911, and carbon copy of letter dated Dec. 11, 1911, attached thereto.)

Q. 143. I show you a bill of the Denivelle Hydraulic Composite Stone Co. dated January 7, 1911, addressed to The Pennsylvinia Tunnel & Terminal Railroad Co.—do you identify that as a bill received and passed through your hands?

A. Yes, sir; it is a minor repair. [283]

Q. 144. It bears a stamped endorsement with your initials, "D. T. W.—office copy"—and that endorsement was made by you? A. Yes, sir.

(Deposition of Daniel T. Webster.)

(Offered in evidence as Defendants' Exhibit 37—Denivelle bill.)

Q. 145. I show you another Denivelle bill dated January 7, 1911, addressed to The Pennsylvania Tunnel & Terminal Railroad Co., and ask if you recognize that as a bill received?

A. That's a duplicate of the previous bill.

Q. 146. A duplicate of the bill—Defendants' Exhibit 37—is it?   A. Yes, sir.

(They will be both fastened together and offered as one exhibit—Exhibit 37.)

Q. 147. I call your attention to a carbon copy of a letter dated October 26, 1911, addressed Denivelle Hydraulic Composite Stone Co., and ask if you signed the original of that letter?

A. Yes, sir.

(Offered in evidence as Defendants' Exhibit 38 —Webster letter of Oct. 26, 1911.)

Q. 148. I show you an original letter from Denivelle H. C. S. Company addressed to McKim, Mead & White, dated October 26, 1911, "Kind attention of Mr. D. T. Webster"—do you recall receiving that letter?

A. I recollect that letter—that's not my [284] notation on it, however. I identify the letter nevertheless.

Q. 149. You remember receiving the letter?

A. Yes.

(Offered as Defendants' Exhibit 39—Denivelle letter of Oct. 26, 1911.)

Q. 150. I show you a document which has been

(Deposition of Daniel T. Webster.)
marked Defendants' Exhibit 4—Bond and Contract
—and ask if you ever saw that document before,
and whether you can identify it?   A. Yes, sir.

Q. 151. And that is the bond and contract given by
the Denivelle Company for its work on the Pennsylvania Station in this city?   A. Yes, sir.

Q. 152. And it is the work which was done under
your supervision as representing the architects,
McKim, Mead & White?   A. Yes.

(Offered in evidence as Defendants' Exhibit 4—
Bond and Contract.)

Q. 153. Now, Mr. Webster, from these papers to
which I have called your attention, I am asking you
particularly to look at Defendants' Exhibit 39—
Denivelle letter—and Defendants' Exhibit 7—Denivelle release. Will you state when the Denivelle
Company completed the installation of its plastering and imitation travertin work in the Pennsylvania Station in New York City?

Mr. LOFTUS.—Objected to as leading and suggestive. [285]

A. Yes, sir; the main contract was completed on
or about November 29, 1910, and the repairs and
other items, as mentioned in Mr. Denivelle's letter,
on or about October 26, 1911.

Q. 154. And these repairs which were completed
on or about October 26, 1911, were they repairs
which were covered by what is known as a "maintenance bond," given by Mr. Denivelle or his company?   A. Yes, they were.

Q. 155. After the Pennsylvania Station was com-

(Deposition of Daniel T. Webster.)

pleted, did you have anything to do with any work done by Mr. Denivelle or the Denivelle Hydraulic Composite Stone Company in connection with the Windsor Street Station at Montreal, Canada?

A. As I stated in one of my letters to you, Mr. Denivelle was doing some imitation stone work in the waiting-room of the Windsor Street Station in Montreal, which my firm in Montreal were architects for; that work had been started before I had gone to Canada.

Q. 156. And that was the imitation travertin in the Windsor Station waiting-room of the Canadian Pacific Railroad in Montreal?

A. No, sir; I corrected that statement in a previous letter; I had forgotten the fact—it was imitation stone—I wrote you afterward about that.

Q. 157. Then Mr. Denivelle did not do any imitation travertin in that Railroad Station in Montreal? [286]

A. No, sir.

Q. 158. Well, after the Pennsylvania job was completed by Mr. Denivelle, did he under your supervision do any other imitation travertin work for you?   A. No, sir.

Q. 159. You represented the architects, McKim, Mead & White, in this imitation travertin work which was being done by Mr. Denivelle in the Pennsylvania Station?   A. Yes.

Q. 160. It was your duty to see that that work was done in accordance with Mr. Denivelle's contract and specifications, was it not?

(Deposition of Daniel T. Webster.)

A. Yes, sir.

Q. 161. Is it your testimony that that work was done in that manner in accordance with his contract and specifications?

A. Except where it was altered as he progressed with his experiments and process of manufacturing his material, with our consent.

Q. 162. Did you pass upon the work or such changes as were made by Mr. Denivelle, so as to be able to approve the work as it was done?

A. After calling the attention of my employers to these changes as they arose, I approved, acting as their agent.

Q. 163. And your testimony is that that work was done in a manner satisfactory to you and your firm as representing the owners of that property? [287]

A. Yes, sir.

Direct examination closed.

Cross-examination.

(By Mr. LOFTUS.)

XQ. 1. Mr. Webster, it has been suggested here that your firm, McKim, Mead & White, would not be likely to undertake any experimental work in connection with the building like the Pennsylvania Terminal, isn't it a fact that various new and experimental things did enter into that building?

A. What do you mean by "experimental things," Mr. Loftus, please?

XQ. 2. New and untried matters of structure and methods?

A. We did several things in the Station that had

(Deposition of Daniel T. Webster.)
never been done before—it was a very unusual building.

XQ. 3. What were several of those things?

A. Let me recall—for instance, around the Station there was a very extensive area of patent light pavement, and the difficulty had always been with patent light work that due to the nature of the construction of the concrete adjacent to the bull's-eyes there would be a certain amount of splitting of the glass due to expansion and contraction. Before we placed a contract for the patent light we were asked by the Pennsylvania Company to make constructions of various kinds of material of that nature which we did, and during the process of making these investigations various schemes were suggested and tried [288] out with a view of preventing the bull's-eyes from distortion, and eventually we adopted a lead ring around the bull's-eyes, and after trying out a section for a period of about 3 or 4 months it was adopted on our recommendation for the full light paving around the Station—is that what you mean—something of that nature?

XQ. 4. Yes?

A. We also tried out different kinds of paint on concrete work; that was more or less of a novelty in those days to get a paint that would withstand heat and contraction, and we directed various manufacturers to submit samples of various kinds of concrete paint, with the result that after a trial the Pennsylvania Company adopted three or four

(Deposition of Daniel T. Webster.)
of these types of paint and the lower section of the
building was painted with these three or four kinds
of material; some of it turned out better than
others.

XQ. 5. Now, this travertin work that Mr. Denivelle did—that I understand was made of white
Portland cement?

A. Yes, the epidermis or outer surface was made
of white Portland cement; the ingredients consisted of 1 to 1 part sand and cement and the backing consisted of half of white cement and sand,
and the final foundation of sand and ordinary
Portland cement.

XQ. 6. How long had white Portland cement been
known at that time?

A. Frankly, I had never heard about white Portland [289] cement until about 1908. It was a
new thing on the market—there had been a cement
imported theretofore called Puzzolan cement which
was quite expensive—and this was supposed to take
the place of Puzzolan - cement and is universally
used for that purpose now.

XQ. 7. And prior to this Pennsylvania Station
job you had never heard of artificial travertin or
had any experience with it?

A. Prior to the Pennsylvania Station I did not
know anything about travertin.

XQ. 8. Either artificial or natural?

A. No, sir.

XQ. 9. Considering the fact that this travertin is
rather porous at its outer surface and considerably

(Deposition of Daniel T. Webster.)

denser in the back portion, also the fact that it was subjected to the vibrations of trains in this Terminal Building, how long a time do you think it would require to keep that in place before its permanency or durability could be determined?

A. Well, that's hard to say. The point was when we closed Denivelle's main contract we asked for an extension of a year's guaranty to determine how good the material was within that period, and it did demonstrate that the vibration and change of temperature affected certain areas, and there were sections that had been repaired.

XQ. 10. But it required considerably longer time than [290] one year to determine whether or not it was a satisfactory construction for that purpose?

A. It has taken longer periods than that to determine whether any artificial stone is good for its purpose. It is a question of perfection in the method of construction and the materials used therein to get a better product, and that is determined by actual periods of time and depending upon the localities where it is installed; that was one of the reasons why McKim, Mead & White were doubtful about using imitation stone in the waiting-room; they had had trouble theretofore with imitation stones that had imitation marble—they were looking for something better.

XQ. 11. And the conditions in this Pennsylvania Terminal were unusual and difficult, were they?

A. They were unusual to the extent that the areas were considerably larger than—larger ex-

(Deposition of Daniel T. Webster.)
pansion in a building and the sizes of the stone had
to be proportionately larger to harmonize with the
architecture.

XQ. 12. Did troubles of vibration enter there,
too?

A. I should attribute part of the trouble to and
the fact that imitation stone affected plastering the
building.

XQ. 13. And these walls, as I understand it, are
not all of the same height, are they?

A. The building varies in height in different
sections. [291.]

XQ. 14. Would that be a factor?

A. No, I would not say so, because the steel is
designed to carry the varying force in the different
sections proportionately, but we did have expansion
and contraction in the steel work and that had to
be taken care of by expansion joints in the steel
itself to allow for give and take—that's going on
constantly.

XQ. 15. That's due to the peculiar construction
of the building?

A. Due to the expansion, contraction and vibration, and especially so in the main concourse; all
the steel being exposed and not protected by
masonry, is subjected to extremes of heat and cold
—must expand and contract—that in turn has its
reaction on the balance of the building.

XQ. 16. What are the peculiar conditions in regard to temperature changes or air currents?

A. There was not so—extreme heat in the build-

(Deposition of Daniel T. Webster.)

ing is regulated to a great extent automatically. If there is a sudden drop in temperature of course there will be a sudden drop in the room but that is corrected automatically by a system of air regulation.

XQ. 17. And this main waiting-room, what is the size of that?

A. I think it is 110 feet high, about 115 feet wide, and 300 feet long, approximately.

XQ. 18. As a matter of fact, you did regard this travertin [292] work as an experiment, didn't you?

A. That's not for me to say; the question of policy of using materials was determined by the firm, and any architect who does not occasionally experiment with new materials would lead a pretty monotonous existence.

XQ. 19. The firm of McKim, Mead & White had a reputation for introducing novelties in building construction, did it not?

A. It did; it was progressive. But it never did so without a trial of the material or getting opinions from experts or others, as to the advisability of using this material. Architecture in general is more or less experimenting with different kinds of materials and models to get the effects the architects wish to obtain.

XQ. 20. Did you have occasion to observe the different methods which Denivelle used in making this travertin?   A. Yes.

(Deposition of Daniel T. Webster.)

XQ. 21. Did he change or vary these methods from time to time?

A. Well, when he first started in, in order that we would have his work under surveillance there was a place allotted on the south side of the arcade in what we called the "Shop Section," where he started in his first development, and from there he was moved over later to the other side of the arcade, and as his work increased and the material requirements expanded we had to move him down to the so-called "Baggage Section," which is a large room, and he was all the time working [293] different kinds of schemes to improve the process, especially to expedite the fabrication of the material. One of his methods was by the use of trays of the size—to duplicate the size of a piece of ashlar, and in this tray there would be a glass bottom, and the tray was arranged on a pivot, the purpose being that when he put his first layer of material in the inspector, as well as myself, would see what was going on by the use of electric lights reflected on the under side of the tray, and see the development or laminations and the coloring effects. That was tried for a while but proved to be rather slow and pretty costly because the glass broke in many cases due to the weight of the material, but he learned many things about the introduction of color and the process of introducing the laminations in this material.

XQ. 22. What is your recollection, Mr. Webster —was this contract awarded to Denivelle because

(Deposition of Daniel T. Webster.)

of low bid or was it because your firm had the belief that he was sufficiently interested in the success of the proposition to see it through?

A. When the bids were taken, as I recollect, to the Fuller Company we verified them and I am sure that the records will show that the Fuller Company were rather doubtful as to Denivelle's ability to carry on a contract of this size, especially due to its novelty, and as they were responsible to a great extent for the progress of the building, they recommended the contract be awarded to McNulty Bros., who I believe would have agreed to reduce their original proposition. That proposition [294] was submitted by our main office to the Pennsylvania Railroad Company and afterward—I don't know how it came about—but there was a consultation between Mr. Gibbs of the Pennsylvania Railroad Company and Mr. Mead, who told me about this—and Mr. Gibbs wrote a letter shortly after this conference to Mr. Mead, suggesting as a matter of fairness that Denivelle's proposition be reconsidered. The major objection the Fuller Company had was the question of financing, but Mr. Denivelle was able to form a company with proper financing and get a bond, so that to a great extent relieved the anxiety with reference to that matter. McKim, Mead & White I believe, in fact I know, were impressed with Mr. Denivelle's personality and artistic temperament, and expected more from him than they would have gotten from the ordinary commercial plastering contractor.

(Deposition of Daniel T. Webster.)

XQ. 23. Where is Mr. Mead at the present time?

A. I do not know. I haven't seen Mr. Mead for a month or so.

XQ. 24. How old a man is Mr. Mead?

A. He must be around 70-odd years—73 years, I think.

XQ. 25. Have you any knowledge of the extent to which artificial travertin is used at the present time?

A. No; I have seen examples around New York City and elsewhere of imitation travertin, so called; it crops up every now and then in the most unexpected places. [295]

XQ. 26. I understood you to say on your direct examination you had some correspondence with Mr. Anderson?

A. Why, Mr. Anderson wrote us several letters and I responded. (Addressing Mr. Anderson.) I think I answered your questions, Mr. Anderson?

Mr. ANDERSON.—I think you did. I should be perfectly willing to submit to counsel for plaintiff, the correspondence which has taken place between Mr. Webster and myself.

Mr. LOFTUS.—Yes, I would like to see it.

XQ. 27. I call your attention particularly to a carbon copy of a letter dated January 19, 1924, addressed to Mr. D. T. Webster, and ask if you received such a letter and from whom?

A. I remember receiving the letter, yes, sir.

XQ. 28. That was signed by whom?

A. I do not—there is no signature on—

(Deposition of Daniel T. Webster.)

Mr. ANDERSON.—I signed that letter.

XQ. 29. I call your attention to a letter dated January 22, 1924, addressed Mr. T. Hart Anderson, and signed Daniel T. Webster—did you write that letter?   A. Yes, sir.

(Mr. LOFTUS.—These two letters to be copied into the record.)

Mr. ANDERSON.—I ask that the whole correspondence be put in evidence. [296]

Mr. LOFTUS.—That's agreeable to me.

(Offered in evidence as Defendants' Exhibit 40— Anderson-Webster correspondence.)

Mr. LOFTUS.—That's all.

Redirect Examination.

(By Mr. ANDERSON.)

RDQ. 1. Mr. Webster, was this contract for artificial travertin or imitation travertin awarded to the Denivelle Company after it had furnished to the architects a satisfactory sample or specimen of imitation travertin?

A. Yes, sir; there was a sample compared with other samples and judged to be better.

RDQ. 2. But your testimony is that a satisfactory sample of imitation travertin had been furnished to the architects before they had decided to grant this contract to Mr. Denivelle?   A. Yes, sir.

RDQ. 3. And in like manner McNulty Bros. submitted a sample of artificial travertin, and Miller submitted a sample of artificial travertin, is that right?   A. Yes, sir.

RDQ. 4. And they all put in bids on this artificial travertin work, is that right?   A. Yes, sir

RDQ. 5. Isn't it true that the Denivelle Company's bid was the lowest bid?   A. Yes, sir
[297]

RDQ. 6. Isn't it also true that if that sample of artificial travertin produced by Mr. Denivelle had not satisfied the architects as to its practicability, and as to the correctness of imitation of travertin, they would not have used imitation travertin in that building?

A. I wouldn't say that. The other samples might have been satisfactory in comparison— purely comparing one sample with the other to get the best results, and Denivelle's sample; he had followed out the specification using white Portland cement—the other hadn't done so. I think McNulty had secured another specification from McKim, Mead & White and wrote me in a letter that he could furnish a sample but he didn't do so at the time he was asked to do so.

RDQ. 7. Do you mean by the last answer that the architects required that this white Portland cement be used?

A. It was part of the proposition, yes.

RDQ. 8. Now, I fear that you misunderstood my next to the last question. That question was intended to get from you a statement as to whether or not the sample submitted by Mr. Denivelle of imitation travertin was sufficient in color and structure to satisfy the architects that they could

(Deposition of Daniel T. Webster.)

use imitation travertin in that Pennsylvania Station? A. It was sufficient.

RDQ. 9· And it was the character of that sample of imitation travertin submitted by Mr. Denivelle, which satisfied the architects that they could use imitation travertin in the [298] Pennsylvania Station?

A. It showed that they could get results by using that method. Now, if you will follow it through, Mr. Anderson, you will see a letter from Mr. Mead to Mr. Gibbs in which he states that the evidence was that imitation travertin could be made, and they expected if the contract was given to Mr. Denivelle, to make that imitation.

RDQ. 10. So that according to your testimony, upon the receipt of that sample of imitation travertin from Mr. Denivelle, the architects were satisfied that they could use imitation travertin in the Pennsylvania Station? A. Yes, sir.

RDQ. 11. If they hadn't been satisfied they wouldn't have used it?

A. That stands to reason, yes, sir. What they would rather have used was real stone, naturally, but it was too expensive.

RDQ. 12. Now, the Pennsylvania Station in any part of the construction which had been designed and specified by the architects was no more of an experiment than any other building designed and constructed by them, was it?

A. By McKim, Mead & White?

RDQ. 13. Yes?

(Deposition of Daniel T. Webster.)

A. Why, no; all buildings where you have architects in that capacity they have to experiment as they go along to determine different materials; to determine ornamentation of [299] models—the whole thing is a process of experimentation. As you go along too there are genuine rules to follow in the general results; where new material comes up for consideration, then one has to be pretty careful before they go on record to recommend a material of that nature.

RDQ. 14. Exactly, and having recommended certain features of construction and ornamentation in that building, it is evidence that they were satisfied that the experiments were finished, isn't that true?

A. No, the experiments would still be carried on to prove what had been done before; that I brought out in my testimony heretofore, sir. It wasn't a hard and fast proposition; when Mr. Denivelle got the contract he started in trying to improve the method of making this material to get a better effect as well as to expedite the making of it.

RDQ. 15. But when that building was finally finished and Mr. Denivelle was paid for it, was that regarded as an experiment by McKim, Mead & White?

A. I don't think so; they were quite satisfied and so stated to Mr. Denivelle.

RDQ. 16. It was in every way according to specifications a complete and satisfactory job?

(Deposition of Daniel T. Webster.)

A. Complete up to that time, yes.

RDQ. 17. An architect wouldn't be justified in paying a bill for an experiment, would he?

A. An architect doesn't pay bills, sir; the bills [300] are paid by the owners with the architect's recommendation, and the architect wouldn't go into a proposition of this nature without the owner's consent.

RDQ. 18. He wouldn't approve a bill unless he was satisfied that so far as that particular building was concerned, it was a complete and efficient job? A. No.

Redirect examination closed.

Recross-examination.

(By Mr. LOFTUS.)

RXQ. 1. Which was the more difficult material to work with, the white Portland cement or the plaster or gypsum, in the making of stone imitation?

A. Why, the white Portland cement was more difficult work.

RXQ. 2. It was a new product at that time?

A. Yes; and took longer to set and had to be handled in view of these different qualities compared with gypsum—

RXQ. 3. But gypsum has been used for making imitation Portland?

A. I don't know anything about that; I had no experience of that nature.

RXQ. 4. Do you recall how any of the other samples submitted by the bidders were made? [301]

(Deposition of Daniel T. Webster.)

A. Well, the Miller sample was made of plaster —it may have been cement—cement. in it—and the McNulty sample was plaster, but he submitted a supplementary sample later on containing cement —presumably white Portland cement—it was a very good sample.

RXQ. 5. Do you know how that was made?

A. I don't know how it was made; it always appeared to me that he had made a cast—got a piece of real travertin—slab—and made a cast by shaping in a mold, and then used that for making a reverse cast for the purpose of casting from the cast an imitation in cement and using the coloring matter of the same.

(By Mr. ANDERSON.)

That's merely an expression of your opinion?

A. There was such a distinct duplication of the holes and the various peculiar markings in the stone, in the model, that it looked like a replica, don't you see? It was very ingenious.

(Mr. LOFTUS.)

RXQ. 6. Did it show any evidence of blow holes?

A. I don't recall any.

RXQ. 7. Such a method would not be practical on a large job like that?

A. I wouldn't say that; that is purely a matter of the manufacturer's opinion—it's up to them to take that chance. [302]

RXQ. 8. Do you know whether or not Mr. Denivelle made repairs or replacements on that travertin job at the Pennsylvania Station even after his contract was completed?

(Deposition of Daniel T. Webster.)

A. Yes. I don't know the exact date but it was after his guaranty expired—he made further repairs.

RXQ. 9. Some time after?

A. Some time after, yes. I happened to notice how he was coming back from Canada, and I stopped into the Station there and I noticed there were some bad looking spots; and I think I dropped him a note or telephoned him that he had to take care of it and he did, without any expense to us.

RXQ. 10. Do you recall what year that was?

A. I don't know when it was—about 1912, I suppose. I associated that with coming back from Canada; I was going back and forth between 1911 and 1912 about once a month.

Mr. LOFTUS.—I think that's all.

Re-redirect Examination.
(By Mr. ANDERSON.)

RRDQ. 1. Such repairs, however, Mr. Webster, are to be expected in any new building, are they not?

A. We had to make repairs in the plastering; there were certain other things had to be repaired.

RRDQ. 2. That's true of any building, is it not? [303]

A. It's true of any building where you have expansion tracks.

Deposition closed.

Signature waived.

Recess. [304]

[Title of Court and Cause.]

Wednesday, March 12, 1924.

DEPOSITION OF DANIEL T. WEBSTER, FOR DEFENDANTS (RECALLED).

DANIEL T. WEBSTER, being recalled as a witness on behalf of the defendants, and being cautioned that the oath previously taken is still binding, in answer to interrogatories propounded by Mr. Anderson, testified as follows:

Q. 1. Mr. Webster, you are the same Daniel T. Webster who has previously testified in this case?

A. Yes, sir.

Q. 2. In your previous testimony you mentioned that possibly your personal files would disclose some correspondence which had taken place while you were working on the Pennsylvania [305] job, have you looked for that file?   A. Yes, sir.

Q. 3. Did you find it?

A. No; I didn't find the file—the letter you referred to—

Q. 4. Do you know where it is?

A. No, I do not; all the correspondence I had on the job was eventually all sent to the main office.

Q. 5. Now, do you recall identifying at your last deposition, certain papers which I showed to you, including letters and copies of letters?

A. In a general way, yes.

Q. 6. Is it your testimony that those letters were written at or about the dates which appear thereon?

A. Yes, sir.

ation closed.

(Deposition of Daniel T. Webster.)

Cross-examination.

(By Mr. LOFTUS.)

XQ. 1. Do you know Mr. Clay M. McClure who just preceded you on the witness-stand?

A. Yes, sir.

XQ. 2. What were his duties in connection with the erection of the Pennsylvania Terminal Station?

A. He was my assistant and was more in touch with the work on the job in a practical way. I attended to the [306] executive and administrative work on the job, and McClure had charge of the inspection, the deputy superintendents reporting to him, and eventually their reports were transmitted through Mr. McClure and reached my desk for final review.

XQ. 3. Did Mr. McClure have anything to do with determining what materials went into this construction?

A. No more than I had. He would make recommendations which I in turn would pass on and submit to the main office.

Deposition closed.

Signature waived.

Adjourned to 2:30 P. M. [307]

[Title of Court and Cause.]

5:00 P. M., Wednesday, March 5, 1924.

Met pursuant to adjournment for recess.

Parties present as before.

It is agreed that Mr. Cooke's deposition may be taken before George H. Emslie, Esq., notary public, and taken down and transcribed by Miss Hoff-

(Deposition of William Steele Cooke.)
man, a stenographer in the employ of Munn, Anderson & Munn.

DEPOSITION OF WILLIAM STEELE COOKE, FOR DEFENDANTS.

WILLIAM STEELE COOKE, a witness produced on behalf of the defendants, having been first duly cautioned and sworn, in answer to interrogatories propounded by Mr. Anderson, testified as follows: [308]

Q. 1. Your full name, Mr. Cooke, is William Steele Cooke?   A. Yes, sir.

Q. 2. How old are you?   A. 45 years old.

Q. 3. And where do you live, Mr. Cooke?
A. 608 Chestnut Street, Roselle Park, N. J.

Q. 4. What is your business, Mr. Cooke?
A. Plasterer.

Q. 5. Were you formerly in the employ of Paul E. Denivelle or his company, Denivelle Hydraulic Composite Stone Company?   A. Yes, sir.

Q. 6. When so employed, did you work with Mr. Denivelle on the Pennsylvania Railroad Station in New York City?   A. Yes, sir.

Q. 7. Did you do any so-called imitation travertin work in the Pennsylvania Station in New York City?   A. Yes, sir.

Q. 8. For Mr. Denivelle?   A. Yes, sir.

Q. 9. And as I understand you, that imitation travertin work which you did for Mr. Denivelle in the Pennsylvania Station was what is known as "run" or applied work, and not cast work.

(Deposition of William Steele Cooke.)

A. I wouldn't use the term "run"—applied work would cover it—"run" is to run with the mold—it's the same thing.

Q. 10. And please state how much of that work you did [309] for Mr. Denivelle in the Pennsylvania Station?

A. Well, only one section—I couldn't just describe the size of it now—from my mind's eye—but the whole operation that I worked on there on the Pennsylvania job was about 6 hours—there were three men working on it—it was a section as I have already stated, where that statue had to go, probably 12 feet high by 10 feet wide.

Q. 11. As I understood your explanation to me, they filled in a niche in the wall and you applied the imitation travertin surface over this part which had previously been a niche in the wall?

A. Exactly.

Q. 12. Now, at the time you did that job, was the rest of the wall surrounding that spot covered with imitation travertin?

A. The upper portion of it was; the lower portion of the wall was the real travertin—we worked down to the real travertin.

Q. 13. And surrounding this niche was imitation travertin?

A. Imitation and real, both—there were columns near it—the real travertin—and there was imitation travertin.

Q. 14. Now, after that job in the Pennsylvania

(Deposition of William Steele Cooke.)

Station, did you do any other imitation travertin work for Mr. Denivelle? A. Yes, sir.

Q. 15. What was the next job you did of imitation travertin? [310]

A. The next job I did was the Goshen job—the Goelet residence at Goshen.

Q. 16. You mean the residence that was built for Mr. Robert Goelet at Goshen, New York?

A. Yes, sir.

Q. 17. And who were the architects on that job, do you know?

A. I can't recall who the architects were on that building, now.

Q. 18. Just what kind of imitation travertin work did you do for Mr. Denivelle on the Goelet house?

A. Applied work—hawk and trowel.

Q. 19. And after working on the Goelet house, what did you do?

A. I left the Goelet house and I came to another residence that Mr. Denivelle was doing at Huntington, New York; and I went to work on that residence for him.

Q. 20. Was there any imitation travertin work in that? A. No, sir.

Q. 21. And how long did you work for Mr. Denivelle or his company? A. Altogether?

Q. 22. Yes.

A. Well, I have worked for Mr. Denivelle from about 1908 till 1915—but that isn't steadily—that was off and on [311] as Mr. Denivelle had business and we were out of a job, we would get a job

(Deposition of William Steele Cooke.)
with Mr. Denivelle if we weren't working for somebody else.

Q. 23. Now, did you work for Mr. Denivelle in California? A. Yes, sir.

Q. 24. Doing imitation travertin work?

A. Yes, sir; imitation on buildings—applied—hawk and trowel.

Q. 25. Exposition buildings? A. Yes, sir.

Q. 26. How long were you in California?

A. From September 1913 till May 1915.

Q. 27. And when did you return to New York?
A. 1915.

Q. 28. What month? A. May, 1915.

Q. 29. Did you work for Mr. Denivelle after you returned to New York? A. Yes, sir.

Q. 30. Did you do any imitation travertin work for Mr. Denivelle after you returned to New York?

A. Yes, sir; 95th Street, in the Astor Market—95th Street and Broadway.

Q. 31. And what kind of imitation travertin work was that?

A. That was applied—hawk and trowel.

Q. 32. Was there any cast imitation travertin in that job? [312]

A. Yes, I think so; the caps and bases of the pilasters were cast—that was the only thing I can recall.

Q. 33. Do you remember how soon after you got back from New York that you worked on that Astor Market job? A. No, I can't recall that.

(Deposition of William Steele Cooke.)

Q. 34. Do you know the name of the builder of that Astor Market job? The contractor?

A. No, sir; I do not.

Q. 35. This imitation travertin work that you did in the Pennsylvania Station for Mr. Denivelle —was that hawk and trowel work?

A. Yes, sir; that was applied with a hawk and trowel, excepting laminations, etc.—we got out under Mr. Denivelle's instructions—as he had instructed us to get the result.

Q. 36. And did you do the same kind of work on the Goelet house? A. Yes, sir.

Q. 37. And did you do the same kind of work on the Astor Market?

A. Well, we had as we went along—we got better at it—we could make a better imitation as time went on—we got his ideas into our heads a little better—what he was wanting, and we could make a better job as we went along.

Q. 38. And in this work which you did for Mr. Denivelle—the three jobs which you have mentioned —was it according to his instructions and under his supervision? [313]

A. No, the Market wasn't under his supervision —he wasn't here. But the Goelet house—

Q. 39. But you did it for him?

A. We did it for him.

Q. 40. What were you going to say about the Goelet house?

A. Well, the Goelet house—we had some—I got in "Dutch" with Mr. Denivelle in the Goelet house

(Deposition of William Steele Cooke.)
because we were getting a certain texture there and he come along and he was changing it and wanted it changed again; and he had different ideas—something he wanted there—and we had to change, particularly the caps and bases. I wasn't there at the time the caps and bases were changed—the texture of them—but I know when I come back—I had to go away to Milwaukee for a couple of weeks—and when I come back they had changed the thing around again.

Q. 41. But all of these jobs were what you have described as "hawk and trowel" jobs?

A. With the exception of a few—in the jobs I spoke of—there wasn't very much cast work.

Q. 42. Was there any cast work on the Goelet job?   A. Yes, sir.

Q. 43. What part was cast?

A. Caps and bases of columns and pilasters.

Q. 44. And that was imitation travertin?

A. Yes, sir. But there wasn't many of them, there were 2 columns in the entrance and I think 4 columns in the   [314]   loggia outside.

Q. 45. Do you remember when you did the work on the Goelet house?   A. Yes, sir.

Q. 46. When was that?   A. That was 1912.

Direct examination closed.

Cross-examination.

(By Mr. LOFTUS.)

XQ. 1. Was this Goelet job completed when you left it?   A. The Goelet job?

XQ. 2. Yes.   A. No, sir.

(Deposition of William Steele Cooke.)

XQ. 3. Work was done there after you left, by Mr. Denivelle? A. Yes, sir.

XQ. 4. Did you see the samples of imitation travertin that McNulty Bros. and Miller submitted for the Pennsylvania Station? A. No, sir.

XQ. 5. How was this work carried on at the Pennsylvania Station—was there a shop there where this imitation travertin was cast?

A. Yes, sir.

XQ. 6. Was that shop open to the public?

A. No, sir. [315]

XQ. 7. Did you have occasion to observe the method used there in casting the travertin?

A. No, sir.

XQ. 8. You were working on the other thing—on the applied travertin? A. Yes, sir.

XQ. 9. Well, then, the method that you used— were they changing from time to time and improving as the work went along? A. Yes, sir.

XQ. 70. He didn't do that small piece of travertin?

A. I did—were you speaking in general in reference to San Francisco?

XQ. 11. Well, in reference to the Pennsylvania Station and the Goelet job particularly.

A. Well, we had—it was changed on the Goelet job—the texture wasn't coming out right and Mr. Denivelle come along there and changed it—the change was made as I already said, while I was in Milwaukee.

(Deposition of William Steele Cooke.)

XQ. 12. How far had the method been worked out when you did the Exposition job?

A. Well, you mean—

XQ. 13. The applied work.

A. The applied work—well, we again changed the applied work in San Francisco; we changed the style of getting it. [316]

XQ. 14. Did you meet either Mr. MacGruer or Mr. Simpson on that job at San Francisco?

A. Yes, sir.

XQ. 15. You know both of them?

A. Very well.

XQ. 16. What were they doing there?

A. They had the contract on Machinery Hall for the plastering of the building and imitation stone.

XQ. 17. Did they do this travertin work on Machinery Hall?   A. Yes, sir.

XQ. 18. Under whose instructions?

A. Under the instructions of Mr. Denivelle's representatives.

XQ. 19. You were one of those representatives?

A. Well, yes, sir.

XQ. 20. Part of your duty was to show these workmen of MacGruer & Simpson how to execute this travertin?

A. On the hawk and trowel—on the applied work.

XQ. 21. Did you have any difficulty with them getting them to follow instructions?

A. Certainly did.

XQ. 22. What was the cause of these difficulties?

A. Well, I will tell you what the principal diffi-

(Deposition of William Steele Cooke.)

culty is in a proposition of that kind—it was entirely new to those men out there and they didn't know the first thing [317] about it and it took them a long while to get on to what we wanted—and that was our chief difficulty—it was getting the men to learn the method of setting the result that we wanted.

XQ. 23. They were opposed to the idea of travertin, were they?

A. All the contractors were opposed to it—made it "hot" for us—very unpleasant job.

XQ. 24. You were with Denivelle prior to the time that he commenced this work on the Pennsylvania Station?

A. Yes, I worked for Mr. Denivelle.

XQ. 25. Did you ever see him doing any experiments around his own shop in connection with travertin?

A. Previous to the Pennsylvania job?

XQ. 26. Yes?

A. No, I never saw him do anything like that.

XQ. 27. Had you heard of travertin before the Pennsylvania job?   A. Never knew of it.

XQ. 28. First time you knew of it?

A. First time I saw it.

XQ. 29. What was your opinion when Denivelle took this Pennsylvania job—this new material—did you think he was taking quite a gamble?

Mr. ANDERSON.—I object to that; it is immaterial what this man's opinion is about the Pennsylvania job. [318]

(Deposition of William Steele Cooke.)

A. I think he was taking an awful chance because it was a thing that was not heard of before—I never knew of it.

XQ. 30. How long have you been in the plastering business? A. 23 years.

XQ. 31. Do you know anything about the extent to which travertin is used now-a-days in the city?

A. In the City of New York?

XQ. 32. Yes?

A. It's used to considerable extent—coming more so every day—why you can take these new apartment houses that are going up through the Bronx there—they are putting it in all the hallways and entrance halls, and show windows all over the city—I am just after finishing a job myself in it on 37th Street and Seventh Avenue.

XQ. 33. How long since you were employed by Denivelle?

A. Since I was directly employed by Denivelle?

XQ. 34. Yes? A. In 1915.

XQ. 35. You haven't been with him since that time?

A. No, sir; I haven't seen him since.

XQ. 36. Did you ever make any repairs or replacements on the travertin in the Pennsylvania Station for Mr. Denivelle? A. No, sir.

XQ. 37. Do you know whether he did make any such repairs or replacements?

A. Yes, I believe there have been men there working [319] off and on at different times.

(Deposition of William Steele Cooke.)

XQ. 38. What's the latest date you recall when such work was done?

A. Well, I couldn't give you a specific date—I couldn't give you a specific year—I did know that there was a time—I was in Goshen—men had been working there doing repair work.

XQ. 39. Are you familiar with the different methods which Denivelle used in making this cast artificial travertin?   A. No, sir.

XQ. 40. All your work was with the other type?

A. Yes, sir; and in the erection of it.

Mr. LOFTUS.—I think that's all.

Cross-examination closed.

Redirect Examination.

(By Mr. ANDERSON.)

RDQ. 1. You say that you instructed the Mac-Gruer & Simpson crowd, representing Mr. Denivelle, as to how to make the imitation travertin on the Machinery Hall in the Exposition grounds in San Francisco?   A. On the walls.

RDQ. 2. That was applied work?

A. What we call with "hawk and trowel."

RDQ. 3. And that was the hawk and trowel work?

[320]   A. Yes, sir.

RDQ. 4. And was that hawk and trowel work the same as you had done in the Pennsylvania Station?

A. No.

RDQ. 5. Different; was it?   A. No.

RDQ. 6. In what way did it differ?

A. Well, in the first place the material was entirely different.

(Deposition of William Steele Cooke.)

RDQ. 7. What material was used on the Exposition Building?   A. Plaster.

RDQ. 8. What material was used in the Pennsylvania Station?   A. Portland cement.

RDQ. 9. What material was used in the Goelet house?

A. That was a cement but just exactly which cement it was I can't say, because the material Mr. Denivelle made up in his factory and shipped to us in bags.

RDQ. 10. What material was used in the Astor Market?   A. Cement.

RDQ. 11. White Portland cement?

A. Colored.

RDQ. 12. Colored Portland cement?

A. Yes, sir.

RDQ. 13. So that your testimony is that the work which you did in California was different from that which you had done in the Pennsylvania Station? [321]

A. Yes, sir; very much so. It was entirely different—the work in the Pennsylvania job was as near as possible an imitation of real travertin while on the Exposition we got travertin but it was nothing like the Pennsylvania job, for the simple reason that we couldn't put in the time, etc., on it, and then he had a different idea that he wanted carried out on those buildings.

RDQ. 14. Have you seen Mr. Denivelle before you came in this room this afternoon—within the last week or 10 days?   A. Yes, sir.

(Deposition of William Steele Cooke.)

RDQ. 15. Where did you see him?

A. I saw him down at the building on Broadway.

RDQ. 16. Did he send for you?

A. No, he came to see me.

RDQ. 17. In your office?   A. 115 Broadway.

RDQ. 18. Job you are working on?

A. Yes, sir.

RDQ. 19. And he talked about this imitation travertin case?

A. Well, he told me he had come into town and that he had a case coming on here in which Mr. MacGruer was interested and I told Mr. Denivelle —I says—Well, Mr. Denivelle, I have seen Mr. Mac-Gruer in this very same building; he has been in to see me, and if I have any testimony to submit, George MacGruer is a friend of mine—I will submit that [322] testimony faithfully and honestly, and I will submit that testimony to the best of my ability.

RDQ. 20. Mr. Denivelle is also a friend of yours?

A. Yes, sir; both of them are.

RDQ. 21. But he did go to see you within the last week or 10 days?   A. Yes, sir.

Deposition closed.

Signature waived.

Adjourned until Thursday at 10:00 A. M. [323]

(Deposition of Louis S. Massimo.)

[Title of Court and 'Cause.]

New York, N. Y. March 6, 1924—10 A. M.

Met pursuant to adjournment.

Present: WILLIAM A. LOFTUS, Esq., Representing the Plaintiff.

T. HART ANDERSON, Esq., Representing the Defendants.

It is agreed that the deposition of Mr. Massimo,
may be taken before George H. Emslie, Esq., a
notary public, and taken down in shorthand and
transcribed by Miss Helen I. Gorman. [324]

DEPOSITION OF LOUIS S. MASSIMO, FOR DEFENDANTS.

Direct Examination.

(By Mr. ANDERSON.)

LOUIS S. MASSIMO, a witness produced on
behalf of the defendants, and having been first duly
cautioned and sworn, testified as follows:

Q. 1. Your full name is Louis S. Massimo?

A. Yes.

Q. 2. How old are you, Mr. Massimo?   A. 58.

Q. 3. Where do you live, Mr. Massimo?

A. Bayside, L. I.

Q. 4. And what is your business, Mr. Massimo?

A. Superintendent for H. W. Miller, Inc.

Q. 5. What business is H. W. Miller, Inc., engaged in?

A. Plain and ornamental plastering and imitations of stones.

Q. 6. How long have you been with H. W. Miller,
Inc.?   A. A little over five ears.

(Deposition of Louis S. Massimo.)

Q. 7. And before that what were you doing?

A. I was in the same capacity with McNulty Bros., Inc.

Q. 8. You mean McNulty Bros., Inc., of New York City?

A. McNulty Bros., Inc., of New York City.

Q. 9. And is H. W. Miller, Inc., also in New York City? [325]　　A. Yes, sir.

Q. 10. Now, how long were you with McNulty Bros., Inc.?　　A. About 15 years.

Q. 11. Covering what period of time?

A. Well, previous to 1918, about 15 years.

Q. 12. That would be about 1903 to 1918?

A. About that.

Q. 13. And what was the business of McNulty Bros., Inc.?

A. Plain and ornamental plastering and imitation of stones.

Q. 14. The same as H. W. Miller, Inc.?

A. Identical.

Q. 15. And before you went with McNulty Bros., Inc., what was your business?　　A. Same business.

Q. 16. On your own account?

A. No, I was with John J. Roberts, another concern of the same class, in the capacity of foreman.

Q. 17. How long were you with John J. Roberts?

A. About five years.

Q. 18. Now just how long have you been associated with the business of plain and ornamental plastering and the imitation of stones?

(Deposition of Louis S. Massimo.)

A. Previous to the five years with John J. Roberts [326] I was with a very old firm here in New York City, H. Berger & Sons, of New York City. They are out of business now. That is the place I had the pleasure of meeting Mr. Denivelle. He worked there with me.

Q. 19. So Mr. Paul E. Denivelle, here present, was a fellow-employee with you in H. Berger & Sons?

A. He was an employee with H. Berger & Sons. That is many years ago.

Q. 20. While you were with McNulty Bros., Inc., did that company furnish a specimen or sample of so-called imitation travertine stone for the Pennsylvania Station? A. Yes, sir.

Q. 21. New York City? A. Yes, sir.

Q. 22. When was that sample of imitation travertine made, and where was it made?

A. About 1909. It was made at Giobbe's shop, under my direction.

Q. 23. And where was Giobbe's shop located?

A. 32d or 33d Street, between Sixth and Seventh Avenues, I think. It might have been 31st Street.

Q. 24. You have said that sample of imitation travertine was made under your supervision and direction? A. Yes, sir. [327]

Q. 25. For what purpose was that made?

A. To put it up at the Pennsylvania Station for the inspection of the architects, McKim, Mead & White.

Q. 26. Where was that specimen of imitation travertine put up in the Pennsylvania Station?

(Deposition of Louis S. Massimo.)

A. In the Arcade of the Penn. Station, leading from Seventh Avenue to Eighth Avenue. On the South side of the Arcade.

Q. 27. What was the form of that specimen which was installed in the Arcade?

A. It was an entablature or cornice; on the main cornice.

Q. 28. In what position was that placed in the Pennsylvania Station?

A. Approximately right over the entrance to the restaurant—the dining-room they call it—as I have stated, on the south side.

Q. 29. How far above the floor was that specimen positioned when it was installed?

A. I guess about 12 or 15 feet.

Q. 30. Was that specimen a mitered piece to fit in the corner?

A. It was. Yes, it was an angle.

Q. 31. At which corner of this Arcade was that McNulty specimen installed, having reference to the points of the [328] compass?

A. On the southwest corner.

Q. 32. At the time the McNulty Bros. specimen of imitation travertine was installed in that Arcade did you see any other samples of imitation travertine being installed?

A. I did. I saw H. W. Miller, Inc.'s sample.

Q. 33. And were there other samples being installed at that time? A. The Denivelle samples.

Q. 34. And Mr. Paul E. Denivelle who is here

(Deposition of Louis S. Massimo.)

present, was he connected in any way with the installation of samples?

A. As far as I know, he was.

Q. 35. Did you see him at the time the sample was being installed?

A. I can't say whether I did or not; I don't remember. I saw his name.

Q. 36. Please tell us the location of the Miller sample and the Denivelle sample with relation to McNulty sample.

A. The Miller sample was on the same side as the McNulty sample; on the east side. The McNulty was on the west side.

Q. 37. Was the Miller sample a mitered or angle piece? A. Yes.

Q. 38. And which corner of the Arcade was the Miller sample in with relation to the points of the compass? [329]

A. I believe it was at the southeast corner.

Q. 39. Now, where was the Denivelle sample installed?

A. The Denivelle sample to my recollection was installed right immediately opposite to these samples that I have described.

Q. 40. Was that a mitred corner section also?

A. I don't remember.

Q. 41. But it was in the same Arcade?

A. The same Arcade, at the same height.

Q. 42. The same distance from the floor?

A. Yes, sir, the same distance from the floor.

Q. 43. Do you know what was the purpose of

(Deposition of Louis S. Massimo.)
these three concerns installing samples of imitation travertine stone in the Pennsylvania Station?

A. Yes, sir, it was for the object of getting the contract to do the entire work of imitation travertine.

Q. 44. Did McNulty Bros., Inc., submit a bid for that work?   A. Yes, sir.

Q. 45. In submitting that bid what did they follow in the way of specifications and drawings?

A. I couldn't tell you.

Q. 46. You don't know?

A. I don't know.

Q. 47. Now, Mr. Massimo, you say this McNulty sample of imitation travertine was made in the Giobbe shops under your [330] instructions. Do you know what that was made of?

A. I do. It was made of a mixture of Keene's cement, and coloring of course.

Q. 48. Now just how was that sample made, if you remember?

A. It was made of crumbly material.   Dry material pressed or cast on a glue mold.

Q. 49. What was its color?

A. White. Of a creamish color. The color of real travertine stone, with veinings, some lighter than the main body and some darker, having surface holes in the strata.

Q. 50. Did McNulty Bros., Inc., get the contract for the Pennsylvania Station?   A. No, sir.

Q. 51. Who did get that contract?

(Deposition of Louis S. Massimo.)

A. The firm of Denivelle.

Q. 52. Did McNulty Bros. remove the sample which they had installed in the Pennsylvania Station?

A. I believe they did, but I do not remember. It was not under my supervision.

Q. 53. Did McNulty Bros., Inc., get paid for submitting and installing that sample?

A. Yes, sir.

Q. 54. By whom were they paid?

A. By the Denivelle concern. [331]

Q. 55. Do you know how much McNulty Bros. received? A. Yes, sir, $200.

Q. 56. Did McNulty Bros. do any work in connection with the Pennsylvania Station?

A. No, sir.

Q. 57. About when was it? I believe you have given me approximately the time but I would like to have it once more, that this sample of imitation travertine was installed in the Arcade of the Pennsylvania Station, by McNulty Bros.?

A. I mailed you a signed statement. You will find the exact time in that document.

Mr. LOFTUS.—Without looking at that document you don't remember that date, is that correct?

Mr. MASSIMO.—Not without looking at it. That date is taken from the record.

Q. 58. What record? A. McNulty Bros., Inc.

Q. 59. Where did you find that?

A. I went to see Mr. Moore, the secretary of McNulty Bros., Inc., and got the accurate date.

(Deposition of Louis S. Massimo.)

Q. 60. And it is that information which you embodied in the statement which you sent to me?

A. Yes.

Q. 61. I show you a statement on the letter-head of H. W. Miller, Inc., dated February 6, 1924. Is that the statement you [332] referred to in your last answer?   A. Yes, sir.

Q. 62. Now, as I understand you, you went to see Mr. Moore concerning the McNulty records. Who is Mr. Moore?

A. He is the bookkeeper of the McNulty Bros., Inc.

Q. 63. Is he located in New York City?

A. Still in the office of McNulty Bros.

Q. 64. Is McNulty Bros., Inc., still in business?

A. No, sir, not in business, but they have an office.

Q. 65. Now, in this statement you say: "In August, 1908, while in the employ of Messrs. McNulty Bros., Inc., New York City, in the capacity of shop superintendent, I was requested to furnish a sample of imitation travertine to be erected for inspection in the Pennsylvania Terminal, New York City." Is the date of August, 1908, the date that you obtained from Mr. Moore?

Mr. LOFTUS.—Objected to as leading and as suggestive.

A. Yes, the date that the sample was made, yes.

Q. 66. Is that the date that you obtained from Mr. Moore?   A. Yes, sir.

Q. 67. Now, having refreshed your recollection by

(Deposition of Louis S. Massimo.)

reference to the records of McNulty Bros., how does that agree with your own recollection?

Mr LOFTUS.—Objected to, as he stated he had no recollection. [333]

A. I believe I said that it was about 1909.

Q. 68. What is your impression now?

A. That it was 1908. The date does not change the fact.

Q. 69. The question now is as to your recollection of the date. Was it 1908 or 1909? A. 1908.

Q. 70. While you were with the McNulty Bros., Inc., did you have anything to do with the construction of the Widener Building in Philadelphia?

A. I did.

Q. 71 What were you doing on that job?

A. I furnished a sample of imitation of travertine to Horace Trunbour, architects of Philadelphia, Pa. The sample was accepted and I was instructed to proceed with the imitation of travertine work of the Widener Arcade.

Q. 72. When was the Widener Building in course of construction and when was it finished?

A. Between April, 1915—it was completed about September, 1915.

Q. 73. What was the character of the imitation travertine which was installed in the Widener Building?

A. Blocks for the walls. Blocks of the size approximately 16 inches high, about 2 feet wide and 1¼ inches thick. [334]

Q. 74. Where did you get these blocks of imita-

(Deposition of Louis S. Massimo.)

tion travertine which were installed in the Widener Building?   A. Made them right on the job.

Q. 75. Now, tell us of what material those blocks were made.

A. White Portland cement mixture, marble dust, and coloring.

Q. 76. Now exactly how were those blocks made?

A. They were made on a cement plate, dividing the size with wood strips the proper thickness, $1\frac{1}{4}$ inch; lay the same on this plate to the size of the block, then oil the surface so that they wouldn't stick to the plate.   Then I had a device of my own which consisted of an ordinary teapot.   I made a mixture of the same material, of lighter color than the body, and liquid form, and poured that into the teapot, and from the spout of the teapot I run horizontal-wise, a line of what we call veinings, varying from $\frac{1}{8}$ of an inch to $\frac{1}{4}$ of an inch in width.   I made these veinings of two colors, one lighter than the body and one darker than the body. Then with a brush I broke the sharp edges of these veinings.   After that I made a mixture of the main-body material very hard or thick, so that it would be in crumbly form, and threw over the entire surface these crumbs.   What we call "semi-dry," and over the entire surface filled the back with the main-body of the material, as I have stated before, composed of white [335] Portland cement, marble dust and coloring material.

Q. 77. Now, you say you poured veins out of this teapot.   Upon what did you pour them?

(Deposition of Louis S. Massimo.)

A. On the table where the castings were to be made from.

Q. 78. And that part of the table would be the face of the mold?

A. That would be the face of the plate or mold.

Q. 79. And that surface you had oiled before pouring the veins?   A. Yes, sir.

Q. 80. Now, what was the purpose of using a brush on this veined matter that you had poured into the mold?

A. So that the veinings would not have a distinct edge, but the edge would blend with the main body of the block, and they would come nearer to the real travertine.

Q. 81. How much of this crumbly material did you put into the mold?

A. Just an even cover—barely covering the entire surface.

Q. 82. Was that put in over the veins that you had laid on the surface?

A. Yes, sir. Also, I would state that it was put in varying the veinings. We intended to form a strata as found in the real travertine. [336]

Q. 83. Now, what was the consistency of the material that you put in after the crumbly layer?

A. It was regular casting consistency, which is similar to very thick cream. Of such consistency that it would spread. It would run.

Q. 84. And then what did you do after that?

A. About forty minutes after that the plate would

(Deposition of Louis S. Massimo.)
be hard enough to lift, and repeat the same operation.

Q. 85. By "plate" in your last answer what do
you mean?

A. The block ready to apply on the wall. A block
as I have stated, 1¼ inches thick and according to
the size required.

Q. 86. Now, having removed that block what was
the appearance of the surface which was against
the surface of the mold?

A. The appearance was similar to the real travertine. In fact, by placing alongside the real travertine it could not be told which was the real and
which was the imitation.

Q. 87. And is that the process you employed in
making the blocks of imitation travertine for the
Widener Building?   A. Yes, sir.

Q. 88. What had been your experience before that
in the manufacture of imitations of various natural
stones?

A. Why, we always obtained a sample of the real
stone and then we tried to imitate it according to
the nature of the stone. Some stones are smooth
and some otherwise. [337]

Q. 89. Well, had you before that made imitations
of natural stones?   A. Yes, sir.

Q. 90. To what extent had you done that?

A. I made the vestibule of the then called Manhattan Hotel, corner of 43d Street and Madison Avenue, in the imitation of lime-stone, when I was in

(Deposition of Louis S. Massimo.)

the employ of H. Berger & Sons, 101 Fourth Avenue. I have already given you the date of that.

Q. 91. Now, had you made imitations of other stones except lime stone?

Mr. LOFTUS.—Objected to as incompetent, immaterial and irrelevant and having no bearing on the issue of this suit.

A. I have.

Q. 92. During your entire experience in the ornamental plastering art, about how many natural stone imitations had you made?

A. Imitation of limestone, imitation of Caen stone, imitation of travertine, imitation of Kato, imitation of Noisette stone, etc.

Q. 93· All of these stones that you have named have smooth surfaces?

A. Some of them have and some have not.

Q. 94. Which ones of those, aside from travertine, have a rough surface or a vermiculated surface? [338]

A. Imitation of Kato stone has the same surface as travertine minus the veinings of color.

Q. 95. What is the natural color of Kato stone?

A. More of a yellowish tint.

Q. 96. And you had made imitations of Kato stone?

A. Only recently. It is a new stone.

Q. 97. Did anyone make any objection to the way in which you were making imitation travertine for the Widener Building? A. Yes, sir.

Q. 98. Who was it?

A. Mr. McNulty handed me a letter coming from

(Deposition of Louis S. Massimo.)
Denivelle, saying that we were infringing on a patent of Mr. Denivelle's, in the Widener Building, and Mr. McNulty referred the case to me.

Q. 99. Then what did you do?

A. I got in touch with Mr. Denivelle on the telephone and asked him to send me a copy of his patent so that I might see to what extent I was infringing on his patent. I might also state that I told Mr. Denivelle, I am now using the very same words, "Mr. Denivelle, you know very well that I made imitation of travertine and other stones long before this time." Mr. Denivelle's answer was: "You might have made the same but if you failed to patent your process you would be the loser if I got a patent on the same."

Q. 100. After that conversation what happened?
[339]

A. I read carefully the copy of this patent and was convinced that I was not infringing on said patent. This patent dwelt mostly on the apparatus formed with a rectangular pot with a line of spouts underneath, which would be used to lay the veinings on the surface, while I used an ordinary teapot, which in my estimation was a better method, so that the lines would not run exactly parallel, because with a teapot each line was put by itself, while with this apparatus the lines would always be in the same position, running perfectly parallel.

Q. 101. Well, what happened after that?

A. I reported to Mr. McNulty and Mr. McNulty made an appointment with Mr. Denivelle to go to

(Deposition of Louis S. Massimo.)

Philadelphia and see for himself that we were not infringing on said patent.

Q. 102. Did Mr. Denivelle go to Philadelphia?

A. Mr. Denivelle didn't go to Philadelphia but he sent his—what I was made to understand was his partner—Mr. Connor, and Mr. Connor, Mr. McNulty and myself went to Philadelphia direct to the working shop in the Widener Building, and saw the men working. Mr. Connor was there to see the complete work. In other words, he saw the making of these blocks from beginning to end, and I explained to him that we were not infringing upon the patent according to the copy I had. Mr. Connor pulled a timetable from his pocket and got the next train, leaving Mr. McNulty and myself on the job.

Q. 13. Now, at the time of this visit of Mr. Connor to [340] the Widener Building in Philadelphia, what kind of blocks did your men make in the way of a demonstration?

A. The same blocks that we were making for the building, as I have heretofore described them; 1¼ inch thick, varying in size according to requirements.

Q. 104. They were blocks of imitation travertine stone? A. Imitation travertine stone.

Q. 105. Now, Mr. Massimo, what is your recollection as to the date of that visit and demonstration which you have just described?

A. Why, the date is between April, 1915, and September, 1915. To my recollection it was around

(Deposition of Louis S. Massimo.)
June, 1915; it was very nice weather when we went there.

Q. 106. And when was your work on the Widener Building finished?   A. September, 1915.

Q. 107. Was the building completely finished at that time?   A. Our work was finished then.

Q. 108. But the building was still under construction?   A. Still under construction.

Q. 109. Did you see any part of the Denivelle work in the Pennsylvania Station while it was being installed?   A. Yes, sir.

Q. 110. What part did you see?   [341]

A. The main waiting-room of the Station.

Q. 111. When it was being installed?

A. Yes, sir.

Q. 112. What was the occasion of your going to the Pennsylvania Station to enable you to see that work?

A. Why, we go to see all work of our competitors. It is the method that we have, so that we can see how other people do the work.

Q. 113. Did you have any difficulty in getting into the Pennsylvania Station while it was in course of erection?   A. No, sir.

Q. 114. Did you at that visit to the Pennsylvania Station see how Mr. Denivelle or his employees were making the blocks of imitation travertine?

A. I did not try to see it. I only saw the complete work.

Q. 115. Now, after that Station was finished, did you go in and look it over?   A. I did.

(Deposition of Louis S. Massimo.)

Q. 116. What is your recollection now as to the time when that Station was finished?

A. I have no recollection. I could not remember the date. I am not so very keen on dates. It was right after the Station was opened. I believe it was 1910.

Q. 117. Did you have any knowledge of any work that was [342] being done in that Station by the Miller Company with whom you are now associated?

A. Yes, sir, I knew that H. W. Miller, Inc., were contractors for all of the plastering work of the Pennsylvania Station, outside of the imitation of travertine.

Q. 118. Mr. Massimo, have you any knowledge of any other use of imitation travertine by anybody between 1910 and 1915 than that which you have mentioned? A. I have not.

Direct examination closed.

Cross-examination.

(By Mr. LOFTUS.)

XQ. 119. Where did you have this conversation with Mr. Denivelle in regard to his patent?

A. I was in the shop of McNulty Bros., Inc.

XQ. 120. Here in New York City?

A. New York City, on the telephone.

XQ. 121. Did you have just one conversation over the telephone? A. Just one conversation.

XQ. 122. You didn't see Mr. Denivelle personally, did you? A. No, sir.

XQ. 123. Did you write him any letters in regard to the subject of patents? [343]

(Deposition of Louis S. Massimo.)

A. If there were any letters written, the firm of McNulty Bros., Inc., did all of the writing.

XQ. 124. You are familiar with Mr. P. H. McNulty's signature? A. I think I am; yes, sir.

XQ. 125. I show you a letter dated June 14, 1915, addressed to Mr. P. E. Denivelle, and signed "P. H. McNulty," and ask you if you can tell us whether or not that is Mr. McNulty's signature.

A. Yes, that is Mr. McNulty's signature, and that is the letter that I asked Mr. McNulty to write to Mr. Denivelle.

Mr. LOFTUS.—I offer the letter in evidence, and ask that it be marked Plaintiff's Exhibit "B" —McNulty letter.

XQ. 126. Now, did Mr. Denivelle in reply to that letter send you a copy of his patent.

A. He sent the firm of McNulty Bros. a copy.

XQ. 127. Did you see that copy? A. Yes, sir.

XQ. 128. What form was it in? Was it a typewritten document or was it printed?

A. I believe it was printed. I couldn't say, but the copy was in my possession, and has been in my possession, until 1919.

XQ. 129. And this Denivelle patent that you saw at that time, had it to do with an apparatus for making travertine? [344]

A. It dwelt mostly on the apparatus.

XQ. 130. Did you understand that it was to be used for the making of travertine? A. Yes, sir.

XQ. 131. Well, now, this document that you saw

(Deposition of Louis S. Massimo.)

at that time, what did it include? Drawings and certain specifications?

A. As far as my recollection goes, I am pretty certain that it dwelt mostly or wholly on an apparatus for making imitation travertine.

XQ. 132. Would you be able to recognize a copy of that drawing if it was shown to you at the present time? A. I think I would.

XQ. 133. I hand you a blue-line print and ask if that is similar to the drawing which you saw at the time above mentioned. A. Yes, sir.

XQ. 134. In other words, at that time you saw a drawing like this blue-print which you have just identified. Is that correct?

A. Yes, sir, that's correct. That coincides with my description of those spouts (indicating) in line, making parallel veinings, while I use an ordinary teapot—each veining singly—by themselves.

XQ. 135. And the veins which are distributed by this apparatus are the veins forming the striations in the travertine? A. Yes, sir. [345]

Mr. LOFTUS.—I ask that the blue-print identified by the witness may be marked Plaintiff's Exhibit "C," for identification.

XQ. 136. Are you a member of the Contracting Plasterers' International Association?

A. No, sir.

XQ. 137. Is your firm, H. W. Miller, Inc., a member of that Association?

A. Why, he is a member through the Employing Plasterers' Association of New York.

(Deposition of Louis S. Massimo.)

XQ. 138. The Employing Plasterers' Association of New York is affiliated with this other association?

A. Yes, sir.

XQ. 139. How do you happen to appear here as a witness, Mr. Massimo, at whose request?

A. Mr. Anderson's request.

XQ. 140. Has Mr. McGruer been around to see you?   A. No, sir.

XQ. 141. You haven't seen Mr. McGruer?

A. No, sir.

XQ. 142. Does your firm, H. W. Meyer, Inc., make and install artificial travertine at the present time?   A. Yes, sir, to a great extent.

XQ. 143. Prior to the Pennsylvania Terminal job had you ever seen or heard of artificial travertine? [346]   A. Not artificial travertine.

Cross-examination closed.

Redirect Examination.

(By Mr. ANDERSON.)

RDQ. 144. I call your attention, Mr. Massimo, to Plaintiff's Exhibit "B," and ask you to note the date of that letter, and state whether it was about the date of that letter that this visit of Mr. Connor, representing Mr. Denivelle, to Philadelphia, where he witnessed your manufacture of imitation travertine, took place?

A. Previous to seeing this letter I said that I

(Deposition of John A. Fincke.)
thought it was about June; now I find that I was
correct.

Deposition closed.

Signature waived.

Recess until 2 P. M.   [347]

[Title of Court and Cause.]

2:00 P. M., March 6, 1924.

Met pursuant to adjournment.

Parties present as before.

It is agreed that Mr. Fincke's deposition may be
taken before Philip D. Rollhaus, Esq., a notary public, and taken down in shorthand and transcribed by
Miss Helen I. Gorman, a stenographer in the employ
of defendants' counsel.

DEPOSITION OF JOHN A. FINCKE, FOR De-FENDANTS.

Direct Examination.

(By Mr. ANDERSON.)

JOHN A. FINCKE, a witness produced on behalf of the defendants, having been first duly cautioned and sworn, testified as follows:

Q. 1. Mr. Fincke, your full name is John A.
[348] Fincke?   A. Yes, sir.

Q. 2. How old are you, Mr. Fincke?

A. 57 years old.

Q. 3. Where do you reside, Mr. Fincke?

A. New York City.

Q. 4. And what is your business?

(Deposition of John A. Fincke.)

A. Well, I term myself a plain and ornamental plasterer.

Q. 5. How long have you been in that business?

A. About thirty-five years.

Q. 6. When one speaks of imitation travertine stone do you know what it is?   A. Yes.

Q. 7. Have you ever made any imitation travertine stone?   A. I have made lots of it.

Q. 8. When did you first make imitation travertine stone?   A. In actual work or experimental?

Q. 9. No, actual work.

A. Well, the first job I did was the Frank E. Campbell Funeral Chapel, Broadway and 66th Street.

Q. 10. Was that cast, or run or applied work?

A. That was cast and hung. It was a coffered [349] ceiling and side walls.

Q. 11. When did you do that Campbell job?

A. As far as memory goes I couldn't say as to whether it is twelve or thirteen years ago.

Q. 12. Twelve or thirteen years age?

A. The records of the contractor will establish that.

Q. 13. Who was the contractor?

A. He was a Chicago man, but the architect was here in the city.

Q. 14. Have you any records which would establish that date?

A. No, I destroyed all that stuff when I moved to my present quarters.

(Deposition of John A. Fincke.)

Q. 15. Where were you located when you did that Campbell job?   A. I was located in 22d Street.

Q. 16. Now, was that imitation travertine in the Campbell job manufactured in your place of business?   A. Yes, sir.

Q. 17. Now, can you tell us just how it was made and what it was made of?   A. Yes.

Q. 18. Please do so?

A. I made a model of the coffer itself. I then [350] put the original veinings on the model. From that I made a glue mold, and from the glue mold I distributed different colored materials.

Q. 19. Just what materials did you employ?

A. Well, the general body is composed of plaster with ground marble. It is a question of color to get in different shades that you want.

Q. 20. Just what do you mean by the term "plaster." What was it made of?

A. Plaster of paris.

Q. 21. And that is what the artificial travertine was made of, that you put in the Campbell chapel?

A. Yes, sir.

Q. 22. How did you obtain the depressions or holes?

A. Well, I made them by making indentations in the model.

Q. 23. The model from which you made the glue mold?   A. Yes, sir.

Q. 24. Did you follow a piece of genuine travertine stone in making these imitations?

A. Yes, naturally.

(Deposition of John A. Fincke.)

Q. 25. And your recollection now is that that was twelve or thirteen years ago?   A. Yes. [351]

Q. 26. What was the name of the architect?

A. Randolph H. Almiroty, 48 West 46th Street.

Q. 27. Was that the first job of imitation travertine work that you did?

A. It was. The first real job.   I had been making a specialty of mantels for quite some time previous to that, and I made antiques of all kinds, and imitation lime stone, Caen stone, etc.

Q. 28. What were those mantels made of?

A. They were made of Keene cement.

Q. 29. How did you mold those?

A. In the same way that I did the Campbell job,

Q. 30. Now, what was the size of the blocks which you installed in the side walls in the Campbell chapel?

A. Well, I should say they were probably an average of—might be 5 feet high by 2 feet 6, or 3 feet wide. The coffers in the ceiling were much thicker.

Q. 31. You mean to say that each block was the size you gave?

A. You take the height of a room and divide it in about two parts and cast it in two sections.

Q. 32. How thick were those sections?

A. In some places they would probably be ¾ and in some places they might be 2 inches.

Q. 33. And were those sections all one tone or were [352] there variations of different tone colors?

(Deposition of John A. Fincke.)

A. Variations. We couldn't very well make the same thing over again. We had to work in free-hand as it were, and each casting would be differ-ent; variety.

Q. 34. And how did you make the different color tones in that casting.

A. By the different color materials we used.

Q. 35. Will you explain just how you applied the different colored materials?

A. In the mold of course. The little holes that form in imitation travertine are in reverse in the molds, and the holes, of course, we always try to get shadowed. Where our mold has all those little upright veins as it were, we would put the different colors along and then back it up with the main body and in that way get more or less of

Q. 36. So that when the casting was set the col-ored lines on all those veins would be a part of the main body, would they? A. Yes.

Q. 37. That is the way you made it? A. Yes.

Q. 38. Do you know what the term "semi-dry" means, in making cast plaster—

A. Well, as far as I know, I should say "semi-dry" would be meant by setting a material and then reducing [353] it to a powder again. I should say that would—that is my conception of it.

Q. 39. You have heard of the use of semi-dry materials in making plaster castings have you?

A. Just what I have stated. We use semi-dry processes to enable them to get different colors, I suppose.

(Deposition of John A. Fincke.)

Q. 40. Did you ever use any so-called semi-dry material in making any of your artificial travertine? A. No.

Q. 41. Are you quite sure that it was twelve or thirteen years ago that you did that Campbell job?

A. I cannot pin it right down, but you can get that information by calling up the architect or getting in touch with Campbell.

Q. 42. What is your best recollection?

A. I can't say one way or the other; it might be twelve or thirteen years.

Q. 43. Do you know when the Pennsylvania Station was built?

A. I recollect when it was built but I cannot state the date.

Q. 44. Was this Campbell job before or after that? A. I should say it was after that.

Q. 45. Did you have anything to do with the work on the Pennsylvania Station? [354] A. No.

Q. 46. Do you recall any other place where you used imitation travertine.

A. Yes, I did a restaurant. I think it was the Fass restaurant. Just what street was it on? It was between Fifth Avenue and Broadway, I know. It was in the old "Judge" Building—I think it was.

Q. 47. When did you do that restaurant?

A. That was probably a year after I did the Campbell job.

Q. 48. You have no records at all, to fix these dates? A. As I say you can get the other.

(Deposition of John A. Fincke.)

Q. 49. Who was the contractor on the restaurant you mention?

A. In fact, I got that job through looking at the Campbell job.

Q. 50. Done at the same time?   A. Afterwards.

Q. 51. How long afterwards?

A. I should say six or eight months afterwards.

Q. 52. When did you move to your present shop, Mr. Fincke?   A. March of last year.

Q. 53. Where was your shop located before that?
[355]   A. At 227 East 22d Street.

Q. 54. How long were you in that shop?

A. I was probably there fifteen years.

Q. 55. And it was in that shop that you did this work, was it?   A. Yes.

Q. 56. And was it in that shop that you made those mantels?   A. Yes.

Q. 57. And you made the mantels as I understand it, before you did the Campbell job?

A. Yes.

Q. 58. Did you see the travertine work in the Pennsylvania Station, after it was opened to the public?   A. Yes.

Q. 59. How long after that was it before you made those mantels?

A. As far as I know I might have made them before. I don't know. I was always more or less dickering in antiques and all kinds of imitations.

Q. 60. Have you made imitations of other stones in addition to the travertine.

A. I have made imitations of every known stone, I guess, there is in the world.

(Deposition of John A. Fincke.)

Q. 61. Well, now, how does the manner of making
your imitation travertine differ, if at all, from making [356] imitations of other stones, which you
have made?

A. No difference except that the colors—and the
fact of their having voids in it.

Q. 62. Was that the first natural stone having
voids in it, that you tried to imitate?

A. No. In making antiques of any kind of stone
we generally try to make it look as if the weather
had eaten into it, and naturally—

Q. 63. As I understand it, where you had to make
a void you did it by making a void with a projection to form that void?

A. Yes, and then we get a lot of voids by air-
pockets in our castings. If a man is careless in
casting he will get air voids, and those air voids
help to make up the imitation of the travertine.

Q. 64. And don't you get air voids whether you
want them or not, in making imitation stones?

A. If you are careless, yes.

Direct examination closed.

Cross-examination.

(By Mr. LOFTUS.)

XQ. 65. Mr. Fincke, do you use that same method
to-day that you have described, namely, the use of a
mold with negative projections?   A. No.

XQ. 66. Do you make artificial travertine at the
[357] present time?   A. Yes, sir.

XQ. 67. What method do you use?

A. I have patented a method of my own.

(Deposition of John A. Fincke.)

XQ. 68. What is that method?

A. It is purely a dry method.

XQ. 69. Dry?   A. Dry method.

XQ. 70. When did that patent issue to you?

A. Oh, I should say about a year ago. It was pending for two years.

XQ. 71. And to-day you use the method described in that patent?   A. Yes, sir.

XQ. 72. Do you happen to know the number or date of that patent?   A. No.

XQ. 73. Had you ever seen any artificial travertine prior to its use in the Pennsylvania Railroad Station?   A. Oh, yes.

XQ. 74. Where?   A. In any   of   the   stone yards.

XQ. 75. Artificial travertine?

A. Oh, not artificial; I thought that you meant original,—oh, the artificial—no, I can't say that I have. [358]   That is, I don't suppose it was called to my attention. I may have seen it, because when that—I am making a statement—when that job was put on the market for estimating, all the firms of New York City were interested in figuring it and making samples for it.

XQ. 76. Did you make a sample for it?

A. No, I wasn't big enough in business at that particular time to think of estimating that size job.

XQ. 77. Do you know how soon after you completed this Campbell Undertaking Chapel that the building was occupied?

A. It was occupied while I was working on it.

(Deposition of John A. Fincke.)

XQ. 78. That was a new building, was it?

A. No, it was alterated.

XQ. 79. What alterations were made there?

A. Floors were changed in height, and partitions were taken down, and the whole building was generally altered to meet the requirements of Frank E. Campbell and his business.

XQ. 80. Who was the contractor on that job?

A. He was a Chicago man. Just what his name is I can't recall. You can get that from the architect. He can give you all that information.

Cross-examination closed.

Deposition closed.

Signature waived.

Adjournment to Friday, March 7, 1924, 10 A. M.
[359]

[Title of Court and Cause.]

New York, N. Y., March 7, 1924—10 A. M.

Met pursuant to adjournment.

Parties present as before.

It is agreed that the deposition of Mr. Cousins may be taken before George H. Emslie, Esq., a notary public, and taken down stenographically and transcribed by Miss Helen I. Gorman, a stenographer in the employ of defendant's counsel.

DEPOSITION OF HENRY A. COUSINS, FOR DEFENDANTS.

HENRY A. COUSINS, a witness called on behalf of the defendants, having been first duly cautioned and sworn, testified as follows: [360]

Direct Examination.

(By Mr. ANDERSON.)

Q. 1. What is your full name, Mr. Cousins?

A. Henry A. Cousins.

Q. 2. How old are you, Mr. Cousins?   A. 66.

Q. 3. Where do you reside, Mr. Cousins?

A. Belleville, N. J.

Q. 4. What is your occupation or profession?

A. Manufacturer of artificial marble, stone and scagliola.

Q. 5. How long have you been in that business, Mr. Cousins?   A. 49 years.

Q. 6. Now, are you in business for yourself?

A. No, I am with H. A. Cousins, Inc.

Q. 7. How long have you been with that corporation?

A. Well, that corporation only dates back from 1917, I think, but I was in business under my own name, personally, up to that time.

Q. 8. In New York City?

A. New York City; same address.

Q. 9. You say you have been in that business for 49 years?   A. Yes.

Q. 10. Give us a brief but comprehensive statement of [361] the history of your business in

(Deposition of Henry A. Cousins.)
connection with the manufacture of artificial stone.

A. I entered business in 1875. In 1879 I joined in partnership a man named Guelton and we carried on business at Brighton, England. In 1882 I started in business in my own name in London, England, and carried on business there until early in '90, when I came to New York City, where I was practically head of the Mycenian Marble Company, continuing with that concern until 1910, when I acquired the goodwill, etc., of the concern and did business in my own name. In 1917 the concern was incorporated under the name of H. A. Cousins, Inc., and is doing business at 524 West 25th Street, this city.

Q. 11. Now, during all that period have you been engaged in the manufacture of artificial stone?

A. Yes. Artificial marble and stone.

Q. 12. Please name some of the artificial stone which you have manufactured during that period?

A. Lime stone, travertine, Caen stone, Kingwood stone, and others.

Q. 13. Which one of these imitations of natural stone could be described as having a honeycombed surface, or as I believe the technical term is, vermiculated surface?

A. Well, one of the most characteristic is travertine.

Q. 14. Is there any other natural stone which you [362] have imitated, having a similar surface?

A. Yes, some lime stones; not exactly similar, because the strong stratification of color is absent.

(Deposition of Henry A. Cousins.)

Q. 15. I had reference of course only to the appearance. Have you imitated any stone other than travertine, having such appearance?

A. Oh, yes, some lime stones having a textured surface or finish.

Q. 16. Now, what materials have you used in the manufacture of those imitations of natural stone?

A. Well, many. Used mixtures composed of plaster and other ingredients; that is, calcine plaster. Some of Portland cement, some of Keen cement.

Q. 17. Were those materials commonly employed for that purpose?   A. Yes.

Q. 18. How long have these materials been used for producing imitations of stone?

A. Since before I can testify to.

Q. 19. Now, coming down to imitations of travertine stone. When did you first make any such imitations?   A. I believe in 1908.

Q. 20. What was the occasion of your making those imitations of travertine stone in 1908?

A. They were made up to a sample of natural stone [363] which was supplied to us, that is, to the Mycenian Marble Company, by the Fuller Company, George A. Fuller Company, in connection with the proposed wall treatment of the Pennsylvania Station.

Q. 21. At whose request were those imitations made?

A. Now, the individual at that time, I can't recall. He was the head of the New York Branch of

(Deposition of Henry A. Cousins.)

the Fuller Company, but at this moment I can't say who he was. I dealt with a Mr. Connors, also, in that connection.

Q. 22. With what concern was Mr. Connors?

A. George A. Fuller Company.

Q. 23. How many specimens of imitation travertine did you make at that time?

A. I made several, but I think only two were submitted.

Q. 24. To whom were they submitted?

A. They were given to the George A. Fuller Company, but I can't say who received them.

Q. 25. Who delivered them?

A. They were delivered by one of our messengers.

Q. 26. What was the purpose of your making those specimens for the George A. Fuller Company?

A. To see how nearly we could imitate the stone which they suggested using.

Q. 27. And in order to make those specimens the Fuller [364] Company furnished you with a piece of the natural travertine stone? A. Yes.

Q. 28. Who supervised the making of those imitations? A. I made them myself.

Q. 29. Of what material did you make those specimens of imitation travertine? A. Keen's cement.

Q. 30. Now, will you state exactly how you made those two specimens or samples of imitation travertine stone for the George A. Fuller Company?

(Deposition of Henry A. Cousins.)

A. Mixtures of colored cements representing the different shades shown in the natural sample were prepared. Certain of the light shades of these were placed in a rubber squeeze bulb which was drawn in nearly parallel lines on a glass table, forming ridges of colored cement standing from 1/8 to 3/16 of an inch high above the glass surface. Certain of the ground color was then taken—I should have stated that these colored cements were mixed, and used while in a plastic condition. After the placing of these parallel lines on the table a portion of the darker colors which really formed the groundwork, was taken on a palette and splashed by means of a bass broom, on the general surface. This, to break up the rigidity of the lines and at the same time to cover [365] somewhat the general ground of the table, being careful, however, to leave certain parts of the table open or clear. Next, granules formed of the ground-colored cements were taken and lightly spread into the fissures left by the lines of color already described. After this, the general ground-color, in a more plastic condition, was spread over the whole mass, with a trowel; it was roughly smoothed out with a trowel, and over the whole mass a cheese cloth was spread, on to which dry cement was deposited, this for the purpose of absorbing the superfluous moisture from the whole mass and rendering it harder. After a time this was taken off and the mass pressed with a trowel in the general direction of the lines, and the mass was then filled to the thickness of about $1\frac{1}{2}$ inches,

(Deposition of Henry A. Cousins.)

which was permitted to harden. When taken up from the glass table it was rubbed with a stone and so finished.

Q. 31. Which surface was rubbed with a stone?

A. The surface that had been in contact with the glass.

Q. 32. And what was the appearance of that surface after it was rubbed with the stone?

A. It was considered by all who saw it, a wonderful imitation of the natural stone.

Q. 33. Well, now, you have not described the appearance of it. Please tell us what it looked like?

A. Well, it looked like the natural stone which had been given to me to work from. [366]

Q. 34. Please describe its appearance.

A. In color it was of a warm, light buff color, with lines of lighter shade running in almost parallel lines, but having in stratified lines a series of indentations and granulations of a lava-like appearance.

Q. 35. Now, you have used the term "ground color" in the description. What do you mean by "ground color"?

A. The color which more nearly represents the general tone of the stone, forming indeed, the major part of the colored mass.

Q. 36. Now in making those samples that you have described were you following any specification or formula given to you by anybody?

A. No, none whatever.

(Deposition of Henry A. Cousins.)

Q. 37. How was it that you made the samples in the manner which you have described?

A. Well, from my practical knowledge of the manipulation of cements I conceived a method which I thought would produce me certain results, and I followed it.

Q. 38. I believe you said you made two such specimens?

A. I know I made more but I submitted two.

Q. 39. That is you delivered two, or caused two to be delivered to the George A. Fuller Comapny?

A. Yes. [367]

Q. 40. What became of those two samples that you delivered to the George A. Fuller Company?

A. I saw them from time to time in the Estimating Department of the George A. Fuller Company's office in the Flatiron Building. Between those times I was informed by the office, and also had other information that they had been given to certain prospective bidders on the job, as standards of the work required.

Mr. LOFTUS.—I move to strike out the latter part of the witness' answer as partly based on hearsay.

Q. 41. Counsel has objected to your answer, on the ground that it is based on hearsay. Have you any direct knowledge as to what use was made of those samples?

A. If personal corroboration is required I guess you can apply to a man named Thomas Coronato, and Michael Noscenti.

(Deposition of Henry A. Cousins.)

Q. 42. The question is, Mr. Cousins, have you any direct knowledge of what use was made of those samples?

A. None except that they told me that they were in Michael Noscenti's shop, and that they used them for the purpose of trying to reproduce the effects obtained in those samples.

Q. 43. Who told you that?

A. Michael Noscenti and Coronato.

Q. 44. They told you, each of them, that they had your [368] samples which you made, in their shops?

A. Coronato at that time was working for Michael Noscenti.

Q. 45. They told you that they had the samples which you had made, in their shop?   A. Yes.

Q. 46. Did you see them in their shop?

A. No, I never was in the shop.

Q. 47. When you submitted those samples to the George A. Fuller Company, did you at the same time bid on the work which was required?

A. Yes, we figured the work and made a bid.

Q. 48. And for what was that bid made. For what work?   A. For the Pennsylvania Station.

Q. 49. Now, before that time had you ever made any imitation of travertine stone.

A. No. I believe that was the first occasion that it had ever been proposed to use it as a decorative material.

Q. 50. And I believe you said that was in 1908?

A. Yes.

(Deposition of Henry A. Cousins.)

Q. 51. Can you fix the date any more definitely than that? A. At present I cannot.

Q. 52. Well, since 1908 have you made any imitations of travertine stone? [369] A. Oh, yes.

Q. 53. When did you next after that date make imitation of travertine stone?

A. Well, I couldn't say offhand, but every few weeks or months.

Q. 54. And for what purpose were those later imitations made?

A. Some of them for samples for distribution on request, and some for work which we actually did.

Q. 55. Well, now, give us the names of some jobs of work which you actually did, where located, and when they were done; I mean imitation travertine jobs.

A. Dental Dispensary, Rochester, N. Y.

Q. 56. When did you do that job?

A. I think that was about 1915 or 1916.

Q. 57. Was there any other job before that?

A. Well, I can't state the dates. We have done quite a number of jobs but I haven't got a list of them. There was a job at Greenwich, a private residence, but I couldn't give you the data as to the name of the owner. I can get it though. Quite a number of small jobs the conditions of which I don't recall, but we were doing it right along.

Q. 58. Have you any records in your establishment which would show such jobs?

A. Some records, yes. The records we have got.

(Deposition of Henry A. Cousins.)

ten [370] rid of beyond a certain point, and they are not available; but I will look into it and see.

Q. 59. Do you remember the name of the contractor and the architect on this Dental Dispensary job in Rochester? What was the name of the architect? A. At this moment I couldn't tell you.

Q. 60. What was the name of the builder?

A. I didn't have anything to do with him, but that can be ascertained easily. I can get that for you.

Q. 61. Who got the contract for the Pennsylvania job?

A. Well, I don't know whether the contract was included in the plastering with the Miller concern or whether it was given separately to Mr. Denivelle.

Q. 62. Do you know who did the imitation travertine work in the Pennsylvania Station?

A. I know it was done by Mr. Denivelle or under his direction.

Q. 63. Did you see that job in course of construction? That is to say, the imitation travertine work at the Pennsylvania Station? A. No.

Q. 64. Have you seen it since it was finished?

A. Oh, yes.

Q. 65. Do you know when it was finished? [371]

A. I may say "No." I imagine about 1911, but I don't know by actual knowledge.

Q. 66. When that Pennsylvania Station was first opened to the public did you go in and look it over?

(Deposition of Henry A. Cousins.)

A. Soon after.

Q. 67. Was the imitation travertine job finished at that time?   A. With some exceptions, yes.

Q. 68. Can you give us approximately the date when you made that inspection of the imitation travertine job at the Pennsylvania Station?

A. No.

Q. 69. About what year was it?

A. I believe 1910 or '11· I am not sure.

Q. 70. Had you, before making those two samples of stone which you delivered to the Fuller Company, made other imitations of stone of the same materials?   A. Oh, yes.

Q. 71. In what manner did you use those same materials in making those other imitations of stone?

A. Well, there were many different kinds of stones made and they would be made according as the conditions would call for. Even travertine is not made by one formula but by many, according to the conditions under which it is to be applied, and general requirements. ·[372]

Q. 72. Has it been your experience for forty-five years or more that there are?

Mr. LOFTUS.—Objected to as leading.

A. Yes.

Q. 73. Did you say that that was a problem which ornamental plasterers and makers of imitation stone, and what might be called "plastic workers" were frequently called upon to figure out and solve?

Mr. LOFTUS.—Same objection; and the further

(Deposition of Henry A. Cousins.)
objection is made that it is irrelevant and immaterial.

A. Oh, yes.

Q. 74. Do you know whether anyone else was called upon to make imitations of travertine for that Pennsylvania job?

A. Of by own knowledge, no; generally, many submitted samples.

Q. 75. On what do you base your last answer?

A. From information received at the office of George A. Fuller, where I was told several times that the other people were months behind me in their results.

Q. 76. Why didn't you get that contract?

A. Well, that was a matter due to financial trouble on the part of my associate at that time, and his exxtreme age, which made him loath to incur the responsibility of large operations at that time. [373]

Q. 77. Do you recall the name of Mr. Nesbit as being one with whom you came in contact in the George A. Fuller Company's organization?

A. Yes, I have met Mr. Nesbit.

Q. 78. Did you have anything to do with Mr. Nesbit concerning these samples?

A. I don't remember.

Q. 79. Have you installed any artificial travertine in the city of New York?   A. Yes.

Q. 80. Give us the names of the jobs if you can?

A. Cunard Building.

Q. 81. Any others?

(Deposition of Henry A. Cousins.)

A. Knickerbocker Building.

Q. 82. Any others?

A. I don't recall others, but there are.

Q. 83. You mentioned Niagara Falls. Did you do a job in Niagara Falls?   A. Yes.

Q. 84. What job was that?

A. Niagara Falls Bank.

Q. 85. Imitation travertine?   A. Yes.

Q. 86. Now, when did you do the Cunard Building in New [374] York City?

A. I believe it would be about 1917 or '18·

Q. 87. Who had the contract for that building?

A. Max Eidlitz, General Contractor.

Q. 88. Was there any genuine travertine used in the Cunard Building?   A. Yes.

Q. 89. What was the imitation travertine which you furnished to the Cunard Building. Can you specify?

A. That consisted of columns, pilasters, wall paneling and ornamental capitals.

Q. 90. Where is this work located. In the main office of the Cunard Office?

A. In the passenger office and the freight office.

Q. 91. Was there any genuine travertine used in the passenger office?

A. I don't recall that there was—yes there was, adjacent to our work.

Q. 92. Was there any genuine travertine used on the walls of the passenger office?

A. No, I think not.

Q. 93. Is it your recollection that the walls and

(Deposition of Henry A. Cousins.)
the other parts you have mentioned; in the main
passenger office, except the floor, is your imitation
travertine?

A. I don't recall that the floor in the passenger
office was stone of any kind. I believe it was wood
or teratza. [375]

Q. 94. There was some genuine travertine stone
however, in the passenger office of the Cunard
Building, was there not?   A. Yes.

Q. 95. Now in regard to the Knickerbocker
Building. What imitation travertine did you furnish for that building?

A. The wall paneling, columns, pilasters, ornamental blocking.

Q. 96. And in what part of the building is this
imitation travertine located?

A. In the first story. Now used as the Knickerbocker Barber Shop. The contractor of the work
was also Mr. Eidlitz.

Q. 97. When did you do that job?

A. I think that was 1918.

Q. 98. Do you recall the size and shape of the two
specimens of imitation travertine which you made
and delivered to George A. Fuller Company in
1908?

A. To the best of my recollection they were about
two feet long by fourteen inches wide and one and
a half inches thick.

Q. 99. Please tell us how you made the imitation
travertine for the Cunard job?

A. That work was made substantially as de-

(Deposition of Henry A. Cousins.)

scribed already as the process used for the production of these samples. [376]

Q. 100. And how did you make the imitation travertine for the Knickerbocker Building job?

A. That also was similar. The process used in the Dental Dispensary was different, as that work was applied in a plastic form.

Q. 101. That is to say, the Cunard job and the Knickerbocker Building job were pre-cast imitations?

A. Yes, pre-cast, and were made in substantially the way described for the production of the samples. The Dental Dispensary job was applied in a plastic form, in which the colors were deposited on oil-cloth by means of a tray on which alternate lines of the different colors were laid. This was then drawn over the surface of the oil-cloth, which was laying on a flat table, the colors sliding over the tray, were drawn throughout the length of the oil-cloth or piece to be made, and this was applied, depositing in its passage a stream of the vari-colored cement to form straight ribbons of the colored cements, which ultimately formed the grounds of the stone to be imitated. This material is then smoothed over with a trowel and cheese-cloth laid thereon, on the top of which is deposited the dry cement for the purpose of absorbing superfluous moisture. When the cheesecloth and the dry cement are removed the work is troweled and then applied to the walls, which have been prepared to receive it, by being [377] leveled. The

(Deposition of Henry A. Cousins.)

striated colors are thus formed, but were, up to the time of application on the wall, without any indentation or texture. This was applied by means of tools made from steel-points embedded in lead holders, which were hammered on the surface to form the indentations or granular depressions so as to imitate the characteristics of the natural stone. The molds, which consisted of cornices, capitals, etc., were made by a metal templet such as used in plastering, on the face of which, however, a muffle having teeth projecting beyond the lines of the contour of the mold, was formed. The mold was then run in colored cements heretofore described, in the ordinary way employed by plasterers for the production of a mold. When this had attained a sufficient hardness the muddle was removed and the full templet used. The molding was then covered with a lighter-colored material and was run over by a complete templet. This gave the lines of different colored cements required. The perforations were then made by means of the same tools described for the flat surfaces.

Recess until 2 P. M. [378]

Met pursuant to adjournment 2 P. M.

Q. 102. Now, you have described, have you, Mr. Cousins, the two methods employed by you, one in making pre-cast imitation travertine, the other in making what might be called "run" or applied imitation travertine? A. Yes.

Q. 103. Now you say that in making applied

(Deposition of Henry A. Cousins.)

imitation travertine the wall is prepared by leveling it. Of what material is the surface wall made?

A. It depends somewhat on the character of the finish. If it is interior we sometimes use Keen cement; sometimes ordinary plaster mortar, or a mixture of Portland cement and an aggregate.

Q. 104. What do you mean by an "aggregate"?

A. A mixture of sand, marble-dust and cement in certain proportions.

Q. 105. Now, you have described certain jobs you did. Please tell us of what materials the wall surfaces were made in those jobs.

A. In the case of the Dental Dispensary the walls were built up with plastering mortar to within one-half inch of the surface, and then about three-eighths of an inch of Keen cement and marble-dust in equal proportions was applied, leaving about three-sixteenths of an inch of thickness for the [379] finished colored coat.

Q. 106. Now, this colored coat to which you refer is the one which was made on the oil-cloth?

A. On the oil-cloth.

Q. 107. What would be the condition of the wall surface regarding moisture at the time you applied this colored coat?

A. There are different conditions under which we sometimes apply the material on to live cement. That is to say, cement applied on the walls at the same time as the work is being prepared on the table, so that each are brought together in a live or semi-plastic condition. In other cases it is ex-

(Deposition of Henry A. Cousins.)
pedient to prepare the walls first, and on the day
of applying the finished coat to wet and brush
over with a solution of the same cement, the walls
already formed.

Q. 108. Well, what method did you employ on
the jobs you have described where you made applied work?

A. The semi-plastic or live method.

Q. 109. Now, you have spoken of the use of a tool
having projections which you say were hammered
into the surface. What was the condition of the
surface at the time this tool was used, as to its moisture?

A. It was of a consistency which would not be
indented by the pressure of the hand, but would
admit of indentations being made with a sharp,
heavy instrument such as I have described. [380]

Q. 110. Now, at the recess we all went down and
looked over the imitation travertine and the genuine travertine in the Cunard Building. What we
to-day observed, does that confirm your testimony
given in the forenoon as to the amount of imitation
travertine work you furnished in that job?

A. Yes, except that I noted that certain parts
had been made by the applied process in the passenger office, which had escaped my recollection
until I had the opportunity to see it.

Q. 111. So that your testimony now is that some
of that imitation travertine was done by what is
called the "applied" process?   A. Yes.

Q. 112. And some by the pre-cast process?

(Deposition of Henry A. Cousins.)

A. Yes.

Q. 113. What is the meaning of the term "isolating" as used in the plastering art or in the manufacture of imitation stone?

A. I presume it alludes to the medium which is applied to a mold to prevent the cast from sticking thereto—such as oil, steric acid, or fluid soap.

Q. 114. Is that a term well known in the plastering art or in the art of manufacturing imitation stone or making pre-cast blocks of cement?

Q. 115. I never heard the term used before in that connection. [381] There is also another isolating medium consisting of a solution of shellac in some cases or a varnish in others, by which it is sought to stop the porosity of the mold from absorbing the moisture of the cast. This is first used and allowed to dry, then the grease, steric acid, or soap applied. In the case of the samples which I described as having been made on plate-glass no such medium is necessary. Any cast will leave plate glass without any such application.

Q. 116. Is it common in this art to apply grease or similar material to the surface of the mold?

A. Yes, some such medium is always used in the case of cast work.

Q. 117. But I believe your testimony is that when it is made on a piece of plate-glass it is not necessary?

A. Plate-glass being the only exception.

Q. 118. The method of producing the lines or veins which you have described as having been em-

(Deposition of Henry A. Cousins.)

ployed by you, was that a common method employed in the plastering art at the time?

A. Those samples? The manner of forming those lines was one of many ways used to produce certain effects in the production of artificial marbles.

Q. 119. At the time you made those samples of imitation travertine for George A. Fuller & Company was that particular manner of forming colored lines in a cast imitation stone a common method? [382]

Mr. LOFTUS.—Objected to as incompetent, irrelevant and immaterial.

A. It was.

Q. 120. Now, you described an operation of using a brush on those lines after you had laid them on the glass surface, did you not? A. Yes.

Q. 121. What is such an operation known as in the plastering art? A. Softening or stippling.

Q. 122. Was that a common, well-known operation in the production of such colored lines in precast blocks of imitation stone at the time you made those samples?

Mr. LOFTUS.—Objected to as incompetent, irrelevant and immaterial.

A. The process is not for the purpose of making lines; it is for softening lines.

Q. 123. Was that a common step for that purpose at the time you made those samples? A. Yes.

Q. 124. In making those samples what was the condition of those lines which you laid upon the

(Deposition of Henry A. Cousins.)

plate-glass at the time you applied this granular material which you mention?

A. The material as applied to the glass was of a density almost as thick as cream cheese—decidedly thicker than heavy cream, the object being to have them well raised [383] above the surface.

Q. 125. Had it become set or hardened before you applied the granular or other material which you refer to? A. No.

Q. 126. Now, what was the condition of this granular material to which you have referred, when you applied it on this glass surface, over the lines, as you have described? A. The condition of it?

Q. 127. Yes.

A. Well, there were several different pieces made. They were made at different times—that is, different ways, and were slightly varied. On some of them the granules were hard; in other cases they were semi-hard.

Q. 128. What were they made of?

A. Of portions of the colored cements such as were used for the general ground of the material—in this case, of colored Keen cement.

Q. 129. Would it be proper to describe that material which was applied—and which you have referred to as "granules" or "granular material"— as of a semi-dry and lumpy consistency?

Mr. LOFTUS.—Objected to as incompetent, irrelevant and immaterial, and as leading.

A. Well, that seems to me a very loose way of describing the sharp little lumps or granules that

(Deposition of Henry A. Cousins.)
are required [384] for the production of the peculiar characteristics of travertine.

Q. 130. In the finished cast would that granular material that you have described show on the surface? A. A very small proportion of it would.

Q. 131. And what was the appearance of it on the surface of the two samples made for the Fuller Company?

A. It had the appearance of a stone having irregular depressions of a granulated character.

Q. 132. Now, you described filling in over this granular material what I believe you called "ground color." How did that act on the material that was already applied to the plate-glass?

A. It filled in generally, the interstices of the material as already laid. Its passage, however, toward the glass would be interrupted to a certain extent by the granulated particles, leaving small holes and depressions surrounding those granules as seen from the finished surface.

Q. 133. What is meant by the term "bonding" in this art of making imitation pre-cast blocks of imitation stone such as you have described? Is it with relation to the backing? Did you ever hear the term "bonding" used in connection with the manufacture of blocks of imitation stone such as you have stated here this morning you have made?

A. Only in the laying up; not in the making of [385] them.

Q. 134. By "laying up" I assume that you mean placing in position on the wall? A. Yes.

(Deposition of Henry A. Cousins.)

Q. 135. Would it be improper to apply the term "bonding" to the effect which this semi-fluid body-colored portion which you pour over the surface of your granules on the striated colored lines has in uniting the whole mixture into one block? Would that be a common use of the term?

A. Well, since it is all one plastic material there is no need for bonding. It consists of an aggregate; the same material, but as in this case, of different consistencies. It might be used in that connection. We do not, however, apply the term with any of the operations of casting one material at a time.

Q. 136. Well, let us assume that after *the* have your colored lines on the glass and your granules on the glass, and the colored lines, you had allowed that mass to dry. What would you have?

A. You wouldn't allow it to dry unless you wanted it to be spoiled.

Q. 137. Why would it spoil?

A. Well, cement is best when one aggregate sets up together. Not when portions of the same aggregate are applied at different times. [386]

Q. 138. So you regard, do you, the colored lines, the granular layer, and the more or less fluid body portion which you pour in, as all one aggregate mass?

A. One general aggregate. The cast is not complete until it is all laid on.

Q. 139. What is the meaning of the term "blotting and drying" as used in the manufacture of cast blocks of imitation stone?

(Deposition of Henry A. Cousins.)

A. That is a process that is always used in the manufacture of artificial marble and is intended to withdraw from the semi-fluid mass a large proportion of the water, so as to make it of a stiffer or harder consistency and permit of its being pressed with a trowel and so increased in hardness.

Q. 140. Did you in making those imitation travertine samples use anything except cement and color?

A. No, cement, color and water.

Q. 141. Is it common to use what is known as an "aggregate" in the manufacture of such imitation stones?

A. That depends on the purpose for which it is required. In outside work, for instance, we use an aggregate formed of Portland cement, silica, quartz, sand and other ingredients to enhance the effects of brilliancy in its translucence or semi-translucence and to reduce the strength of the Portland cement itself. [387]

By Mr. ANDERSON.—Counsel for the defendants requires counsel for plaintiff to state which of the claims of the patent in suit plaintiff intends to rely on in this case.

By Mr. LOFTUS.—In view of the short notice of this request plaintiff's counsel is unwilling at this time to definitely commit himself as to all of the claims which will be relied upon. In any event, however, claims 1, 2, 5, 9 and 10 will be relied upon.

Q. 142. Mr. Cousins, have you studied a printed Patent Office copy of the Denivelle patent No. 1,212,-331, January 16, 1917?   A. Yes.

(Deposition of Henry A. Cousins.)

Q. 143. Have you a copy of that patent with you?
A. Yes.

Q. 144. As one skilled in this art, will you explain what you understand to be disclosed in that patent, and whether you understand it, and if you have any reason to criticise the disclosure of that patent please do so; and in your criticism you may refer, and I ask you to refer specifically to any portion of that patent, by page and line, which you may at any time be referring to?

A. In the description after the preamble, section 1, line 68 and on, describing the surface which is prepared or greased, this is a sample device commonly used by plasterers and others, in casting any objects in plaster or cement, and is not novel. Next, as to the veinings. This is in the second paragraph, from line 75 on; it states that the colored cements [388] in a semi-liquid state is poured from a receptacle such as described in this patent, through a series of nozzles that produce jets by gravity. This is a most impractical if not impossible suggestion, in that if the jets are to be maintained the density of the material will have to be so light and thin that a mere smear will be produced after the first. That is to say, a cement mixed in a semi-liquid condition will at first flow very rapidly, and in order to form lines must be propelled very quickly over the mold or surface which it is required to cover. This force will of course be reduced as the receptacle becomes empty and the flow will become a series of droppings instead of lines. Further, in

(Deposition of Henry A. Cousins.)

practice, cement quickly loses its flow from such a
receptacle, on account of the precipitation of the
coarser parts of the cement to the bottom, and the
flow will cease altogether, although the receptacle
may be nearly full, or in any case, the lines so
formed will not be of the sharp, raised character
which will bear the application of the coarser lumpy
formation afterwards described in the patent. The
striating of the colors is a process which is used
and has been used for many years in the manufacture of artificial marble. The receptacle was probably never used by Mr. Denivelle, or anyone else,
more than a couple of times before being deposited
under the work-table, or in the dump. The stippling, under paragraph 3, line 95, same page, is a
process used in the manufacture of artificial marble,
except that the artificial marble workers usually
employ a bass brush [389] having greater elas-
ticity, which admits of a greater modulation of
effect.

No. 4269

United States

Circuit Court of Appeals

For the Ninth Circuit. 2

Transcript of Record.

(IN TWO VOLUMES.)

AUL E. DENIVELLE,

Appellant,

vs.

acGRUER & SIMPSON, a Copartnership, and
GEORGE SMITH MacGRUER and ROB-
ERT MORTON SIMPSON, Individually,
and Sometimes Doing Business as Mac-
GRUER & CO.,

Appellees.

VOLUME II.
(Pages 353 to 693, Inclusive.)

Upon Appeal from the Southern Division of the
United States District Court for the
Northern District of California,
Third Division.

No. 4269

United States

Circuit Court of Appeals

For the Ninth Circuit.

Transcript of Record.

(IN TWO VOLUMES.)

PAUL E. DENIVELLE,

Appellant,

vs.

MacGRUER & SIMPSON, a Copartnership, and
GEORGE SMITH MacGRUER and ROB-
ERT MORTON SIMPSON, Individually,
and Sometimes Doing Business as Mac-
GRUER & CO.,

Appellees.

VOLUME II.
(Pages 353 to 693, Inclusive.)

Upon Appeal from the Southern Division of the
United States District Court for the
Northern District of California,
Third Division.

(Deposition of Henry A. Cousins.)

Paragraph 4, line 100 and on, page 1, the next step, which is described as a mixture of different or similarly colored cements reduced to a semi-dry and lumpy consistency by hand or otherwise, is a method that has been used for hundreds of years in the production of scagliola, a description of which would be very similar to that given in this patent, namely, scagliola is produced mainly by the making up of colored cements into stiff particles or masses which are broken up into larger or smaller particles, as the case requires, into and over which other colored material *or* poured. This process, again, is not by any means novel. This applies also to paragraph 5, page 2, under the head of "Bonding."

Same page, paragraph 6, the blotting or drying is a process used in the manufacture of artificial marble and most artificial stones. In all cases, usually, however, by first applying a cheesecloth or other material on to the mass of colored cements already formed, on to which dry cement is sifted or thrown, which after a time is removed and the work pressed, for the purpose of hardening the same.

Also, the next paragraph, 7, page 2, under the head of "Reinforcement." Reinforcement of some kind or other is almost always employed in the casting of any plastic or cement castings, either by means of burlap, fibre, wood or [390] metal, and is therefore not novel. Taking it step by step I only find one novelty and that is in the receptacle marked "C" in the illustration.

(Deposition of Henry A. Cousins.)

Q. 145. Mr. Cousins, I call your attention to the
paragraph numbered "1," which you will find beginning with line 85 and ending with line 94 on page
2 of the Denivelle patent. Please read that paragraph and state whether you understand it.

A. Oh, yes, I understand that paragraph.

Q. 146. You understand it, do you? A. Yes.

Q. 147. Does the step or steps set forth in that
paragraph 1, to which I have called your attention,
relate to what has been described as a pre-cast block,
or does it relate to applied or run work?

A. To applied work, and is the method by which
practically all plastering is done.

Q. 148. How about the materials therein specified;
are they common materials for such work?

A. Those are common materials for such purpose.

Q. 149. And were they common at the time this
patent was issued? A. Oh, yes.

Q. 150. And how long before that patent was
issued were those materials common for that kind
of work?

A. During my personal experience of forty-nine
[391] years they have always been the same.
Those materials have always been in use and so
employed. Previous to that plaster of paris and
Portland cement were used for a still further period
for this purpose and in that manner, Portland cement having been introduced fifty years, probably,
previous to this patent.

Q. 151. I call your attention to paragraph 2, beginning with line 95 and ending with line 112 on

(Deposition of Henry A. Cousins.)

page 2 of the Denivelle patent. Do you understand what is set forth in that paragraph?

A. I understand what is set forth, yes.

Q. 152. Is that intended to set forth a step in the manufacture of a pre-cast piece of imitation stone or applied or run surface?

A. Applied or run surface.

Q. 153. What would be the result of following the step or steps set forth in that paragraph?

A. That would have the effect of a surface covered with a colored mixture of cement, plaster or magnesites.

Q. 154. Do you understand that the effect produced would be of one solid color or vari-colored.

A. It would be of one solid color such as ordinarily employed in plastering where the finish is required to be tinted, as it is called, and is frequently done. [392]

Q. 155. I call your attention to the following paragraph, 3, beginning with line 113, on page 2, of the Denivelle patent, and ask you whether or not you understand that relates to a pre-cast block of imitation travertine stone or an applied or run process of making an imitation of stone?

A. Well, to an applied process of doing something.

Q. 156. Assuming that the step or steps set forth in paragraph 3 to which I have called your attention were followed what result would be obtained?

A. Well, you might get a smeary effect of mixed

(Deposition of Henry A. Cousins.)
colors, depending on the care with which it was carried out.

Q. 157. Have you noticed that that paragraph states that it is for the purpose of providing light horizontal striated lines or veins of different colors or tones of color in the finished result? A. Yes.

Q. 158. Do you think that effect would be produced?

A. If very nicely done you *might such* an effect.

Q. 159. What would you say as to the novelty of that step or steps set forth in paragraph 3, at the time this patent was applied for?

Mr. LOFTUS.—Objected to as incompetent, irrelevant and immaterial and not proper mode of proof, [393] and on the further ground that any attempt to discuss the elements or steps of this patent piecemeal is improper.

A. I would say it is not novel, as it is part of a process frequently employed in the production of striated stones, such as limestone, sandstone and others.

Q. 160. In making your last answer have you taken into consideration that that paragraph refers, as you have stated, to a process employed in producing applied or run surfaces?

A. Paragraph 3 applied to a run or applied process.

Q. 161. I call your attention to paragraph 4, which begins with line 128 at the bottom of page 2. Please read that carefully and state whether you understand it.

(Deposition of Henry A. Cousins.)

A. This process describes the impressions to be made with a slender brush with stiff bristles applied with a series of alternating sharp jabs, and pressure. This method is also one that is not novel and is used in the production of textured stones other than travertine, and which were commonly made long before the introduction of travertine into this country, to my knowledge.

Q. 162. Did you ever use it?

A. I cannot say that I have, in that I did not apply myself to the manufacture of artificial stone till a later date.

Q. 168. What do you mean by a "later date"? [394]

A. I don't think I did any textured stone in this country previous to 1908.

Q. 164. What kind of imitations of stone would that step set forth in paragraph 4 be useful in?

A. Well, I can't say what it would be useful for other than the making of a light texture such as we have in some limestones, but it certainly would not produce very accurately the characteristics of travertine.

Q. 165. As you understand the Denivelle patent, does that step 4, paragraph 4, refer to the applied or sun surface, or to the pre-cast block?

A. To the applied or run.

Q. 166. I next call your attention to paragraph 5, beginning with line 9 on page 3. Please state whether you understand what is set forth therein.

A. Well, the trowel application would naturally

(Deposition of Henry A. Cousins.)

flatten that surface out. Would tend to close up the depressions made.

Q. 167. You understand what is set forth in paragraph 5?

A. Oh, yes; but as to its providing an undercut quality, that can scarcely be maintained in practice.

Q. 168. Did you ever see that step tried out in the manufacture of applied surfaces in imitation stone?

A. Oh, yes, I have done it myself. [395]

Q. 169. I call your attention to paragraph 6, beginning with line 19 of page 3 of the Denivelle patent. Please read it and state whether you understand what is set forth therein. Is that step descriptive of applied or pre-cast work?

A. Applied and run work.

Q. 170. Would that step produce the result which is set forth in paragraph 6? A. I say yes.

Q. 171. I call your attention to paragraph 7 of the Denivelle patent, beginning with line 31, page 3; do you understand what is set forth in that paragraph?

A. Yes.

Q. 172. Does that relate to applied or run work or pre-cast work? A. To applied work.

Q. 173. I call your attention to paragraph 8, beginning with line 43 on page 3 of the Denivelle patent. Do you understand what is set forth therein?

A. Yes.

Q. 174. Does that relate to applied or run work or pre-cast work?

A. To what is known as run work.

Q. 175. Run work? A. Yes. [396]

(Deposition of Henry A. Cousins.)

Q. 176. Was that step new with the Denivelle patent?

A. No. All molded work is made by means of such a templet.

Q. 177. I call your attention to the Denivelle patent, to those parts beginning with paragraph 1, line 68, page 1, and ending with line 66, page 2. Does that part of the Denivelle patent describe applied or run work, or pre-cast work?

A. That is pre-casting.

Q. 178. You know what the claims of the patent are, do you? A. Yes.

Q. 179. Please read claims 1, 2, 5, 9 and 10 (I will mark them for you), of that Denivelle patent, and state whether or not you understand those claims, and which of them, if any, apply to run or applied work or pre-cast work; that is, indicate to your mind that they relate to run or applied work or pre-cast work?

Mr. LOFTUS.—I object to any interpretation of this witness as to the meaning of these claims, on the ground that the patent claim is solely for the court to construe. It is not within the province of this witness.

A. Claims 1, 2 and 5 relate to pre-cast work. Claim 9 covers either cast or applied work. It is too indefinite to decide which is meant. Claim 10 covers laid up work. [397]

Q. 180. Laid up work? A. Laid up work.

Q. 181. What do you mean by that? Pre-cast?

A. No, laid up on the wall.

(Deposition of Henry A. Cousins.)

Q. 182. It is described however, as a combination form of differently toned thin layers of strata. It does not seem to describe in any way the processes which have been given in the preceding methods.

Q. 183. I call your attention to claim 10 and to the following language: "formed of differently-toned thin layers of strata, the said layers only partly connected one to the other, in such manner as to leave serrated voids in striated formation between said layers." What do you understand is meant by that passage?

A. I have said I don't understand it to relate to the processes already described in the patent, but something very indefinitely described, giving a result which one might desire but could not obtain from any of the processes described for laid up work or work laid in place, that is to say, on the wall.

Q. 184. Well, assuming that it was intended to describe a pre-cast job what would that language mean to you?

A. It would perhaps more nearly describe the process in that it speaks of thin layers of strata which in the pre-cast is attempted to be described by the laying down [398] of certain lines of certain colored materials, and then the filling in of the voids. I take it, however, that it is meant to cover the second process, as described from line 67, page 2 and on.

Q. 185. I call your attention to claim 9. Do you understand that claim.

(Deposition of Henry A. Cousins.)

A. I think I understand what it means to say, but I could not really interpret from it any of the foregoing processes described.

Q. 186. Do you mean the processes described in the patent? A. In the patent, yes.

Q. 187. Why doesn't that claim 9, to your mind describe any of the processes set forth in the specification of that patent?

A. The mass of cementitious material one surface of which is shaped and striated and formed with irregularly spaced depressions, that might be construed as covering the pre-cast. It certainly does not describe the laid up process. The striae constituting the exposed portions of shallow inlays of uniformly colored cement, probably attempts to describe the run work.

Direct examination closed.

Cross-examination.

(By Mr. LOFTUS.)

XQ. 188. What is the meaning of "striae," Mr. Cousins? A. The lines of stratification. [399]

XQ. 189. Would that mean the colored veins?

A. It would mean both in this instance, since the cavities run in the same direction as the colored stratifications.

XQ. 190. What do you understand is meant in claim 10 by a natural stone of sedimentary origin?

A. A stone formed by a depositary system, so to speak, by which a sediment is left from time to time, and the deposit which accumulating, forms into a striated mass.

(Deposition of Henry A. Cousins.)

XQ. 191. What are the different natural stones
of sedimentary origin that you are familiar with?

A. Limestone, sandstone; of course travertine,
etc.

XQ. 192. As I understood from your direct examination, prior to 1908 you were not engaged in the
manufacture of artificial stone of texture.

A. I may say that prior to 1908 I was so full of
artificial marble I never gave much attention to
bidding on stone work, but travertine was never
at that time considered as a stone, it was considered as a marble, and part of our business, and we
reproduced it in the same way that we made an
artificial marble, not as a stone—to which, by-the-
way, it is more nearly allied than a stone.

XQ. 193. What distinction do you draw between
a stone and marble?   [400]

A. Well, of course, they are both lime, but there
is a depositary origin. Marbles are formed by different means, as stones are, and the structure of
this travertine is so allied to marble—in that it
takes a good polish. There is where a stone generally departs from marble. A stone does not as a
rule take a polish and a marble does. The composition nevertheless of each being very similar
chemically.

XQ. 194. What do you mean by a stone or marble
of texture?

A. A stone or marble of texture is one in which
there is that stratification. Most marbles are con-
glomerates.

(Deposition of Henry A. Cousins.)

XQ. 195. You don't wish to convey to the Court that prior to the time of this Pennsylvania Station that artificial stone or marble had been made, containing this stratification and having the colored veins and also the numerous small undercut voids or depressions?

A. Not exactly the same. Different stones, as with marbles, have their different characteristics and color. That, I believe, was the first introduction of travertine to this country.

XQ. 196. Did you actually make a bid on that Pennsylvania Station for the travertine work?

A. We did.

XQ. 197. With whom was that bid filed? [401]

A. I couldn't say. I believe it would be sent in in the ordinary course. I wasn't familiar with the office work at that time.

XQ. 198. When was that bid submitted to the Fuller Company?

A. It would ordinarily have gone into the Fuller Company. I know I made up the figures—checked off the quantities and made up the figures.

XQ. 199. Do you recall what the amount of that bid was?   A. I couldn't at this time.

XQ. 200. Approximately?

A. I couldn't say at this time.

XQ. 201. You didn't erect the samples in the station did you?   A. No.

XQ. 202. I believe you stated the samples were made of Keen's cement?   A. Yes.

XQ. 203. What material was used in the artificial

(Deposition of Henry A. Cousins.)
travertine that went into the station, which Mr.
Denivelle installed?

A. Well, I couldn't say what he used. I have
never gone into it. It wasn't Keene's cement.

XQ. 204. It was not? A. It was not. [402]

XQ. 205. Did you know that the architects required that contract to be executed in white Portland cement?

A. I know that. I have done many jobs for the
same architects, which were specified to be done
in Portland cement. (They have left it to me
to make it in whatever material I did.)

XQ. 206. Your answer is "Yes"? A. Yes.

XQ. 207. You knew that? A. Yes.

XQ. 208. You don't know where those samples
are at the present time? A. No.

XQ. 209. How long since you have seen them?

A. Probably not since 1909 or '10·

XQ. 210. How large were these samples?

A. Well, as I remember, about two feet, roughly,
by about 14 or 15 inches, and about one and a half
inches thick.

XQ. 211. Were they just plain, flat slabs?

A. Plain, flat pieces. They were similar in thickness, and I believe in width, but probably twice the
size of the sample given us to imitate.

XQ. 212. There were no ornamental features on
them? A. No.

XQ. 213. Did you ever try to use a receptacle
like [403] the one shown in the drawings of the
Denivelle patent?

(Deposition of Henry A. Cousins.)

A. No. Not of that particular form. We have receptacles that we use in the manufacture of artificial marble, but which don't depend on gravity as the force for propulsion.

XQ. 214. Tell us what this scagliola is?

A. It is an imitation, or a process which is used to reproduce the effects and characteristics of colored, artificial marbles.

XQ. 215. Does it contain this texture that you have—referred to?

A. In some cases. But it is the process that I spoke of as being identical with that by which scagliola was formed. Scagliola is a mass formed of plaster. A mixture of plaster and glue, and water of course, and this makes a mass of different colors which is brought to a very stiff consistency. It is then crumbled up into small and large particles, and so on, and is spread out on the table according as the marble will require. In some cases on the actual mold; in others just spread out roughly, and the thinly mixed material which forms the face is then thrown in among it to unite the particles and form the veins.

XQ. 216. Are there any of these undercut voids present in scagliola?

A. Unless those which are left for the purpose of being filled in with colors. [404]

XQ. 217. Well then, the final surface is one of smooth dense surface? A. Yes.

XQ. 218. In what way are these facts arranged in this scagliola?

(Deposition of Henry A. Cousins.)

A. That depends on the artist. They are arranged to as nearly approximate the effects of the marble as possible, by the artist; just as with paint one man will paint a beautiful picture and another one spoil a fence.

XQ. 219. What was the first artificial limestone or sandstone which you made?

A. Oh, I have made artificial limestone and sandstone probably in the '70's.

XQ. 220· You are acquainted with Mr. Denivelle are you' not?

A. Well, yes, as a member of the Employers' Association.

XQ. 221. Are you a member of the Contracting Plasterers International Association?

A. Indirectly. The firm is.

XQ. 222. What action have they taken in connection with this present suit?

A. I don't know.

XQ. 223. At whose invitation do you appear here as a witness? [405]

A. I guess Mr. Anderson is responsible for my being here; certainly not any association.

XQ. 224. Has Mr. MacGruer been to see you?

A. I saw Mr. MacGruer with Mr. Anderson.

XQ. 225. Did Mr. MacGruer or Mr. Anderson point out to you that it would be to your interest to assist in trying to defeat this patent?

A. Certainly not. I am not personally interested. I told Mr. Anderson that I was not interested, in the beginning.

(Deposition of Henry A. Cousins.)

XQ. 226. You make and instal imitation travertine at the present time, in your business, do you not? A. Yes; that is, the firm does.

XQ. 227. What is your position with the firm?

A. I am not a member of the firm.

XQ. 228. You are simply an employee?

A. No, not even that.

XQ. 229. What are you then?

A. Nothing, except that I do assist them sometimes by personal intercourse with prospective clients.

XQ. 230. Are you employed on a salary?

A. No.

XQ. 231. In what way are you remunerated for your services? A. At present not at all. [406]

XQ. 232. What did you have to do with the travertine work that went into the Cunard Building?

A. I superintended it.

XQ. 233. How much time did you devote to that work? A. Oh, considerable.

XQ. 234. Did you receive anything for your services there? A. Oh, yes.

XQ. 235. You recognize it as a fact, do you not, that the artificial travertine in the Cunard Building is an infringement of this Denivelle patent?

Mr. ANDERSON.—I object to that as calling for an interpretation of the scope of the patent. The witness does not claim to be a patent expert.

Mr. LOFTUS.—Well, he has been reading from the claims here.

A. No. Part of that work was done by a pro-

(Deposition of Henry A. Cousins.)

cess absolutely different from any described in that patent.

XQ. 236. To what part do you refer?

A. That in the passenger office.

XQ. 237. The work which you term "applied"?

A. Yes; and further, I note that this is dated "1917." I made the original samples in 1908.

XQ. 238. For this Cunard Building?

A. No, the original samples I am speaking of.

XQ. 239. Is this firm that you are connected with [407] a corporation?   A. Yes.

XQ. 240. Where is it incorporated?

A. New York.

XQ. 241. You are not an officer?   A. No.

XQ. 242. Has this patent been discussed in any of the meetings of the Employees' Association?

A. I have not attended a meeting in probably five or six years, and I don't know of a single discussion or utterance regarding it.

XQ. 243. Are you being reimbursed for your time here as a witness?

A. I leave that to Mr. Anderson.

XQ. 244. It is immaterial to you whether you receive anything or not?

A. Well, I would surely expect that my time is compensated for.

XQ. 245. When did you enter business in this country?   A. In this country?

XQ. 246. Yes.   A. Early in 1890.

XQ. 247. You have been in business here in New York continually since that time?

(Deposition of Henry A. Cousins.)

A. Yes.　[408]

XQ. 248· And the first job of artificial travertine which you installed was that at Niagara Falls?

A. No, that was comparatively recent.

XQ. 249. That was one of the first, was it?

A. No, there were several others. I will have to have that looked up.

XQ. 250. You know I suppose, a man by the name of Frank Whipple?　　A. Yes.

XQ. 251. Was he ever employed by you?

A. Yes.

XQ. 252. When?

A. Well, I couldn't tell you. I think about 1916 or '17·

XQ. 253. Who was the general contractor on the Cunard Building; Mark Eidlitz?　　A. No.

XQ. 254. Did the Mark Eidlitz Company have anything to do with that Cunard Building?

A. No.

XQ. 255. Did the Mark Eidlitz Company have anything to do with the Knickerbocker Building?

A. Yes.

XQ. 256. Do you know Mr. Daniel T. Webster, who is with that company? [409]　　A. Oh, yes.

Cross-examination closed.

No redirect examination.

Signature waived.

Adjournment until Monday, March 10, 1924, at 10 A. M.　[410]

(Deposition of Tommaso V. Coronato.)
[Title of Court and Cause.]

2:00 P. M., Monday, March 10, 1924.

Met pursuant to adjournment.

Present: WILLIAM A. LOFTUS, Esq., on Behalf of Plaintiff,

T. HART ANDERSON, Esq., on Behalf of Defendants.

It is agreed that this deposition may be taken before George H. Emslie, Esq., notary public, and taken and transcribed by Miss Hoffman, a stenographer in the employ of Munn, Anderson & Munn.

DEPOSITION OF TOMMASO V. CORONATO, FOR DEFENDANTS.

TOMMASO V. CORONATO, a witness produced on behalf of defendants, having been first duly cautioned and sworn, in [411] answer to interrogatories propounded by Mr. Anderson, testified as follows:

Q. 1. Your full name is Tommaso V. Coronato?
A. Yes, sir.

Q. 2. How old are you?   A. 50.

Q. 3. Where do you live?
A. Staten Island—Rosebank, S. I.

Q. 4. And what is your business?
A. Artificial marble work.

Q. 5. How long have you been engaged in that business?
A. It will be 34 years this coming August.

Q. 6. You were at one time in the employ of Henry A. Cousins?

(Deposition of Tommaso V. Coronato.)

A. It was the Mycenian Marble Company.

Q. 7. Was Mr. Cousins connected with that company? A. He was the superintendent.

Q. 8. When did you work for the Mycenian Marble Company?

A. I guess—well, I started the 9th day of August, 1890, and I left there—must be 1908—no, it must be 1907.

Q. 9. Now, Mr. Coronato, it is important to some extent that you fix the date as near as you can, when you left the employ of the Mycenian Marble Company.

A. I cannot; but I have been away 22 months before I come back—yes, that was this month in March, 1908, I come [412] back to business, so I was with him—

Q. 10. Do you mean that in March, 1908, after having been away 22 months, you again entered the employ of the Mycenian Marble Company?

A. That's right.

Q. 11. Now, what do you know, if anything, about samples of imitation travertine stone which *may* have been made by Mr. Cousins or the Mycenian Marble Company?

Mr. LOFTUS.—Objection is made to the question and to any testimony relating to an alleged prior use or prior invention within the knowledge of this witness, for the reason that no notice has been given in the answer or otherwise, as required by the statute.

A. I state that I saw that sample in the Fuller

'(Deposition of Tommaso V. Coronato.)'
Company, and I was told that Mr. Cousins made the
sample.

Mr. LOFTUS.—I move to strike the latter part
of the witness' answer on the ground that it is based
on hearsay.

Q. 12. Now, as I understand you, you saw at the
office of the Fuller Construction Company a sample
of imitation travertin stone which you were told had
been made by Mr. Cousins, is that right?

A. That's true.

Q. 13. Now, what was the occasion of your visit
to the office of the Fuller Construction Company,
and who did you see there, do you remember? [413]

A. I don't know—it was one of the clerks—I don't
know who it was—I don't know the name, either.

Q. 14. Well, what did you go there for?

A. To see the sample—to see the travertin stone.

Q. 15. Who sent you there?

A. I went with the employer—

Q. 16. Whose employer?

A. Nickman & Noscenti.

Q. 17. Were you at that time working for Nickman & Noscenti? A. Yes, sir.

Q. 18. Was this before you went back to work for
Cousins? A. Oh, yes.

Q. 19. How long before?

A. I can't state the time—I am not sure on that.

Q. 20. Well, was it before you went to work with
Nickman & Noscenti?

Mr. LOFTUS.—Objected to as leading.

(Deposition of Tommaso V. Coronato.)

Q. 21. Was it before you went to work for Noscenti?

A. Did I see the sample—

Q. 22. Yes.

A. Well, I was working with Noscenti at that time, then, that I see—while I was working with Noscenti—I didn't see it before.

Q. 23. Well, what was the purpose of your going to the Fuller Company's place with Mr. Noscenti? [414]

A. To show me the sample so I can copy it and give it to McNulty, because they would figure on this job, and they were asking to make a sample for them—

Q. 24. You mean that you were going to make a sample for McNulty Bros.

A. That's what I understood—make a sample for the shop then they can give it to McNulty and show what we can produce—I suppose that was the idea.

Q. 25. Now, what did you see at the Fuller Company's place of business?

A. I saw the real marble sample—real travertin—whatever you want to call it—and the artificial travertin.

Q. 26. How big a piece was the artificial travertin that you saw there?

A. Must have been between a foot by 18 inches—something like that.

Q. 27. Did you make at that time a sample of imitation travertin?

A. Yes, sir; when I went back I started right in.

(Deposition of Tommaso V. Coronato.)

Q. 28. What did you do with that sample?

A. It was left in the shop and one of the two—I don't know whether it was Mr. Nickman or Mr. Noscenti, took that to McNulty Bros.—that's all I know about the sample.

Q. 29. What did you understand your sample was to be used for?

A. For that Pennsylvania Station. [415]

Q. 30. Now, you went back to the Mycenian Marble Company?   A. Yes, sir, I went back there.

Q. 31. In March, 1908?   A. March, 1908.

Q. 32. When you went back there, did you work on any imitation travertin for that company?

A. No, sir.

Q. 33. Did you see anyone else working on imitation travertin there?   A. No, sir.

Q. 34. Did you see any specimens of imitation travertin there?   A. Mr. Noscenti?

Q. 35. Did you see any specimens of imitation travertin in Mr. Cousins' place of business?

A. I didn't take particular notice that time because I went away to Chicago right away.

Q. 36. Oh, you went out to Chicago after you went back to Mr. Cousins?   A. Yes.

Q. 37. For him?   A. Yes; for him.

Q. 38. Now, how long did you stay with Mr. Cousins after that?

A. That I can't tell you—I broke away twice from him. [416]

Q. 39. How long have you been with your present concern?   A. It will be four years in August.

(Deposition of Tommaso V. Coronato.)

Q. 40. And before that, who did you work for?

A. For Mycenian Marble Company—with Cousins.

Q. 41. Now, did you ever make any other imitation travertin except that first specimen that you talked about?   A. Then, or lately?

Q. 42. At any time?

A. Make right now a job—

Q. 43. Tell us how you made that first sample?

A. Well, I lay—I send a boy out to procure me some sand—generally in the shop we have a glass table, or cement table, or slate table—well, I clean one of the corner of the cement table, and I lay the sand on—then I take a stick and make those lines—divide—so it will be a clearer space between the sand and the table—then I mix the color, two shade, and I put that on with a trowel—gauging trowel—after I fill that up, take cheesecloth and dry it up with some material which is called Keene's cement—take the cheesecloth and the brush—it will show the water will come up—and put on back again—dry it again; then I take two pieces iron or wood—one or the other—and I back up that thickness with the same material; next morning I take it off and I brush the same out; and there was the holes in it—

Q. 44. Now, what did you do with these two pieces of iron you talked about?   [417]

A. Well, that's for the thickness, see (indicating), put on the edge of the table, then pass rod over to make that thickness—

(Deposition of Tommaso V. Coronato.)

Q. 45. They were not any part of the imitation travertin, were they?   A. No, sir.

Q. 46. You simply used those as a marginal edge for the material that you were working, is that right?

Mr. LOFTUS.—Objected to as leading.

A. That is, the thickness that you wanted to make it.

Q. 47. Now, that was the first piece of artificial travertin you made?

A. That was the first one, yes, sir.

Q. 48. Now, did you make it after that?

A. I didn't bother any more.

Q. 49. Well, you have made it since, haven't you?

A. Lately, yes.

Q. 50. All right, tell us how you made it lately.

A. I made it out of plaster of paris; and I made it out of cement; and Portland cement—now which one do you want to know?—it's the same process, anyhow.

Q. 51. Well, tell us how you made it.

A. Well, I have two different colors—two shades—I lay them on a table, and I have a comb made out of rubber or leather or—what do you call this board—compo board— [418] cut the teeth out, just like a comb—and I pass it along anyway I want it, and I break those lines with a little bit of a brush—

Q. 52. Now, what did the comb do to the material that you laid on the table?

A. That's to divide the color—so it would be a

(Deposition of Tommaso V. Coronato.)
solid mass—as you see, my finger (indicating),
when it pass the spot, it would be the line—

Q. 53. It would cut it up into lines?

A. Cut it up into lines.

Q. 54. Then what did you do?

A. Then I have a small brush—break away so
I don't have it so solid—then I have the same material—make stiff, hard—whatever you want to call it
—and make it crumbly—and then I lay it on, well,
over this line—then I will take with the same material soft and put it on top, gently, then as I said, I
take the cheesecloth—when it was well filled up—take
cheesecloth and dry it up twice—then I will break
it up the thickness that I want—5⁄8 of an inch—
3⁄4 of an inch—whatever is necessary.

Q. 55. Now, those two processes you have mentioned, how did you come to use those?

Mr. LOFTUS.—Objected to as incompetent, irrelevant and immaterial.

A. Well, experimenting in my own way—I
haven't seen it at all, but I tried to make out my
own way; I haven't [419] seen anyone do it—
I don't know, how could I explain why I make it
that way?

Q. 56. But that is the way you believe it should
be done, is it—these two ways that you made it?

A. Well, I guess each one got his own way to
do it—some other men have a different idea to do
it but this is the easiest for me—I never see any
other easy way to do it—could be that marble could
be done just the same.

(Deposition of Tommaso V. Coronato.)

Q. 57. Now, have you in your business experience made any imitations of stone?

A. Imitation stone or travertin?

Q. 58. Any kind of stone?

A. Yes, I made some Caen stone—but no holes in it.

Q. 59. How did you make that?

A. Well, I use marble dust and plaster with the colors in whatever shade you want—put some relardo so the plaster don't cut—some people use glue —some people use, what they call it, oxblood— and I use common stuff, what they call it—it's a patent process—neetstuff.

Q. 60. Well, have you made any other imitations except Caen stone?   A. I said artificial marble?

Q. 61. You made artificial marble?

A. Yes, in colors.

Q. 62. Well, tell us how you made the artificial marble?

A. That all depends what color you want me to [420] explain—yellow, red—

Q. 63. Well, how did you work the materials?

A. You have a superfine Keene's cement, like white lead, like a painter use—then you use color. I am not an expert on it—that's all I know.

Q. 64. Now, you're building up a piece of artificial marble—tell us how you do it?

A. Put different shade of colors in pot; mix it to any different shades—then you have a silk in the sand—threads or silks—that stuff prepared whatever shade that you want—put the silk in that—then

(Deposition of Tommaso V. Coronato.)

you have holes or—whatever it may be—pull the threads out—put it right across the table whatever shape you want it.

Q. 65. Well, what's on those ribbons—strings—that you talk about?   A. Stain.

Q. 66. What's it made of?

A. Out of water and color.

Q. 67. What do you have on the table when you use this?

A. Nothing on the table—clear, like this glass here, now.

Q. 68. Now, what's the next step in making artificial marble?

A. Put different shades of colors in, on top of those threads; then same process; when it's all filled take these threads off and put some color where those threads come out— [421] maybe stronger or weak—whichever you want—whatever colors going to be represented—then same process—dry them up and back them up with coarse skeins—whatever thickness you like.

Q. 69. Your description might be clear to Mr. Morkel because he is engaged in the business, but this has got to be read by a Judge 3,000 miles away from here, who perhaps has never seen a piece of artificial marble made, and so I wish you would tell that Judge, without leaving out anything, just what you do to make a piece of artificial marble?

A. That's just as clear as I can explain to you—I can't say—It isn't clear? Well, I don't know—

Q. 70. Well, what I got from you was that you had

(Deposition of Tommaso V. Coronato.)

a lot of colored cords; that you started with a lot of colored pieces of string or silk.

A. That's as far as you understood?

Q. 71. Yes? Now, you laid those on the table, did you?　A. Laid them on the table, yes.

Q. 72. And what was that for?

A. To make a vein in the marble.

Q. 73. Now, having laid those on the table, what did you do?　A. Put the color on top of it.

Q. 74. What do you mean by "color"?

A. Different shade or color.

Q. 75. What was it made of?　[422]

A. Out of Keene's cement.

Q. 76. Now, you got the colored cement on top of the cords—now what do you do?

A. When that is all filled in, cover up those strings—we call the face—and take the cords out.

Q. 77. And pull the cords out?

A. Yes; and we fill that in with different color, whatever it is supposed to be—rub and smooth it over a little—then we put the cheesecloth to dry a little—

Q. 78. Well, now, in smoothing it over, what did you use?　A. A trowel.

Q. 79. And when that set, it is a piece of marble, is it—imitation marble?

A. Well, smooth it over—dry it with coarse skein twice—rub a little bit cement on with these coarse skeins, and put the burlap in to enforce it; and you use iron rods or wood, whatever it may be, and back

(Deposition of Tommaso V. Coronato.)

it up to certain thickness you require—⅝ of an inch—¾ of an inch—whatever you require.

Q. 80. And what do you back it up with?

A. With Keene's cement—there's two kinds, white and coarse.

Q. 81. Then you let it set?   A. Let it set.

Q. 82. Now, having set, what does the face look like? [423]

A. Well, it is smooth—it is representing the marble that you want to make—then it's got to go to rubbing it—

Q. 83. Why do you rub it?

A. Why do we rub it? Well, to take the gloss out so the color will come out better—to take the veneer off, practically, so the color will come out—and then we brush it with the material upon it to fill all those pores when they come out—

Q. 84. What pores?

A. Pores in the model itself—

Q. 85. In the imitation stone that you made?

A. Imitation marble, yes.

Q. 86. Is that in the face of it?   A. In the face.

Q. 87. What would cause that?

A. It's in, well, pressed in.

Q. 88. And so, in order to make it look like a piece of marble you have to fill in all those pores and polish it, is that it?

A. Then you have got to rub it three times until you come to a finer surface.

Q. 89. How long have you used that process?

(Deposition of Tommaso V. Coronato.)

A. How long? Since I've been in business.

Direct examination closed.   [424]

Cross-examination.

By Mr. LOFTUS.—Without prejudice to the objection heretofore entered on the ground of lack of notice, I will ask this witness a few questions:

XQ. 1. The samples of travertin which you said you made while in the employ of Nickman & Noscenti, were according to your understanding turned over to McNulty Bros.?

A. As far as I understand.

XQ. 2· With what concern are you now employed?

A. John Wise & Company.

XQ. 3. What is their address?

A. 587 Eleventh Avenue.

XQ. 4. Can you name any places where you have recently installed artificial travertin?   A. Yes.

XQ. 5. Please do so.

A. There is one on 42nd Street—I don't remember the number—19 I think it is, or 26—I am not sure; it is on the uptown side—Wise Shoe Store; then Young's Hat Store at Broadway and 37th Street; there is another one in Brooklyn, but I don't know the address; there are two up on 125th Street and 7th Avenue, same firm, Wise Shoe Store. I am doing a job now in Pawtucket, R. I., Church of our Lady of Consolation. That's all at present.

XQ. 6. Who asked you to appear here as a witness?   A. Mr. Anderson.   [425]

XQ. 7. Anyone else?   A. No, sir.

(Deposition of Tommaso V. Coronato.)

XQ. 8. Now, these jobs that you have just mentioned, which you have done for John Wise, have all been installed recently, is that correct?

A. Yes.

XQ. 9. And while you were with H. A. Cousins you did not do any travertin work, is that correct?

A. No; no travertin work; made some sample, that is all.

XQ. 10. Well, that sample you made while you were with Nickman & Noscenti, is that correct?

A. Well, it was a different company—made one there, yes—went to McNulty, as far as I know.

XQ. 11. Did you make any while you were with Mycenian Marble Company?

A. Yes, I made some—

XQ. 12. Made several—some?

A. That's in the office—still there, I think.

XQ. 13. Still there in Cousin's place?

A. Against the wall.

XQ. 14. When did you make those samples for Cousins?   A. Must have been about 6 years ago.

XQ. 15. Six years ago?   A. Yes.

XQ. 16. How many different kinds of methods have you [426] tried in your experiments with artificial travertin? Have you tried several different ways of making it?

A. Well, I tried three or four ways—practically the same thing—come out the same thing anyhow.

XQ. 17. When was the first occasion when you ever saw any artificial travertin used in a building?

(Deposition of Tommaso V. Coronato.)

A. I haven't seen any till the Pennsylvania Station.

XQ. 18. You never had seen anything prior to that time, installed in a building?   A. No.

XQ. 19. Do you know who did that artificial travertin work in the Pennsylvania Terminal?

A. I was told Denivelle did it.

XQ. 20. Do you know Mr. Denivelle?

A. I think I saw him once or twice.

XQ. 21. Do you know Mr. Frank Whipple?

A. Frank Whipple?

XQ. 22. Yes?   A. No, sir.

XQ. 23. William Cooke, do you know him?

A. William Cooke, is that the Vice-President—? No, I don't know him.

XQ. 24. Have you met Mr. Adolph Giobbe?

A. No, sir.

XQ. 25. You don't know him?   [427]

A. No. . This Frank—what did you say his name was?   I thought because this name seemed familiar —I wanted to know (name repeated).   No, I don't know him.

Mr. LOFTUS.—I have nothing further.

Redirect Examination.

(By Mr. ANDERSON.)

RDQ. 1. Mr. Coronato, you have stated that you made some samples of artificial travertin for Mr. Cousins or his company, and that you believe they are still there—when did you last see them?

(Deposition of Tommaso V. Coronato.)

A. I haven't seen them since I left him four years ago.

RDQ. 2. Were they there when you left four years ago?

A. Yes, sir; well, I tell you, you know between slack times we were trying to fill up the time—trying to make something for the office—I think they are still there.

RDQ. 3. And when did you make those?

A. Must have been six years ago.

RDQ. 4. That would be around 1918?

A. Something like that.

Redirect examination closed.

Recross-examination.

(By Mr. LOFTUS.)

RXQ. 1. One question, Mr. Coronato — prior to the time that you made these samples for Mr. Cousins, which you say was [428] six or eight years ago, had anyone else there in Mr. Cousins' shop, to your knowledge, made any artificial travertin stone? A. Not to my knowledge.

Mr. LOFTUS.—That's all.

Re-redirect Examination.

(By Mr. ANDERSON.)

RRDQ. 1. When you went back to work for Mr. Cousins in March, 1908, did you tell him about making a sample of imitation travertin while you were with Nickman & Noscenti?

Mr. LOFTUS.—Objected to as incompetent, irrelevant and immaterial.

(Deposition of Tommaso V. Coronato.)

A. I think I did—I wouldn't swear to it.

RRDQ. 2. Did you tell him about seeing a sample of imitation travertin which he had made, at the Fuller office?

Mr. LOFTUS.—Same objection.

A. I saw that—I told him that I seen it.

RRDQ. 3. And what did he say about that, anything?

Mr. LOFTUS.—Same objection.

A. He said, "How do you like it?"

RRDQ. 4. Did he tell you anything about his making it?

Mr. LOFTUS.—Same objection.

A. Yes.

RRDQ. 5. Did he tell you why he had made it?

Mr. LOFTUS.—Same objection.

A. For the purpose that a big job was coming along— [429] the Pennsylvania Station.

RRDQ. 6. Did he talk over with you that big job that was coming along?

Mr. LOFTUS.—Same objection.

A. Yes, sir.

RRDQ. 7. What did he tell you about that big job?

Mr. LOFTUS.—Same objection.

A. Well, it was a big job coming along—telling different matters—because I didn't pay much attention—I was not much interested in it—so they say big job coming and what to do—where they would get the men, etc. I didn't generally pay

(Deposition of Frank John Morkel.)
much attention to it—was not interested in that
anyhow.

Deposition closed.

Signature waived.   [430]

[Title of Court and Cause.]

3:30 P. M., Monday, March 10, 1924.

It was agreed that this deposition may be taken
before George H. Emslie, Esq., notary public, and
taken and transcribed by Miss Hoffman, a stenographer in the employ of Munn, Anderson & Munn.

DEPOSITION OF FRANK JOHN MORKEL, FOR DEFENDANTS.

FRANK JOHN MORKEL, a witness produced
on behalf of defendants, having been first duly
cautioned and sworn, in answer to interrogatories
propounded by Mr. Anderson, testified as follows:

Q. 1. Your full name is Frank John Morkel?

A. Yes.   [431]

Q. 2. How old are you, Mr. Morkel?   A. 48.

Q. 3. Where do vou reside?

A. 521 East 67th reet, New York City.

Q. 4. And what is our business?

A. Ornamental plasterer.

Q. 5. How long have you been in that business?

A. To the best of my recollection, since about
June 1891—33 years.

Q. 6. Mr. Morkel, do you know what I mean when
I refer to imitation travertine?   A. Yes, sir.

(Deposition of Frank John Morkel.)

Q. 7. Did you ever make and install any imitation travertine? A. Yes, sir.

Q. 8. When did you first make and install imitation travertine?

A. Purely travertine—imitation travertine—was at the Cambridge Library, Mass., the year of 1914.

Q. 9. Was that cast or applied work? A. Both.

Q. 10. Will you kindly tell us how the cast imitation travertine was made for that Cambridge Library?

A. Most of the pieces which we cast were of an ornamental nature, like, for instance, large cartouches and ornaments of similar nature. The casts of those ornamental [432] features were indentured in the plaster model, the indentures of the travertine showing the holes, and that portion we put right into the model—we cut into the model to be reproduced in the cast, and to help along to get the sharp undercut effect of these various smooth holes, the material that the ornament was cast of was gauged very thick and stiff to produce what we call in the trade, "blow holes," which went to give the sharp effect in the castings.

Q. 11. Now, what were those castings made of?

A. Those were—for the Cambridge job they were plaster work—plaster with a small addition of Keene's cement; added to that there was sand—silica sand; plaster, and the cement with the additional colors added to it, that is, small amount of umber and yellow ochre, to give the desired colored effect. The molds were greased to allow the ma-

(Deposition of Frank John Morkel.)

terial to come away freely from the glue—from the gelatine glue; there were three shades of the material used to make the veining which were laid in strata to imitate the real stone; a facing of about ¼ to ⅜ of an inch was put over the entire mold, and the same was backed up with plaster to make 'the required thickness and strength necessary for handling, which was on the average about ¾ to 1 inch thick. The casts were then allowed to set and become hard in mold, and then were moved, and it was then ready to ship to job.

Q. 11. And those were the casts used on the Cambridge Library, were they? [433]   A. Yes, sir.

Q. 12. When was that job done?   A. In 1914.

Q. 13. What month, do you know?

A. I coudn't tell you that; I would have to refer to the files for that, at the office.

Q. 14. Who was the architect on that job?

A. Trumber of Philadelphia. Mr. Mertz was the supervisor.

Q. 15. And who was the contractor?

A. That I couldn't tell you offhand; I would have to refer to the files.

Q. 16. Now, tell us how the applied imitation travertine work was done on that Cambridge job?

A. The applied imitation travertine on the job was what we call three-coat work. On the wire lath was the ordinary scratch coat, which is the first coat; then the browning, which is the second coat; then the finish coat, about ⅜, was the travertine; the same was applied with a hawk and trowel simi-

(Deposition of Frank John Morkel.)

lar to any plastering job, that is, the mixed travertin with the colors—the additional colors added to
it—was applied on with a hawk and trowel; then
the men took a small tool—what they call the
plasterer's small tool, anl put small indentures to
create a sort of veining for the colored—or striping
which the natural travertin has, and they fill those
[434] with a lighter mixture of travertin—lighter
and a darker mixture, three shades being used; then
they have a small wire brush—while this was slow-
setting stuff they were putting on—set in about 4
hours—then with a small wire brush they effected
these small holes which the travertin has, to give
it the porous nature; after the same had become
stiff somewhat, they would run over that with their
trowel to smooth down the face, which also removed
the small burrs caused by the wire brush. That
practically finished the travertin.

Q. 17. Well, now, have you done any other imitation travertine work, other than the Cambridge
Library?

A. I was going to mention—we done a job the
year previous—1913—of porous stone called St.
Quentin stone, which was almost—that is, the St.
Elmo Club at New Haven—we done a job there
which they called St. Quentin stone, which has almost the same nature as travertin with the exception that it does not run in veins or strata—the
coloring effect—the holes or conglomeration running every which way.

(Deposition of Frank John Morkel.)

Q. 18. How did you make that St. Quentin imitation?

A. The texture and color are similar to travertin; the process we used there was almost the same as on the Cambridge Library, only that there were no shades of color—it was one solid color throughout; the holes were cast there by simply gauging the stone thick—gauging the material very thick and taking some of the same material and forming crumbs, by simply drying the material, putting more to it, drying it—the same [435] as on crumbs—the consistency almost the same as on crumb cake; putting them first down on the face of the mold, and then filling in behind—

Q. 19. With what?

A. With the same material which cast the face of the stone; then it would be of a porous nature. This job was all cast and applied an inch and a half thick in slabs to the wall.

Q. 20. And that was the St. Elmo Club at New Haven?

A. Yes, sir; that to the best of my knowledge was in 1913. I didn't bring my data with me on those various jobs—I didn't know what it was for—

Q. 21. Did you make those cast slabs of imitation St. Quentin stone at the St. Elmo Club?

A. I had a man to go there and cast it on the job. I broke him in to do the work in the shop and send him on the job—it was cast right on the job and applied to the walls.

Q. 22. Did you use a mold?

(Deposition of Frank John Morkel.)

A. Just a flat table—flat board—that we cast on; we smoothed it off perfectly clean with kerosene and oil, and that was used for a mold.

Q. 23. And how did you get these slabs the right size and shape?

A. That was simply framed in with wood strips to give the required thickness; the slabs were various sizes, and they were simply tacked down on the board to keep the material from spreading, which gave the size that was necessary. [436]

Q. 24. What was tacked on the board?

A. The inch and a half strips which are framed in to form a square or oblong, according to what size stone was needed. The board was greased with what we call in the trade, "scagliola," which is a sort of candle grease mixed with kerosene.

Q. 25. What was that done for?

A. That was done so that the material doesn't stick to the mold.

Q. 26. Now, is it your testimony that the surface of these slabs of imitation St. Quentin stone is of the same appearance except for the striated lines, as imitation travertin?

Mr. LOFTUS.—Objected to as calling for an opinion and conclusion of the witness, and not the best evidence.

A. Yes, sir; I believe they have that in the previous testimony.

Q. 27. Now, since this Cambridge Library job, have you made any other imitation travertin?

A. Made it practically from then on; there is

(Deposition of Frank John Morkel.)

hardly a year past that I didn't do half a dozen jobs, practically, since then.

Q. 28. Was the Cambridge Library the first imitation travertin job done by you?   A. Yes, sir.

Q. 29. Do you remember the imitation travertin work done in the Pennsylvania Station?   [437]

A. I hadn't seen it until it was all completed.   I hadn't seen it, in fact, until several years later; I had no cause to be over that way—

Q. 30. You had nothing to do with that job, did you?   A. No, sir.

Q. 31. Did you have anything to do with a job of imitation travertin work in the Biltmore Hotel in New York City?

A. At the time the Biltmore was built?

Q. 32. Yes?   A. No, sir.

Q. 33. Did you have anything to do with a job of imitation travertin work, said to be in the Vanderbilt Hotel, New York City?   A. No, sir.

Q. 34. Are you familiar with the term which is some times used in the plastering art, of "semi-dry" material?   A. Yes, sir.

Q. 35. What does that mean?

A. Semi-dry is partially wet, partially dry. Why, semi-dry, I should say, is something like the crumbs on cake; you see, it is just damp material that you can take in your hands and just run that way (indicating) and it would crumble up.

Q. 36. Have you ever used any such material in the manufacture of imitation stone?

A. Yes, sir.   [438]

(Deposition of Frank John Morkel.)

Q. 37. It is used extensively in Portland cement work, semi-dry?

A. All pressed—what they call "dry pressed." It is all semi-dry, just moist, very little bit—so that you can take it and just squeeze it, so (indicating), and then take and break it—that's the way we would test it.

Q. 38. Is that a common material to use in making imitation stone?

A. Why, semi-dry, it only refers to your mixture. You can make semi-dry of plaster, Keen's cement, Portland cement—it's a term expressing how you gage your stuff. If you gage it thick or fluid—it's simply a term of expressing the way you want your material gaged, that is, the semi-dry process. If I tell a man to make a cast in Portland cement, he will ask me whether I want it wet or semi-dry; if I say dry-pressed to the man, he will know that it is to be semi-dry—that's a term that's used.

Q. 39. What would be the reason for using semi-dry material?

A. To give you the semi-porous effect of limestone, as when I use it in the fluid state—the cement —I get a cut-clean face similar to this glass here (indicating), as smooth as the object which I remove it from, whereas if I press it semi-dry or dry-pressed I get the sandy textures that limestone has—

Q. 40. How long have you known that to be a fact? [439]

A. Practically as long as I have been in the busi-

(Deposition of Frank John Morkel.)

ness. You see, we do all sorts of imitations—artificial marble, limestone, caenstone, etc. We also
make all sorts of imitation stones; I've been with
them—been making it for the last 33 years—artificial marbles of all sorts; caenstone, limestone,
Kingwood stone, travertin and stones of similar
nature.

Q. 41. How is an imitation marble made?

A. An imitation marble is made—it all depends
on what marble you imitate; if you take, for instance, we will state, a sienna marble, that has lots
of veining. The first process would be to get a glass
table—a large slab of glass which is prefectly
cleaned off, and a slight coat of grease put over
same so that the cement will not stick to the face;
the glass table is used as a mold. The next process
is to take silk strings; the strings are on an average
about 30 inches long—they come in the hank, the
same as wool or other material of that nature.
Those strings are tightened to small strips of wood
about 12 inches long. The silk is spread across,
tightened at each end to these strips—these short
strips—so that a man can handle them and stretch
these silks. The strings are then dipped into the
color necessary to get the effect of the marble that's
to be copied. The colors are water colors that are
used with a slight addition of cement to make same
harden; the strings—the silk strings—are then
[440] dipped into these various colored mixtures
and laid across the face of this glass table, which
are to form the veining for the marble; then here

(Deposition of Frank John Morkel.)

and there additional color is added; for instance, spots as large as 10-cent or 50-cent pieces, which the real marble has, are also added to the face of this glass slab; then the body color of the marble which is mixed in a cement to a stronger consistency, is then placed over the entire surface, covering the entire glass slab; then a little dry cement is .put into the sieve which also has the same color as the wet material, added to it, and it is gently dried— the wet cement face is gently dried from sieving this dry cement over it; when it reaches that consistency these silk strings are drawn upward through this self cement so that the colors run right clean through the adjacent cement; then a little more dry stuff is sieved over it, and the same is gently troweled down; over that we have another mixture of the same colored cement which is put on probably about a quarter of an inch thick. The same process then takes place, of drying. The drying then is done with cheesecloth which is spread over, and dry cement is put on probably a half inch thick, which absorbs all the moisture of the lower cement, causing it to become hard and firm; then it is troweled out smooth and hard to get this as compact as possible, to avoid as many blow holes as possible; then the back of that is reinforced with a coarse mixture of cement, which probably makes the cast and all about [441] 5/8 thick, which is the general usage for the artificial marble; the same is left on for about 24 to 48 hours according to the way it sets. It is then removed from the

(Deposition of Frank John Morkel.)

glass slab and turned over, and the face will be found porous due to the fact that we could not press too firmly, as it would mingle our colors of the veining one into the other; we then have a coarse rubbing stone—the marble is rubbed down, which opens up still more of the porous veins; then a thin cement is made of the same color as the marble and these holes are all filled in with a brush; it is taken and brushed in, and a piece of wood is used—a soft piece of wood is used—a sort of a scrubber, like, and it is manipulated back and forth until these holes are all filled in—these small holes; then it is rubbed off with this piece of wood until it becomes clean; the same is allowed to harden again for about 24 hours, and the same process is gone through, that is, rubbed and refilled. It takes two or three of these same operations to make the face compact so that it will take a polish. The polish is then according to what the party wants—where it is a stone polish it is done with a green hard stone of fine texture and water is used, and is polished similar to what real granite is. If that polish is not desired, then a French polish is put on which is of shellac, alcohol and linseed oil, similar to what is put on pianos, which causes the high polish which is seen on artificial marble. [442]

Q. 42. How long has that process which you described, been known to the plastering trade?

A. As long as I have been in the business—33 years. I believe it's an old art—I believe it has been in use previous to that, in Europe.

Direct examination closed.

(Deposition of Frank John Morkel.)

Cross-examination.

(By Mr. LOFTUS.)

XQ. 1. Mr. Morkel, you testified some time ago in a case entitled, "Los Angeles Lime Company and Paul E. Denivelle, Plaintiffs, vs. E. Ceriat," involving a patent issued to said Paul E. Denivellle for the manufacture of artificial travertin, is that cor rect?   A. I did, yes, sir.

XQ. 2. I notice the record in that case, namely, the record on appeal No. 3,532, gives your name as Frank Markel—that should be Frank Morkel?

A. Yes, sir; see, my name is confused so much with Merkel because it's spelled somewhat similar, but it isn't—it's Morkel.

XQ. 3. In that deposition you told about a job of artificial stone you made for the Temple Emanu-El at 76th Street and Fifth Avenue, New York City, about 1892?   A. Yes, sir.

XQ. 4. Should that be Temple Emanu-El or Temple Beth-El? [443]   It is on the southeast corner of Fifth Avenue and 76th Street.

A. Beth-El. That was in 1892—that was a sienna marble.

XQ. 5. Is that sienna marble? Isn't it also known as scagliola?

A. Well, scagliola is simply a different process. You see, the marble which I described is an imitation marble done with string. The scagliola practically to-day isn't made on account of the expense; you see, scagliola was taken by lumps; the cement was made thick—all in pieces—and then pulled and

(Deposition of Frank John Morkel.)

pressed together; and then a pull was taken and you dug out and you filled your veining from the rear. You see, the string marble is a cheaper process and is more satisfactory. You can get a more artistic job with the string marble than you can with scagliola, and the scagliola is still more porous—it's on account of the stone being thick and pressed together; it takes more pressure to fill that and send it through. Scagliola to-day is practically unknown; it isn't made much, in fact in my time it wasn't made much—the scagliola—very little of it.

XQ. 6. Well, now, this marble or stone in Temple Beth-El here in the city, it is a perfectly smooth and polished stone, is it not?

A. Yes, sir; imitation of sienna marble.

XQ. 7. It is as smoth as that glass top on the table? A. Yes, sir. [444]

XQ. 8. And it contains little fine strings of colored material or cement? A. Yes, sir.

XQ. 9. In other words, it lacks what is termed "texture" which is the outstanding characteristic of artificial travertin, is that correct?

A. Yes, sir.

XQ. 10. Now, you have told about the work you did at the St. Elmo Club in New Haven, and referred to it as the artificial St. Quentin stone—where does the natural St. Quentin stone come from?

A. That I can't say; I believe it is imported—sort of a volcanic stone. I have the sample still up at the shop; it is composed of little threads

(Deposition of Frank John Morkel.)

which seem to me to be a volcanic stone, similar in nature to the travertin.

XQ. 11. You would call this travertin a volcanic stone?

A. Yes, sir; to the best of my knowledge I would call that a volcanic stone.

XQ. 12. How long have you known of the use of St. Quentin stone in this country for building purposes?

A. That was my first job and the last—this St. Quentin stone—I haven't used it since.

XQ. 13. Now the pores in that St. Quentin stone are not undercut pores, are they?　A. Yes, sir.

XQ. 14. That was a cast job on the St. Elmo Club, was it? [445]

A. Yes, sir; that was a cast job.

XQ. 15. And the pores were formed by indentures on the mold?

A. No, sir; it was cast on a flat table. I was going to say that it was similar to that semi-dry, by having the stuff thick and dry and then cast the indentures in the face.

XQ. 16. Well, then, the only kind of molds you used on the St. Elmo job were glass?

A. No; we made them on smooth wood tables— they were just small tables—we used wood—we at all times did like that in the Grand Central Station —the class of imitation stone which was all cast on wood molds.

XQ. 17. But St. Quentin stone lacks the striations that are　present in the Roman travertin?

(Deposition of Frank John Morkel.)

A. Yes, sir; otherwise it is similar; it has one color.

XQ. 18. But on the job which you did on the Cambridge Memorial Library—there you did use molds?

A. Molds, both ways; also the plain work was done with a hawk and trowel and some of the mold parts were cast; then all the architecture was cast.

XQ. 19. And what were these molds made of that you used on the Cambridge job?

A. Plaster molds and gelatine molds. [446]

XQ. 20. And did these molds have the pores formed in them—the projections formed in them?

A. On the ornamentation.

XQ. 21. In other words, projections were formed on these molds which cast the pores or voids in the finished material?

A. Yes, sir; but in addition to that we helped along to get the sharp undercut with the semi-dry process.

XQ. 22. In other words, such a mold will not form an undercut void?

A. They will; but just as the previous witness here stated, these little templets or art projections tear away on the gelatine which makes the cast appear dull, so we help along with the semi-dry process, but these indentures help to give the even finish you see on this conglomeration of holes— then we get the strata through that by having it in the marble.

(Deposition of Frank John Morkel.)

XQ. 23. Did you ever have occasion to observe a job of so-called artificial travertin at an undertaking establishment here in the City, at 66th & Broadway, known as the Campbell Mortuary Chapel?   A. No, sir.

XQ. 24. You are not familiar with it?

A. No, sir; never seen it.

XQ. 25. Now, when you did this work on the Memorial Library in Cambridge, Mass., how near was the building to completion when you completed your work?   [447]

A. I never was on the job?

XQ. 26. You never were at the job?

A. You see, I always broke a man in who I sent there—I had a man by the name of Frank Anderson, and I broke him in and he took charge of it; of course the casts were made in the shop and some of the mold parts which we shipped there.

XQ. 27. Do you know the full name of that Library—is it the Harvard Collegiate Library?

A. I believe it is the Harvard Memorial Library.

XQ. 28. Is it named for a Mr. Weidner? Weidner Memorial Library?

A. I believe to the best of my knowledge it is the Weidner Memorial Library, Cambridge.

XQ. 29. Now, if it should appear that that Weidner Memorial Library was first opened and dedicated on the 24th of June, 1915, would that change your testimony in regard to the date when you did this artificial travertin work there?   A. No, sir.

(Deposition of Frank John Morkel.)

XQ. 30. You still would believe that you did it in 1914?

A. I could look up the files at the office.

XQ. 31. You have not as yet loked up those dates?

A. Our bookkeeper did; he gave me the dates because I naturally couldn't remember— [448]

XQ. 32. So that all you know now is what your bookkeeper told you in regard to this date?

A. Yes, sir; see, that would easily be possible because some of these jobs run a year or a year and a half; we were down on the Dering job in Miami for about a year and four months.

XQ. 33. How large a job was this Cambridge Library?

A. It was quite a large job—quite a big job.

XQ. 34. What is your position with the Klee-Thompson Company?   A. Superintendent.

XQ. 35. The Klee-Thompson Company is doing artificial travertin work at the present time, is it?

A. Yes, sir.

XQ. 36. What methods do they use in such work?

A. All methods, according to the prices you receive for the jobs — cheap job you use naturally cheaper methods.

XQ. 37. You do put in cheap jobs too, do you?

A. Yes, sir, naturally if you get a store they are not going to pay the same price that a mansion would on Fifth Avenue.

XQ. 38. Are you familiar with an organization known as the Contracting Plasterers International Association?   A. No, sir.

(Deposition of Frank John Morkel.)

XQ. 39. What is some times called the Master Plasterers? [449]

A. I don't believe our firm belong to it.

XQ. 40. Whom have you talked to in regard to this case? A. Mr. Anderson.

XQ. 41. Was Mr. MacGruer around to se you?

A. Yes, he was around.

XQ. 42. Did you talk to him? A. Yes, sir.

XQ. 43. Did he tell you that if Denivelle won this suit that your firm would likely be held as infringers? A. No, sir.

XQ. 44. He didn't say that?

A. No, sir; he simply asked me when we done our travertin; how long ago—and questions similar to what you have asked me.

Mr. LOFTUS.—I think that's all.

Deposition closed.

Signature waived.

Adjourned to 10:30 A. M., Tuesday, March 11, 1924. [450]

[Title of Court and Cause.]

New York, N. Y., March 11, 1924—10:30 A. M.

Met pursuant to adjournment.

Present: WILLIAM A. LOFTUS, Esq., Representing the Plaintiff.

T. HART ANDERSON, Esq., Representing the Defendants.

It is agreed by counsel that Mr. Moore's deposition may be taken before George H. Emslie, Esq., a notary public, and taken down in shorthand and

(Deposition of Peter G. Moore, Jr.)
transcribed by Miss Helen I. Gorman, a stenographer in the employ of counsel for [451] the defendants in this case.

DEPOSITION OF PETER G. MOORE, JR., FOR DEFENDANTS.

Direct Examination.

(By Mr. ANDERSON.)

Q. 1. Mr. Moore, what is your full name?

A. Peter G. Moore, Jr.

Q. 2. How old are you?   A. 49 years.

Q. 4. Where do you reside?   A. Bogota, N. J.

Q. 5. And what is your occupation or profession?

A. Well, I am an accountant by profession, and at the present time I am Manager of the McNulty Estate.

Q. 6. How long have you been Manager of the McNulty Estate?

A. Since the bankruptcy of the firm of McNulty Bros.

Q. 7. That is McNulty Bros., Inc., of New York?

A. New York, yes.

Q. 8. When did that firm go into bankruptcy? What year?

A. June 27, 1916. At the present time I am still Treasurer of the old McNulty Bros. Company. The Trustee has retained my services as Treasurer.

Q. 9. So that McNulty Bros., Inc., is still in the [452] hands of Receivers, and being settled?

A. Trustee.

(Deposition of Peter G. Moore, Jr.)

Q. 10. Who is the trustee?　What is his name?

A. Francis L. Kohlman.

Q. 11. Does McNulty Bros., Inc., still retain an office?

A. Well, I have all their books in their old office, No. 551 West 52d Street.　The office of the Trustee is at 27 Cedar Street.

Q. 12. So that the books and records of McNulty Bros., Inc., are still in their old office in this city?

A. In this city, yes.

Q. 13. In order to fix certain dates in connection with work which I understand was done by McNulty Bros., Inc., in connection with the Pennsylvania Railroad Station in this city, and the Biltmore Hotel in this city, it would be necessary for you to consult the books in the office, would it?

A. Yes, sir.

By Mr. ANDERSON.—Counsel for defendants now request that an immediate adjournment be taken to the former office of McNulty Bros., Inc., No. 551 West 52d Street, New York City, for the purpose of permitting this witness to examine the books in continuing his deposition.

The deposition of Mr. Moore is continued at the office of McNulty Bros., Inc., 551 West 52d Street, New York City.　[453]

Q. 14. Mr. Moore, you have laid out on the table some books of McNulty Bros., Inc.?

A. Yes.

Q. 15. Just what are those books?

A. They are the ledgers, the journal, the cash

(Deposition of Peter G. Moore, Jr.)

register, and two ledgers, cash and accounts receivable and payable ledgers.

Mr. MOORE.—I want to correct the date that I gave as to when McNulty Bros. went into bankruptcy. It was 1918 and not 1916.

Q. 16. What period of time is covered by these books you have here?

A. The years 1909, 1912 and 1914.

Q. 17. Who was the bookkeeper at that time?

A. I was the bookkeeper at that time.

Q. 18. Did you make the entries in these books now before us? A. Yes, sir.

Q. 19. Are there any entries in these books showing the building of the Widener Building in Philadelphia? A. Yes, sir.

Q. 20. Now, examine the books and tell us just what the books show concerning the building of the Widener Building in Philadelphia?

A. I am now referring to another book; the contract [454] register, which shows that we took the contract on April 21, 1914, from the George A. Fuller Company, amounting to $112,500.

Q. 21. What does the book show concerning the completion of the Widener Building?

A. The building was practically completed in September, 1916, although there was work done, small patching work, until May, 1917 in the following year. The contract was started on June 4th, the first labor was June 4, 1914.

Q. 22. Now, what is the entry in your contract ledger showing when you obtained the contract for the Widener Building? How does the entry read?

(Deposition of Peter G. Moore, Jr.)

A. "1914-4-21," under the heading "Contract, $112500." The witness explains: The number "660" is the number of the slip which was made out when we made the contract, and delivered to the bookkeeping department.

Q. 23. Did you make the entry in that contract ledger, which you have just read?

A. Yes, sir, I did.

Q. 24. How do you know that is the Widener Building work?

A. Because the page is headed "Widener Bldg. Philadelphia."

Q. 25. Now, you have read from a cost journal and ledger certain dates which indicate when the work on the Widener [455] Building was started. Please read those entries on the record.

A. June 4, 1914, labor $30.25.

Q. 26. How do you know that is the Widener Building?

A. It is headed on the page, "Widener Home Building." It was first called in the office "Widener Home," but later we called it the "Widener Building," as you see here from the entry (indicating).

Q. 27. That is the same building?

A. Yes, sir, same building.

Q. 28. Now, what is the entry that indicates when the work was practically completed? Please quote that on the record.

A. September 28, 1916, pay-roll $11,975.01.

Q. 29. Now, in between those dates in the journal

(Deposition of Peter G. Moore, Jr.)

and ledger are there entries running right along relating to the Widener Building job?

A. I have an entry here of $2300.42.

Q. 30. What date?

A. This is a summary of pay-rolls between the 5th of October and the 28th of December, 1916.

Q. 31. But the first entry you read was in 1914, wasn't it?   A. Yes, sir.

Q. 32. Well, between that entry and the one which indicates the completion of the Widener Building are there entries [456] right along on the work, in that book?   A. Yes, sir, every week.

By Mr. ANDERSON.—The books are offered for examination by counsel for plaintiff.

Q. 33. Now, what do your books show concerning the manufacture and installing of à sample of travertine by McNulty Bros. in the Pennsylvania Station?

A. Practically nothing—Oh, in the Pennsylvania Station—I have the cost. of the work.

Q. 34. Read the entry.

A. December 8, 1908, A. Giobbe, $50. December 18, A. Giobbe, $100. December 31st, modeling and casting, $28.37.

Q. 35. And those all refer to December, 1908?

A. Yes. February 5, 1909, John P. Kane, $2.80. C. L. Miller & Company, February 5, 1909, $1.38.

Those are in 1909—February is. June 8, 1909, A. Giobbe, $200. A total cost of $382.55.

Q. 36. Now, what makes you believe those entries relate to the manufacture and installing of a speci-

(Deposition of Peter G. Moore, Jr.)
men of travertine by McNulty Bros., Inc., in the Pennsylvania Station?

A. My journal entry on page 123, which says "Order covering artificial stone." [457]

Q. 37. Anything else?

A. That's all. What I gave you there was the amount agreed by Denivelle as payment of this work. Denivelle Hydraulic Composite Stone Company.

Q. 38. How much is the amount of that entry?

A. $200.

Q. 39. What does that indicate?

A. That indicates that he owed us $200 for the manufacturing of artificial stone.

Q. 40. When was that $200 paid?

A. My ledger shows that it was paid June 3, 1909, which is verified from the cash register, page 72.

Q. 41. Read the entry on page 72 of the cash register?

A. June 3d, Denivelle Hydraulic Composite Stone Company, Pennsylvania Terminal, $200.

Q. 42. So your testimony is that the Denivelle Hydraulic Composite Stone Company paid McNulty Bros., Inc., the sum of $200 on that date? For what?

A. For the manufacture of a sample of stone submitted by us to Warren & Wetmore, architects.

Q. 43. Warren & Wetmore? Where do you get that name, Mr. Miller?

A. My recollection of the order. I may be mistaken in that.

(Deposition of Peter G. Moore, Jr.)

Q. 44. Does the book show that that payment was made [458] for work submitted to Warren & Wetmore? A. No, it does not.

Q. 45. Have you any entry showing when that sample of stone was made by Giobbe? A. No.

Q. 46. Only the dates on which we gave the money. I should judge it was in the neighborhood of May, 1909.

By Mr. ANDERSON.—The books last referred to by the witness are offered for the inspection of counsel for plaintiff.

Q. 47. Did McNulty Bros., Inc., have anything to do with the Biltmore Hotel in New York?

A. We were the contractors; subcontractors on the plastering work.

Q. 48. Who was the general contractor on that job? A. George A. Fuller Company.

Q. 49. Do the books show the amount of the McNulty contract on the Biltmore Hotel? When it was received and when the work was done?

A. I submit you the contract itself.

Q. 50. This document you have handed me is the contract between McNulty Bros., Inc., and George A. Fuller Company, relating to the Biltmore Hotel?

A. Yes, sir.

Q. 51. Mr. Moore, is it necessary that you preserve this document as a part of the record of your company? Can [459] you let me have it?

A. We have no further use for it. If you will give me a receipt for it.

By Mr. ANDERSON.—The contract produced

(Deposition of Peter G. Moore, Jr.)
by the witness is offered in evidence as "Defendants'
Exhibit 42, McNulty Bros. Contract for Biltmore
Hotel."

Q. 52. The signature here, and the endorsement,
McNulty Bros. The signature of McNulty Bros.,
Inc., by P. H. McNulty, President, you recognize
that as the signature of Mr. P. H. McNulty?

A. I do.

Q. 53. Mr. McNulty is now deceased?

A. Now deceased.

Q. 54. What is your testimony concerning when
the Biltmore Hotel was finished by McNulty Bros.?

A. September, 1914.

Q. 55. And in September, 1914, McNulty Bros.,
Inc., had completed their contract at the Biltmore
Hotel?   A. Yes, sir.

Q. 56. Your information for your last answer you
have obtained from one of your records here?

A. From the cash register.

Q. 57. And what is the entry that gives you that
information? Read it on the record.

A. "Labor, September 24th, $126.50." [460]

Q. 58. Is that the last entry in your books concerning the McNulty Bros., Inc., contract with the
Biltmore Hotel?

A. The last labor entry on the book is November
6, 1914.

Q. 59. How do you harmonize your statement last
given with your answer?

A. There is a small amount of patching done
after a building is occupied.

(Deposition of Peter G. Moore, Jr.)

Q. 60. I assume, therefore, that your last answer shows an entry for a small patching job?

A. Yes.

Q. 61. Of your own knowledge, do you know whether or not McNulty Bros., Inc., did in the Biltmore Hotel any so-called imitation travertine work?

A. I do not. We had some artificial stone in the nature of Caen stone and what we call Botticini marble.

Direct examination closed.

Cross-examination.

(By Mr. LOFTUS.)

XQ. 62. Was Mr. Giobbe regularly in the employ of McNulty Bros. in 1909?

A. From time to time.

XQ. 63. What were his duties?

A. He was an ornamental man. He was a Frenchman and we occasionally employed him to make bits of stone—imitation [461] stone.

XQ. 64. Do your books show that he worked for some time for you in 1909?

A. Not as a business man. That is, he worked for us as a mechanic. That I know only from memory. I could prove it by pay-rolls, but I am afraid the pay-rolls are not now in existence. But at the time he did the Pennsylvania Hotel he was trying to start a business of his own—I don't mean "Hotel," I mean Station.

XQ. 65. What, if anything, do you know of your own knowledge, about the making of these samples of artificial travertine?

(Deposition of Peter G. Moore, Jr.)

A. Only from what I have seen the men in the shop turn out.

XQ. 66. In connection with what job have you seen them turn out artificial travertine?

A. The Pennsylvania Terminal.

XQ. 67. What particular man in your shop did that work?   A. Mr. Massimo.

XQ. 68. What part did Mr. Giobbe have to do?

A. Mr. Giobbe submitted a panel for Mr. Massimo, and also samples.

XQ. 69. Do you know anything about any artificial travertine made for McNulty Bros., Inc., by a concern know as Nickman & Noscenti? [462]

A. They never made any for us.   They used to do our artificial marble work.   That is my recollection. I am only speaking from memory.

XQ. 70. Of what materials was this artificial travertine sample made, which you state was for the Pennsylvania Railroad?

A. A composition of cement and colors.

XQ. 71. What kind of cement?

A. Portland cement.

XQ. 72. Following the making of this sample which you state was made in 1909 the next job of artificial travertine with which McNulty Bros., Inc., had anything to do was the Biltmore Hotel, was it?

A. I don't know anything about what was done in the line of manufactured stone in the Biltmore. I do know that we had travertine work on the Widener Building in Philadelphia, but I don't know

(Deposition of Peter G. Moore, Jr.)
the quantity or extent of the work. It was all made
on the building in Philadelphia.

XQ. 73. Do you know what became of those samples which McNulty Bros., Inc., placed in the Pennsylvania Terminal? A. No, I do not.

Cross-examination closed.

No redirect examination.

Deposition closed.

Signature waived. [463]

[Title of Court and Cause.]

New York, N. Y., March 11, 1924.

Met pursuant to adjournment.

Parties present as before.

It is agreed that the deposition of Mr. Clough may
be taken before George H. Emslie, Esq., a notary
public, and taken down stenographically and transcribed by Miss Helen I. Gorman, a stenographer in
the employ of defendants' counsel.

DEPOSITION OF WALTER H. CLOUGH, FOR DEFENDANTS.

WALTER H. CLOUGH, being produced as a
witness on [464] behalf of the defendants, and
having been first duly cautioned and sworn, testified
as follows:

Direct Examination.

(By Mr. ANDERSON.)

Mr. LOFTUS.—Objection is made to the taking
of this deposition, on the ground that no notice of
the same has heretofore been given.

(Deposition of Walter H. Clough.)

Mr. ANDERSON.—I deem it unnecessary to argue a question of this kind at this time. Counsel for plaintiff undoubtedly knows that it is absolutely unnecessary to give the names of every witness who is examined by a party to a cause. Whether or not the deposition is admissible under the notice depends upon whether or not it relates to some piece of work which has either been pleaded in the defendants' answer or set up in the notice.

Q. 1. Your full name, Mr. Clough, is Walter H. Clough?   A. Yes.

Q. 2. How old are you Mr. Clough?

A. 53 years.

Q. 3. And where do you reside?

A. Montclair, N. J.

Q. 4. What is your business or profession, Mr. Clough?   A. General contractor.

Q. 5. Were you formerly connected with the George A. Fuller Company of New York City?

A. Yes, sir.

Q. 6. When, and in what capacity?

A. From about 1900 until the fall of 1916. Superintendent of construction, Manager of the Philadelphia office, Assistant General Manager in charge of New York construction, [465] and First Vice-President.

Q. 7. Do you recall that the George A. Fuller Company constructed the Pennsylvania Station in New York City?   A. Yes, sir.

Q. 8. Did you have anything to do with that construction?   A. Yes, sir.

(Deposition of Walter H. Clough.)

Q. 9. In what capacity?

Q. 10. I was the chief executive in charge, for the George A. Fuller Company.

Q. 11. In that capacity you had supervision of the work of construction in the Pennsylvania Station?

A. Yes, sir.

Q. 12. Is it your knowledge that the Denivelle Hydraulic Composite Stone Company did any work in connection with that Pennsylvania Station

A. Yes, sir.

Q. 13. Do you recall just what work was done by that company?

A. They furnished imitation travertine stone for certain portions of the building.

Q. 14. I show you a file of documents, the first document of which appears to be a letter from the Denivelle Hydraulic Composite Stone Company, dated March 9, 1909, to the George A. Fuller Company, New York City, and the last document [466] in the file appears to be a copy of a contract between the Denivelle Hydraulic Composite Stone Company and the George A. Fuller Company, made on the 5th day of March, 1909. This file comprises altogether, including the manuscript covers, fifty-three sheets of paper all secured together by four large paper fasteners, which at the back pass through brass washers. Will you kindly examine that file of papers and state whether you can identify them, and whether there is anything on those papers which enables you to identify them, and if so, state what the file is.

(Deposition of Walter H. Clough.)

A. Yes, I recognize some of the papers.

Q. 15. Are they all stamped with a stamp which you recognize?

Mr. LOFTUS.—Objected to as leading.

A. As a matter of fact, I don't think they are, but most of them are. There is one (indicating) that certainly isn't. (The letter of March 19th to George A. Fuller Company, from Denivelle.) Copy of letter to the Denivelle Company, from the Fuller Company, March 11, 1909. Copy of memorandum for Nesbit, dated March 5th. Letter March 9th to McKim, Mead & White, from C. W. Wilson & Company. Stamped, but I don't recognize the stamp. March 5th to McKim, Mead & White, signed by Joseph Osgood; stamped, but I don't recognize the stamp. Copy of a letter dated February 2d, to McKim, Mead & White, from Denivelle, which is not stamped. Copy of letter [467] March 5th to McKim, Mead & White, and signed "D. H. King, Jr.," which is not stamped. Another letter to McKim, Mead & White, March 5th, signed by Frank O. Roe, which is not stamped. Bond from the National Surety Company, which is not stamped but which is referred to in the contract.

Q. 16. The contract attached, do you recognize that contract?   A. Yes, sir.

Q. 17. Did you have anything to do with the making of that contract?

A. I executed it for the Fuller Company.

Q. 18. And that is your signature, representing the Fuller Company, on that contract?

(Deposition of Walter H. Clough.)

A. Yes, sir.

Q. 19. Now, on the other papers in that file do you find any specimens of your own handwriting?

A. Yes, sir.

Q. 20. There are some papers which are stamped with a rubber stamp?   A. Yes, sir.

Q. 21. Do you recognize that stamp as a stamp of the George A. Fuller Company?

A. Yes, sir.

Q. 22. You recognize all of them?   A. Yes. [468]

Q. 23. Now, having examined that file would you state that that constituted a part of the archives of the George A. Fuller Company, in connection with the building of the Pennsylvania Railroad Station?

Mr. LOFTUS.—Objected to as leading.

A. Yes, sir.

Q. 24. This first letter from the Denivelle Hydraulic Composite Stone Company, dated March 9, 1909, do you recognize that letter? Do you remember that letter?

A. I have no special recollection of this particular letter. I know that we had letters of this nature, and this apparently is a letter that I had seen, but there is no special mark on it that brings back to my mind that that is a particular letter that I had seen before, but we have letters of that kind which have been the basis of our negotiations.

Q. 25. Would you say that that letter was the basis of the negotiation for that Denivelle contract?

A. Subject to the qualification I have just made,

(Deposition of Walter H. Clough.)

because of these stamps up here (pointing to stamps on the letter).

Q. 26. Now, what was the custom of the Fuller Company in preserving contracts and letters in connection with a contract? Was it customary to fasten them together in the manner in which that file is fastened together?

A. All papers which bore directly on the contract; [469] that is to say, on the conditions of the contract, the material to be furnished, the prices at which they were to be furnished, and the time at which the contract was to be done, were collected together and attached to the contract. Some of them were of a formal nature and some of informal nature. That is to say, that would account for some of those memorandums in those papers.

Mr. ANDERSON.—The file of fifty-three sheets of paper which has been shown the witness and which has been referred to, is offered in evidence as "Defendants' Exhibit 40—Fuller File."

Mr. LOFTUS.—The Exhibit is objected to as incompetent, irrelevant and immaterial, and on the further ground of lack of identification.

Q. 27. Mr. Clough, you do identify that file of papers, do you not?

A. I identify portions of the file of papers. Those without stamps I said I could not identify.

Q. 28. But otherwise you identify those papers?

A. Yes.

Q. 29. As part of the Fuller files?

A. Yes, sir.

(Deposition of Walter H. Clough.)

Q. 30. Do you recall Mr. Clough, that in addition to the bid received from the Denivelle Company, the Fuller Company received bids for imitation travertine work in the Pennsylvania Station, from other concerns? [470] A. Yes, sir.

Q. 31. Do you recall that before passing on those bids, the bidders submitted and installed specimens of imitation travertine, made in accordance with the instructions of the architect? A. Yes, sir.

Q. 32. I show you "Defendants' Exhibit 7—Denivelle Release," and ask you what the giving of such a Release indicates concerning the completion of the contract?

Mr. LOFTUS.—Objected to for lack of foundation.

A. The Release shows, first of all, that it was paid in full, stating the amount of money which Denivelle received from the Fuller Company, and that in view of having received all the money they released and discharged the Fuller Company from all claims, liens and demands of every kind and character, arising, or to arise out of or in connection with the said contract, on March 5, 1909, and the Release further shows that they agreed to repair and make good any fault or damage in the work which will appear within one year. Those are the essential points.

Q. 33. The giving of such Release indicates what, as to the condition of the contract—of the work?

A. First that the work was completed in accord-

(Deposition of Walter H. Clough.)
ance with the contract and to the satisfaction of
the builders and the architects. [471]

Q. 36. Does the giving of a maintenance bond indicate that the work is incomplete?　　A. No, sir.

Q. 37. Is a maintenance bond customarily given
in work of this kind?

A. Not generally. It is not unusual for them to
be asked for.

Q. 38. And what does such a bond usually cover?

A. Why the maintenance of the work installed.
If any defects occur within the limit of the bond
they are to be repaired without cost to the owners
or contractors.

Q. 39. And excepting for the repair of such imperfections as might arise during that period the
job is complete, is it not?　　A. Yes, sir.

Q. 40. Did you have anything to do with deciding
that the Denivelle Company was to get this contract?

A. I undoubtedly was consulted and I undoubtedly had a good deal to do with it. I don't recall
all that transpired. The reason I say that is that
that was my office—my job.

Q. 41. Other conditions being satisfactory, would
it be safe to assume that Denivelle got this job because he was the lowest bidder? [472]

Mr. LOFTUS.—Objected to as leading.

A. Yes. I want to qualify, if I may.

Mr. ANDERSON.—Go ahead.

A. Other conditions are seldom the same among
the various contractors, and there are a great many

(Deposition of Walter H. Clough.)

things that enter into the letting of a contract and affect the judgment of the man in charge of making the award.

Q. 42. Have you any recollection at this time as to whether or not Denivelle was the lowest bidder on this Pennsylvania job?   A. No, sir.

Direct examination closed.

Cross-examination.

(By Mr. LOFTUS.)

XQ. 43. Prior to the introduction of artificial Travertine in the Pennsylvania Station had you ever seen such material in use?

A. I don't recall.

XQ. 44. Do you recall who submitted samples of artifical travertine other than Denivelle, in connection with this Pennsylvania Station?

A. There were several. I remember Miller did, and I think McNulty did.

XQ. 45. Have you any recollection as to the character of those samples?   [473]   A. No, sir.

XQ. 46. Do you recall how they compared with the Denivelle sample?   A. No, sir.

XQ. 47. What was done with the samples submitted by Miller and McNulty?

A. I don't recall.

XQ. 48. What material was used in the construction of those artificial travertine in the Pennsylvania Station?   A. I don't recall.

XQ. 49. Was it white Portland cement?

A. I can't recall it.

(Deposition of Walter H. Clough.)

XQ. 50. Do you know whether or not Denivelle made any repairs or replacements of this artificial travertine in the Pennsylvania Station after the work was installed and completed?

A. No, sir; I don't remember.

Cross-examination closed.

Redirect Examination.

(By Mr. ANDERSON.)

RDQ. 51. Mr. Clough, did the George A. Fuller Company build the Biltmore Hotel in New York City?   A. Yes, sir.

RDQ. 52. When was that hotel finished?

A. It was opened to the public New Year's Eve, 1914. [474]

RDQ. 53. Did the Fuller Company put imitation travertine in the Biltmore Hotel?

A. I think so.

RDQ. 54. Do you recall where that was put?

A. No, sir.

RDQ. 55. Do you recall that McNulty Bros., Inc., had anything to do with the building of the Biltmore Hotel?

A. They had the subcontract for plastering.

RDQ. 56. You say the hotel was opened on New Year's Eve, 1914. When was your work finished there?

A. Well, we had mechanics in the building for several months after that, but the work was substantially completed the night it was opened to the public.

Redirect examination closed.

Deposition closed.

(Deposition of Clay M. McClure.)

[Title of Court and Cause.]

11:00 A. M., Wednesday, March 12, 1924.
Met pursuant to adjournment.

Present: WILLIAM A. LOFTUS, Esq., on Behalf
of Plaintiff.
T. HART ANDERSON, Esq., on Behalf of Defendants.

It is agreed that this deposition may be taken
before George H. Emslie, Esq., notary public, and
taken down in shorthand and transcribed by Miss
Hoffman.

DEPOSITION OF CLAY M. McCLURE, FOR DEFENDANTS.

CLAY M. McCLURE, a witness produced on behalf of the defendants, having been duly cautioned
and sworn, in answer [476] to interrogatories propounded by Mr. Anderson, testified as follows:

Mr. LOFTUS.—Objection is made to the taking
of this deposition on the ground of lack of proper
notice.

Q. 1. Your full name, Mr. McClure, is Clay M.
McClure?   A. Yes, sir.

Q. 2. How old are you, Mr. McClure?   A. 56.

Q. 3. Where do you reside?

A. That's a hard question to answer—my official
home is in Maryland—Camp Parol—I am temporarily located at 208 West 56th Street, New York
City.

(Deposition of Clay M. McClure.)

Q. 4. And what is your business or profession?

A. Architecture.

Q. 5. Were you formerly associated with the firm of McKim, Mead & White, Architects, New York City?   A. Yes, sir.

Q. 6. During what period of time were you with McKim, Mead & White?

A. With them for six years beginning at the beginning of operation of the erection of the Pennsylvania Station and terminating with the completion of the Post Office Building—the exact years I am unable to say—I think it was 1908 or 1907—until 1913.

Q. 7. By the Post Office Building you mean the building directly west of the Pennsylvania Station in New York City? [477]   A. Yes, sir.

Q. 8. In the erection of the Pennsylvania Station just what were your duties?

A. I was Superintendent in charge of the erection of the building in the field—did you say Post Office or Station?

Q. 9. Pennsylvania Station?

A. That's correct.

Q. 10. As such Superintendent, were you on the ground while that building was in course of erection?   A. Constantly.

Q. 11. You were associated with Mr. Daniel T. Webster in that work, were you?   A. Yes, sir.

Q. 12. And he also was a representative of McKim, Mead & White,

(Deposition of Clay M. McClure.)

A. Yes, sir; General Superintendent.

Q. 13. Do you recall the use of imitation Travertin in the construction of the Pennsylvania Station?

A. I do.

Q. 14. Who was that work done by, do you know?

A. The Denivelle Imitation Stone Company or some such name—I can't recall the official name—it was done almost wholly by Mr. Denivelle.

Q. 15. Do you refer to Paul E. Denivelle?

A. Yes. [478]

Q. 16. Did you have anything to do with considering or approving the bids for that work?

A. No, sir.

Q. 17. As a preliminary to adopting imitation travertin in that work, what was done, do you know?

A. Specifications were submitted by the office of McKim, Mead & White—I think written by Mr. John Holske, their present specification writer—for imitation travertin work, on which several were invited to prepare—submit—samples for this work, the result of which 3, as I remember, contractors prepared and put up samples as they understood it from this specification; one of which was Denivelle; the other was Miller; and the other was McNulty—their official names I am not giving.

Q. 18. Did you have anything to do with the installation of those samples?

A. No; I indicated the place where they would be placed.

(Deposition of Clay M. McClure.)

Q. 19. And where were they placed?

A. They were placed on the south wall of the foyer or lobby between the arcade, general waiting-room, lunch room and dining room.

Q. 20. Do you mean the arcade leading in from Seventh Avenue?   A. Yes, sir.

Q. 21. Now, after those samples were installed, what [479] happened?

A. They were inspected by the office and many others including myself.

Q. 22. What office?

A. Of McKim, Mead & White.

Q. 23. You said office, or officers?

A. By office I mean the members of the firm and employees of the office of McKim, Mead & White; I think perhaps everybody examined them in that vicinity—they were somewhat of a curiosity.

Q. 24. Now, it has been contended by Mr. Denivelle that the imitation travertin work which he did in the Pennsylvania Station was nothing but an experiment, what have you to say concerning that contention?

Mr. LOFTUS.—That's objected to as calling for an opinion and conclusion of the witness, and on the further ground that the Court has already decided that such work was an experiment.

Mr. ANDERSON.—You can answer that.

A. I think to refer to it as experimental work is very foolish; very sad. It was the beginning, so far as I know, of the imitation work, and in a

(Deposition of Clay M. McClure.)

sense might be referred to as such. We now make it much better but it would never have been allowed to be put in there if we didn't think it was something more—more definite—more than an experiment. It was intended to be a fair and square proposition, and we [480] were satisfied that it was such or it would have never gone in, I am confident. We believed then, as we still believe, that it was a fair representation of the stuff—the real travertin stone from Italy. I don't think that McKim, Mead & White could be induced to place that, or any other product, in a building of such magnitude and monumental nature, on a purely experimental basis; they might try it on a small insignificant house where the display, etc., is of small moment, but on the other hand, on a building of this character, I think it was out of the question.

Mr. LOFTUS.—I move to strike the answer on the ground that it is based largely on conjecture.

The WITNESS.—If you care to, I could give you a parallel case as an illustration of what is an experiment, and one which would show they were opposed to such a thing on the same building.

Q. 25. I would like to have that?

A. To illustrate the point, the use of Monel metal was offered and even advocated by the railroad authorities themselves, as a covering for the roofs, substituting copper, lead or other material of that nature. McKim, Mead & White opposed the idea purely on the ground that it was of an experimental

(Deposition of Clay M. McClure.)

nature, dealing with a metal that they knew nothing about. However, this was later used, but it was solely with the understanding that the Railroad authorities themselves [481] would bear any blame that might come from it. They did not object, however, to using this on some small building for experimental purposes.

Q. 36. You were telling me this morning that in some other case this Pennsylvania job had been attacked as an experiment, will you kindly tell us about that case?

Mr. LOFTUS.—Objected to on the ground that the question is indefinite, particularly in what is meant by the Pennsylvania job?

Mr. ANDERSON.—You can answer it, Mr. Mc-Clure.

Q. I was called as a witness in a suit brought by Bessie Winn—she is an actress—claiming damages for injuries received in falling down the steps leading from this same foyer or lobby, between the lunch and dining room to the general waiting-room, which are built of real travertin. It was claimed that these steps had been made from unknown material; were temporary or experimental in material, design, ond other things. It was proven to the satisfaction, I think, of all present, that they were not experimental, either in material or design, the material being the same as that used in the building of St. Peter's at Rome, and many other monumental buildings; they having stood the test of many years; that the design was highly monumental and sub-

(Deposition of Clay M. McClure.)
stantial and built in the best way we know how—as
evidence it still stands.

Mr. LOFTUS.—I move to strike the answer on
the ground that it apparently is based on hearsay, and the further ground [482] that if it is
desired to prove the issues in the case referred to,
or conclusions of the Court, this is not the proper
mode of proof.

Q. 27. If there was anything in the nature of an
experiment in connection with the installation of
artificial travertin in the Pennsylvania Station by
the Denivelle Company, what was that experiment?

Mr. LOFTUS.—Objected to as leading, and calling for an opinion and conclusion of the witness;
also for lack of proper foundation.

A. I don't think it was ever looked upon by the
firm, and surely not by myself, other than a reasonably simple matter to make an imitation of travertin
out of the mixture of lime, cement, sand, coloring
matter, etc. I don't think any architect would
consider that a difficult matter at all. We believed
that it could be done—that some might do it better
than others—it is not unusual at all to make samples of nearly all things prior to installing them;
the temporary feature of the same, or the manufacture and installation of the travertin as that,
was out of the question, in my mind.

Mr. LOFTUS.—I move to strike the witness'
answer as not responsible to the question.

Q. 28. Would you regard the production and in-

(Deposition of Clay M. McClure.)
stallation of those samples by Miller, Denivelle and
McNulty as an experiment?   [483]

Mr. LOFTUS.—Objected to as calling for an
opinion and conclusion of the witness.

A. I do not.

Q. 29. So that I conclude that your opinion is
that so far as the installation of imitation travertin
in the Pennsylvania Station is concerned, there was
no experiment whatsoever?

Mr. LOFTUS.—Objected to as leading and suggestive, and calling for an opinion and conclusion
of the witness; and immaterial, irrelevant and incompetent.

A. No experiment to my mind whatsoever.

Direct examination closed.

Cross-examination.

(By Mr. LOFTUS.)

XQ. 1. Under whose directions or instructions
did you work on this Pennsylvania Terminal, Mr.
McClure? In other words, who was your superior,
or to whom did you have to report?

A. McKim, Mead & White.

XQ. 2. Any particular member of that firm?

A. No; Mr. Kendall, Mr. Richardson, as members
of the firm; and Mr. Fenner; also Mr. Mead—I
reported to from time to time.

XQ. 3. Was your work done entirely independent
of Mr. Webster's work?

A. No, sir; he was not a member of the firm, that
I [484] know of.

(Deposition of Clay M. McClure.)

XQ. 4. Well, did you have any particular connection with Mr. Webster on that work?

A. I did.

XQ. 5. Was he your chief, or were you his chief?

A. He was the General Superintendent.

XQ. 6. Was that regarded as a more important position than your work?   A. It certainly was.

XQ. 7. Did you come under the direction or instructions of Mr. Webster on this work?

A. I did. If you had modified that "member of the firm" I would have given you that answer in the first place; he was at no time that I remember, a member of the firm—

XQ. 8. In other words, you worked under Mr. Webster on this Pennsylvania job?

A. Yes; I didn't seek to evade your question.

XQ. 9. You are an architect by profession?

A. I am.

XQ. 10. Are you actively engaged in that profession at this time?   A. I am.

XQ. 11. Prior to the use of this artificial travertin in the Pennsylvania Terminal, had you ever heard of its being used in any building construction? [485]

A. I never had heard of the imitation nor the real prior to its use in that building.

XQ. 12. Of what materials was this artificial travertin made that was used in the Pennsylvania Terminal by Mr. Denivelle?

A. It was made of sand; more than one kind of

(Deposition of Clay M. McClure.)
cement; lime; coloring; and others; the exact proportions and ingredients, I do not know.

XQ. 13. Are you sure there was any lime used in it? A. I am reasonably sure.

XQ. 14. You don't know definitely or positively as to that?

A. I don't recall now, but I think there was. I do not know that there were two or more kinds of cement.

XQ. 15. What were those cements?

A. I don't recall now what they were.

XQ. 16. What do you know about the uses and properties of white Portland cement at that time, namely, the year 1909?

A. Why, it was generally used where you wanted to get a lighter color in the finish.

XQ. 17. Was it a new product at that time or had it been long in use?

A. It had been in use for years before.

XQ. 18. How many years, to your knowledge?

A. I haven't the slightest idea.

XQ. 19. Ten years? Twenty years?

A. I haven't the slightest idea. [486]

XQ. 20. Why did you say it had been known and used? A. I only think so.

XQ. 21. Well, that's what I would like to find out, Mr. McClure—what you know of your own knowledge, and what you are merely guessing at?

A. I am sorry, I can't answer. I don't know how to say any more.

XQ. 22. You mentioned the use of Monel metal

(Deposition of Clay M. McClure.)

in connection with this Pennsylvania Terminal—do
you know of any other devices or materials of a new
and untried nature which were incorporated in
this Pennsylvania Terminal?

A. No; I don't recall any now. The materials
were used, possibly, in little different ways on some
occasions, in some places, but they had been used
before.

XQ. 23. You have stated, Mr. McClure, that you
did not regard the use of this artificial travertin
as an experiment, just tell us what your idea or
definition of an experiment is?

A. My idea of an experiment is something that
you are not quite confident or sure will stand the
test for which you propose using the particular
thing; until it has passed that point I would consider it an experiment—experimental.

XQ. 24. How could you be sure before this artificial travertin had been in use for some time, that
it would stand up under the vibrations present in
this Railroad Station, and withstand the varying
temperatures occurring therein, considering the
fact that it contained these various kinds of [487]
cement; that it was to some extent porous and filled
with voids; and that there were no precedents to go
by, as regards this particular artificial body?

A. By the knowledge gained in the beginning, we
have learned to know that the mixture of flour,
water, etc., in the proper proportions and baked
under the proper conditions will make bread; likewise do we know that the mixture of cement, sand,

(Deposition of Clay M. McClure.)
lime, etc., will make that material suitable for the
coverings of walls, floors, etc. By that knowledge
do I know that these things would function in a
similar way.

XQ. 25. You don't regard the fact that this artificial travertin was partially porous and filled with
voids as being of any importance in this connection?

A. No.

XQ. 26. You would ignore that factor in your
deductions as to the durability of the product, would
you?

A. I would make the material of sufficient richness to take care of it, if I felt that that would
affect it any; I would probably add a little bit more
cement if I felt that way, but the ordinary mixture
of cement, as we use it, is sufficient to take care of
that, in my opinion.

XQ. 27. For your information, Mr. McClure, I
will say that this artificial travertin was made of
white Portland cement—did you know about the
properties and actions of white Portland cement at
this particular time? [488]

A. Yes; as we know that of the other cements.

XQ. 28. You don't consider white Portland cement as being any different from ordinary Portland
cement, do you?   A. We do not.

XQ. 29. Well, I am asking you; you mean by
"we" that you do not?

A. I do not. It's a standard; it's an axiom; it's
just the same as anything else that we know—like
in our tests it has to meet those requirements, the

(Deposition of Clay M. McClure.)
same as the grey Portland cement; in other words, to my mind that's an axiom—in the trade it is so—it has to meet the same physical test as the grey cement.

XQ. 30. Are you aware of the fact that white Portland cement was a comparatively new product at this time?   A. Yes.

XQ. 31. But you would consider that as immaterial in connection with determining the durability of any artificial stone made from this material?

A. Yes, when I had been satisfied that it was cement, and if not equal to, virtually equal to, the grey Portland cement which we used and use now, and possibly used in the days of Rameses, why, I should say, yes.

XQ. 32. How long a test would you want to subject any cementitious material to to satisfy your mind that it was durable and would meet the conditions called for in a railway terminal?   [489]

A. Anywheres from 7 minutes to 30 days.

XQ. 33. And after 7 minutes or 30 days you would feel satisfied in your own mind that the material would stand up under these conditions and give satisfaction for a period of 50 years, would you?

A. Yes, sir.

XQ. 34. And that is the rule you follow in your practice as an architect?

A. I am trying to see how that fits in here—if you ask if I would have any hesitancy in using it, I would say no, but I follow many principles. There are many rules; I will say "No" to the rule—

(Deposition of Clay M. McClure.)

let that be my answer to that. I have no rule for any one thing that will apply to others—as applicable to cement, yes.

XQ. 35. Do you feel qualified, Mr. McClure, to express an opinion concerning the behavior and durability of cementitious materials?

A. Most assuredly, I do.

XQ. 36. I noticed the other day in a publication —I think it was the "Literary Digest," where a concrete building of some three or four stories in height, crumbled into ashes in a period of about 24 hours?   A. Quite possible.

XQ. 37. What is your explanation of that?

A. I would have to examine the material before I could express an opinion; I might hazard a point which would   [490]   probably not be far from the answer or the true conditions.

XQ. 38. Can you give us any reason why this might occur?   A. Oh, yes, sir.

XQ. 39. What would be your explanation of it?

A. It might be the insufficient quantity of cement; poor quality of cement; poor quality of sand; poorly mixed; poorly placed; forms struck too soon; and other things, too numerous to mention, any one of which would be enough.

XQ. 40. Has such a thing ever happened within your experience?

A. Not as you have stated it; nothing quite so bad —as bad as that—in 24 hours, to go to ashes. I have heard of some very disastrous things, though—very sad.

(Deposition of Clay M. McClure.)

XQ. 41. Now, these steps or floors that you testified about in the prior suit, they were not of artificial travertin, were they?

A. I didn't testify about any floor or steps.

XQ. 42. They were not of artificial travertin, were they? A. They were not.

XQ. 43. So that, as I understood your answer, the fact that the natural travertin had been known for many years and had been used in large buildings in Rome, definitely proved that the natural travertin was not an experiment, is that correct?

A. Yes. [491]

XQ. 44. Supposing these steps had been made of artificial travertin, was there any precedent that you could refer to as proving the nonexperimental character of it? A. No.

XQ. 45. Do you recognize any unusual conditions present in the Pennsylvania Terminal which are not present in the ordinary dwelling-house or similar building? A. Yes.

XQ. 46. What are those conditions?

A. Too numerous to mention—thousands of them.

XQ. 47. Would they be likely to affect the durability of an artificial stone product? Would it be a factor in any way?

A. Not any more so than the other things.

XQ. 48. In this Pennsylvania Terminal, the matter of vibration is a factor to contend with, is it not?

A. Taken into consideration with everything that went into it, size and unusual proportions—every-

(Deposition of Clay M. McClure.)

thing to avoid—against difficulty due to vibration, expansion and contraction, as far as possible. In other words, the whole of the thing was built more substantially than is ordinarily the custom, including all things. I would rather not—I would like to have "all things" stricken out.

Mr. ANDERSON.—Strike out "all things."

XQ. 49. Do you know Mr. Paul E. Denivelle?
[492]

A. I do.

XQ. 50. Did you have occasion to observe the work going on in Mr. Denivelle's shop in connection with the manufacture of this artificial travertin?

A. I did; many, many times.

XQ. 51. And where was this work done?

A. Chiefly in the Station building.

XQ. 52. What part of the Station building?

A. At the level of the general waiting-room floor, in what is known as the "baggage-room" section.

XQ. 53. Was that set apart for Mr. Denivelle's use?   A. It was.

XQ. 54. Just what did you see going on in this shop which Mr. Denivelle had in the baggage-room.

A. Saw him making imitation travertin stone.

XQ. 55. How did he proceed to make this imitation travertin stone? What steps were employed?

A. Oh, he mixed the different ingredients heretofore named in the way that he and we all thought would represent imitation travertin stone, and cast them, and later put them up in the building in the

(Deposition of Clay M. McClure.)

place, in the order and manner, not unlike that of setting of interior stone work.

XQ. 56. Well, can you give us any further details as to how he proceeded in placing this material in the mold, and what steps were gone through?

A. Yes, sir; I could tell you—it would take a [493] week to tell you all I know about it. I think that covers the point sufficiently.

XQ. 57. No, I would like to have you tell us just what the particular steps were?

A. I would rather not tell you; it is too tedious; I haven't the patience.

Mr. ANDERSON.—But he is entitled to have that, Mr. McClure; briefly, how Denivelle made those—

A. I have said it's a mixture of those ingredients that go into it.

XQ. 58. Is that the best answer you can give, Mr. McClure?

A. At the present time, yes; to tell you just how this was done would take a long time.

Mr. ANDERSON.—Well, the question is whether you can tell us, and if you can, the Court is entitled to your answer.

A. Well, to my mind the question is answered; to tell just exactly how these different things were blended by using rubber bags and sifting the stuff on in different layers and different thickness, first one kind of cement and then another, preparing a background, then putting the face on it, and all that stuff is mechanical; making the voids, etc.

(Deposition of Clay M. McClure.)

XQ. 59. How did he make those voids, Mr. Mc-Clure?

A. He prepared that using dry stuff in places, which came out later and were not incorporated in the finished product.

XQ. 60. Then do I understand that he had a dry stuff [494] that was subsequently removed from the finished product leaving these holes or voids?

A. I don't wish to convey the idea that I know all the secrets and formulas, or exactly how this was done; there were many different ways attempted in which to get the work—to go ahead—and new ideas came to Mr. Denivelle as to how best this could be done.

XQ. 61. Well, then, is it your testimony that Mr. Denivelle employed many different methods during this time?

A. I might go so far as to say—yes—I would say that same was prepared, cast and finished, and set in the building as independent stones—was applied directly to the surface of the wall as you would apply plaster, and then marked off and finished to represent travertin.

XQ. 62. What were the steps of finishing which gave it the appearance of travertin in working with this applied material?

A. I don't recall just now.

XQ. 63. In your practice as an architect, have you had occasion since the time of the Pennsylvania Terminal, to make use of artificial travertin?

A. Yes, sir.

(Deposition of Clay M. McClure.)

XQ. 64. In what instances?

A. The last of which was in the Park Lane Building.

Mr. ANDERSON.—Park Lane Apartment Hotel in New York City? [495]

A. On the eastern side of Park Avenue between 48th and 49th Streets—Schultz & Weaver, Architects.

XQ. 65. Were you connected with Schultz & Weaver? A. I was. Superintendent.

XQ. 66. How long since you severed your connection with Schultz & Weaver?

A. About four months.

XQ. *69.* Were you a partner or an employee?

A. An employee.

XQ. 70. What, if anything, did you have to do in connection with the Los Angeles Biltmore Hotel of which Schultz & Weaver were architects?

A. Nothing.

XQ. 71. You knew about the job, did you not?

A. Yes.

XQ. 72. And that is the job which is involved in this present suit, you so understand that, do you?

A. No.

XQ. 73. You didn't know that?

A. I don't. I have heard in a way that Mr. Denivelle was doing that. I don't know what the suit's about now excepting trying to establish the priority of the manufacture, making or conceiving or getting the travertin—I didn't know it was associated with

(Deposition of Clay M. McClure.)

a suit on any particular thing—I didn't know about
it at all.   [496]

XQ. 74. Have you ever met Mr. MacGruer of San
Francisco?   A. No, sir; not to my knowledge.

XQ. 75. At whose request do you appear here as
a witness?   A. Mr. Anderson's.

XQ. 76. Is he the only one that you have ever
talked to regarding this matter?   A. No.

XQ. 77. What others?

A. Daniel Webster—Daniel T. Webster.

XQ. 78. When did you talk to Mr. Webster regarding this travertin patent?

A. Three or four days ago.

XQ. 79. Any others, aside from Mr. Anderson
and Mr. Webster?   A. Not that I recall.

XQ. 80. Did the question of this travertin patent
ever come up while you were with Schultz &
Weaver?   A. No, sir; not in my presence.

XQ. 81. Just what were your particular duties on
this Pennsylvania Terminal? You have told us that
you were superintendent, but can you not give us a
better idea what duties you had to perform?

A. I have answered that question; the usual duties
of a superintendent in charge of a building.

XQ. 82. I would like to have you tell us what the
usual duties of a superintendent in charge of such
a building consist of?   [497]

A. He has charge of everything.

XQ. 83. How many such superintendents were
there on this Pennsylvania Terminal?

A. I don't recall.

(Deposition of Clay M. McClure.)

XQ. 84. More than one?   A. Yes.

XQ. 85. Was the work of these superintendents divided into departments?   A. Yes.

XQ. 86. What department did you have?

A. I had them all.

XQ. 87. Well, then, as I understood you, Mr. McClure, you had charge of all these different departments—full charge in connection with the Pennsylvania Terminal?

A. Yes, sir; all of which was under Mr. Webster, as General Superintendent.

XQ. 88. You have given us a temporary address, namely, 208 West 56th Street, New York City, what business do you carry on at that address?

A. I sleep there; no business whatever.

XQ. 89. Where is your place of business?

A. 17 West 46th Street, with John Russell Pope, Architect.

XQ. 90. And how long have you been connected with John Russell Pope?   A. About three months. [498]

XQ. 91. How long were you connected with Schultz & Weaver?   A. About six months.

XQ. 92. Prior to that time, what did you do?

A. With York & Sawyer.

XQ. 93. Architects?   A. Yes.

XQ. 94. How long were you connected with York & Sawyer, Architects?   A. About a year.

XQ. 95. Prior to that time, what did you do?

A. Farm.

XQ. 96. Farmer?   A. Yes.

(Deposition of Clay M. McClure.)

XQ. 97. How long were you engaged in farming?

A. About three years.

XQ. 98. Prior to that time, what were you doing?

A. Practicing architecture.

XQ. 99. With what concern?

A. McClure & Harper.

XQ. 100. How long were you with McClure & Harper?   A. About four years.

XQ. 101. Prior to that time what were you doing?

A. Palmer, Hornboster & Jones.

XQ. 102. That last firm—architects? [499]

A. Yes. I left out—where does that fit in—? Following McClure & Harper I was one year with the Construction Division of the Army at Washington.

XQ. 103. In your direct examination you stated that these samples of artificial travertin placed in the Pennsylvania Terminal were a curiosity, just tell us why they were regarded as a curiosity?

A. As samples of anything almost—of stone, iron, bronze or other things are brought in they are looked upon and viewed in a curious way; in such a manner were these samples of the imitation travertin curious.

XQ. 104. What became of those samples, do you know?

A. They were retained for a period as samples representing the material; the ultimate disposition I don't recall.

XQ. 105. Did they remain on the wall of the building?

(Deposition of Clay M. McClure.)

A. They did not.

XQ.106. How soon were they taken down after they had been erected?   A. I don't recall that.

XQ. 107. What was the shape of these samples?

A. They were a section of the entablature or cornice of the arcade or lobby.

XQ. 108. Do you know why Denivelle was given the contract for the artificial travertin in the Pennsylvania Station?   [500]

A. Two reasons, I guess; one is simply meeting the requirements according to the architect's idea; second, dollars and cents, or cheapness.

Mr. LOFTUS.—I think that's all.

Redirect Examination.

RDQ. 1. When these samples were installed, what officials of McKim, Mead & White inspected them, do you remember?

A. I don't remember, but I haven't a doubt but what Mr. Kendall and Mr. Richardson did.

RDQ. 2. Well, while this building was in course of construction, did the members of the firm of McKim, Mead & White make visits to that building?

A. Yes, sir.

RDQ. 3. And was that true while this Denivelle artificial travertin work was going on?

A. Oh, yes; that was going on quite a period.

RDQ. 4. In your experience as an architect, is this method of securing samples and passing thereon, a common thing?

A. Quite common; quite the practice.

RDQ. 5. And why is that done?

(Deposition of Clay M. McClure.)

A. Well, it sometimes seems foolish, especially when we have a model made for such a thing as a Corinthian cap, where Corinthian caps date back, so far back that we hardly know when, we still seek to make and do have incorporated for every job of any consequence, a new model made of a [501] Corinthian cap, and yet a Corinthian cap is supposed to be a Corinthian cap—they do differ slightly from another.

RDQ. 6. But why is this procedure usually adopted?

A. So that the particular Corinthian cap or sample of other material may fit in the particular place to please this particular condition and architect.

RDQ. 7. Does the question of the strength or durability of the material have anything to do with this custom? A. Yes, sir.

RDQ. 8. Do you know whether or not those samples which had been submitted by Denivelle and McNulty Bros., and Miller were subjected to any test to determine their strength or durability.

A. None other than a suitable examination, that I know of; sufficient, however, to satisfy the architects.

Mr. LOFTUS.—I move to strike the latter part of the witness' answer as dealing with an opinion and based upon conjecture.

RDQ. 9. It is quite usual, isn't it, Mr. McClure, for architects to take into consideration all the condi-

(Deposition of Samuel L. Kriney.)
tions present in deciding to use any particular material in the construction of a building?

A. Yes, sir.

Redirect examination closed.

Deposition closed.

Signature waived.   [502]

[Title of Court and Cause.]

New York, N. Y., March 12, 1924.

Met pursuant to adjournment.

Present: WILLIAM A. LOFTUS, Esq., Representing the Plaintiff.

T. HART ANDERSON, Esq., Representing the Defendants.

It is agreed by counsel that the deposition of Mr. Kriney may be taken before George H. Emslie, Esq., a notary public, and taken down in shorthand and transcribed by Miss Helen I. Gorman, a stenographer in the employ of counsel for defendants in this case.   [503]

DEPOSITION OF SAMUEL L. KRINEY, FOR DEFENDANTS.

Direct Examination.

(By Mr. ANDERSON.)

SAMUEL L. KRINEY, a witness produced on behalf of the defendants, having been first duly cautioned and sworn, testified as follows:

Q. 1. Your full name, Mr. Kriney, is Samuel L. Kriney?   A. Yes, sir.

Q. 2. How old are you, Mr. Kriney?

(Deposition of Samuel L. Kriney.)

A. 50 years old.

Q. 3. Where do you reside?

A. Plainfield, N. J.

Q. 4. I am a member of the firm of Fellows, Kelly & Kriney, plastering contractors.

Q. 5. How long have you been a member of that firm?   A. For about two years.

Q. 6. And before that who were you with.

A. Why, I was with various contractors since the death of Mr. McNulty.

Q. 7. Were you formerly in the employ of McNulty Bros., Inc.?   A. Yes, sir.

Q. 8. How long were you with McNulty Bros. Inc.?

A. Why, I should say about 15 years. [504]

Q. 9. Covering what period?

A. It seems to me that I went to work for them in 1902—until 1917.

Q. 10. While you were with McNulty Bros. do you remember that concern making and installing a sample of artificial travertine in the Pennsylvania Station?   A. Yes, sir, I do.

Q. 11. Did you have anything to do with that sample?

A. I supervised the erection of that sample.

Q. 12. By that you mean you supervised the installation of it in the Pennsylvania Station?

A. Yes, sir.

Q. 13. Was it a slab, or what form was it in?

A. It was a cast form taken out of a mold. Cast in a mold.

(Deposition of Samuel L. Kriney.)

Q. 14. Was it what is know as a "mitered" sample? A. Yes, sir, it was a corner of a cornice.

Q. 15. Now, did you install that in the Pennsylvania Station? A. Yes, sir.

Q. 16. Where, in the Pennsylvania Station?

A. Right to the left of the entrance going into the waiting-room on the upper level. The street level off of Seventh Avenue, at the head of the stairs going into the waiting-room, on the left-hand side. The entrance to the cafe there. [505]

Q. 17. Now, where was that sample made? Do you know?

A. Why, I suppose it was made in our shop. It came from our shop.

Q. 18. Do you know where it was made?

A. That part I couldn't swear to. It was shipped to the building in one of our trucks. Gotten out under the direction of Mr. Cousins, and Mr. Giobbe was the man who claims he made the sample, and he was on the job at the time the sample was installed.

Q. 19. After you installed that sample in the Pennsylvania Station did you see it again?

A. Yes, sir.

Q. 20. Do you know how long it remained there?
A. I couldn't say.

Q. 21. Well, now, did you work on any other job for McNulty Bros, where imitation travertine was used?

A. We did the Widener Building in Philadelphia.

Q. 22. Were you on that job.

(Deposition of Samuel L. Kriney.)

A. I occasionally dropped in on that job.

Q. 23. Did you have anything to do with that job?

A. No, other than that it was under my supervision, but I didn't go down there very often. I was on the job several times.

Q. 24. Was imitation travertine used in the Widener Building? [506]

A. Considerable.

Q. 25. Did McNulty Bros. have any other job there, other than the Widener Building, in which imitation travertine was used, at that time, or since?

A. Why, I don't just remember. I know that we used it in vestibules and places of that kind, but just where, I can't recall.

Q. 26. Do you know where that imitation travertine which was used in the Widener Building was made?   A. No, sir, I couldn't say.

Q. 27. Did you have anything to do with the building of the Vanderbilt Hotel in New York City?

A. No, sir.

Q. 28. What do you know of the use of imitation travertine in the Pennsylvania Station?

A. Why, all I know is that the imitation travertine was used throughout, and I understood at the time we put up our sample, Mr. Miller, Mr. Denivelle and ourselves put up three samples, all put up in this one place, and as I understand it our sample was rejected because the base was plaster. That was as I remember it now. The reason that Denivelle's sample was accepted, was that it had

(Deposition of Samuel L. Kriney.)
a Portland cement base and that is the way I understand it now. I don't remember it. So we lost the job and of course we were awful busy and I wasn't interested, only I know they cast a great deal of it [507] and applied a lot of it by hand.

Q. 29. You didn't have anything to do with the construction of the Pennsylvania Station?

A. No, sir, not a thing.

Q. 30. Now, what is your recollection as to when you installed this sample in the Pennsylvania Station?

A. Well, I just can't remember that date.

Q. 31. Not the year?

A. No, I don't. Hardly—I can't call it off. I would have to look it up and I didn't think to look it up. I don't just remember it. It seems to me it was along about '10 or '11· I am not sure—I can't say—I just can't call the date.

Direct examination closed.

No cross-examination.

Deposition closed.

Signature waived. [508]

[Title of Court and Cause.]

New York, N. Y., March 12, 1924.

Met pursuant to adjournment.

Present: WILLIAM A. LOFTUS, Esq., Representing the Plaintiff.

T. HART ANDERSON, Esq., Representing the Defendants.

It is agreed by counsel that the deposition of Mr.

(Deposition of Randolph H. Almiroty.)

Almiroty may be taken before George H. Emslie, Esq., a notary public, and taken down in shorthand and transcribed by Miss Helen I. Gorman, a stenographer in the employ of counsel for the defendants in this case. [509]

DEPOSITION OF RANDOLPH H. ALMIROTY, FOR DEFENDANTS.

Direct Examination.

(By Mr. ANDERSON.)

RANDOLPH H. ALMIROTY, a witness produced on behalf of the defendants, having been first duly cautioned and sworn, testified as follows:

Q. 1. What is your full name, Mr. Almiroty?

A. Randolph H. Almiroty.

Q. 2. How old are you?   A. 47.

Q. 3. Where do you reside?

A. In New Rochelle, N. Y.

Q. 4. What is your occupation or profession?

A. Architect.

Q. 5. How long have you been an architect?

A. Twenty-five years.

Q. 6. Did you design the Campbell Funeral Church on Broadway near 66th Street?

A. Yes, sir.

Q. 7. Was any imitation travertine surface finish applied to the walls of that church?

Mr. LOFTUS.—Objection is made to any testimony relating to this particular job, on the ground of lack of proper notice.

A. Yes.

(Deposition of Randolph H. Almiroty.)

Q. 8. Who did that imitation travertine work?

A. John A. Finck. [510]

Q. 9. When was that done?

A. Between 1915 and '16·

Q. 10. When did you say that was finished?

A. About August, 1916.

Q. 11. Before that job was done had you known of the use of imitation travertine stone in any big job in this city?   A. O, yes.

Q. 12. What big job do you recall?

A. The Pennsylvania Station.

Q. 13. Do you know who did that job in the Pennsylvania Station?   A. Yes, Denivelle.

Q. 14. Do you refer to Paul E. Denivelle?

A. Yes.

Q. 15. Do you know him?   A. Yes, very well.

Q. 16. How long have you known him?

A. I have known him for twenty years.

Q. 17. Did you know him at the time that job was being done?   A. Yes.

Q. 18. Did he tell you anything about that job at the time he was doing it? [511]

A. He told me considerable.

Q. 19. Just tell us as nearly as you can, what he told you about that job?

A. He told me that he had secured the contract and was very glad of it, because it was a big one, and he hoped to make a reputation on it, etc. He said he had gotten the job because of the sample of travertine that he had submitted to the architects, which they had accepted and approved. Later on

(Deposition of Randolph H. Almiroty.)

he took me through the building and showed me the working process of construction, and erection, etc.

Q. 20. Did he tell you about samples submitted by anybody else in competition for that job?

A. My recollection is that he stated that his sample had been selected from a number submitted by other contractors in the same field.

Q. 21. Do you know who the others were who submitted samples?

A. Well, I only recollect McNulty and Miller, and I think possibly Durkin—that I wouldn't say for certain.

Q. 22. Do you refer to Patrick J. Durkin of this city? A. Yes, New York City.

Q. 23. Do I understand you to say that Mr. Denivelle took you in and showed you how he was making imitation travertine for the Pennsylvania Station? [512]

A. He explained to me how it was done.

Q. 24. At the time he was doing the job?

A. At the time the work was going on; yes.

Q. 25. You had nothing to do with that job, did you? A. No, nothing.

Direct examination closed.

Cross-examination.

(By Mr. LOFTUS.)

XQ. 26. How does this artificial travertine in the Compbell Mortuary Chapel compare with the artificial travertine in the Pennsylvania Terminal, as to color and texture?

(Deposition of Randolph H. Almiroty.)

A. Well, that is a broad question. I should say that it was primarily the same color, and as far as the texture was concerned it approximates it to a varied degree in different pieces. Some pieces maybe more than others, and of course the scale of it is all very much smaller than the scale of it in the Pennsylvania Station.

XQ. 27. Do you know how that travertin in the Campbell Mortuary Chapel was made? What method was used?

A. There were various methods used. Some of it was made right in the place, so to speak, and some of it was made in the shop. Some of it was partly made in the shop, and finished at the building. You mean as to the mechanical method by which it was made?

XQ. 28. Yes. [513]

A. Some of it was cast on marble slabs, and in those stones where we felt we desired a little more marking, a little bit more character, that was done by hand at the building afterwards, and those stones where we felt that the markings were all right we didn't touch. Some places where we had a vaulted ceiling—we had quite a number of vaulted ceilings —where it was impractical to use a casting—most of the markings were made afterwards by hand, at the building, but in the straight slab work on the walls, that was cast in the shop, and as I say, if we wanted to give it a little bit more character that was done afterwards by hand at the building.

(Deposition of Randolph H. Almiroty.)

XQ. 29. What produced the voids in the slabs that were cast on the marble?

A. Well, there were various methods used for that. Sand was used to some extent and Mr. Fincke developed his own process afterwards, in connection with that work, to produce the voids, and I think water was used at one time very satisfactorily. At one time air was used. Various methods were experimented with to produce the best results, but I think on the whole sand was found to be the most feasible.

Q. 30. Does that artificial travertine in the Campbell establishment appear to you to have the same undercut features in the voids as were present in the Pennsylvania Terminal Station? [514]

A. In certain stones, yes; not in all of them.

XQ. 31. Would you say that the artificial travertine in the Campbell establishment contained those veins or striations that were present in the Pennsylvania Station? A. O, yes, I would say so.

XQ. 32. Have you seen that work in the Campbell establishment recently?

A. No, I haven't been there for—O, I guess, since about 1919.

XQ. 33. I ask that question because I had occasion to see that material *with* the last few days and I was unable to find the stratifications there. Is it possible they would fade out?

A. It might have faded out, depending on how much color was used. If it was under a strong light it might fade out.

(Deposition of Randolph H. Almiroty.)

XQ. 34. Was that the only job of artificial travertine that you had to do with, namely, this Campbell job?   A. As far back as that, yes.

XQ. 35. You have done some since that?

A. O, yes, we have done quite a lot of it.

Cross-examination closed.

Deposition closed.

Signature waived.

Adjournment to.March 13, 1924, at 2 P. M.   [515]

[Title of Court and Cause.]

New York, N. Y., March 13, 1924.

Met pursuant to adjournment.

Parties present as before.

It is agreed that Mr. Liva's deposision may be taken down before George H. Emslie, a notary public, and taken down in shorthand and transcribed by Miss Helen I. Gorman, a stenographer in the employ of defendants' counsel.

DEPOSITION OF PHILIP LIVA, FOR DEFENDANTS.

PHILIP LIVA, a witness produced on behalf of defendants, and having been first duly cautioned and sworn, testified [516] as follows:

Mr. LOFTUS.—The taking of this deposition is objected to on the ground of lack of notice.

Direct Examination.

(By Mr. ANDERSON.)

Q. 1. Your full name, Mr. Liva, is Philip Liva?

A. Yes.

(Deposition of Philip Liva.)

Q. 2. How old are you, Mr. Liva?   A. 49.

Q. 3. Where do you live?

A. I live at 228 Prospect Avenue, Brooklyn, N. Y.

Q. 4. What is your business?

A. Plastering, imitation of stone, decorative, all lines of plaster work.

Q. 5. How long have you been in that business?

A. Since I was twelve years of age.

Q. 6. Where did you start?   A. In Italy.

Q. 7. How long have you been doing that work in this country?

A. In this country, twenty years.

Q. 8. With whom?

A. I worked for Davis Brown when I come in this country. Then I started to work for Hammerstein & Denivelle [517] when they were partners together. Then I worked for McNulty Bros., and P. J. Durkin where I am now.

Q. 9. When did you work for Hammerstein & Denivelle?   A. I think since 1907 to 1909.

Q. 10. What work did you do for Hammerstein & Denivelle in 1907 to 1909?

A. Other plaster work on buildings, and mold maker and model maker in the shop.

Q. 11. Did you do any work on the Pennsylvania Railroad Station in this city?

A. Not on the building but in the shop.

Q. 12. What did you do in the shop?

A. I made some molds for the travertino job.

Q. 13. What travertine job?

(Deposition of Philip Liva.)

A. On the Pennsylvania Railroad.

Q. 14. You mean Station?   A. Yes.

Q. 15. Do you know Mr. Denivelle?   A. O, yes.

Q. 16. What is his first name, do you remember?

A. I don't know.

Q. 17. What did he have to do with the work on the Pennsylvania Station?

A. Well, he supervised the shop and building, [518] But I was supposed to have charge of the shop just for that job, and they turned over and they put somebody else in my place, and I worked for three or four weeks more in the shop and quit.

Q. 18. When you say you made molds what do you mean?

A. We had a full-size from the architect—

Q. 19. Full-size what. Full-size drawing?

A. Yes.

Q. 20. Then we copied from the drawing—we run some cornice and make some molds and then they cast the travertine in.

Q. 21. Did you make any casts of travertine for Mr. Denivelle?   A. No.

Q. 22. Did you make any samples of travertine?

A. I made samples for myself in my own idea, in my own time.

Q. 23. What did you do with the samples you made?

Mr. LOFTUS.—The question is objected to, as the purpose of this testimony is to prove prior invention by others. The question is also objected to on the ground of lack of evidence.

(Deposition of Philip Liva.)

Q. 24. What did you do with the samples you made?

A. The samples I made, I don't have results I expect, because in Italy I make some imitation travertino and I made in Stockholm, Switzerland, but we use different materials, [519] and in that time there when I came in this country I started to work for him I never know the materials which they have in this country, and I find in the shop different materials that we have in the old country, so I never was able to get the sample out like I have in the old country.

Q. 25. What was the reason that you tried to make these samples of imitation travertine?

A. Because I see the imitation travertino they do there don't come really close to the natural.

Q. 26. And so you thought you would try your hand at it?

A. I know I did better before and I tried my own idea, but I don't have the same results, because I don't have the same material.

Q. 27. What material did you make this sample of that you made here?

A. Sand, white Portland cement—

Q. 28. Did you see any travertine blocks being cast while you were with Denivelle?

A. Yes, sure.

Q. 29. What were they made of?

A. Sand and Portland cement, on a glass table.

Q. 30. Did you know why they were being made?

A. I don't understand.

(Deposition of Philip Liva.)

Q. 31. Did you know for what purpose they were being made? [520]

A. The beginning, when he had the job in the Pennsylvania Station he tried to have good system to put out the work correct for the purpose for that job there, for the Pennsylvania Station.

Q. 32. How long did you stay with him after he went to work on that job?

A. I don't remember—maybe five or six weeks, four or five—three or four.

Q. 33. How many people were working on those samples of travertine?

A. When I was there, there were only me and the laborer.

Q. 34. What was your position in the shop?

A. I used to take charge of the shop. I never had charge of the shop, because we never start in that moment, but I was there every day, and we worked to make something but really I never established the wages and conditions to take charge of the shop.

Q. 35. These samples that you made, were they made in the Denivelle shop? A. Yes.

Q. 36. Was Mr. Denivelle on work on samples too?

A. Yes, he worked in samples too, in a private room. We don't know what he is doing.

Q. 37. Did you see the samples that Mr. Denivelle [521] made?

A. I think he regulated only the color.

(Deposition of Philip Liva.)

Q. 38. After you left Mr. Denivelle did you ever see him?

A. I worked for him in 1913 again in Holyoke, Mass., on Mrs. Skinner's residence.

Q. 39. Was there any travertine work in that Skinner house?

A. Artificial stone, but different work. No, it was different work.

Q. 40. What kind of artificial stone?

A. Something like Caen stone; yellow stone, only the yellow color.

Q. 41. Did you have anything to do with making that stone in Mrs. Skinner's residence?

A. I was in charge of the job. I see the material. He was in California but his partner run the shop.

Q. 42. What was his partner's name?

A. I don't know; the last partner he had. He kept the business here. When the house was finished they bust up.

Q. 43. Do I understand that the cast stone used on the Skinner house was made in New York? The material?

A. The material? We cast the stone but the material was sent from New York.

Q. 44. How did you do it? [522]

A. Mixed up the material with water, and threw it in on the mold. We had a model; we make the mold and put the material in. A regular plaster— it was the same thing. Every kind of artificial stone is different color, but the effect is the same.

(Deposition of Philip Liva.)

Q. 45. You didn't go to California, did you?

A. No.

Q. 46. Who are you with now?

A. P. J. Durkin.

Q. 47. How long have you been with Mr. Durkin?

A. Six years.

Q. 48. While you have been with Mr. Durkin have you done any imitation travertine work?

A. Sure.

Q. 49. Cast work?   A. Cast work.

Q. 50. Applied work?

A. Applied work, but we use different systems and different material than Denivelle.

Q. 51. You are sure of that?

A. Positive. We use natural stone. We reproduce the travertin from natural stone.

Q. 52. You mean by taking a cast from a piece of natural stone and then make molds from that cast?

A. We take the mold from the natural stone and [523] then from the mold. We cast the imitation stone and we use different material than I use there in the shop when I am there. We use different treatment. He don't give the same treatment we give. We give now on our stone when it is finished and dried.

Q. 53. Did you make any imitation travertine stone in Italy?

A. Sure. I make in Italy and in Stockholm.

Q. 54. What materials did you use?

A. Same materials we use here in P. J. Durkin's shop. Plaster, Keene cement and marble dust.

(Deposition of Philip Liva.)

Q. 55. Is that what you are using in P. J. Durkin's shop? A. Yes.

Q. 56. Why did you leave Mr. Denivelle's employ?

A. I left him because I have a foreman—Italian foreman, and I was assistant,—and I don't know, he had some argument with him and he left the firm and he went with McNulty Bros. and he call me and I went with him.

Q. 57. What is his name? A. Commolli.

Q. 58. Do you know Mr. Massimo? A. Yes.

Q. 59. Was Mr. Massimo with McNulty Bros. when you went there? A. Yes. [524]

Q. 60. Did you go with McNulty Bros. after you left Mr. Denivelle? A. Yes.

Q. 61. Was McNulty Bros. making any artificial travertine? A. Sure, they make it.

Q. 62. For what jobs did they make artificial travertine?

A. In Boston, in New York, in Philadelphia—all over the country, but I never worked in that job except in Boston in imitation travertin for McNulty Bros.

Q. 63. What was the Boston job that McNulty Bros. did? A. Orpheum Theatre.

Q. 64. When was that done?

A. 1914 or 1915, between that time.

Q. 26. Was that artificial travertine? A. Yes.

Q. 66. Sure of that?

A. Sure. We received the material from the shop and we cast over there, and Massimo sent the man from New York to cast travertino there on

(Deposition of Philip Liva.)

the job, on the building, and I was in that building with Commolli, and Commolli was foreman and I was his assistant on that building.

Q. 67. That is the Orpheum Theatre in Boston?

A. Yes.

Direct examination closed.   [525]

Cross-examination.

(By Mr. LOFTUS.)

XQ. 68. Do you remember any job that McNulty Bros. did in Philadelphia, known as the Widener Building?

A. I know that they had a big job there in Philadelphia in travertino.

XQ. 69. Was this Orpheum Theatre in Boston later than the Widener Building in Philadelphia?

A. No, I think it was before.

XQ. 70. Have you looked it up to verify the date?

A. Well, I was four years out from New York, and I come in town for a day or two and then I had to go out again, and I was all the time up north— Buffalo, Syracuse, Utica, Boston, all the places there. I come down for two or three days and then I got to go back again for a new job. Maybe I was here for a week for four weeks; so I don't remember.

XQ. 71. Well now, the first job of artificial travertine that you did for McNulty Bros. was in Boston, was it?

A. When I worked where there was imitation travertino was in Boston?

(Deposition of Philip Liva.)

XQ. 72. Have you done any artificial travertine work since that? A. Sure.

XQ. 73. What jobs have you done since then?

A. I do Ambassador Hotel in New York; then for [526] P. J. Durkin I do 290 Park Avenue between 48th and 49th Streets.

XQ. 74. For Durkin?

A. For Durkin. I do for this job here Park-Lane, 48th and 49th Streets, 299 Park Avenue, and I do a job before I left Denivelle, in Oyster Bay for him; a vestibule in travertino. I went there Saturday, Sunday and Monday; I was all alone.

XQ. 75. Now, this job that you did for Denivelle in Oyster Bay, whose place was it?

A. I don't remember. I was there on Saturday with a foreman and I worked until twelve o'clock. After twelve o'clock we went for a lunch and I took my tools and I had to work overtime, because on Tuesday morning—possibly on Monday—I had to come back to New York—so that I never had time to take care of—before I finish my job.

XQ. 76. What was the foreman's name?

A. Commolli.

Q. 77. What material did you use in this Oyster Bay job?

A. They sent it from the shop, except I mixed up—I gaged up and applied on the wall, and stippled with a brush, and went over with a trowel like we had on the Ambassador Hotel. Some is cast and some is applied. In 290 Park Avenue, same thing;

(Deposition of Philip Liva.)

some is cast and some is applied. Except here in 299 Park Avenue all is cast. [527]

XQ. 78. Well now when you tried these experiments, in the Pennsylvania Station, did you find that this white Portland cement did not give you good results?

A. No. It did not give good results. I never had the results I expected, in that material, so I gave it up.

XQ. 79. It was very difficult material was it?

A. Yes.

XQ. 80. And who changed it afterwards?

A. Denivelle himself. He changed three or four times.

XQ. 81. Changed what?   A. The material.

XQ. 82. What material was finally used in the Pennsylvania Station in making the artificial travertine?

A. Well, he used Carbay sand, red sand, white sand; he used some plaster also.

XQ. 83. What kind of plaster?

A. I don't know, because he had special laborers and give each a quantity of the material they have to use to mix up. So when the men in the shop they receive the material they don't was able to know what kinds of material they mix up. It was impossible.

XQ. 84. So that you don't know that white Portland cement was used in the making of the travertine in the Pennsylvania Station? You don't know that? [528]

A. No, I can't say sure, because he tried, begin-

(Deposition of Philip Liva.)

ning, a few kinds of material, and finally he finds
something, which Vinati, he find some material more
convenient to use, and they mix up and send it
there, to the shop. They mix up on second floor
and they send up on the top floor.

XQ. 85. Well, now, how much of that travertine
had been put in place in the Pennsylvania Station
when you left the job?

A. I think they just started, and I don't think
there was anything in place except that casting.
A few pieces of cornice and arches.

XQ. 86. Then your friend quit Denivelle and went
to work for McNulty Bros. and you went with him?

A. This friend time I worked for Denivelle he was
out in the building, but not on the Pennsylvania
Station. He was in some place else, and in that
time I worked in the shop, and when he quit he
called me and I went with him. In the shop there
was this fellow Vinati here, the same fellow who
is now in California with him.

XQ. 87. Did you make any artificial travertine
in McNulty's shop after you went to work for
McNulty?

A. I never make the composition. They send
the composition from the shop but we cast in
Boston, we erect on the building. We receive the
material all ready prepared, from the shop here.
Just now we have a job in Syracuse, [529] and
I send the job all ready for the men when they got
to go to work.

XQ. 88. How long had you been in the United

(Deposition of Philip Liva.)

States before this travertine work was done in the Pennsylvania Station?

A. Well, I am in this country since 1904, 19th of January, and I work for Davis Brown first, I think about twenty-two months—about two years. Then I work for Denivelle. We work on the Manhattan Theatre and a few jobs, but I don't remember now exactly how long I was before the Pennsylvania Railroad start.

XQ. 89. Well, before you worked on this Pennsylvania Station job, had you ever seen any artificial travertine in the United States?

A. Well, I know, there was a friend of mine—I don't know where he is now, but I know he made in Boston an applied not cast—

XQ. 90. Well, you didn't see that job in Boston, did you?

A. No, but I know he made it, because he write to me if I want to go there in business with him, and I know here in New York there was more people they do that artificial stone, because it is now a new thing. Many people from all countries they come over and they know to make artificial travertino, but really close to the natural. [530]

XQ. 91. Close to the natural?

A. Yes. Because in Italy we have stone in museum—any kind of stone we wish to have, just to go there and pick up the color and study the system to make it. In fact, I had to make marble in Palarmo and I went to the museum for three or four days to try—because I had to make an altar

(Deposition of Philip Liva.)

in the church and I had to get more close to the natural as possible, so I went to the museum—and there in museum in Italy we have every kind of stone; any kind of stone.

XQ. 92. Well, now, do you make artificial travertine in your employment by Durkin, at the present time?   A. Yes.

XQ. 93. What is the last job of artificial travertine you have done?

A. Park-Lane Building, 299 Park Avenue; not finished yet.

XQ. 94. You are doing that at the present time? A. Yes.

XQ. 95. How are you making that travertine in the Park-Lane Building. What method do you use?

A. Well, we pour the glue on the real stone, and we get the form from the real stone, then I add a quantity to mix up the material, and I give the material prepared to the men and they mix up the job like a plaster, any kind of material, and they feed in on the mold.   [531]

XQ. 96. In other words, you use a mold which is made of glue?

A. Yes, what Denivelle never used. In the times when I was there I never see any glue mold, only plaster mold.

XQ. 97. Who was it who asked you to come here as a witness?

A. I don't know. This gentleman (pointing to Mr. Anderson), this morning, in P. J's office. He

(Deposition of Philip Liva.)

asked me about this question here about Denivelle, and P. J. gave me a ticket and say "Go down there, this office, and make a statement."

XQ. 98. Do you mean P. J. Durkin?

A. P. J. Durkin. He told me to come down here, three o'clock.

Cross-examination closed.

Redirect Examination.

(By Mr. ANDERSON.)

RDQ. 99. Do you know the job—did you ever see the travertine job in the Lord & Taylor Building here in New York?

A. No. I don't go in any building because I get enough shopping in our building—I got no time to go somewhere else.

Redirect examination closed.

Deposition closed.

Signature waived.   [532]

[Title of Court and Cause.]

New York, N. Y., March 13, 1924—2:30 P. M.

Met pursuant to adjournment.

Parties present as before.

It is agreed that Mr. Hopkins' deposition may be taken before George H. Emslie, Esq., a notary public, and taken down in shorthand and transcribed by Miss Helen I. Gorman, a stenographer in the employ of defendants' counsel.

DEPOSITION OF WALTER L. HOPKINS, FOR DEFENDANTS.

WALTER L. HOPKINS, a witness called on behalf of the defendants, and having been first duly cautioned and [533] sworn, testified as follows:

Mr. LOFTUS.—Objection is made at this time to the taking of this deposition, on the ground of lack of notice.

Direct Examination.

(By Mr. ANDERSON.)

Q. 1. Your full name is Walter L. Hopkins?

A. Yes, sir.

Q. 2. How old are you, Mr. Hopkins?

A. 44.

Q. 3. Where do you reside?

A. 875 West 181st Street, New York City.

Q. 4. What is your occupation or profession?

A. Architect.

Q. 5. How long have you been in the architectural profession? A. 25 years.

Q. 6. Are you in business for yourself or associated with some other concern?

A. I am associated with Warren & Wetmore.

Q. 7· How long have you been associated with Warren & Wetmore?

A. Since 1901, I think—about 22 years. [534]

Q. 8. Were Warren & Wetmore the architects of the Vanderbilt Hotel in this city?

A. They were, sir.

(Deposition of Walter L. Hopkins.)

Q. 9. Did you have anything to do with the Vanderbilt Hotel job?   A. Yes, sir.

Q. 10. Just what?

A. I had charge of the preparation of all the drawings, and of the construction of the building itself after the drawings had been prepared.

Q. 11. From that I take it that you were on that job while the job was under construction?

A. Yes, sir, from the beginning.

Q. 12. Do you recall any artificial travertine work in the Vanderbilt Hotel?

A. Yes, sir the walls of the bar were of imitation travertine stone.

Q. 13. Do you know who did that imitation travertine stone work in the bar of the Vanderbilt Hotel?

A. Well, the general contractor, the general plastering contractor was a man named Davis Brown, and it is my recollection that he sublet all the imitation stone work to a man named Denivelle.

Q. 14. Do you refer to Paul E. Denievelle? [535]

A. Yes, I think that was his first name.

Q. 15. How large a room is this bar-room?

A. Well, I should say—that's rather hard to answer—I should say it was 30 feet by 50 feet.

Q. 16. 30 feet by 50 feet?

A. Possibly—yes, around that.

Q. 17. And what portion of the walls were covered with travertine?

A. All the walls from the floor to the vaulted ceiling.

(Deposition of Walter L. Hopkins.)

Q. 18. And that is the work that was done by Denivelle or his company?   A. Yes.

Q. 19. Now, when was that Vanderbilt Hotel job done?

A. It was open to the public, as I recall it, on the 31st day of December, 1911.

Q. 20. Were you present at that opening?

A. I was.

Q. 21. Is it your testimony that this bar-room was finished at that time with the imitation travertine on the walls?

A. Yes, sir, the bar was entirely completed.

Q. 22. Was any part of the Hotel Vanderbilt regarded as an experiment, by your firm of architects?

Mr. LOFTUS.—Objected to as incompetent, irrelevant and immaterial, and calling for an opinion [536]   of the witness, and on the further ground of lack of proper foundation.

A. No.

Q. 23. Before this imitation travertine finish was decided upon for the Vanderbilt Hotel had you seen any specimens of imitation travertine done by the Paul E. Denivelle Company?   A. Yes, sir.

Q. 24. Where?

A. In the Pennsylvania Station.

Q. 25. What was the occasion of your seeing that imitation travertine in the Pennsylvania Station?

A. Well, I don't recall. I travel on the Pennsylvania lines a great deal. I don't think I made any special trip there to look at it but it was a

(Deposition of Walter L. Hopkins.)
very important building and most architects went
to see the Station—as part of their business life.

Q. 26. Do you know the occasion or reason for
putting artificial travertine in the bar-room of the
Vanderbilt Hotel?

Mr. LOFTUS.—Objected to as icompetent, irrelevant and immaterial.

A. The reason that that particular material was
used was in order to provide a wall that would be
permanent and require no upkeep and to provide
a proper contrast with the ceiling which is tiled.

Q. 27. That travertine work in the Vanderbilt
Hotel bar was not regarded by you or your firm
as an experiment, was it? [537]

Mr. LOFTUS.—Objected to as incompetent, irrelevant and immaterial, as leading, and, on the further ground of lack of foundation.

A. Certainly not.

Q. 28. Supposing a contractor demands and receives payment in full for a job, and the architects
authorize payment of his bill. What does that indicate, concerning that job?

A. It indicates that the work has been finished
according to the plans and specifications, and to the
satisfaction of the architects.

Direct examination closed.

Cross-examination.

(By Mr. LOFTUS.)

XQ. 29. Mr. Hopkins, just what were your duties
in connection with the erection of the Vanderbilt
Hotel?

(Deposition of Walter L. Hopkins.)

A. I was the designer. I mean to say I made all the sketches and did all the work of the designing, and superintended the preparation of the working drawings. There were various times when different numbers of men were working on the drawings, sometimes five, sometimes ten, I should say, and as the building progressed it was my duty to superintend the construction, particularly that part of the construction which applied to the decoration rather than the structural part of it. The man in charge of the structural portions of the [538] building was a man named Roselle. That is to say, he had charge of the steel work and the walls and the mechanical equipment, but my function was to superintend the erection of the ornamental portions of the building. All the marble work, decorative woodwork, etc.

XQ. 30. Whose idea was it to introduce artificial travertine in this Vanderbilt Hotel?

A. Well, that is rather difficult. Mr. Wetmore talked the building over and all my designs were submitted to Mr. Wetmore, and they were discussed with him, and I cannot say whether it originated with me or with Mr. Wetmore.

XQ. 31. In any event the installation of this artificial travertine in the Vanderbilt Hotel had to be approved by Mr. Wetmore.

A. Yes, all my designs and my suggested use of materials were approved by Mr. Wetmore.

XQ. 32. Well, don't you remember that it was Mr. Wetmore who suggested this use of artificial travertine?

(Deposition of Walter L. Hopkins.)

A. No, I really don't. I made a great many different designs for various rooms and they were the result of several conferences with Mr. Wetmore. I really can't say that he suggested it.

XQ. 33. Why do you say, Mr. Hopkins, that the reason for introducing artificial travertine in the bar-room of the Vanderbilt Hotel was for the purpose of obtaining something [539] of a permanent nature and which required no expense of up-keep? A. Because that's why it was put there.

XQ. 34. Well, didn't I understand you to testify that you do not recall who was responsible for introducing that material in this hotel? A. Yes.

XQ. 35. Then, how are you able to say, or assign any reason for the introduction of that material there?

A. Well, it was our idea when we did the Vanderbilt, to get away from old-established customs, and the Vanderbilt Hotel has a great many innovations in it, and had we been willing to spend the money we would have probably put real travertine stone there. That would have been too expensive.

XQ. 36. Now, in testifying here, Mr. Hopkins, you have used habitually, the plural, as if you were speaking for the firm of Warren & Wetmore, and what we are trying to arrive at is what you know; your own personal knowledge. So, I will ask you again if you do recollect, personally, who was responsible for introducing this artificial travertine?

A. I really can't answer that, because—

(Deposition of Walter L. Hopkins.)

XQ. 37. Well, not knowing, then, who was responsible for using the artificial travertine in the Vanderbilt Hotel, you, personally, would be unable to testify why it was introduced. Isn't that true?
[540]

A. Well, I don't think that follows, necessarily. That is, if I may be permitted to say so, I guess it is rather a curious way to testify, but I think that in general it was my idea to have it, although it has been so long a time that I don't really recall that detail. Mr. Wetmore and I have a habit of working together and we talk things over very freely and at great length. We make different suggestions, and I couldn't testify that the idea was mine, and I couldn't testify that the idea was his.

XQ. 38. Now, leaving out all conjecture and any attempt to speak for the firm of Warren & Wetmore, and confining yourself to what you know of your own knowledge, can you truthfully testify here, under oath, that this artificial travertine was installed in this Vanderbilt Hotel solely for the purpose of permanency and saving upkeep?

A. I think I can testify to that, yes, because the thesis, as you may say, that we started with was to have that all through the hotel. For instance, the doors are all steel; the bases around the walls of all bedrooms are all—a very unusual construction. The building at the time of its erection was a very unusual building. There is absolutely no wood of any description that entered into its construction anywhere. What is known as the Della Robia room

(Deposition of Walter L. Hopkins.)
was done in terra cotta and with panels painted on canvas, so that there was no upkeep. The reason that I feel that I can testify [541] to that, no matter whether it was suggested by me or by Mr. Wetmore is that that was our object throughout the entire building.

XQ. 39. Well, just what do you understand when you use the word "permanency"? Do you mean a fireproof material?

A. No, I can't say that—it doesn't require painting or patching up as plaster does or as woodwork does.

XQ. 40. Well, now, why should plaster require patching up and artificial travertine should not?

A. Well, the stone is harder, and then, if it should crack it doesn't matter, because it's part of the—the real stone cracks, but it doesn't require any painting as plaster does.

XQ. 41. Of what material was this artificial travertine made which was put in the bar-room of the hotel?

A. Well, that I can't answer, because I didn't ask Mr. Denivelle and he didn't volunteer the information, and I felt that it was more or less of a secret process of his and I didn't ask.

XQ. 42. How do you know that it is harder than ordinary plaster? A. Well, you can feel it.

XQ. 43. You don't know by what process the artificial travertine is made which Mr. Denivelle installed—

A. I don't know the ingredients. I don't know

(Deposition of Walter L. Hopkins.)

[542]　the various materials or their proportions, but I saw it put on the walls and I am very familiar with the method of applying.

XQ. 44. What is that method?

A. It is put on to what we call a scratch coat, such as an ordinary plasterer's scratch coat of cement, and then the ingredients—whatever they may be— are mixed and applied with a trowel, just as you would plaster a wall, then there are certain holes put in by a man who is skillful at that kind of thing, with a little instrument, after which the surface of the travertine is smoothed over with a trowel and lines representing the joints between the stones are ruled in with a tool called a jointer.

XQ. 45. Now, in this artificial travertin in the Vanderbilt Hotel bar are there any veins or striations, and if so, how are they applied?

A. I don't believe there are any striations. In fact, I am sure there are not.

XQ. 46. Do you know whether Davis Brown sublet this artificial travertine job to Mr. Denivelle?

A. No, sir, I don't.

XQ. 47. You testified here that nothing which entered into the construction of the Vanderbilt Hotel was in the nature of an experiment. Will you please give us your definition of "experiment."?
[543]

A. Well, an experiment, I should say, in connection with building materials would be the use of a material that was unknown and untried.

XQ. 48. How long would you say it would have to

(Deposition of Walter L. Hopkins.)
be tried to be outside the definition of an experiment?

A. Well, I don't think anyone could answer that question. I mean, you can't tell.

XQ. 49. Maybe one period of time for one kind of material and a different period of time for another material? In other words, it varies?

A. Well, yes, I suppose you could say that. We have frequently used new materials, or at least we try to do it—and we generally know what we are doing when we use them.

XQ. 50. In other words, you do as other architects of prominence do. You try to promote progress, and at the same time you do not undertake any dangerous experiments.

A. Yes—we watch our step.

XQ. 51. Is that correct?

A. Yes. I think that's a fair way of putting it.

XQ. 52. I think you have said that there were many innovations introduced in the Vanderbilt Hotel? A. Yes, sir.

Cross-examination closed.

Redirect Examination.

(By Mr. ANDERSON.)

RDQ. 53. Do you mean to testify that an architect [544] would adopt a new material without having satisfied himself that it was proper material to use for the job upon which he was going to use it?

A. Well, I don't know about other architects, but we wouldn't. We have in our office more or less of

(Deposition of Walter L. Hopkins.)

a department which you might say is a research department and it is the duty of this department to keep in touch with new methods and new materials that develop, and we carefully keep records and statistics about all kinds of building materials of every description. That is in charge of Mr. Munzell.

RDQ. 54. So that when you have investigated a material you are reasonably sure—

A. We try to be. Occasionally we make a mistake.

RDQ. 55. Now, before putting this imitation travertine in the bar of the Vanderbilt Hotel had you seen any imitation travertine work?

Mr. LOFTUS.—That is objected to, as the witness has already answered.

A. Yes, sir.

RDQ. 56. What work had you seen before that?

A. The most prominent work to my recollection was the Pennsylvania Railroad Station. I was thinking of the Biltmore, of which we were the architects, but the imitation stone in that was Caen stone. [545]

RDQ. 57. How was that Caen stone applied in the Biltmore Hotel? Do you know?

A. Yes. The only difference between travertine and Caen stone was the difference in the ingredients and the roughening of the surface of the travertine.

RDQ. 58. Otherwise, they were the same structurally?

Mr. LOFTUS.—Objected to as leading.

(Deposition of Walter L. Hopkins.)

A. Otherwise they were the same structurally. They were applied to the wall in the same manner, with a trowel.

RDQ. 59. But to get the travertine finish they punch it full of holes and then plaster it?

Mr. LOFTUS.—Objected to as leading.

A. Yes, sir.

Redirect examination closed.

Recross-examination.

(By Mr. LOFTUS.)

RXQ. 60. You have testified, Mr. Hopkins, that the Vanderbilt Hotel was opened to the public December 31, 1911. I want to ask you how you fixed that date?

A. Why, one of the men in the office looked it up.

RXQ. 61. Did you look it up?   A. No, sir.

Mr. LOFTUS.—I move that the witness' answers as to the date of the opening of the Vanderbilt Hotel be stricken, on the ground of hearsay.   [546]

Recross-examination closed.

Re-redirect Examination.

(By Mr. ANDERSON.)

RRDQ. 62. What is your recollection as to that date?

A. Well, I am frank to say that I wouldn't have been able to answer the exact date and the year if it hadn't been looked up. If I hadn't been told.

RRDQ. 63. Were you present at the opening?

A. Yes, sir, but it was some time ago, and I have been present at other openings, and I wouldn't have

(Deposition of Walter L. Hopkins.)

been able to answer with any certainty unless it had been looked up.

RRDQ. 64. And it was looked up for you?

A. Yes, sir.

Re-redirect examination closed.

Deposition closed.

Signature waived. [547]

[Title of Court and Cause.]

New York, N. Y., March 15, 1924—5 P. M.

Met pursuant to adjournment.

Parties present as before.

It is agreed that Mr. Durkin's deposition may be taken before George H. Emslie, Esq., a notary public, and taken down in shorthand and transcribed by Miss Helen I. Gorman, a stenographer in the employ of defendants' counsel.

DEPOSITION OF PATRICK J. DURKIN, FOR DEFENDANTS.

PATRICK J. DURKIN, a witness produced on behalf of defendants, and having been first duly cautioned and sworn, testified as follows: [548]

Direct Examination.

(By Mr. ANDERSON.)

Q. 1. Your full name is Patrick J. Durkin?

A. Yes, sir.

Q. 2. How old are you, Mr. Durkin?

A. 57 years.

Q. 3. Where do you reside?

A. 102 West 183d St., New York City.

(Deposition of Patrick J. Durkin.)

Q. 4. What is your business?   A. Plasterer.

Q. 5. How long have you been in the plastering business?   A. 35 years.

Q. 6. Are you in business on your own account.

A. Yes, sir.

Q. 7. How long have you been in business on your own account?   A. About 20 years.

Q. 8. Do you know Paul E. Denivelle?

A. Yes, sir.

Q. 9. Did Paul E. Denivelle ever do any so-called artificial travertine work for you?   A. Yes, sir.

Q. 10. What was that job that he did for you?

A. The Evans Museum. The Evans Dental Parlor, [549] some call it, but the Evans Museum, it was known as.

Q. 11. Where is the Evans Museum located?

A. It is in Philadelphia. I don't know just the street now.

Q. 12. Was that work given to Mr. Denivelle or to some company with which he was associated?

A. Yes, sir.

Q. 13. What was the name of the company?

A. The Denivelle Hydraulic Stone Company, I think it is. I don't know whether it is incorporated or not.

Q. 14. Was that imitation travertine work which Mr. Denivelle or his company did for you in connection with the museum in Philadelphia what is known as cast work or applied work?

A. Most of it was applied work. There was some of it cast work.

(Deposition of Patrick J. Durkin.)

Q. 15. When was that done?

A. I couldn't say without I refer to—I couldn't tell you the date exactly.

Q. 16. You have records in your office showing that? A. Yes, I have.

Q. 17. What is this record that I show you, entitled "Ledger"? Is that one of your office records?

A. Yes, sir.

Q. 18. From an examination of that record can you [550] tell when Mr. Denivelle did the work for you. Now, you may refer, if you want to, to this page taken from some book, but first tell what that page is. Is it from one of your books in your office?

A. Yes. Taken from one of my books.

Q. 19. And what is that book used for, that that page was taken from? A. Records of bills.

Q. 20. And this was taken from a bill-book?

A. This is a bill that we paid to Denivelle.

Mr. ANDERSON.—The bill identified by the witness reads as follows:

(By the WITNESS.—I think you had better correct that name. I thought it was the Evans Museum. I see from this bill it is the Thomas W. Evans Museum.)

Q. 21. I assume, Mr. Durkin, that you want to preserve this bill which was taken from one of your records, but I would like to borrow it, if you have no further use for it. I will return it to you after the trial of this case.

A. Well, you may have it.

(Deposition of Patrick J. Durkin.)

Mr. ANDERSON.—The bill identified by the witness is offered in evidence as "page from Durkin's bill-book, Nos. 151 and 152. Exhibit 42."

Q. 22. Now, Mr. Durkin, I call your attention to a bill pasted on that page, purporting to be from the Denivelle Hydraulic Composite Stone Company, with the item "July 9th, to contract, $7000," dated December 16, 1914. There further [551] appears on that bill "Thomas W. Evans Museum, Philadelphia, Pennsylvania." Was that a bill rendered to you by the Denivelle Company? A. Yes, sir.

Q. 23. What does that cover?

A. It covers travertine work on the Evans Museum.

Q. 24. When was that work done? Possibly you may want to refer to your ledger.

Mr. LOFTUS.—Can't you tell us when the work was done without referring to the ledger?

Mr. DURKIN.—I couldn't, no, sir.

(Witness refers to ledger.)

A. Evidently this was done in 1914.

Q. 25. You are referring now to the items appearing at the top of page 414 of your ledger, which I presume— A. You can have it—

Q. 26. Do you mean I can borrow this whole book?

A. You can borrow the whole book or cut—

Q. 27. You mean to say that you will give me permission to cut from this ledger of yours page 414?

A. Well, I suppose that I shouldn't, but I don't see that it's any harm. I had a lot of books de-

(Deposition of Patrick J. Durkin.)
stroyed in the fire and I presume that the contract
of this particular job has been destroyed. [552]

Mr. ANDERSON.—Well, I will take advantage
of your offer, and I now cut from your ledger, page
414.

Mr. DURKIN.—Which I hope you will return.

Mr. ANDERSON.—I will return it to you at the
end of the trial.

Mr. ANDERSON.—I now offer the page in evidence, as page 414, cut from Durkin's ledger-book,
Exhibit 43.

Q. 28. Now, Mr. Durkin, the entries on Defendants' Exhibit 43, what do they show?

A. It shows the dates of payments made to the
Denivelle Company.

Q. 29. On what job?

A. On the Evans Museum; Thomas W. Evans
Museum.

Q. 30. Can you state when that job was done by
the Denivelle Company for you on the Evans Museum?

(Witness refers to Exhibits 42 and 43.)

A. That was work done in the early spring of
1914.

Q. 31. And when was it completed?

A. I would say around—I am not positive of this
—about September or October.

Q. 32. What year? A. The same year.

Q. 33. 1914? A. 1914.

Q. 34. And the amount of that work was $7000?
[553]

(Deposition of Patrick J. Durkin.)

A. $7000; yes, sir.

Q. 35. Did you pay the Denivelle Company for that job?   A. Yes, sir.

Q. 36. Who was the architect of that job?

A. I would have to refer to—I think it was a Philadelphia architect, but I don't recollect.

·Q. 37. Did you have the contract for the whole building?   A. Yes, sir.

Q. 38. That is the plastering work?

A. Yes, sir.

Q. 39. Who was the building contractor, or construction company?

A. Pomeroy Construction Company.

Q. 40. How did it happen that you went to the Denivelle Company to do that work for you?

A. Well, the architect wanted him to do it, and the builder didn't want to let us the job without we agreed to let Denivelle do the work.

Q. 41. Do you know why the architect and builder wanted Denivelle to do the work?

Mr. LOFTUS.—Objected to as incompetent, irrelevant and immaterial, and as calling for an opinion and the conclusion of the witness.

Q. 42. Do you know why they insisted that Denivelle do the work?

A. Well, I presume because he was competent and [554] and had done other work similar to it, and supposed to be what they wanted.

Q. 43. How did you get that impression?

A. Because we couldn't get the job to do ourselves, and we would like to have done it but they

(Deposition of Patrick J. Durkin.)
thought Denivelle was better prepared—was able
to do the work—on account of having a record of
doing other work of that character.

Q. 44. You are positive that it was an imitation
of travertine stone that Denivelle did on that job for
you?   A. Yes, sir.

Direct examination closed.

Cross-examination.
(By Mr. LOFTUS.)

XQ. 45. Do you happen to know, Mr. Durkin,
when that Thomas W. Evans Museum was completed and opened to the public?

A. I really don't know that. I should know.
Perhaps I would know if I could go into the records a little more closely. I could find out, but I
do not know the exact dates.

XQ. 46. There has been offered in evidence as Defendants' Exhibit 42, a page from Durkins' order-
book, which consists of a sheet of paper on which
is pasted an invoice from Froment & Company; an
invoice from the New Jersey Wire Cloth Company,
and three bills or invoices bearing the names of
Denivelle H. C. S. Company. What do you know
about these [555] records of your own knowledge, Mr. Durkin?

A. Of my own knowledge I know I recognize the
handwriting of the bookkeeper I had.

XQ. 47. Otherwise you know nothing about them.
Is that correct?

XQ. 48. Well, I know that I paid the money out
toDenivelle on those. I cannot recollect the amount

(Deposition of Patrick J. Durkin.)

—I know the New Jersey Wire Cloth Company who I had been doing business with on several jobs—I don't think that would apply to that—we didn't use their material there.

XQ. 49. Did you use any material from Froment & Company? A. I don't suppose we have.

XQ. 50. Now, I call your attention to the statement bearing the address of Denivelle H. C. S. Company, dated December 16, 1914, and reading "July 9, to contract $7000." What year does that refer to? A. That would refer to 1914 I believe.

XQ. 51. In the same column, above the word "July" appears the numeral "1913." That appears to be a mistake, doesn't it, and should read "1914," according to your other records?

A. I suppose that would be 1914.

XQ. 52. That appears to be a mistake?

A. Yes, it does. [556]

XQ. 53. Now, having in mind, Mr. Durkin, the date of your last payment to Denivelle for this work in connection with the Thomas W. Evans Museum, what would you say was the time of completion of Denivelle's contract?

A. If my recollection is correct, it would be in the fall of 1914.

XQ. 54. I notice on this ledger page which is offered in evidence as "Defendant's Exhibit 43,— Page from Durkin's ledger," some entries as late as February 17, 1915, and April 9, 1915, would that refresh your memory in any way with reference to the date of completion of Denivelle's work?

(Deposition of Patrick J. Durkin.)

A. Well, you can understand that there may be some question about the completion of the work and the date of payments. While he may have been paid very promptly I cannot remember, but I remember that it was quite some time after before we got a settlement on the job after the date of completion of our work when we got payment, and like a good many other people I didn't have too much money, and he didn't get paid any too quickly after. I don't know—I shouldn't say—how soon after the job was completed. This wouldn't give me any idea of how early or how long before that date the job was completed, but it seemed to me it was in the fall—early in the Fall of 1914.

XQ. 55. Well, now, what do these items appearing on this page from your ledger, Defendant's Exhibit 43 represent? [557]

A. The dates—the items and payments.

XQ. 56. Any thing else?

A. Why I don't see that there is anything else only payments.

XQ. 57. Who keeps those records?

A. The bookkeeper.

XQ. 58. Have you ever seen this page before?

A. Yes, I have.

XQ. 59. When?

A. It may have been five or six years ago—seven years ago.

XQ. 60. What was the occasion?

A. Passing through the books. I didn't have any particular object in view at all.

(Deposition of Patrick J. Durkin.)

XQ. 61. Where does your bookkeeper get the data for making these entries?   A. From contracts.

XQ. 62. Is it your opinion that the entries on both sides of the page represent payments to Denivelle?

A. This is the contract. It doesn't seem to be kept by a very clever bookkeeper, and I am not a bookkeeper myself, but this seems to be the amount of the contract here; $7000, at the top of page 414, at the right-hand side.

XQ. 63. What are the figures underneath that $7000 entry. What do they represent? [558]

A. That seems to be an extra order. They seem to be extra orders.

XQ. 64. You are referring now to the entries appearing under the entry of $7000, to wit: $60.82 dated August 4th, 1914; $191.75 dated December 16, 1914; and $5.00 dated December 16, 1914. Those you think represent additional work over and above the contract?   A. That is what I would say.

XQ. 65. Would that convey anything to your mind with relation to the time when Denivelle completed his work? Wouldn't it be as late as December 16, 1914?

A. Well, it may have been done previous to that, but evidently that is the date that he got the order.

XQ. 66. That is the date that Mr. Denivelle received the order from you to do this extra work?

A. Perhaps not to do it, but he had done the work —evidently that is what it is—that he had gotten this verbal order, perhaps, to do the work, but it

(Deposition of Patrick J. Durkin.)

would seem to me that that job was completed—it is an easy matter for us to find that out, if you choose. I know that we can find that out very easily, the date when that museum was opened.

XQ. 67. I know when it was opened, Mr. Durkin. What I am trying to find out is what you know as to the date when Denivelle did the work. As a matter of fact, the museum was opened in February, 1915. [559]

A. Well, I know that we were working there during the Summer and the early Fall. We had completed our work I thought, before any cold weather set in.

XQ. 68. But it is probable that Denivelle had to do some additional work there in December of 1914; and that is borne out by your records?

A. I do not think it was as late as that.

XQ. 69. I understand that you know what those records are?

A. Well, it is very hard—I am not very well up on mathematics myself and it is pretty hard to tell those records. I didn't look them over, only casually to-day.

XQ. 70· Well now, since this transaction here in connection with the Evans Museum, what jobs of artificial travertine have you had to do with?

A. Since this job—why about the first job was the Commodore Hotel.

XQ. 71. In New York? A. Yes, sir.

XQ. 72. And you did that work on your own account and with your own organization?

(Deposition of Patrick J. Durkin.)

A. Yes, sir.

XQ. 73. What particular employee of yours executed that work in the Commodore Hotel? [560]

A. Why, there were different men working at it. Many of the plasterers worked at it.

XQ. 74. Have you done any since the Commodore Hotel?

A. Yes, I have done some since then. Done some work at 299 Park Avenue; Ambassador Hotel, and other work—I don't remember just where.

XQ. 75. Well now, you have seen this artificial travertine in the Pennsylvania Station in this city?

A. Yes, sir.

XQ. 76. Had you ever seen any artificial travetine prior to that time?

A. I don't remember that I did.

Cross-examination closed.

Redirect Examination.
(By Mr. ANDERSON.)

RDQ. 77. Do you recall that Mr. Anderson cut out of your order book, this morning, the page Exhibit 42, numbered 151 on one side and 152 on the other?

A. I may be a little deaf—but you (pointing to Mr. Anderson), are the gentleman that did it.

RDQ. 78. You saw me cut it out?   A. Yes, sir.

RDQ. 79. At the time I cut that page out, were the various pages which are now attached to it, attached thereto?   A. Yes, sir.

Redirect examination closed. [561]

(Deposition of Patrick J. Durkin.)

Recross-examination.

(By Mr. LOFTUS.)

RXQ. 80. Did Mr. MacGruer of San Francisco call to see you a couple of months ago, Mr. Durkin?

A. Yes, sir.

RXQ. 81. In connection with that matter?

A. Why, in connection with a case he has got on with Denivelle in California, I understand.

RXQ. 82. Did he point out to you at that time that the Denivelle patent, if the Courts should sustain it, would hinder you in your work?

A. Well, he mentioned something about it.

RXQ. 83. Was that matter taken up in your association known as the Employing Plasterers' Association?

A. I believe it was, but I wasn't there at that meeting.

Recross-examination closed.

Deposition closed.

Signature waived.

Adjournment is taken to the office of Davis Brown, 306 East 40th Street, New York City, at 10:30 A. M., March 14, 1924. [562]

10:30 A. M., Friday, March 14, 1924.

Met pursuant to adjournment.

Present: WILLIAM A. LOFTUS, Esq., on Behalf of Plaintiff,

T. HART ANDERSON, Esq., on Behalf of Defendants.

It is agreed that this deposition may be taken before George H. Emslie, Esq., notary public, and

DEPOSITION OF DAVIS BROWN, FOR DE-FENDANTS.

DAVIS BROWN, a witness produced on behalf of the defendants, examined at his place of business by agreement of [563] counsel, in answer to interrogatories propounded by Mr. Anderson, testified as follows:

Q. 1. Your full name, Mr. Brown, is Davis Brown?   A. Yes, sir.

Q. 2. How old are you Mr. Brown?   A. 50.

Q. 3. Where do you reside?

A. 1148 Fifth Avenue.

Q. 4. What is your business?

A. Plastering contractor.

Q. 5. How long have you been in that business?

A. Actively engaged as employer?

Q. 6. No, in the business generally?

A. 32 years.

Q. 7. You are now with Davis Brown, Inc.?

A. Yes, sir.

Q. 8. How long has that company been in existence?

A. The business is in existence about 27 or 27 years; it was not a corporation then.

Q. 9. How long has it been a corporation?

A. 1912 as a corporation.

Q. 10. And you have been associated with it during the whole period?

A. Entire period of time.

Q. 11. You know Paul E. Denivelle?

A. Yes, sir; I do. [564]

(Deposition of Davis Brown.)

Q. 12. How long have you known him?

A. I know Mr. Denivelle, I should say for 30 years; 29 to 30 years.

Q. 13. And where did you first meet Mr. Denivelle?

A. When I was an apprentice boy at the trade at the shop of J. & J. Morrison in 42d Street, between 2d and 3d Avenues; Mr. Denivelle was working there as an employee at that time.

Q. 14. You know, do you, that Mr. Denivelle or the Denivelle Hydraulic Composite Stone Company did some imitation travertine stone work in the Pennsylvania Station?

A. Yes, I do know that; I do know that Paul Denivelle done it. I don't know that it was a Hydraulic Company or whatever you say there; I only knew him at that time as Paul Denivelle.

Q. 15. Did you bid on that work in the Pennsylvania Station?   A. On the plastering contract?

Q. 16. Yes.   A. I have no recollection of that.

Q. 17. Do you know whether others in addition to Mr. Denivelle or his company bid on that travertin work in the Pennsylvania Station?

A. Yes, I do know that; I do know of that.

Q. 18. Do you know who did bid on that work? [565]

A. Yes; McNulty Bros. was one concern, and H. W. Miller was the other concren.

Q. 19. Now, did you see any samples or specimens of imitation travertin which were installed in the Pennsylvania Station?   A. Samples only?

(Deposition of Davis Brown.)

Q. 20. Yes?

A. I don't positively recollect, but I have visited the building at a certain stage of the work—while it was in progress—I have seen some samples laying around.

Q. 21. What was the occasion of your visiting the Pennsylvania Station during the progress of the work?

A. It was because in those days we had what we called an Arbitration Board—any complaint had to be brought before the Arbitration Board composed of, I believe, 5 employers and 5 journeymen for adjustment. The labor unions representing the journeymen made a complaint that the plastering contractor, Mr. Miller, was violating some of the rules of the agreement, and for that purpose, to examine this violation, a committee was appointed, and I was one of that committee to examine the work in conjunction with the journeymen who were also appointed on the same committee, to see what the violation was.

Q. 22. Now, on the occasion of the visit of that committee to the Pennsylvania Station, was Mr. Denivelle at work on his imitation travertin contract? [566]   A. Well, I don't remember that.

Q. 23. But your testimony is that on the occasion of that visit you saw some samples of imitation travertin in that Station.

A. Yes, I did; because we met Mr. McNulty's man on the building—his name is Calhoun—and he was at that time his foreman on the job, I believe,

(Deposition of Davis Brown.)

and he talked on the job in a general way—showed us around the building—he showed us some samples —something I can't testify to positively because I 'don't remember—that time there was a lot of talk on the subject—I believe he has showed me some samples but I am not so sure on that.

Q. 24. Do you recall whether those samples were in place or installed in the building, or were they—?

A. No, they just were loose pieces—he just showed us loose samples, only he was a little disappointed because he didn't get the job because he thought his sample was just as good as the other one.

Q. 25. Now, did Paul Denivelle or his company do any imitation travertin work on any of your jobs?

A. Why, I had a case where I gave him a small job—the Vanderbilt Hotel—I had a contract for that building and after it was about 70 to 80% finished they decided to have a bar-room on the south—on the northwest corner of the street—this would be the southwest corner of the building— lower [567] room—and they asked me for an estimate to finish up these walls in travertin material, which I did; and they awarded me the work, Possibly about $1,000 worth on the job—and I was prepared to go on with it, but the president of the Ojev Company, Mr. Gray,—that was the contracting company—informed me that Mr. Wetmore would like to have Mr. Denivelle do that travertin work for me.

(Deposition of Davis Brown.)

Q. 26. Mr. Wetmore was one of the firm of Warren & Wetmore? A. Yes.

Q. 27. Architects of the Vanderbilt Hotel?

A. Yes; that was an expression of the president of the building company, that Mr. Wetmore would like to have Mr. Denivelle do that work for me, to be sure.

Q. 28. Now, you had the entire plastering contract for the Vanderbilt Hotel?

A. Entire building, yes.

Q. 29. And was that the only work which Mr. Denivelle did for you in that Vanderbilt Hotel?

A. That's all.

Q. 30. And that is the bar-room?

A. He applied only the finish coat because I put on the preparation—the browning coat—on all the walls, and filled it out—so that this material was applied only ¼ or ⅞ of an inch.

Q. 31. And that was imitation travertin, was it?

A. Imitation travertin. [568]

Q. 32. Did you pay Mr. Denivelle for that work?

A. Oh, yes.

Q. 33. Now, when did he do that Vanderbilt bar-room for you?

A. Well, the information I got—inasmuch as I have no records—was opened December 31, 1911—so that bar-room was positively done a month or so ahead of that, because it was one of the last things we did there.

Q. 34. Who represented the architects on that Vanderbilt job?

(Deposition of Davis Brown.)

A. Mr. Hopkins was one—I don't know his first name—and another one, the superintendent for the architects—was Mr. Russell. Yes, Russell was for the construction end and Mr. Hopkins was for the design end. These two men were there almost every day for hours.

Q. 35. Now, you spoke about some date which you obtained from records, are there any records in your office here concerning the Vanderbilt job?

A. None whatsoever.

Q. 36. What is your personal recollection now as to the time when Mr. Denivelle did that work for you in the Vanderbilt bar?

A. I can only go by—I am told—I think that's correct—that December 31, 1911, they opened the hotel. Therefore this room was done practically almost towards the very end—that was November, possibly October—October [569] because after that they had to put in the fixtures and all that thing, and still be ready for December 31st; so possibly it was October or November of 1910.

Q. 37. 1910?

A. 1911—because, as I am informed, that the hotel was opened December 31, 1911, so that means we did it 1911—around October.

Mr. LOFTUS.—Where did you get that information—December 1911, Mr. Brown?

A. Where I got that information? We done a job—Lord & Taylor—in 1912, finished in 1913—I know that we have done the Vanderbilt possibly two years prior to that—a year or two years ahead

(Deposition of Davis Brown.)

—I know it was done prior to that—the only way to find out is to see the manager, Mr. Brown—his name was Brown too—that's an easy matter to find out about any building—as to completion and the like—can be easily found out, and I have no records on this case, but that is what I am told that this is when it was completed.

Mr. LOFTUS.—And you had no recollection until you got this data from Mr. Brown on the Vanderbilt Hotel?

A. I didn't say I went to Mr. Brown. I say that anyone can find out by going to the place or to the architect's office, or I can call up some of my colleagues who were working there, and possibly they may have the records.

Q. 38. How do you account for the fact that you have no [570] records in your office on the Vanderbilt job?

A. There is no way to account for it excepting moving about—we done this office over, and we had files collected for 25 or 30 years, and it was high time to get rid of them, and throw them away.

Q. 39. You got rid of them?

A. Yes, the job was finished and paid, and we are no more interested in it.

Q. 40. Now, you spoke of the Lord & Taylor job, was that imitation travertin? A. Yes.

Q. 41. How big a job was that?

A. That was a huge contract.

Q. 42. I mean the imitation travertin work.

A. Yes.

(Deposition of Davis Brown.)

Q. 43. How extensive was that job in the Lord
& Taylor building?

A. Well, the entire main floor is travertin—very
large proposition—almost as big as the Pennsylvania.

Q. 44. Did Mr. Denivelle do that work for you?

A. No, we did it ourselves, and the architects
were satisfied.

Q. 45. Now, when did you do the Lord & Taylor
building?

A. Some time ago I got in touch with the architects and they have their records, and I was told
that the job was finished early in 1913, so it was
done in the winter of 1912–13. [571] I remember
it was the winter-time because I had about 70 sala-
manders heating the place—it's a very large floor.

Q. 46. Now, did you regard the imitation travertin work in the Vanderbilt Hotel which Mr. Denivelle did for you, as an experiment?

Mr. LOFTUS.—Objected to as irrelevant, incompetent, and no proper foundation has been laid.

A. Why, not at all, because he has done a job
which the architect liked, and he thought he can
do it maybe better, and he wanted Mr. Denivelle
to do the work—there's no experimenting about
that—experimenting is done when a man is preparing samples; that is the time when he is experimenting.

Q. 47. You would say, then, that if there was
any experiment in connection with any building

(Deposition of Davis Brown.)
job, that experiment ends when the man submits a satisfactory sample, with his bid, perhaps?

Mr. LOFTUS.—Objected to as leading.

A. When a man bids—or after he bids—he makes his sample first at the shop, and he does his experimenting there—for the color—for the materials— for the general principle—then he is carrying on his work with experiments. But when a contract is awarded to a man because an architect wants him —because the architect has seen his work, then that's beyond the experimental stage.

Direct examination closed. [572]

Cross-examination.

(By Mr. LOFTUS.)

XQ. 1. Have you any recollection as to when the Lord & Taylor building was opened?

A. The exact date?

XQ. 2. Approximately.

A. Why, it was opened early in 1913.

XQ. 3. How do you fix that date?

A. I fix that date because the architect who gave me the contract—he gave it to me over the phone, as to the date of my contract, and also when the building was finished, and they were moving while we were still on the job.

XQ. 4. That Lord & Taylor building was at 424 Fifth Avenue, in this city?

A. It's between 38th and 39th Streets, on Fifth Avenue, running towards Sixth, possibly 200 feet or so—I don't know how many feet.

XQ. 5. I show you a letter on the stationery of

(Deposition of Davis Brown.)

Lord & Taylor, and signed by A. C. McMaster, Vice-President, giving the date of the opening of the Lord & Taylor building as February, 1914, would that change your answer in any way regarding the date of opening?

A. The only way I would change my answer is —I will call up the architect for your information because I am only going by recollection of information which I received here [573] some months ago, and my secretary just told me that the information we received—she said was 1913—and it may be possible it is 1914; now if you wish the exact information on that I can do the very thing which you have done here—by inquiring I can get this information the same way as you can—my recollection cannot go back for 8, 9, 10 years and give the exact date. If this man says 1914, no doubt he is right; maybe my recollection is wrong.

XQ. 6. Are we to understand, also, Mr. Brown, that you have no exact records or definite recollection as to the date of opening of the bar-room of the Vanderbilt Hotel, is that correct?

A. Not personally, except what I was given by information—I know—the only sharp recollection I have is this—that I do remember that the Vanderbilt was done at least a year or two ahead of the Lord & Taylor—I remember that—but as to the date when it was done, I don't know, except that I was told it was opened December 31st, and that is a matter easy to verify.

XQ. 7. Well, now, what material was used in the

(Deposition of Davis Brown.)

manufacture of artificial travertin which went into the bar-room of the Vanderbilt Hotel?

A. For the backing or for the facing?

XQ. 8. Well, throughout.

A. Well, I done the backing—I prepared the backing for it—that's the only thing I can tell you —what I used [574] there—what was used for the finish is immaterial for me—I was not so much interested what they used because they can use what they like—one can use Keene's cement or Portland cement—that is immaterial—all the same except as to strength.

XQ. 9. Now, is this travertin work cast work or what is called applied work?

A. In that Vanderbilt Hotel?

XQ. 10. Yes.

A. Some of it applied and some of it cast.

XQ. 11. Do you know what methods or steps Denivelle used in making the cast material in the Vanderbilt bar?

A. What method he used in making it?

XQ. 12. What method or steps?

A. Well, the cast parts he made in the shop.

XQ. 13. Yes; and do you know what steps he or his workmen used in connection with the applied work in the Vanderbilt?   A. Why, yes.

XQ. 14. How was that work done?

A. Applied with a trowel—using a trowel—applying the material in a plastic condition; jointed on to the required size as the architect wanted; using little brush—as that—digging the holes in—

(Deposition of Davis Brown.)

the usual proceedings—that is there is no—there can be no two ways to do it—there is only one way 'to do applied work—apply to the joints [575] while it is plastic to be sure to cut the joints even after it is hardened up, but you got to put in the holes while the material is in a plastic condition—just while it commence to get its initial setting—it is cast—make it ready in the shop and ship it to the building and set it in position.

XQ. 15. Prior to the use of artificial travertin in the Pennsylvania Station, had you ever seen or heard of artificial travertin?

A. No, sir; I did not. I believe that was the first time that genuine stone was really brought over by the architects, as far as I can understand.

XQ. 16. Well, now, you have stated that your idea of an experiment is the making of samples; that after the samples have been made and examined, the experimental stage is over—did I understand you correctly?

A. To a very large extent—once you get into the building—it is one thing to make a sample, possibly a yard or 2 or 3 feet large—and you have to improve on your method as you go into a job— when you do it on a large surface,—sometimes the sample that we make in the shop is just the initial method and proportion—but it is a constant—there is room constantly to improve on our class of work, and we try to improve on it.

XQ.17. Well, now, you could not tell merely from the making of a small sample of artificial travertin

(Deposition of Davis Brown.)

whether or not such material, if applied to a large room like the Pennsylvania [576] waiting-rooms, would stand up and be satisfactory, could you?

A. Oh, yes; knowing the material used—knowing what background is to receive it.

XQ. 18. Do you know what material was used in the manufacture of the artificial travertin in the Pennsylvania Station?   A. No, sir.

XQ. 19. Supposing some of the ingredients there were new, then you would not be able to tell what satisfaction this artificial travertin would give, until it had been in place for some time, isn't that true?

A. Well, if there would be a secret process to making a piece of stone like that—of course we couldn't tell what's in the material unless we have it analyzed—but I may say to you this—that any way this imitation was made—whether it is travertin or limestone, or brownstone or marble—there are three materials that they generally use—one is plaster, next is Keene's cement, and the third is Portland cement.

XQ. 20. Is that a white Portland cement?

A. White or grey—it depends on the color scheme or design you want to get—now, if I want to get a dark surface produced I can use more darker than light material, whereas if I have to manufacture or imitate a light stone—soft, creamy finish— according like this—I must use a light Portland cement—light materials. I can always darken up a light material but I can never lighten up a dark

(Deposition of Davis Brown.)

material—that [577] is common knowledge to the trade or to an ordinary mechanic here—just what he ought to use I don't have to tell him that, because if I do, he is no mechanic.

XQ. 21. But, as a matter of fact, white Portland cement was used in the artificial travertin that went into the Pennsylvania Station? A. Yes.

XQ. 22. Now. wasn't white Portland cement rather a new product at that time?

A. Well, I don't know that it was any new product; as to the white Portland, there was one branch of the white Portland which I think they called a "builder's" white Portland cement, and a new company was getting it out, but we have used white Portland cement, I think, from the day or a few days after they were able to put it on the market, on various stucco jobs, because we have wanted a white stucco finish in place of that greyish looking finish—the artists have taken an immediate fancy to it, to use a white colored Portland—and we use it for exterior stucco work and in hardening up a surface—it was used in six months after the manufacturers put it on the market—and I think that—

XQ. 23. How long ago was that?

A. It was called Blank's Portland Cement—the company went out of existence. We can get all that data by calling up the Atlas Portland Cement headquarters—just as soon as the Blank Company got their cement out—what they [578] called a

(Deposition of Davis Brown.)

"builder's cement"—naturally the Atlas Cement Company got into the market and tried to make something just like theirs, which they did, and where Carrere & Hastings was the architects they wanted Blank's Portland cement, because as I believe, one of the mechanics—I don't know whether he is still a partner or not—he was one of the agents of the white Portland cement and naturally he introduced it in the architect business, and naturally it was a good material and he was determined to use it, and where a firm like Carrere & Hastings and McKim, Mead & White—wherever they start with a new material the others simply follow in line—that's all it is—but we used that white Portland cement, I am sure, shortly after it was put on the market.

XQ. 24. Well, now, you do recognize certain unusual conditions in connection with a large room like the Pennsylvania waiting-room, such as vibrations from the trains and temperature changes and the high walls, that would make it difficult to determine whether or not this new material would stand up until it had been in place for some time, is that true, Mr. Brown?

A. I recognize nothing, sir; it doesn't make any difference how big or how small—whether you got a railroad running on the top, railroad on the sides, or railroad on the bottom—we use exactly the same material, the same method, and apply the same way, and the results are the same, because if there is such a vibration that there should be a crack, you can

(Deposition of Davis Brown.)

use any kind of material in our industry at all, and it [579] will crack—and if there is no vibration and no shrinkage in the walls, and nothing to disturb the plastic conditions, it will stay up, because—remember one thing at all times—the plastic material is not applied to a building to hold it together; it is only put on as a veneer, as a cleaning-up proposition—to decorate it, that's all. I done the New York Central Building job, and we had the engineers there when something happened, and they realized only too well it made very little difference what they would use, except material made out of rubber, which gives, then it would pull any way you like without more damage—but any plastic material is plastic, whether it is plaster, cement or Portland—always.

XQ. 25. Well, those conditions present there in the Pennsylvania Station would be liable to cause cracking, would they not?

A. More than in a building where there is an absolutely solid foundation and no danger of vibration—that's natural—but when it comes on to that point of cracking—I will take you, if you like, into that bar-room—it isn't a bar-room any more, it's a lunch-room—I drop in there once a year if I happen to be in the neighborhood and naturally I look at my work—how it stands up—and I want to tell you that bar-room is cracked so that you—

XQ. 26. That is the travertin portion?

A. It is; cracked, badly cracked, and the only thing you got to do, I did, and I examined the con-

(Deposition of Davis Brown.)

ditions when [580] they did no more business there—and still it was cracked. It can't be helped; certain materials will crack under certain conditions and under other conditions they will stand up. We have a very peculiar line to deal with. Sometimes we are called in on a job, and they will say, "Look at the ceiling is cracked." Ten experts come in and they all try to testify why it's cracked, and no one of them is right.

XQ. 27. But have you seen any artificial travertin work recently that would stand up and not crack?

A. Yes, I did; yes, and we do have it. Those who know how to use materials and those who know what kind of materials to use, oh, yes. I will take you into the Vanderbilt bar-room, which is a room possibly twice as big as this room, or 2½ times, and it is full of cracks. I will take you over to the Lord & Taylor building—I haven't examined the work for some time, but I question to find any cracks there—they were using different kind of materials. It is essential to use a material for the under coat first; clean off the outer coat so that while it is modeled it should give a little if possible, not immediately crack like glass; glass is—of course I am speaking to you, Mr. Loftus, from the mechanic end of it because I am a mechanic myself at the trade.

XQ. 28. Yes, that is why I am asking you these questions, Mr. Brown.

A. I am trying to give them to you just as I find them—just as I know them. [581]

XQ. 29. Well, now, considering that artificial

(Deposition of Davis Brown.)

travertin is more or less porous and filled with voids
near its outer surface, and the back wall is rather
dense, is that a condition that would be likely to
cause warpage or cracking, due to uneven expansion
or contraction?

A. No more than under any other circumstances
because travertin itself, or what you see—the coloring and the holes in it—is only a matter of about a
quarter of an inch—as long as it is applied to the
ground coat it will only crack when the ground coat
cracks—unless the travertin is applied in a fashion
that may be the ground coat is too smooth or too dry,
then of course there is not so much suction there to
bind the two materials together; then it is liable to
loosen up and crack—that condition will come up
on that wall—come up with any material in that
vicinity—make no difference whether it is plaster;
but we know from information, for instance, that in
plastering—that the finish coat which is only about
1/8 of an inch thick, scratches off from the browning
for the reason it might have been two weeks after
applying the browning coat, or too dry, or maybe
dust settled on it and the careless mechanic applies
it without dusting off, and after the material is dry
it creates a vacuum between the two and you get
that hollow—here (indicating)—

XQ. 30. Well, the material which forms the outer
layer of this artificial travertin is a semi-dry material, is it not? [582]

A. No, you mix it exactly the same way as you
mix plaster, or you mix Keene's cement—you got

(Deposition of Davis Brown.)

to have water in it—its got to be absolutely plastic because if it isn't you are not able to put it on.

XQ. 31. Well, how do you get the voids or pores?

A. The little holes?

XQ. 32. Yes.

A. Oh, it is a simple process—take a whiskbroom or a little brush and push it in and then scratch it off.

XQ. 33. Well, you are referring now to the applied work?   A. Yes.

XQ. 34. But I had in mind the cast work?

A. For cast work you always have to have a model. Now, then, when we have a model, assuming—here's a piece of travertin now—we are using it for a paper weight—assuming I want to make exactly like this here—I want to cast 100—I will make a model like this, and if I believe that I want to imitate the holes in this stone, I take my modeler or crumbler and make these little holes in it; then I make my form off that—the matrix—I can demonstrate now, upstairs, in a few minutes—if you look at the glue mold—

XQ. 35. You use a glue mold in your work, do you?

A. Just with travertin; that depends upon what I am to do. We have no hard and fast rules; whenever you consider one imitation you use one; for another you use other one. But I try to just tell you, now, you see—I don't care what you [583] fellows think—I am a disinterested party in this matter, but when it comes to that somebody tells me

(Deposition of Davis Brown.)

that it is a patent—why, when I was an apprentice boy some 32 years ago—my boss was a Scotchman, Morrison—his father was a plasterer—why, if anybody would have told you you can't do something in our line, why, it would be ridiculous. Why, my old boss and his father, who was a contracting plasterer, why, he loved this plastering—in this art we love it —we can do anything; we can do anything—anything at any time; why, we have the most wonderful mechanics in our branch. Now, then, getting back to these holes, then I have a model with the holes— the only thing I can do to get in the holes is—made with knobs in it—pour it into the molds—the material shows up in the rear—it shows upon the inch of the material—then cast—set up in the building.

XQ.36. In other words, the mold of which you cast the travertin has little projections on it which form the pores or voids in the cast product, is that correct?

A. Well, you do it in a different fashion—it will be possibly clearer. Then when we do a wall—when we want to do a wall of this size—we want to do it in imitation travertin—we go to work and do this— we go to the genuine stoneman who manufactures, or rather who cuts the genuine stone, and we buy from him 8 or 10 slabs and use that for a model, then we copy it about as near perfect as natural, as [584] long as color which we put into the plastic material is matching the genuine stone, as near as it is possible to deceive the human eye, but other times again, we take a slab of stone, about that size

(Deposition of Davis Brown.)

(indicating), and make a model out of it, and one of the mechanics upstairs—he is a little better mechanic than the other—he will try to dig in these little holes to match as near the genuine stone as can be done by human hands, and then we use it for a model—we are doing it very frequently.

XQ. 37. Well, the result of that would be to produce a great many slabs which were identical in appearance, would it not?

A. Oh, that is the reason we go to work and get the genuine stone, for instance, for a wall of that size we order a half a dozen stones, so it doesn't look much alike, because if we only get one stone and represent it and set it up on the wall, it would look too mechanical—that's where the skill of the mechanic comes in—to use his brains.

XQ. 38. Well, now, where you are casting travertin under such a method as you have described, is it possible to get the under-cut effect in the voids?

A. If you cast it out of a glue mold, yes, decidedly yes; any kind of glue gives; can demonstrate it to you upstairs in about a half an hour, if you care to look at it.

XQ. 39. Do you get an under-cut effect if the mold is a wooden mold? [585]

A. We never use wooden molds except on very rare occasions, and in wooden molds you can get an under-cut if you make your wooden molds in so many pieces—it can be done, but it is an expnesive way and therefore we use a mold which is more practical and cheaper, because our work is done

(Deposition of Davis Brown.)

mostly on competition, and a man never gets it who is the higher, but usually the man who is the lower and responsible.

XQ. 40. What other jobs of artificial travertin have you made since the Lord & Taylor building?

A. I should say we done—I don't know how many —a great many. I don't know—we can look those things up; we can look back for the last 3 years, possibly 4 years, I don't know; of course this information—in case Mr. Denivelle finds out—we got to pay him a royalty—I am not worrying about that— I haven't got enough money to pay it; now, we have done it right along; it is very rarely that we are without a job of that character—all of us—not only I or my concern—most capable contractors who do this work, they do it all the time; there isn't a contractor in the entire union who is no more or less familiar with the manufacture of this material; and some of them are more familiar with it—out of 3,000 men that is saying something—I don't have to take it and find out which men I am going to put on this work—they all know it—only some of them are swifter and smarter than others.

XQ. 41. Prior to the use of artificial travertin in the Pennsylvania Station, had you ever seen or made any artificial [586] stone or marble containing striations or veins, and having these under-cut voids in its outer surface?

A. Yes; but if you ask me, on the other hand, whether I was trying to *imitation* travertin, I say no. We have made all kinds of artificial marble

(Deposition of Davis Brown.)

work and artificial stone work, molded, ornamented and otherwise.

XQ. 42. But not of the characteristic which I have mentioned there in my question, that is, the stone with striations or veins, and containing these undercut voids?

A. You mean voids or moldings and the like? Try to be a little more specific so I can answer accordingly, because void can mean in my mind anything—if I make a molding which is like this—this is the surface—yes, I made those if it is what the architect wants, and we do it accordingly, whatever his design is.

XQ. 43. Well, you understand what I mean by voids or pores in connection with travertin, do you not?

A. Well, if you use the word travertin I will give you one answer, but if you use the word travertin you only say with dents and the like—I have done all kinds of imitation stone work, and was an apprentice boy at the trade when we were doing imitation work on all kinds of drums whenever the architect had any special calls for it.

XQ. 44. But nothing in the nature of travertin?

A. No, sir. [587]

Redirect Examination.

(By Mr. ANDERSON.)

RDQ. 1. Mr. Brown, you are absolutely certain that Mr. Denivelle did this artificial travertin work for you in the Vanderbilt Hotel? A. Oh, yes.

(Deposition of Davis Brown.)

RDQ. 2. And that he was paid for it?

A. Yes, I paid him for it.

RDQ. 3. Now, you spoke about the Terminal building job; do you mean the Grand Central Terminal?

A. Grand Central Terminal, yes, sir; you see, the Grand Central Building is done in two parts; the section from 45th Street—no, from 43d Street to 45th Street is what they call the north half, and from 43d to 42d Street is the south half, which is the main station; the north half is the office building—we had the contract for this huge building.

RDQ. 4. Office building?   A. Yes.

RDQ. 5. Was there any imitation cast stone in that building, in the north half?   A. No.

RDQ. 6. You didn't do any imitation stone work, did you?

A. No, not my firm—Klee-Thomson Company did the main station.

RDQ. 7. Did you ever make any imitation Caen stone?   [588]   A. Oh, yes; yes, sir.

RDQ. 8. Would you say that a block of imitation Caen stone, except for the surface finish, was substantially the same as a block of imitation travertin?

Mr. LOFTUS.—That's objected to as incompetent, irrelevant, immaterial, and calling for an opinion and conclusion of the witness, and not the best evidence.

A. I would say there is no difference between the two—the finish of the surface—we got to make it the same way—same identical thing—doesn't matter

(Deposition of Davis Brown.)

whether it is limestone, Caen stone, anything—its got to be done the same way—same mechanics doing it.

RDQ. 9. Now, in your business, was it common to make imitations of Caen stone, limestone, and the other stones, before the Pennsylvania Station was done.

Mr. LOFTUS.—Same objection.

A. Yes; we have been making always imitation materials.

RDQ. 11. Now you mentioned the fact that Mr. Paul Denivelle called upon you recently—what was the object of his call—what did you discuss?

A. Well, Mr. Anderson—I would take that as a social call, and whatever can come out of it—I don't think I care to testify—I don't think you have the right to ask me that question, Mr. Anderson. [589]

RDQ. 12. Well, Mr. Brown, I appreciate the fact that your friendship for Mr. Denivelle possibly leads you to believe that you shouldn't disclose the subject of that call, but if it related to this litigation, I think it is material to the Court.

A. Now, Mr. Anderson, a man comes to my house —I haven't seen him for many, many years, and we have what I would call a social call, but notwithstanding that it is natural to talk what is on his mind—if it was brought out I would be very much embarrassed—if I would have done what Denivelle really wanted me to do—have lunch with him—I wouldn't hesitate to tell you, to testify, but I couldn't afford to leave my home—I wish, Mr. An-

(Deposition of Davis Brown.)

derson, you leave my personal, social and friendly conversation which I had with him out of this.

RDQ. 13. Do you object to saying whether or not the conversation related to this litigation?

A. No, we spoke on the subject quite some; I would say that because he gave me a part of his printed matter—he showed me, I believe—the Appellate Court out in San Francisco; he asked me to read it over carefully to see what interesting reading matter it was.

Redirect examination closed.

Recross-examination.

(By Mr. LOFTUS.) [590]

RXQ. 1. Do you know Mr. McGruer, the defendant in this case, a San Francisco man?

A. Yes, I met him.

RXQ. 2. He was in to see you, too?   A. Yes.

RXQ. 3. A couple of months ago?

A. Well, I couldn't tell you—getting me down to dates—maybe it's 2, 3, 4 months ago—I couldn't tell you; he was in here. I met once Mr. Schultz, you know who he is—Schultz & Weaver, architects for that hotel out west.

RXQ. 4. The Biltmore Hotel in Los Angeles?

A. Yes; that's the man. I met him on the train; he lives in Scarsdale, and I lived up on the line, or used to in those days; we went home together, and he approached me on the subject—this very job— what I think of the situation. Well, it was just a casual conversation, and I think Schultz mentioned

(Deposition of Davis Brown.)

it to me, among others, that Paul Denivelle submitted a ridiculously high figure for the work or something on that order; I wasn't in those days interested in the matter at all—just listened to him— he made the statement that time, I think his figure was around $45,000 or something like that—I don't know what the work was worth, so I couldn't tell him it was low, high or indifferent.

RXQ. 5. Do you think you could locate a letter dated March 15, 1923, written by MacGruer & Simpson to you?   [591]

A. March 15, 1923?

RXQ. 6. Yes.

A. I think we could, what is the nature of the letter—you got a copy of it?

RXQ. 7. I haven't a copy of MacGruer & Simpson's letter to you, but I have a copy of your reply to them, which they embodied in an affidavit signed by Mr. MacGruer and filed in this suit—I will show you a copy of your reply.

A. I think we can find that—I am unable to find the letter called for at this time because the one having charge of my files is not at present in the office. I feel sure that I can find this letter, and I will be glad to mail you the original.

RXQ. 8. You do recognize this copy which I showed you and which is embodied in an affidavit entitled, "Affidavit of George S. MacGruer on Motion for Preliminary Injunction"?

A. Yes, I recognize that letter; I remember writing such a letter.

(Deposition of Davis Brown.)

Mr. LOFTUS.—That's all.

Re-redirect Examination.

(By Mr. ANDERSON.)

RRDQ. 1. When was this visit to you by Mr. Denivelle, was it recently?

A. I think it was last Saturday.

RRDQ. 2. Last Saturday? That would be Saturday, the [592] 8th day of March? A. Yes.

Examination closed.

Deposition closed.

Signature waived.

Counsel for the respective parties visited the hotel Vanderbilt and interviewed one of the assistant managers and the chief porter, both of whom said they had been with the Vanderbilt Hotel from a time previous to its opening, and both of whom declared that the hotel was informally opened for a reception or private view on the 9th day of January, 1912, and that on the 10th day of January, 1912, it was opened for the reception of guests.

It is agreed that if these witnesses were called to testify, they would testify as above.

The taking of depositions on behalf of the defendants, of witnesses more than 100 miles from the place of trial, and under the Order of the Court and Notice hereinbefore referred to, is concluded. [593]

County of New York,
State of New York,—ss.

I, Philip D. Rollhaus, a notary public in and for the county of New York, State of New York, do hereby certify that pursuant to the stipulation of counsel for the respective parties in the case of Paul E. Denivelle vs. MacGruer & Simpson, et al., now pending in the District Court of the United States for the Northern District of California, Southern Division, on the 3d day of March, 1924, I took the deposition of Carl Henry Meyn on behalf of the defendants, and that by agreement of counsel the said deposition was taken down in shorthand and transcribed by Miss Florence Hoffman; and on the 6th day of March, 1924, I took the deposition of John A. Fincke on behalf of the defendants, and that by agreement of counsel the said deposition was taken down in shorthand and transcribed by Miss Helen I. Gorman; both depositions having been taken in the offices of Munn, Anderson & Munn in the Woolworth Building in the city of New York, county and state of New York; the said depositions were taken in the presence of William A. Loftus, Esq., of counsel for the plaintiff, and T. Hart Anderson, Esq., of counsel for the defendants; that before the taking of the depositions each of said witnesses was first duly cautioned and sworn by me, to tell the truth, the whole truth and nothing but the truth; and that Exhibit 1 was introduced in evidence as appears from the record which I hereby [594] certify, which said exhibit I have marked and certified as indicated by the record; and by stipulation of counsel the signature of the respective witnesses to the depositions was waived.

I am not of counsel, nor related by blood or mar-

riage to any of the parties in this proceeding, and
I am not interested in any manner whatsoever in
the outcome thereof.

IN WITNESS WHEREOF I have hereunto set
my hand and affixed my seal, this 22d day of March,
1924.

[Seal]   PHILIP D. ROLLHAUS,

Notary Public, Kings County, No. 250. Certificate
    Filed in New York County No. 67. Kings
    County Register's No. 5050. New York
    County Register's No. 5124. [595]

County of New York,
State of New York,—ss.

I, George H. Emslie, Esq., a notary public in and
for the county of New York, State of New York,
do hereby certify that pursuant to the stipulation
of counsel for the respective parties in the case of
Paul E. Denivelle vs. MacGruer & Simpson, et al.,
now pending in the District Court of the United
States for the Northern District of California,
Southern Division, beginning the 3d day of March,
1924, and on the 4th, 5th, 6th, 7th, 10th, 11th, 12th,
13th, 14th and 15th days of March, 1924, I took the
depositions of Richmond H. Shreve, Burt L. Fenner,
Vance W. Torbert, Frank A. Whipple, Julius F.
Gayler, Daniel T. Webster, William Steele Cooke,
Louis S. Massimo, Henry A. Cousins, Tommaso
V. Coronato, Frank J. Morkel, Peter G. Moore,
Jr., Walter H. Clough, Clay M. McClure, Samuel
L. Kriney, Randolph H. Almiroty, Philip Liva,
Walter L. Hopkins, Davis Brown and Patrick J.
Durkin on behalf of the defendants, the depositions

of all of the witnesses, with the exception of Peter G.
Moore, Jr., and Davis Brown, having been taken
in the offices of Munn, Anderson & Munn in the
Woolworth Building in the city of New York,
county and State of New York, and that by stipulation and agreement of counsel, the depositions of
Peter G. Moore, Jr., and of Davis Brown were
taken at the places of business respectively, of
those witnesses, in the said city, county and State of
New York; and that by agreement of counsel the
depositions of Richmond H. Shreve, Julius F. Gayler, Louis S. [596] Massimo, Henry A. Cousins,
Peter G. Moore, Jr., Walter H. Clough, Samuel L.
Kriney, Randolph H. Almiroty, P. 'ip Liva, Walter L. Hopkins and Patrick J. Durkin, were taken
down in shorthand and transcribed by Miss Helen
I. Gorman, and that the depositions of Burt L.
Fenner, Vance W. Torbert, Frank A. Whipple,
Daniel T. Webster, William Steele Cooke, Tommaso V. Coronato, Frank J. Morkel, Clay M. Mc-
Clure and Davis Brown, were taken down in shorthand and transcribed by Miss Florence Hoffman;
the said depositions were taken in the presence of
William A. Loftus, Esq., of counsel for the plaintiff, and T. Hart Anderson, Esq., of counsel for
the defendants; that before the taking of the depositions each of said witnesses was first duly cautioned and sworn by me, to tell the truth, the whole
truth and nothing but the truth; and that the several exhibits were introduced in evidence as appears from the record which I hereby certify, which
said exhibits I have marked and certified as indi-

cated by the record; and by stipulation of counsel the signature of the respective witnesses to the depositions was waived.

I am not of counsel, nor related by blood or marriage to any of the parties in this proceeding, and I am not interested in any manner whatsoever in the outcome thereof.

In witness whereof I have hereunto set my hand and affixed my seal this 22d day of March, 1924.

[Seal] GEORGE H. EMSLIE,

Notary Public, Bronx County, No. 10. Certificate Filed in New York County No. 58. Bronx County Register's No. 38. New York County Register's No. 4053.

[Endorsed]: Filed Apr. 2, 1924. [597]

[Title of Court and Cause.]
Tuesday, April 22, 1924.
REPORTER'S TRANSCRIPT.

[598]

[Title of Court and Cause.]
Tuesday, April 22, 1924.
Counsel Appearing:

For Plaintiff: CHARLES E. TOWNSEND, Esq., WLLIAIM A. LOFTUS, Esq.

For Defendant: T. HART ANDERSON, Esq.

Mr. TOWNSEND.—May it please the Court:

This is a patent case. It is somewhat unusual as far as patent cases go in, first, that the patent has already been adjudicated and held valid by our Circuit Court of Appeals in a case that came up from Los Angeles and reported in 270 Fed. 155. I will later hand you up a printed copy of the decision.

The COURT.—Well, that makes it easy.

Mr. TOWNSEND.—Yes, I think so. And, secondly, it relates to a subject matter that is of more than ordinary interest, because it played such an important part in the great exposition held here in 1915, the Panama-Pacific Exposition. If your [599] Honor was an attendant at that exposition you will recall the wall surfacing of the buildings—

The COURT.—I did not have that pleasure.

Mr. TOWNSEND.—The surfacing of all the structures at that fair, a fair in which the original building program involved something like $17,-000,000 worth of structures. All those structures were surfaced with this so-called artificial travertine. Artificial travertine, as the name implies, is a simulated stone of the original Roman travertine. Our Court of Appeals decision speaks of the subject of travertine, and its origin, it being dug from the river or near the River Tiber. When exposed to the air this travertine hardens and becomes, when properly finished, a very beautiful and a very enduring material for wall surfacing. The Coliseum is one of the monumental structures.

I will refer briefly to the origin of it. The decision referred to discusses the origin of it. It

seems that along in 1909 and 1910, at the time of
the building of the great Pennsylvania Station in
New York, a $50,000,000 job, the architects, Mc-
Kimm, Mead & White, desired, in the building of
the station, itself, to use something that had never
been used before, and something architecturally
and artistically that had never been done before or
attempted before. That was to use travertine in
the great halls and waiting-rooms of that station.
But the cost of natural travertine was almost pro-
hibitive. So Mr. Denivelle, the patentee and the
plaintiff, here, was called in by McKimm, Mead &
White and asked if he thought he could produce an
artificial stone or plastic material which would
simulate the natural travertine. As a result of
that invitation, Mr. Denivelle set about doing something that he did not know when he [600]
started out to do it just what could be done; but he
produced some samples in the course of several
months trials which, while not entirely satisfactory
at that time to Mr. Denivelle, far surpassed the expectations of the architects. They said they would
go ahead on that, that they saw the practicability of
it. Bids were called for for the production of such
a work. Several big contractors in the country, including S. W. Miller, of New York, and McNulty
Bros. & Co., were among the bidders. They were
submitted samples, they were shown a piece of
original travertine and were asked to see if they
could approach it in artificial form. None of the
samples passed muster except Mr. Denivelle's. As
a result, the contract was awarded to Mr. Deni-

velle, in the face of great opposition from everyone, practically, but the architects, because not only was this a new thing and it was going into a monumental structure, and there was a fear that it might not endure, but there was, of course, the large financial feature whether Mr. Denivelle and his company could carry it through. The job there in the Pennsylvania Station involved a contract of something like $125,000 ultimately. That job was completed and while the station was first opened to the public in the early part of 1910, Mr. Denivelle's work still continued there, although he had his original work erected, the matter was in such an experimental state, they were changing the work as they went along, feeling their way to see which would be the best method, they were working with new products—white Portland cement and other things which made even the outcome of such work highly conjectural in Mr. Denivelle's mind. So, as I say, his work on that station, taking care of that, and the upkeep, continued along until 1912 or 1913. [601]

In 1912 the Exposition was under way, and they were about to begin building. Some of the architects who had seen this work of Mr. Denivelle in the Pennsylvania Station, called the matter to the attention of the Exposition authorities, who were looking for something new in the way of World's Fairs. They had had white stuff—white-colored plastic effects at St. Louis and at Chicago. The terrible cost of painting them and keeping them looking white during the short time that the exposition lasted was a big question with them, and it was one of the serious financial drawbacks attached to those expositions. Furthermore, the Exposition people here wanted something new. So that in the end of 1912, in December, Mr. Denivelle came to the Coast, at the invitation of the Exposition authorities, told them what he believed he could produce, and that he had put this work in the Pennsylvania station, and that as an arcitecturally enduring matter it was a question of time as to how it was going to come out. However, it so impressed the authorities that they agreed to adopt the Denivelle method of surfacing the Exposition buildings with artificial travertine, as it early became known by that name.

Artificial travertine is characterized in this way, by its peculiar surface of striations or veins running through it in conjunction with voids. It has a roughened surface, as it were; it has a surface pitted or filled with voids which give it, with the striations, and with the peculiar tan coloring of the stone, a very distinctive appearance and a very pleasing color effect.

The contracts were signed up with the various contractors on the various buildings to have this work done. One of the [602] first things that Mr. Denivelle was confronted with when he was put in charge of all of this work was to see that his ideas were carried out. He met with great opposition from the contractors. They said, "You can't do that, that is an impossible thing to do." But

Denivelle showed them samples, and said that it is possible if you will only follow my instructions.

Among those who were directly interested in this matter as contractors, and who did the Machinery Hall building, were these defendants, MacGruer & Simpson. They were awarded the contract for the plastering, a subcontract, from Anderson & Co., who had the general contract for the erection of the building. There were various difficulties, not only that arise on every job, but that particularly arose on this job. As time went on, it required a great deal of persuasion to get these contractors, including these defendants, to do what Mr. Denivelle wanted. The work on that building was completed along in the early part of 1914. The building was accepted in the spring of 1914.

So we have here, in the first place, these defendants learning this patent process—which was not then patented, but an application for patent had been filed, and then later their infringement in connection with the case to which I will shortly refer.

The patent here immediately in suit was not filed until October of 1915, but, as I say, a previous application had been filed, in about the middle of 1913, after Mr. Denivelle came to the coast.

The Court thoroughly considered the effect of the Pennsylvania work in the decision to which I have referred in 270 Fed. 155, and they found that that work was not a public use in the [603] sense of the statute, but a use by the public. There was a distinction, which was brought to the Court's attention, that a use by the public is not always a public use in the sense of the statute. So the Court carefully reviewed the evidence in regard to the Pennsylvania Station, and found that that did not come within the inhibition of the statute, that the work was largely in an experimental state, as far as Mr. Denivelle was concerned during the Exposition.

What has been astonishing, your Honor, is this: That here is a building material which first tried in any way and appearing anywhere in the world back in 1910 has only to-day, some fourteen years afterwards, begun to be recognized as a standard or a regular and satisfactory finish. Mr. Denivelle had all the prejudices to overcome in those early days.

We have here in 1922 the defendant taking upon itself to put this patented process into the Los Angeles Biltmore Hotel. Now, before I take that up, I want to refer a little to the nature of the process. I will show your Honor a little booklet entitled, "Wall Surfaces of the Exposition," which was in the Los Angeles case, and which was considered by the Circuit Court of Appeals, and is quoted in the opinion of the Circuit Court of Appeals—

Mr. ANDERSON.—Do you propose to offer that in evidence, Mr. Townsend?

Mr. TOWSEND.—I shall. I am just showing his Honor for a moment the opinion of the Circuit Court of Appeals also.

I do not think it is necessary to take the time of the Court in reading the opinion, because your Honor will do that. As I say, they reviewed the early history. They quote Mr. Marquardt, who was the assistant director of works at the exposition.

He [604] was really the man who built the Exposition,—and also his little article here.

I would like to show the Court now some photographs which were before the Court before—

Mr. ANDERSON.—I object to this, your Honor, unless these are offered as exhibits.

The COURT.—Yes. When the time comes we will receive them.

Mr. TOWNSEND.—These are illustrative of the buildings at the fair. They will show you how the material appears when photographed.

The COURT.—Just what have we here—the trial as to the validity of the patent?

Mr. ANDERSON.—Yes, your Honor.

The COURT.—Well, proceed with your opening statement. I assume that is what you are making.

Mr. TOWNSEND.—Yes, your Honor. In 1923, at the time of the building of the Los Angeles Biltmore Hotel, the plaintiff and the defendants were in consultation in regard to the use of the patented process. The defendants were fully aware of the patents. There was a conference, in which it was stated that Mr. Denivelle would submit a proposition or a bid to the defendants, who had the general contract for this artificial travertine work, and for all the plastering work on the Biltmore Hotel. They wrote to Mr. Denivelle and asked him what his price would be to do certain work. He replied what it would be. Nothing further came of it. The defendants proceeded, and they put this artificial travertine in. We will show that it follows the same process, it is closer to Mr. Denivelle's

than was the process followed by the defendants in
the Los Angeles suit. So we think there is nothing doubtful about the question of infringement.
[605]

Now, just one more word with regard to the
matter of defense of invalidity, or anticipation, or
whatever it may be. All that the defendants have
done in the mass of testimony they have taken back
East, some 23 depositions, is to prove with more
particularity the very things that we admitted were
done on the Pennsylvania Station. They have
proven a date definitely that we stated was approximate. They have proven the same character of
work which we admitted had been done. So there
is no new defense offered here. It will be quite
apparent the moment you begin to hear the depositions read, or read them, that they have produced
not one iota of new defensive material that was not
before the Court before.

In the History of the Exposition by Mr. Frank
Morton Todd, it is said, in Vol. 1, page 351:

"If we were asked to designate the most important single item of the Expositon color
scheme, we should be tempted to say it was the
imitation travertine plaster that covered the
exterior walls and formed the general background. Its softness and richness and per-
vasive warmth characterized the whole scene
and gave the Exposition distinction over all
others. It was the first time such a thing had
been done, and it constituted a bold and most
successful departure from the white-marble

tradition. Columns and ornaments were modeled in this material, and all decoration had to harmonize in color with it. There was a good critical opinion that the tint, being under control, was more beautiful than that of the genuine.

"Travertine is that light buff, porous, sedimentary lime stone of which the Vatican and St. Peter's, with its peristyle are built, as well as many of the Renaissance churches of Rome, and almost all the Imperial City's fountains and monumental stairways. Its tint is warm and rich, and it's porous surface [606] gives it an interesting and a pleasing texture. It is a relief from the dead monotony of marble, and in the bright sunshine of California, as in that of Central Italy, its color would restfully absorb a great deal of light. For background, nothing better could have been devised, and it was consistently carried through the Exposition construction. In fact, this was a 'travertine' city.

"The interior of the Pennsylvania Railway Station at New York had been finished in part with a plaster of this shade and softness of surface, which enriched and beautified it wonderfully. This was employed by the New York architectural firm of McKimm, Mead & White and Mr. William Symmes Richardson of that firm had suggested it for the Exposition. It was early determined by the Architectural Commission and the Directors, that the background of the Exposition palaces should be of this similar material, and for the purpose Paul E. Denivelle was called into service, as he had been connected with the Pennsylvania Station work. He came to San Francisco in December, 1912.''

And further, in Vol. 3, page 23:

The COURT.—Are you offering these in evidence now?

Mr. TOWNSEND.—I will offer them later; yes, sir.

The COURT.—I am not saying whether they are competent, or not, but I think all of this had better be left until the progress of the trial. You are making your opening statement now.

Mr. TOWNSEND.—I though it was a convenient place to bring it in. I should say this, in closing: When the plaintiff learned, after considerable lapse of time, that the defendants had proceeded with the artificial travertine work in the Biltmore Hotel, an effort was made for some time to find out [607] exactly what they were doing. The work was carried on behind closed doors, and it was only by a workman who worked there and who Mr. Denivelle knew, it was only through him that he was able to get a couple of samples which are here in evidence as Plaintiff's Exhibits ''A'' and ''B'' as samples of the work done by the defendants in connection with the Biltmore job. With that information, this suit was filed and an application for a preliminary injunction prayed and heard on full presentation of affidavits by both sides by the late

Judge Van Fleet, who, on August 3d, after hearing both sides, said: "In my mind, there is no question about infringement, and an injunction shall issue." So a preliminary injunction was issued, and is still in effect.

The other factors in connection with the case will develop, I believe, as we proceed.

I want to say in regard to that case in Southern California, it was very stubbornly contested, and all the evidence introduced there substantially covers all the defenses that are made here.

I shall first offer some exhibits, physical and documentary. I offer as Plaintiff's Exhibit—

Mr. ANDERSON.—I object to the offer of an exhibit in the absence of proof showing what it is.

The COURT.—I don't understand that anything is offered yet. Proceed, Counsel.

Mr. TOWNSEND.—I offer, as Exhibit 1, the sample which was marked Exhibit "A" on the Motion for Preliminary Injunction. It was submitted in connection with an affidavit as a sample of artificial travertine made by the defendant. No claim was made on the hearing of that motion that that was not a genuine sample, and it not being denied, we have assumed that it was [608] admitted. We will submit it to you now, Mr. Anderson, and if you have any question about it you can so state.

Mr. ANDERSON.—All right. I might admit it if you give me an opportunity to see it.

Mr. TOWNSEND.—Very well, here it is.

Mr. ANDERSON.—My client says he cannot identify this.

Mr. TOWNSEND.—Then I ask that it be marked for identification.

The COURT.—I have not just understood this: Is there an objection made to this?

Mr. ANDERSON.—Yes, your Honor, I object to the exhibit unless it is proven what it is.

The COURT.—Yes, certainly, that is a proper objection. I simply wanted to hear what your objection was.

Mr. TOWNSEND.—I will ask for a ruling, your Honor, in face of the fact that it was not denied before.

The COURT.—I don't think that would make it admissible. They might have admitted it merely temporarily, perhaps as a matter of strategy. That is permissible. Can you prove it now?

Mr. TOWNSEND.—Not now. I will have to pass that for the present, your Honor.

The COURT.—Very well. I think the objection is good.

Mr. TOWNSEND.—I will withdraw that. I will now offer Exhibit 1 what was attached to the defendant's affidavits on the preliminary injunction as their Exhibit 3 in conjunction with the affidavit of F. L. Tovani, the affidavit being dated July 27, 1923, Tovani saying—

Mr. ANDERSON.—I object to his reading from the affidavit, your Honor.

The COURT.—Well, I will hear what he wants to read. [609]

Mr. TOWNSEND.—"That Exhibit 3, forming part of this affidavit, is a sample of imitation travertine made by affiant in accordance with the method used by defendant in constructing the Los Angeles Biltmore Hotel.'' That is an admission against interest, your Honor.

The COURT.—And you say the defendant offered that in connection with an affidavit?

Mr. TOWNSEND.—Yes, your Honor.

Mr. ANDERSON.—I will withdraw my objection. We can stipulate that this is what it purports to be, a sample of the defendant's stone. We will admit that.

Mr. TOWNSEND.—Very well, that is admitted.

(The document was marked Plaintiff's Exhibit 1.)

The COURT.—This is a sample of the defendant's work, what you were using in that hotel: Is that the idea?

Mr. ANDERSON.—Yes, sir.

Mr. TOWNSEND.—As Plaintiff's Exhibit 2, I offer Defendant's Exhibit 5 on the preliminary injunction hearing, forming part of the affidavit of Mr. Delaney dated August 1, 1923, and referred to on page 6, lines 16 and 17 as being a specimen of defendant's product.

Mr. ANDERSON.—Well, we have one; what is the use of having more than that?

The COURT.—There is no objection. Admitted.

(The document was marked Plaintiff's Exhibit 2.)

Mr. ANDERSON.—We will admit that it is the defendant's product.

Mr. TOWNSEND.—And as Plaintiff's Exhibit 3,

I offer the original Denivelle patent in suit, No. 1,212,331, as of January 16, 1917. This was Exhibt 1 in the Los Angeles suit.

(The document was marked Plaintiff's Exhibt 3.)

[610]

As Exhibit 4, I offer a certified copy of the file-wrapper of the patent just referred to, which was Exhibit 16 in the Los Angeles suit.

Mr. ANDERSON.—That is the patent in suit, is it?

Mr. TOWNSEND.—Yes.

(The document was marked Plaintiff's Exhibit 4.)

As Exhibit 5, I offer a certified copy of the judgment-roll in the Los Angeles suit.

The COURT.—It is admitted. Was that a suit between the same parties?

Mr. TOWNSEND.—No, your Honor, it was a suit between the plaintiff and a party named Ceriat, and there was another defendant in another case, and the two cases were consolidated and tried together. The present defendants were not parties to that suit.

(The document was marked Plaintiff's Exhibit 5.)

I next offer a certified copy of the transcript of record before the Circuit Court of Appeals in that suit, and ask that it be marked Plaintiff's Exhibit 6.

(The document was marked Plaintiff's Exhibit 6.)

I next offer a certified copy of the deposition taken in that case of one Frank Morkel.

Mr. ANDERSON.—Isn't that included in the record on appeal?

Mr. TOWNSEND.—The record on appeal is in narrative form. This is merely the certified copy of the complete deposition. I have done that because, in showing the history of that case, it is well to point out that Morkel has also testified in the present case on behalf of the defendants.

(The document was marked Plaintiff's Exhibit 7.)

I next offer a certified copy of the deposition of F. J. [611] McNulty, given in that Southern California case.

(The document was marked Plaintiff's Exhibit 8.)

Now, as illustrative of the procedure followed in the plaintiff's process, and further illustrating the exhibits which were before the court in that Los Angeles case, I am going to offer a mold in which the stuff is sometimes cast. This mould was Exhibit 3 in the Los Angeles case; I now offer it as Plaintiff's Exhibit 9 in this case.

(The mould was marked Plaintiff's Exhibit 9.)

And as Plaintiff's Exhibit 10, I offer a can which is used for veining; that was Exhibit 4 in the Los Angeles case.

(The can was marked Plaintiff's Exhibit 10.)

In the Los Angeles case we had two exhibits of natural travertine, which were 5 and 11 in that case; I offer them now and ask that they be marked, respectively, in this case, as Plaintiff's Exhibits 11 and 12.

(The exhibits were marked, respectively, Plaintiff's Exhibits 11 and 12.)

Mr. ANDERSON.—For what purpose are these exhibits offered?

Mr. TOWNSEND.—They are offered showing the complete record, and as—

Mr. ANDERSON.—In order that the Court may be able to compare the first case with this one. Is that the idea?

Mr. TOWNSEND.—In order to show what new defenses are introduced here over and above the defense that were introduced before.

Mr. ANDERSON.—No objection to them for that purpose.

Mr. TOWNSEND.—As Exhibit 13, I offer the little booklet that your Honor has, Wall Surfaces of the Exposition; that was Exhibit 10 in the Los Angeles case. A duplicate of that [612] is attached to the affidavit offered by the defendants on the motion for preliminary injunction, the affidavit of J. Harry Blohme, architect. Mr. Blohme says in his affidavit—

Mr. ANDERSON.—I object to counsel quoting from an affidavit. The witness' was not under examination and cross-examination; in other words, he was not being orally examined.

The COURT.—The theory on which you are offering this is the same, an admission against interests?

Mr. TOWNSEND.—Yes, your Honor, an affidavit used on the hearing for the preliminary injunction, as an admission against interest.

The COURT.—And they used it there?

Mr. TOWNSEND.—Yes, your Honor.

The COURT.—It will go in the record over the

objection. If not competent or material, the Court will give it no consideration. If the case goes up to the Circuit Court of Appeals it will not have to be sent back merely because that was not admitted.

(The document was marked Plaintiff's Exhibit 13.)

Mr. TOWNSEND.—Regarding this booklet, Mr. Blohme, in his affidavit, on page 2, beginning line 24, says:

> "That to the best of affiant's knowledge and belief Exhibit No. 7 forming part of this affidavit is one of the original copies of said publication and is so identified by affiant."

Mr. ANDERSON.—What is this for?

Mr. TOWNSEND.—You don't question, Mr. Anderson, but what your Exhibit 7 is a duplicate of the exhibit just offered?

Mr. ANDERSON.—That is correct.

Mr. TOWNSEND.—As Plaintiff's Exhibit 14 I offer a slab [613] of artificial travertine. It was in evidence in the Los Angeles cases as Ceriat Exhibit "A," being a slab of the infringing artificial travertine in that case. It is offered for the same purpose as the other one.

Mr. ANDERSON.—That is, for the purpose of comparison only.

(The sample was marked Plaintiff's Exhibit 14.)

Mr. TOWNSEND.—And as Plaintiff's Exhibit 15, a slab of defendants' infringing travertine, a demonstration made in open court; in that case it was marked Exhibit "F."

(The sample was marked Plaintiff's Exhibit 15.)

Now, as Plaintiff's Exhibit 16, I offer a copy of the opinion that is reported in 270 Fed. 155. I merely offer that for the convenience of the court.

(The document was marked Plaintiff's Exhibit 16.)

I shall now read from some of the affidavits of the defendants offered on the hearing of the preliminary injunction, on the same basis, being admissions against interest. I will begin reading from the affidavit of John H. Delaney, dated August 1, 1923, and filed in this court, page 2, line 21:

"That he knows of an imitation of travertin as made by the plaintiff patentee; that plaintiff's stone or artificial travertin consists of a striated or veined substance made by arranging or forming upon a greased mold, a series of narrow lines of colored plastic material in imitation of veins; depositing upon said lines or veins and upon the exposed surfaces of the mold between the veins a suitable material of such texture and consistency as will leave numerous small voids of exposed surfaces out of contact with the material, and then binding together the veining material and the void-forming material with a moist plaster material, and allowing the mass to set and harden; that the so-called void-forming material is [614] of a loose, lumpy character."

Page 3, line 13:

"That affiant has labored for several years to bring into existence an imitation travertin that would meet commercial or trade requirements not heretofore overcome in the material of the plaintiff.''

Page 5, beginning line 4:

"That well knowing these old processes and with full knowledge of the defects and imperfections attendant the production of imitation material of plaintiff's character, affiant set about to eradicate these imperfections and to produce a material in closer simulation of natural Roman travertine and to provide a plastic substance which is very porous and rough and which will be provided with a surface having undercut cavities or voids in true conformity with the natural voids or cavities of the so-called Roman travertin; that affiant had among other things the creation of a novel and new and useful composition of matter wherein these cavities can be more or less consistently formed upon the exposed surface of the finished product.''

Line 24, the same page:

"That essentially speaking, applicant makes use of an old and well-known mold characterized by features of common knowledge; that he greases this mold as is also well known; that he then places upon the surface thereof plastic substances, which, while in a moist state, are combed or otherwise treated to produce veins, so to speak; that he then introduces to the surface thus treated granules of calcium carbide, and finally spreads upon the aforesaid constituents a plastic mass which gives to the structure a form of backing; that this backing is applied while in a moist state, and that incident [615] thereto a chemical action is set up which causes the chemical carbide to assume a gaseous state and explode and thereby produce upon the surface of the finished product a plurality of cells, pockets or voids of an under-cut character. Affiant states that through this process and by the very inherent qualities of the chemicals employed the mass of material or lumpy matter employed in plaintiff's patent is entirely eliminated with a functional departure from plaintiff's patent as to arise to the dignity of a new and patentable invention."

Next I will read from the affidavit of F. J. Traits, offered on behalf of the defendants on the motion for the preliminary injunction. He says he is a general contractor and engineer, vice-president of the Scofield Engineering Construction Co., general contractors for the erection of the Biltmore Hotel, in the city of Los Angeles, County of Los Angeles, State of California.

On page 2, line 4, he says:

"That after due investigation, they decided to award this work to MacGruer and Simpson, not because they were the lowest bidder, but because it was thought they would most certainly finish on time, and because of their reputation for doing good work; that, after this intention was explained to the architect, the Architect requested that we make another effort to get from the plaintiff a firm bid for the above work, the Architect being acquainted with the plaintiff and not with the defendants; that in pursuance of this request, and as a matter of accommodation to the Architect, we did ask the plaintiff again for a firm bid covering the above work, that they never did receive from him a complete bid so as to enable us to consider letting the work to him; that the price he did [616] submit for a portion of the work was out of range with other prices in our possession, and therefore unusable; that at no time was there any possibility of awarding this work to the plaintiff.''

Now I will read from the affidavit of the defendant Simpson, filed in Jnuary of this year, in connection with a proposed motion of the defendant to increase the bond.

Mr. ANDERSON.—Your Honor, I object to that. Here is a motion we have not had an opportunity to try it yet, we have not argued it, and that is left open for argument. Now, he proposes to read from an affidavit that we filed in support of that motion. If he wants to argue the motion, I am perfectly willing to argue it, because I think we ought to have an increased bond.

Mr. TOWNSEND.—This is an affidavit on file in this court. It is an admission against interest.

The COURT.—Oh, yes, if it will rise to the dignity of an admission I think it should be heard. The objection is overruled. If not competent or material the Court will disregard it in its decision.

Mr. ANDERSON.—I do not care for it at all,

except that it takes too much time to dispose of this case.

Mr. TOWNSEND.—Beginning on page 1, Mr. Simpson says that at the time this suit was instituted he put on an extra force and worked overtime.

Also that at the time of the injunction they had a contract involving $287,000, and that their profits would have amounted to $43,000.

The next is from the affidavit of Mr. MacGruer, the defendant, made in New York, dated December 29, 1923. I desire [617] to read from page 4. (Reads.)

DEPOSITION OF GEORGE SMITH MAC-GRUER, FOR PLAINTIFF.

GEORGE SMITH MacGRUER, called for the plaintiff, sworn.

Mr. TOWNSEND.—Q. Mr. MacGruer, you are one of the defendants in this case? A. I am.

Q. I show you a letter, apparently on the letterhead of your firm and apparently signed by you, dated June 19, 1922, and addressed to the plaintiff, Mr. Denivelle, and I ask you if you recognize that letter, having written it? A. I do.

Q. Do you recognize your signature attached thereto? A. I do.

Mr. TOWNSEND.—I offer this letter as Plaintiff's Exhibit 17. I suggest it might be copied into the record for convenience.

(The letter was marked Plaintiff's Exhibit 17 and is as follows:)

PLAINTIFF'S EXHIBIT No. 17.

(Letter-head of MacGruer & Simpson.)

"San Francisco, Cal., June 19, 1922.

"Mr. P. E. Denivelle,

280 Golden Gate Ave.,

San Francisco, Calif.

"Dear Sir:

"We have been awarded the contract for all metal furring, lathing, plastering, artificial stone, etc., on the New Biltmore Hotel, Los Angeles, California, per the plans and specifications of Messrs. Schultze and Weaver, Architects, New York City.

"Under the terms of this contract it is proposed to use a cast artificial Travertine Stone in certain portions of the building, namely:

"Basement elevator lobby and stairways adjacent as covered by Addendas 2 and 3.

"Ground floor, architraeve at Telephone Room. [618]

"Main Hotel Lobby, including the elevator lobbies on ground and first floors.

"First Floor Dining Room.

"The above, at present, covers all of the cast artificial Travertine Stone according to the terms of our contract.

"We are in receipt of a letter from the Scofield Engineering and Construction Company enclosing a copy of letter from your Attorney, notifying them of the existence of a certain patent held by you for this character of work and asking them to take the matter up so as to avoid any unnecessary complications in the event that it is the intention to use your process for the manufacture of this cast artificial Travertine Stone.

"In keeping with the above and also our interview with you and your Attorney Mr. Townsend, at the office of Mr. C. L. Patton, our Attorney, on the 16th, may we ask under what terms we can have the privilege of using your process as covered by your Patent #1,212,331 and dated January 16, 1917, so that your interests may be protected?

"As there is a possibility of certain portions of the above-enumerated work to be changed to artificial stone of another character other than cast artificial travertine, may we request, when submitting your proposal or terms, that you segregate same in the following manner:

"1. A price for the right to use your process under the terms of a license for this particular building for the work now contemplated.

"2. A lump sum bid including all metal furring necessary for the erection of the cast artificial Travertine Stone as enumerated above.

"3. A separate bid for the furnishing of all cast artificial Travertine Stone as covered by Proposal #2. This bid is [619] not to include the erection or pointing of same.

"4. A separate bid for the Main Lobby and Elevator Lobbies as shown on Ground and First Floor plans.

"5. A separate bid on Proposal #4 for the furnishing of this and not including the metal fur-

(Deposition of George Smith MacGruer.)
ring, erection and pointing for the Main Hotel Lobby
and Elevator Lobbies on Ground and First Floor.

"6." A separate bid for the dining-room.

"7. A separate bid for the basement elevator
lobby and Stairway.

"8. A separate bid for dining-room in keeping
with Proposal #4.

"9. A separate bid for the Basement Lobby and
Stairway similar to proposal #5.

"Kindly forward us this information at the earliest possible moment and oblige,

"Very truly yours,
"MacGRUER & SIMPSON.
"GEORGE MacGRUER."

In the second paragraph from the bottom of page
one of this letter you state:

"We are in receipt of a letter from the Scofield Engineering and Construction Company
enclosing a copy of letter from your Attorney,
notifying them of the existence of a certain
patent held by you for this character of work
and asking them to take the matter up so as
to avoid any unnecessary complications in the
event that it is the intention to use your process
for the manufacture of this case artificial travertine Stone."

Have you that letter from the Scofield Company?

A. I think we have the copy. They only enclosed
a copy. I informed you of that, I think, at the
meeting in Mr. Patton's office. This letter was
written subsequent to your interview with me.
[620]

(Deposition of George Smith MacGruer.)

Q. That is referred to in the next paragraph of this letter, and I will refer to that in just a moment. Have you the original Scofield letter referred to in the paragraph I have just read?

Mr. ANDERSON.—No, we have not that letter.

Mr. TOWNSEND.—Have you the copy of my letter to the Scofield Company which they sent you with that letter?

Mr. ANDERSON.—Yes, here it is.

Mr. TOWNSEND.—Q. Your counsel has just handed me a copy and states he believes that is the copy that came from the Scofield Company at that time: Is that your recollection?

A. That is my recollection.

Q. However, that copy has some notations on it that were not on my letter.

A. That was made by Mr. Scofield, himself. That was inter-office communication.

Q. I have here a carbon of a letter I sent them. Will you accept my copy in lieu of that?

A. After I compare it.

Q. Yes, assuming the body of the letter is the same.

A. Yes, assuming the body of the letter is the same.

Mr. TOWNSEND.—Subject to any correction that may be found I will offer my own true copy, it having no notation upon it.

The COURT.—Copy of what?

Mr. TOWNSEND.—Of the letter I wrote to the general contractors in Los Angeles.

(Deposition of George Smith MacGruer.)

The WITNESS.—It is in effect the same.

The COURT.—And by Scofield sent to the defendant?

Mr. TOWNSEND.—Yes, your Honor.

The COURT.—What is the object of the offer?

Mr. TOWNSEND.—The object is to show notice.

Mr. ANDERSON.—A copy of the original of which was sent to the defendant. We make no objection that it is a carbon.   [621]

Mr. TOWNSEND.—We ask that it be copied in the record and marked our Exhibit 18.

(The letter was marked Plaintiff's Exhibit 18 and is as follows:)

PLAINTIFF'S EXHIBIT No. 18.

"May 24th, 1922.

"Scofield Engineering & Construction Co.,

Pacific Finance Bldg.,

Los Angeles, Cal.

Attention: Mr. E. H. Scofield.

"Gentlemen:

Re: Paul E. Denivelle Travertine Patents.

"Mr. Denivelle has laid before me the facts and circumstances in connection with his proposal to do the artificial travertine work in connection with the Los Angeles Biltmore Hotel pursuant to the plans and specifications submitted by you, and has also shown me your wire advising that the contract for this work had been let to other parties.

"You are, I suppose, conversant with Mr. Denivelle's patents covering this character of work, and the further fact that these patents have not only been upheld, but broadly construed by the United States Circuit Court of Appeals for this Circuit.

"Manifestly, Mr. Denivelle cannot stand by and see his patents infringed with impunity. Inasmuch as he has but one licensee authorized to do this work and this licensee has no right to sub-license others, we are, therefore, desirous of knowing at once to whom the contract for this work has been let.

"In the event of not hearing from you within a reasonable time, we shall assume that the work contemplated is unauthorized as far as Mr. Denivelle is concerned, and that the letting of the contract constitutes a threat to infringe, giving legal cause for court action.

"While it is not the desire of Mr. Denivelle to engage [622] in litigation, and then only as a last resort, he must have his patent rights respected, particularly where a lifetime of effort on his part has been directed to the bringing of this process to perfection, and in view of the money and time already expended in litigating and upholding these patents. On the other hand, it is assumed that you do not desire to involve your client nor yourselves in unnecessary litigation, the only result of which would be to cause them and yourselves added expense and delay in the event the process of injunction is invoked.

"It is hoped that a full and frank discussion of these matters at this time will have the effect of

(Deposition of George Smith MacGruer.)
removing any misunderstandings that may exist on the part of any of the parties concerned.

"Yours very truly,

"CHAS. E. TOWNSEND,

"CET:GMR. Attorney for Paul E. Denivelle."

Q. At the bottom of the letter of June 19, 1922, Exhibit 17, page 1, you say:

"In keeping with the above and also our interview with you and your Attorney, Mr. Townsend, at the office of Mr. C. L. Patton, our Attorney, on the 16th, may we ask under what terms we can have the privilege of using your process as covered by your patent #1,212,331 and dated January 16, 1917, so that your interests may be protected?"

Will you tell us about that interview?

A. The reason for the writing of that letter came partly from your suggestion and Mr. Patton's. I was influenced by your letter, which I considered was intimidation to the general contractor and to throw obstacles in my way to complete the contract.

Mr. TOWNSEND.—I move, your Honor, that the opinion part of the answer be stricken out as not responsive and as expressing an opinion. [623]

The COURT.—If that is in the answer, let it be stricken.

Mr. TOWNSEND.—Q. What was said and done at that meeting on the 16th?

A. Nothing beyond the fact that you tried to impress upon me that Denivelle had a valid patent, which I questioned.

(Deposition of George Smith MacGruer.)

Q. And as a result of that interview you submitted this?

A. As a result of that interview, at your suggestion, along with Mr. Patton's, I wrote this letter, so that we could get down to a basis of possibly arriving at some conclusion.

Q. Did you get a reply from Mr. Denivelle?

A. I did, I received a firm bid.

Q. Have you the original letter from Mr. Denivelle?

A. I think it has been submitted.

Mr. ANDERSON.—Here it is.

Mr. TOWNSEND.—Q. Your counsel has submitted a letter—two letters, the first of three pages and the second of one sheet. The first one is dated June 26, 1922, from Mr. Denivelle to your firm, and the second being dated June 28, 1922, similarly signed and addressed. I ask that these be marked and received in evidence respectively as Plaintiff's Exhibits 19 and 20, and copied into the record at this point.

(The letters were marked, respectively, Plaintiff's Exhibits 19 and 20. Plaintiff's Exhibit 19 is as follows:)

PLAINTIFF'S EXHIBIT No. 19.
(Letter-head of Paul E. Denivelle.)

June 26, 1922.

"MacGruer & Simpson,
266 Tehama Street
San Francisco, Calif.

"Gentlemen:

"Re: New Biltmore Hotel, Los Angeles.

"In accordance with your letter of June 19 defining the portions of above building in which it is proposed to use cast imitation travertine stone, am submitting herewith my figures [624] for furnishing and erecting the work complete for the following as described in your letter.

" 'Basement elevator lobby and stairways adjacent as covered by Addendas 2 and 3.'

" 'Ground Floor, architraeve at Telephone Room.'

" 'Main Hotel Lobby, including the elevator lobbies on ground and first floors.'

" 'First Floor Dining Room.'

"As to the enumerated schedule contained in your other communication with several requests numbered 1 to 9, I do not see my way clear to supply all of the information requested. I have given considerable thought to these different requests with the following conclusions:

"*Request No. 1.* 'A price for the right to use your process under the terms of a license for this particular building for the work now contemplated.'

"I cannot see my way clear to quote you acceptable terms for license at this time as this would involve a division of responsibility for the ultimate result in the work.

"*Request No. 2.* 'A lump sum bid including all metal furring necessary for the erection of the cast artificial travertine stone as enumerated above.'

"This is complied with in the bid contained herewith.

"*Request No. 3.* 'A separate bid for the furnishing of all cast artificial travertine stone as covered by Proposal #2. This bid is not to include the erection or pointing of same.'

"This likewise involves a division of responsibility which for practical reasons cannot be granted as said imitation travertine stone is never completed as a fabricated article until it has been erected and finished.

"*Request No. 4.* 'A separate bid for the Main Lobby and Elevator Lobbies as shown on Ground and First Floor plans.' [625]

"A separate figure for this is furnished herewith.

"*Request No. 5.* 'A separate bid on proposal #4 for the furnishing of this and not including the metal furring, erection and pointing for the Main Hotel Lobby and Elevator Lobbies on Ground First Floor.'

"Cannot be complied with for the same reasons as pertaining to No. 3.

"*Request No. 6.* 'A separate bid for the Dining Room.'

"A separate bid is contained herewith.

"*Request No. 7.* 'A separate bid for the Basement Elevator Lobby and Stairway.'

"A separate bid is contained herewith.

"*Request No. 8.* 'A separate bid for Dining Room in keeping with Proposal No. 5.'

"Cannot be complied with for the reasons pertaining to No. 3.

"*Request No. 9.* 'A separate bid for the Basement Lobby and Stairway similar to Proposal #5.'

"Cannot be complied with for the reasons pertaining to No. 3.

"I submit herewith my proposal to furnish, execute, and erect (Including any incidental furring required therefor) my No. 4 Special imitation travertine stone finished and complete in every respect per the aforesaid schedule and according to your request No. 2 comprising that portion of your contract for the sum of FORTY–ONE THOUSAND FIVE HUNDRED ($41,500.00.) DOLLARS.

"Contained in the foregoing are the following amounts, which, if separated would be as follows:

Request No. 4, Main Lobby and Elevator

    Lobby $25,000.00

Request No. 6, Dining Room 18,000.00

Request No. 7, Basement Elevator Lobby

    and Stairway 2,000.00

"The foregoing figures do not include any models of [626] ornament which I understood are to be provided by others under the head of modeling.

"In complying with your request and submitting figures as above, it is, of course, without prejudice to the fact that the artificial travertine which I contemplate using is not only covered by patent on the product but the method as well is also protected.

Inasmuch as this is a patented article, I cannot concede that it is open to public bidding.

"On the other hand, the fact that the Product and Method are patented has had no bearing on the figures given you above.

"As previously explained to you, my object in patenting my Artificial Travertine and my Process was primarily to protect the architect and his clients who see fit to use this material, and to guarantee and to maintain the standard of quality as well as to prevent, by legal means, cheap and unworthy imitations. For the same reason I have felt justified in exercising proper precautions and restraint in the issuance of licenses.

"It is understood as a part of this proposal that, in the event of its acceptance, I shall be awarded all imitation travertine that shall be contained in your contract and as there may be some deductions therefrom, likewise shall I be awarded any portions as may be added later.

"Trusting that the above may be acceptable to both yourselves and your clients, I remain,

"Very truly yours,

"PED:W.   PAUL E. DENIVELLE."

(Plaintiff's Exhibit 20, on the letter-head of Paul E. Denivelle, is as follows:)

(Deposition of George Smith MacGruer.)
PLAINTIFF'S EXHIBIT No. 20.

"June 28, 1922.

"MacGruer & Simpson
266 Tehama Street
San Francisco, Calif.

"Gentlemen: [627]

"Re: New Biltmore Hotel, Los Angeles.

"Please be advised that in my proposal of the 26th I omitted to specifically state that I did not include scaffolding, my reason being that it was obvious that you would require scaffolding for ceiling. It would be a useless added expense for me to include it likewise.

"Very truly yours,
"PED:W.   PAUL E. DENIVELLE."

The COURT.—Are these for the purpose of notice?

Mr. TOWNSEND.—Notice and negotiations and it bears on the question of deliberate infringement.

Q. How soon after the letters to which we have referred did you begin the work on the Biltmore?

A. It was months afterwards, some considerable long time.

Q. And the work was in progress at the time the suit was brought?

A. The work was in progress; it was practically completed.

Mr. TOWNSEND.—That is all.

Cross-examination

Mr. ANDERSON.—Q. Did you have any conver-

(Deposition of George Smith MacGruer.)
sation with Mr. Denivelle at this meeting that Mr.
Townsend has asked you about?

A. The only conversation was a sort of cross
questioning back and forth, in which he intimated
to me that I was going to go along and that I knew
of his patent, and I stated that I didn't think he
had a patent, and I was still of that opinion. He
stated, "You have been doing this thing for a long
time and you have been trying to get around this
patent for a long time." I said, "I don't see any
need of getting around the patent, I don't think
there is any patent.

Q. And at that time had you devised your process, the process of making the artificial travertine
which you employed in the [628] Biltmore
Hotel?

A. We had, and Mr. Denivelle's licensee in Southern California had been in our office and had seen
it.

Q. And did you so advise Mr. Denivelle at that
interview?

A. We did advise his licensee, and his licensee
told us he did not think Mr. Denivelle's patent was
worth much based on this process.

Redirect Examination.

Mr. TOWNSEND.—Q. When you say you did
not believe that Mr. Denivelle had a patent, what
do you mean by that?

A. I didn't believe he had a valid patent.

Q. You knew that he had a patent?

A. I knew that he had a patent, yes.

(Deposition of George Smith MacGruer.)

Q. And you knew of the litigation that had been held over the patent?

A. I knew in a general way, yes.

Q. You didn't mean to infer in your cross-examination that you mentioned to us that you had gotten up a process which you thought—

A. I said I mentioned it to your licensee, who visited my office.

Q. Well, we don't know anything about that. I am talking about this meeting.

A. Yes, we did tell you in the office of Mr. Patton.

Q. Do you mean to say—

A. I certainly did.

The COURT.—Let counsel finish his question.

Mr. TOWNSEND.—Q. Do you mean to say that you mentioned to Mr. Denivelle and myself that you had applied for a patent?

A. No, we did not say we applied for a patent. If you will recall the conversation, Mr. Townsend, when I stated to Mr. Denivelle that we were now trying to get away from the semi-dry process, and we believed we had done it, Mr. Denivelle put a menacing finger toward me and said, "You have been doing this for a long time, but you won't get away with it." [629]

Q. As far as you went at that time was this: You stated to us you were trying to get around the Denivelle patent.

A. I said we were trying to get away from the semi-dry process which I stated to you at that time

(Deposition of George Smith MacGruer.)
was the only thing I thought he had of any possibility in his patent, if the patent was valid.

Q. You did not state to us at that time that you had filed an application, did you?

A. No, it was not necessary.

Q. What I want to make clear is this: You did not show us any sample of what you had.

A. We showed your licensee prior to that interview.

Mr. TOWNSEND.—I move that that be stricken out, your Honor, as not responsive.

A. (Continuing.) He was representing the Denivelle people.

The COURT.—Let it stand. It is not worth while striking it out. If it is not competent or material the Court gives it no consideration. Proceed with your questioning.

Mr. TOWNSEND.—Q. Did you show us any samples that you had?

A. We could not show it in the office of the attorney, he didn't ask for it.

Q. You didn't show it?

A. We didn't show it there.

DEPOSITION OF PAUL E. DENIVELLE, FOR PLAINTIFF.

PAUL E. DENIVELLE, called for the plaintiff, sworn.

Mr. TOWNSEND.—Q. You are the plaintiff in this case, Mr. Denivelle?   A. I am.

(Deposition of Paul E. Denivelle.)

Q. Do you know the defendants, or either of them? A. I know them both, yes.

Q. When did you first become acquainted with them?

A. In the latter part of 1913 and 1914, mainly.

Q. Did they do any artificial travertine work on any of the P. P. [630] I. E. buildings?

A. On Machinery Hall, yes.

Q. When was that work done?

A. That was begun, their part of it was begun in the latter part of 1913, and completed in 1914.

Q. Under whose direction was that work done?

A. Under mine and the demonstrators that were under me.

Q. Did you come in contact with these gentlemen, or either of them, or with the workmen during that work? A. Very frequently.

Q. Will you tell us of your relations and contact with the defendants at that time?

A. Well, the first contact that I had with them was due to the fact that the men under me whom we sent them for preliminary instruction and co-operation came back and reported to me that they were not getting it, and I naturally went over to see them and tried to aid them, and that was the beginning of our negotiations, toward their being taught that which they said later to the exposition was totally impossible. They seemed to think that I was a dreamer, that I did not know what I was talking about, that I was seeking to do things which they seemingly did not understand.

(Deposition of Paul E. Denivelle.)

Mr. ANDERSON.—I object to that.

The COURT.—That is not involved here. He has gone far enough. You had better question him.

Mr. TOWNSEND.—Q. Did you meet with co-operation or did you meet with opposition on their part in putting your process into effect?

A. Opposition, mainly.

Mr. ANDERSON.—I object to that as asking for an expression of opinion. He should state what happened, in order that your Honor may draw the conclusion as to whether he met with co-operation or opposition.

The COURT.—You are not suing for any breach of contract, or anything? [631]

Mr. TOWNSEND.—No.

The COURT.—What do you want to show?

Mr. TOWNSEND.—This is to show information on the part of the defendant of the travertine process.

The COURT.—You may show that.

Mr. TOWNSEND.—I think that is shown sufficiently.

Q. At the close of the Exposition, were there any particular ceremonies in connection with the work that you had done?

Mr. ANDERSON.—I object to that as immaterial, irrelevant and incompetent to any issue in this case.

The COURT.—What is the object?

Mr. TOWNSEND.—Public recognition. It will not take but a moment.

(Deposition of Paul E. Denivelle.)

The COURT.—Let him answer. If not material or competent it will not be regarded.

A. There was on the 18th of March, 1915.

Mr. TOWNSEND.—Q. What was it?

A. The president of the Exposition set aside the 18th, the afternoon of the 18th as Travertine Day, for the purpose of doing me honor for my contribution to the Exposition.

Q. Did you receive any especial note of recognition?

A. I was presented, after addresses by the various heads, including the President, an address by the president of the Exposition, with a bronze plaque testifying to my services.

Q. Anything additional to that?

A. Well, that was the objective. There were testimonial addresses made, as I say, by the various heads of the Exposition; as I remember, the chief architect especially made a very complimentary address, more or less deserved, possibly.

Q. I thought there was a medal in connection with it?

A. I said a bronze plaque; later I received the Gold Diploma of [632] the Exposition, and the highest honors that the Exposition could award, namely, the gold medal.

Q. Have you put your process in practice in this city in any large or extensive way, and if so, where, and what.

A. Yes, first in the Civic Center Library, in San Francisco, and since then in the Federal Reserve

(Deposition of Paul E. Denivelle.)
Bank Building, in the Anglo Bank Building, and
some others; those are the outstanding features.

Q. What is the extent, speaking in money terms,
of the job that was recently done in the Anglo
Bank?   A. Around $110,000, I think.

Q. For the artificial travertine?

A. For the artificial travertine work—mainly constituting artificial travertine work.

Q. Have you a sample of the artificial travertine
you placed in any of these buildings, in court?

A. I have one I placed in the Civic Center
Library, a typical piece. That is a typical piece
taken from the work which was being done at the
time in the Civic Center Library.

Q. Is this one of the original slabs made for that
work?

A. It is one of the original slabs made for that
work.

Q. What date was that?

A. That was in the latter part of 1913.

Q. The Civic Center Library?

A. The Civic Center Library—oh, no, I mean
1916, and the early part of 1917.

Mr. TOWNSEND.—I offer this slab just referred
to as Plaintiff's Exhibit 21.

(The slab was marked Plaintiff's Exhibit 21.)

Q. Have you a sample of natural travertine?

A. Yes, I have one here in court.

Mr. TOWNSEND.—This slab referred to is of-
ered as Plaintiff's Exhibit 22.

(Deposition of Paul E. Denivelle.)

(The slab was marked Plaintiff's Exhibit 22.)
[633]

The COURT.—They are in wood frames?

A. Yes, they are in wood frames.

Mr. TOWNSEND.—They are hard to handle otherwise they are liable to break.

The WITNESS.—Especially the natural ones are liable to break; that is a typical piece of Roman travertine, the natural Roman travertine.

Q. Have you read or have you heard read the extracts to which I referred from the depositions of the defendants relating to the Biltmore job and the process followed by the defendants in providing the artificial travertine for that job?

A. I have.

Q. Have you seen the Biltmore Hotel?

A. I have.

Q. Since it was finished?

A. Since it was finished.

Q. How recently?

A. About 30 days ago, I think, about the 19th of last month, the 19 of March.

Q. Have you been familiar with the artificial travertine, so-called artificial travertine that was made by defendant Ceriat in the Los Angeles cases referred to and held to be an infringement?

A. Yes.

Q. Exhibits 14 and 15 which were Exhibits "A" and "F" in the Los Angeles case, do you recognize those? A. I believe I do.

Mr. ANDERSON.—If they are in fact Exhibits

(Deposition of Paul E. Denivelle.)

"A" and "F" in the previous case the record will show it.

Mr. TOWNSEND.—I want to know if this witness recognizes them as exhibits in that case.

A. I do.

Q. Have you examined the defendants' work on the Biltmore job illustrated by Exhibits 1 and 2 here in evidence?   A. I have.

Q. On the hearing of the motion for preliminary injunction to which we have referred, which was heard before Judge Van Fleet, did you make samples according to your process for the purpose [634] of that case?

A. I submitted samples.

Mr. ANDERSON.—I object to that as not material.

Mr. TOWNSEND.—They are filed in court and I am asking him if he made them.

The COURT.—It is a mere preliminary question. He may answer. The objection iss overruled.

Mr. TOWNSEND.—I show you what were marked on the preliminary motion proceedings as Plaintiff's Exhibits "C" and "D," and ask you if you recognize those as your work?

A. I do.

Mr. TOWNSEND.—I will ask that the former Exhibit "C" be marked and received in evidence in this case as Plaintiff's Exhibit 23.

(The exhibit was marked Plaintiff's Exhibit 23.)

Mr. ANDERSON.—Were they exhibits in the motions for preliminary injunction?

(Deposition of Paul E. Denivelle.)

Mr. TOWNSEND.—Yes.

Mr. ANDERSON.—Filed by the plaintiff?

Mr. TOWNSEND.—Filed by the plaintiff with the clerk. And Exhibit "D" I ask to be marked Plaintiff's Exhibit 24.

(The exhibit was marked Plaintiff's Exhibit 24.)

Q. Now, will you please refer to these various samples of artificial travertine here before you and compare them as to the manner of production, texture, and general effect when in place as a wall surface, and in this connection I direct your attention particularly to Exhibits 1, 2, 14, 15, 21, 22, 23 and 24.

A. They are all examples of the same process or method, they are the same in kind; they are different varieties, in results, but substantially the same in so far as their characteristics are concerned. They vary in degree, only. Do you want me to analyze them?

Q. Yes, please.

A. They are all constructed with what you call [635] a cementitious structure the object of which is to create a certain decorative quality of wall surface, and the characteristics of each are a series of veins or stria that are laid on a mould or form and separated either by means of a brush or directly poured from a spout or a series of spouts or other device, and then a dry or semi-dry or crumply type of material interposed over these veins and especially in the surface between the veins, and then backed by a cementitious mass or plastic substance

(Deposition of Paul E. Denivelle.)
that will bind the veins in part with the binding
material, and sometimes they are backed with a
solid substance for greater reinforcement, but those
are the principal characteristics.

Q. How about the wall surface effect when
erected?

A. The wall surface effect when erected of each
and every one of them being taken in large areas,
for instance, they have a certain decorative effect
that has come to be recognized as of especial value
under the head of texture. They all more or less
have a certain artistic quality in varying degrees,
and that has been found desirable from the standpoint of architects and the public at large.

Q. What have you to say in regard to the production of the slabs, either of your own method or
the Ceriat method, or the present defendants'
method, in producing voids?

A. The voids in each and every case are produced by the use of a lumpy substance that is placed
over these veins in such manner as to keep certain
portions of the mould out of contact with the
material itself, and then, as I say, afterwards being
bound together by cementitious or plastic substance
that is interposed over the back of the vein.

Q. Do you recall how the work was done in the
Ceriat case, the Los Angeles case?

A. I do. [636]

Q. Just briefly explain.

Mr. ANDERSON.—I object to having this witness testifying to something that is in the record

(Deposition of Paul E. Denivelle.)

in one of the exhibits that has been introduced in this case, a certified copy of the record.

Mr. TOWNSEND.—I withdraw the question.

Q. Do you know what the method of Ceriat was?

A. I do.

Q. Take the defendants' suggested method of using calcium carbide on veins and then backed up with material, and state your comparison of that to the method that you have employed and do employ.

A. It is substantially the same. In the preliminary work, in travertine, I tried similar substances such as quicklime, such as unslacked lime in a crumbly form; I also tried bicarbonate of soda, which had been partly dampened so as to become lumpy.

Mr. ANDERSON.—I object to what this witness has tried. The question is whether any of these things are made in accordance with thiss patent, not what he has tried to do, or what he has done outside of his patent.

Mr. TOWNSEND.—May the witness answer the question and not be interrupted?

Mr. ANDERSON.—I object to its going into the record.

The COURT.—I think you may proceed briefly. So far as not competent, the Court will not regard it.

A. I will try to be as brief as possible. I repeat that they are all substantially the same in method and process, they are created by the same

(Deposition of Paul E. Denivelle.)

means, the same steps, and there is practically no variation except in the degree of the result. There may be a slight variation in the method, but the steps to the result are exactly. the same. I don't know as I could make it [637] any clearer than that.

Q. When working with a brush or a can provided with spouts, or with a brush or a cone, will you briefly tell us how you proceed to form the vein and whether or not there is any difference?

Mr. ANDERSON.—That is explained in his patent and I object to it.

The COURT.—He may proceed.

A. We place the so-called vein material in a can —this is one example; I have others; at the exposition we had another type. It is poured over the form in this manner so as to provide a series of separated lines on the mould.

Mr. TOWNSEND.—Q. These lines are of colored cement?

A. These lines are all colored of a cementitious nature.

Q. But of a little different color than the body?

A. Slightly different color. The objective usually is to provide a slightly different color or tone than the body material of the mass. They are afterward sometimes, as in this instance and that—

Q. You mean, I presume, exhibits 1 and 2

A. Yes—they are separated more definitely by means of a brush or a cone, or something which will divide this into more definite lines. Oevr that

(Deposition of Paul E. Denivelle.)

is placed a crumply or lumpy mass sprinkled in varying degrees of thickness—these steps follow in a
certain type of sequence, so that the surface material will begin to set sufficiently so that it may hold
its form; as I say the crumply mass is then placed
on top of these veins and then a cementitious material is again placed over this mass and the voids,
of course, are produced by the fact that the crumply
material or lumpy material has kept the mould out
of contact, it being made this way.

Q. With the surface down?

A. Yes, with the surface down— [638] that
this lumpy material has kept that material out of
contact with the face of the mold, and it provides
a series of voids of varying degree, in accordance
with the method manipulation that has been
adopted, and the skill of course of the operator.

Q. If you used lumpy unslacked carbide, do I
understand that that keeps the cementitious back
out of contact with the face of the mould?

A. Yes, absolutely.

Mr. ANDERSON.—I object to that as leading.

The COURT.—Yes, but I think he may answer.

A. It keeps it out of contact with the face of
the mould.

Mr. TOWNSEND.—Is it clear to your Honor,
that in making the slab it is face down?

The WITNESS.—It is inverted.

The COURT.—It was not. Now that you say
it, it is clear.

The WITNESS.—I tried to make that clear.

(Deposition of Paul E. Denivelle.)

The COURT.—Very well, proceed.

Mr. TOWNSEND.—They take a mould, as the witness has explained.

The WITNESS.—Of that kind.

Mr. TOWNSEND.—Like Exhibit 9 here.

Q. Now just run through it for the Court.

A. Taking the mould, there are sides to this mould which are not in place at the present time; they are somewhere in court. There are detachable sides to this mould, and if you place one of them in place his Honor will understand what it means. These are the mould parts, and they are placed in their respective positions, where they belong. I think that belongs here. These are adjustable detachable sides; the material being placed in this can or receptacle is poured over the face of the mould with a certain degree of speed in operation, according to the density [639] of the striae, or veins, as they have been called. Then sometimes we develop these lines before introducing the crumply material by separating them, either longitudinally or along their path, and furthermore, for greater refinement, use brushes and break up these lines before introducing the crumply material, in order to produce serrated edges so that they will not be as regular as is sometimes shown in some of these samples, for example, to produce the refinement that occurs here.

Q. In Exhibit 21, of the Civic Center Library?

A. Yes, which, of course, resembles the natural travertine more closely and is a very much more

(Deposition of Paul E. Denivelle.)

refined product. As I say, it is according to the skill of the operator as to what his result will be, and as to the proper application of the method or otherwise.

Q. Having drawn your lines, will you explain the next step?

A. The next step is to sprinkle this lumpy material and then over that to place a cementitious material to bind the whole thing in part so as to form a porous structure, that is, partly solid and partly porous, the object being to produce a certain decorative quality. It has a series of serrated voids of varying consistency and gives the impression, when properly executed, of being voids that continue clear through the mass, as is represented in the natural Roman travertine stone, which sometimes has these voids go through the mass to such an extent that you can hardly handle the piece, as is the case in this.

Q. In regard to the meeting on June 16, 1922, in Mr. Patton's office, at which time, the correspondence shows, Mr. MacGruer, and yourself, and others were present, will you briefly tell us what took place, and the object of that meeting? [640]

A. Mr. MacGruer wanted to find out under what arrangement he could proceed with his work, and do it in accordance with my patent, he seemingly having no other method of doing it at that time. He wanted to know if he could go ahead on a royalty basis, and we discussed the question of royalty, but I pointed out to him that my main object was to

(Deposition of Paul E. Denivelle.)

maintain a standard of quality in connection with my product, so as not to depreciate the value of my patent or my patented product, and that that was my main interest, and for that reason I could not consent at that time, and I told him that I was not satisfied that he could produce a product that would be satisfactory in its standard to me, and that would not depreciate the value of my product. As a result of that conference, he asked me to submit a bid for the travertine portion of his contract on the Biltmore Hotel, and I told him if he would put his request in writing so that it would be definite in form, I would endeavor to do so, which he later did, and I submitted a bid accordingly.

Q. Did you receive any reply to that letter submitting a bid?

A. I have no recollection of his having given it any notice.

Q. As far as you know, there was no reply?

A. My files do not show any reply.

Q. As I understand, if you had given him a license to do the work and pay a royalty, it would have meant that he would have done the work: Is that right?   A. Exactly.

Q. And to that you had objection?

A. I did for the reason stated.

Q. That you desired to maintain the standard of quality?   A. Absolutely.

Mr. TOWNSEND.—That is all.   [641]

(Deposition of Paul E. Denivelle.)

Cross-examination.

Mr. ANDERSON.—Q. You have given licenses, however, under your patent, have you not?

A. I have, Mr. Anderson.

Q. You have?   A. Yes.

Q. To whom?

A. When you say "given," you mean arranged for a license?

Q. Yes.   A. Yes.

Q. To whom?

A. Oh, I don't know that I could recall; my principal licensee and the only one of importance was the concern down in Los Angeles who were co-plaintiffs with me in the former case.

Q. They had a license?

A. They had a license to manufacture and produce under my patent.

Q. At this conference in Mr. Patton's office, did not Mr. MacGruer tell you that he had been working to devise a method of making artificial travertine which would be outside of your patent?

A. Not in any such language, or not conveying any such impression.

Q. Do you mean to say that he did not convey to you the idea that he thought he could make travertine regardless of your patent, something that would not be within your patent?

A. I would not be surprised as to what he thought, but he did not make any such statement.

Q. I ask you whether he conveyed that idea to you.   A. No, not to my recollection.

(Deposition of Paul E. Denivelle.)

Q. Now, do you know how these defendants made their imitation travertine in the Biltmore Hotel job? A. I do.

Q. Will you describe it to the Court?

A. Well, I think I have once.

The COURT.—Describe it again. I am not clear in my recollection of it.

A. All right. They laid a series of lines [642] or veins on an upturned mould surface—poured or laid—they afterwards divided these lines with a cone or something of that sort. They then used a lumpy calcium carbide in crumply form and sprinkled it over these veins and over that they poured the binder or a coat of cementitious plaster; in this instance, it was plaster that was used, colored plaster, over these veins, to bind the surface mass, and then I believe they backed it up with fiber plaster of paris reinforcement.

Q. You did not see the defendants make it in that way, did you? A. Personally, no.

Q. Now, what is the action of calcium carbide, assuming that was used by the defendants, in the manner in which you have described?

A. Calcium carbide would, when coming in contact with the moisture, proceed to start slacking, and by the time that that cementitious mass that had been placed over it had set or stiffened up, which might be anywhere from twenty minutes to an hour or more, that slacking process would have left an ash in these holes or voids, and by this slacking process or this decomposition of the calcium

(Deposition of Paul E. Denivelle.)

carbide these voids would automatically be left in the surface by keeping the surface of the mould out of contact with the material that constituted the slab.

Q. Do you think that is the primary object of using calcium carbide?   A. I certainly do.

Q. Is it true, Mr. Denivelle, that calcium carbide generates a gas?

A. Undoubtedly it does for illumination purposes, mainly.

Q. I mean in the process as used by the defendants.

A. I do not believe that was the object.

Q. I asked you, do you understand that its action was to generate a gas?   A. In part, yes.

Q. And that generated gas pours along the surface in contact [643] with the face of the mould and up into the mass, does it?

A. It may to some extent. I question it very much. I do not think it would act very differently from what I said.

Q. You won't admit that the calcuim carbide being acted upon by the moist plaster body generates a gas quick by its expansion, pours along the surface of the mass and into the surface and forms this volcanic effect?

A. I question that. It may in a minor degree.

Q. Did you ever try it?

A. Not calcium carbide, no. I have tried other substances that have the same action.

Q. You are prepared to admit, however, Mr.

(Deposition of Paul E. Denivelle.)

Denivelle, that this calcium carbide which you call a loose, lumpy material—I understand that is what you meant by referring to it as loose, lumpy material?   A. Yes.

Q. Is entirely consumed and does not remain as a part of the cast block: Isn't that true?

A. It becomes an ash.

Q. And the ash blows out or is washed out of the openings after the block is set?   A. It should be.

Q. So that it forms no part of the completed cast block?

A. I think in part it does remain—it does not slack perfectly; frequently it forms a part of the cast block. I have found evidences in the defendants' samples of pieces of carbide that were unslacked and were part of the mass.

Q. That would not form a void, would it?

A. Not in that particular instance; it would be a part of the mass, just as the loose crumply material might.

Q. In other words, if you threw a lot of pebbles on the face of the mould and then poured in your plaster body, you would not call that a piece of travertine made in accordance with your process?

A. Not necessarily. It might make a piece as good as [644] some of these that we have here.

Q. But the fact that the pebbles were loose and lumpy, they would not give the porous effect, if you poured your plastic mass over the pebbles, would it?

(Deposition of Paul E. Denivelle.)

A. It depends whether they kept the surface of the mould out of contact with the material.

Q. Wherever there was a pebble, the surface of the material would be out of contact with the plastic material upon the opposite side of that pebble, from the face of the mould, would it not?

A. In part—possibly alongside of it.

Q. That would not make artificial travertine, would it?

A. It might make as good samples as some of these.

Q. You want the Court to understand, do you, that taking a mould and laying on the face of it some lines of plastic cement, and then laying between those lines some loose pebbles, and then pouring into that mould the plastic body mass that you would thereby produce a piece of material imitating travertine?

Mr. TOWNSEND.—If your Honor please, I object to that as a hypothetical question. The patent has to do with loose, crumply material.

The COURT.—I know, but he is cross-examining now to determine the expert's knowledge of the method. He may answer.

A. I mean to say, Mr. Anderson, if I can make it clear, that I could take any loose, lumpy, crumbly material or any material of that sort and produce as good replicas of travertine as some of these exhibits here. Is that plain?

Q. That may be very interesting, but it is not an answer to the question.

(Deposition of Paul E. Denivelle.)

The COURT.—Read it.

(Last question repeated by the reporter.)

A. Pebbles used in the same sense could be made to produce a [645] certain type of void if placed between.

Q. You still have not answered my question.

A. If the material that was placed in back of these pebbles was sufficiently stiff it might produce a similar result. I am not going to say it will produce travertine, necessarily, no.

Q. You know it would not, don't you?

A. I don't know anything of that sort, Mr. Anderson.

Q. You do know something about your patent, however, don't you?

A. I did not hear the question?

Q. You do know something about your own patent, don't you?   A. I hope so.

Q. Now, the loose, lumpy, crumbly material intended to be set forth in your patent is made of cement and plaster, is it?

A. If found the most desirable medium, yes.

Q. What did you intend to define by that term in your patent?

Mr. TOWNSEND.—Your Honor, that is not cross-examination. We have not asked him anything about the patent. The patent is in evidence. He was put on to prove certain specific facts. This transgresses the bounds of cross-examination.

Mr. ANDERSON.—It seems to me you covered a broad, wide field. You started in from the very in-

(Deposition of Paul E. Denivelle.)

ception of this work in New York and carried him out here and gave him a gold medal and hung a sash on him. It seems to me I have considerable latitude on this cross-examination.

The COURT.—I think he may answer. He has been asked to compare these processes and methods of making these different samples. He may inquire. In so far as not competent or not material the Court will give it no consideration in making up its decision. For the sake of the record the objection will be overruled and an exception noted. [646]

Q. Do you want to see the patent, or do you remember it? A. No.

The COURT.—Well, proceed.

A. I meant to provide a mixture of a cementitious mass that would contain just sufficient moisture to keep it from becoming plastic and so as to create what would form more or less what Mr. Anderson has just called pebbles, which when placed over this would leave a certain part of the portions of the mould between these veins out of contact with material acted as a binder. Is that an answer, your Honor?

Mr. ANDERSON.—Q. And that crumbly material remains in and forms part of the completed casting, does it not?

A. In part only. We always have to clean off a certain residue of that crumbly material from the mould after we have removed the cast. We have

(Deposition of Paul E. Denivelle.)
to especially where a coarse mixture is used, such as
in some of these exhibits, as this one, for instance.

Mr. TOWNSEND.—21.

A. We had to clean the mould of the excess of
crumbly material; a portion of it became a part of
the mass, not exactly all of it.

Mr. ANDERSON.—Q. You did clean the moulds?

A. I removed from the moulds the residue of the
excess of the crumbly material between those veins
that had not become a part of the mass.

Q. By the term "mould" you mean the cast?

A. That upturned form would represent the
mould. That does not become a part of the cast,
if you want to put it that way.

Q. So that when you take a cast out you find on
the surface of the mould a few particles of plaster:
Is that it?

A. Especially where the texture is coarse—not
necessarily a few particles.

Q. But this loose, crumbly material that you put
in over the [647] veins is intended to become a
part of that cast block of travertine, is it not?

A. That portion which is to give a certain characteristic becomes a part of the mass, and the rest
drops out and leaves voids that would not otherwise occur.

Q. Now, in the defendants' process, however, the
only thing left of this so-called loose, crumbly material, calcium carbide, is ash, is it not?   A. Yes.

Q. When you brush out or wash out the ash, none

(Deposition of Paul E. Denivelle.)

of the loose, crumbly material is left on the cast block?

A. Unless there are unslacked portions of calcium carbide.

Q. That is an improbability, that such would be left, isn't it?

A. Not necessarily; they are quite common.

Q. You came out here from New York for what purpose?

Mr. TOWNSEND.—If your Honor please, we did not go into the early history, earlier than 1913, when I asked him when he had first met the defendant. I do not believe that the inquiry should go back of that at the present time. It may be that we will want to go into that part of the history in rebuttal if the gentleman impeaches the finding of our Circuit Court of Appeals.

The COURT.—I do not know as to whether you asked the witness about his coming out.

Mr. TOWNSEND.—I did not.

Mr. ANDERSON.—That was in your statement.

Mr. TOWNSEND.—That was in my statement.

The COURT.—It might have been in counsel's statement. There was nothing about it in the interrogation of the witness. He started off with contact between the parties at the fair buildings in 1913 and from there on.

Mr. ANDERSON.—I would like to have an answer to the question.

The COURT.—I will sustain the objection as not proper cross-examination. [648]

(Deposition of Paul E. Denivelle.)

Mr. ANDERSON.—Does your Honor rule it out?

The COURT.—Yes.

Mr. ANDERSON.—I note an exception.

The COURT.—It will be noted.

Mr. ANDERSON.—I am through with my cross-examination.

Redirect Examination.

Mr. TOWNSEND.—Q. Mr. Denivelle, in the artificial travertine of defendants that you have seen in place in the Biltmore Hotel, have you seen any evidences of remaining calcium carbide in the voids?

A. Quite some.

Mr. TOWNSEND.—That is all.

Recross-examination.

Mr. ANDERSON.—Q. Just a loose ash?

A. No, hard lumps.

Q. Are you sure of that?   A. Absolutely.

Mr. TOWNSEND.—Plaintiff rests.

The COURT.—Proceed with the defense.

Mr. ANDERSON.—If your Honor please: Your Honor has not been shown the patent in suit, nor has it been explained to you. It undoubtedly may seem strange that we come out here after this patent *has sustained* by the Court of Appeals for this Circuit and we still attack the validity of this patent practically on the same job of work that was involved in the prior case, but we have taken testimony to prove what was insufficiently treated in the prior case; that this Pennsylvania job was done by Mr. Denivelle before he came to California in 1913; the fact that it was completed in 1909 or 1910 was a public use and a sale by that embodiment of his invention. The only evidence in that prior case wherein this Pennsylvania job is characterized as an experiment, is that of Mr. Denivelle, [649] himself. You can look through that record from start to finish and the only evidence you will find in which anyone says that this was an experiment was that of Mr. Denivelle.

Now, this application for patent was filed in October, 1915, and the depositions which we have taken will conclusively prove the conditions under which Mr. Denivelle obtained that Pennsylvania contract in competition with other bidders, bidding on specifications that were prepared by the architects and furnished to him, calling for artificial travertine; and when the job was finished and he got his money, he came out here to California, but before coming out here, based upon this monumental job which he did in the Pennsylvania Station, he was called upon by other contractors to do other work of the same kind, which he did; and that work being done more than two years before he filed his application.

Now, I desire to offer in evidence the depositions which we have taken in New York, the first being the deposition of Jacob M. Krafft; the deposition of Carl Henry Meyn, taken in New York, the deposition of Richmond H. Shreve, taken in New York, the deposition of Burt L. Fenner, taken in New York, the deposition of Vance W. Torbert, taken in New York, the deposition of Frank A. Whipple, taken in New York, the deposition of Jules F. Gayler, taken in New York, the deposition of Daniel T. Webster, taken in New York, the deposition of William Steele Cooke, taken in New York, the deposition of L. S. Massimo, the deposition of J. A. Fincke, the deposition of H. A. Cousins, the deposition of Tommaso V. Coronato, the deposition of Frank John Morkel, the deposition of Peter G. Moore, Jr., the deposition of Walter H. Clough, deposition of Clay M. McClure, deposition of Samuel L. Kriney, deposition of [650] Randolph H. Almiroty, deposition of Philip Liva, deposition of Walter L. Hopkins, deposition of Davis Brown, deposition of Patrick J. Durkin.

I also offer the various exhibits which are referred to in some of these depositions, and which were offered at the time the depositions were taken. The first exhibit is a copy of the specifications for artificial stonework for the Pennsylvania Terminal Station in New York. That is Defendant's Exhibit 1. Also some correspondence, contract, etc. And I want to offer a certified copy of the file-wrapper and contents of an abandoned application of Paul E. Denivelle, No. 782,671, August 2, 1913. There was some reference made in the other case to this abandoned application, and I think we ought to know what it is.

(The document was marked Defendants' Exhibit 25.)

Now, completing my brief opening, I will say that our defense is that this patent is invalid because it was put on sale and in use more than two years before the application was filed; that claims 9 and 10 of this patent known as article claims are invalid, because they were introduced in his application while the application was pending in Washington, after it had been filed, without a supplemental oath, those two claims containing, as we contend, a departure from the invention as originally disclosed in this application. And, third, that so far as the process claims are concerned, and if the article claims or product claims 9 and 10 can be regarded to be valid, they must be, as we think, valid because they are made in a certain way, and assuming that these claims might under any possibility be held to be valid, we do not infringe these claims. [651]

Now, your Honor has heard how the defendants make this artificial stone. The defendants make the lines of their plastic material on the surface of the mould, then lays particles of calcium carbide in between these lines, then puts over the filling of plastic material the body part, and the dampness in the body part, acts upon this calcium carbide, causing a gas to be generated, which expands and pours along the surface and up into the material itself, so that when you take it off and out of the mold you have a formation that looks like artificial travertine; it looks like travertine.

Now, does your Honor want me to read these depositions? They are quite long.

The COURT.—Perhaps you can tell me the substance of them as you go along. I suppose these New York depositions are largely to prove public use.

Mr. ANDERSON.—Yes.

The COURT.—Taken on notice and cross-examination?

Mr. ANDERSON.—Exactly. I will read first the deposition of Carl Henry Meyn.

Mr. TOWNSEND.—Your Honor, this witness Meyn was not noticed as provided by the statute, so his testimony may only go to show the so-called state of the art, and not for the purpose of anticipation.

Mr. ANDERSON.—Do you mean I did not put his name in the notice I sent to you of taking depositions?

Mr. TOWNSEND.—I am speaking of the answer. I do not know whether it was in the notice, or not, that you sent of the taking of depositions, but it was not set up in the answer as provided by Section 4920 of the Revised Statutes.

Mr. ANDERSON.—I submit that it is not the law that we [652] put the names of witnesses in the answer.

The COURT.—I will hear it, and so far as competent it will be given consideration, and not otherwise. The law point can be settled later.

(Thereupon counsel stated the substance of the deposition.)

Mr. ANDERSON.—I will next take up the deposition of Burt L. Fenner.

(Thereupon counsel stated the substance of the deposition.)

I will now take up the deposition of Daniel T. Webster.

(Thereupon counsel stated the substance of the deposition.)

The COURT.—We will take an adjournament now until to-morrow at ten o'clock A. M.

(An adjournment was here taken until to-morrow, Wednesday, April 23, 1924, at 10 o'clock A. M.) [653]

[Title of Court and Cause.]
Wednesday, April 23, 1924.
Thursday, April 24, 1924.

REPORTER'S TRANSCRIPT.

INDEX.

[654]

Wednesday, April 23, 1924.

(Thereupon counsel proceeded with the reading of the depositions.)

Mr. TOWNSEND.—In response to the demand of plaintiff, defendant has produced a carbon of the letter purporting to be written by MacGruer & Simpson, on March 15, 1923, to Davis Brown, Inc., New York, which reads as follows:

PLAINTIFF'S EXHIBIT No. 27.

"March 15th, 1923.

"David Brown, Inc.,
    306 East 40th St.,
        New York, N. Y.

"Gentlemen:

"We are taking the liberty of writing you in search of information with reference to the manufacture of Artificial Travertine. We are at present executing a very large building, namely the new Biltmore Hotel at Los Angeles, Calif., from plans and specifications prepared by Schultze & Weaver, Architects, of New York.

"In connection with these operations we have received notice from a patentee by the name of Paul E. Denivelle of a threat to infringe his patent. The said Paul E. Denivelle you will recall was originally associated with the firm of Hammerstine & Denivelle in New York City. He now operates here on the Pacific Coast and claims the exclusive patent rights for the manufacture of artificial travertine. On this point however we do not agree as we have manufactured considerable artificial travertine, but we never thought it was a material of sufficient merit to warrant the taking of a patent. There is no doubt about the validity of the patent granted the said Paul E. Denivelle, but the question in our minds at the present time [655] is the settlement of the question whether he has the sole right to manufacture artificial travertine and bar any other concern from manufacturing same by a process other than the one covered by his letters patent.

"We have been advised through our many friends in the building business that your firm executed the artificial travertine in the department store of Lord and Taylor, on which operations were started in the year 1913, and completed in the year 1914. Will you kindly advise us of the exact date of these operations, also if you have any further data on this point prior to this time. It will be of great value to us, and may possibly be of great service to you in the event that you should be placed in the same position as we find ourselves at present. To be truthful we are not seriously alarmed over the situation, although it is very annoying and embarrassing.

"For your further information we may state that our General Superintendent has applied for a patent for the use and manufacture of a novel method of manufacturing travertine, and we have no hesitancy in stating same will be granted. This method is the most simple and practical method we have yet seen in operation, the edifying part of this being that it makes the additional cost of manufacure of artificial travertine, over the regular method of casting, very small.

"We would thank you very kindly if you will forward us this information without delay, so that it will help us in the event we are threatened with a suit in this connection.

"Thanking you in advance, we are,
                "Very truly yours,
                    "MacGRUER & SIMPSON,
"MacG/GM.   By."

We offer that as plaintiff's Exhibit 27. [656]
(The letter was marked Plaintiff's Exhibit 27.)

We offer in evidence the reply of Davis Brown,
Inc., dated March 27, 1923, which reads as follows:

PLAINTIFF'S EXHIBIT No. 28.

(Letter-head of Davis Brown, Inc.)

"New York, March 27th, 1923.

"MacGruer & Simpson,
    266 Tehama Street,
        San Francisco, Cal.

"Gentlemen:

"We are very sorry for the delay in not answering yours of the 15th inst. any sooner but the writer
has been out of town for a few days so take this
opportunity to reply as quickly as possible as we
realize the importance of your letter.

"As to the date of the Lord & Taylor store, where
we have executed the plastering including the imitation travertine work it has been started in the year
of 1913 and completed the following year.

"As to the claim of Paul E. Denivelle that he has
the sole right to manufacture imitation travertine,
I have heard of that but of course we are all doing
this work in the City of New York and disregarding such a claim as there is no secret about the
manufacturing whether it is applied in the building
or cast in the shop and set up in slabs in the building.

"The fact is that here we are constantly called
upon to make imitations of the various marbles and
stones an architect may fancy to use in his opera-

tions and I dare say that the making of these artificial stones has developed to quite an art besides forming a fair size of our business but at no time would any one man claim the sole right to manufacture any imitation stone. [657]

"You also mention in your letter that you have improved on the method of making artificial travertine. This simply shows that you are also progressing and taking an interest in the manufacture of improving this part of our work which we all here are constantly trying to improve upon and that you are also trying to take a patent on your new method.

"In connection with this, isn't it a fact that all stones are created by God Almighty and you and I and all of us trying to make a poor imitation of His work at its best therefore I maintain that we are doing the infringing on His work but as long as He is not objecting we are simply trying to imitate His work and I do not know why any other manufacturer of artificial stone should make claims for patents.

"I recollect some thirty (30) years ago when I was working at the trade as an apprentice boy for the old firm of James J. Morrison whose father was even a plasterer, they have manufactured in those days all sorts of imitation stones very successfully but never looked for the sole rights therefore we believe and maintain that a patent to be claimed by Paul E. Denivelle even if he received such a patent from my point of view is absurd.

"In closing, I wish you the very best of success.

"Sincerely yours,

"DAVIS BROWN."

We offer that as Plaintiff's Exhibit 28.

(The letter was marked Plaintiff's Exhibit 28.)

(An adjournment was here taken until to-morrow, Thursday, April 24, 1924, at ten o'clock A. M.) [658]

Thursday, April 24, 1924.

Mr. ANDERSON.—I offer in evidence copy of United States Patent granted to John Henry Delaney, No. 1,468,343, dated September 18, 1923.

Mr. TOWNSEND.—That patent is objected to as immaterial, irrelevant and incompetent. It is just a recently issued patent.

The COURT.—It would seem so, but it will be admitted over the objection and an exception wil be noted. If not entitled to any consideration the Court will give it none.

(The patent was marked Defendant's Exhibit 29.)

Mr. ANDERSON.—I offer in evidence copy of United States patent No. 247,262, dated September 20, 1881, granted to J. W. McKnight.

(The patent was marked Defendant's Exhibit 30.)

I also offer copy of United States patent No. 982,029, dated January 17, 1911, issued to C. H. Bellemy.

(The patent was marked Defendant's Exhibit 31.)

I offer copy of United States patent 886,124, dated April 28, 1908, issued to John C. Henderson.

(The patent was marked Defendants' Exhibit 32.)

I offer copy of United States patent No. 651,657, dated June 12, 1919, issued to J. Eshe.

(The patent was marked Defendants' Exhibit 33.)

I offer copy of United States patent No.262,603, dated August 15, 1882, granted to John W. McKnight.

(The patent was marked Defendants' Exhibit 34.)

I offer copy of United States patent No. 978,616, dated December 13, 1910, issued to J. Mitats.

(The patent was marked Defendants' Exhibit 35.)

[659]

I offer copy of United States patent 978,617, dated December 13, 1910, issued to J. Mitats.

(The patent was marked Defendants' Exhibit 36.)

I offer what purports to be a photographic copy from the United States Patent Office of a British patent, No. 12468, of 1893, granted to Groetsch & Frush. Have you any objection to that, Mr. Townsend?

Mr. TOWNSEND.—No objection on the ground that it is a copy, but we reserve our objection to all of these on the ground that they are immaterial, irrelevant and incompetent.

(The patent was marked Defendants' Exhibit 37.)

Mr. ANDERSON.—I offer what purports to be a photographic copy from the records of the United States Patent Office of British patent No. 2011, of 1903, issued to Zermak and another.

(The patent was marked Defendants' Exhibit 38.)

Mr. ANDERSON.—I ask counsel whether it is admitted that the Denivelle Hydraulic Composite

Stone Company was a corporation of New York, and was the company with which Paul E. Denivelle was associated, and which company took the contract for the imitation travertine work in the Pennsylvania Station.

Mr. TOWNSEND.—I understand that that is the fact.

The COURT.—Very well, that will be admitted.

DEPOSITION OF GEORGE S. MacGRUER, FOR DEFENDANT (RECALLED).

GEORGE S. MacGRUER, recalled for the defendant.

Mr. ANDERSON.—Q. Mr. MacGruer, with what firm are you associated?

A. MacGruer & Simpson.

Q. What is the business of that firm?

A. Contractors for marble furring, lathing, plastering, ornamental plasterer and artificial stones, and artificial marbles of all kinds. [660]

Q. Is that firm located in San Francisco?

A. It is.

Q. How long has that firm been in existence?

A. It has been in existence since about 1909, the name changed from MacGruer & Co. and later I operated the firm individually, in the absence of my partner in Canada, and on his return we became associated together and we carried along without filing partnership papers, and recently we filed the regular copartnership papers.

Q. How long have you been in this business, Mr. MacGruer?

(Deposition of George S. MacGruer.)

A. I have been identified with the plastering business since the year 1899. I have been brought up in the business, my father being a plasterer.

Q. And where did you start in in this business?

A. In Dundee, Scotland.

Q. When did you come to this country?

A. In the year 1905.

Q. Where did you start in this country?

A. In New York City.

Q. When did you come to California?

A. In the year of 1907.

Q. And you have been here ever since?

A. Yes, sir.

Q. Your firm did some work in connection with the exposition buildings in San Francisco, California?

A. We done the first palace at the Exposition.

Q. You did what?

A. We had the contract for the first palace, the Machinery Hall, at the Exposition grounds.

Q. And that was Machinery Hall?

A. Yes.

Q. When did you begin work on that building?

A. In the early part of 1913. The contract was awarded in the late fall, December; I think; the records will show it; in December of the year 1912.

Q. You got the contract in 1912?

A. Through W. W. Anderson & Co., the general contractors, and I think our name appears in the records as being one of the subcontractors bidding with [661] them on that portion of the work.

(Deposition of George S. MacGruer.)

Q. W. W. Anderson & Co. had the contract for erecting that building, and your firm had a sub-contract with them?   A. That is correct.

Q. Under that subcontract, what work did you do on that building?

A. All the plain and ornamental plastering, which was specified under the heading of colored staff and plaster.

Q. And was that the outer walls of that building?

A. That was all the outer walls surrounding the Machinery Palace.

Q. When did you complete your work on that building?

A. That would have to be determined by the records, Mr. Anderson.

Q. You could not tell us at this time?

A. No, not offhand, but I think the building was finally accepted some time in the early part of 1914.

Q. You met Mr. Paul E. Denivelle on that work, did you not?   A. I did.

Q. In what capacity was he on that work?

A. When we bid on the job there was in the specifications an addenda that followed the speci-fications, the original specifications, in which they were to adopt a color scheme. They had a building called the Service Building, and that was before the grounds of the Exposition were enclosed—there was a service building or administration building in which—

The COURT.—Just a moment. Read the ques-tion.

(Deposition of George S. MacGruer.)

(Question read by the reporter.)

Now, just answer the question.

A. But it is all leading up to it, your Honor.

The COURT.—But we don't want too much matter leading up to it. Just answer the question directly.

A. As I understood, he was to collaborate and assist. He was [662] employed by the Exposition Company in the capacity of what we generally call on a building a superintendent.

Mr. ANDERSON.—Q. What did he do in connection with the work which you were doing there?

A. Nothing more than any general superintendent would do.

Q. What was that?

A. That was to come down and see that the work was carried out according to the plans and specifications.

Q. Did he, or any of his assistants, instruct you and your workmen as to how this plaster work was to be done on that building?

A. If I can recall the exact incident, Mr. Denivelle arranged for a meeting with my partner on the grounds, at Machinery Hall, for a Sunday morning. I think the first demonstration of what they wanted to try to put across, which was not specified, was done that Sunday morning.

Q. And you were not there?

A. No; my partner, Mr. Simpson, was there.

Q. Of your own knowledge, was Mr. Denivelle

(Deposition of George S. MacGruer.)

active in instructing your workmen concerning the work on that Machinery Hall?

A. Yes, intermittently.

Q. He showed them how it should be done?

A. Well, at that time it was very much of an experiment with himself, because hehad never used plaster.

Q. That work was done in plaster?

A. Yes, sir.

Q. You have not stated yet whether he did instruct your workmen as to the effect he wanted to be produced on that Machinery Hall.

A. He did try and instruct them.

Q. You heard Mr. Denivelle testify the other day concerning some bank buildings in San Francisco; do you recall the names of those bank buildings?

A. Yes, the Anglo Paris Bank and the Federal Reserve.

Q. We visited those two bank buildings yesterday morning, [663] didn't we?   A. We did.

Q. Did you see any imitation travertine work in those two buildings   A. No, there is no—

Mr. TOWNSEND.—Now, I object to what this witness means by imitation travertine, or the work on the buildings he refers to, or who did the work. I think a proper foundation should be laid as to who did the work at any particular building he visited; for instance, it might have been work done in 1900, and that would be wholly immaterial here.

Mr. ANDERSON.—These are the two buildings

(Deposition of George S. MacGruer.)
that Mr. Denivelle testified he did in this city, using imitation travertine.

The COURT.—The objection is overruled, and an exception will be noted; if not material, the Court will give it no consideration.

Mr. ANDERSON.—Q. Was there any imitation travertine in those two bank buildings?

A. No, sir.

Q. What kind of plaster or imitation stone work did you find in those two buildings?

A. It was a color texture finish; it is not done in simulation of travertine. It is made in the usual method, and the same successive steps as are employed in the manufacture of artificial marble, the only difference being at the finish, that to get the texture it is sand blasted before any indentations or voids are put in—

Mr. TOWNSEND.—Now, just a moment. I move that the answer be stricken out, your Honor, on the ground that there is no foundation laid, it is merely the opinion of the witness, he didn't do the work, and it is self-serving; it does not appear that he knows how it was done.

The COURT.—Well, it may stand; if not competent the Court will give it no consideration. [664]

Mr. ANDERSON.—Q. Then it is your testimony that the texture surface in those two buildings was produced by sand-blasting operation?

A. Yes, after the work was installed in place.

Q. Your firm caried out the contract for the im-

(Deposition of George S. MacGruer.)
itation travertine in the Biltmore Hotel, in Los
Angeles?   A. It did.

Q. Was that a pre-cast job?   A. It was.

Q. I want you to tell the Court just how that
work was done.

A. You want the successive steps leading up to
the manufacture of the stone.

Q. Yes.

A. Well, the mould is prepared in the usual way.
It is known in the art for years and years—even
before I was born.

Q. How was it prepared?

A. By having the desired model of what you want
to duplicate; then you grease the mould, which
forms the isolator. After that you take your
colored mix and splash that in on the mould with
a whisk broom. Then we took a rubber comb and
combed the lines, to get the veins.

Q. What would be the effect of combing the
material that you splashed on the surface of the
mould?

A. That would be to run the colors together to
get the simulation of the stone that you would want
to follow.

Q. Then what do you do?

A. Then we take calcium carbide and throw that
in between the veins.

Q. On the surface of the mould?

A. Yes, on the surface of the mould.

Q. And that had been prepared by the combing
operation?   A. Yes.

(Deposition of George S. MacGruer.)

Q. Then what do you do?

A. Then we take the body mix or the backing-up material, and we put that in over the mass.

Q. And what happened to it all?

A. Immediately the moisture touches the calcium carbide it explodes, and it keeps exploding while the material is setting, and it keeps foaming and bubbling up through, forming hole; then we back it up with the fiber and [665] plaster, and any reinforcing that is necessary, according to our specifications, and allow the same to set.

Q. And where was that process devised?

A. That was devised in our own shop.

Q. By whom?

A. By J. H. Delaney, with our assistance.

Q. Was Delaney an employee of yours?

A. He was. He was our general superintendent.

Q. Can you tell us when he devised that process?

A. I think is was either the early part or the latter part of April; the application to the Patent Office will show the date.

Mr. TOWNSEND.—We object to that, your Honor. The application would be the best evidence of when it was filed.

The COURT.—Yes, I think so, but he may answer; if it is at all at variance with the application, the application, of course, will control.

Mr. ANDERSON.—Q. That was John Henry Delaney? A. It was.

Q. Now, what is your testimony as to when he devised that process in your shop?

(Deposition of George S. MacGruer.)

A. Well, immediately after we bid on the contract we started making experiments. We do with all materials that we—

The COURT.—Now, just answer the question as it is put to you. Read the question.

(Question read by the reporter.)

A. I would say from April to May.

Q. In what year?

A. In the year 1922, I think it was.

Mr. ANDERSON.—Q. And that is the John H. Delaney who took out the patent No. 1,468,343?

A. Yes.

Q. And that is the way you made the imitation travertine for the Los Angeles Biltmore Hotel?

A. It was.

Q. At the time you did that work, was Delaney experimenting in [666] your shop on this process?

A. That and others. It was his duty to carry out any experiments that we brought forward to him.

Q. Did he work for you on that Biltmore job?

A. He did.

Q. Now, let us get back to the Exposition once more. How many plastering contractors, approximately, were at work on those buildings?

A. Well, I think that pretty nearly every one in the Master Plasterers Association, and others; I would say possibly around 100.

Q. In other words, your firm did only one building?

(Deposition of George S. MacGruer.)

A. No, sir, we done numerous buildings.

Q. You did?   A. Yes.

Q. And other contractors did other buildings?

A. Yes.

Q. The same character of work?

A. The same character of work.

Q. Was it your understanding that Mr. Denivelle had supervision of all of that kind of work on the Exposition grounds?

A. There was some agreement with the Exposition Company that any building done in the Exposition grounds was subject to the general supervision of the Exposition authorities and Mr. Denivelle, naturally, being employed by the Exposition Company, naturally had that sort of supervision that would come under that plan.

Q. When you got this contract for the Biltmore job, what happened, so far as Mr. Denivelle and his patents are concerned?

A. Nothing beyond the letter that Mr. Townsend sent to Mr. Scofield.

Q. That letter to Mr. Scofield—Scofield was the general contractor there, was he not?   A. Yes.

Q. Scofield sent that letter to you?

A. Scofield sent me a copy.

Q. Then what did you do?

A. I was asked by Mr. Scofield to [667] take up the matter with my counsel, who at that time was C. L. Patton, now deceased. After discussing it with Mr. Patton, in view of the letter that Mr.

(Deposition of George S. MacGruer.)

Townsend had sent to Mr. Scofield, we arranged for an interview.

Q. And you had that interview?

Mr. TOWNSEND.—If your Honor please, we again make demand for that letter from the Scofield Company to the witness. I made a demand in writing before the trial. They have already furnished us here on the trial a copy of my letter, a copy of which Scofield sent them. Somehow or other, they have not furnished the letter from Scofield. We ask for that now.

Mr. ANDERSON.—We have not that letter, your Honor. I will tell you what we have, and I will promise to get it if we have not got it here with me: We have a copy of that letter furnished to us by Scofild. I think we have it. If we have it I will produce it.

Mr. TOWNSEND.—I understood that to be an original letter.

Mr. ANDERSON.—We have not got that letter. We have looked for it and we have not found it. If Mr. Scofield sent us a carbon copy of that letter I will produce it.

Mr. TOWNSEND.—Have you interrogated Mr. MacGruer as to whether he is able to furnish a copy of my letter but not a copy of the letter which accompanied it?

Mr. ANDERSON.—No.

The WITNESS.—That was a carbon copy of the letter sent by Mr. Townsend to the Scofield Construction Company and it contained notations of

(Deposition of George S. MacGruer.)
interoffice communication. I think all that letter said in the body of it was: "Herewith please find letter which is self explanatory." Of course, that letter would be in the files of the Scofield Construction Company in Los Angeles. If it is necessary we could have that letter; we could [668] have the Scofield people send us another copy.

The COURT.—Well, gentlemen, proceed with the examination.

Mr. ANDERSON.—Q. At this interview, what took place?

A. At the interview Mr. Patton and Mr. Townsend talked back and forward, as counsel do, and then—

Q. Was Mr. Denivelle there?

A. Mr. Denivelle was there, yes, sir.

Q. And you were there? A. Yes.

Q. Did you have any conversation with Mr. Denivelle at that interview?

A. Oh, just a few remarks.

Q. Did you tell him at that interview anything about this Delaney process?

A. I told him that we were doing something that we thought had no bearing on his patent.

Q. When did that interview take place?

A. The letter shows the date; I don't just happen to remember it.

Q. The letter from Mr. Townsend?

A. My letter to Mr. Denivelle.

Q. At this time you had this contract for the Los Angeles Biltmore Hotel.

(Deposition of George S. MacGruer.)

A. We had already signed and executed bonds.

Q. These specimens that have been introduced in evidence here purporting to be and admitted to be specimens prepared by the defendant, none of them are such specimens as were prepared to go into a building, are they?

A. At the time of the hearing of the motion for the injunction, they were prepared down at 266 Tehama Street to show the result of action of calcium carbide.

Q. And they were not prepared to show what they actually put in a building? A. No.

Mr. TOWNSEND.—Now, I object to that, your Honor, as leading. I think that is a good objection to this question, your Honor.

The COURT.—Well, if that were to be recognized as a vice in this case, we wouldn't have very much in on either side, I am afraid. It is leading, but the answer would be expected, [669] anyway. He has answered. Proceed.

Mr. ANDERSON.—Q. I show you a specimen of plastic material; when was that made, and by whom?

A. That was made yesterday evening by myself.

Q. What is it made of?

A. It is made of ordinary common plaster-of-paris that is sold every day to the trade.

Q. How did you get that surface that appears there?

A. We just took a plain piece of plaster slab and took a knife or wood chisel and we cut two or three

(Deposition of George S. MacGruer.)

grooves on the plaster slab and then shellacked it, and then we put the isolator or grease on, and then we took the calcium carbide and shook it into the grooves, and then simply took the plaster-of-paris and mixed it up and poured it on the mould.

Q. And that mixture was with water?

A. Yes.

Q. That is all that was done?

A. Yes, and after it was allowed to set and it was removed from the mould we held it under a faucet, turned on the faucet, and I put my thumb on it to get pressure under the water, and that is the result.

Q. What did you hold it under the water for?

A. To wash the ash of the calcium carbide to form the verniculations.

Mr. ANDERSON.—I offer this as an exhibit to show the operation of calcium carbide on this plastic material.

Mr. TOWNSEND.—Objected to as immaterial, irrelevant and incompetent, as a self-serving exhibit, and made in a private demonstration. The lack of weight to be given to such demonstrations is well known to your Honor.

The COURT.—It will be admitted over the objection; if not competent, the Court will give it no consideration.

(The exhibit was marked Defendants' Exhibit 39.)

Mr. ANDERSON.—Q. Now, I am going to show

(Deposition of George S. MacGruer.)
you another piece of plastic material; will you state
to the Court what [670] that is?

A. That is a piece of common plaster, máde in
the same way, except that we did not resort to
the washing out process; it is left just as the action
of the calcium carbide leaves it.

Q. In other words, this piece is made in the same
way as the other piece, except that you left the ash
in?

A. Yes, and that the carbide is a little denser.

Mr. ANDERSON.—I offer that in evidence.

Mr. TOWNSEND.—The same objection.

The COURT.—The same ruling.

(The exhibit was marked Defendants' Exhibit
40.)

Mr. ANDERSON.—Q. You had nothing to do
with the former suit on this patent, did you, the
suit against Nye and Ceriat?

A. Nothing whatever.

Q. And you did not testify in that case?

A. No.

Mr. TOWNSEND.—I think counsel could get
his answer from the witness without asking questions that are so pre-eminently leading.

'The COURT.—Well, these are matters over which
there is no dispute. I don't think that is an objectionable form when they only pertain to such
matters. Of course, as to other matters, there are
leading questions that are asked.

Mr. ANDERSON.—Q. You visited New York in
December, 1923, did you not?   A. I did.

(Deposition of George S. MacGruer.)

Q. For what purpose?

A. To find out prior uses of artificial travertine.

Q. What did you do there?

A. I interviewed many people connected with the plastering industry.

Q. Can you mention some?

A. I interviewed Mr. Durkin; I interviewed Davis Brown; I interviewed Mr. Fenner, of McKim, Mead & White; I called at the office of Carrerer & Hastings, but I can't just recall the name of the gentlemen who had charge [671] of the specifications, but they said they would have the records looked up and give me the definite information—I think it was a Mr. Ward. He finally turned out some specifications. I said I understood that Paul E. Denivelle had executed some artificial travertine—

Mr. TOWNSEND.—I object to these conversations, your Honor; that is not responsive to the question.

The COURT.—Objection sustained.

Mr. ANDERSON.—Have you named all that you interviewed?

A. No. I interviewed Mr. Holland, of Ward & Wetmore; I also interviewed Mr. Schultz, of Schultz & Weaver, architects.

Q. Were they the architects for the Biltmore Hotel?

A. Yes, they were. Mr. Weaver telephoned to a Mr. Brandt, saying that he was sending me down with a letter of introduction, and if they had any

(Deposition of George S. MacGruer.)
records which would be of any value in connection with the information that I was seeking, to show me all that he could.

Q. Mr. Brandt was connected with the Fuller Company? A. Yes.

Q. And the Fuller Company were the general contractors on the Pennsylvania Station job?

A. Yes.

Q. You also interviewed that witness from Washington, Mr. Julius Krafft? A. Yes.

Q. There has been an intimation in this record that you sought the assistance and got a promise of the assistance of a certain plasterers association: Tell us about that.

A. I have received no offer of assistance from any plasterers association other than the moral support of the San Francisco Plasterers Association. I also interviewed the association in Chicago, and Mr. Ream called a meeting of the members, at which I was present, and I stated my mission. [672]

Q. What was your mission?

A. My mission was to find out from any member there if they had made any artificial travertine of a prior date to the patent in question.

Q. As a matter of fact, who was paying the expenses of this litigation, so far as the defendant is concerned? A. MacGruer & Simpson.

Mr. ANDERSON.—Now, if your Honor please, I hoped to have a specimen of our work here, but

(Deposition of George S. MacGruer.)

it is not here yet. Subject to that I will close my direct examination.

The COURT.—Cross-examine.

Mr. ANDERSON.—Oh, yes, it is here now, your Honor; I find that it has just been brought in.

Q. I call your attention to a slab of plastic material: What is that slab?

A. That is color plaster.

Q. Does that represent the work MacGruer & Simpson did in the Biltmore Hotel job Los Angeles?

A. It does—a degree, of course.

Q. What is it made of?

A. It is made of plaster-of-paris.

Q. All of the work of the Biltmore Hotel was a plaster job, was it?   A. It was.

Q. Was that slab made in the same way that you have described to the court, by the use of calcium carbide?   A. It was.

Mr. ANDERSON.—I offer that in evidence as a specimen of the work done by the defendants in the Biltmore job.

Mr. TOWNSEND.—The same objection as to the previous exhibits, your Honor.

The COURT.—The same ruling.

(The specimen was marked Defendants' Exhibit 41.)

Mr. ANDERSON.—Q. What was your knowledge of the use of white Portland cement in the plaster trade?

A. It is a material that has been used for long, long, and many years. [673]

(Deposition of George S. MacGruer.)

Q. When did you first use it?

A. My first use of white Portland cement was in a house when I was an apprentice boy, in Monifieth, which is about ten miles from Dundee, Scotland.

Q. What year was that?

A. That would be about the year 1901.

Q. You have used also the so-called brown Portland cement?

A. When I came to San Francisco in 1907 I worked on a building on Market Street, for A. Knowles, the plasterer, and we did a white cement finish on the side of a facade, using a cement called the LaFarge.

Q. How long have you used dark colored Portland cement?

A. Oh, I have used that ever since I went into business.

Q. What is your testimony concerning the relative properties of those two cements?

A. The dark Portland cement is always more durable than the white.

Q. What dictates the use of the white, or the brown, or *vice versa*?

A. Well, it is more pleasing to the eye, and it is easier to get color experiments with the white, because if you use a gray the amount you had to use to bring it back to the color desired would practically neutralize the cement.

Q. The job on the Exposition building was a plaster job, was it?

(Deposition of George S. MacGruer.)

A. It was a plaster job. There were minor pieces done in cement.

Q. On the Machinery Hall which you did, how was the wall surface finished?

A. The main portions of it were done with plaster-of-paris, just the ordinary hardwall plaster, colored.

Q. How was that put on?

A. By the usual method, with a hawk and trowel.

Q. How was the verniculated surface formed?

A. On the applied surface it was done with a brush. After the wall was brought to [674] the proper line, it was stippled.

Q. What do you mean by "stippled"?

A. We take a brush and jab the holes along in irregular lines; then we take another little brush and break it in between; then we finally trowel it over.

Q. Will you mention some of the large jobs which have been done by your firm in the city of San Francisco?

Q. We have done the Bank of Italy Building; the Matson Navigation Building; we are now doing the artificial marble and art plaster in the California Palace of the Legion of Honor.

Q. What was the work you did in the Matson Building?

A. It was done in a sort of an imitation marble; it was just a color scheme. It does not represent any true marble.

Q. What was the amount of that contract?

(Deposition of George S. MacGruer.)

A. The amount of that contract will run over $100,000.

Q. What are you doing in the Legion of Honor Building?

A. We are doing six special rooms out there.

Q. And what is the amount of that contract?

A. The amount of that contract is just under $50,000.

Q. That is not imitation travertine?

A. No, that is done to simulate buff San Saba.

Q. Marble?   A. Marble.

Q. And what was the Bank of Italy work?

A. That is a sort of imitation marble, with no particular marble in mind—just a pleasing effect to the architect on a color scheme.

Q. What was that contract?

A. That contract was in the neighborhood of about $93,000 or $94,000, including the extras.

Q. Did you have any conversations or negotiations with Mr. Denivelle's licensee in Los Angeles concerning the Biltmore job?   A. Yes, I did—

Mr. TOWNSEND.—Just a moment. That is immaterial and not [675] binding on this plaintiff.

The COURT.—That might remain to be seen. Is there any defense of that sort?

Mr. TOWNSEND.—A mere licensee is not an agent, your Honor, taken in the sense of agency.

The COURT.—I understand that. I will hear it. If not material or competent the Court will, of course, ignore it.

(Deposition of George S. MacGruer.)

Mr. ANDERSON.—Q. State the substance of those negotiations. First of all, tell us who was that party?

A. Mr. Malone. I also talked with Mr. Roth, and with Mr. Perry Sawyer; they all represented Mr. Denivelle.

. Q. Did they so tell you? A. Yes, sir.

Q. Now, tell us those negotiations.

A. Mr. Sawyer called on Mr. Scofield numerous times and asked Mr. Scofield to use his influence to see if we could not get together. At the suggestion of Mr. Scofield, while I was in Los Angeles, I went to see Mr. Sawyer and Mr. Roth; I also talked with Mr. Malone. Mr. Malone, at a subsequent date, called at my office with, I think it is Percy Stewart—

The COURT.—Well, did anything come of this? Is there anything in it that is material? I don't care to hear it if there is not.

Mr. ANDERSON.—I don't know that there is, your Honor; I withdraw the question.

Q. Where did you get the materials that you used on the exposition grounds?

A. We bought some from the Pacific Portland Cement, and we bought some from the Arden Plaster Company.

Q. Did you buy any from the Exposition officials, themselves?

A. No, not direct, execpt that they served us with some color.

Q. You mean they sold you the color?

(Deposition of George S. MacGruer.)

A. Yes, sir.

Q. At the time you put in your bid at the Exposition, you had [676] seen a specimen on the service building of what is called imitation travertine? A. It did not so specify.

Q. But at the present time we know that as imitation travertine? A. Yes.

Q. And that was a sample specimen, was it, for the plaster contractors to look at?

A. Yes. It was specified as colored staff, and colored plaster, and that is what caused all the trouble, because it was misrepresented.

Mr. TOWNSEND.—I move that that be stricken out, about any misrepresentations.

The COURT.—I think that may be stricken.

Mr. ANDERSON.—Q. But it did have the color of this imitation travertine? A. It had one color.

Q. One color? A. Yes.

Q. No lines in it? A. No lines in it.

Q. Did you put lines in the work that you did on the Exposition?

A. The stipples formed in the plastered surface. By the lines, I mean it did not have no veins formed in different colors.

Q. Did you form any veins in the work that you did on the Machinery Hall? A. On the cast work?

Q. On the cast work? A. Yes.

Q. But not on the walls? A. No, sir.

Q. Frank L. Whipple, who gave a deposition in case, was here a representative of Mr. Denivelle on that exposition work?

(Deposition of George S. MacGruer.)

A. He was under Mr. Denivelle.

Q. And also Mr. Cook? A. Yes, sir.

Mr. ANDERSON.—That is all on direct.

The COURT.—Cross-examine.

Cross-examination.

Mr. TOWNSEND.—Q. Mr. MacGruer, taking these various [677] samples of plaster cast before you, for instance, Plaintiff's Exhibits 1 and 2 and Defendants' Exhibits 39, 40 and 41, and these two samples which are not yet in evidence, but which were exhibits "A" and "B" on the preliminary injunction, will you state which. if any of those seven samples, most nearly represents, according to your best recollection, the erected artificial travertine in the Biltmore Hotel?

A. Well, I would say that these three are nearer, and some of these for the plain wall surfaces.

Mr. ANDERSON.—You included these two, Mr. Townsend?

Mr. TOWNSEND.—Your Honor, counsel ought not be permitted to suggest matters to the witness in that way. I don't believe that is proper.

The COURT.—His query was that you included them. It was not to the witness. However, the Court takes note of anything that might affect the testimony.

Mr. TOWNSEND.—Q. By "these three," you refer to the one marked exhibit "B" on the back, and to exhibits 2 and 1?

A. Yes, these three, and some like this.

(Deposition of George S. MacGruer.)

Q. You mean exhibit 41?

A. Yes. All stones will vary. No two men make the same piece alike.

Mr. TOWNSEND.—In regard to this sample which the witness referred to, and which on the preliminary injunction was exhibit "B," I ask that that be marked Plaintiff's Exhibit 42.

(The sample was marked Plaintiff's Exhibit 42.)

Q. Do you recall having any specimens in place in the Biltmore that will correspond to exhibit "A"?

A. No, I don't recall it. The job was a large job, and there is bound to be quite a variance in all the pieces.

Q. Did you yourself make, by your own hand, either of the exhibits that you have introduced this morning, 39, 40, 41? [678]

A. Yes, I made these two.

Q. You made those? A. Yes.

Q. Did you, on the Biltmore job, perform the manual labor of casting?

A. No, I don't have time to perform the manual labor on the job.

Q. Your answer is no. A. My answer is no.

Q. Prior to the receipt of the letter which I sent Mr. Scofield, and which the Scofield Company sent to you and which we have referred to, had you had notice of the Denivelle patent here in suit?

A. No, we had no notice.

Q. Was that the first time you had ever heard of it, do you mean? A. What do you mean by that?

(Deposition of George S. MacGruer.)

Q. Just what I say.　A. Just say it again, then.

Q. Do you mean to say that you had never heard of the Denivelle patent prior to the receipt of the Scofield correspondence in early June?

A. I knew of the Denivelle patent at the time that you or your representative called on our Mr. Simpson in connection with the Santa Fe Building.

Q. When was that?

A. Well, you can get that from the records; it was somewhere, I think, between 1915 and 1916.

Q. I don't know the transaction you are referring to, but you believe that as early as 1915 or 1916 Mr. Denivelle either had a patent or was getting a patent on it—you knew that then, did you?

A. Yes, and Mr. Denivelle was at that time advised that we did not think it was a valid patent.

Q. Just stick to my question: Did you or did you not at that time know of the Denivelle patent, or that he was applying for a patent?

A. He so stated, that he had a patent pending.

Q. When did you first hear of the patent after it was issued? It was issued, you know, early in 1917.

A. I don't believe　[679]　that he ever did bring it to my notice after that.

Q. Won't you please answer the question, if you can?　A. I am trying to.

Q. When did you first hear of this patent after it was issued?

A. I don't believe that I had any particular definite date.

(Deposition of George S. MacGruer.)

Q. You knew of the litigation at the time it was going on in Los Angeles against Ceriat, did you not?

A. No, I didn't. If I had, I possibly might have tried to help the defendant.

Q. At present your best recollection in regard to the patent is when you got this letter from Scofield, in May or June, 1922, enclosing a copy of my notice to which we have referred?

A. That was my first official notice.

Q. Were there any others in New York that you interviewed besides the names that you have given, in regard to testifying or giving testimony or information?

A. Yes; I must have interviewed quite a few, but I do not have them all down on my finger tips.

Q. Will you be good enough to mention those that you called upon?

A. I went to the Master Plasterers Association meeting, and I met, I think, the representatives of Roberts, I just forget his name offhand. Maybe I have a memorandum.

Q. Do not take too much time.

A. I would like to be specific if I can. I saw Mr. Jacobson, I saw Mr. O'Rourke, I saw Mr. Reum in Chicago, I saw Mr. McNulty in Chicago.

Q. That is to say, the McNulty who testified in the Ceriat Case?

A. No, I think that was his brother. I would not be positive.

(Deposition of George S. MacGruer.)

Q. Do you know the initials of the one you saw in Chicago?

A. I think T. J. died. I think that is the one that you have reference to.

Q. You were introduced to the Master Plasterers Association by Mr. David Brown, who testified for you, were you not? [680]

At his invitation I was invited to the meeting. I also saw Mr. Thompson, of the Klee Thompson Company. I also saw Mr. Fields, of Kenneth Murchinson, architects. I went to see him with reference to work that they had done on the St. Elmo Club, at New Haven, Conn. Their business is at 101 Park Avenue. I also went to see York & Sawyer; I tried to see Mr. Benedict, but he was busy, and I saw Mr. Colleen. I also went to Humphries & Peters, at 218 East Forty-fifth Street—Mr. Braid was the representative of Roberts. I also went to see John Finck. I did not see Mr. Price, of the Durastone Company, but I talked to him over the phone, and Mr. Price told me that he furnished the travertine materials or some of them to Mr. Denivelle for the Pennsylvania Depot. I called on Mr. Brand, of the Fuller Company, and he showed me a job, pointed out of his window of his office, that Mr. Denivelle contracted for, he called the American Art Gallery at 23d Street and Fifth Avenue, which consisted of applied travertine with a few small pieces of cast slabs. It has now been destroyed, the building has been renovated and the travertine work removed. That building was lo-

(Deposition of George S. MacGruer.)

cated next to the Bartholdi Hotel. I also called
on Mr. Whipple, and I called on Mr. William Cook;
I just forget the location of the building that I saw
Mr. Cook in, but it was somewhere downtown.

Q. That is immaterial. You can give that later
if you want to. I would not want to take the time
of the Court. You practically saw every witness,
of course, that you called?

A. That is what I went for to New York, to find
out information.

Q. And you saw a great many others?

A. I am trying to give you every one in rota-
tion as I saw them.

Q. I will take your word that you saw a great
many others. Now, passing on to another topic.
At the time of the Exposition, [681] you mentioned two of the names that you bought travertine
material from, and you were interrupted by your
counsel. Were there any others you were going to
mention that you bought from?

A. I was. We bought plaster from the Nephi
Company. We had a contract with them to furnish us with plaster, white plaster, f. o. b. cars at
either Seventh or Ninth and Brannon, whatever
the spot is.

Q. You bought a large quantity from them?

A. We bought a large quantity, and they later
were furnished with a formula from the Exposition
Company to furnish us colored material, at a later
date, after a lot of experiments had been made by
ourselves, with the assistance of Mr. Denivelle.

(Deposition of George S. MacGruer.)

Q. When is it your recollection that you made the contract with Mr. Anderson, or the W. W. Anderson Company?

A. I think it was finally approved in January, 1913, but the records will show that.

Q. How soon after the approving of that contract did you proceed to erect the plaster and travertine upon Machinery Hall?

A. I think the records of the Exposition Company will give you the definite date; I could not recall back to 1913 the exact date, but we did it; the Exposition Company had a thorough way of keeping records, and they can tell you about the date.

Q. You are satisfied that the records at the Exposition would correctly represent them?

A. Well, they ought to.

Q. I am asking you your memory; you said your recollection was that as to certain things you thought you began early in 1913.

A. I think that we began somewhere around March; we were ordered by the Exposition Company to erect a shop on the shop; we erected a shop, as you come right down the bottom of Fillmore Street, where the Machinery Hall was placed over [682] there, right about, I would say, about the middle of the Machinery Palace, we erected a cast shop there.

Q. Do you recall when you were through and out of the Machinery Building, completely?

A. No, I was sick at that time. I had a very severe illness at that time.

(Deposition of George S. MacGruer.)

Q. And who was conducting the business, your partner, Mr. Simpson? A. My partner.

Q. You were conducting the business then as MacGruer & Co.? A. Yes.

Q. Was Mr. Simpson the company part of it? A. Yes.

Q. And you have not any independent recollection as to any of these dates when the contract was signed, or when you began work, or when you quit the job?

A. I have an independent recollection of this, that we started to make some of the ornamental features, which are now shown in that book of Wall Surfaces of the Exposition, and particularly with reference to that Greek fret with the little rosette on it, which would be little in comparison to the size of the piece, but I couldn't give you the exact dimensions of the rosette, and Mr. Denivelle came down there on a Sunday morning, if I can recall the incident correctly—

Q. (Intg.) I was only thinking of dates, unless you have the date I don't care for it.

A. It was around some time after Mr. Denivelle came back from New York; he can recall that.

Q. He made several trips to New York, you know. Was that in April or July?

A. He came out there, I think it was some time around April.

Q. Now, were you interested financially or otherwise in the suit that W. W. Anderson Company

(Deposition of George S. MacGruer.)

brought against the Exposition Company for an additional payment? A. I should say we were.

Q. You took quite an active part in that litigation, didn't [683] you A. Why wouldn't I?

Q. You did, didn't you? A. We did.

Q. You were vitally interested in the outcome of that litigation, were you not? A. Yes.

Q. And you are familar with the proceedings that were had there? A. Yes, I am.

Q. Do you remember the title of the suit?

A. W. W. Anderson Company vs. The Panama Pacific International Exposition.

Q. Right here in the Superior Court of the City and County of San Francisco?

A. Murasky's court.

Q. Before Judge Murasky? A. Yes.

Q. In Department 2?

A. I don't know what department, Judge Murasky, anyway.

Mr. TOWNSEND.—I will say, your Honor, the Superior Court has been kind enough to let us have some orginal exhibits that were in that file to which I referred. I simply want to state where the records came from.

Q. I will ask you if you can identify some of these papers. Do you recognize that as the original Anderson contract, an agreement between W. W. Anderson & Company and the Exposition Company, dated January 29, 1913, and the signature of W. W. Anderson, by Dan R. Wagner?

(Deposition of George S. MacGruer.)

A. Yes, but the bids were in December.

Q. I am speaking now of the date of the signing of the contract. You recognize this? You will observe on the face of this that was an exhibit in that case, No. 58,122, Department 2, Plaintiff's Exhibit 1.

A. Well, I have no doubt that is correct.

Q. In connection with your answer you may take into account the two-page memorandum marked "Addenda, Machinery Building, December 16, 1912," in that this addenda will supersede and [684] take precedence over the second paragraph of Page 52, and the third and fourth paragraphs of Page 53.

The COURT.—What is the object?

Mr. TOWNSEND.—To identify the contract and to fix the date of the contract. Using this Exposition matter as a matter of alleged prior use, it is quite important to show that it was of a later date.

Mr. ANDERSON.—When was the contract executed?

Mr. TOWNSEND.—The contract was executed on January 29, 1912.

Mr. ANDERSON.—That is good enough for us.

Mr. TOWNSEND.—And there is an addenda of December 16, 1912.

Mr. ANDERSON.—We will take that.

Mr. TOWNSEND.—I will ask that that addenda be copied in the record.

(The addenda is as follows:)

"ADDENDA.

"MACHINERY BUILDING.

"December 16, 1912.

"This addenda will supersede and take precedence over the second paragraph of Page 52, and the third and fourth paragraphs of Page 53.

"All exterior plain surfaces where covered with metal lath or sheeting lath shall receive a thin scratch coat of ordinary lime mortar mixed with a proportion of fibre, gauged with the necessary quantity of plaster of paris. On the scratch coat shall be applied a finish coat composed of a colored plaster mixture, ready mixed which shall be used as supplied by the manufacturer with only the addition of water and a percentage of Ocean Beach sand in the proportion of two (2) parts plaster mixture and one (1) part of sand. This finish coat [685] shall be stippled with brushes and treated in a certain manner as will be directed by the authorized representative of the Director of Works for the purpose of obtaining exact texture required and to match examples which are in place on the exterior of the Service Building at the Exposition Grounds. All portions which are not passed as satisfactory by the said representative of the Director of Works must be removed and replaced in a satisfactory manner.

.   .   .   .

"All the above ornamental work and cast surfaces shall be cast of colored materials, as supplied by manufacturers, which must match when completed, the plain portions of building. The texture voids

(Deposition of Paul S. MacGruer.)

and stratified perforations in moldings and ornamental portons will be produced by the use of materials of semi-liquid and semi-dry form, so applied in
the molds during the progress of casting, as to produce exact nature of texture throughout all portions
in uniform manner. The back of said casts must
be reinforced with the necessary amount of fibre or
burlaps to insure against breakage in handling.

"All casting and ornamental work must be executed and turned out on the promises in sheds supplied by the Contractor.

"The Director of Works will have a representative, who in turn will have demonstrators in charge
of the entire work to collaborate and assist the Contractor in producing the necessary results, both in
the shop and building work, and their instructions
must be followed as the work progresses. Any castings which are condemned by the said representatives of the Director of Works cannot be erected and
must be replaced by satisfactory examples."

Q. I will show you a letter of MacGruer & Company, signed by MacGruer & Company, by R. Simpson, dated March 6, 1913, and ask you if you recognize that letter?   A. Yes. [686]

Mr. TOWNSEND.—I will just call attention to
the first paragraph:

"Referring to the contract for plastering
Machinery Hall now awaiting signature and de-
livery, we have been advised by you that Hoff
& Hoff, Putman & Gorsuch"— and others—
"would be satisfactory modelers."

Then on another page.

(Deposition of Paul S. MacGruer.)

"We trust that you will be able to make this satisfactory to the Exposition people, as we feel that we cannot, in justice to ourselves, yield this point and allow them to name the firm to do our modeling."

Then, again:

"If we are allowed to proceed in our own manner, we assure you that we will turn out a job that will be entirely satisfactory to the architects, the contractors, and the public generally."

The WITNESS.—Which we did.

Q. You recognize this letter of April 17, 1913, signed by Robert Simpson? A. Yes.

Q. To W. W. Anderson & Co.? A. Yes.

Q. It is dated April 17, 1913, and says, among other things:

"It is imperative that we get some definite information so as to enable us to proceed without delay on our portion of the work," etc.

Mr. ANDERSON.—What is the date of that?

Mr. TOWNSEND.—The date of that is April 17, 1913.

Q. And this one of June 18, 1913, where it says:

"We would also like if you would take up the matter of the finish for the exterior work and find out if there has been any definite arrangement as to how the plain surfaces on the machinery hall are to be finished, as we would like to be informed [687] as to whether we will prepare to follow the letter of the specifica-

(Deposition of Paul S. MacGruer.)

tions, which requires lime mortar for the first
coat and a color plaster for the finish."

Do you identify that?

A. Yes, there was a change every day.

Q. You recognize this letter of July 9, 1913, from
MacGruer & Co., R. Simpson, to W. W. Anderson,
"Re Machinery Hall: We wrote you under date of
July 7th, asking for information regarding the
formula of the colors used in the plaster in the casting of staff work. We have not yet received any information bearing upon this question."

A. Yes. They would not allow us to make our
own formulas, they said they would furnish them
themselves.

Q. Do you recognize this as being a copy of one
of your original letters, on your own letter-head,
MacGruer & Co., per ——, R. S., "Re Machinery
Hall," dated July 17, 1913, to W. W. Anderson &
Co., "While it has always been our intentions to
use Nephi plaster on this building, we do not intend
to allow any manufacturers to supply us with colored plaster until they meet a competitive market
price."

A. Yes, but we had already arranged for a contract price, and the Exposition people had informed
us that they would supply us colored material which
would not cost us but a certain percentage, and after
they worked the back alley to have the manufacturer
supply this, there was an increase of about $3 a ton.

Q. Have you seen this letter which was Exhibit
99 in that suit 58,122, from H. D. Connick, Director

(Deposition of George S. MacGruer.)

of Works, to W. W. Anderson & Co., under date of September 6, 1913?

A. We had no reason to get that letter, because that is addressed to W. W. Anderson, and is not for our files, unless it came directly to our office.   [688]

Q. Do you know Mr. Connick?

A. No, not particularly.

Q. Would you know about the letters from W. W. Anderson to the P. P. I. E. Company?

A. No, we had no access to their files.

Q. You know Dan R. Wagner's signature?

A. Yes, I know his signature.

Q. This is a letter of September 6, 1913, to the Director of Works,—"We wish to notify you that on September 6 we received our first car of scratch coat for the exterior plastering and a few days previous received our first car for exterior finish plain stucco work."

Mr. ANDERSON.—I object to that letter, it has not been connected up with McGruer & Co.

Mr. TOWNSEND.—I realize that technically that is true.

Q. Here is a copy of a letter that you wrote Anderson—MacGruer & Co. did.

A. Unless you show me the original I will not say. You show me the original, and then we will talk about it.

Q. We have here an original exhibit introduced in that suit, to which this witness was a party, Defendant's Exhibit 105, from Anderson to the Director of Works:

(Deposition of George S. MacGruer.)

"We hand you herewith a copy of a letter
from our plaster contractors, which explains
several things you undoubtedly wish to know."

I believe that the original of that would be in the
custody of this gentleman, or under his control; it
was offered by him, and his privies in that suit, and
I think it should be received with some force and
effect.

The COURT.—Proceed.

Mr. ANDERSON.—I suggest, your Honor, that
it ought to be shown just how this gentleman was
interested in that suit.   [689]

Mr. TOWNSEND.—Did you sue Anderson?

A. No, we did not sue Anderson. Anderson was
financially embarrassed; otherwise, we would have
had quite a suit with Anderson.

Q. Did you sue the Exposition Company?

A. No, Anderson brought us in to help him in
that suit against the Exposition Company.

Mr. TOWNSEND.—He was vitally interested in
this suit. The money was due to both of them.

Q. You were not a party to that suit?

A. Anderson owed us a lot of money, but he was financially embarrassed.

Q. You recognize this paragraph—this is a letter
of September 18, 1913, from MacGruer & Co., signed
"MacGruer & Co., George MacGruer," to W. W.
Anderson & Co., and it says:

"At present we are experiencing great difficulty in getting proper shipments of casting
plaster to facilitate the work, and have been

(Deposition of George S. MacGruer.)

compelled this day, at ten A. M., to lay off all of our castors, pending the arrival of more casting plaster. We may state, however, that we have tried another brand of casting plaster, which was approved by the Exposition Company, and found it to be very unsatisfactory and in no way any use to us for any heavy castings,'' etc.

"We may also state that we have consulted with Mr. Denivelle in regard to testing still another brand of casting plaster, with a view of pushing ahead this work, providing the material is satisfactory, and Mr. Denivelle has consented that we bring out a few tons and try the same on small castings with a view of obtaining results, and we expect shipment of same late this afternoon or early A. M. to-morrow.''

Q. Do you recognize the tone and tenor of that letter?

A. There would be lots of letters along that line, because we had to answer or send letters of that character— [690]

Mr. ANDERSON.—What is your purpose, to show that the work was going on at that date?

Mr. TOWNSEND.—Progressing.

Mr. ANDERSON.—What is your contention as to the completion of that work?

Mr. TOWNSEND.—We will get at that in a moment.

Mr. ANDERSON.—We will agree on it.

The COURT.—It is a waste of time to go over

(Deposition of George S. MacGruer.)
innumerable letters, if that can be agreed upon.
Can't you tell us when that was?

The WITNESS.—The work was started, as I
stated, in 1913, and finished in the fall of 1914; the
records show the completion.

Mr. TOWNSEND.—This building, instead of
being started in the early part of 1913 or the latter
part of 1912 was started in September.

The COURT.—It can be proven other than by an
innumerable number of letters.

Mr. TOWNSEND.—May I just use one more?
There are two letters of the witness bearing on the
question of experimentation, over the signature of
this witness.

The COURT.—Proceed.

Mr. TOWNSEND.—Q. Do you recognize this
letter, Mr. MacGruer, signed by you, addressed to
W. W. Anderson, on your letter-head, dated October
8, 1913? I say, is that your signature?

A. I won't say unless I read it.

The COURT.—Whose letter is this?

A. It is my own letter.

Q. Did you sign it?   A. I did.

The COURT.—Very well, proceed.

Mr. TOWNSEND.—Did you sign this letter dated
October 8? Does it bear your signature?

A. Yes. That is my signature. [691]

Mr. TOWNSEND.—The first letter I referred to
reads as follows—it is signed by this defendant:

"Re Plastering Contract Machinery Hall.

(Deposition of George S. MacGruer.)

"Having proceeded and covered considerable area of the plain surfaces of the Machinery Hall, and in view of copy of letter dated December 29th, from the Exposition Company, over signature of William Waters, Superintendent of Construction, that certain joinings in this work are unsatisfactory and will be required to be scraped or otherwise rubbed down, we may state that as this work has been under the personal supervision of Mr. Denivelle and his staff, at all times, and his instructions being followed, we will refuse to do any fixing to the said portions unless we receive payment for same, and only on the receipt of a written order covering such.

"We will, however, be pleased to co-operate with Mr. Denivelle to try to avoid certain joinings, but owing to the vastness of areas involved, it would be impossible for us to try to keep same from showing after connecting one day's work to another.

"We may also state that if Mr. Denivelle will come on the scaffolding and show us by the use of the trowel how to avoid this unseemly joining and providing, after he has finished same without any scraping or rubbing down, he can hide any vertical or horizontal jointing or connections, we will be only too please to correct the portions of the building to which exception has been taken. Awaiting an early reply, we remain,

"Yours very truly,
"MacGRUER & CO.,
"GEORGE MacGRUER."

(Deposition of George S. MacGruer.)

The WITNESS.—Which he was never able to do.

Mr. TOWNSEND.—We have here this other letter of October 8, 1913:

"Now that we have proceeded far enough with our work to [692] arrive at a basis of the additional cost which has been pressed upon us, and of which you are well aware our contract does not call for, we now advise you that we will demand to be compensated for all the experimental work we have been doing for the Exposition Company. Also the additional cost of executing in our casting the imitation of travertine stone, which necessitated the breaking up of our molds so that they would lie in a horizontal position to receive the veining process.

"We are being compelled to try and match the jointing of the staff or imitation travertine stone work with one of the colored plasters, together with some unfibered hardwall, according to some formula or instructions given by Mr. Denivelle or his representatives, and so far we have been unable to get the desired result which is easy to understand in the face of the fact that we are being asked to match a combination of colors in our staff or imitation travertine stone with practically one colored plaster"

The last paragraph:

"We may say we are following the method of mixing of materials and entirely as directed, and we are finding the burden of expense is being placed on our shoulders which should be borne by the Exposition Company, as we are being used solely for

(Deposition of George S. MacGruer.)
experimental purposes, which is not in accordance
with the terms of our contract.''

Q. And accompanying that was a bill, is that
correct, for services in experimental work, $500?

A. They never paid it.

Q. Is that correct, on that memorandum that you
sent? A. We made out the bill.

Q. For services in experimental work $500?

A. Yes, but they did not pay it. They said it
was part of our contract.

Mr. TOWNSEND.—To fix the date of completion, this is [693] another one of these original
exhibits, and is dated March 18, 1914:

"Notice of Completion of Work Contract No. 24:

''Notice is hereby given that the work to be done
under a certain contract dated on the 29th day of
January, 1913, by and between the Panama Pacific
International Exposition Company, a corporation,
therein designated The Exposition Company, and
.W. W. Anderson Co., therein designated Contractor,
and filed for record in the office of the Recorder of
the City and County of San Francisco, State of
California, on the 31st day of January, 1913, was
completed on the 10th day of March, 1914.''

A. Yes, but our work was finished prior to that.

Q. That is when that building was completed?

A. The records will show that.

Q. You accept that as the record?

A. If it is the official record, yes.

Mr. TOWNSEND.—Any question about that?

(Deposition of George S. MacGruer.)

Mr. ANDERSON.—No, none at all, but Mr. Mac-Gruer says his work was completed before that.

Mr. TOWNSEND.—Q. Did I understand you to say that the sample on the Service Building from which you worked did not show any veins?

A. I said that the sample on the Service Building was a plain wall surface, stippled. It was placed, if I can recall it—

Q. Just state how that was done.

A. It was stippled, I told you.

Q. Did it have veins? A. It had no vein.

Q. How many colors did it have?

A. It only had the one main color, the same as we used practically throughout our work on the Machinery Hall.

Q. How many colors did that sample have?

A. That sample had [694] one color.

Q. It had voids? A. It had stipples.

Q. Do you know how that was done?

A. It was done with a brush.

Q. Did you see it done?

A. No, it was put up there for the bidders, especially designed as an example of the work to be executed.

Q. The plain wall surface of the Exposition Building had no veins in them?

A. I said the plain wall surface of the Machinery Building had no veins.

Q. How was that effect obtained, of voids?

A. By stippling with a brush.

(Deposition of George S. MacGruer.)

Q. It is your recollection that there were no veins in that work? A. I know there were not.

Q. How many colors did the wall surfaces of the Machinery Building have?

A. The formula was made up of a series of colors that formed one body color.

Q. Do you know how many colors appeared in contrast upon the surface?

A. There would be but one main color, if you used one colored material.

Q. How many colors appeared on the surface of this building, particularly the Machinery Hall Building that you saw? A. On the plain surface?

Q. Yes.

A. I told you that it had one body mix, that it had one color.

Q. Did you do any work in which there were veins or striae? A. In the cast work, yes.

Q. In the cast work?

A. Yes, but not on the applied surface.

Q. You did a very large amount of cast work?
A. I certainly did.

Q. You did not do much work yourself?

A. Well, no, that would be impossible for one man to do something like that.

Q. Did you observe how they did that work, how they made the [695] veins? A. Yes.

Q. What did they have to do it by?

A. They had lots of methods.

Q. What did they use in making the veins?

(Deposition of George S. MacGruer.)

A. Sometimes they used a can, an ordinary can, and sometimes they used a special spouted can, which was furnished by the Exposition Company, for which they charged rental.

Q. And you used a brush?

A. We used a stippling brush. We later developed another method ourselves with a brush.

Q. On the Exposition?   A. Yes.

Q. You used both the pouring can, with spouts, and you used a brush to make a vein?   Just answer "Yes" or "No."

A. I said yes, we used pouring cans and we used ordinary cans.

Q. Do you recognize this receptacle as such a device as was used on the Exposition?

A. I ought to.

Q. You rented a great many of these from the Exposition Company, did you not?

A. We were forced to rent them. We did not want them, but we were forced to.

Mr. TOWNSEND.—I ask that this be marked Plaintiff's Exhibit 43.

(The receptacle was marked Plaintiff's Exhibit 43.)

Q. You did not mention Mr. Delaney at that interview in June, 1922, in Mr. Patton's office, did you?

A. No, why should I mention Mr. Delaney?

Q. You did not mention that he had any process?

A. Why should I?

Q. Did you or did you not?   A. No, I did not.

Q. You did not tell us what your method was?

(Deposition of George S. MacGruer.)

A. No.

Q. Why, if you had a method developed at that time, did you write the letter a few days later to Mr. Denivelle asking him for a bid or a royalty basis under his patent for the work on the Biltmore Hotel?

A. Because it was suggested by Mr. Scofield, [696] it was also suggested to me by Mr. Patton as possibly the easiest way out, and the cheapest way out, to get through with a large contract, and I impressed upon Mr. Patton that I did not want to enter into any agreement that would place my rights in jeopardy, and Patton said to me, "Well, anyhow, go ahead and write him the letter and see what comes of it."

Q. So at the time you wrote that letter, and you got Mr. Denivelle's reply, you did not intend to act under it at all?

A. I so told him at the meeting.

Q. You put Mr. Denivelle to the trouble of figuring in good faith, and you had no intention of even considering his bid?   A. He had already—

Q. (Intg.) Just answer my question.

A. He had already submitted his figures, and he did not have to waste any time figuring any more.

Q. Read the question.

(Last question repeated by the reporter.)

A. He wasted no time, he had already figured the job.

Q. Is that the best answer you can give?

A. Yes.

(Deposition of George S. MacGruer.)

Q. As a matter of fact, you did not intend to consider his bid?

A. No, I did not, unless it was of such a nature that it would save me any expense.

Q. Have you a sample of the carbide as you used it?   A. I believe we could produce one.

Mr. ANDERSON.—Do you want us to make a demonstration here?

Mr. TOWNSEND.—No.

Q. Have you some commercial carbide?

A. Yes, we have some here.

Q. In the form that you use it?   A. Yes.

Q. That is unslacked carbide?   A. Yes.

Mr. TOWNSEND.—I believe the Court will take judicial cognizance of the characteristics of calcium carbide? [697]

The COURT.—I should think so.

Mr. ANDERSON.—I suggest that we might stipulate it is—

Mr. TOWNSEND.—Here is a box they have produced, and I will submit it to the Court and offer it in evidence as Plaintiff's Exhibit 44.

Mr. ANDERSON.—Can't we stipulate on the record that the texture surface in the defendants' work is produced by the action of calcium carbide when subjected to moisture in the generation of a gas which bores the holes and apertures in the surface of the material?

Mr. TOWNSEND.—We prefer to stand on the sworn record.

The COURT.—Any further cross-examination?

(Deposition of George S. MacGruer.)

Mr. TOWNSEND.—No.

The COURT.—Redirect, if any.

Redirect Examination.

Mr. ANDERSON.—Q. Mr. MacGruer, this spouted can, Plaintiff's Exhibit 43, did you use these cans on the exposition work?

A. We were forced to use them.

Q. Did you use them?

A. Yes, and we later discarded them.

Q. You discarded them?   A. Yes.

Q. And after that what did you use?

A. We used an ordinary can with a few holes punched in it.

Q. What was the amount of this Biltmore job?

A. The amount of the Biltmore, as contracted for, was $406,509—there may be a variation in the odd figures, but that was about it.

Q. When was that job completed by you?

A. It was completed just prior to the opening of the Biltmore, which was October, 1923.

Q. When did you start that job?

A. The actual work started somewhere around November, 1922.

The COURT.—Your next witness. [698]

Mr. ANDERSON.—I will call Mr. Denivelle.

DEPOSITION OF PAUL E. DENIVELLE, FOR DEFENDANTS (RECALLED).

PAUL E. DENIVELLE, recalled for defendants.

Mr. ANDERSON.—Q. Mr. Denivelle, that is not

(Deposition of Paul E. Denivelle.)
imitation travertine in the two bank buildings that
you mentioned the other day, is it?

A. They are both an idealization of imitation
travertine.

Q. But it is not what we all know as imitation
travertine in this case?

A. I have not any idea what you knew as imitation travertine, Mr. Anderson. I repeat, it is an
idealization of imitation travertine; in other words,
an evolved development of the idea of naturaliz
travertine.

Q. You want the Court to understand that the
two jobs were done in accordance with your patents?

A. I absolutely do.

Q. You used a sand blast on those jobs, did you
not?

A. After they were erected and put up, and the
imitation travertine had been constructed in the
slabs, yes.

Q. That sand blast was for what purpose?

A. For the purpose of taking off the mold scum,
what we call mold scum that appears on the surface.

Q. For the purpose of forming holes, was it not?

A. No; they were made according to my process
absolutely, and I have many witnesses to that if it
is necessary.

Q. The process of your patent, as I understand it,
is directed, according to your understanding, to pre-
cast work alone, is it not?

Mr. TOWNSEND.—That is a matter for the

(Deposition of Paul E. Denivelle.)

Court to construe, and the patent is the best evidence.

The COURT.—He may inquire, of course. The patent will [699] stand or fall according to its language. He may answer.

A. There is one patent that provides for the precast work and another for the applied work.

Mr. ANDERSON.—But this patent is for precast work? A. Which patent?

Q. The one here in suit. A. Yes.

Mr. ANDERSON.—That is all

Mr. TOWNSEND.—No cross-examination.

The COURT.—Any further witnesses for the defendants?

Mr. ANDERSON.—I would like to make that demonstration, if there is any question in your Honor's mind as to the action of this calcium carbide.

The COURT.—I have no objection if you do it timely, that is all. Have you closed your case?

Mr. ANDERSON.—Yes.

The COURT.—It might be done during the argument, or at the time of the argument. Any rebuttal by the plaintiff?

Mr. TOWNSEND.—Short rebuttal.

The COURT.—Are you ready to make that test?

Mr. ANDERSON.—Yes.

The COURT.—How long will it take?

Mr. ANDERSON.—About 15 minutes.

The COURT.—You may do it as part of your case now.

(Deposition of Paul E. Denivelle.)

Mr. ANDERSON.—I will do it as part of my case. But first I will recall Mr. Denivelle for a few questions.

DEPOSITION OF PAUL E. DENIVELLE, FOR DEFENDANTS (RECALLED).

PAUL E. DENIVELLE, recalled for defendants.

Mr. ANDERSON.—Q. You made an affidavit in this case on the 14th of July, 1923, which I show you, did you?

A. This is [700] not my signature, so I don't know just how I can identify it.

Mr. TOWNSEND.—What is it you want?

Mr. ANDERSON.—That is a copy furnished to the defendants' counsel in the case.

The COURT.—I have no doubt counsel will identify it if served by him.

Mr. TOWNSEND.—I have no reason to question that those are correct copies that were served on the preliminary injunction.

The COURT.—Are the originals in the files?

Mr. ANDERSON.—Yes. I would like to read portions into the record

"The patented process comprises briefly, the production of striated or veined artificial stone structure by depositing upon a prepared surface, as, for instance, a mould which has been suitably greased or lubricated, a series of narrow lines of colored plastic material in simulation of veins; depositing upon said lines or veins and upon the exposed surfaces of the mould between the veins a suitable material of such texture and consistency as will leave numerous small voids or portions of said exposed surfaces out of contact with the material, and then binding together the veining material and the void-forming material with a moist plastic, and allowing the mass to set.''

I will further read:

"The tools or apparatus for performing the different steps and producing the patented product are of any suitable sort and are very simple, consisting simply of a greased or prepared mould, upon the surface of which the veining is first run or let out by suitable means as either a can with a pouring spout or spouts, or, as affiant frequently practices the work, with a divided brush, which is adapted to be dipped into a suitable [701] material and then drawn in lines over the surface of the mould.''

Further reading from Mr. Denivelle's affidavit:

"The intrinsic merit of the objection has found expression in a large, practical way, in its extensive use by affiant in the monumental structure of the Pennsylvania Railroad Station in New York City, and the wall surfacing of the buildings of the Panama Pacific International Exposition in San Francisco; this work in each instance being under the personal supervision of affiant, the patentee.''

"Affiant has also applied his process and product of the patent in suit to many other monumental buildings, including the San Francisco Public Library in the Civic Center, the Federal Reserve Bank, and the Anglo-California Bank Building, all in San Francisco; the Union Station, Ottawa, Canada; and in various other places. The contract for the Pennsylvania Station work alone involved an expensive scheme of interior decoration never before attempted; while the Panama Pacific International Exposition work involved exterior treatments subject to weather conditions."

Further reading from Mr. Denivelle's affidavit:

"Affiant further states that he is well acquainted with the defendants, George Smith MacGruer, and Robert Morton Simpson, and each of them; that said defendants acting under the direction of affiant became thoroughly familiar with affiant's patented process and product aforesaid during the building of the Panama Pacific International Exposition, particularly during the years 1913 and 1914, when the said defendants, under the direction of affiant, applied affiant's patented process and product as an exterior covering for the walls of the Machinery Hall at the Panama Pacific International Exposition; that [702] said artificial travertine so used on said Machinery Hall was applied by the workmen employed by the said George Smith MacGruer and Robert

(Deposition of Paul E. Denivelle.)

Morton Simpson, and was done under the supervision and instruction of affiant and assistants.

"Affiant further shows that there is no known method of commercially producing artificial travertine except by plaintiff's patented method, and on information and belief affiant states that the said Scofield Engineering & Construction Company and these defendants and the architect for the said Los Angeles Biltmore Hotel knew such to be the fact."

Mr. TOWNSEND.—I can shorten this reading by stipulating that the whole affidavit go in. I will offer the balance of it.

(The affidavit reads as follows.)

(Here follows affidavit of Paul E. Denivelle on motion for preliminary injunction.) [703]

Mr. ANDERSON.—Q. Now, Mr. Denivelle, you did not see in process of manufacture the specimens which have been introduced here as plaintiff's exhibit as representative of the defendants' work on the Biltmore Hotel, did you?

A. I did not see them made, you say?

Q. Yes.

A. I did not see them made personally, no.

Q. And you do not claim to have seen the defendants' work in process of construction in the Biltmore Hotel? A. No.

Q. Would you say that was a copy of the specification from which you prepared your estimate and bid for the Pennsylvania work, referring to Defendants' Exhibit 1?

(Deposition of Paul E. Denivelle.)

A. I believe it would be.   The cover at least represents so.

Q. Defendants' Exhibit 1?   A. Yes.

The COURT.—Is it in evidence already?

Mr. ANDERSON.—Yes.

Q. Does this exhibit 40—a—is there any doubt, Mr. Denivelle that the letter of March 9 constitutes your bid for the Pennsylvania [704] job?

A. It seems to be O. K.; I presume it is correct.

Q. That is the contract which you executed for the Pennsylvania job, is it?   A. Yes.

Q. This letter of April 4, 1912, forming part of Defendants' Exhibit 2, is that your bid for the Robert Goelet house?

A. Yes, I recognize it as such, sent out by the company of which I was a member.

Q. These bills dated August 4, 1914, and December 16, 1914, pasted on the back of a page, when it was formerly page 152 of a scrap book, which is entitled Defendants' Exhibit 42, are these bills rendered by your company for work done in Philadelphia?

A. I believe they are correct.   Of course, I could not identify this and that.

Q. You did that work?   A. I did.

Q. That was imitation travertine work?   A. Yes.

Q. The Goelet house was imitation travertine work?

A. In a very small part as represented by the bed.

Q. But you did some imitation work on the Goelet house?   A. There was some, I believe.

(Deposition of Paul E. Denivelle.)

Q. Mr. Denivelle, on April 4, 1912, this is the bid to Carrere & Hastings for the Goelet house?

A. Yes.

Q. And among the references appearing at the left of your letter-head is Pennsylvania Station, Seventh Avenue and Thirty-second street, New York; that is intended to refer to the travertine work that you did at the Pennsylvania Station?

A. Whatever I did on that.

Q. On April 4, 1912, that work was completed, was it?

A. No, I do not think so, not quite. It went on that date.

Q. You had fulfiled your contract, however, by that date?

A. The bulk of the contract, but it was not completed, as has been pointed out.   [705]

Q. This bid forming part of Defendants' Exhibit 40–A, dated March 9, 1909, that was preceded by a bid of December 28, 1908, was it not?

A. Is that an "8"?

Q. Isn't it?

A. I would not say, as it has been punched over.

Q. This is your signature on that letter?

A. I do not question the signature at all.

Q. It is dated December 28, is it not?   A. Yes.

Q. 1908?

A. I could not say about the "8"; that is punched over.

Q. That was a revised bid for artificial travertine in the Pennsylvania Station addressed to

(Deposition of Paul E. Denivelle.)

George A. Fuller & Co. by your company, or by you as its representative?   A. Yes.

Q. This letter dated July 20, 1908, forming part of Defendants' Exhibit 5, signed "Hammerstein & Denivelle Company by P. E. Denivelle," do you recognize that signature?

A. I recognize that signature.

Q. Then that is a bid to George A. Fuller Company for imitation travertine work?

The COURT.—Are these already in evidence and proven in connection with some deposition?

Mr. ANDERSON.—Yes.

The COURT.—What is the necessity of having this witness confirm it, then?

Mr. ANDERSON.—You do recognize that?

A. I recognize that signature, I stated.

Mr. ANDERSON.—That is all.

Mr. TOWNSEND.—No questions.

(A recess was here taken until two o'clock P. M.)
[706]

AFTERNOON SESSION.

Mr. ANDERSON.—Your Honor, I proposed to make a demonstration in the courtroom; I want to convince your Honor as to the action of calcium carbide. But the consumption of this calcium carbide creates a gas and would leave an odor in the courtroom that would be objectionable. I would like to avoid that demonstration if I can. For that reason I asked my adversaries if they would agree that the white substance that now fills the apertures or honeycombed sections of Exhibit 40 is no part of the cementitious material employed in the manufacture of that exhibit, but is the ash developed by the burning of the calcium carbide and is removed either by washing it or brushing it out after the cast is made. If they will make that concession I can avoid the demonstration.

Mr. TOWNSEND.—The difficulty with stipulating to that is that we don't know how that was made. From what they said, it was made differently from the process that was practiced at the Biltmore.

Mr. ANDERSON.—We do not contend that it was made according to the process we used on the Biltmore job. That is the process we used to get the honeycombed effect.

Mr. TOWNSEND.—We contend that the honeycombed effect is gotten by the action of the carbide on the material.

Mr. ANDERSON.—This piece was made last night and was immediately washed out.

The COURT.—Well, we have had testimony in the record about that. I think that so far as that is concerned your record is sufficient.

Mr. ANDERSON.—I am a little surprised that they will not concede that proposition. Your Honor undoubtedly knows the action [707] of calcium carbide.

The COURT.—I have the same general knowledge that anyone else has. Have you any further evidence?

Mr. ANDERSON.—No, your Honor. We rest.

The COURT.—Any rebuttal.

Mr. TOWNSEND.—Counsel and I have stipu-
lated, to avoid the necessity of calling a witness, to
the fact that the Wiedner Memorial Library at Harvard, referred to variously in the testimony as the
Cambridge Memorial Library, or the Harvard Memorial Library, was dedicated on Commencement Day,
June 24, 1915, and was thereafter open to the public.

Mr. ANDERSON.—I agree to that.

Mr. TOWNSEND.—I had a college book which
also showed the picture of the Library, in case your
Honor desired to look at it.

Now, with regard to the early history of the invention, and its development through the Pennsylvania stages as might be given by Mr. Denivelle if
he were called for that purpose to show how he took
the matter up and how the inspiration came to him,
that can be avoided, unless your Honor desires that
information, by reason of the testimony we have
already had on the subject of the Pennsylvania
development, and concerning which there is no real
controversy, and by reason of the findings of the
Circuit Court of Appeals of this Circuit in the case
we have already referred to as the Los Angeles case,
reported in 270 Fed. 155. On pages 8 and 9 of the
opinion which we have filed as an exhibit in this
case, Judge Ross goes at length into that. Unless
you think there is some reason for me to call Mr.
Denivelle and have him repeat that story, I am
inclined to rest and take it as a finding by the Court
of Appeals.

(Deposition of Paul E. Denivelle.)

The COURT.—I assume that these statements in this opinion are found in the evidence in that case which you have introduced. [708]

Mr. TOWNSEND.—Yes, your Honor.

The COURT.—Then certainly it is before the Court in one way or another.

Mr. TOWNSEND.—Yes, your Honor, and, therefore, it is not necessary for me to repeat it?

The COURT.—I would not think so.

Mr. TOWNSEND.—Very well, your Honor. I have two or three questions to ask Mr. Denivelle on another point.

DEPOSITION OF PAUL E. DENIVELLE, FOR PLAINTIFF (RECALLED IN REBUTTAL).

PAUL E. DENIVELLE, recalled in rebuttal.

Mr. TOWNSEND.—Q. In the deposition of Lever, here offered in evidence by the defendant, appears, on page 12 of that deposition, in answer to question 74 on that page appearing, the following:

> "I do a job before I left Denivelle in Oyster Bay for him, a vestibule in travertine; I went there Saturday, Sunday and Monday; I was all alone."

Will you tell us what the facts are in regard to any Oyster Bay job at any time that you may have done?

A. To say the least, he is absolutely mistaken. The statement is in actuality untrue. There was no travertine in Oyster Bay that was done before the Pennsylvania Station. That was a plain, smooth,

(Deposition of Paul E. Denivelle.)
concrete white-faced block proposition, as I remember it.

Q. Did I understand you to say the Oyster Bay job was done before the Pennsylvania Station?

A. Considerably before, by several years.

Q. Lever said that he was a foreman in your employ at one time; did you ever have a foreman by the name of Lever?

A. I never had a foreman by the name of Lever.
[709]

Q. He said that he had worked with a man named Camolli, and that he left when Camolli left. Who was Camolli?

A. Camolli was a foreman for me on the Manhattan Opera House in New York; he was discharged prior to the completion of that job for dishonesty—inaccuracies in connection with knocking down on the wages of the men. As I say, he was discharged prior to the completion of that job. That was opened to the public in December, 1906.

Q. Reference has been made to a sample or samples for the Exposition which were in place at the Service Building, samples for the men to follow. Will you tell us how the sample or samples were made, when they were made, and by whom?

A. They were made by me, assisted by a plasterer who applied the coats of colored plaster. I colored these coats, made up the formulas and went up on the scaffold and instructed him how to apply the coats, and then with my own devices I jabbed the indentures or the voids into the surface while it

(Deposition of Paul E. Denivelle.)

was in a plastic state, producing what appeared to be the stratiae, the voids and veinings. One of these was on the exterior of the portico, or the portico face, we will say, and the other was on the rear wall of the portico—both of them outside the building.

Q. Did either of those samples have veinings in them?

A. Yes. I recall distinctly that one of them had veins of a different color, the one under the portico. They were both submitted by me to the exposition as a suggestion of what I might bring about in the exposition, and for the benefit of the architects.

Q. How was the surface on Machinery Hall done, and what effects did you get, and when I say you I mean MacGruer & Company working under you?

A. That was done in almost identically the same manner. We provided the tools, or the brushes, which we made in my experimental station back of the building, provided [710] those incidentals, don't you know, which had to have a certain personality. We showed them and kept showing them the method of jabbing these brushes. It is a very crude proposition, but I have one in my bag, a remnant, as it were. These were jabbed into the plastic surface while it was soft, after it had been applied, to the thickness of approximately one-quarter of an inch. It produced the undercut effect and the striated effect that the walls of the buildings of the exposition had.

Q. You referred to brushes: Have you a brush?

(Deposition of Paul E. Denivelle.)

A. It was very simple. It was a thing of this type, which we had to improvise from a completed brush of a certain width. We sheared them, and then we split these with nippers, we just cut these out in a certain irregular fashion, so that when jabbed into the material they would produce a sort of an accidental quality of voids in irregular spacing, etc.

Mr. TOWNSEND.—I ask that this brush be marked as Plaintiff's Exhibit 45.

(The brush was here marked Plaintiff's Exhibit 45.)

Q. What was the effect accomplished by the plastic material itself and these voids upon the wall surfaces of the Machinery Building?

A. The base color, naturally, is contained in the material. This jabbing effect produces a shadow in varying degree, hence darkening the general appearance of the wall, we will say, that this material constituted. In other words, you can take a buff wall and before it has been jabbed it is absolutely a plain, smooth, buff wall; after you have jabbed these shadows into it, as we instructed them, it changed both the variation in color, by the introduction of a black or a gray in varying quality representing the shadow, and the basic coat, which was the color; controlling that in a varying form [711] and jabbing this horizontally—it is jabbing, it is erroneously named "stippling"—jabbing these brushes in the form of indentations in this manner, it produced an under-cut quality after the trowel

(Deposition of Paul E. Denivelle.)

had again been passed over. You must understand that this jabbing process is a repeated one over the same area, in other words, over the same section, you keep jabbing it and retroweling it so as to get this vein striated effect. You cannot get it otherwise. You cannot get it by jabbing it and then letting it alone.

Q. And is that done in a horizontal way or is it in a mass way?

A. In a horizontal direction generally, in not too stultified and stiff a manner. The character of it is due to the degree of skill in the manipulation of it.

Q. Will you give us an idea of the thickness you make your artificial travertine?

A. You mean the pre-cast?

Q. Yes.

A. They would approximate one inch with their backing; that relating to the texture, itself, may be half an inch in thickness, in accordance with the degree of coarseness that is required, or depth that is required in the voids.

Q. If you were to use white Portland cement for the surfacing, what would you back that up with?

A. I would back it up with common Portland, as is shown in that slab there.

Q. Is there any difference in price between white Portland cement and common cement?

A. Oh, yes, there is a great difference. I think the present market rate on white Portland cement

(Deposition of Paul E. Denivelle.)
is around $11, and on common Portland it runs around $4. I think that approximates it.

Q. Can you tell us the approximate value or price or cost per square foot of your artificial travertine, as compared with natural travertine?

A. Yes, I think I can. Taken in plain [712] surface, in plain walls, the cheapest, that is, the least expensive type of the natural, that would probably cost, erected in place, $6 per square foot.

Q. The witness is referring to No. 22 as the natural travertine. Is that correct?

A. Yes, if that is the number. That is the natural. The other approximates, on the wall, and, as I say, in a plain surface, $1 to $1.25 per square foot. However, the moment you get into molded forms, that is, moldings, cornices, and ornaments, the disparaging difference is very much greater between the natural and the artificial, because the moment they have to mill and form moldings in the natural, it is extremely expensive, whereas, by the process of reproduction in the artificial we make them at a cost that is comparatively nominal. So that while we have represented the difference between the two slabs in price, taken on a job, and one executed in natural and the other, taking the Pennsylvania, for instance, in artificial, they would have run into millions of dollars to have produced there what I did artificially.

Mr. TOWNSEND.—That is all.
The COURT.—Cross-examine.

(Deposition of Paul E. Denivelle.)

Cross-examination.

Mr. ANDERSON.—Q. And that is true of almost any imitation of a high-grade building stone, isn't it, there would be the same disparagement in cost as between the genuine stone and a plaster representation?

A. There would be a similar difference in cost, a ratio of difference.

Q. Now, was it your testimony, Mr. Denivelle, that this specimen—

A. (Intg.) Pardon me, Mr. Anderson: To answer your question more fully, since you have asked it, there is this difference between natural travertine and the ordinary other stones, there is a [713] great loss in natural travertine in getting any degree of selection whatever, because it runs from an impossible spongy type; in other words, to get one stone out of that slab—that was gotten out of a slab that was five feet square, referring to exhibit 22. A good part of the rest of it is a specimen of travertine. It is a very fine specimen. You might have to go very far if you proposed to select the travertine for the purpose of your job.

Q. And this specimen you have here is a very fine selected specimen, isn't it?

A. I beg your pardon, Mr. Anderson, you are referring to the wrong one.

Q. Well, I am referring to whichever one it is. That is a very fine specimen, isn't it?

A. That is a very nice specimen.

(Deposition of Paul E. Denivelle.)

Q. This courtroom here has a great deal of beautiful marble in it, has it not?

A. It has a great deal of marble in it, yes.

Q. They do, in practice now, and have for years, have they not, imitated marble of this character?

A. That is a well-known fact.

Q. And the imitation of the marble made of plaster would cost very, very much less than the genuine marble?

A. It would not be an imitation of this marble if it were made of plaster, because you could not polish it, you could not get the surface.

Q. Well, whatever you make marble imitation of —I am not technical about the materials; you have seen good imitations of this marble, haven't you?

A. Yes.

Q. And made of cementitious material?

A. Yes.

Q. And so if this marble in this courtroom were made of cementitious material it would be a very much cheaper job than the natural stone, would it not?   A. Undoubtedly it should be.

Q. This specimen that you put on the Administration Building [714] over here at the World's Fair, and which you have referred to—

A. Pardon me, on the Service Building.

Q. Yes, on the Service Building, when did you put that there?

A. In December, 1912, on my first arrival in San Francisco.

Q. Then you came back early in 1913?

(Deposition of Paul E. Denivelle.)

A. That is correct, in April.

Q. And you came out here under contract with the exposition authorities to show these workmen out here, including these defendants, how to make imitation travertine?   A. Absolutely.

Q. And you did that?   A. I did that.

Q. And you got paid for it?

A. Why, most assuredly. I received a salary; I was under a salary, subject to specified conditions, which I specified.

Mr. ANDERSON.—That is all.

Mr. TOWNSEND.—Plaintiff rests.

Mr. ANDERSON.—Does your Honor desire us to sum up this afternoon?

The COURT.—Oh, yes, this afternoon, if you are going to do it at all.

Mr. ANDERSON.—Will I have the first say?

Mr. TOWNSEND.—No, the plaintiff has the opening, I suppose. Isn't that customary, your Honor?

The COURT.—I don't know. You should know in patent suits what is the usual practice.

Mr. TOWNSEND.—Inasmuch as we are the plaintiffs in the action we have the opening.

The COURT.—I will give you equal time, so far as that is concerned. We have two and a half hours before five o'clock. You ought to be through by that time; perhaps you can finish in one hour on a side. [715]

Mr. TOWNSEND.—I think we can finish it this

afternoon, your Honor, and we can argue it now and do away with the necessity of briefs.

The COURT.—Very well, you may proceed.

(Here follows argument.)

[Endorsed]: Filed Apr. 26, 1924.　[716]

[Title of Court and Cause.]

DECISION.

Los Angeles Lime Co. vs. Nye, 270 Fed. 155, this Circuit, sustained the validity of the patent and claims involved in this suit, and therein sufficiently appear details of process and patent.

In the instant suit, however, the evidence is widely variant from that in the former suit, and requires a contrary decision. It now appears that claims 9 and 10 for the product of the process, were added to the application theretofore filed, by amendment without oath. The application was for a process alone, neither disclosed nor claimed invention of its product, and the absence of an oath avoids the patent to the extent of said claims.

See Steward vs. Co., 215 U. S. 168.

Westinghouse etc. Co. vs. Co., 290 Fed. 664.

The subject of the process, artificial or imitation stone, is older than and is the instrument of the most ancient recorded history.

It always was and now is made of plastic, cementitious materials, and in moulds shaped or cast in infinite form. Long prior to any time material herein, it was common knowledge that in color, texture, appearance, the artificial could be made in fair simulation of any natural stone. The state of the art rendered its production a matter of craftsmanship more than of invention, and architects desiring any new imitation, commonly referred to makers of artificial stone to produce it. In casting artificial stone, the workmen early discovered that failure to render sufficiently plastic the material or to carefully [717] press it in close and firm contact with the surface of the mould, resulting in voids, pockets, pits or holes in or on the surface of the cast. If a smooth surface was desired, these were defects to be repaired by filling. In imitation of limestone and lava rock, these voids, pockets, pits or holes were necessary and by design were produced by the very process that otherwise was unintended carelessness. And this intentional and skilful porosity of the cast, to simulate the like of Roman travertine limestone, is the process of the patent in suit.

In 1906 the architects of the Pennsylvania Depot in New York, Messrs. McKlm, Mead & White, determined that a large amount of the artificial stone for interior finish therein should be imitation of travertine, natural travertine had been contracted for in some quanity but was too costly to warrant its use to the extent desired.

At that time the imitation, if known, was not used in this country, and perhaps the same was true of the natural stone. Some of the latter received for the depot; artificial stone makers were as a matter of course requested to submit samples of

imitations of it, and they in like fashion did
so. Five samples were thus submitted, accompanied
by formal bids to make and install, by five different
makers, one of whom was this plaintiff. The evidence is that at least several of the samples other
than plaintiff's were made by the methods hereinbefore described. All these samples were deemed
satisfactory, but plaintiff's was the best and his
price the lowest. There was hesitancy, however,
to accept his bid, instead of some other, until his
financial ability to perform was assured. This
done, on March [718] 5, 1909, plaintiff formally
contracted to make and install in said depot, cast
and applied artificial or imitation travertine in
large amount and for a consideration of $109,000.
At no time had plaintiff given expression to aught
indicating experimental nature of the work, that it
was other than in ordinary course of an artificial
stone maker's trade, or that he doubted its practi-
cality or his ability to do the work in a competent
manner and to a successful result.

In behalf of his due performance, he furnished
a surety company bond in sum $50,000. The con-
tract with additions was performed and in consideration plaintiff received $125.000. When completed
in Nov. 29, 1910, plaintiff undertook to repair and
maintain the travertine for one year, gave bond to
that effect, and for a further consideration to him
of $3,500. During that year some inconsiderable
repairs were made. In 1911 plaintiff made and
installed imitation travertine in the barroom of the
Vanderbilt Hotel, New York, for a consideration

of $1,000. In 1912 and 1913 he did the like in the Goelet residence, New York. Some objection was interposed to evidence of this, for that no statutory notice of this prior public use had been given. None was necessary, the statue not applying to use by the patentee himself or to evidence of his admission, for therein is no surprise, nor to the testimony of witnesses.

Plaining etc. Co. vs. Keith, 101 U. S. 493.

During 1912 and 1913, plaintiff was advertising his "artificial Roman Travertine" accomplishment in the Pennsylvania depot. Early in 1913 a large amount of imitation travertine was made and installed in and upon the buildings of the San Francisco exposition, pursuant to [719] an arrangement with plaintiff to teach the process to the various contractors who so used it, and for which plaintiff stipulated a price which was paid.

The evidence indicates that in all the foregoing plaintiff had no conception of a new discovery or process, tho he may have believed he had invented new instruments to operate it. Aug. 2, 1913, he filed application subsequently abandoned, for a patent for instrumentalities—"apparatus or device whereby surfaces simulating various kinds of marble or other stone" may be produced. And not until Oct. 20, 1915, did he file application for the patent in suit. The evidence in the former suit gave to plaintiff's activities, the appearance of experimentation in respect to the process. Accordingly it was held that of process and product had not been public use for more than two years prior to the lication to which was cited Elizabeth vs. Co.,

97 U. S. 126. The evidence herein is otherwise,
clearly discloses public use for the period aforesaid,
and brings this suit within the analogy of Root vs
Ry., 146 U. S. 210, and of International etc. Co. vs.
Gaylord, 140 U. S. 55. As in the Root case, here
was advertisement and extensive operation of the
process in ordinary trade and business, barter and
sale of its product, devotion of it to practical and
public use, and only in remote degree suggestive of
experimentation. And as in the International case,
here was extensive and compensated teaching of the
process, likewise ordinary public use. Nothing appears to differentiate imitation travertine in characteristics and essential qualities from other well
understood artificial stone, and to require any extraordinary experimentation. All the circumstances
negative experiment and affirm ordinary uses.
[720]

More than two years public use having been
clearly established, the burden was plaintiff's to
prove by full, unequivocal and convincing evidence
that the use was experimental only.

Smith etc. Co. v. Sprague, 123 U. S. 264.

Therein he failed.

If the process was a new discovery and patentable, by use and sale plaintiff must be held to have
abandoned it to the public and to have incurred the
ban of the statute, § 4886 R. S.

The patent is invalid and the suit is dismissed.

Decree accordingly.

April 28, 1924.

BOURQUIN, J.

[Endorsed]: Filed Apr. 29, 1924. [721]

[Title of Court and Cause.]

DECREE.

This cause coming on for trial at the March Term of this Court on the 22d day of April, 1924, on the pleadings, proofs and the various exhibits introduced in evidence on behalf of the respective parties, and the Court being fully advised in the premises:

Now upon due consideration thereof, it is hereby:

ORDERED, ADJUDGED AND DECREED that letters patent of the United States No.1,212,331, dated January 16th, 1917, being the patent in suit, issued to Paul E. Denivelle, plaintiff, is, as far as claims 1, 2, 5, 9 and 10 are concerned (being the only claims charged to be infringed), invalid by reason of public use and sale more than two years before the application for the patent in suit was filed; that claims 9 and 10 of said patent are void by reason of the absence of a Supplemental Oath.

It is further ORDERED, ADJUDGED AND DECREED that the temporary injunction heretofore allowed be and the same is dissolved and the bill dismissed.

BOURQUIN.

Dated: May 1, 1924, San Francisco, California, 1924.

[Endorsed]: Filed and entered May 1. 1924. [722]

[Title of Court and Cause.]

PETITION FOR ORDER ALLOWING APPEAL.

To the Honorable Court, Above Entitled:

The above-named plaintiff, Paul E. Denivelle, conceiving himself aggrieved by the Decree filed and entered on the first day of May, 1924, in the above-entitled cause, does hereby appeal therefrom to the United States Circuit Court of Appeals, for the Ninth Judicial Circuit for the reasons and upon the grounds specified in the assignment of errors, which is filed herewith, and prays that this appeal may be allowed, that a citation issue as provided by law, and that a transcript of the record, proceedings, exhibits and papers, upon which said Decree was made and entered as aforesaid, duly authenticated, may be sent to the Circuit Court of Appeals for the Ninth Circuit, sitting at San Francisco.

And your petitioner further prays that an Order be made staying all further proceedings in this Court and fixing the amount of security which the plaintiff shall give and furnish upon such Appeal and that the transcript of evidence [723] taken in open Court and in the form of question and answer and depositions taken pursuant to Statute, in the form of question and answer, be embodied in the transcript of record on Appeal.

CHAS. E. TOWNSEND,

WM. A. LOFTUS,

Solicitors and Counsel for Plaintiff.

Dated: May 5th, 1924.

ORDER ALLOWING APPEAL.

The foregoing petition for appeal is allowed upon the Petitioner filing a bond in the sum of two hundred and fifty dollars ($250.00), with sufficient sureties, to be conditioned as required by law.

IT IS FURTHER ORDERED that the transcript of evidence taken in open court on final hearing and in the form of question and answer and depositions taken pursuant to Statute, in the form of question and answer, be embodied in the transcript of record on Appeal.

FRANK H. RUDKIN,
Judge.

Dated: May 5th, 1924.

[Endorsed]: Filed May 5, 1924.   [724]

[Title of Court and Cause.]

ASSIGNMENT OF ERRORS.

Now comes the plaintiff in the above-entitled cause and files the following assignment of errors upon which he will rely upon the prosecution of the appeal in the above-entitled cause, from the Decree made by this Honorable Court on the 1st day of May, 1924.

(1)   That the said United States District Court for the Northern District of California, Third Division, erred in dismissing the Bill of Complaint.

(2)   That the said United States District Court for the Northern District of California, Third Di-

vision, erred in finding that the said Denivelle Patent No. 1,212,331 in suit did not involve novelty.

(3) That the said United States District Court for the Northern District of California, Third Division, erred in finding that the said Denivelle Patent No. 1,212,331 in suit does not involve invention.

(4)· That the said United States District Court for the Northern District of California, Third Division, erred in [725] finding that the said Denivelle Patent No. 1,212,331 in suit is void for prior use and/or sale.

(5·) That the said United States District Court for the Northern District of California, Third Division, erred in not finding the patent valid and infringed with respect to claims 1, 2, 5, 9 and 10 sued on, and each of them, and which were the only claims in issue.

(6) That the said United States District Court for the Northern District of California, Third Division, erred in failing to find that the plaintiff was entitled to an accounting for, damages and profits for infringement of said Letters Patent No. 1,212,331.

(7) That the said United States District Court for the Northern District of California, Third Division, erred in failing to make temporary injunction permanent, restraining the further infringement of said Letters Patent No. 1,212,331.

(8·) That the said United States District Court for the Northern District of California, Third Division, erred in not holding that the authority of the Circuit Court of Appeals for the Ninth Circuit, expressed in the case of this plaintiff et al. vs Nye et al. (270 Fed. 155), sustaining the validity of the patent and the claims involved in that suit, was controlling in this suit.

(9) That the said United States District Court for the Northern District of California, Third Division, erred in holding that the Vanderbilt Hotel and Goelet jobs, and either of them, had been properly pleaded in accordance with Section 4920 under the authority of Planing etc. Co. vs. Keith, 101 U. S. 493.

(10) That the said United States District Court for the Northern District of California, Third Division, erred in [726] holding that the facts of the present case brings this suit within the analogy of Root vs. Ry., 146 U. S. 210 and/or of International etc. Co. vs. Gaylord, 140 U. S. 55, and not within the doctrine of the Elizabeth Paving Case, 97 U. S. 126.

(11) That the said United States District Court for the Northern District of California, Third Division, erred in holding that the plaintiff abandoned the invention to the public.

CHAS. E. TOWNSEND,
WM. A. LOFTUS,
Solicitors and Counsel for Plaintiff.

Dated, May 2d, 1924.   ,

[Endorsed]: Filed May 5, 1924.   [727]

[Title of Court and Cause.]

ORDER ALLOWING WITHDRAWAL OF ORIGINAL EXHIBITS.

On motion of Chas. E. Townsend, Esq., solicitor for plaintiff, and good cause appearing therefor, it is by the Court now ordered:

That all exhibits, physical and documentary, in the above-entitled case, both plaintiff's exhibits and defendants' exhibits, including models, drawings, copies of patents, books and printed publications, and which are impracticable to have copied or duplicated, be, and they are hereby allowed to be withdrawn from the files of this court in said case and transmitted by the Clerk of this Court to the United States Circuit Court of Appeals for the Ninth Circuit as a part of the record upon appeal for the plaintiff herein to the said Circuit Court of Appeals; said original exhibits to be returned to the files of this court upon the determination of said appeal by said Circuit Court of Appeals.

FRANK H. RUDKIN,
Judge.

Dated, May 2d, 1924.

[Endorsed]: Filed May 5, 1924. [728]

[Title of Court and Cause.]

PRAECIPE FOR TRANSCRIPT ON APPEAL.

To the Clerk of the United States District Court:

Please incorporate the following papers, documents and exhibits in the transcript of record on appeal in the above-entitled cause, omitting title of cause and omitting copying of all documentary exhibits:

(1) Bill of complaint.

(2) Amended answer.

(3) Order to show cause.

(4) Notice of motion and motion for preliminary injunction.

(5) Affidavit of Paul E. Denivelle on motion for preliminary injunction, dated July 14th, 1923.

(6) Affidavit of P. V. Koyse on motion for preliminary injunction, dated July 11th, 1923.

(7) Affidavit of D. R. Wagner, dated July 31st, 1923, for defendants on motion for preliminary injunction.

(8) Affidavit of F. J. Twaits, dated July 27th, 1923, for defendants on motion for preliminary injunction.

(9) Affidavit of Leonard Schultze, dated July 28th, 1923, for defendants on motion for preliminary injunction. [729]

(10) Affidavit of Eric Lange, dated July 31st, 1923, for defendants on motion for preliminary injunction.

(11) Affidavit of Frederick L. Tovani, dated July 27th, 1923, for defendants on motion for preliminary injunction.

(12) Affidavit of Thos. Lawrence, dated July 26th, 1923, for defendants on motion for preliminary injunction.

(13) Affidavit of Stephen Vida, dated July 31st, 1923, for defendants on motion for preliminary injunction.

(14) Affidavit of J. Harry Blohme, dated August 1st, 1923, for defendants on motion for preliminary injunction.

(15) Affidavit of John H. Delaney, dated August 1st, 1923, for defendants on motion for preliminary injunction.

(16) Order for preliminary injunction dated August 3d, 1923.

(16a) Preliminary injunction dated August 4, 1923.

(17) Injunction bond dated August 2d, 1923.

(18) Answer to plaintiff's interrogatories dated February 16th, 1924.

(19) Opinion of the United States Circuit Court of Appeals for the Ninth Circuit—Los Angeles Lime Co. et al. vs. Nye et al., on the patent in suit, being Plaintiff's Exhibit 16.

(20) Opinion of District Judge Bourquin, dated April 28th, 1924 (filed April 29th, 1924).

(21) Decree dated May 1st, 1924.

(22) Transcript of the entire record of all proceedings and testimony in full in the exact words of the witnesses, including depositions, except the deposition of Plaintiff Paul E. Denivelle appearing at pages 103–123, incl. of the daily transcript; the same already having been copied and printed above in item No. 5.

(23) All exhibits in the case, both physical and documentary.

(24)   Plaintiff's petition for order allowing appeal
       and order allowing appeal.
(25)   Assignment of errors.   [730]
(26)   Order allowing withdrawal of original ex-
       hibits.
(27)   Bond on appeal.
(28)   Citation.
(29)   This praecipe.

CHAS. E. TOWNSEND,

WM. A. LOFTUS,

Solicitors and Counsel for Plaintiff.

Dated May 1st, 1924.

Service of copy of the within praecipe for transcript on appeal, admitted this 23d day of May,
A. D. 1924.

R. M. J. ARMSTRONG,

T. HART ANDERSON,

Of Counsel for Defendants.

[Endorsed]:   Filed May 23, 1924.   [731]

[Title of Court and Cause.]

BOND ON APPEAL.

KNOW ALL MEN BY THESE PRESENTS:
That I, Paul E. Denivelle, of the city and county
of San Francisco, State of California, as principal,
and the Fidelity and Deposit Co. of Maryland, a
corporation, created, organized and existing under
and by virtue of the laws of the State of Maryland,
as surety, are held and firmly bound unto the above-
named appellees, MacGruer & Simpson (a co-part-

nership), and George Smith MacGruer and Robert
Morton Simpson, individually, and sometimes doing business as MacGruer & Co., in the sum of Two
Hundred Fifty Dollars ($250.00), in lawful money
of the United States of America, for the payment
of which well and truly to be made unto the said
appellees, their heirs, executors, administrators, successors and assigns, we bind ourselves, our heirs,
executors, administrators, successors and assigns,
jointly and severally, firmly by these presents, con-
ditioned that

WHEREAS, on the 1st day of May, 1924, in the
Southern [732] Division of the United States
District Court for the Northern District of California, Third Divison, in a suit pending in that court,
wherein Paul E. Denivelle was the plaintiff and
said MacGruer & Simpson (a copartnership) and
George Smith MacGruer and Robert Morton Simpson, individually, and sometimes doing business as
MacGruer & Co., were the defendants, numbered
on the Equity Docket as 1,078, a decree was rendered, which said decree was against the said Paul
E. Denivelle; and

WHEREAS, said Paul E. Denivelle having obtained an appeal to the United States Circuit Court
of Appeals for the Ninth Circuit, to reverse the
said decree, which said decree was entered in the
said United states District Court on the 1st day of
May, 1924, and an appeal allowed, and citation
directed to the said appellees, citing and admonish-
ing them to be and appear at a session of the United

States Circuit Court of Appeals for the Ninth Circuit.

NOW, THEREFORE, the condition of this obligation is such that if the above-named appellant shall prosecute said appeal to effect and answer all costs, if he fails to make his plea good, then the above obligation to be void; else to remain in full force and virtue.

PAUL E. DENIVELLE,

Principal.

FIDELITY AND DEPOSIT CO. OF

MARYLAND.

[Seal]   By C. K. BENNETT,

Surety.

Attorney-in-fact.

E. K. AVELOW,

Agent.

Dated: May 6th, 1924.

Approved:

FRANK H. RUDKIN,

Judge.

[Endorsed]: Filed May 8, 1924. [733]

[Title of Court and Cause.]

CERTIFICATE OF CLERK U. S. DISTRICT COURT TO TRANSCRIPT OF RECORD.

I, Walter B. Maling, Clerk of the District Court of the United States, in and for the Northern District of California, do hereby certify the foregoing seven hundred and thirty-four (734) pages, numbered from 1 to 734, inclusive, to be 'ull. true and correct copies of the record and proc 'dings in the above-entitled suit as enumerated in tl praecipe for record on appeal, as the same rem:as of record and on file in the office of the clerk f said court, and that the same constitutes the recrd on appeal to the United States Circuit Court ofAppeals for the Ninth Circuit.

I further certify that the cost of 'ie foregoing transcript of record is $257.25; that said amount was paid by the plaintiff and that the riginal cita_ tion issued in said suit is hereto anneed.

IN WITNESS WHEREOF, I have hereunto set my hand and affixed the seal of said I strict Court this 17th day of June, A. D. 1924.

[Seal]   WALTER B. MALING,
Clerk United States District Court for 1e Northern
     District of California.   [734]

CITATION ON APPEAL

UNITED STATES OF AMERICA,—ss.
The President of the United States, T MacGruer & Simpson (a Copartnership) :nd George Smith MacGruer and Robert Morta Simpson, Individually, and Sometimes Doing Business as MacGruer & Co., GREETING:

You are hereby cited and admonishe to be and appear at a United States Circuit Court of Appeals for the Ninth Circuit, to be holden at 1e City of San Francisco, in the State of Califoria, within

thirty days from the date hereof, pursuant to an order allowing an appeal, of record in the Clerk's Office of the United States District Court for the Northern District of California, Southern Division, wherein Paul E. Denivelle is appellant, and you are appellees, to show cause, if any there be, why the decree rendered against the said appellant, as in the said order allowing appeal mentioned, should not be corrected, and why speedy justice should not be done to the parties in that behalf.

WITNESS, the Honorable FRANK H. RUD-KIN, United States Circuit Judge for the Ninth Judicial Circuit, this 5th day of May, A. D. 1924.

FRANK H. RUDKIN,

United States Circuit Judge.   [735]

Service of a copy of the within citation on appeal admitted this 8th day of May, 1924.

T. HART ANDERSON,

Solicitor for Defendant-Appellee.

[Endorsed]: Equity—No. 1078. United States District Court for the Northern District of California, Southern Division. Paul E. Denivelle, Appellant, vs. MacGruer & Simpson (a Copartnership) and George Smith MacGruer and Robert Morton Simpson, Individually, and Sometimes Doing Business as MacGruer & Co. Citation on Appeal. Filed May 8, 1924. Walter B. Maling, Clerk. By J. A. Schaertzer, Deputy Clerk.

———

[Endorsed]: No. 4269. United States Circuit Court of Appeals for the Ninth Circuit. Paul E.

Denivelle, Appellant, vs. MacGruer & Simpson, a Copartnership, and George Smith MacGruer and Robert Morton Simpson, Individually, and Sometimes Doing Business as MacGruer & Co., Appellees. Transcript of Record. Upon Appeal from the Southern Division of the United States District Court for the Northern District of California, Third Division.

Filed June 17, 1924.

F. D. MONCKTON,

Clerk of the United States Circuit Court of Appeals for the Ninth Circuit.

By Paul P. O'Brien,

Deputy Clerk.

———

In the Circuit Court of Appeals for the Ninth Circuit.

No. 4269.

PAUL E. DENIVELLE,

Plaintiff-Appellant,

vs.

MacGRUER & SIMPSON (a Copartnership) and GEORGE SMITH MacGRUER, and ROBERT MORTON SIMPSON, Individually, and Sometimes Doing Business as MacGRUER & CO.,

Defendants-Appellees.

ORDER RELIEVING APPELLANT FROM PRINTING DOCUMENTARY EXHIBITS.

GOOD CAUSE APPEARING, it is hereby ordered that the appellant may be relieved from printing the original documentary exhibits in this case, provided the appellant appropriately arranges and binds said original documentary exhibits in convenient form with numbered pages, for the consideration of the Court.

HUNT,
Judge.

Dated: July 10th, 1924.
CET:FVC.

[Endorsed]: No. 4269. In the Circuit Court of Appeals for the Ninth Circuit. Paul E. Denivelle, Plaintiff-Appellant, vs. MacGruer & Simpson et al., Defendants-Appellees. Order Relieving Appellant from Printing Documentary Exhibits. Filed Jul. 10, 1924. F. D. Monckton, Clerk. By Paul P. O'Brien, Deputy Clerk.

No. 4269

IN THE

United States Circuit Court of Appeals

For the Ninth Circuit

. DENIVELLE,

                          Appellant,

VS.

UER & SIMPSON (a copartnership) and
GE SMITH MACGRUER and ROBERT
TON SIMPSON, individually, and some-
s doing business as MacGruer & Co.,

                          Appellees.

On Denivelle
for
Artificial Tra
No. 1,212,3
Dated, Janua
1917.

BRIEF FOR APPELLANT.

CHAS. E. TOWNSEND,
WM. A. LOFTUS,
      Attorneys for Appellant.

Subject Index

Table of Cases Cited

No. 4269

United States Circuit Court of Appeals

For the Ninth Circuit

———

L E. DENIVELLE,

Appellant,

vs.

GRUER & SIMPSON (a copartnership) and EORGE SMITH MACGRUER and ROBERT ORTON SIMPSON, individually, and some- mes doing business as MacGruer & Co.,

Appellees.

On Denivel fo Artificial T No. 1,21 Dated, Jan 191

BRIEF FOR APPELLANT.

———

STATEMENT.

This is an appeal by plaintiff below from a decree entered pursuant to an opinion rendered by his Honor Judge Bourquin holding the patent in suit invalid and dismissing the bill.

The patent sued on, No. 1,212,331, issued January 16th, 1917, application filed October 20th, 1915, for Artificial Travertin, has already been before this Court and held valid, on, we respectfully submit, substantially the same state of facts, in the case of *Los Angeles Lime Co. and Paul E. Denivelle v. C. L. Nye* (and same plaintiffs v. *E. Ceriat*), No. 3,532, 270 Fed. 155.

The present suit was brought July 16th, 1923. On motion for preliminary injunction the late Judge Van Fleet issued a restraining order *pendente lite*. The case was tried before Judge Bourquin on the 22nd, 23rd and 24th days of April, 1924.

Judge Bourquin's decision appears in the present record at pages 674 to 678; the final decree at page 679.

The claims in controversy are the same as in the former suit, (or as we shall term it, "the Los Angeles suit"), and are as follows:

"I. A process for the manufacture of striated artificial stone structures which comprises depositing upon a prepared surface of desired form a series of narrow layers of plastic material, depositing upon said layers and upon the exposed surfaces there-between a suitable material of such texture and consistency as will leave numerous small portions of said exposed surfaces out of contact with said material, binding together said layers and said material with a fluid cement, and allowing the mass to set.

"2. A process for the manufacture of striated artificial stone structures which comprises depositing upon a prepared surface of desired form a series of narrow layers of plastic material of a certain color, depositing upon said layers and upon the exposed surfaces there-between a suitable material of a different color and of such texture and consistency as will leave numerous small portions of said exposed surfaces out of contact with said material, binding together said layers and said material with a fluid cement, and allowing the mass to set.

"5. A process for the manufacture of striated artificial stone structures, which consists in preparing a mold of suitable outline with an isolator, forming veins of plastic material over this prepared surface, depositing loose, lumpy material over the veining to provide pockets, binding the pocket-forming material with the veining material, and leaving certain pockets exposed on the surface adjacent to the mold surface.

"9. A cementitious structure suitable for decorative purposes comprising a mass of cementitious material at least one surface of which is shaped and striated and formed with small irregularly spaced depressions, the striae constituting the exposed portions of shallow inlays of uniformly colored cement.

"10. A cementitious combination for decorative use such as a finish for exterior or interior building walls and ceilings, which combination is formed of differently toned thin layers or strata, the said layers only partly connected one to the other in such manner as to leave serrated voids in stratified formation between said layers, said layers and voids existing only adjacent to the surface but giving an appearance, when erected, of extending through the depth of the mass, the resulting decorative surface simulating that of a natural stone structure of sedimentary origin."

The basis of the Trial Court's decision in the instant case is briefly:

1. That the product claims No. 9 and No. 10 of the Denivelle patent are void because added subsequent to the filing of the application by amendment without the formality of a Supplemental Oath. (Note that the Court did not hold that the insertion

of these claims was not disclosed in the original specification and drawings as filed.)

2. "Public use" within the meaning of the Statute by this plaintiff and in the Pennsylvania Station in New York City. (This it will be revealed was the main defense in the Los Angeles suit.)

The bill is in the usual form for a patent infringement suit, except that it set up the prior adjudication of this Court (Paragraph IX, R. 5-6).

The defendants by their amended answer (R. 10-19) admitted the prior adjudication but claimed newly discovered evidence. They admit (Paragraph 7, R. 12):

> "* * * that the plaintiff has requested them not to infringe the aforesaid letters patent, and to account to plaintiff for the alleged infringement thereof, but they deny that they have ever infringed said letters patent, and accordingly refused to cease employing the process used by them, as upon the advice of counsel learned in the law, they are assured that what they have been doing in and about the manufacture of artificial travertine, in nowise constitutes an infringement of any valid claim of the said patent, and in fact that, notwithstanding the decision of the Court of Appeals referred to in paragraph 'IX' of the bill of complaint, the said letters patent are invalid for reasons known to the plaintiff."

In their amended answer they set up some twenty-three patents as alleged anticipation (13 R. 15-16).

At the trial (R. 602-603) the defense offered seven of these patents and two British patents, concerning which no notice pursuant to the Statute (R. 920) had been given. None of these patents were accompanied by any explanation in aid of the Court. Not a word was said about these patents or any of them on argument. The Trial Court apparently ignored them.

The defendants in the amended answer (Paragraph 14—R. 16) also set up a prior publication entitled "Limestones and Marbles" but this was withdrawn by bill of particulars (R. 83), filed February 18th, 1924.

The answer in Paragraph 15 further set out the names of a considerable number of alleged prior users, several of whom were called to testify to the work done by Mr. Denivelle in the Pennsylvania Station prior to his introducing his method to the Panama-Pacific International Exposition. The list includes many, in fact most of the so-called prior users noted in the previous Los Angeles suit, and includes at least one deponent, Morkel, for defendants (R. 387) who deposed to a like effect in the Los Angeles case (see Transcript of Los Angeles Record, Exhibit 6, R. 544; certified copy prior deposition Morkel Exhibit 7, R. 545).

PRELIMINARY INJUNCTION GRANTED BY THE LATE JUDGE VAN FLEET.

On the filing of the present bill a preliminary injunction was prayed for and on full hearing was granted August 4th, 1923 (R. 79), by the late Judge Van Fleet.

The defendants appeared and vigorously contested the motion, filing voluminous and elaborate affidavits which are reproduced in this record for the purpose here; first, to show the completeness of the defendants' showing before Judge Van Fleet; second, as admissions against interest.

Two of the plaintiff's affidavits in support of the Motion for Preliminary Injunction are reproduced in this record: affidavit of P. E. Denivelle (R. 23-46); and P. V. Keyse (R. 46-51).

Reference is made to these affidavits and particularly that of Mr. Denivelle for a somewhat more detailed description of the patented invention.

Defendants' affidavits, considered as admissions, show:

(1) Proof of infringing product (Tovani R. 59; Delaney 74-75).

(2) Wilful infringement (Twaits R. 54; Tovani R. 59; Blohme R. 67-68; Delaney R. 74).

(3) That the Denivelle process was in an admittedly experimental stage *in late 1913* at the time the work was going on at the Panama-Pacific International Exposition (Wagner R. 52).

(4) That defendants while claiming that Denivelle's Artificial Travertin is not and cannot be patentable, nevertheless they profess to have created in *their* infringing product "a novel and new and useful composition of matter wherein these cavities can be more or less consistently formed upon the exposed surface of the finished product" (Delaney affidavit, R. 74) upon which they claim to have issued a patent (Delaney patent No. 1,468,343, dated September 18th, 1923—Defendants' Exhibit 29, R. 602, but which patent says nothing in fact about "artificial Travertin" or "veining").

DEFENDANTS' EASTERN DEPOSITIONS.

On the joining of issues the defendants proceeded by stipulation to take the depositions of some twenty-three different witnesses in New York City and Washington, D. C. to show that the work was done by Mr. Denivelle on the Pennsylvania Railroad Station in New York City during the years 1909 to 1912, inclusive. These depositions appear in full in the record (R. 83 to 530, inclusive), and support plaintiff's view as embodied in your Honors' opinion in the Los Angeles case. The substantial and material parts of these depositions are later quoted herein.

ASSIGNMENT OF ERRORS (R. 681-683).

On this appeal plaintiff urges in brief that it was error for the Trial Court:

(1) To dismiss plaintiff's bill, because of any of the alleged defenses of lack of novelty, lack of invention, prior use, sale, or abandonment.

(2) In not finding the patent valid and infringed as to claims 1, 2, 5, 9 and 10, and each of them and awarding an accounting.

(3) In disregarding the prior adjudication of this Court sustaining the patent.

(4) In erroneous application of the law to the facts.

THE PARTIES.

The patentee is known to this Court from the opinion in the Los Angeles suit (270 Fed. 155).

His work at the Panama-Pacific International Exposition in San Francisco in 1915 has become known, recognized, admired and imitated far beyond the limits of this city and State.

His other and more recent work in this city embraces such monumental structures as the Public Library in the Civic Center, the Federal Reserve Bank and the Anglo Bank, the latter a recent job totaling about one hundred and ten thousand dollars' ($110,000.) (R. 572).

The defendants, MacGruer and Simpson are "contractors for marble furring, lathing, plastering, ornamental plasterer and artificial stones, and artificial marbles of all kinds'' (R. 604). They were the sub-contractors for plaster work on Machinery Hall at the San Francisco 1915 Exposition under W. W. Anderson & Co., the general contractors for that building (R. 605).

Without going into details at present, it is sufficient to say that under the supervision and assistance of Mr. Denivelle, the plaintiff, they were obliged reluctantly to carry out Mr. Denivelle's plans and ideas for treatment of Machinery Hall in Artificial Travertin. The work was done and accepted by the Exposition authorities on March 18th, 1914 (R. 647). To the same effect see MacGruer testimony (R. 606).

As showing the novelty of the Process to such experienced men supposedly skilled in the art as the defendants, as late as *October 8th, 1913,* the witness MacGruer identifies a letter of protest he wrote the Exposition authorities, wherein defendants said (R. 646-647):

"Now that we have proceeded far enough with our work to arrive at a basis of the additional cost which has been pressed upon us, and of which you are well aware our contract does not call for, we now advise you that we will demand to be compensated for all the *experimental work* we have been doing for the Exposition Company. Also the additional cost of executing in our casting the *imitation of travertine stone,* which necessitated the breaking up of our molds so that they would lie in a horizontal position to receive *the veining process.*

"We are being compelled to try and match the jointing of the staff or imitation travertine stone work with one of the colored plasters, together with some unfibered hardwall, according to some formula or instructions given by Mr. Denivelle or his representatives, and so far we *have been unable to get the desired result* which is easy to understand in the face of the fact that we are being asked to match a combination of colors in our staff or imitation travertine stone with practically one colored plaster."

The last paragraph:

"We may say we are following the method of mixing of materials and entirely as directed, and we are finding the burden of expense is being placed on our shoulders which should be borne by the Exposition Company, as *we are being used solely for experimental purposes,* which is not in accordance with the terms of our contract" (italics ours).

At R. 608 MacGruer testified:

"Well, at that time (1913) *it was very much of an experiment with himself,* because he had never used plaster" (italics ours).

Daniel R. Wagner, a former member of W. W. Anderson Co., made an affidavit for these defendants in opposition to the motion for preliminary injunction (R. 51-53) in which he said (R. 52):

"* * * that the said MacGruer & Simpson, *in order to carry out the provisions and specifications of the contract* awarded as aforesaid, *prepared samples of artificial travertin for the approval of the Director of Works of said Exposition* and in conformity with the terms of said contract awarded to said Mac-

Gruer & Simpson; that he knows it to be true
that in order that this work could be satisfactorily carried out by said MacGruer & Simpson, in accordance with said contract, *it was
necessary that said MacGruer & Simpson carry
on costly and expensive experiments* in order
to cause said imitation travertin to meet the
full approval of the said Director of Works in
charge of the Panama-Pacific International
Exposition;"

and

"* * * that this work was duly performed
by the said MacGruer & Simpson after *costly
experiments* on their part and that it consisted
in *imitating Roman travertin in conformity
with the specifications* provided by said Panama-Pacific International Exposition" (italics
ours).

At R. 607 MacGruer said:

"A. As I understood, he was to collaborate
and assist. He was employed by the Exposition Company in the capacity of what we generally call on a building a superintendent."

And R. 613:

"There was some agreement with the Exposition Company that any building done in the
Exposition grounds was subject to the general
supervision of the Exposition authorities and
Mr. Denivelle, naturally, being employed by the
Exposition Company, naturally had that sort
of supervision that would come under that
plan."

Time passed until the building of the Los Angeles
Biltmore Hotel in Los Angeles in 1922 and 1923.

MacGruer testified (R. 653):

"The amount of the Biltmore, as contracted for, was $406,509—there may be a variation in the odd figures, but that was about it."

* * * * * * *

"It was completed just prior to the opening of the Biltmore, which was October, 1923."

* * * * * * *

"The actual work started somewhere around November, 1922."

NOTICE TO DEFENDANTS.

On May 24th, 1922, plaintiff's attorney addressed a letter to the Scofield Engineering & Construction Co., the General Contractor of the Hotel, appearing at R. 557 to 559, and reading as follows:

"Gentlemen:

"Re: Paul E. Denivelle Travertine Patents.

"Mr. Denivelle has laid before me the facts and circumstances in connection with his proposal to do the artificial travertine work in connection with the Los Angeles Biltmore Hotel pursuant to the plans and specifications submitted by you, and has also shown me your wire advising that the contract for this work had been let to other parties.

"You are, I suppose, conversant with Mr. Denivelle's patents covering this character of work, and the further fact that these patents have not only been upheld, but broadly construed by the United States Circuit Court of Appeals for this Circuit.

"Manifestly, Mr. Denivelle cannot stand by and see his patents infringed with impunity. Inasmuch as he has but one licensee authorized to do this work and this licensee has no right to sub-license others, we are, therefore, desirous of knowing at once to whom the contract for this work has been let.

"In the event of not hearing from you within a reasonable time, we shall assume that the work contemplated is unauthorized as far as Mr. Denivelle is concerned, and that the letting of the contract constitutes a threat to infringe, giving legal cause for court action.

"While it is not the desire of Mr. Denivelle to engage in litigation, and then only as a last resort, he must have his patent rights respected, particularly where a lifetime of effort on his part has been directed to the bringing of this process to perfection, and in view of the money and time already expended in litigating and upholding these patents. On the other hand, it is assumed that you do not desire to involve your client nor yourselves in unnecessary litigation, the only result of which would be to cause them and yourselves added expense and delay in the event the process of injunction is invoked.

"It is hoped that a full and frank discussion of these matters at this time will have the effect of removing any misunderstandings that may exist on the part of any of the parties concerned.

"Yours very truly,
"CHAS. E. TOWNSEND,
"Attorney for Paul E. Denivelle."

Subsequently, on June 6th, 1922, at the solicitation of the defendants, a meeting was arranged at the offices of the late C. L. Patton, attorney for defendants, in San Francisco, at which were present the plaintiff and his present counsel, the defendant MacGruer and Mr. Patton.

On June 19th, 1922, defendants wrote plaintiff as follows (R. 553-555):

PLAINTIFF'S EXHIBIT No. 17.

(Letter-head of MacGruer & Simpson.)
"San Francisco, Cal., June 19, 1922.
"Mr. P. E. Denivelle,
   280 Golden Gate Ave.,
      San Francisco, Calif.
"Dear Sir:
   "We have been awarded the contract for all metal furring, lathing, plastering, artificial stone, etc., on the New Biltmore Hotel, Los Angeles, California, per the plans and specifications of Messrs. Schultze and Weaver, Architects, New York City.

   "Under the terms of this contract it is proposed to use a cast artificial Travertine Stone in certain portions of the building, namely:

   "Basement elevator lobby and stairways adjacent as covered by Addendas 2 and 3.

   "Ground floor, architraeve at T e l e p h o n e Room.

   "Main Hotel Lobby, including the elevator lobbies on ground and first floors.

   "First Floor Dining Room.

   "The above, at present covers all of the cast artificial Travertine Stone according to the terms of our contract.

   "We are in receipt of a letter from the Scofield Engineering and Construction Company enclosing a copy of letter from your Attorney, notifying them of the existence of a certain patent held by you for this character of work and asking them to take the matter up so as to avoid any unnecessary complications in the event that it is the intention to use your process for the manufacture of this cast artificial Travertine Stone.

"In keeping with the above and also our interview with you and your Attorney, Mr. Townsend, at the office of Mr. C. L. Patton, our Attorney, on the 16th, may we ask under what terms we can have the privilege of using your process as covered by your patent No. 1,212,331 and dated January 16th, 1917, so that your interests may be protected?

"As there is a possibility of certain portions of the above-enumerated work to be changed to artificial stone of another character other than cast artificial travertine, may we request, when submitting your proposal or terms, that you segregate same in the following manner:

"1. A price for the right to use your process under the terms of a license for this particular building for the work now contemplated.

"2. A lump sum bid including all metal furring necessary for the erection of the cast artificial Travertine Stone as enumerated above.

"3. A separate bid for the furnishing of all cast artificial Travertine Stone as covered by Proposal No. 2. This bid is [619] not to include the erection or pointing of same.

"4. A separate bid for the Main Lobby and Elevator Lobbies as shown on Ground and First Floor plans.

"5. A separate bid on Proposal No. 4 for the furnishing of this and not including the metal furring, erection and pointing for the Main Hotel Lobby and Elevator Lobbies on Ground and First Floor.

"6. A separate bid for the dining-room.

"7. A separate bid for the basement elevator lobby and Stairway.

"8. A separate bid for dining-room in keeping with Proposal No. 4.

"9. A separate bid for the Basement Lobby and Stairway similar to proposal No. 5.

"Kindly forward us this information at the earliest possible moment and oblige,

"Very truly yours,
"MacGruer & Simpson.
"George MacGruer."

(Italics ours.)

Concerning the interview on June 16th, 1922, and the writing of this letter to Denivelle Mr. MacGruer says (R. 559):

> *"The reason for the writing of that letter came partly from your suggestion and Mr. Patton's.* I was influenced by your letter, which I considered was intimidation to the general contractor and to throw obstacles in my way to complete the contract" (italics ours).

And (R. 560):

> "As a result of that interview, at your suggestion, *along with Mr. Patton's,* I wrote this letter so that we could get down to a basis of possibly arriving at some conclusion.
> "Q. Did you get a reply from Mr. Denivelle? A. I did, I received a firm bid," (italics ours).

On June 26th, 1922, Mr. Denivelle wrote at length (R. 561-565) a letter (Plaintiff's Exhibit 19) and submitted bids and conditions specifying, according to one proposition of defendants, a sum of forty one thousand five hundred dollars ($41,500); and, according to another requested proposition, forty-five thousand dollars ($45,000).

To quote some noteworthy and commendable excerpts from this letter Mr. Denivelle said (R. 561-562):

"*Request No. 1.* 'A price for the right to use your process under the terms of a license for this particular building for the work now contemplated.'

"I cannot see my way clear to quote you acceptable terms for license at this time as this would involve a division of responsibility for the ultimate result in the work."

*　　　*　　　*　　　*　　　*　　　*　　　*

"*Request No. 3.* 'A separate bid for the furnishing of all cast artificial travertine stone as covered by Proposal No. 2. This bid is not to include the erection or pointing of same.'

"This likewise involves a division of responsibility which for practical reasons cannot be granted as said imitation travertine stone is never completed as a fabricated article until it has been erected and finished."

(R. 563-564):

"In complying with your request and submitting figures as above, it is, of course, without prejudice to the fact that the artificial travertin which I contemplate using is not only covered by patent on the product but the method as well is also protected. Inasmuch as this is a patented article, I cannot concede that it is open to public bidding.

"On the other hand, the fact that the Product and Method are patented has had no bearing on the figures given you above.

"As previously explained to you, my object in patenting my Artificial Travertine and my process was primarily to protect the architect and his clients who see fit to use this material, and to guarantee and to maintain the standard of quality as well as to prevent, by legal means, cheap and unworthy imitations. For the same reason I have felt justified in exercising proper precautions and restraint in the issuance of licenses."

As showing wilful infringement and deliberate contempt for this Court's solemn opinion expressed in the Los Angeles suit concerning the validity of plaintiff's patent, defendant MacGruer on the stand admitted, on cross-examination by his own counsel concerning the June 16th, 1922 conference (R. 566):

> "The only conversation was a sort of cross-questioning back and forth, in which he intimated to me that I was going to go along and that I knew of his patent, and I stated that I didn't think he had a patent, and I was still of that opinion. He stated, 'You have been doing this thing for a long time and you have been trying to get around this patent for a long time.' I said, 'I don't see any need of getting around the patent, I don't think there is any patent'."

On further direct examination (R. 567) MacGruer testified:

> "Mr. TOWNSEND. Q. Do you mean to say that you mentioned to Mr. Denivelle and myself that you had applied for a patent?
>
> "A. No, we did not say we applied for a patent. If you will recall the conversation, Mr. Townsend, when I stated to Mr. Denivelle that we were now trying to get away from the semi-dry process, and we believed we had done it, Mr. Denivelle put a menacing finger toward me and said, 'You have been doing this for a long time, but you won't get away with it'."
>
> *　　*　　*　　*　　*　　*　　*
>
> "I said we were trying to get away from the semi-dry process which I stated to you at that time was the only thing I thought he had of any possibility in his patent, if the patent was valid."

MAINTENANCE OF HIGH STANDARD OF QUALITY OF WORK CHIEF AIM OF PLAINTIFF.

Mr. Denivelle's account of the interview is given at (R. 581-582):

"Mr. MacGruer wanted to find out under what arrangement he could proceed with his work, and do it in accordance with my patent, he seemingly having no other method of doing it at that time. He wanted to know if he could go ahead on a royalty basis, and we discussed the question of royalty, but I pointed out to him that my main object was to maintain a standard of quality in connection with my product, so as not to depreciate the value of my patent or my patented product, and that that was my main interest, and for that reason I could not consent at that time, and I told him that I was not satisfied that he could produce a product that would be satisfactory in its standard to me, and that would not depreciate the value of my product. As a result of that conference, he asked me to submit a bid for the travertine portion of his contract on the Biltmore Hotel, and I told him if he would put his request in writing so that it would be definite in form, I would endeavor to do so, which he later did, and I submitted a bid accordingly."

Further, on the point of deliberate infringement see the affidavit of F. J. Twaits of the Scofield Engineering-Construction Company (R. 53-54):

(R. 54)

"That after due investigation, they decided to award this work to MacGruer and Simpson, not because they were the lowest bidder, but because it was thought they would most certainly finish on time, and because of their reputation for doing good work; that, after this intention was explained to the architect, the *architect requested that we make another effort to get from the plaintiff a firm bid for the above work, the architect being acquainted with the plaintiff* and not with the defendants; that *in pursuance of this request, and as a matter of accommodation to the architect,* we did ask the plaintiff again for a firm bid covering the above work; that they never did receive from him a *complete* bid so as to enable us to consider letting the work to him; that the price he did submit for a portion of the work was out of range with other prices in our possession, and therefore unusable; that *at no time was there any possibility of awarding this work to the plaintiff"* (italics ours).

Under such circumstances suit was eventually inevitable though it was many months before work actually began on the Travertin portions of the Hotel.

MacGruer says (R. 653) that work began in November, 1922, and was completed "October 1923" (this latter date would be subsequent to the issuance of the preliminary injunction by the late Judge Van Fleet on August 4th, 1923).

During the interim between the June conference and correspondence and the beginning of work on the Biltmore it was quite apparent defendants were striving desperately to find some way to "get around" the patent, thereby acknowledging its merit. After the infringing work was commenced by the defendants it was carried on with such secrecy that it became very difficult to secure evidence as only trusted employees of defendants were admitted to the building (see the affidavit of Keyse, R. 46). In fact, it was defendants' own affidavits that offered the best proof of infringement and so convinced the late Judge Van Fleet that to his mind not only was the patent valid but its infringement clear beyond doubt.

––––

INDUCEMENT TO INFRINGE GREAT ON ACCOUNT OF SAVING EFFECTED.

The desire of architects to use real Travertin would naturally be prompted by its known artistic merits, enhanced no doubt by its comparative rarity in building use, due to its extremely high cost.

By the same token it would seem obvious for architects and builders to seek to employ an imitation, having due regard for faithfulness in reproduction, permanence, durability, cost, etc.

Six dollars a foot for Natural Travertin against one for the Patented ARTIFICIAL.

As to the comparative costs between the natural and the patented imitation we are told by Mr. Denivelle (R. 670):

> "Taken in plain surface, in plain walls, the *cheapest,* that is, the *least expensive* type of the natural, that would probably cost, erected in place, $6 per square foot.
>
> * * * * * * *
>
> "The other (the imitation) approximates, on the wall, and, as I say, in a plain surface,

$1 to $1.25 per square foot. However, the moment you get into molded forms, that is, moldings, cornices, and ornaments, the disparaging difference is very much greater between the natural and the artificial, because the moment they have to mill and form moldings in the natural, it is extremely expensive, whereas, by the process of reproduction in the artificial we make them at a cost that is comparatively nominal. So that while we have represented the difference between the two slabs in price, taken on a job, and one executed in natural and the other, taking the Pennsylvania, for instance, in artificial, they would have run into *millions of dollars* to have produced there what I did artificially" (italics ours).

But to obtain a correct and enduring imitation of Travertin Stone, quite apparently presented to those skilled in the art difficulties far beyond those that plasterers and ornamental stone artificers had met with in imitation of ordinary smooth marbles.

This, no doubt, was due in large measure to the peculiarities of Travertin.

As Mr. Denivelle points out (R. 671):

" * * * there is this difference between natural travertine and the ordinary other stones, there is a great loss in natural travertine in getting any degree of selection whatever, because it runs from an impossible spongy type; in other words, to get one stone out of that slab—that was gotten out of a slab that was *five feet square,* referring to exhibit 22. A good part of the rest of it is a specimen of travertine. It is a very fine specimen. You might have to go very far if you proposed to select the travertine for the purpose of your job."

And then followed a rather humorous mistake on the part of defendants' counsel, but which only emphasized the merit of the Denivelle invention and the artistic perfection of his process.

> "By Mr. ANDERSON. Q. And this specimen you have here is a very fine selected specimen, isn't it?
>
> "A. I beg your pardon, Mr. Anderson, you are referring to the wrong one.
>
> "Q. Well, I am referring to whichever one it is. That is a very fine specimen, isn't it?
>
> "A. That is a very nice specimen."

In other words, so perfect was the Denivelle specimen of imitation Travertin (Exhibit 21) that it was confused by defendants' counsel with the *Natural* Travertin (Exhibit 22).

Comparing such work by the patentee with the crude, garish, but nevertheless striking counterfeit work of these defendants represented by Exhibits 1 and 2, quite justified the fears of Mr. Denivelle when he wrote these defendants on June 26th, 1922 (R. 564):

> "As previously explained to you, my object in patenting my Artificial Travertine and my Process was primarily to protect the architect and his clients who see fit to use this material, and to guarantee and to maintain the standard of quality as well as to prevent, by legal means, cheap and unworthy imitations. For the same reason I have felt justified in exercising proper precautions and restraint in the issuance of licenses."

THE DENIVELLE PATENT.
Plaintiff's Exhibit 3.

The Denivelle patent issued January 16th, 1917, on an application filed October 20th, 1915; this application being in continuation and substitution of an earlier application filed August 2nd, 1913, Ser. No. 782,671, Defendants' Exhibit 25, R. 594. Under the law the patentee is entitled to this filing date with respect to any question of public use (*Union Carbide Co. v. American,* 172 Fed. 120, 130).

The patent in suit is for the manufacture of Artificial Stone in simulation of Roman Travertin. The patent embodies the invention in two forms:

(A) The form in controversy in which the method as practiced is for casting separate articles later to be set in place; the so-called "cast" method and here involved; and

(B) The form representing the method as practiced for surfacing structures already in place; the so-called "applied" method, not here involved, method (B) being covered by a separate patent not here in issue.

The patented process like most processes resides in a series or succession of steps taken in a certain order of arrangement and applied to certain materials to produce a desired result. The result of the process is a building slab having much the surface texture of natural Travertin, but, of course, the patent is not to be judged by how close it approaches natural Travertin. It is primarily an artificial stone of distinctive characteristics which the trade through plaintiff's efforts and success, has come to recognize as a new product.

The patent describes how the process is practiced with prerequisite exactness; the nature of the process and of the resulting product being aptly illustrated by the claims charged to be infringed, and previously quoted herein.

The patentee, by way of illustrating his invention, describes the necessary tools. These tools are very simple, consisting merely of a can (Plaintiff's Exhibit 10, R. 545) with a pouring spout for applying the veining in suitable fashion, and a suitably greased or prepared mold, upon the surface of which the veining is first run. The grease prevents the slab from sticking to the mold.

In practice the veining is sometime broken up, serrated or otherwise varied or even produced by means of a suitable stiff split brush (Plaintiff's Exhibit 45, R. 668).

Over this veining a cloddy, or lumpy material, very much of the consistency of mortar, is spread to form the pockets, or, as the patent says: depositing upon the exposed surfaces of the mold

> "a suitable material of such texture and consistency as will leave numerous portions of said exposed surfaces out of contact with the material."

This lumpy material produces the voids adjacent to the finished surface, "but giving an appearance when erected of extending through the depth of the mass"; to use the phraseology of claim 10.

The final step of the process is backing up this veining and the lumpy, void-forming material with suitable cementitious backing so that when the mass is allowed to set the veins and pocket-forming material and backing will be knit into a solid, durable mass, forming an artificial stone slab which can be set up in position as a wall surface or covering.

The only difference between defendants' procedure as we will see, and plaintiff's, is that after the defendants *grease* the mold and provide the *veining,* they scatter a *lumpy* substance (calcium carbide) in *dry* form over the veins and then quickly pour on a moist *cementitious binder* or backing, which latter, after giving up some of its water to slack the carbide or pocket-forming material, binds the mass together (e. g. Denivelle claim 2).

COMMERCIAL AND ARTISTIC MERIT OF THE INVENTION.

The intrinsic merit of the invention has found expression in a large practical way in its extensive use by the patentee-plaintiff in the monumental structures of the Pennsylvania Railroad Station in New York City, the wall surfacing of the buildings of the Panama-Pacific International Exposition, The Civic Library, Federal Reserve Bank and other large structures in San Francisco; this work in each instance being under the personal supervision of plaintiff, the patentee.

The work on the Pennsylvania Station comes in for chief consideration in this case just as it did in the Los Angeles case but with this difference: here the showing is even more favorable to the plaintiff in establishing that as far as the patented process was concerned it was "experimental" and in a state of development and trial on Denivelle's part and of uncertainty on the part of everyone coming in contact with its use and proposed use and continued so for a long time thereafter.

As we have already seen and as we will further show, the defendant MacGruer was, as late as October, 1913, bitterly complaining of his "costly experiments" with the Denivelle Process in order to fulfill his contract in Machinery Hall. What evidence could possibly be stronger?

Your Honors in the Los Angeles case referred to and quoted the article by Mr. A. H. Markwart, Assistant Director of Works at the Panama-Pacific International Exposition, entitled "Wall Surfaces of the Exposition" (Exhibit 13, Book of Exhibits). Mr. Markwart says that when the Denivelle plan was first proposed to the Exposition authorities in December, 1912, that

> "Experienced Exposition contractors pronounced the texture and colored exterior as

impossible of accomplishment, and many of the Western gypsum mills looked *unfavorably upon the proposal,* so for a time the *artistic success of the Exposition was threatened by the attitude of both of these necessary factors"* (italics ours).

One of these "factors" was the contracting firm of MacGruer & Simpson, the defendants.

Mr. Markwart gives full credit to Mr. Denivelle, plaintiff, for his great contribution to the success of the Exposition.

Indeed, it may well be said that to Mr. Denivelle, plaintiff, is attributable that rare distinction of having created a new industry.

It is quite natural that an innovation in wall surfacings meeting with such success and against tremendous odds should sooner or later find imitators. It is such imitation that has resulted in the present litigation.

INFRINGEMENT AGGRAVATED BY INFERIOR IMITATION.

Much the same situation prevails here respecting the character of defendants' infringement, that did in the Los Angeles case: Both infringements, there and here, represent a damagingly inferior grade of work.

In the Los Angeles case the defendant Ceriat's work in the Grauman Theater was so much inferior to the genuine Denivelle product that it not only created an impression unfavorable to artificial Travertin but induced the late Judge Trippett to remark after viewing the job of that defendant:

"I don't think it is very pretty * * * If I was building a building, I would not use the stuff that is in there, I will tell you that." (At page 84 of Transcript of Los Angeles record—Exhibit 6.)

We have only here to compare the samples of defendants' (MacGruer and Simpson) work (Exhibits 1 and 2) admitted to be Biltmore Hotel specimens * with the Denivelle Civic Center Library specimen of *artificial* Travertin, (Exhibit 21, R. 572). Then compare Exhibit 21 with the *natural* Travertin sample (Exhibit 22, R. 573) and, in turn, the latter with MacGruer and Simpson's samples (Exhibits 1 and 2).

Of course, by the same degree that MacGruer & Simpson's work is better than the defendant Ceriat's in the Los Angeles case, they are just that closer to the Denivelle patent. Nevertheless both instances emphasize the point of Mr. Denivelle's prophecy already quoted but bearing repetition (R. 581-582):

"I pointed out to him (MacGruer) that my main object was to maintain a standard of quality in connection with my product, so as not to depreciate the value of my patent or my patented product, and that that was my main interest, and for that reason I could not consent at that time, and I told him that I was not

---

* Tovani Exhibit 3 (R. 60), being present Exhibit 1 *supra* (see R. 542): Delaney Exhibit 5 (R. 75-76), being present Exhibit 2 *supra* (see R. 543).

satisfied that he could produce a product that would be satisfactory in its standard to me, and that would not depreciate the value of my product.''

We submit that the bungling workmanship on the part of these defendants aggravates rather than condones their offense; for most certainly the defendants doing the work in a slovenly manner has not avoided the patent.

"No man is permitted to evade a patent by simply constructing the patented thing so imperfectly that its utility is diminished'' (*Walker on Patents,* Section 376).

Such a colorable variation or change is merely evidence of an attempt at evasion by narrowing the function of usefulness of the device infringed (*Blake v. Robertson,* 94 U. S. 728, 24 L. Ed. 245; *Whitely v. Fedner* (C. C.), 73 Fed. 486).

As was said in the case of *Sewell v. Jones,* 91 U. S. 171:

"To constitute an infringement, the thing used by the defendant must be such as substantially to embody the patentee's mode of operation, and thereby attain the same kind of result as was reached by his invention. It is not necessary that the defendant should employ the plaintiff's invention *to as good advantage* as he employed it, or that the result should be the same in *degree;* but it must be the same in *kind''* (italics ours).

And in *Tilghman v. Procter,* 102 U. S. 707, 26 L. Ed. 279, 289:

"The defendants seeing the utility of the process, and believing that they can use a method somewhat similar without infringing Tilghman's patent, put a little lime into the mixture, and find that it helps the operation, and that they do not have to use so high a degree of heat as would otherwise be necessary. Still, the degree of heat required is very high, at least a hundred degrees above the boiling point; and a stronger boiler or vessel is used in order to restrain the water from rising into steam. Can a balder case be conceived of an attempted evasion and a real infringement of a patent?"

We direct your Honors' attention to the cover of the booklet, "Wall Surfaces of the Exposition", supra, the illustrations therein and the Civic Center Library sample Exhibit 21 as indicating what artificial Travertin should and does look like when done properly.

――――

THE DEFENSES.

(1) Lack of Invention and Novelty:

Reading the decision (R. 674) of the Honorable Trial Judge gives the impression at the outset that His Honor deemed the subject-matter of the Denivelle patent of least doubtful patentability and novelty (R. 674-675).

It is believed that this disinclination to recognize that such an invention was patentable, even in the face of your Honors' decision to the contrary, led the Honorable Trial Judge in the instant case (as it did the Trial Judge in the Los Angeles case) to view the defenses with more liberality than otherwise would have been accorded them or that they deserved, and to hold that the patentee had merely substituted "intentional and skillful porosity" for hitherto "unintended carelessness" (R. 675).

This Court's previous decision, of course, settles that point adversely to these defendants.

But that it may not be made to appear that there was lacking in the Los Angeles record the definite defense of "lack of novelty" we have only to direct your Honors' attention to the mass of testimony in the Los Angeles record (Exhibit 6) on the point to see that that defense there was continually emphasized by showing the old practice of careless workmen producing voids in concrete and other plastic substances, and arguing therefrom that there was no invention in the Denivelle process and product (see testimony of Mr. Denivelle, page 76 of Exhibit 6; Ernest Marden, page 91, same; Frank Markel, page 112, same;—also see deposition in full Exhibit 7 Defendants' Book of Exhibits; F. J. McNulty, page 115).

The following from our brief in the Los Angeles case (pages 52-54) sufficiently answers the criticism of the Honorable Trial Judge:

> "We have the authority of the Supreme Court to the effect that *a process patent can only be anticipated by a similar process* (Carnegie Steel Co. v. Cambria Company, 185 U. S. 403, 46 L. Ed. 968, 981).

> "That case also establishes that accidental practice of any step or group of steps does not constitute an anticipation.

"ACCIDENTAL USE IS NOT AN ANTICIPATION.

"It would seem almost unnecessary to cite cases to refute the defense that the accidental and detrimental formation of blow-holes in forming smooth-surfaced, artificial stones in the prior art deprive the Denivelle Process of novelty.

" 'Mere accidental resemblance to the patent in suit without a known performance of the functions of the patented process is not sufficient to establish anticipation' (*Topliff v. Topliff*, 145 U. S. 156).

" 'To anticipate a patent the inventive thought of the later device must have been present in the mind of the inventor' (*Clough v. Gilbert,* 106 U. S. 166).

"*Raisin Seeder Case,* 182 Fed. 59 (C. C. A. 9th Cir.);

"*Los Alamitos Sugar Co. v. Carroll,* 173 Fed. 280 (C. C. A. 9th Cir.).

"It has even been held that a drawing in a mechanical patent which incidentally shows a similar arrangement of parts in a later patent, where such arrangement is not essential to the first invention and was not designed nor adapted and used to perform the function which it performs in the second invention, is not a bar to the grant of a valid subsequent patent, (Minising Paper Co. v. American Sulphite Pulp Co., 228 Fed. 700), citing numerous cases including Tilghman v. Proctor, 102 U. S. 707, where it was held that prior accidental production of the same thing, when the character and function were not recognized until the invention of the later patent, does not effect an anticipation.

"See also:

"*Hillard v. Fisher Book Typewriter Co.*, 159
Fed. 439 (C. C. A. 2nd. Cir.);

"*Byerley v. Barber Asphalt Paving Co.*, 230
Fed. 997;

"*Pieper v. S. S. White Dental Mfg. Co.*, 228
Fed. 39 (C. C. A. 7th Cir.);

"*Maxheimer v. Meyer*, 9 Fed. 460.

"THE DEFENDANTS TAKE OCCASION TO URGE THE
LACK OF UTILITY OF THE INVENTION.

"The fact that a patent has been infringed by
a defendant is sufficient to establish its utility,
at least as against the defendant (*Lehnbeuter v.
Holthaus,* 105 U. S. 84, 96)."

**(2) Defense That Lack of Supplemental Oath Voided Claims
9 and 10:**

This defense is a technical one and not favored by
the Courts. It is, of course, based on the showing in
the *File Wrapper* of the patent in suit.

The *identical certified copy* of the Denivelle File
Wrapper and Contents that was used in the Los
Angeles case is here in evidence as Plaintiff's Exhibit 4 (R. 544). Likewise, this File Wrapper appeared in printed form in the volume of Exhibits
in the Los Angeles case page 209.

Notwithstanding those facts the Honorable Trial
Judge said (R. 674):

"In the instant suit, however, the evidence is
widely variant from that in the former suit, and
requires a contrary decision. It now appears
that claims 9 and 10 for the product of the

process, were added to the application theretofore filed, by amendment without oath.''

In further criticism of claims 9 and 10 Judge Bourquin said (R. 674):

"The application was for a process alone, neither disclosed nor claimed invention of its product, and the absence of an oath avoids the patent to the extent of said claims.''

Aside from the fact that this Honorable Court of Appeals has affirmatively found the patent valid *on a full record of all proceedings had before the Commissioner,* it may nevertheless be appropriate for us to show, briefly, what the facts are as to original disclosure and make such reference to cases as seem applicable and controlling.

In the first place it is not unusual but eminently proper to include claims for *process* and *product,* as well as *apparatus* in one and the same application and patent (*Walker* (Fifth Edition) Section 176, page 223).

A patent for the product of a process is for substantially the same invention as the process itself; so that the insertion of a claim for the *product* is not a departure from the original invention.

To quote Mr. Justice Bradley in *Powder Co. v. Powder Works,* 98 U. S. 136; 25 L. Ed. 77, 82:

"In another case, arising on the original patent of Goodyear (Goodyear v. R. R. Co.) reported in 2 Wall., Jr., 356, Mr. Justice Grier used this expression: 'The p r o d u c t and the process constitute one discovery.' The product in Goodyear's invention was the direct result of the process. They were parts of one invention and, except in imagination, could no more be separated from each other than the two sides of a sheet of paper, or than a shadow from the body that produces it."

See also:

> *Downes v. Teter Heany Co.,* 150 Fed. 122, 3 C. C. A. (1st Syllabus) and citing *Mosler Safe Co. v. Mosler,* 127 U. S. 361;
>
> *Asbestos Co. v. Johns Manville Co.,* 184 Fed. 620-631;
>
> *Williams v. Miller,* 107 Fed. 290;
>
> *Camp Bros. v. Portable Wagon & Dump Elevator Co.,* 251 Fed. 603;
>
> *Westinghouse v. Metropolitan,* 290 Fed. 661;
>
> *Wheeler v. Rinelli,* 295 Fed. 717.

As the Court said (page 727) in the last menioned case:

"The mere fact that there was no claim for the method in the application when it was filed, and that one was added by amendment without a new oath does not make the patent invalid. John R. Williams Co. v. Miller, DuBrul & Peters Mfg. Co. (C. C.) 107 Fed. 290.

"The real test is: Does the applicant by the amendment present a conception materially different from or enlarged over that shown by the original application? and, if he does not, no supplemental oath is necessary. Camp Bros. & Co. v. Portable Wagon Dump & E. Co., 251 Fed. 603, 163 C. C. A. 597.

"Claim 1 of the patent in suit, in my opinion, is fairly derivable from the sworn disclosure of

the original specification, and therefore no supplemental oath was required to sustain the
amendment adding claim 2, which eventually
became claim 1. Westinghouse E. & Mfg. Co. v.
Metropolitan E. Mfg. Co. (C. C. A.) 290 Fed.
661.''

As far as the Trial Court's criticism pertains to
the ministerial acts of the Commissioner of Patents
determining that claims 9 and 10 were *not* new matter, it seems answered by the observations of your
Honors in *Kitchen v. Levison*, 188 Fed. 658, 661,
where it was said:

> "From the reissuance of the patent it is to
> be presumed that the law was complied with,
> and the proceedings can only be impeached for
> fraud. In Seymour v. Osborne, 11 Wall. 516-
> 543 (20 L. Ed. 33), it was said:
>
>> " 'Where the commissioner accepts a sur-
>> render of an original patent, and grants a new
>> patent, his decision in the premises in a suit
>> for infringement is final and conclusive and is
>> not re-examinable in such a suit in the Circuit
>> Court unless it is apparent upon the face of the
>> patent that he has exceeded his authority, that
>> there is such a repugnancy between the old and
>> the new patent that it must be held as matter
>> of legal construction that the new patent is not
>> for the same invention as that embraced and
>> secured in the original patent.' "

Asbestos *Shingle Slate & Sheathing Co., et al., v.
Johns-Manville Co.,* supra, the patentee had originally obtained a patent with claims covering a
process for making asbestos shingles. He reissued
this patent and added other claims covering the

product resulting from the process. The patent was attacked on the ground that the reissue was not for the same invention as the original. In over-ruling this contention the Court said (page 631):

> * * * "The grounds for reissue were within the discretion of the commissioner. His ruling that Hatschek's failure to include his product was due to accident, inadvertence, or mistake is not reviewable here on the facts. Seymour v. Osborne, 11 Wall. 516, 20 L. Ed. 33; Russell v. Dodge, 93 U. S. 460, 23 L. Ed. 973; Topliff v. Topliff, 145 U. S. 156, 12 Sup. Ct. 825, 36 L. Ed. 658. The only question which can arise is as to the identity of the two inventions. Claim 7 is limited to the product of precisely the process described. That product is the same invention as the process itself. James v. Campbell, 104 U. S. 356, 26 L. Ed. 786; Powder Co. v. Powder Works, 98 U. S. 136, 25 L. Ed. 77. It is quite true that in both these cases the rule is laid down *obiter*, but it is quite deliberate, citing a decision of Mr. Justice Grier in Goodyear v. Central Ry. Co. of N. J., 2 Wall., Jr., 356, Fed. Cas. No. 5,563, and I should feel bound by it as authority even if it did not seem true in principle. In other countries it is even unnecessary to claim the product separately, nor would it have been less desirable had our own law developed in the same way."

This Court held in *Singer v. Cramer*, 109 Fed. 652, (9th C. C. A.) an inventor may amend his specification so as to include therein all the advantages within the scope of his invention.

The original Denivelle drawings and specification sufficiently show and suggest the claims finally made as fully to justify the latter (*Hobbs v. Beach*, 180 U. S. 383, 396; 45 L. Ed. 586, 593).

CLAIMS 9 AND 10 NO DEPARTURE FROM THE ORIGINAL SPECIFICATIONS OF DENIVELLE.

But, turning to the Denivelle patent, and remembering that the specification is substantially as originally filed, it would seem most obvious that the process claims themselves describe the manner of manipulation of the various substances used, as would necessarily lead one to visualize a product having the very characteristics of claims 9 and 10.

This is made further apparent by the following from the patent (page 1, lines 32-38):

> * * * "*to produce in the cast* or positive taken from said mold, form, etc., automatically as a result of the progressive steps and special application, *a certain striated form of texture porousness in simulation of a stone known as 'travertin' or 'Roman travertin'* " (italics ours).

This, of course, presupposes a knowledge of the surface characteristics of "Roman Travertin" the voids, striae, texture, etc. The *method of imitation* described and claimed by Denivelle necessarily differentiates from the *natural Travertin* in the very particulars of claims 9 and 10. Otherwise, of course, there would be no novelty in the product to begin with. But the patentee in his· specification says further (page 1, lines 44-54):

> "The second method involves the use of the above colored materials in a certain definite and

novel manner during their direct application to a wall or ceiling, or similar surface, and before the set or crystallization is complete, *in order that the resulting surface may have a colored striated or porous surface in simulation of travertin or Roman travertin texture or stone of similar striated porousness*; this form of use and effect being an innovation" (italics ours).

Continuing, the patentee says (page 1, lines 55-56):

"The drawings illustrate the application of the invention simply in a schematic manner."

The drawings, of course, are part of the specification and the claims are to be read with each.

Then under the heading of "Forming Pockets" beginning page 1, line 10, the product is necessarily portrayed with greater detail and the patentee concludes that paragraph as follows (page 2, lines 1-10):

"This is for the purpose of preventing the next coating of step (5) from entirely enveloping, by gravity or seepage, the intent of said operation (4). *Coating 4 is so applied and is of such loose lumpy consistency as to provide in the finished surface of the cast a porous, pocket-like appearance between the striated poured lines or veins 3, described in operation (2)* (italics ours).

And, again (page 2, lines 20-25):

"This fluid cement makes a bond to fill the voids in the loose lumpy layer 4, except for the pockets, that forms on the surface and serves to bind the portion of the surface produced by operation (2) with that of the semi-dry layer of operation (4)."

In describing process B, the patentee says (page 3, lines 10-18):

"This is for the *purpose of producing the greater porosity in texture markings required in the finished result*; the form and nature of the bristles producing a jagged series of depressions, *horizontally striated formation*, and the trowel's pressure reducing the width of these depressions, together with providing an undercut quality to the stippling it would not otherwise have" (italics ours).

And, finally (page 3, lines 34-42):

* * * * "to leave a straight smooth surface of different color tones produced by the variegated striated veins and the shadows of the depressions, such as are characteristic of Roman travertin or stone commonly known as 'travertin'."

THE LAW GOVERNING SUPPLEMENTAL OATHS.

Among the original claims presented in the Denivelle application were the following:

"2. A process for the manufacture of striated artificial stone structures, which consists in preparing a mold of suitable outline with an isolator, forming veins of plastic material over this prepared surface, depositing loose, lumpy material over the veining to provide pockets bonding the pocket-forming material with the veining material, and leaving certain pockets exposed on the surface adjacent to the mold surface."

"6. A process for the manufacture of striated artificial stone structures, which consists in the preparation of the surface of the article to be treated and laying a soft background thereon, veining the same with a plastic material, stippling the veining, and trowelling the same.''

These claims present broadly the idea of casting an artificial Travertin and also applying the same in position upon a wall. They set forth a method which, if followed, would produce the artificial structure set forth in the claims of the Denivelle Patent.

As was said in *Crucible Steel Co. of America v. Heller Bros. Co.*, 291 Fed. 175, (Pages 177-178):

> "An amendment within the scope of the origiginal specification and a limitation and narrowing of the original claim may be made after the death of the inventor, so long as the invention is the identical invention sworn to. De La Vergne Machine Co. v. Featherstone, 147 U. S. 209, 229, 13 Sup. Ct. 283, 37 L. Ed. 138.
> "The case of George Cutter Co. v. Metropolitan Mfg. Co. (C. C. A.) 275 Fed. 158, and Del Turco v. Traitel Marble Co., unreported, need no discussion. The decisions do not go to the extent claimed for them by the defendant, and do not and cannot in any way alter the rule of law above stated. *The applicant for the patent, in his original application having sworn to a broader claim that that finally allowed, was properly not required by the Patent Office to make an additional oath*" (italics ours).

In the case of *Mine & Smelter Supply Co. v. Braeckel Concentrator Co. et al.*, 197 Fed. 897, 900 (italics ours):

> "3. We come now to the third defense, especially emphasized in argument and brief. This is that in the specification and claims in issue the patentee made a substantial departure from the application originally filed, introduced

new matter, a new function, and described an entirely different invention, all unaccompanied by a new or supplemental oath; for which reason, it is contended, the patent, especially as to the claims in issue, is void. *It should be remembered that this patent duly issued carries with it the presumption of regularity. It is presumed that the commissioner did and exacted what the law required him to do and exact, and the burden is upon the alleged infringer to overcome this presumption.* The statute does not, in terms, demand that the oath required should be in writing, and it has been held that such a requirement is not implied. In Hancock Inspirator Co. v. Jenks (C. C.) 21 Fed. 911, Judge (afterwards Justice) Brown said:

'*There is nothing in the act requiring this oath to be in writing,* and, notwithstanding the existence of the supplementary application, verified by the attorney, *it is possible that the patentee appeared personally before the commissioner and made the requisite oath in his presence.* The commissioner, having general jurisdiction of the subject, is presumed to have complied with all the requirements of the law before issuing the patent. Indeed, the courts have gone so far as to hold that the presence in the files of the Patent Office of a paper purporting to be an oath, but void for want of a *jurat,* will not defeat the patent.'

"At this hearing Mr. Justice Matthews sat and concurred in the decision. So far as appears in the case at bar, *counsel for defendants rely upon the single fact appearing in the record that the file wrapper and contents introduced in evidence do not disclose the presence of a supplemental oath* to the amended specification and claims.

"In Hoe v. Kahler (C. C.) 25 Fed. 271, 279, Mr. Justice Blatchford, sitting at circuit, held

that the mere failure of the file wrapper and
contents to disclose whether the application was
properly verified or not was not sufficient to rebut the presumption that the commissioner required and received a proper preliminary oath.
He says:

'*The affirmative probative force of a paper
in a file wrapper, to show the existence of its
contents, is one thing, but its negative probative force, to show that a paper or a fact not
shown by anything in its contents did not exist,
is quite a different thing.* The fact that papers
known to have existed, and which properly belong in a file wrapper, are missing therefrom,
is a fact of such frequent occurrence in patent
suits as to have become a matter of judicial
cognizance.'

"To the same effect, see American Steel
Foundries v. Wolff Truck Frame Co. (C. C.)
189 Fed. 601, 602. It does not appear that the
defendant has sufficiently rebutted the presumption raised by the issuance of the patent."

And at pages 902-903:

"It will be conceded that amendments, within the scope of the original oath and of the invention described in the original specification,
are allowable and do not require additional veri-
fication. De La Vergne Refrigerating Mach.
Co. v. Featherstone, 147 U. S. 209, 13 Sup. Ct.
283, 37 L. Ed. 138. In determining whether matter introduced into an application by way of
amendment is new matter, the original drawings
are to be understood with such variations in
form, shape, and proportions as common sense
and mechanical skill in that art would suggest.
Michigan Cent. R. Co. v. Consolidated Car-
Heating Co., 67 Fed. 121, 14 C. C. A. 232. The
Court said:

'This carries the doctrine to its verge, and if the original drawings and specifications fail to indicate to those familiar with the art, and having the mechanical skill peculiar thereto, the device which is introduced by the amendment, then the patent does not include that device.'

"If they do so indicate, then they are sufficient. It is obvious here that both the specification and drawings indicate the device, the function, and mode of operation, and any one possessing common sense and mechanical skill in that art could construct and operate the machine described. * * *

"Where new specifications and claims are filed in which the invention is stated much more in detail, and with much fuller and more accurate language than before, this does not necessarily expand the original claims beyond the scope of the invention, *particularly where the original drawings and specifications suggest the claims finally made.* Hobbs v. Beach, 180 U. S. 383, 396, 397, 21 Sup. Ct. 409, 45 L. Ed. 586.

"The principle invoked by counsel for defendant usually arises where an applicant for a patent amends and limits his claims and specifications to meet objections of the Patent Office; whereby, in order to get his patent, he accepts one with a narrower claim than that contained in his original application. In such case, he is bound by the claim of the patent as issued. Hubbell v. United States, 179 U. S. 83, 21 Sup. Ct. 24, 45 L. Ed. 95; Brill v. St. Louis Car Co., 90 Fed. 666, 33 C. C. A. 213. And where an applicant for a patent, after his application has been rejected and lain dormant for years, during which time the art has made rapid progress, amends the same, and on the basis of such amendment makes claims of a different character, it is the duty of the Court to scrutinize the patent issued carefully to see that it has not been enlarged in scope beyond the invention disclosed in the original application. Heston-ville, M. & F. Pass. Ry. Co., et al., v. McDuffee, et al., 185 Fed. 798, 109 C. C. A. 606" (italics ours).

The language of the Court of Appeals of the Sixth Circuit in the case of General Electric Co. v. Cooper Hewitt Electric Co., 249 Fed. 61, 54, 161 C. C. A. 121, 124, is in point:

"The claims, as issued, are made to depend in part upon these things not originally specified. Hence it is plausibly argued that the insertion was of new matter and was vital to the invention as patented; and thereupon it is said that the patent is void. Railroad v. Sayles, 97 U. S. 554, 563, 24 L. Ed. 1053; Railroad v. Consolidated Co. (C. C. A. 6) 67 Fed. 121, 129, 14 C. C. A. 232. This view overlooks the substance of the invention, as disclosed in the original specification and drawing. The rule is that insertions by way of amendment in the description or drawing, or both, do not hurt the patent, if the insertions are only an amplification and explanation of what was already reasonably indicated to be within the invention for which protection was sought—'something that might be fairly deduced from the original application.' Hobbs v. Beach, 180 U. S. 383, 395, 21 Sup. Ct. 409, 45 L. Ed. 586; Cleveland Co. v. Detroit Co. (C. C. A. 6) 131 Fed. 853, 857, 68 C. C. A. 233; Proudfit Co. v. Kalamazoo Co. (C. C. A. 6) 230 Fed. 120, 123, 144 C. C. A. 418; Cosper v. Gold, 36 App. D. C. 302. When we seek to apply this rule in this case, we first observe that the alleged new matter was not only permitted by the Patent Office, but was required, because an element claimed was not shown or sufficiently described. *The Patent Office has a strict rule on this subject. It fully recognizes that new matter must not be permitted and it is constantly engaged in defining what is and what is not new matter.*

The application of the rule must, of necessity, be more or less arbitrary, and the presumption of correctness which attends Patent Office rulings must apply with especial force to this class of ruling; and most peculiarly is that true when the applicant has only complied with the demands which the Patent Office made'' (italics ours).

In Cleveland Foundry Co. v. Detroit Vapor Stove Co., 131 Fed. 853, 68 C. C. A. 233, the Court said:

"If an inventor comes to better understand the principles of his invention while his application for a patent is pending, an amendment of his claims to conform thereto does not introduce any original matter nor enlarge his invention, and it is within his legal right."

See also *Proudfit Loose Leaf Co. v. Kalamazoo Loose Leaf Binder Co.,* 230 Fed. 120 (6th C. C. A.).

We submit that this defense is without merit and should be overruled.

(3) Defense of Prior Use.

Manifestly, the Trial Court gave this phase of the case the most attention. It apparently based its conclusions on *parts* of the *correspondence* in evidence touching the literal letting of the contract for the Artificial Travertin in the Pennsylvania Station but overlooked other and material parts of the correspondence showing that the *doubts of the architects and contractors* were not focussed alone on this patentee's limited financial standing; but *that any form of Travertin (natural or imitation)* was of an *experimental nature* (see correspondence appearing in Book of Exhibits). By these same letters as we shall point out more in detail, the samples of *imitation* stuff submitted raised in the minds of the architects and contractors for the Railroad grave doubts as to *"quality"* and *"as to permanency under varying temperatures"*; and as to whether it would *"wear satisfactorily"* on surface *"with which the public will come directly in contact"* (letters M & W, October 15th 1908, page 22, Book of Exhibits).

The defense seems to have entirely overlooked the real bearing of these letters, as well as others, to which we shall refer. This correspondence shows better than by anything we had in the Los Angeles case the true significance of Mr. Denivelle's statement in the former record (Exh. 6, p. 169): "The conditions—the materials were new, had never been used before * * * It was regarded as an experiment from the very beginning."

SUMMARY OF DEFENDANTS' EVIDENCE ON THE DEFENSE OF PRIOR USE.

It is interesting to note that we have in this record a glimpse of some of the things that went on behind the scenes in connection with the Pennsylvania job that were not available at the time of the former trial, and which go to show the interest with which this new invention, this new idea of Denivelle appealed, not only to the architects, to the general contractors, but to the Pennsylvania Railroad authorities themselves. For instance, the President of the Pennsylvania Terminal Company was so impressed with the idea of getting such a novelty and such a useful thing into that building, in the way of imitation travertin, according to the Denivelle process, that Mr. Rea, their President, appealed to McKim, Mead & White, through Chief Engineer Gibbs of the Railroad Company, to give Denivelle a chance, as he thought that here was something worthy of following, quoted post (Gibbs' letter of February 4th, 1909, Defendants' Exhibit 8, Book of Exhibits, page 30).

The Court will take judicial notice of the fact that with building materials it takes years of use sometimes to demonstrate their practical durability and value.

Among some of the difficulties that naturally occur to the mind of the Court and which must have confronted the Pennsylvania Railroad authorities and architects, as well as the inventor, and which, as the evidence shows, did confront them, may be mentioned the following: vibrations of trains and surface travel; expansion and contraction of the materials forming the artificial stone structure; durability as against liability to disintegrate; liability of joints opening up by chemical effect of the joint material; stability of colors; lasting uniformity of effect throughout, including texture and color; the tendency or lack of tendency to efflorescense or exudation of salts forming a powdery surface so often noticeable in artificial structures, due to loss of water by crystallization. (See McNulty letter quoted post.)

Manifestly, there could be said to have been no "public use" in Mr. Denivelle's case until such time as his work had passed beyond the experimental stage and it had been proved that the work was durable and permanent beyond question. Who could say in 1912 or 1913 whether one year, or five years, or fifty years were sufficient proof? Looking at the work from the year 1924 it has turned out a masterful success. It certainly could not have been said to be a success in 1910 before it was even fairly started, nor even when it was completed late in 1911 or 1912.

Regarding the experimental work of Denivelle, it is to be borne in mind that this experimental work which was carried on over into the Exposition is of itself evidence of a high degree of invention.

> *Okmulgee Window Glass Co. v. Window Glass Mach. Co.*, 265 Fed. 626, 635, C. C. A. 8th Circuit.

Defendants contend, however, that there is "new evidence" here as to public use not before this Court in the former Los Angeles case. It, therefore, becomes incumbent to see just what this alleged "new evidence" is and compare it with the proofs in the Los Angeles suit.

Defendants rely on the following alleged uses (though several are not pleaded) and some were later withdrawn as shown to be *too late* in point of time; (bearing in mind the date of the Denivelle application as *October 20, 1915,* filed in substitution and continuation of his original application of *August, 2, 1913,* Exhibit 25 R. 594).

(1) Pennsylvania Station.

(2) Ottawa Station, Canada (not available as a defense even if proven, as occurring in a Foreign Country, U. S. R. S. 4923).

(3) Montreal Station. Not travertin at all (R. 265) and defense later withdrawn.

(4) Vanderbilt Hotel Bar, New York City, (proofs unsatisfactory but shown to be by some method more akin to the *"Applied* Method B" of patented *Process* not here involved; while as to the Vanderbilt *product* the architect, Hopkins, for the Vanderbilt Hotel testifies (2 R. 481-482):

"XQ. 41. Of what material was this artificial travertine made which was put in the bar-room of the hotel?

"A. Well, that I can't answer, because I didn't ask Mr. Denivelle and he didn't volunteer the information, and I felt that it was more or less of a secret process of his and I didn't ask. * * * I don't know the ingredients. I don't know the various materials or their proportions, but I saw it put on the walls and I am very familiar with the method of applying. * * * It is put on to what we call a scratch coat, such as an ordinary plasterer's scratch coat of cement, and then the ingredients—

whatever they may be—are mixed and applied with a trowel, just as you would plaster a wall, then there are certain holes put in by a man who is skillful at that kind of thing, with a little instrument, after which the surface of the travertine is smoothed over with a trowel and lines representing the joints between the stones are ruled in with a tool called a jointer.

"XQ. 45. Now, in this artificial travertin in the Vanderbilt Hotel bar are there any veins or striations, and if so, how are they applied?

"A. I don't believe there are any striations. *In fact I am sure there are not"* (italics ours).

This, of course, is not the "cast" method in suit of claims 1, 2 and 5, and without "striations" or "veins" there is no prior use of any sort of the *product* claims 9 and 10.

(5)   Widener Memorial Library at Harvard (too late as not open to the public and not dedicated until Commencement Day, *June 24th, 1915*) (R. 664).

(6)   Widener Building, Philadelphia, (not completed until September, 1916, (R. 407, Q. 21) a year *after* the patent in suit was applied for).

(7)   Campbell's Funeral Church (too late, August, 1916) (R. 455, Q. 10).

(8)   Evans Museum, (too late, 'September or October," 1914, (R. 490, Q. 31) besides use not proven according to established standards of necessary proof beyond a reasonable doubt).

(9)   ·Goelet job, (too late; building not completed and accepted until Spring of 1914 (Gayler R. 227, 236, R. D. Q. 91), besides this was mostly "applied

process B" of patent not in issue (R. 286, Q. 18);
the only cast work, according to Mr. Cooke R. 289
being:

> "Caps and bases and pilasters. * * *
> "But there wasn't many of them, there were
> 2 columns in the entrance and I think 4 columns
> in the loggia outside."

The process was still experimental even on this
small job for says Cooke (R. 288-289):

> "Well, the Goelet house—we had some—I got
> in Dutch with Mr. Denivelle in the Goelet house
> because we were getting a certain texture there
> and he come along and he was changing it and
> wanted it changed again; and he had different
> ideas—something he wanted there—and we had
> to change, particularly the caps and bases. I
> wasn't there at the time the caps and bases
> were changed—the texture of them—but I know
> when I come back—I had to go away to Mil-
> waukee for a couple of weeks—and when I
> come back they had changed the thing around
> again."

And R. 290:

> "Well, we had—it was changed on the Goelet
> job—the texture wasn't coming out right and
> Mr. Denivelle come along there and changed it
> —the change was made as I already said, while
> I was in Milwaukee."

These several uses will be taken up in more detail.

As a matter of fact the Pennsylvania Station
job is the only one requiring serious attention.

DENIVELLE'S FORMER TESTIMONY ON GENESIS AND DEVELOPMENT OF THE INVENTION ACCEPTED AS BEING BEFORE THE COURT IN THIS CASE.

At pages 664 and 665 of the present Record on Appeal appears the following:

"Mr. TOWNSEND. * * * Now, with regard to the early history of the invention, and its development through the Pennsylvania stages as might be given by Mr. Denivelle if he were called for that purpose to show how he took the matter up and how the inspiration came to him, that can be avoided, unless your Honor desires that information, by reason of the testimony we have already had on the subject of the Pennsylvania development, and concerning which there is no real controversy, and by reason of the findings of the Circuit Court of Appeals of this Circuit in the case we have already referred to as the Los Angeles case, reported in 270 Fed. 155. On pages 8 and 9 of the opinion which we have filed as an exhibit in this case, Judge Ross goes at length into that. Unless you think there is some reason for me to call Mr. Denivelle and have him repeat that story, I am inclined to rest and take it as a finding by the Court of Appeals.

"The COURT. I assume that these statements in this opinion are found in the evidence in that case which you have introduced.

Mr. TOWNSEND. Yes, your Honor.

"The COURT. Then certainly it is before the Court in one way or another.

"Mr. TOWNSEND. Yes, y o u r Honor, and, therefore, it is not necessary for me to repeat it?

"The COURT. I would not think so."

The foregoing was acquiesced in by the defendants without objection. Mr. Denivelle was at all times present in Court and, in fact, became the next witness. Defendants c o u l d h a v e challenged Mr. Denivelle by cross-examination if they wished to attempt to impeach his testimony in the former suit. As it is, the above ruling of the Trial Court that Mr. Denivelle's testimony was already before the Court and need not be repeated makes that testimony a part of the record in this case.

Sufficient of Mr. Denivelle's testimony concerning the patentee's version of the early history and development of the invention is quoted in your Honors' previous opinion as not to require repetition.

The long excerpt from Mr. Denivelle's testimony quoted in the opinion 250 Fed. at page 161, appears at pages 77 to 79 of the Los Angeles Record (Exhibit 6).

As we shall point out later, the testimony of the witnesses called by the present defendants, particularly Webster, Fenner, Whipple, Cook and Mac-Gruer, corroborates Mr. Denivelle and adds substantial basis for this Court's opinion in the former suit.

This Court will remember that in the former suit the Trial Court by the late Judge Trippett, refused to allow Mr. Denivelle to go into details as to what caused the Pennsylvania Station job to be considered experimental in character. Thus in that case at page 80 (Exhibit 6) Mr. Denivelle was asked by his counsel:

"Q. Was there a ready acceptance of your proposal to use artificial travertin on the Pennsylvania station?

"A. No, absolutely not.

"Q. Will you just tell what difficulties you encountered in having it adopted?

"Mr. FORD. I object to that, your Honor,—

"The COURT. The objection will be sustained.

"Mr. TOWNSEND. This goes to the novelty of the invention, your Honor, and it is always pertinent where you can see that the difficult and new thing has of being received, that it is the very best evidence of its novelty. The complete story would just show this, that it was a new thing and an entirely novel proposition.

"The COURT. Well, suppose it was novel there. It has nothing to do with this case. Here is a patent upon a certain method of producing it."

And at pages 81-82:

"Q. After the work was done and in place in the building, was your work done? A. My work was not done, no.

"Q. Did you know, and did the officials who had the responsibility for this work, accept this work the moment that the last trowel of material had been applied and the last slab in place there, or were there conditions involved? A. Not at all.

*   *   *   *   *   *   *

"Q. Did you know whether or not that material was going to be durable after it was placed on the walls there? A. Absolutely not.

*   *   *   *   *   *   *

"The COURT. I don't see what it has got to do with it.

"Mr. TOWNSEND. I am going to show that this work was not a so-called public use, in the sense of the statute, and this is the only way we can show it.

"The COURT. Well, under claims 9 and 10?

"Mr. TOWNSEND. Under claims 9 and 10, 1, 2 and 3 there, the use of this material——

* * * * * * *

"The COURT. This just relates to the process.

"Mr. TOWNSEND. Yes, your Honor, the practice of the process. In other words, to bring it, your Honor, within the doctrine of Elizabeth vs. The Paving Company. You know the paving blocks, where the blocks had to be in position, and were left to be worn off a number of years. That is, I am meeting one condition of apparent defense, and this is a good opportunity and time to bring out just exactly when this was done.

"The conditions of traffic there in New York City, the different expansive action of material used, had to undergo careful supervision. So I will ask, did you have to supervise and investigate this artificial travertin that you had put in the Pennsylvania station after you had erected it?"

And, again, pages 166 and 167 (Exhibit 6):

"Q. Well, what process of making it, how did you make it? A. Well, the process varied really from the beginning to the end. Start in one way and ended up in another. * * * We put in a material that was harder than the veins, as I explained. We started by forcing it through screens. * * * And put it on the molds like soft spaghetti. * * * Then that later evolved—all the way through, that job it was an experimental stage, and the steps were changed as the work progressed all the time. * * * In other words, we had to seek more economical methods from the beginning to the end."

And pages 168 to 170:

"Q. (By Mr. TOWNSEND.) After that work was actually erected, was your duty in regard to it at an end?

"Mr. FORD. Objected to as immaterial. A. It was not.

"The COURT. I don't understand, Mr. Townsend, what in the world you are trying to get at. * * * It seems to me you are wasting time most absurdly, the way it looks to me.

"Mr. TOWNSEND. Well, I regret it has that appearance.

"The COURT. It does have that appearance to me.

"Mr. TOWNSEND. I want to show you that this work, being of such character, required constant attention and inspection, and for a long period of time, and that the work was not of such character that the moment it was fabricated it became a complete thing.

*   *   *   *   *   *   *

"Q. (By Mr. TOWNSEND). State what those reasons were.

"Mr. FORD. Objected to as immaterial.

"The COURT. Go ahead and state them briefly. Overruled.

"A. Well, the conditions—the materials were new,—had never been used before.

"The COURT. Now, you stated that on direct examination.

"The WITNESS. Well, the architect and the Pennsylvania Railroad, both, were not satisfied that this work would stand up. * * * Because it was regarded as an experiment from the very beginning.

"Q. (By Mr. TOWNSEND). What were the factors, if any, that entered into the experimental stage of it?

"Mr. FORD. Objected to as immaterial.

"The COURT. Sustained. Now, you cannot ask a question along that line any more, Mr. Townsend."

As we shall later point out, the testimony there sought to be offered on the subject is corroborated by the very evidence, documentary as well as oral, offered by the defendants in this case.

THE DEFENSE OF PUBLIC USE IN THE LOS ANGELES RECORD.

Turning to the Los Angeles record for the purpose of seeing what has already been adjudicated, the Amended Answer there, as shown by the Judgment Roll (Exhibit 5 herein, and Paragraph V, pages 31-33, Exhibit 6) alleged:

"* * * that plaintiff's assignor, Paul E. Denivelle, manufactured artificial stone structures of the kind set forth in said alleged application for patent of said invention, at the Pennsylvania Railroad Station in New York City, in the year 1908; that artificial stone structures have been manufactured and sold by McNulty Bros. Co., of Chicago, Illinois, on the Widener Building, Philadelphia, Pa., in June, 1914, and in the City of Chicago, during the past twenty-five years; that such artificial stone structures have been manufactured and sold by H. W. Miller, Inc., of New York City, for over twenty years last past; that such artificial-stone structures have been manufactured and sold by P. J. Durcan, Inc., of New York City, for over fourteen years last past; that such artificial stone structures have been manufactured and sold by Massimo-Hutter Co.

of New York City, in New York City, different parts of the United States and Canada for twenty-five years last past; that such artificial stone structures have been manufactured and sold by John J. Roberts Co., of New York City, in the State of New York and in other parts of the United States for over twenty years last past; that such artificial stone structures have been manufactured and sold by Klee-Thompson Co., of New York City, for more than ten years last past; that such artificial stone structures have been manufactured and sold by H. A. Cousins, Inc., of New York City, for over forty years last past in the City of New York and throughout the United States; that said method described in said patent of plaintiff and its said assignor has been in general use of the trade for over twenty-five years last past throughout the United States; that this defendant is informed and believes, and upon such information and belief alleges, that the process alleged to have been invented by said Paul E. Denivelle is described in Miller's Plastering Book, published more than sixty (60) years ago.''

Later the Los Angeles defendants gave notice of taking depositions to support the above defenses of the following witnesses in New York and Chicago (see Exhibit 6, pages 39-41, and notices accompanying Plaintiff's Exhibits 7 and 8 herein, most of the witnesses being called by the present defendants:

> Frank Morkel (deposition in present case R. 387);
>
> H. A. Cousins (deposition in present case R. 387);

H. W. Miller (deposition in present case R. 387);

P. J. Durkin (deposition in present case R. 387);

L. S. Massimo (deposition in present case R. 387);

Jos. W. Bard (deposition in present case R. 387);

Davis Brown (deposition in present case R. 387);

F. J. McNulty (deposition in present case R. 387).

Morkel (or Markel) (see page 111, Exhibit 6; for full transcript of his deposition in Question and Answer see Exhibit 7 herein) testified as to work on Temple Emanu-El in New York City; the St. Elmo Club, New Haven; the Harvard Memorial Library, Cambridge; and as to the "lack of invention" generally in his opinion of the Denivelle Process.

Morkel as a witness here again (2 R. 387-404) and practically repeats his former story.

McNulty in the Los Angeles case (pages 113, Exhibit 6; for full transcript see Exhibit 8) testified (page 117) to doing the Widener Building, supra, in Philadelphia in 1914 by McNulty Bros. and to certain conferences with Mr. Denivelle concerning the same; also to work on the Pennsylvania Station in New York City "prior to 1910" (page 119, Exhibit 6); also as to the "lack of invention" in the witness' opinion in the Denivelle patented Process and Product.

Mr. Denivelle was called by the defendants in the Los Angeles case (page 72, Exhibit 6) to testify at length concerning the work on the Pennsylvania Station.

Mr. Marden was called in the Los Angeles case (page 84, Exhibit 6) to show the contribution to the art by H. W. Miller Co., one of the three final competitors on the Pennsylvania Station; these three being H. W. Miller Co., McNulty Bros. and the present plaintiff. The witness Marden was also called to testify in the Los Angeles case to "absence of invention", in his opinion, in the Denivelle Process and Product (page 91, Exhibit 6).

––––––––

THE LOS ANGELES RECORD RE—PENNSYLVANIA STATION USE.

At page 84 of the Los Angeles Record (Exhibit 6), Ernest Marden testified:

"Witness is an ornamental plasterer, living in Los Angeles, and in the business for twenty-eight years, first in New York City, worked there up to 1909, since then he has been in Los Angeles. He was employed by Miller the plasterer, in New York City in 1909 and recalled the building of the Pennsylvania Railroad station."

(Page 85, Exhibit 6):

"Witness stated that he had made samples for the Railroad, using wet methods. In making the samples submitted, he used semi-dry for the voids.''

(Page 86, Exhibit 6):

"The WITNESS. We first were told to go to work and make this from a sample sent from McKim, Mead & White's office, a sample slab, and told to proceed and make samples. One was a cornice and the others were slabs. We then went to work and made molds in various forms, some in gelatine molds and some in plaster molds or hard molds.

"The veins were laid with a funnel-shaped or irregular with spoons, any way we could pick them up, sometimes done with a funnel, with a corrugated funnel, a piece of tin corrugated on the edges, in order that the colors would blend together as they were laid. We next put in semi-dry.

"A. The semi-dry is so you can handle it so it won't run, so you can squeeze it in your fingers without running, is what we call the semi-dry. Then we lay that into it, and that forms the pockets, also gives it the depth. And when we laid on our wet stuff on the veins, we laid it on carelessly, uniform somewhat, to get out parallel lines with the veins, but we don't try to avoid airholes on the surface, as we would in other work.''

(Pages 88-9, 90, Exhibit 6):

"Q. Mr. Mardon, did you see any imitation or what was purported to be imitation of travertin stone in the Railroad buildings of the Pennsylvania Road in New York City in 1910?

"Witness saw only the sample in the building itself and did not see the building afterwards. He left before the travertin was started. All the samples that were presented as represented by the different firms were all similar to

one another. * * * On the H. W. Miller
sample, we used plaster of paris, sand and color.
Plaster of paris is a cementitious material.
These samples for pockets, or so-called airholes and veins, all were different colors, all
the way through, about three different colors.
It is difficult to describe these colors here. They
were trying to get as near the color of the
natural travertin stone as possible. The colors
were put into the cement. There were differently
toned thin layers or strata and voids of the
stratified formation between the layers. * * *
Miller & Co. of New York submitted samples
at that time to the Pennsylvania station. Witness was one of the persons employed by them
at that time.

" 'Q. Describe the process they used. What
was the process, that is, H. W. Miller, of New
York City?'

" 'A. We first made a mold or a sample plate
by putting strips on a marble bench, instead
of building up a special mold, such as is described here; putting strips around the bench
to form the thickness. We then greased that
marble bench or mold, and then we took our
different colors—the three colors, or four colors
it might have been—three colors, I remember,
and made our veinings. Sometimes we made it
with a trowel, sometimes we took a scoop and
corrugated the sides and formed our veins all
along. And then we took the semi-dry material
and threw along the lines of those veins promis-
cously all over that; and after that, we filled it
up with the body and scraped it off on the back
of the mold.'

"For pouring, witness says that they just
took a piece of tin or zinc that they had 'laying
around the shop, and just turned it up on the
edges, and just bent the edges all along so as
to let the different colors flow into one another,
and lay it along there by moving it irregularly,

as the veins in the natural would show irregularly.'

"The object was to get the color of the veins not too even all the way through. After veining we threw in the semi-dry."

And on cross-examination Mr. Marden testified concerning the work of his firm on the Pennsylvania Station Job (pages 91 to 94 of Exhibit 6):

"Witness was a mechanic in the ornamental plaster department of Miller & Company. Witness is an all-round ornamental plasterer. He and others worked on the samples. Witness personally, possibly made five or six or a half dozen plates or more for the purpose of seeing which one would be the best in our coloring matters. For coloring they used ochers—yellow, blue, a little green, and sienna. Witness states he was working on the sample off and on for about two weeks, myself, personally. These samples were about three feet long, and some of them about 18 inches long. * * * Witness thinks that Miller Brothers delivered six or seven samples to the Pennsylvania station, one a section of a cornice.

"As to the size of these samples, witness says: 'Well, to my recollection now—of course, it is ten years or more ago—I should judge that sample piece of the cornice alone would be around four feet long. I am not sure it wasn't a mitered piece. I am not positive, but I know there was a piece of cornice submitted, and the cornice, I should judge, would be around a three foot depth to my best recollection.'

"Various methods were used in making these samples. The method described on direct examination was one of witness' methods of making it.

"Q. And you were experimenting on certain methods and other men in the shop there were experimenting on other methods; is that right?

"A. That is right.

"Q. And you experimented on behalf of Miller Brothers on a variety of methods?

"A. That is right.

"Q. There was evidently some question among the officials of Miller Brothers as to just what would be the best method to employ in making a sample to be submitted; is that true?

"A. It was just a question of what would be a practical way of doing it, if we got the job to do."

"A. There was no decision as to what method would have been used while the samples were in abeyance, and also the contract to be let.

"Witness stated that there was one sample already up submitted by McNulty Brothers of New York and he believed Mr. Denivelle had a sample there too."

Frank Markel in the Los Angeles case testified (see page 111, Exhibit 6):

"My name is Frank Markel, residence 337 East 40th Street, New York City; business, ornamental plasterer. I have been in such business about twenty-seven years and am familiar with the process of manufacturing imitation stone simulating travertin stone, or marble. I first made such artificial stone at Temple Emanuel at 76th St. and 5th Ave., in New York City about 1892. This job was done by Clay Brothers of New York City, for whom I was working at the time."

And (page 112, Exhibit 6) Marden said:

"The first sample I made of travertin stone was at St. Elmo Club at New Haven, August first to October first, 1913, and another job at Memorial Library, Cambridge, Mass., in the summer of 1914. The Cambridge job we used gelatin moulds. After being greased the mixture was made of colored cement to imitate real Travertin, three different colors were used for same, the putty bulb being used for each color.''

T. J. McNulty, of McNulty Bros. Co. was a witness in the Los Angeles case.

He testified (page 113, Exhibit 6):

"T. J. McNulty, 627 Melrose St., Chicago, a contractor specializing in plaster work, cement work, fire proofing and sculpture work.''

(Page 116, Exhibit 6):

"McNulty Bros. Co., outside of Chicago, have offices in Pittsburg and Cleveland. My brothers, McNulty Bros., of New York, knew Paul E. Denivelle.''

(Pages 117-118, Exhibit 6):

"Q. In June, 1914, when McNulty Bros. Inc. of New York were doing the Whitney building in Philadelphia, Mr. Denivelle raised the question that the McNulty Bros. Inc. of New York were infringing on his patent. Mr. Massemoe, who is in the employ of the McNulty Bros. Company was making the imitation stone and he requested that Mr. McNulty, Mr. Massemoe and Mr. Denivelle go into Philadelphia and see the process that was in use there. Mr. Connors, who was then a partner of Mr. Denivelle's, Mr. McNulty and Mr. Massemoe visited Philadelphia and saw the process that was in use, and after Mr. Connors saw the process he turned around and walked away, and did not express himself in any way.''

(Page 119, Exhibit 6):

"The buildings in which artificial stone was used prior to October, 1915, are the Whitney Building, in 1914, Edgewater Beach Hotel in 1914, also the San Francisco Fair buildings. There were also a number of bank buildings that have been done in travertin since 1914.

* * * * * * *

"The structures done in travertin prior to 1910 were the interior main waiting-room of the Philadelphia Station in New York City. The work on the Philadelphia Station was commenced in 1905 and finished in 1908."

At pages 72-74 (Exhibit 6) Mr. Denivelle, called as a witness for the defendants, testified as follows:

"In 1909 or 1910, subsequent to conversations in reference to the matter, witness received an invitation from the Pennsylvania Railroad Company to submit samples and bids on imitations of marble for their building in New York City. A great many other plastering firms were invited to make samples and submit bids, including Miller and McNulty. Witness saw the samples, that these other firms submitted and each sample was a cementitious structure in imitation of veining and each of them had pockets. There were a great many competitors but witness did not know how many submitted samples. He did know, however, that the competition ranged all the way from producing travertin chemically—by a chemical decomposition—to methods which he used. Some time succeeding that, his bid was accepted on the job.

"Witness first made samples long before anyone submitted bids, the process then used being somewhat different from the present, concerning which witness says: 'I used a method of taking the material and pressing it through a screen; first laying the veins and then taking the material in a sort of putty-like consistency, and pressing it through a screen, so that it came out as it were like spaghetti, and then depending upon a certain settlement, by gravity, of its forming the result; but my first sample was different from that, even.' In making these early samples sometimes witness used the mold and sometimes there were bench samples made on a horizontal surface, the surface being isolated by the use of some oily or greasy compound, then the veining was applied by pouring. * * * In the beginning, witness did not use loose, lumpy material. Witness did not use loose lumpy material until 'about the very latter part of the progress of that Pennsylvania station; on towards its completion.' Witness had men in there in 1912. The use of loose, lumpy material occurred in 1911. Witness' work on the Pennsylvania Station was completed the latter part of 1912.

"After completing the Pennsylvania Station witness did not make any more artificial travertin for some time. As to the next job witness says: 'I am not sure as to whether it was in the entrance of the American Art Galleries or the Evans College at the University of Pennsylvania'. Witness employed other men in making the artificial travertin at other places. Witness knows because he brought some to the Exposition.

"Witness brought his process of making artificial travertin to the Exposition authorities of the Panama-Pacific International Exposition in San Francisco on December 12, 1912, slightly before he applied for a patent."

Mr. Denivelle, called again in rebuttal for plaintiffs in the Los Angeles case, testified (page 167, Exhibit 6):

"The final competitors on the Pennsylvania Station were McNulty Brothers, H. W. Miller and witness. Witness knew the character of the specimen that was submitted to the Pennsylvania Station by Miller. It was made by a series of sausages of the material that was laid of different colors, which was laid on the slabs and pressed together sideways, and then tamped down and backed up. There was another sample that was furnished by Miller after the competition had ended; in fact, after the three competitors had delivered their samples.

"It was a white slab of white Portland cement, which was the only one of the other competitors that complied with the instructions or specifications of the competition, which stipulated that the samples were to be made with white Portland cement. And I protested this sample at the time, because it had been delivered one week after the ending of the competition; and secondly, on the claim that an examination would show that it had been cast from a negative form of a real natural piece of travertin. * * *

"This sample furnished by Miller cast from natural travertin was rejected. This Miller is the same party referred to by the witness, Mardon."

And (page 171, Exhibit 6):

"Witness stated he knew the facts in connection with the statement in the deposition of McNulty on behalf of defendant and with reference to the Widener or Whitney building in Philadelphia and the purported visit to have been made by Mr. Connors, a partner of Mr. Denivelle, with certain members of the firm of McNulty and Company in New York.

"Witness stated that the occurrence was in June, 1915 and not in 1914 as stated by McNulty.

"Witness fixes the date by a letter he wrote to Mr. Townsend, his counsel, complaining of McNulty's infringement and asking for advice and counsel's reply thereto. These letters are in evidence as Plaintiffs' Exhibits 14 and 15."

And on cross-examination in that case Mr. Denivelle testified (page 173, Exhibit 6):

"Q. And when did the public first begin to go through that Pennsylvania Railroad station?

"A. Well, long before the building was completed.

"Q. It was in 1910, wasn't it?

"A. I have no means of proving that, but I would not be surprised that a portion of the station was used long before our work had even fairly progressed."

That there was no misunderstanding in the former suit as to the Artificial Travertin put into the Pennsylvania Station in 1910 by Mr. Denivelle meeting the calls of the product claims 9 and 10 of the patent in suit, is seen from the rigid cross-examination of Mr. Denivelle in that case at page 173 (Exhibit 6).

In conclusion, the Court there said (page 175, Exhibit 6):

"The COURT. If you take time. I want you to state the evidence, as to whether or not this patent was dedicated to the public by the Pennsylvania station, and you gentlemen can state the evidence through the briefs."

Yet this Court held that despite the showing of actual user, which was never denied, it was not of

*such a character as to fall within the inhibition of
the statute or adversely to affect the validity of the
Denivelle patent.*

That there was no uncertainty as to the actual
reality of the Pennsylvania Station's use of Artificial Travertin by the Denivelle Process is seen
further by the publication "Wall Surfaces of the
Exposition" by Mr. Markwart, of the Exposition
Company (Exhibit 13 here and Exhibit 10 in the
Los Angeles case), particularly where Markwart
said (pages 1 and 2):

"Roman Travertine was first artificially represented in the new Pennsylvania Station in
New York City by Mr. Paul E. Denivelle, the
originator and supervisor of the Exposition
plastic scheme. McKim, Mead & White, the
architects of the structure, used the natural
travertine for a decorative wainscoting in the
passenger waiting room, but this material was
too costly for use on the entire walls and
vaulted ceilings of this room, and it occurred
to them that a suitable imitation would make
an agreeable substitute for the great portion of
the wall area above the wainscoting. Mr. Denivelle, a happy combination of the artist and
artisan, undertook this important work and
carried it out successfully.

"The work done in the Pennsylvania Station
was in 1910 and captures the admiration of all
who see it. Therefore, at the suggestion of
Messrs. McKim, Mead & White, the Division
of Works engaged Mr. Denivelle in position of
Supervisor of Texture and Modeling in order
that there might be assured a successful plaster
exterior, with due regard to its practicability,
originality, color and texture. In this capacity
Mr. Denivelle carried out the plastic scheme and

superintended the making of architectural models to the end that the proper interpretation was given to the architect's work, and by this arrangement all instructions to modelers were given through one source. Mr. Denivelle was attached to the Bureau of Building Construction and the Departments of Architecture and Color and Decoration, and co-operated extensively with the Department of Sculpture."

Continuing, Mr. Markwart said:

"But there was a difference between the use of a few tons of colored cement plaster cast blocks over the comparatively limited interior wall area in the Pennsylvania Station and the use of a gypsum product on the wood-sheathed exterior area of all the buildings upon the Exposition grounds. When twenty-five to thirty thousand tons of material were to be used, a widely different problem was presented. Experienced Exposition contractors pronounced the textured and colored exterior as impossible of accomplishment, and many of the Western gypsum mills looked unfavorably upon the proposal, so for a time the artistic success of the Exposition was threatened by the attitude of both of these necessary factors. However, Mr. Denivelle, fortified with the knowledge obtained by the solution of a similar problem, believed that the Exposition plastic scheme might be made successful if the plaster manufacturers could be interested. In this connection he succeeded in convincing Dr. Will L. Ellerbeck, the head of the Nephi (Utah) Plaster and Manufacturing Company, of the feasibility of the process. Dr. Ellerbeck's special technical training in the mineral earth industries and his extraordinary facilities from a mill-operating standpoint made him a valuable adjunct to the scheme, and while the hope of anticipated profits may have spurred him on to some extent, it must be said in all fairness and without detracting from others, that his co-operation with Mr. Denivelle was a potent factor in bringing about the successful result.''

And on page 5 Mr. Markwart pays this tribute to Mr. Denivelle's genius:

"In conclusion, it may be stated that while Mr. Denivelle was not engaged as either an artist or architect, nor as a sculptor, yet he must be mentioned among the first of those who contributed to the artistic success of the Exposition. His studies at the Paris Louvre and the instructions he received at the Geneve Beaux Arts in design and modeling, together with his extensive practical experience in New York, peculiarly fitted him to perform the work in question. It is conceded by all that the rare quality of the artificial Travertine dove-tailed admirably into the beautiful color scheme of Mr. Jules Guerin. An engineer may be presumptuous to offer an artistic appreciation, but it appears to the writer that here, there and everywhere about the Exposition the suggestions of Mr. Denivelle were of great value, for there was an intimate relation of his work in the fountains, the vases, the lighting standards, the modeling and the sculpture and here and there in the color scheme. And that he played an important role in assisting those in charge of special features cannot be denied, and this assistance is no doubt appreciated by the architects and those of the Division of Works, perhaps more than by the general public.''

From the foregoing it is quite evident that lack of invention by "accidental use," and "prior use" by the patentee in the Pennsylvania Station in 1910, were the main defenses and were fully tried out and decided by this Court against the defendants.

The holding of this Court was that while there was undoubtedly in the Pennsylvania Station case a "use by the public" extended beyond the statutory two year period, nevertheless this use was, under the circumstances, not in legal effect a "public use" (*Elizabeth v. Paving Co.,* 97 U. S. 126).

Now in the present case the defendants have presented the same defenses, only elaborated with cumulative effect. The evidence is the same in kind, varying only in degree.

THE PRESENT RECORD.

There is this notable distinction between the present case and the former Los Angeles case: We have here powerful defendants, who have enlisted every argument and agency that they could think of or whip into line, and have used every means that they could to defeat what every architect and plastering contractor now recognize as an extremely valuable contribution to their business. Plaintiff is confronted here by what we may correctly characterize as a gigantic attempt and a conspiracy to rob him of what this Court said was a meritorious invention, and which the evidence shows it to be. The evidence further shows the great stakes for which these defendants are playing.

ADMITTED BIAS AND SELF INTEREST OF DEFENDANTS' WITNESSES.

This conspiracy to rob the plaintiff and defy this Court's solemn decree is shown in many ways and in many instances in the record.

(1)   Correspondence in June, 1922 (already quoted supra), between Mr. Denivelle and the defendant, MacGruer, regarding the Los Angeles Biltmore job.

(2)   The brazen defiance of the former decree upholding the patent, by defendant MacGruer on the stand (R. 559):

> "Mr. TOWNSEND.   Q.   What was said and done at that meeting on the 16th?
> "A.   Nothing beyond the fact that you tried to impress upon me that Denivelle had a valid patent, which I questioned."

(R. 566):

> "The only conversation was a cort of cross-questioning back and forth, in which he intimated to me that I was going to go along and that I knew of his patent, and I stated that I didn't think he had a patent, and I was still of that opinion. He stated, 'You have been doing this thing for a long time and you have been trying to get around this patent for a long time.' I said, 'I don't see any need of getting around the patent, I don't think there is any patent'."

(R. 567-568):

> "I said we were trying to get away from the semi-dry process which I stated to you at that time was the only thing I thought he had of

any possibility in his patent, if the patent was valid.''

This was said with full knowledge by the witness of this Court's prior decision upholding the patent and as showing studied disregard by this defendant for patents in general (see his cross-examination R. 629) :

"Q. I don't know the transaction you are referring to, but you believe that as early as 1915 or 1916 Mr. Denivelle either had a patent or was getting a patent on it—you knew that then, did you?
"A. Yes, and Mr. Denivelle was at that time advised that we did not think it was a valid patent.''

(3) MacGruer defied his lawyer and the general contractors as well, who apparently advised defendants to get a license from Denivelle (see quotation supra).

(R. 560) :

"As a result of that interview, at your suggestion, along with Mr. Patton's, I wrote this letter so that we could get down to a basis of possibly arriving at some conclusion.
"Q. Did you get a reply from Mr. Denivelle?
"A. I did, I received a firm bid.''

(R. 624) :

"Mr. ANDERSON. Q. Did you have any conversations or negotiations with Mr. Denivelle's licensee in Los Angeles concerning the Biltmore job? A. Yes, I did—''

(R. 625) :

"A. Mr. Malone. I also talked with Mr.

Roth, and with Mr. Perry Sawyer; they all represented Mr. Denivelle."

*   *   *   *   *   *   *

"A. Mr. Sawyer called on Mr. Scofield numerous times and asked Mr. Scofield to use his influence to see if we could not get together. At the suggestion of Mr. Scofield, while I was in Los Angeles, I went to see Mr. Sawyer and Mr. Roth; I also talked with Mr. Malone. Mr. Malone, at a subsequent date, called at my office with, I think it is Percy Stewart—"

(R. 651):

"XQ. Why, if you had a method developed at that time, did you write the letter a few days later to Mr. Denivelle asking him for a bid or a royalty basis under his patent for the work on the Biltmore Hotel?

"A. Because it *was suggested by Mr. Scofield, it was also suggested to me by Mr. Patton as possibly the easiest way out,* and *the cheapest way out,* to get through with a large contract, and I impressed upon Mr. Patton that I did not want to enter into any agreement that would place my rights in jeopardy, and Patton said to me, 'Well, anyhow, go ahead and write him the letter and see what comes of it.'

"XQ. So at the time you wrote that letter, and you got Mr. Denivelle's reply, you did not intend to act under it at all?

"A. I so told him at the meeting.

"XQ. You put Mr. Denivelle to the trouble of figuring in good faith, and you had no intention of even considering his bid?

*   *   *   *   *   *   *

"A. He had already submitted his figures, and he did not have to waste any time figuring any more."

*   *   *   *   *   *   *

"XQ. Is that the best answer you can give?
"A. Yes."

(R. 652):

> "XQ. As a matter of fact, you did not intend to consider his bid?
>
> "A. *No, I did not,* unless it was of such a nature that it would save me any expense" (italics ours).

(4) The affidavit of F. J. Twaits, the Engineer for the Biltmore Hotel contractors, already quoted supra (R. 54).

(5) Affidavit of John H. Delaney on motion for preliminary injunction (R. 74).

(6) Activity of these defendants in enlisting sympathy. Thus MacGruer testifies (R. 618-620):

> "Mr. ANDERSON. Q. You visited New York in December, 1923, did you not? A. I did."
>
> * * * * * * *
>
> "A. To find out prior uses of artificial travertine.
>
> * * * * * * *
>
> "A. I interviewed many people connected with the plastering industry.
>
> "A. I interviewed Mr. Durkin; I interviewed Davis Brown; I interviewed Mr. Fenner, of McKim, Mead & White; I called at the office of Carrerer & Hastings, but I can't just recall the name of the gentlemen who had charge of the specifications, but they said they would have the records looked up and give me the definite information—I think it was a Mr. Ward. He finally turned out some specifications.
>
> * * * * * * *
>
> "I interviewed Mr. Holland, of Ward & Wetmore; I also interviewed Mr. Schultz, of Schultz & Weaver, architects.
>
> "Q. Were they the architects for the Biltmore Hotel?
>
> "A. Yes, they were. Mr. Weaver telephoned

to a Mr. Brandt, saying that he was sending me down with a letter of introduction, and if they had any records which would be of any value in connection with the information that I was seeking, to show me all that he could.

*   *   *   *   *   *   *

"I have received no offer of assistance from any plasterers association other than the moral support of the San Francisco Plasterers Association. I also interviewed the association in Chicago and Mr. Ream called a meeting of the members, at which I was present, and I stated my mission."

And on cross-examination (R. 630):

"I went to the Master Plasterers Association meeting, and I met, I think, the representatives of Roberts, I just forget his name off hand.

*   *   *   *   *   *   *

"I saw Mr. Jacobson, I saw Mr. O'Rourke, I saw Mr. Reum in Chicago, I saw Mr. McNulty in Chicago."

(R. 631):

"At his invitation I was invited to the meeting. I also saw Mr. Thompson, of the Klee Thompson Company. I also saw Mr. Fields, of Kenneth Murchinson, architects. I went to see him with reference to work that they had done on the St. Elmo Club, at New Haven, Conn. Their business is at 101 Park Avenue. I also went to see York & Sawyer; I tried to see Mr. Benedict, but he was busy, and I saw Mr. Colleen. I also went to Humphries & Peters, at 218 East Forty-fifth Street—Mr. Braid was the representative of Roberts. I also went to see John Finck."

(R. 632):

* * * "I also called on Mr. Whipple, and I called on Mr. William Cook;

* * * * * * *

* * * "You practically saw every witness, of course, that you called?

"A. That is what I went for to New York, to find out information."

(7) Previously, as seen at R. 598, 599, MacGruer ad written to at least one of his most important nd valuable witnesses, Davis Brown, a letter as ollows:

PLAINTIFF'S EXHIBIT No. 27.

"March 15th, 1923.

"David Brown, Inc.,
 306 East 40th St.,
  New York, N. Y.

"Gentlemen:

"We are taking the liberty of writing you in search of information with reference to the manufacture of Artificial Travertine. We are at present executing a very large building, namely the new Biltmore Hotel at Los Angeles, Calif., from plans and specifications prepared by Schultze & Weaver, Architects, of New York.

"In connection with these operations we have received notice from a patentee by the name of Paul E. Denivelle of a threat to infringe his patent. The said Paul E. Denivelle you will recall was originally associated with the firm of Hammerstine & Denivelle in New York City. He now operates here on the Pacific Coast and claims the exclusive patent rights for the manufacture of artificial travertine. On this point however we do not agree as we have manufactured considerable artificial travertine, but we never thought it was a material of sufficient merit to warrant the taking of a patent. There

is no doubt about the validity of the patent
granted the said Paul E. Denivelle, but the
question in our minds at the present time is
the settlement of the question whether he has
the sole right to manufacture artificial travertine and bar any other concern from manufacturing same by a process other than the one
covered by his letters patent.

"We have been advised through our many
friends in the building business that your firm
executed the artificial travertine in the department store of Lord and Taylor, on which operations were started in the year 1913, and completed in the year 1914. Will you kindly advise
us of the exact date of these operations, also
if you have any further data on this point
prior to this time. It will be of great value to
us and may possibly be of great service to you
in the event that you should be placed in the
same position as we find ourselves at present.
To be truthful we are not seriously alarmed
over the situation, although it is very annoying
and embarrassing.

"For your further information we may state
that our General Superintendent has applied
for a patent for the use and manufacture of a
novel method of manufacturing travertine, and
we have no hesitancy in stating same will be
granted. This method is the most simple and
practical method we have yet seen in operation,
the edifying part of this being that it makes
the additional cost of manufacture of artificial
travertine, over the regular method of casting,
very small.

"We would thank you very kindly if you will
forward us this information without delay, so
that it will help us in the event we are threatened with a suit in this connection.

"Thanking you in advance, we are,
"Very truly yours,
"MacGruer & Simpson,.
"MacG/GM.   By."

(8) On March 27th, 1923 (see Exhibit 28, R. 600), Mr. Brown wrote MacGruer & Simpson in which is reflected generally the attitude of not only this witness but most of the other witnesses for the defense (all admitted infringers) open defiance to any patent or any Court opinion that stands in the way of their getting a job.

Brown candidly wrote (R. 600-602):

"As to the date of the Lord & Taylor store, where we have executed the plastering including the imitation travertin work it has been started in the year of 1913 and completed the following year.

"As to the claim of Paul E. Denivelle that he has the sole right to manufacture imitation travertin, I have heard of that but of course we are all doing this work in the City of New York and disregarding such a claim as there is no secret about the manufacturing whether it is applied in the building or cast in the shop and set up in slabs in the building.

* * * * * * *

"You also mention in your letter that you have improved on the method of making artificial travertine. This simply shows that you are also progressing and taking an interest in the manufacture of improving this part of our work which we all here are constantly trying to improve upon and that you are also trying to take a patent on your new method.

"In connection with this, isn't it a fact that all stones are created by God Almighty and you and I and all of us trying to make a poor imitation of His work at its best therefore I maintain that we are doing the infringing on His work but as long as He is not objecting we are simply trying to imitate His work and I do not know why any other manufacturer of artificial stone should make claims for patents.

"I recollect some thirty (30) years ago when I was working at the trade as an apprentice boy for the old firm of James J. Morrison whose father was even a plasterer, they have manufactured in those days all sorts of imitation stones very successfully but never looked for the sole rights therefore we believe and maintain that a patent to be claimed by Paul E. Denivelle even if he received such a patent from my point of view is absurd.

"In closing, I wish you the very best of success.

"Sincerely yours,
DAVIS BROWN."

(9) Not only was this defendant MacGruer active in interviewing prospective interested witnesses and priming them, but his counsel sought to cultivate opinion unfavorable to Denivelle.

For instance, see the letter to Mr. Webster of January 19th, 1924, from counsel for defendants (Book of Exhibits, page 198), in which appears:

"I am representing MacGruer & Simpson of San Francisco, who have been sued on the Denivelle patent for the manufacture of artificial travertine, a copy of which I am enclosing for your information.

*   *   *   *   *   *   *

"*I think you will agree with me that this patent is a menace to the building trade generally. In fact, Denivelle, by means of this patent, has already caused considerable trouble on the Pacific Coast and will cause further trouble in New York unless the patent be invalidated*" (italics ours).

It is only too evident how such artful suggestion

would produce a fruitful crop of witnesses unfavorable to any patent, particularly where self interest intervened.

Mr. Webster showed, however, by the tenor of his reply that he was not in sympathy with the evident conspiracy to fleece the plaintiff, for he says in a letter dated January 22nd, 1924 (Book of Exhibits, page 200):

"Jan. 22, 1924.

"Mr. T. Hart Anderson,
  "c/o Messrs. Munn, Anderson and Munn,
    "233 Broadway, New York.
"Dear Sir:
  "In reply to your inquiry of Jan. 19th, in regard to the question of Artificial Travertin: To the best of my knowledge and belief, the Denivelle process of making Artificial Travertin originated during the erection of the Pennsylvania Railroad Station in New York City, where I was assigned as General Superintendent by the Architects, Messrs. McKim, Mead & White.
  "Italian Travertin, for interior architectural finish, had never been used in this country until it was adopted by Messrs. McKim, Mead & White for the Pennsylvania Railroad Station, and as it was not feasible to utilize the real material throughout for all the wall surfaces and for the ornamental cornices and caps of the columns and pilasters in the Main Waiting Room and Arcade, due to the expense, the Architects decided to try duplicating the real marble with Artificial Travertin.
  "Experiments were made by Mr. Denivelle and other competing plastering contractors and sizable samples were erected for examination, by each of the concerns interested, with the final result that *Mr. Denivelle's material was selected as being the best submitted, both with*

regard to color, texture and *durability, due to
the process and materials used in its fabrication,* and the contract for this work, therefore,
was awarded to Mr. Denivelle for all the Imitation Travertin required in the Pennsylvania
Station Building.

"Shortly after the completion of the Pennsylvania Terminal Building I left the employ of
Messrs. McKim, Mead & White to become associated with the Firm of Barott, Blackader &
Webster, architects in Montreal, so I do not
know whether Mr. Denivelle undertook any
other contracts for the fabrication of Imitation
Travertin in New York City; but he did some
very satisfactory work for us in Montreal, on
the Windsor Station Waiting Room, for the
Canadian Pacific Railroad.

"Afterwards I learned that he had been requested to take charge of the Imitation Travertin for the exterior finish of the Exposition
Buildings in San Francisco.

*"I do not agree with you that if Mr. Denivelle
has a valid patent for the fabrication and installation of Imitation Travertin that such a
patent is a menace to the Building Trade generally—as you state in your letter.*

*"I believe Mr. Denivelle to be the originator
and exponent of Imitation Travertin, and is entitled to the credit due to his knowledge and
experience.*

> "Yours very truly,
> (Signed) D. T. WEBSTER."

(Italics ours.)

Mr. Webster, moreover, was given the tribute of
praise by counsel for defendants at the time the
depositions were read in Court as being "a very fair
witness, although a friend of Mr. Denivelle".

THE DOCUMENTARY EVIDENCE IN THE PRESENT CASE SUSTAINS THIS COURT'S FORMER DECISION IN FAVOR OF THE DENIVELLE PATENT.

We are indebted to defendants for having produced here much of the early correspondence bearing on the work on the Pennsylvania Station. In addition to fixing dates, it shows of itself conclusively what Mr. Denivelle said in the former trial that "it was regarded as an experiment from the very beginning" (page 169, Exhibit 6).

As early as July 20th, 1908, Denivelle, as President of Hammerstein & Denivelle Company, addressed a letter to the Geo. A. Fuller Co., General Contractors for the erection of the Pennsylvania Station, which letter is in evidence as Defendants' Exhibit 5, page 2, Book of Exhibits, in which he proposed to do certain work for a gross sum of $167,000, saying in part:

> "Said work to be made in our composite granite and Roman travertine in cast, individual slabs and blocks separated and divided at every joint, cast at least 2" in thickness and composed of materials with a White Portland Cement base by an accurate method and process that guarantees uniform results; producing not an imitation but an exceedingly durable and true substitute for real Travertine and granite *without the slightest danger of flaking or disintegration.* The finished surface to be clean and smooth, but without polish.
>
> "The above work to be as per our understanding, and to the entire satisfaction of the Architect, for the sum of $167,100.00 one hundred and sixty-seven thousand one hundred dollars.
>
> "We shall expect you to furnish main scaffold

in general waiting room and arcade'' (italics ours).

Evidently there were several changes in plans and specifications, because on August 31st, 1908, a new proposal was submitted by Mr. Denivelle (see letter, Defendants' Exhibit 5, page 5, Book of Exhibits) and reading (italics ours) :

"New York, Aug. 31, 1908.
"In re Pennsylvania Terminal
"Revised Estimates.
"George A. Fuller Co.
"Gentlemen :
"We propose to furnish and erect complete in above building, according to revised plans and specifications the entire *artificial Travertine* made on the same basis as our sample and later samples to be submitted, for the sum of— one hundred seventy-three thousand nine hundred ten dolls. ($172,910.00).
"You will note that our estimate is based on reinforced form of cement stone cast in individual blocks with a high grade white *portland cement composition forming the face.* This in our estimation is the only basis for producing an indestructable material for the purpose required and far superior in every way to Keene's cement or any other gypsum product. Kindly note the above in considering our estimates.
"We have not considered the alternative of using a soft material above points of contact, as the difference in cost will hardly compensate for the loss in durability.
"It might be well to add that we will be in position to thoroughly prosecute this contract should it be awarded us from both financial and practical view points.
"Truly yours,
"HAMMERSTEIN & DENIVELLE CO.,
"W. 5th St., New York,
"PAUL E. DENIVELLE, President.''

Note that neither letter gives any description of the process or indication of the appearance of the product. Denivelle evidently felt he could do the job. He was seeking hard to get the opportunity to try.

On October 2nd, 1908, the architects, McKim, Mead & White, wrote Mr. Geo. Gibbs, Chief Engineer for the Pennsylvania Railroad Company a letter, which is in evidence as Defendants' Exhibit 6, page 20, Book of Exhibits, in which five parties are mentioned as submitting samples "of varying merit" with bids likewise varying, *from $107,800 by Mr. Denivelle's firm to $432,000 by one Lilienthal;* the architects noting caution by adding,

> "before rendering final decision *we wish to further investigate the quality of the samples submitted as to permanency under varying weather conditions.*"

On October 15th, 1908, the architects again wrote Mr. Gibbs (Defendants' Exhibit 6, page 22, Book of Exhibits) along similar lines to the last letter but going more into a discussion of the *doubts in their minds* not only as to relative financial worth of the several bidders, but, more particularly, into the question of *whether any of the so-called imitations were capable of satisfactory demonstration under the test of time and permanency,* and whether the production of the *small sized samples* could insure the carrying of the quality forward on a *large scale.* For example, they say:

> "Samples have been made by the various firms submitting figures, which are of *varying merit.*

As the nature of this work, however, demands
a careful consideration of the *quality* of the
samples submitted, as well as the relative
amount of cost, it would seem to us *advisable
to delay action* in the awarding of this contract
until larger sized samples can be obtained, and
their *quality investigated* as to *permanency* under *varying temperatures"* (italics ours).

Nothing could more strongly emphasize the "experimental" field that they were all delving in.

This is stressend in the very next paragraph:

"While we are in general well satisfied with
the samples of artificial Travertine which we
have been able to obtain *as to color and general
appearance, we feel that the surfaces with which
the public will come directly in contact will not
wear satisfactorily,* and therefore *recommend
the substitution of real stone* in the Arcade section, and for an additional course at the north
and south ends of the General Waiting Room,
in the passages leading to the Restaurant, Lunch
Room and Barber Shop" (italics ours).

This is the doubt supreme; that while it *looks* all
right at a distance, take no chances on the public
touching it, but put in the natural stone!

Continuing in this letter we see that the architects,
the undoubted leaders in America if not in the world
in this line, viewed even the use of *natural* travertin
in this country and in such building as *"of an experimental nature",* saying:

"Originally we hesitated to ask your Company
to purchase any more Travertine as we felt
that the ordering of large quantities of this
stone from quarries in Italy, considering the

difficulties of transportation, was *of an experimental nature.*"

However, in view of the saving to be made by the use of "miscellaneous marble plastering and artificial Travertin" contemplated in parts of the building, they say:

" * * * it would therefore seem to us that the use of *real material* in this section is a *conservative recommendation* in conformity with the dignity of your undertaking.

"If your Company thinks favorably of this *recommendation,* the arcade stone can be ordered at once and installed during the coming winter, and the *awarding of the artificial stone contract can then be postponed for some time* (inasmuch as the work will come mainly in the General Waiting Room) *pending further investigation of the samples, as outlined in the first part of this letter*" (italics ours).

Note "postponement" of award of artificial stone Contract "pending further investigation of the samples".

In the next paragraph they go on to say, in effect, that although it will cost thousands of dollars additional to use the natural stone where the public may possibly touch or come in close contact with the walls, that they *prefer to do that than take chances with an unknown, untried material,* for they say:

"Messrs. Batterson & Eisle estimate the cost of the Travertine for the sections above referred to, which includes all the stone work in the Arcade up to the level of the pilaster caps, and the additional course in the entrance to the Restaurant and the north and south ends of the General Waiting Room, as $23,248.40."

McNULTY BROS. DID NOT COMPLY WITH THE SPECIFICATION BUT DENIVELLE DID.

On December 28th, 1908, McNulty Bros., by J. M. Krafft, wrote the architects, attention Daniel T. Webster (see letter Defendants' Exhibit 6, page 28, Book of Exhibits), as follows:

> "Referring to our estimate of December 22, 1908 for Artificial Travertine stone work required in Pennsylvania Terminal Station, New York City, and in further explanation of the sample installed by us in Arcade at your request.

> "We desire to state that we will absolutely guarantee to make all of this work as hard as may be required by you. We will instantly remove any work which does not meet with your approval.

> "It is pointed out that in the sample in place it has been our chief object to show our ability to imitate this stone; the ingredients used in the hardening of the material do not interfere with the aesthetic features of the imitation in any one particular.

> *"We have not followed your request to submit a sample made of white portland cement,* because the short time allowed for the execution of this work precludes its use, aside from the *possibility of efflorescence* * *due to certain ingredients contained in this material"* (italics ours).

Note that McNulty Brothers, Inc. admit the difficulties of trying to handle "white portland cement"; the "short time" "precludes its use"—"aside from

---

* "Effloresce * * * chem. To become powdery, wholly or in part, and lose crystalline structure through loss of water of crystallization on exposure to the air: to become covered with a crust of saline particles left by evaporation, as the ground" (Standard Dictionary).

the possibility of efflorescence due to certain ingredients contained in this material"! And yet this "short time" must have been months and months! Still they couldn't do it.

The Mr. Krafft who signed this letter (vice-president of McNulty Bros., R. 88) was a willing witness for the defendants here to show there was nothing unusual nor experimental about this Pennsylvania Station job (Krafft deposition, beginning R. 86).

Mr. Daniel T. Webster mentioned was also a witness (R. 237-281) but, knowing more about the process and the actual realities of the case, took sharp issue with the defense and showed that the Pennsylvania Station job was *one series of experiments and uncertainties from beginning to end.* His testimony will be considered in detail later.

The written records show that the years 1909-10 still found things in an experimental stage.

The Railroad Company, real party in interest, intervened by its vice-president, Mr. Rea, and, as seen by the letter of Mr. Gibbs to Mr. Mead, of McKim, Mead & White of February 4th, 1909 (Defendants' Exhibit 8 (R. 249), page 30, Book of Exhibits) demanded that Denivelle be given a square deal, and that his was the *best* sample as well as his bid being the lowest; this letter being as follows:

"Letterhead of Pennsylvania Tunnel and
Terminal Railroad Company.
"10 Bridge St., New York.
"February 4th, 1909.
"Personal.
"Mr. William R. Mead,
"McKim, Mead & White,
"160 Fifth Ave., New York City.
"Dear Sir:
"Relative to the imitation Travertine marble
for the Pennsylvania Station, regarding which
you wrote me January 27th, I forwarded your
letter to Mr. Rea on January 29th endorsing
your recommendation and asking for authority
to close the contract. On the 30th I received
the following telephone message from Mr. Rea:
" 'Referring to your letter of 29th instant
regarding Travertine contract; I am not satisfied to approve of the recommendation covering
the award of this contract until you, from an
independent standpoint, have established the
fact that the Denivelle Composite Stone Company, *who made the best sample and are the
lowest bidders,* have not the financial ability to
carry on the work both well and expeditiously,
and secondly, that H. W. Miller Incorporated,
the second best bidder, is not able to satisfactorily perform the work. The Denivelle
Composite Stone Company, of which I know
nothing, has at least some practical sympathy
from my standpoint, *because of the labor and
expense they have undergone to give us the best
sample of artificial stone,* and, therefore, they
are *entitled to a fair chance* in this matter. The
process of elimination is too severe without
further investigation.'
"This was taken up with you by Mr. George
R. Rea, and I believe a conference was held on
the second instant.
"I, personally, feel as Mr. Rea expresses it,
that if Denivelle is competent to carry out the

contract he should be given a chance to do so, as an opportunity of this kind is one that does not come to a young man very often. However, we must protect the Railroad Company's interests in the completion of the Station and must of course rely upon the Fuller Company's and your own judgment as the final thing. I understand that since the original bid was made that Denivelle has incorporated a company with some financial backing, and this may alter your conclusions.

"I shall be very glad, therefore, if you will look into the question again and give me your advice in view of present circumstances (italics ours).

"Very truly yours,
"GEORGE GIBBS,
"Chief Engineer."

"P/GG/LBH

The Contract was let finally to Denivelle's Company for $109,378.00 and bears date of March 5th, 1909, accepted April 18th, 1909 (Defendants' Exbibit 40A, Book of Exhibits, page 106).

This Contract provided among other things (Paragraph 9) "that any imperfections and defects should be made good within one year after completion".

A bond of $50,000.00 was required (Book of Exhibits, page 120).

Concerning the lettering of the Contract Mr. Webster, a witness for defendants, testified (R. 269):

"The point was when we closed Denivelle's main contract *we asked for an extension of a year's guaranty to determine how good the material was* within that period, and *it did demonstrate that the vibration and change of tem-*

perature affected certain areas, and *there were sections that had been repaired.*

"XQ. 10. But it required considerably longer time than one year to determine whether or not it was a satisfactory construction for that purpose?

A. It has taken longer periods than that to determine whether any artificial stone is good for its purpose. It is a question of perfection in the method of construction and the materials used therein to get a better product, and that is determined by actual periods of time and depending upon the localities where it is installed; *that was one of the reasons why McKim, Mead & White were doubtful about using imitation stone* in the waiting-room; they had had trouble theretofore with imitation stones that had imitation marble—they were looking for something better" (italics ours).

In a letter of May 25th, 1910 (Defendants' Exhibit 20, Book of Exhibits, page 153), from the architects to the Geo. A. Fuller Co. the uncertainties attendant on the work were adverted to:

"We notice many open joints between stones and where *patches have fallen off this work,* occurring particularly on the upper section of the walls and arches. These defects should be rectified at once; furthermore the domes of the concourse entrance show cracks and these should also be repaired.

"The ashlar on the west wall of the west wall of the General Waiting Room has *never properly dried out* and we would be obliged if you would investigate and *advise us as to the reason for this,* and also as to the best method to accelerate the drying.

"We would be obliged if you would procure from Denivelle Hydraulic Composite Stone Company copy of guarantee as called for in clause 9 of their contract, same to be dated from August 1st, 1910 and run for a period of one year'' (italics ours).

The job proved a financial loss to the Denivelle Co. but it was completed and release signed November 19th, 1910 (Defendants' Exhibit 7, Book of Exhibits, page 137), but this release, at the recommendation of the architects, *carried the unusual clause of a guarantee of future personal attention* by Denivelle.

Thus Webster (R. 255-256):

"Q. 106. I hand you a document which is marked Defendants' Exhibit 7—Denivelle Release—and ask you if you ever saw that document before; if so, when and where?

"A. Yes, this is the one, but I confused the word 'release' with 'guaranty'; that is what we call a guaranty bond for fulfillment of a contract and maintenance of same.

"Q. 107. You wouldn't call that a release?

"A. It is in fact—it is a release—but I was revolving in my mind—I know we insisted on a guaranty.''

Meanwhile and leading up to the guaranty embodied in the release, Mr. Denivelle wrote Mr. Webster on September 9th, 1910 (Defendants' Exhibit 28, Book of Exhibits, page 159), in which he said:

"We would be pleased if our bare labor and expense cost balance through this excess payment of $3500, but we value it doubly as an expression of your recognition of the writer's efforts to fulfill the confidence which Messrs. McKim, Mead & White, did show at the time this extremely difficult contract was awarded. Regarding the understanding desired to effect that writer 'will personally look after the work during coming year and give it his best advice and assistance in keeping it up to its present condition.' I *would therefore pledge myself to regard this as a distinct agreement of the writer's personal services and advice during coming year, this pledge to operate in addition to the general ground covered by this company's surety bond,* in consideration of the said proposed payment to us of thirty-five hundred dollars (italics ours).

"Very truly yours,
(Signed) PAUL E. DENIVELLE."

Concerning this release and guaranty Mr. Fenner, the architect from McKim, Mead & White's office said (R. 185-186):

"I don't know whether those specifications provide that the contractor shall be responsible for damage due to defective material or faulty workmanship for any given period; it is our usual custom to insert such a paragraph in all specifications *but this form of release including the requirement that the contractor continue to maintain the work for a given period and devote his own time to that, is somewhat unusual —I don't recall any other case in our practice where just that course has been followed*" (italics ours).

During 1911 various repairs and replacements were made by Denivelle, as seen by Denivelle Company's bills to the Railroad Company of January 7th, 1911 (Defendants' Exhibit 37, Book of Exhibits, pages 171 and 172), and bill marked "Approved December 12, 1911" (Defendants' Exhibit 36-A, Book of Exhibits, page 169, R. 262), confirmed by letter of the Denivelle Company to the architects dated

October 26th, 1911 (Defendants' Exhibit 39, Book of Exhibits, page 174), in which it is said:

> "We beg to report that for the *past three weeks* we have had men at the above building, touching up the various spots, joints, etc., pointed out by you. In addition, we have in the *past year from time, to time* had men touch up certain little defects which may have appeared. We therefore, hereby make application for payment of the $3500.00, which was to accrue after the 15th date present month" (italics ours).

Naturally these defects were not going to be magnified by Denivelle's Company when they were so anxious to receive the money due them.

But Mr. Whipple, one of the witnesses for the defense, says (R. 206-207):

> "XQ. 18. Now, would the fact that this artificial travertin was made partly porous and partly solid be likely to cause trouble in warpage or flaking off?
>
> "A. I know that was one of our troubles— *it would peel off in places.*
>
> *   *   *   *   *   *   *
>
> "I know that *if a stone is put up green and dries, it is liable to peel off.* We *had a lot of that difficulty*—a stone would be set up there and maybe in a few days you would come back and a *part of the face would be off.*
>
> *   *   *   *   *   *   *
>
> "—it *looked all right but you come back and find a part of the face dropped off for some reason or other.*
>
> "XQ. 22. There were unusual conditions there in that Station on account of vibration— was that one of your troubles?
>
> "A. That was the great trouble there—it was the *vibration*" (italics ours).

Mr. Whipple says (R. 207) he was informed by Mr. Denivelle on Denivelle's return from Montreal and prior to their departure for California to begin work on the Exposition buildings that men were on the Pennsylvania Station as late as *April, 1913,* making repairs. While this is, strictly speaking, hearsay the evidence was given without objection from the witness' counsel and there is no reason whatever to doubt the truthfulness of the statements.

This brings us now to consider the oral testimony on the subject of just how far the Denivelle invention was found in practice to be in the nature of an experimental undertaking.

The oral testimony substantiates former decision of this Court that work experimental and exploratory—test of time only criterion.

THE PENNSYLVANIA STATION 1909-1912.

Of the 23 witnesses called by defendant and examined by deposition, practically all of them pay Denivelle the tribute of being the originator of artificial Travertin; at least that it was an unknown *product* until its use in the Pennsylvania Station.

Thus architect Shreve testifies (R. 164):

"XQ. 65. What was the first artificial or composite travertine that you ever heard of or saw; where was it used?

"A. I don't think it is possible for me to answer that question accurately at this time. The first I remember was work done at the Pennsylvania Station, which I understand Mr.

Denivelle had done, but at that time I had not met him, and I don't recall that situation clearly enough to state anything about it in detail."

BURT L. FENNER (R. 168-186): Mr. Fenner as a member of the firm McKim, Mead & White, testifies to the novelty of the proposition of using artificial Travertin in the Pennsylvania Station.

The Court's attention is called in conection with Mr. Fenner's deposition, to the grossly leading (if not misleading) and argumentative questions propounded by counsel for the defense on direct examination. Thus (R. 180-1):

"Q. 70. Mr. Denivelle, in a suit in California, has testified that that work he did in the Pennsylvania Station was an experiment. Would Mc-Kim, Mead & White cause to be installed on a building designed and constructed under their direction—permit an experiment to be put in such a building?

"Mr. LOFTUS. Objected to as calling for an opinion and conclusion of the witness.

"A. Why, the question is just what 'experiment' means. Certainly the *preparation of samples was an experiment, for to the best of my knowledge nothing of the sort had ever been attempted before.* As a result of the samples, McKim, Mead & White and the officers representing the Railroad Company felt sufficient confidence in the result to warrant McKim, Mead & White in recommending its use to the Railroad Company and the Railroad Company in agreeing to its use and making the contract. It is obvious that both the Railroad Company and McKim, Mead & White felt pretty certain that they were going to get a successfnl result, and they wouldn't have been justified in trying what I understand as an experiment on so large a scale, *and yet until the work was completed and had stood certain tests of time and use, no one could be certain that the results indicated from the samples would actually be brought about in reality.*

"Q. 71. That's true also of almost every building construction, isn't it?

"A. It's true of every new material, I should say, but not of every building construction. We know perfectly well what the result of laying up a brick wall is going to be, or putting in an ordinary plastered ceiling, but *here is a new material* with *no data, no precedent to enable anybody to determine with any accuracy, certainty or finality what the result would be.* The evidence produced by the samples convinced us all that we should get *a satisfactory result*" (italics ours).

Evidently, however, the defense got more than it bargained for because whatever Mr. Denivelle's testimony in the California suit might have been, the witness evidently showed that the work was from the beginning of an experimental character and could only be proven otherwise by "certain tests of time and use".

We are reminded of the words of the Supreme Court:

"When the subject of invention is a machine, it may be tested and tried in a building either with or without closed doors. In either case, such use is not a public use, within the meaning of the statute, so long as the inventor is engaged, in good faith, in testing its operation. He may see cause to alter it and improve it, or not. His experiments will reveal the fact whether any and what alterations may be necessary. *If durability is one of the qualities to be attained, a long period, perhaps years, may* *be necessary to enable the inventor to discover whether his purpose is accomplished.* And though during all that period he may not find that any changes are necessary, yet he may be justly said to be using his machine only by way of experiment; and no one would say that such a use, pursued with a bona fide intent of testing the qualities of the machine, would be a public use within the meaning of the statute. * * * Whilst the supposed machine is in such experimental use, the public may be incidentally deriving a benefit from it. If it be a grist mill, or a carding machine, customers from the surrounding country may enjoy the use of it by having their grain made into flour, or their wool into rolls, and still it will not be in public use, within the meaning of the law." (*Elizabeth v. Am. Nich. Pavement Co.,* 97 U. S. 126, 134.) (Italics ours.)

DANIEL T. WEBSTER (R. 237-284 inc.): Mr. Webster no doubt was the most important witness for the defense because of his greater familiarity with what went on in Mr. Denivelle's line on the Pennsylvania Station.

He testifies (R. 238-9-40):

"I was delegated by McKim, Mead & White to act as general superintendent for the architects at the site. * * *

"I first met Mr. Denivelle around 1909. * * *

"Why, as I recollect, he was requested by McKim, Mead & White to make some samples of imitation stone using a new material, at that time known as white Portland cement, and he was asked to get in touch with me to see the real stone; it was the first time I met him. * * *

"The *architects had been in a quandary* as to getting the proper kind of material for the finishing out of the balance of the wall surfaces

where real travertin had not been contracted
for due to its expense. * * *

"The first sample Mr. Denivelle made, I remember, was a small piece; that had been instigated, I think, by Mr. Mead, who was senior
member of the firm, asking Mr. Denivelle to try
and see what he could do using this white Portland cement—that small sample I saw after it
had been completed."

That Denivelle's work was one of constant change
and experiment and improvement is abundantly
shown by this witness whom we find not only to be
eminently fair and well informed, but one of the few
witnesses called for the defendants who did not seem
to have been stampeded by the appeal that the
"Denivelle patent is a menace."

Thus we have at R. 266 following (all italics
ours):

"Q. 161. Is it your testimony that that work
was done in that manner in accordance with his
contract and specifications?

"A. Except where it was altered as *he progressed with his experiments* and process of
manufacturing his material, with our consent.

"Q. 162. Did you pass upon the work or such
changes as were made by Mr. Denivelle, so as to
be able to approve the work as it was done?

"A. *After calling the attention of my employers* to *these changes* as they arose, I approved, acting as their agent."

and on cross-examination (R. 266 and following):

"A. *We did several things in the Station
that had never been done before*—it was a very
usual building. * * *

"XQ. 5. Now, this travertin work that Mr
Denivelle did—that I understand was made of
white Portland cement?

A. Yes, *the epidermis or outer surface was made of white Portland cement;* the ingredients consisted of 1 to 1 part sand and cement and *the backing consisted of half of white cement and sand,* and the final foundation of sand and ordinary Portland cement."

THIS THIN "EPIDERMIS" OF POROUS CEMENT OF DIFFERENT CONSISTENCY FROM BACKING, A CAUSE OF PEELING.

Artificial Travertin having a thin surface coat of *one material* and besides being full of holes or vermiculations (honey-combed) and a backing or ground coat of *another material,* naturally presents a different problem than where the mass is of homogeneous material throughout with a *smooth* outer surface. The witness Brown touches on the subject but quickly shies off (see R. 515-516):

"XQ. 29. Well, now, considering that artificial travertin is more or less porous and filled with voids near its outer surface, and the back wall is rather dense, is that a condition that would be likely to cause warpage or cracking, due to uneven expansion or contraction

"A. No more than under any other circumstances because travertin itself, or what you see —the coloring and the holes in it—is *only a matter of about a quarter of an inch*—as long as it is applied to the ground coat it will only crack when the ground coat cracks—*unless the travertin is applied in a fashion that may be the ground coat is too smooth or too dry, then of course there is not so much suction there to bind the two materials together:* then it is liable to loosen up and crack—that condition will come up on that wall—come up with any

material in that vicinity—make no difference
whether it is plaster; but we know from information, for instance, that in plastering—that
the finish coat which is only about ⅛ of an inch
thick, scratches off from the browning for the
reason it might have been two weeks after applying the browning coat, or too dry, or maybe
dust settled on it and the careless mechanic applies it without dusting off, and after the material is dry it creates a vacuum between the
two and you get that hollow—here (indicating)——" (italics ours)

Previously Brown testified (R. 503) that the material of the "finish coat" was only "¼ or ⅞ of an
inch". Of course Brown was speaking of the Vanderbilt job which was not a cement job. The finish
coat of the Pennsylvania job being of white Portland cement, we can see the force of Mr. Whipple's
statements as to the difficulty met with on this Pennsylvania job of the outer skin "peeling off" (R.
206-7, already quoted).

WHITE PORTLAND CEMENT WAS NOT ONLY A NEW MATERIAL, BUT ARTIFICIAL TRAVERTIN WAS WHOLLY NEW.

Mr. Webster says (R. 268-7):

"Frankly, I had never heard about white
Portland cement until about 1908. It was a
new thing on the market * * *

"Prior to the Pennsylvania Station I did not
know anything about travertin."

* * * * * * *

"The point was when we closed Denivelle's
main contract *we asked for an extension of a*

year's guranty to determine how good the material was within that period, and *it did demonstrate that the vibration and change of temperature affected certain areas, and there were sections that had been repaired."*

nd again (R. 279):

"RXQ. 1. Which was the more difficult material to work with, the white Portland cement or the plaster or gypsum, in the making of stone imitation?

"A. Why, the white Portland cement was more difficult work. * * * and took longer to set and had to be handled in view of these different qualities compared with gypsum——"

Concerning conditions the witness said (R. 69-70):

"They were unusual to the extent that the areas were considerably larger than—larger expansion in a building and the sizes. of the stone had to be proportionately larger to harmonize with the architecture.

"XQ. 12. Did troubles of vibration enter there, too?

"A. I should attribute part of the trouble to and the fact that imitation stone affected plastering the building * * *

"Due to the *expansion, contraction* and *vibration,* and especially so in the main concourse; *all the steel being exposed* and not protected by masonry, is subjected to extremes of heat and cold—must expand and contract— that in turn has its reaction on the balance of the building."

———

CONSTANT EXPERIMENTATION.

At R. 278 he says:

*   *   *   *   *   *   *

" * * * all buildings where you have architects in that capacity *they have to experiment* as they go along to determine different materials; to determine ornamentation of models —*the whole thing is a process of experimentation.* As you go along too there are genuine rules to follow in the general results; where new material comes up for consideration, then one has to be pretty careful before they go on record to recommend a material of that nature.

* * * * * * *

" * * * *the experiments would still be carried on to prove what had been done before;* that I brought out in my testimony heretofore, sir. It wasn't a hard and fast proposition; *when Mr. Denivelle got the contract he started in trying to improve the method of making this material to get a better effect as well as to expedite the making of it.*"

As indicating some of the change and experiments practiced by Denivelle, Mr. Webster says (R. 272):

"A. Well, when he first started in, in order that we would have his work under surveillance there was a place allotted on the south side of the arcade in what we called the 'Shop Section,' where he started in his first development, and from there he was moved over later to the other side of the arcade, and as his work increased and the material requirements expanded we had to move him down to the so-called 'Baggage Section,' which is a large room, and he was all the time working *different kinds of schemes to improve the process, especially to expedite the fabrication of the material.* One of his methods was by the use of trays of the size—to duplicate the size of a piece of ashlar, and in this *tray* there was *arranged on a pivot, the purpose being that when he put his first layer of material in the*

inspector, as well as myself, would see what was going on by the use of electric lights reflected on the under side of the tray, and see the development or laminations and the coloring effects. That was tried for a while but *proved to be rather slow and pretty costly* because the *glass broke* in many cases due to the weight of the material, but *he learned many things about the introduction of color* and the *process of introducing the laminations* in this material.''

and (R. 273) :

"When the bids were taken, as I recollect, to the Fuller Company we verified them and I am sure that the records will show that the *Fuller Company were rather doubtful as to Denivelle's ability to carry on a contract of this size, especially due to its novelty,''* etc.

Denivelle's sample was better.

Mr. Webster says (R. 275) :

"RDQ. 1. Mr. Webster, was this contract for artificial travertin or imitation travertin awarded to the Denivelle Company after it had furnished to the architects a satisfactory sample or specimen of imitation travertin?

"A. Yes, sir; *there was a sample compared with other samples and judged to be better.''*

This is further emphasized (R. 276) :

"RDQ. 6. Isn't it also true that if that sample of artificial travertin produced by Mr. Denivelle had not satisfied the architects as to its practicability, and as to the correctness of imitation of travertin, they would not have used imitation travertin in that building?

"A. I wouldn't say that. The other samples might have been satisfactory in comparison— purely comparing one sample with the other to get the best results, and Denivelle's sample: *he had followed out the specification using white Portland cement—the other hadn't done so.* I think McNulty had secured another specification from McKim, Mead & White and wrote me a letter that he could furnish a sample but he didn't do so at the time he was asked to do so."

Mr. Webster says *Denivelle had men in the Pennsylvania Station as late as 1912* and after his guaranty expired (R. 280-1):

"RXQ. 8. Do you know whether or not Mr. Denivelle made repairs or replacements on that travertin job at the Pennsylvania Station even after his contract was completed?

"A. Yes. I don't know the exact date but it was after his guaranty expired—he made further repairs. * * * I happened to notice how he was coming back from Canada, and I stopped into the Station there and I noticed there were some bad looking spots; and I think I dropped him a note or telephoned him that he had to take care of it and he did, without any expense to us. * * *

"A. I don't know when it was—about 1912, I suppose. I associated that with coming back from Canada; I was going back and forth between 1911 and 1912 about once a month."

In this Mr. Webster is corroborated by Mr. Cooke who says (R. 294):

"XQ. 38. What's the latest date you recall when such work was done?

"A. Well, I couldn't give you a specific date—I couldn't give you a specific year—I did know that there was a time—I was in Goshen—men had been working there doing repair work."

The Goshen job was not let until the late spring of *1912* before Cooke went to California.

FRANK A. WHIPPLE (R. 194-219): Witness has been in the plastering business over 40 years, and worked for Mr. Denivelle on the Pennsylvania Station and later at the Exposition and on various other jobs.

He testifies (R. 206) to the novelty of Artificial Travertin prior to the Pennsylvania Station:

"XQ. 15. Prior to this Pennsylvania job had you ever seen any artificial travertin?
"A. No, sir."

His testimony as to the troubles with the material "peeling off" after set in place has already been quoted supra. And further (R. 218) he testifies:

"RXQ. 1. As I understand from your testimony, Mr. Whipple, there were changes and improvements being constantly made in this process from the time that you did the Pennsylvania Station until the time of the work in California?
"A. Yes, lots of changes—lots of improvements.
"RXQ. 2. Now, unless this material would stand up under varying temperature changes, and withstand the vibrations of this railroad station for 4 or 5 years, it wouldn't be of much account?
"A. No, it would have to be pretty strong material to stand there.
"RXQ. 3. Was there any way of finding out whether it would stand up, except to put it in place?

"A. I don't know that there was any other way unless you put it there and see what it would do.

"RXQ. 4. No way of testing it in the shop, was there?

"A. Don't see how you could because that would be under different conditions.

"RXQ. 5. You would have no way of imitating these vibrations, would you?

"A. Well, I don't know of any—no more than you could tell whether this house was going to crack or not——"

RECENT IMITATIONS DETRIMENTAL TO DENIVELLE'S PATENTS AND REPUTATION.

Thus says Whipple (R. 210):

"A. I see a great deal of it every day I go out. I saw a new job today—I never heard tell of it before—I went up to get a new automobile license—got into a door and there was a hallway of applied travertin.

"XQ. 49. How does that work compare with the travertin work that was done by Denivelle while you were in his employ?

"A. I would call it rotten what I saw today —it's a disgrace to call it that—but they try to imitate it."

WILLIAM STEELE COOKE (R. 284-296): Mr. Cooke's familiarity with the early history of the Denivelle process and his admitted lack of bias and interest, although called for the defense, shows him a most important witness for the plaintiff.

On redirect, having been asked if he had talked with Mr. Denivelle about the case, he replied (R. 296):

"Well, he told me he had come into town and that he had a case coming on here in which Mr. MacGruer was interested and I told Mr. Denivelle—I says—Well, Mr. Denivelle, I have seen Mr. MacGruer in this very same building; he has been in to see me, and if I have any testimony to submit, George MacGruer is a friend of mine—I will submit that testimony faithfully and honestly, and I will submit that testimony to the best of my ability."

Mr. Cooke is a plasterer formerly employed by Mr. Denivelle on the Pennsylvania Station and at the Exposition and elsewhere in connection with the installation of Artificial Travertin. As shown by the excerpts supra from his testimony concerning the work on the Goelet job at the Exposition, the Denivelle process was undergoing constant change.

As to present day extent of use of artificial Travertin Mr. Cooke testifies (R. 293):

"XQ. 31. Do you know anything about the extent to which travertin is used nowadays in the city? * * *

"A. It's used to considerable extent—coming more so every day—why you can take these new apartment houses that are going up through the Bronx there—they are putting it in all the hallways and entrance halls, and show windows all over the city—I am just after finishing a job myself in it on 37th Street and Seventh Avenue."

This only goes to show how essential has been the "test of time and use" referred to by Mr. Fenner in convincing architects and the public that Artificial

Travertin *in 1924* had finally passed the experimental stage.

Clay M. McClure (R. 425-448): Aside from the fact that this witness had not been noticed according to Section 4920, U. S. R. S. (objection, R. 425), his testimony is of interest in several particulars.

He admits that Artificial Travertin was a novelty prior to the Pennsylvania Station job. Thus (R. 428) (all italics ours):

> "It was the beginning, so far as I know, of the imitation work, and in a sense might be referred to as such" (i. e. as an experiment).

And (R. 433):

> "XQ. 11. Prior to the use of this artificial travertin in the Pennsylvania Terminal, had you ever heard of its being used in any building construction?
> "A. I *never had heard of the imitation nor the real prior to its use in that building.*"

And in answer to Q. 23 concerning the samples, he says (R. 428):

> "I think perhaps everybody examined them in that vicinity—they were somewhat of a *curiosity.*"

That the Denivelle work was *considered experimental at the time* is most naively testified to by this witness. Thus (R. 429-430):

> "A. To illustrate the point, the use of Monel metal was offered and even advocated by the railroad authorities themselves, as a covering for the roofs, substituting copper, lead or other

material of that nature. McKim, Mead &
White opposed the idea purely on the ground
that it was of an experimental nature, dealing
with a metal that they knew nothing about.
However, this was later used, but it was solely
with the understanding that the Railroad authorities themselves would bear any blame that
might come from it. They did not object, however, to using this on some small building for
experimental purposes.''

And then we have this "Travertin" illustration
directly in point (R. 430):

"Q. 36. You were telling me this morning
that in some other case this Pennsylvania job
had been attacked as an experiment, will you
kindly tell us about that case? * * *

"A. I was called as a witness in a suit
brought by Bessie Winn—she is an actress—
claiming damages for injuries received in falling down the steps leading from this same
foyer or lobby, between the lunch and dining
room to the general waiting room, which are
built of *real travertin. It was claimed that
these steps had been made from unknown material; were temporary or experimental in material, design, and other things.* It was proven
to the satisfaction, I think, of all present, that
they were not experimental, either in material
or design, the material being the same as that
used in the building of St. Peter's at Rome,
and many other monumental buildings; they
having stood the test of many years; that the
design was highly monumental and substantial
and built in the best way we know how—as
evidence it still stands.''

On cross-examination (R. 438-439) we have the
following from Mr. McClure:

"XQ. 36. I noticed the other day in a publication—I think it was the 'Literary Digest,' where a concerete building of some three or four stories in height, crumbled into ashes in a period of about 24 hours?

"A. Quite possible. * * *

"XQ. 39. What would be your explanation of it?

"A. It might be the insufficient quantity of cement; poor quality of cement; poor quality of sand; poorly mixed; poorly placed; forms struck too soon; and other things, too numerous to mention, any one of which would be enough. * * *

XQ. 45. Do you recognize any *unusual conditions present in the Pennsylvania Terminal* which are not present in the ordinary dwelling-house or similar building?

"A. *Yes.*

"XQ. 46. What are those conditions?

"A. *Too numerous to mention—thousands of them.* * * *

"XQ. 48. In this Pennsylvania Terminal, the matter of vibration is a factor to contend with, is it not?

"A. Taken into consideration with everything that went into it, size and unusual proportions—everything to avoid—against *difficulty due to vibration, expansion and contraction,* as far as possible. In other words, the whole of the thing was built more substantially than is ordinarily the custom, including all things. I would rather not—I would like to have 'all things' stricken out."

The superficiality, bias and hostility of this witness is evidenced by his feigned ennui on cross-examination (see XQ.'s 56-58, R. 440-1) and by the fact that he has recently been connected with Schultze and Weaver, the architects primarily responsible for the infringement herein complained of in the Los Angeles Biltmore Hotel (R. 443).

JACOB M. KRAFFT (R. 86-116): Witness Krafft (who as vice-president for McNulty Bros. wrote the letter of December 28th, 1908, quoted supra and admitted the McNulty sample was *not* of cement because they did not know what effect efflorescence might have, etc.), says (R. 90):

> "As I recall it there were four concerns invited to *experiment* with the producing of a satisfactory imitation of a stone known as travertine stone, and to erect a sample in place in the Pennsylvania Station, on the condition that a bid for the work had to be submitted simultaneously with the sample, and that the successful bidder would be obliged to pay to each of the other contractors submitting a sample the sum of $200" (italics ours).

And (R. 110):

> "I supervised *all attempts* in this imitation, practically daily, until the sample was past a point of perfection where I decided it was good enough to put in here as an exhibit" (italics ours).

This amount of $200.00 is thus explained on cross examination (R. 110-111):

> "XQ. 75. What was the purpose of that payment, if you know?
> "A. That was according to the terms of the contest, if you choose to call it a contest, that the successful bidder on this work was to pay each of the other contestants the sum of $200 for the sample—for the expense incurred in making the sample.
> *   *   *   *   *

"XQ. 77. The $200 did not fully reimburse you for your expenses?

"A. No; not on our part.

"XQ. 78. Your expenses were a great deal more than that?

"A. Yes, sir.

"XQ. 79. In other words, it was sort of a consolation prize; is that correct?

"A. A booby prize."

As showing bias and self interest of this witness see the following (R. 103):

"XQ. 19. You didn't tell him anything about what the Master Plasterers' Association was going to do?

"A. Yes, sir.

"XQ. 20. What did you tell him about that?

"A. I told him they were going to take it up and come into court alongside of MacGruer and Simpson. * * *

"XQ. 22. And you were going to retain other counsel?

"A. Yes, sir."

And (R. 104-105):

"We do not believe Mr. Denivelle has any patent right in this patent.

"XQ. 36. In other words, you take issue with the Court of Appeals for the Ninth Circuit, do you?

"A. If that is what it means, we do.

"XQ. 37. But if the patent is good you do infringe it, do you not?

"A. We have to admit it then. * * *

"XQ. 41. I notice that this letter refers to a letter written by you on the 31st of December, 1923. What was the occasion of your writing to Mr. P. G. More under that date?

"A. A request by Mr. MacGruer that we assist him to the best of our possible ability in handling this case, and furnish with our information the exact dates on which work had been taken and performed; and without reference to the books I could not possibly give him them" (italics ours).

The letter referred to appears at R. 115-116 and concludes:

"*We are equally anxious to assist in a successful defense of this case,* as it will be for the interest of the trade in general, and we would ask you to forward the information requested above as promptly as possible."

In spite of all this the testimony is more favorable to the plaintiff than the defendants.

CARL HENRY MEYN (R. 119-148):

The witness Meyn says he was superintendent for H. W. Miller, Inc., one of the unsuccessful bidders on the Pennsylvania Station, and claims he was in charge of the manufacture of the samples (R. 123) but his bias and self-interest as an infringer and his being anxious to help the defendants is apparent on cross-examination (R. 139).

As to "experimentation" by the Miller Company, this witness testifies (R. 124):

"Q. 33. Did you have anything to follow in making that sample that you installed?

"A. Yes, sir, a sample of natural travertin stone which was given us by the architects.

"Q. 34. What was the object of the Miller Company making and installing that sample?

"Mr. LOFTUS. Objected to as calling for an opinion and conclusion of the witness.

"A. The samples were to be made with a view to getting a very large contract for that type of imitation stone which was to be installed in that building and on which we were to submit estimates with the samples.''

And R. 126-127:

"We were given a sample of the real stone from which we first made an impression; from this impression we then cast various veins of colored plaster composition. *We then tried a method of reproducing the veinings and holes of the natural stone in a plaster cast, and we then cast from that. We tried casting the veins on marble slabs,* using salt to obtain the holes, which *salt we later washed out. We made crumbs* of semi-dry material which we spread on the slab, over which we then poured the veins to back it up with the body color of the material.''

The Court will note the vice of leading questions repeatedly propounded to this witness by his counsel—a fault which vitiates or greatly weakens the testimony of all the witnesses for defendants and where the nature and purpose of the intended examination is kept in mind.

Louis S. Massimo (R. 297-316): The witness Massimo is at present superintendent for H. W. Miller, Inc. (apparently should be H. W. Meyer, Inc., R. 316) but formerly with McNulty Bros. He adds nothing constructive to the case one way or the other except to show that his present employer is an infringer and that Artificial Travertin was a novelty prior to the installation in the Pennsylvania Station (R. 316).

"XQ. 142. Does your firm, H. W. Meyer,

Inc., make and install artificial travertin at the present time?

"A. Yes, sir, to a great extent.

"XQ. 143. Prior to the Pennsylvania Terminal job had you ever seen or heard of artificial travertin?

"A. Not artificial travertin."

HENRY A. COUSINS (R. 327-370): Cousins is another witness noticed in connection with the defense of the Los Angeles suit but was not called there, claims to be a manufacturer of artificial stone and scagliolo for forty-nine years and yet the first intimation of Travertin stone ever attempted by him was, as he says; "I believe in 1908" (R. 329) "in connection with the proposed wall treatment of the Pennsylvania Station." The witness doesn't even remember for whom he did the job (R. 329).

As to the novelty of artificial Travertin at that time he testifies (R. 334):

"Q. 49. Now, before that time had you ever made any imitation of travertin stone?

"A. No. *I believe that was the first occasion that it had ever been proposed to use it as a decorative material*" (italics ours).

He was apparently a stranger to the process after that for many years; evidently awaiting the "test of time and use" for he testifies, after urging by his counsel (R. 335):

"Q. 55. Well, now give us the names of some jobs of work which you actually did, where located, and when they were done; I mean imitation travertin jobs.

"A. Dental Dispensary, Rochester, N. Y.

"Q. 56. When did you do that job?

"A. I think that was about 1915 or 1916.

"Q. 57. Was there any other job before that?

"A. Well, I can't state the dates. We have done quite a number of jobs but I haven't got a list of them. There was a job at Greenwich, a private residence, but I couldn't give you the data as to the name of the owner. I can get it though. Quite a number of small jobs the conditions of which I don't recall, but we were doing it right along."

And R. 338:

"Q. 79. Have you installed any artificial travertin in the city of New York?

"A. Yes.

"Q. 80. Give us the names of the jobs if you can?

"A. Cunard Building. * * * Knickerbocker Building. * * * Niagara Falls Bank.

"Q. 85. Imitation travertin?

"A. Yes.

"Q. 86. Now, when did you do the Cunard Building in New York City?

"A. I believe it would be about 1917 or '18·"

This is enough to indicate the witness' self-interest as an apparent infringer.

In this connection it is worthy of note that Cousins when he actually began to employ artificial Travertin in 1916-1917 *employed one of Mr. Denivelle's former expert workmen, Mr. Whipple* (R. 369).

TOMASO V. CORONATO (R. 370-387): Coronato was a former employee of Cousins and is a present day infringer (R. 376-377). Artificial Travertin was new with Coronato prior to the Denivelle job in the Pennsylvania Station (XQ. 17, R. 383).

That the manufacture of artificial Travertin is not as simple and obvious as the defense would lead the Court to believe is seen even by this witness' testimony in trying to tell how he set about to make a sample in early days (R. 377):

> "Well, experimenting in my own way—I haven't seen it at all, but I tried to make out my own way; I haven't seen anyone do it—I don't know, how could I explain why I make it that way? * * *
>
> "Well, I guess each one got his own way to do it—some other men have a different idea to do it but this is the easiest for me—I never see any other easy way to do it—could be that marble could be done just the same."

FRANK JOHN MORKEL (R. 387-405): This witness' testimony is a substantial repetition of his former testimony in the Los Angeles suit and need not be reviewed further.

So much for the Pennsylvania Station job. We submit except for its cumulative effect, it is consistent with and supports the record in the Los Angeles case.

WALTER H. CLOUGH (R. 415-424): Objection made to lack of notice under Section 4920 U. S. R. S. (R. 415). This witness was a general contractor formerly employed by the Geo. A. Fuller Co. on the Pennsylvania Station job (R. 417). His testimony adds nothing to that already given except to show (XQ. 43, R. 423) that artificial Travertin was a novelty as far as he recalls at the time of the Pennsylvania Station. His recollection is hazy and his knowledge of the correspondence to which his attorney assiduously seeks to lead him is shown by this (R. 419):

> "A. I have no special recollection of this particular letter. I know that we had letters of this nature, and this apparently is a letter that I had seen, but there is no special mark on it that brings back to my mind that that is a particular letter that I had seen before, but we have letters of that kind which have been the basis of our negotiations."

SAMUEL L. KRINEY (R. 449-453): Kriney is a plastering contractor formerly with McNulty Bros. His testimony simply shows that some sort of a sample was installed by McNulty on the Pennsylvania Station and that later he did infringing Travertin work for McNulty on the Widener Building, in Philadelphia (R. 451). This job is shown by others to have been done in 1915 and 1916 and completed after full notice of Denivelle's pending patent application.

PHILIP LIVA (R. 459-473): Witness was a plasterer, born in Italy, and in this country about twenty years (R. 460); formerly worked for Davis Brown, another witness, but now with P. J. Durkin, another witness (R. 465) doing artificial Travertin. Liva claims he worked for Denivelle, but the latter denies it (R. 666).

The only material part of this witness' testimony is extremely favorable to plaintiff as showing the inherent difficulties of successful manufacture of artificial Travertin, the necessity of experiment and the secrecy practiced by Denivelle on the Pennsylvania Station. Thus answer to Q. 24, R. 462:

> "The samples I made, I don't have results I expect, because in Italy I make some imitation travertino and I made in Stockholm, Switzerland, but we use different materials, and in that time there when I came in this country I started to work for him I never know the materials which they have in this country, and I find in the shop different materials that we have in the old country, so I never was able to get the sample out like I have in the old country."

That he was not successful in his attempt to make Travertin by the Denivelle method is seen from his testimony (confirmed later by Durkin) that *today* he makes the imitation from a *negative of natural Travertin.*

(472):

> "XQ. 95. How are you making that travertin in the Park-Lane Building. What method do you use?
> "A. Well, we pour the glue on the real stone, and we get the form from the real stone, then I add a quantity to mix up the material, and I give the material prepared to the men and they mix up the job like a plaster, any kind of material, and they feed in on the mold.
> "XQ. 96. In other words, you use a mold which is made of glue?
> "A. Yes, what Denivelle never used. In the times when I was there I never see any glue mold, only plaster mold."

As to the experimental work of Denivelle on the Pennsylvania Station Liva says on direct (R. 461):

"A. Well, he supervised the shop and building, but I was supposed to have charge of the shop just for that job, and they turned over and they put somebody else in my place, and I worked for three or four weks more in the shop and quit."

And R. 463:

"Q. 36. Was Mr. Denivelle on work on samples too?

"A. Yes, he worked in samples too, in a private room. We don't know what he is doing."

MATERIALS NEW AND DIFFICULT TO HANDLE.

Liva testifies (R. 469):

"XQ. 78. Well now when you tried these *experiments*, in the Pennsylvania Station, did you find that this white Portland cement did not give you good results?

"A. No. It did not give good results. *I never had the results I expected, in that material, so I gave it up.*

"XQ. 79. *It was very difficult material was it?*

"A. *Yes.*

"XQ. 80. And who changed it afterwards?

"A. Denivelle himself. *He changed three or four times.*

"XQ. 81. Changed what?

"A. The material.

"XQ. 82. What material was finally used in the Pennsylvania Station in making the artificial travertine?

"A. Well, he used Carbay sand, red sand, white sand; he used some plaster also.

"XQ. 83. What kind of plaster?

"A. I don't know, because he had special laborers and give each a quantity of the material they have to use to mix up. So when the

men in the shop they receive the material *they
don't was able to know what kinds of material
they mix up. It was impossible"* (italics ours).

The remarkable thing about all this testimony is
that besides confirming the proofs in the Los Angeles case and decision of this Court favorable to the
patent, it shows that whereas here was an admittedly
new and highly meritorious building material
brought to the attention of architects and others supposedly skilled in the art as far back as 1910 and
1911; yet it is only within the *past 3 or 4 years* that
it has become recognized as a standard or regular
and satisfactory finish. It has taken *fourteen* years
to demonstrate the "test of time and use". Denivelle had all the prejudices to overcome in those
early days. The defendants and the host of other
infringers then standing on the side lines, now seek
to destroy what Denivelle has built up, and to reap
the benefits of his toil, teachings and experience;
and to do this all in the face of the previous holding
of this Honorable Court (on substantially the same
state of facts as here presented) that the patent was
and is valid.

OTTAWA STATION.

As to the Ottawa Station, defendants admit it is
not offered as "prior use":

(R. 198-199).

"Q. 38. And did you install imitation travertin in that station?

"Mr. LOFTUS. The question is objected to on the ground that any use of this invention in a foreign country is incompetent, irrelevant and immaterial. Further objection is made on the ground of lack of proper notice.

"By Mr. ANDERSON. *Obviously this evidence is not offered to prove any prior use;* it is mainly offered to show Mr. Denivelle's activities in the installation of imitation travertin, particularly after the Pennsylvania job had been completed, and in support of the defense that Mr. Denivelle himself had put his alleged invention into public use more than two years before he filed his application for patent. A. Well, yes'" (italics ours).

Section 4923, U. S. R. S., bars such a defense:

"Whenever it appears that a patentee, at the time of making his application for the patent, believed himself to be the original and first inventor or discoverer of the thing patented, the same shall not be held to be void on account of the invention or discovery, or any part thereof, having been known or used in a foreign country, before his invention or discovery thereof, if it had not been patented or described in a printed publication."

This Ottawa work, however, was different from that in the Pennsylvania Station, for says Whipple (R. 205):

"Now, in your work at Ottawa, did you use a white Portland cement? A. No.

"XQ. 12. What did you use there?

"A. I don't know what it was; it wasn't a Portland cement; it was either Keene's cement or plaster combination, or something like that.

"XQ. 13. Anyway, it was different from the Pennsylvania job?

"A. It looked the same, but it was different."

And at R. 207 the same witness says:

"XQ. 26. And when you went to work on the Ottawa job you changed that mode to one of applying it with a trowel?

"A. There was very little cast work on the Ottawa job.

"XQ. 27. What parts were cast there?

A. There were some molded bases and some fluted columns and Corinthian caps; the cornices were all made in place, and all the plain surfaces, ordinary particles, pilasters, etc., were all made in place."

And (R. 211) in answer to RDQ. 5 he said:

"We discovered a different brush when we got up there to give it more of a natural look that we didn't have in the Pennsylvania job."

And:

"RDQ. 10. And is your testimony also that the cast imitation travertin which was employed in the Pennsylvania Station, and that which was employed in the Ottawa Station were exactly the same in construction and appearance?

"Mr. LOFTUS. Objected to as leading and suggestive.

"A. They had the idea—as to a copy of real travertin they had the same color, but as for the construction I don't know as they were the same, for this reason, that Portland cement would be backed up with Portland cement, and a plaster proposition or gypsum proposition would be backed up with fibre and plaster."

WINDSOR STATION, MONTREAL, WAS NOT TRAVER-TINE AT ALL.

See Whipple, R. 200 (italics ours):

"Q. 50. Did you also work on a job which Mr. Denivelle had in Montreal, Canada? A. Travertin?

"Q. Yes?

"A. No, I never did any travertin in Mon-treal—other imitations though, but *not traver-tin*. I worked for Mr. Denivelle but not on travertin work.

"Q. 52. What job did you have in Montreal for Mr. Denivelle? A. Well, the Windsor Sta-tion.

"Q. 53. What kind of work was that?

"A. That wasn't artificial stone—I think they called it "Yorkshire" or "Limestone".

(R. 265):

"Q. 156. And that was the imitation in the Windsor Station waiting-room of the Canadian Pacific Railroad in Montreal?

"A. No, sir; I corrected that statement in a previous letter; I had forgotten the fact—it was imitation stone—*I wrote you afterward about that.*

"Q. 157. *Then Mr. Denivelle did not do any imitation travertin in that Railroad Station in Montreal?*

"A. *No, sir.*

"Q. 158. Well, after the Pennsylvania job was completed by Mr. Denivelle, did he under your supervision do any other imitation traver-tin work for you? A. No, sir."

THE VANDERBILT HOTEL JOB.

WALTER L. HOPKINS (R. 474-486): Witness is an architect and testifies as to the work on the Vanderbilt Hotel which he says was opened to the public December 31st, 1911, (Q. 19, R. 476).

While, he says, there was a small job of Artificial Travertin on the barroom (a comparatively small space 30′x50′ (R. 475) and he thinks that this job was done by Denivelle under Davis Brown (Q. 13, R. 475), nevertheless he doesn't know the ingredients used nor the process practiced and doesn't believe there *are any striations* on the Vanderbilt job (see XQ. 45, R. 482) (all italics ours):

> "XQ. 45. Now, in this artificial travertin in the Vanderbilt Hotel bar are there any veins or striations, and if so, how are they applied?
> "A. *I don't believe there are any striations. In fact, I am sure there are not.*"

At R. 481 he testifies:

> "XQ. 41. Of what material was this artificial travertin made which was put in the barroom of the hotel?
> "A. Well, that I can't answer, because I didn't ask Mr. Denivelle and he didn't volunteer the information, and I felt that it was more or less of a *secret process* of his and I didn't ask.

Manifestly without striations, i. e., veins, it is not imitation travertin by whatever process produced.

Witness' idea of an "experiment" in architecture is rather interesting as he says (R. 482):

> "Well, an experiment, I should say, in connection with building materials would be the *use of a material that was unknown and untried.*

Denivelle's materials as we know were new and untried as was the process itself (Webster, supra).

Previously Hopkins stated (R. 479, XQ. 35):

> "A. Well, it was our idea when we did the Vanderbilt, to get away from old-established customs, and the Vanderbilt Hotel *has a great many innovations in it,* and had we been willing to spend the money we would have probably put real travertine stone there. That would have been too expensive."

And on redirect (R. 483-484):

> "RDQ. 53. Do you mean to testify that an architect would adopt a new material without having satisfied himself that it was proper material to use for the job upon which he was going to use it?
>
> "A. Well, I don't know about other architects, but we wouldn't. *We have in our office more or less of a department which you might say is a research department* and it is the duty of this department *to keep in touch with new methods and new materials that develop,* and we carefully *keep records and statistics about all kinds of building materials* of every description. That is in charge of Mr. Munzell.
>
> "RDQ. 54. So that when you have investigated a material you are reasonably sure——
>
> "A. We try to be. *Occasionally we make a mistake"* (italics ours).

DAVIS BROWN (R. 499-526): This willing, voluble and admittedly hostile witness whose correspondence with the defendants has already been quoted, was noticed in the Los Angeles case but not called. He testifies here to the limited character and poor quality of the Vanderbilt job (R. 502-3):

> "A. Why, I had a case where I gave him a small job—the Vanderbilt Hotel—I had a contract for that building and after it was about 70 to 80% finished they decided to have a bar-

room on the south—on the northwest corner of
the street—this would be the southwest corner
of the building—lower room—and they asked
me for an estimate to finish up these walls in
travertin material, which I did; and *they awarded me the work,* possibly *about $1000 worth on
the job*—and *I was prepared to go on with it,
but the president of the Ojev Company,* Mr.
Gray,—that was the contracting company—*informed me that Mr. Wetmore would like to have
Mr. Denivelle do that travertin work for me.*
* * *

"A. Yes; that was an expression of the
president of the building company, that Mr.
Wetmore would like to have Mr. Denivelle do
that work for me, to be sure * * *" (italics
ours).

The Vanderbilt job an "applied method" job not
here in issue.

Denivelle did only a part of the work Brown tells
us (R. 503) :

"A. He applied only the finish coat because
I put on the preparation—the browning coat—
on all the walls, and filled it out—so that *this
material was applied only* ¼ *or* ⅞ *of an inch*"
(italics ours).

As to the condition of that work Brown says on
cross-examination (R. 514-5) :

"I will take you, if you like into that bar-
room—it isn't a bar-room any more, it's a lunch-
room—I drop in there once a year if I happen
to be in the neighborhood and naturally I look
at my work—how it stands up—and *I want to
tell you that bar-room is cracked* so that you—
"XQ 26. That is the travertin portion?
"A. It is; *cracked, badly cracked,* and the
only thing you got to do, I did, and I examined

the conditions when they did no more business there—and still it was cracked. It can't be helped; *certain materials will crack under certain conditions and under other conditions they will stand up.* We have a very peculiar line to deal with. Sometimes we are called in on a job, and they will say, 'Look at the ceiling is cracked.' Ten experts come in and they all try to testify why it's cracked, and no one of them is right" (italics ours).

And then he contrasts this with the Lord & Taylor job done by witness only a year or two later, but using again *different materials* and he says (R. 515):

"I will take you into the Vanderbilt barroom, which is a room possibly twice as big as this room, or 2½ times, and *it is full of cracks.* I will take you over to the Lord & Taylor building—I haven't examined the work for some time, but I question to find any cracks there— *they were using different kind of materials.* It is essential to use a material for the under coat first; clean off the outer coat so that while it is modeled it should give a little if possible, not immediately crack like glass; glass is—of course I am speaking to you, Mr. Loftus, from the mechanic end of it because I am a mechanic myself at the trade" (italics ours).

Concerning the Vanderbilt job the architect has already told us (R. 482, XQ. 45 and A):

"XQ. 45. Now, in this artificial travertin in the Vanderbilt Hotel bar are there any veins or striations, and if so, how are they applied?

"A. *I don't believe there are any striations. In fact, I am sure there are not*" (italics ours).

Of course, if there are no striations it does not meet the product claims 9 and 10, and since the Vanderbilt job was admitted an "applied" process "B" job and not a "cast" job it does not meet the process claim in suit and hence this defense should be disregarded.

Witness' naive admission of self-interest is seen at R. 520:

"XQ. 40. What other jobs of artificial travertin have you made since the Lord & Taylor building?

"A. I should say we done—I don't know how many—a great many. I don't know—we can look those things up; we can look back for the last 3 years, possibly 4 years, I don't know; of course this information—*in case Mr. Denivelle finds out—we got to pay him a royalty*—I am not worrying about that—*I haven't got enough money to pay it;* now, we have done it right along; it is very rarely that we are without a job of that character—all of us—not only I or my concern—most capable contractors who do this work, they do it all the time; there isn't a contractor in the entire union who is no more or less familiar with the manufacture of this material; and some of them are more familiar with it—out of 3,000 men that is saying something—I don't have to take it and find out which men I am going to put on this work—they all know it—only some of them are swifter and smarter than others" (italics ours).

Witness is forced to admit that there is a difference between doing a small sample and doing a large job; and by his testimony shows the evident existence of experimentation on Denivelle's part through all this early work. Thus (R. 510):

"XQ. 16. Well, now, you have stated that your idea of an experiment is the making of samples; that after the samples have been made and examined, the experimental stage is over—did I understand you correctly?

"A. To a very large extent—once you get into the building—*it is one thing to make a sample*, possibly a yard or 2 or 3 feet large—*and you have to improve on your method as you go into a job*—when you do it on a large surface, —sometimes the sample that we make in the shop is just the initial method and proportion —but it is a constant—there is room constantly to improve on our class of work, and we try to improve on it."

LORD & TAYLOR JOB, 1914.

Brown testifies Denivelle had nothing to do with this job (Q. 44, R. 506) as it was done by Brown without apparent knowledge of Denivelle.

The loose hearsay testimony of this witness, Brown, is illustrated by the following (R. 506):

"Q. 45. Now, when did you do the Lord & Taylor building?

"A. Some time ago I got in touch with the architects and they have their records, and I was told that the job was finished early in 1913, so it was done in the winter of 1912-13.

On cross-examination he says (R. 507):

"A. I fix that date because the architect who gave me the contract—he gave it to me over the phone, as to the date of my contract, and also when the building was finished, and they were moving while we were still on the job."

His uncertainty is manifested in his answer to the next question but one:

"XQ. 5. I show you a letter on the stationery

of Lord & Taylor, and signed by A. C. Mc-
Master, Vice-President, giving the date of the
opening of the Lord & Taylor building as February, 1914, would that change your answer in
any way regarding the date of opening?

"A. The only way I would change my answer is—I will call up the architect for your
information because I am only going by recollection of information which I received here
some months ago, and my secretary just told me
that the information we received—she said was
1913—and it may be possible it is 1914; now if
you wish the exact information on that I can
do the very thing which you have done here—
by inquiring I can get this information the same
way as you can—my recollection cannot go back
for 8, 9, 10 years and give the exact date. If
this man says 1914, no doubt he is right; maybe
my recollection is wrong."

Aside from the fact there is no proof whatever as
to how the Lord & Taylor job was done it is sufficient to show as above that it was subsequent to
Denivelle's invention and within two years of Denivelle's application and hence must be dismissed from
consideration.

———

HARVARD MEMORIAL LIBRARY, 1914-1915.

This defense was before this Court in the Los
Angeles suit (see Markel's testimony, Exhibit 6,
page 112). It is disposed of in this case now by the
stipulation appearing at II R. 664 herein:

"Mr. TOWNSEND. Counsel and I have stipulated, to avoid the necessity of calling a witness,
to the fact that the Widener Memorial Library
at Harvard, referred to variously in the testi-

mony as the Cambridge Memorial Library, or the Harvard Memorial Library, was dedicated on Commencement Day, June 24, 1915, and was thereafter open to the public.

"Mr. ANDERSON. I agree to that."

WIDENER BUILDING, PHILADELPHIA, 1916.

This defense was also before this Court in the Los Angeles case: McNulty deposition Exh. 6, pages 117-8, and Denivelle, page 171.

PETER G. MOORE, JR. (R. 405-415): was called by the defendant to identify certain records in connection with the Widener Building in Philadelphia. That use by McNulty, however, is too late to be available for the defense in any manner, shape or form.

The *contract was let April 21, 1914* (Q. 20, R. 407) and in answer to Q. 21 he shows the *job was not completed until September, 1916,* long after the present Denivelle application for patent was filed. Moore says (R. 407):

"The building was practically completed in September, 1916, although there was work done, small patching work, until May, 1917, in the following year. The contract was started on June 4th, the first labor was June 4, 1914."

That of course disposes of the Widener defense.

CAMPBELL'S FUNERAL CHAPEL, 1916.

JOHN A. FINCKE (R. 317-326), a plasterer, testified that he did the above job for an architect named
Almiroty (R. 320), later called as a witness, but can
give no dates.

RANDOLPH H. ALMIROTY (R. 454-9), an architect,
testifies that the Campbell job was finished "about
August, 1916" (Q. 10, R. 455).

That the Campbell job in 1916 was *largely experimental* (see ans. XQ. 29, R. 458):

> "Well, there were *various methods used* for
> that. Sand was used to some extent and Mr.
> Fincke developed his own process afterwards,
> in connection with that work, to produce the
> voids, and I think water was used at one time
> very satisfactorily. At one time air was used.
> *Various methods were experimented with to
> produce the best results,* but I think on the
> whole sand was found to be the most feasible"
> (italics ours).

The job was evidently a very poor one (R. 458):

> "XQ. 32. Have you seen that work in the
> Campbell establishment recently?
> "A. No, I haven't been there for—O, I
> guess, since about 1919.
> "XQ. 33. I ask that question because I had
> occasion to see that material *with* the last few
> days and I was unable to find the stratifications
> there. Is it possible they would fade out?
> "A. It might have faded out, depending on
> how much color was used. If it was under a
> strong light it might fade out."

This witness a recent imitator also (R. 459):

> "XQ. 34. Was that the only job of artificial

travertin that you had to do with, namely, this Campbell job?

"A. As far back as that, yes.

"XQ. 35. You have done some since that?

"A. O, Yes, we have done quite a lot of it."

THOMAS W. EVANS MUSEUM, PHILADELPHIA
(Late 1914).

PETER J. DURKIN (R. 486-498): This witness was noticed but was not called in the Los Angeles case.

Witness is a plasterer; knows Denivelle (R. 487) and worked for him on Evans Museum in Philadelphia in *1914* (R. 489): "about September or October" (Q. 31, R. 490); which, of course, is too late for any defensive purpose whatever. Besides, the job was mostly an *applied* method (Q. 14, R. 487) (probably "Method B" of the patent and not here involved anyhow).

That artificial Travertin was still a novelty note that the *architects insisted Denivelle do it!* (R. 491):

"Q. 40. How did it happen that you went to the Denivelle Company to do that work for you?

"A. Well, the architect wanted him to do it, and the builder didn't want to let us the job without we agreed to let Denivelle do the work. * * *

"Q. 42. Do you know why they insisted that Denivelle do the work?

"A. Well, I presume because he was competent and had done other work similar to it, and supposed to be what they wanted.

"Q. 43. How did you get that impression?

"A. Because we couldn't get the job to do ourselves, and we would like to have done it but

they thought Denivelle was better prepared—
was able to do the work—on account of having
a record of doing other work of that character."

He like so many of the other witnesses, testifies to
the novelty of artificial Travertin on the Pennsylvania Station (R. 497):

"XQ. 75. Well now, you have seen this artificial travertine in the Pennsylvania Station in
this city?
"A. Yes, sir.
"XQ. 76. Had you ever seen any artificial
travertine prior to that time?
"A. I don't remember that I did."

THE GOELET JOB.

This was a small job, a portion only of which was
done in imitation of Travertin by the "applied"
method and too late in time.

RICHMOND H. SHREVE (R. 149-167): Witness is
an architect; one of the firm of Carrere & Hastings,
Shreve, Lamb & Blake who did the Goelet house at
Goshen, New York, in 1912-1914.

He says (R. 153-154-155):

"A. I dealt with the contract, gave the
orders for the work, knew of the reports of its
being executed, and subsequently saw it in place.
I did not personally see Mr. Denivelle's organization at work on it.
* * * * * * * *
"A. I saw the work in place, complete, in the
fall of 1913, on a visit which I made to Mr.
Goelet's house. I do not know more than that
as to the time in which it was executed.

"Q. 26. And that is the imitation travertine work supposed to have been executed by Mr. Denivelle or his company?

"A. Yes.

* * * * * * * *

"Q. 32. Is there anything in those papers to show when Mr. Denivelle completed his work— or the Denivelle Company?

"A. No, nothing that I see here."

And R. 163:

"XQ. 60. On this visit that you have just referred to, which you made with Mr. Torbert, either in the fall of 1913 or the spring of 1914, how near to completion was the Goelet home? Had it been furnished as yet? Was it occupied?

"A. My recollection is that it was finished and that some of the property of the owner was in it, but I do not think that it had been finally or fully occupied and taken over.

GOELET HOUSE ON PRIVATE GROUNDS REMOVED FROM THE PUBLIC.

"XQ. 61. And how far from a street or thoroughfare were these buildings that contained the Denivelle travertine? Were they close to the street or some distance back?

"A. They were on the large property which Mr. Goelet owns there, on the top of the hill, facing the lake, and perhaps two or three hundred yards from any highway."

Manifestly such testimony, even if it described the process and product of the patent claims, is wholly insufficient under the rule of "proof beyond a reasonable doubt" to defeat a duly issued patent. As a matter of fact the memorandum of payments to the

Denivelle Company, produced by this witness
(R. 107) shows that the final payment was not made
until *June 9th, 1914.*

VANCE W. TORBERT, (R. 187-193): Witness is an
architect formerly with Carrere & Hastings and was
resident superintendent on the Goelet job from
"about the middle of May until the middle of December, 1913" (R. 188).

(R. 189) :

"Q. 16. And what was the condition of the
job when you went on it?
"A. The main house was practically completed except for the interior finish, and the
surrounding terraces were just being started in
construction.
"Q 17. And the work on the surrounding
terraces which was being started, was that being
done by Mr. Denivelle or his company?
"A. Only the stucco and imitation travertin.
"Q. 18. Do you recall just what work Mr.
Denivelle did which you might call imitation
travertin?
"A. Yes, sir.
"Q. 19. What was it?
"A. Railings of the terraces and the coping
of the four-court wall about the driveway entrance."

The imitation Travertin *in 1913* was a novelty
with this witness, for he says (R. 190):

"Q. 24. Had you see any imitation travertin
before that Goelet house was constructed?
"A. I don't recall that I had."

He does not know definitely whether Denivelle
had finished the job or not (R. 190) for he says:

"Q. 29. When you left there in December, 1913, had Mr. Denivelle finished his work on that house?

"A. So far as I recall; if there was work done subsequent to my time I don't know of it."

The house was not occupied (used) until after December, 1913, which, of course, was within the two year period preceding the final application for the Denivelle patent but considerably subsequent to the original application of Denivelle filed in August, 1913. The witness testifies (R. 191) :

"XQ. 2. Well, then, it was occupied some time after December, 1913, is that right?

"A. Yes, sir."

The job was not according to the process in suit but was by the "applied method". The witness says (R. 191-192) :

"A. I have particular recollection of the manner in which the terrace wall railing was formed, and that is, it was run in a plastic form and the moldings were shaped by means of a template.

"XQ. 8. In other words, these moldings were run in place, were they?

"A. That's right, and of course after they were run they used a wire brush or some such stiff instrument to pick out little spots and create the imitation of the travertin."

JULIUS F. GAYLER (R. 220-237) *architect with Carrere & Hastings on the Goelet House:* His testimony, while largely based on memory, shows that the Artificial Travertin was a very minor feature and as a prior use is too late.

He testifies (R. 221):

"Q. 12. Can you state when that Goelet house was begun and when it was finished?

"A. No. I can't state, excepting that I know it was finished, from my recollection, I am reasonably positive of this, it was completed before February, 1914, that date being in my mind because then I went to Europe, and the house was completed before I went."

(R. 222):

"Q. 17. And just what contract was given to Mr. Denivelle or his company?

"A. Stuccoing the entire exterior of the house in pink stucco, with certain features in imitation travertin stone. He also had further contracts for various work and approaches, which were ordered later."

The artificial Travertin comprised (R. 223):

"The features around the front door and certain features around the windows, the exact nature of which I do not recall.

* * * * * * *

"A. Some work on the terrace, handrail and balustrade. He also did the stuccoing around the entrance court, and my impression is that there was an imitation travertine coping on this terrace wall, but I am not sure of it."

And, again, (R. 236):

"RDQ. 90. When was Mr. Denivelle's job on the house completed?

"A. That I cannot state definitely, because *the payments on the house and the other work were carried on together.*

"RDQ. 91. When you left in February, 1914, what was the condition of that Denivelle job on the Goelet property?

"A. To the best of my recollection the work

on e wa s aroun e e rance court was stl to be done'' (italics ours).

The Pennsylvania Station job was evidently a novelty with the witness when undertaking the Goelet job in 1912 because in negotiating the Contract with Denivelle (R. 227) his attention was called to the Pennsylvania Station and that he visited and inspected the Pennsylvania Station before letting the Contract (R. 228).

And at R. 234 he testifies:

"XQ. 83. Had you ever heard of artificial or imitation travertine prior to seeing it in the Pennsylvania Station? A. No."

The Goelet job again was different from the Pennsylvania Station, for says Gayler (R. 229):

"Q. 56. How did that imitation travertine work which was installed in the stair hall, compare as to structure, materials and appearances, with the imitation travertine work which Mr. Denivelle had done on that Goelet job?
"A. *The material was different* because it was inside work. The finished appearance of it was practically the same as that on the outside. So Mr. Hastings said and so I said.
"Q. 57. What material was employed in that imitation travertine work in the stair hall?
"A. The base was plaster of paris with coloring matter."

And (R. 230):

"Q. 61. How did the job which Mr. Denivelle and his company executed under the Goelet contract compare with the work which he called your attention to in the Pennsylvania Station, as to color, appearance, and otherwise?
"A. It was quite a little different. It was done

in a simpler manner. *I do not know how the result achieved in the Pennsylvania Station was arrived at, but it must have been a more complicated method than that used in the Goelet house and exterior,* where they used, so Mr. Denivelle informed me, cement, with coloring matter, and obtained the texture by means of various tools, in a manner similar to that I described as used in the entrance hall by the Harriman Industrial Corporation" (italics ours).

* * * * * * *

"The color was similar, at a distance of say, 30 to 35 feet, the appearance would be practically the same; as you got nearer you could see the difference. The work was not so finely done."

That the Goelet job was a small affair (R. 234):

"A. To the best of my recollection it was a hall about 30 feet square and 25 feet high, with one window and two doors, including the trim of the doors and including the cornice."

Concerning the Goelet job and its importance in the progressive development of the invention to a state of perfection justifying application for the patent Mr. Cooke testifies (R. 286):

"Q. 18. Just what kind of imitation travertin work did you do for Mr. Denivelle on the Goelet house?

"A. Applied work—hawk and trowel."

And R. 288:

"Well, the Goelet house—we had some—I got in 'Dutch' with Mr. Denivelle in the Goelet house because we were getting a certain texture there and he come along and he was changing it and wanted it changed again; and we had different ideas—something he wanted there—and we had to change, the time the caps and bases were changed—the texture of them—but I know when

I come back—I had to go away to Milwaukee
for a couple of weeks—and when I come back
they had changed the thing around again. * * *
"Caps and bases of columns and pilasters
* *

"But there wasn't many of them, there were
2 columns in the entrance and I think 4 columns
in the loggia outside."

And (R. 290):

"Well, we had—it was changed on the Goelet
job—the texture wasn't coming out right and
Mr. Denivelle come along there and changed it
—the change was made as I already said, while
I was in Milwaukee."

The point of all these small jobs, particularly
where the work was entrusted to Denivelle is simply
this: Prominent architects in New York no doubt
had been watching the results achieved by Denivelle
in the Pennsylvania Station and for a considerable
period of years recognized the experimental status
of the invention, so that when a chance came to try
the use of Artificial Travertin, and after the architects had specified its use and awarded the Contract,
they and the *owners insisted that the contractors
should sublet to Denivelle* this particular part of the
job, small though it was; being prompted, no doubt,
by the fear that because of the incomplete and experimental stage of the invention they could not
safely entrust the work to anyone except the originator of Artificial Travertin, Mr. Denivelle.

It is obvious from the above testimony quoted that

architects and builders of prominence recognized this incomplete and experimental status, for *had it been otherwise then any plasterer of ordinary skill could have been relied upon to carry out the work.*

This was notably emphasized and confirmed by the experience at the Exposition. The defendant, MacGruer, on the stand admitted (R. 608) that at the time Denivelle was at the Exposition in 1913 and 1914 "It was very much of an experiment with himself". Indeed, MacGruer sent the Exposition Company a bill for $500.00 in October, 1913, for experimental work done by him in trying to carry out the Denivelle idea (R. 646-647).

PANAMA-PACIFIC INTERNATIONAL EXPOSITION, 1913-1914.

Coming now to the Exposition work of Denivelle and these defendants in 1913 and 1914, the Court will be impressed by the fact that the patented process was still in a state of experimentation and that Denivelle was not only changing, developing and perfecting his method, but he was having the greatest difficulty in getting people, and particularly these defendants, to understand what he was after. This is seen not only by the testimony given here in open Court by Mr. Denivelle but by the defendant MacGruer himself and by the correspondence which is in evidence passing between the MacGruer Company and the Exposition authorities, supplemented by the defendants' depositions of Whipple and Cooke.

Mr. Denivelle testified (R. 569) that his meeting and contact with the defendants was in the latter part of 1913 and 1914 in connection with defendants' work on the Machinery Building at the Exposition. He says (R. 569-570):

> "Well, the first contact that I had with them was due to the fact that the men under me whom we sent them for preliminary instruction and co-operation came back and reported to me that they were not getting it, and I naturally went over to see them and tried to aid them, and that was the beginning of our negotiations, toward their being taught that which they said later to the exposition was totally impossible. They seemed to think that I was a dreamer, that I did not know what I was talking about, that I was seeking to do things which they seemingly did not understand. * * *
>
> "Mr. TOWNSEND. Q. Did you meet with co-operation or did you meet with opposition on their part in putting your process into effect?
>
> "A. Opposition, mainly."

MacGruer testifies on his own behalf (R. 606) that the building "was finally accepted some time in the early part of 1914".

Continuing he says (R. 606):

> "When we bid on the job there was in the specifications an addenda that followed the specifications, the original specifications, in which they were to adopt a color scheme."

(This addendum appears at R. 637 and 638 and is dated December 16th, 1912.)

Mr. Whipple testifies (R. 201) (italics ours):

"Q. 59. And when did you go to California for Mr. Denivelle?

"A. I left here the 10th day of April, 1913.

* * * * * * *

"A. When we first went there we *did a lot of experimenting*.

* * * * * * *

"A. My position there was to supervise the applied work, also to supervise the erection of the staff of imitation travertin".

And R. 208-209:

"XQ. 28. You know the defendants in this case, MacGruer and Simpson? A. Yes, sir.

"XQ. 29. When did you become acquainted with them? A. In 1913 when we reached California.

"XQ. 30. Did they do any work on the Exposition Buildings? A. Yes.

"XQ. 31. What work did they do?

"A. They were doing Machinery Hall when we got there.

* * * * * * *

"When they got started they were under Mr. Denivelle and myself—*Mr. Denivelle first gave them instructions*.

* * * * * * *

"And we also had *another man who taught them how to cast it*.

* * * * * * *

"Well, *everyone seemed to be bucking against it* when they went there—*every contractor*—they just seemed to see how rotten they could do the thing—*they wanted to drive it out if they could*—

"XQ. 39. In other words, they were opposed to the idea of artificial travertin?

"A. They were opposed to it strong.

"XQ. 40. Was the work delayed and made more difficult on that account?

"A. The only thing—I would have to condemn it and they would have to do it over.

"XQ. 41. You found it necessary to condemn a great deal of the work?

"A. Condemned quite a little in the start, and when they saw they had to do it over they straightened out and tried to do it passable.

"XQ. 42. Mr. MacGruer felt at one time that he would be able to stop the use of this travertin on the Exposition work, did he?

"A. Well, not Mr. MacGruer alone—all the contractors.

"XQ. 43. What did they say or do in that connection?

"A. Well, they said they wouldn't be dictated to by us and they called a meeting of all the employees in the Service Building to try to have our supervision stopped, saying that we wanted too good a job done" (all italics ours).

This job was different again from the Ottawa and Pennsylvania jobs, for says Whipple (R. 213):

"RDQ. 19. Was that applied and imitation travertin which was being installed by Mr. Denivelle on the Exposition Buildings in California of the same character as that which you had done at Ottawa and in the Pennsylvania Station?

"A. It was the same character but of a coarser texture."

And (R. 214-215):

"RDQ. 25. Now, you went there as representing Mr. Denivelle, to instruct MacGruer and Simpson and the other contractors how to make this imitation travertin, is that right?

"A. And to get a good material to stand outside.

"RDQ. 26. You went there to instruct them how to make imitation travertin, did you? A. Yes, sir.

"RDQ. 27. And did you give them instructions as how to make travertin? A. Yes sir.

"RDQ. 28. And did you see that they made it according to your instructions? A. Yes, sir.

"RDQ. 29. And did you instruct them according to Mr. Denivelle's instructions to you? A. Yes, sir.

"RDQ. 30. Now, was it your understanding that aside from the difference in the material used, you were following the instructions under which the Travertin had been installed in the Pennsylvania Station? A. No.

* * * * * *

"RDQ. 32. Was it done the same way?

"A. For the applied work we used a different brush again—when we got there we used a different brush altogether than we had ever used."

The proposition was "entirely new" to these defendants in 1913. Mr. Cooke, on whom largely devolved the job of teaching the process to the defendants at the Exposition, says (R. 291-292) (italics ours):

"XQ. 21. Did you have any difficulty with them getting them to follow instructions?

"A. Certainly did.

"XQ. 22. What was the cause of these difficulties?

"A. Well, I will tell you what the principal difficulty is in a proposition of that kind—*it was entirely new to those men out there and they didn't know the first thing about it and it took them a long while to get on to what we wanted*—and that was our chief difficulty—it was *getting the men to learn the method* of setting the result that we wanted."

* * * * * * *

"*All the contractors were opposed to it*—made it "hot" for us—very unpleasant job."

Constant change says Mr. Cooke (R. 291):

"XQ. 12. How far had the method been worked out when you did the Exposition job?

*   *   *   *   *   *   *

"A. The applied work—well, *we again changed the applied work in San Francisco; we changed the style of getting it.*"

And, again (R. 294):

"RDQ. 4. And was that hawk and trowel work the same as you had done in the Pennsylvania Station?
A. No."

And (R. 295):

"*It was entirely different*—the work in the Pennsylvania job was as near as possible an imitation of real travertin while of the Exposition we got Travertin but it was nothing like the Pennsylvania job, for the simple reason that we couldn't put in the time, etc., on it, and then he had a different idea that he wanted carried out on those buildings."

The highly experimental character of the process as late as the fall of 1913 is no better illustrated anywhere than by the letter of these defendants of October 8th, 1913, appearing at R. 646-647 already quoted herein.

The progress of the work is in a large measure indicated by excerpts from the correspondence passing between defendants and the Exposition authorities (R. 642-648) as shown at R. 647 "notice of completion of work dated March 18, 1914". The building was completed on the 10th day of March,

1914. As a prior use this defense is not available as it is within the two year period.

As to Denivelle's connection with the work we have already quoted MacGruer (R. 607) supra.

The record shows that the W. W. Anderson Company, general contractors for the Machinery Building sued the Exposition Company (R. 634-635) in the Superior Court for the City and County of San Francisco in which suit these defendants took an active part. The correspondence herein referred to forms part of the records in that case and the letters read from on behalf of the plaintiff were duly identified by the defendant MacGruer.

When we take this with the admission above quoted at R. 608 of MacGruer:

> "*Well at that time it was very much of an experiment with himself,* because he had never used plaster*",

we must conclude that the finding of this Court in the Los Angeles case more than justifies a like finding here and that while there was "a use by the public" of the invention in various instances and at various places under varying conditions, there was not a *public use* within the meaning of the statute.

USE BY THE PUBLIC VS. PUBLIC USE.

It is possible that the Honorable Trial Judge confused "use by the public" with "public use". "Use by the public", as shown by the following cases, even for more than two years before application for patent, is a very different thing than "public use" beyond the statutory period:

> *Elizabeth v. Pavement Co.,* 97 U. S. 126; L. Ed. 1000;
>
> *Warren Bros. Co. v. City of Owosso,* 166 Fed. 309 (C. C. A. 6th Cir);
>
> *Campbell v. The Mayor of New York,* 9 Fed. 500;
>
> *Emery v. Cavanagh,* 17 Fed. 242;
>
> *Innis v. Oil City Boiler Works,* 22 Fed. 780;
>
> *Railway Register Mfg. Co. v. Broadway & Seventh Ave. R. Co.,* 26 Fed. 522;
>
> *Harmon v. Struthers,* 43 Fed. 437;
>
> *Campbell v. Mayor of New York,* 47 Fed. 637;
>
> *Westinghouse Elec. & Mfg. Co. v. Saranac Lake Elec. L. Co.,* 108 Fed. 221;
>
> *Bryce Bros. Co. v. Seneca Glass Co.,* 140 Fed. 171;
>
> *American Caramel Co. v. Thomas Mills & Bro.,* 149 Fed. 743;
>
> *Penn Electrical & Mfg. Co. v. Conroy,* 159 Fed. 943;
>
> *International Telephone Mfg. Co. v. Kellogg Switch Board & Supply Co.,* 171 Fed. 651;
>
> *Edison v. Allis-Chalmers Co.,* 191 Fed. 837.

In view of the consideration given this subject in the Los Angeles case, the upholding of plaintiff's views therein would seem to make it unnecessary to repeat or reargue the subject here. We believe it would be sufficient to call the Court's attention to plaintiff's brief in that case on the subjects "The Law as to Public Use", "Divisional Applications", and "Continuing Applications", as set out at pages 67 to 80, inclusive thereof.

To this we might add the following from *Walker*, Section 94:

> "If the inventor uses his invention for profit, and not by way of experiment, that is a public use, *unless actual use resulting in profit is necessary to show the inventor how to perfect his invention,* and unless he does perfect it in accordance with the teachings of such use.

> "Experimental use is never public use within the meaning of the statute, if it is conducted in good faith for the purpose of *testing the qualities of the invention,* and for no other purpose not naturally incidental to that. In such a case it is immaterial whether the experimental use disclosed a necessity for improvement, or disclosed no such necessity; and it is also immaterial whether the use was conducted with secrecy or not. It may, indeed, have been had in the open air, and have continued every day for several years, and have been known to hundreds of persons, and have *incidentally inured to the profit of the user and of the public,* and still not be a public use, within the meaning of the statute, *if the nature of the invention was such that only long-continued out-door use could show whether the invention possessed utility, or show in what respects, if any, it required to be improved.* In the case of a patented machine designed to manufacture articles the inventor may make as many articles as are necessary to enable him to observe and remedy the defects in his machine, and he is *not thus brought within the statute* merely beceause the articles, them-

selves, may be perfect, or because he makes the best possible use of them *by selling them.*

"The liberal ideas which underlie the decision just cited will doubtless be applied to every variety of invention, as occasion serves, and will be found elastic enough to cover every meritorious case. Indeed, Judge John Lowell went still further in the direction of liberally allowing scope to experimental use, and decided that such use is not public use within the meaning of the law, where, in order to test its comparative as well as its absolute utility, and in order to convince others of its merit, an inventor allows them to use his invention after he has himself become satisfied that it is useful.

"If, however, the nature of the invention is such that the inventor is obliged to put it into the hands of others for crucial experiment, he may sell specimens to those others for that purpose, and *such a sale will not be obnoxious* to the law now under consideration. * * *

"But where a specimen of an invention is built or made to order, it is *not on sale* until it is *completed, delivered* and *accepted"* (italics ours).

That last sentence would apply to the Goelet job and others.

"* * * the use of an invention by the inventor himself, or by another person under his direction, by way of experiment, and in order to bring the invention to perfection, has never been regarded in this court as such a public use as under the statute defeats his right to a patent." (*Smith & Griggs Mfg. Co. v. Sprague,* 123 U. S. 249, 31 L. Ed. 141, 144.)

"A use necessarily open to public view, if made in good faith, solely to test the qualities of the invention, and for the purpose of experiment, is not a public use within the meaning of the statute." (*Egbert v. Lippmann,* 104 U. S. 333, 336.)

Defendants, however, in the instant case, lean on *Root v. Third Ave. R. R.,* 146 U. S. 221, to support their case as against the *Elizabeth Pavement* case. Aside from the very distinct difference between the inventions involved on the one hand in the *Root* case and on the other hand in the *Pavement* and *Denivelle* cases, it is to be noted that in *Root v. Third Ave. Railroad* the inventor made no attempt to observe and study the structure after it had gone into use. He did not recognize any necessity for improvement, nor did he make any improvements.

The Court said:

"At the time he had no present expectations of making any material changes in it. He never made or suggested a change in it after it went into use and never made an examination with a view of seeing whether it was defective or could be improved in any particular."

ROOT V. THIRD AVE. PREVIOUSLY CONSIDERED BY THIS COURT AND FOUND NOT APPLICABLE.

In the Los Angeles case in the Petition for Rehearing on behalf of the appellees therein, strenuous effort was made by the said appellees to impress upon this Court that the Denivelle situation should be measured by *Root v. Third Ave.* case, rather than by the case of *Elizabeth v. Pavement Co.* (See the said Petition for Rehearing, pages 22 to 40, inclusive.)

_____

INFRINGEMENT.

Little needs be added to what has already been said to show infringement if the Court finds the patent valid. Judge Van Fleet on preliminary injunction was quickly convinced that the process and product of the defendants infringed the Denivelle claims in issue. The trial Court, while expressing no opinion on the subject, was apparently of the opinion that the only escape for the defendants was the annihilation of the Denivelle patent.

It is obvious that defendants' method is only a colorable variation of the defendants' process. Defendants' work, exemplified in Exhibits 1 and 2, shows that their process results in a *product* conforming in every way to the calls of claims 9 and 10.

What the defendant does is, briefly, this: He takes a mold and greases it or applies an *isolator* just as the Denivelle patent calls for. Over this greased or isolated surface he runs veins or irregular lines of a cementitious fluid mixture of different color from the background. This is the *veining* process. Over this veining process he scatters a *lumpy material* which happens to be dry carbide. Over this lumpy material he then applies a *backing of a different consistency,* of *cementitious material* which has the effect, when the entire job is done, of *binding the mass together* and producing the desired result.

Delaney's affidavit (R. 69-77), filed by the defense in opposition to the motion for preliminary injunction, may be construed as an admission of infringement as he described defendants' infringing process in the following language, beginning top R. 75:

"* * * that essentially speaking, applicant makes use of an old and well known mold characterized by features of common knowledge; that he *greases his mold* as is also well known; that he then places upon the surface thereof plastic substances, which, while in a moist state, are *combed or otherwise treated to produce veins,* so to speak; that he then introduces to the surface thus treated *granules of calcium carbide,* and finally *spreads upon the aforesaid constituents a plastic mass which gives to the structure a form of backing;* that this backing is *applied while in the moist state,* and that incident thereto a chemical action is set up which causes the chemical carbide to assume a gaseous state and explode and thereby produce upon the surface of the finished product a plurality of cells, pockets, or voids of an undercut character" (italics ours).

Continuing, Delaney says:

"* * * that through the changes inaugurated by affiant's principle the ultimate product is in closer keeping with the natural Roman travertin, and is light, strong and durable, and is thin so that it may be advantageously used in a manner not true to the commercial usages of plaintiff's product. That a specimen of this last-mentioned product herewith is produced and marked for identification in Defendants' Exhibit 5."

(This "Exhibit 5" is Plaintiff's Exhibit 2 herein) (R. 543).

At R. 74 DeLaney says concerning his infringing product:

> "that affiant had among other things the *creation of a novel and new and useful composition of matter wherein these cavities can be more or less inconsistently formed upon the exposed surface of the finished product* and by means of or through the assistance of chemical instrumentalities which function for the purpose aforesaid and which subsequently become entirely obliterated by chemical reaction so as to never constitute any homogeneous part of the completed mass, and thereby ultimately give to the' commercial or finished product a condition or quality not heretofore experienced or found in substance of common knowledge, or in such substance as could be produced in any manner, shape or form through knowledge gained from plaintiff's patent" (italics ours).

It might be true that defendants' product is indeed an improvement (which it is not) over the patented product, but, that, at best, would only be a matter of *degree,* and, as this Court knows, would not avoid infringement.

> *Winans v. Denmead,* 15 How. 330;
> *Sewall v. Jones,* 91 U. S. 171.

CONCLUSION.

We submit that the defenses, "prior use and sale", "public use", "lack of invention", lack of "supplemental oath", and all the others, should be overruled as without merit and under the doctrine of *stare decisis.*

It has often been held that there is not, in the common law, a maxim more eminently just and promotive of the public convenience than that of *stare decisis*. This is particularly so in patent cases affecting the validity of the patent, where the patent, the question and the evidence are substantially the same, as is the case here when compared with the record in the former Los Angeles case.

A decent respect for the stability of decision and of vested business interests such as plaintiff has in this patent, should under all the circumstances of the case justify your Honors in reversing the Trial Court.

As said in *Bradley Co. v. Eagle Co.*, 58 Fed. 721; 7 C. C. A.

> "The former decree is not the act of the party, but the solemn adjudication of a judicial tribunal. So far as the party is concerned, he may be permitted to waive the former recovery in his own behalf; but the peace and good order of society are likewise concerned, that there shall be an end to litigation, and that the courts should not be twice vexed with the same controversy, when that controversy has once been solemnly adjudicated. Marsh v. Pier, 4 Rawle, 288; Kilheffer v. Herr, 17 Serg. & R. 319."

We submit that the decree should be reversed and plaintiff's patent held valid and infringed with costs to appellant.

Dated, San Francisco,
October 22, 1924.

Respectfully submitted,
CHAS. E. TOWNSEND,
WM. A. LOFTUS,
Attorneys for Appellant.

United States Circuit Court of Appeals

FOR THE NINTH CIRCUIT.

Paul E. Denivelle,
    Plaintiff-Appellant,
 	
vs.
 	
MacGruer & Simpson (a copartnership) and George Smith MacGruer and Robert Morton Simpson, individually, and sometimes doing business as MacGruer & Co.,
    Defendant-Appellees.
	Appeal
	No. 4269.

BRIEF FOR DEFENDANTS-APPELLEES.

T. Hart Anderson,
Attorney for Defendants-Appellees.

Munn, Anderson & Munn, of New York, N. Y.,
Of Counsel for Defendants-Appellees.

INDEX.

United States Circuit Court of Appeals

FOR THE NINTH CIRCUIT.

PAUL E. DENIVELLE,
    Plaintiff-Appellant,

vs.

MacGRUER & SIMPSON (a copartnership) and GEORGE SMITH MacGRUER and ROBERT MORTON SIMPSON, individually, a n d sometimes doing business as MacGRUER & Co.,
    Defendant-Appellees.

Appeal No. 4269.

BRIEF FOR DEFENDANTS-APPELLEES.

May it Please the Court:

The patent here involved has heretofore been before the United States District Court in the Southern District of California, Southern Division, in two suits entitled *Los Angeles Lime Co. & Paul E. Denivelle* v. *Nye*, and *Los Angeles Lime Co. & Paul E. Denivelle* v. *Ceriat*. Those suits were tried together, and in the District Court as in the present suit, a decree was entered for the defendants. On appeal this Honorable Court reversed the decree in the prior suits and held the patent to be valid over the defense of public use and sale by the patentee more than two years before he filed his application for patent.

(The decision of this Honorable Court is published in Vol. 270, Fed. Rep., page 155.)

In the present suit, as in the former suits, the District Court for the *Northern* District of California, Southern Division, has entered a decree for the defendants on the defense that the patentee made a public use and sale of his invention more than two years before he filed his application for patent, and in addition that certain claims are not supported by the oath of the patentee.

Other Defenses.

In addition to the foregoing defenses the defendants here pleaded and offered evidence to show that there was no invention in the subject matter of the patent; that there was no patentable novelty therein; and that in addition to the public use and sale which had been made by the patentee, others had made and used the invention more than two years before the application for patent was filed and that the invention had been abandoned by the patentee (Record, p. 679).

The Decree.

In the opinion of the District Court it was held that: "The patent is invalid and the suit is dismissed" (record, p. 678). While that was the only conclusion which could have been reached by the court below on the record (we submit with all deference to the prior decision of this Honorable Court), yet on the contention of plaintiff's counsel that only claims 1, 2, 5, 9 and 10 were at issue, the decree entered found such claims only to be invalid, because of the public use and sale of the subject matter thereof more than two years before the application for patent was filed, and in addition that claims 9 and 10 were void by reason of the absence of a supplemental oath.

The Evidence in the Former Suit.

This Honorable Court, in its opinion in the former suit, as published in the *Federal Reporter,* quotes at length the testimony of Denivelle the patentee, in which he characterized his work on the Pennsylvania Station in New York, upon which is mainly based the defense of prior use and sale, as an "experiment"; and it was his testimony *alone, absolutely uncorroborated* and *unsupported,* which described this Pennsylvania Station job *as an experiment.*

The Evidence in Present Suit.

In the present case we still find *only* the testimony of Denivelle *uncorroborated,* and this notwithstanding these defendants had taken the depositions of the architects and builders connected with this Pennsylvania Station work, and workmen employed thereon, and other contractors for whom Denivelle had done similar work shortly after he had done the Pennsylvania Station work, and after the defendants had produced and introduced in evidence numerous *documentary exhibits,* all showing conclusively that not only had Denivelle offered for sale and sold a specimen of his work, as exemplified by the Pennsylvania Station job, more than two years before he filed his application for patent, but that he had been *one of many* who had entered *competitive samples* for this Pennsylvania Station job accompanied by competitive bids *based on the same specifications,* and as in the case of any other competitive bidding, he had received the contract because he had named the lowest figure for the job.

In the present case also Denivelle, although testifying at the trial, *says nothing about the Pennsylvania Station job being an experiment,* notwithstanding that all these depositions for the defendants had been taken bebefore he went on the stand, *and not a word of testimony was introduced on behalf of the plaintiff to rebut the testimony given by the defendants' witnesses.* Presumably the plaintiff in the present case was content to rest upon the decision of this Honorable Court, holding that this Pennsylvania Station job, which had been done by Denivelle more than two years before he applied for his patent, was but an experiment; but we feel convinced that when the testimony of the architects, builders and workmen employed in and about the Pennsylvania Station work, and in and about other imitation travertine stone work done by Denivelle in connection with other jobs, shortly after he finished the Pennsylvania Station job, and all more than two years before he applied for his patent, is carefully considered, *this Honorable Court will not hesitate on this record to reverse its prior decision and affirm the decree of the District Court.*

A Word As to the Printed Record.

The printed record in this case on appeal is rather unusual so far as counsel for the defendants' experience goes in the Federal Appellate Courts of nearly every circuit, in that there has not been reproduced a single documentary exhibit, not even a printed copy of the patent in suit nor of the patents of the prior art introduced by the defendants; nor the file wrapper and contents of the Denivelle patent in suit and of the Denivelle abandoned application for patent; nor the very important documentary exhibits introduced by the defendants during the taking of the various depositions of witnesses in New York, comprising among other things, a copy of the specifications prepared by McKim, Mead & White for the Pennsylvania Station job, upon which Denivelle based his bid, and the correspondence between Denivelle and the architects, McKim, Mead & White, and the builders, George F. Fuller Construction Co., and the correspondence with other contractors and the Fuller Co., and the release executed by Denivelle when the Pennsylvania Station job was completed by him; all of which, instead of being reproduced in this printed record is, at the request of plaintiff-appellant, and by order of the court, not reproduced and printed, but are simply required to be arranged and bound in a convenient form with numbered pages, for the consideration of the court.

While these very important parts have been omitted from the printed record, yet for some unexplained reason there is to be found in that printed record not only the opening statement of counsel for the plaintiff (beginning at page 530 and extending to page 552)—which statement cannot of course be regarded as evidence in the case, nor any part of the record on appeal —but there has been included and printed the proceedings, in the matter of the preliminary injunction including the Notice of Motion for Preliminary Injunction, the Order to Show Cause and the numerous affidavits in connection with that Motion, *none of which*, excepting the affidavit of Paul E. Denivelle (printed at pp. 23-45 of the record), were introduced as exhibits in the case in the court below. We do not know for what purpose the proceedings on the motion for preliminary injunction (with the exception of the Paul E. Denivelle affidavit) appear in this printed record, but as they can do no harm we have concluded to proceed with the preparation of our brief and argue this appeal without taking exception thereto.

The Documentary Exhibits of the Greatest Importance.

The documentary exhibits introduced by the defendants are of the greatest importance in this case, and we impress upon this Honorable Court the advisability of giving them careful consideration even though there be but one copy which must be shared by all of the members of this court in the consideration of this appeal.

We also desire to call attention to the fact that these exhibits were introduced at the time the several depositions were taken in New York and Washington, D. C., and numbered consecutively as defendants' exhibits. These numbers do not appear in the order or number of exhibits which were introduced at the trial, with the result that the numbers on some of the exhibits in the case will be duplicated, but defendants' exhibits as numbered at the time they were introduced, may be readily identified by referring to the depositions in connection with which they were introduced.

Patent in Suit Invalid Because of Two Years' Prior Use and Sale.

We think it advisable to take up this defense first because it is our belief that it is quite sufficient and that this court will find it sufficiently proven in this case to warrant the reversal of its previous findings in connection with this Denivelle patent, and the affirmance of the decree of the court below, in fact the amendment of that decree to hold that the entire patent is invalid without the necessity of studying the evidence concerning the other defenses.

Requirements of a Valid Patent.

Under the Revised Statutes (Section 4886), a person to be entitled to a patent must have invented or discovered a new and useful art, machine, manufacture of composition of matter, or a new and useful improvement thereon; the invention must not have been known or used by others in this country before his invention or discovery thereof; it must not have been patented or described in any printed publication in this or any foreign country before his invention or discovery thereof, nor more than two years before the filing of the application for the patent; it must not have been *in public use or on sale in this country for more than two years prior to the application; and it must not have been abandoned.* If any of these things have occurred, then no valid patent can be obtained. If the thing for which a patent is sought be a mere expedient not arising to the dignity of an invention, no valid patent can be obtained; if the thing be not new or useful, no valid patent can be obtained; if it were known or used by others in the United States before its alleged invention or discovery by the one who seeks a patent, no valid patent can be obtained; if before the date of its alleged invention it had been patented or described in a printed publication, either in the United States or a foreign country, no valid patent can be obtained; or if it had been so patented or described more than two years prior to the application for patent, even if this be not before the claimed date of invention, no valid patent can be obtained; and if the alleged inventor or others put the alleged invention in public use or put it on sale in this country more than two years before the date of the application for patent, even though it be not more than two years before the claimed date of invention, no valid patent can be obtained; and if, finally, one who makes an invention abandons it—and abandonment may—be determined by his actions in and about the alleged invention—no valid patent can be obtained.

In the present case the proof introduced by the defendants shows conclusively that the patentee Denivelle—if, for the sake of argument he can be regarded as having made an invention put it into public use and effected a sale of a specimen of it more than two years before he filed his application for patent, and also his actions in and about the same were such as to prove that he abandoned it, as will be hereinafter set forth.

The Pennsylvania Station Job.

There can be no question that the imitation travertine stone in the Pennsylvania Station was constructed and installed in accordance with the Denivelle patent. Denivelle himself says:

> "The intrinsic merit of the invention has found expression in a large practical way in its extensive use by affiant in the monumental structure of the Pennsylvania Railroad Station in New York City * * *" (record p. 28, Denivelle's affidavit of July 14, 1923).

This being so, the question arises—When did Denivelle make a public use of that alleged invention, or when did he make a sale of it? Either a public use or a sale, or *an offer to sell*—one or the other—more than two years before he filed his application, is quite sufficient. This Pennsylvania Station job may be regarded either as a sale of a specimen of his invention, or it may be regarded as a public use of his alleged invention, or both a public use and sale.

Dènivelle or His Company, Denivelle Hydraulic Composite Stone Company, Was One of Four Competitive Bidders for This Work.

Denivelle and his company and the other bidders were furnished by the architects or the general contractors, George F. Fuller Construction Company, with complete specifications upon which they were to make their estimates and submit their bids. Each of the contestants was required to, and did submit, and install a sample of of the work, *prepared in accordance with the specifications,* at the time their bids were submitted. The contract was awarded to Denivelle or his company, and he was required to and did in fact put up a bond to insure the performance of the contract in accordance with the terms thereof, which *required the work to be completed within a specified time.* All of this took place in 1909, while his application for patent was not filed until Oct. 20, 1915.

These proceedings, we submit to this honorable Court, constitute not only on the part of Denivelle and his company, an offer to sell a specimen of his alleged invention, but on the part of the other bidders as well, and at the time the contract was awarded to the Denivelle Co. he and his company then and there made an actual sale of a specimen of his invention. He completed his work, was paid in full therefor, and executed the required release, and his invention was at once put into public use.

It is unnecessary to consider what took place before this contract was awarded to Denivelle. It is unnecessary to determine whether or not Denivelle's alleged conversation with Mr. Mead of the firm of McKim, Mead & White, as quoted in the published decision of this Honorable Court in the prior cases, actually took place or not. It is immaterial to determine whether Mr. Denivelle or some of the others *first made a satisfactory sample of imitation travertine which convinced the architects and builders that they could use imitation travertine.* It is immaterial to discuss the alleged difficulty of the problem submitted or claimed to have been submitted by the architects to Denivelle. Regardless of who produced the first satisfactory sample—regardless of who first convinced the architects that they could use imitation travertine—Denivelle and his company, the successful bidder, offered to do this work *in accordance with specifications prepared by the architects,* and did it, and was paid for it in 1909 or 1910. And he was one of four who were prepared to do the same job at that time, *in accordance with the same specifications,* and having done it and receiving payment for it, he has the effrontery to characterize that job as an *experiment. There may have been an experiment connected with that job, but if so it was not Denivelle's. Denivelle took a contract under certain specifications, completed the work, and was paid for it.* Such experimenting as was done occurred before the specifications were prepared, and *were for the purpose of satisfying the architects that they could use imitation travertine.*

Imitation travertine may never have been produced before McKim, Mead & White conceived the idea that they would like to use it. In fact, it appears that genuine travertine had never been used in this country before this Pennsylvania Station job. Such experimentation as took place was among those to whom McKim, Mead & White appealed, to submit specimens of imitation travertine *long before the specifications were*

written, long before the contract was awarded, in order
that *they* might know that a *satisfactory* imitation of
travertine could be produced. When they were convinced that it could be produced, then their specifications
were prepared, and Denivelle and his company, among
others, were invited to submit bids. One of the witnesses testified that nearly every modeling plasterer in
the City of New York was engaged in producing specimens of imitation travertine for the architects, McKim,
Mead & White.

We submit the evidence shows conclusively that all
experimentation to determine the practicability of
imitation travertine for this work had ceased at the
time McKim, Mead & White prepared their specifications and invited Denivelle and his company and others
to submit bids thereon. At that time McKim, Mead
& White were satisfied that a satisfactory imitation
of travertine could be produced and that they could
employ it in the Pennsylvania Station.

A Brief Review of the Testimony Submitted By Defendants.

BURT L. FENNER.

Mr. Burt L. Fenner is a member of the firm of Mc-
Kim, Mead & White, the architects who designed and
supervised the construction of the Pennsylvania Station.
He has been associated with McKim, Mead & White
since 1891 and became a member of the firm in January,
1906, (record Q 7, p. 169).

Mr. Fenner identified Defendants' Exhibit 3 as the
specifications prepared in the office of McKim, Mead &
White (Q 15, pp. 169-170).

He testified that he was familiar with the artificial
travertine installed by Mr. Denivelle in the Pennsylvania
Station (record Q 11, p. 169).

Mr. Fenner identified the contract between the Denivelle Co., and the George A. Fuller Company, and the bond, introduced in evidence as Defendants' Exhibit 4—Bond and Agreement (Q 23, 30, pp. 171-3).

Mr. Fenner also testified concerning the documentary exhibits obtained from the files of McKim, Mead & White, introduced in evidence as "Defendants' Exhibit 5," in which there should be eleven sheets, all held together by a paper clip, this exhibit comprising correspondence between McKim, Mead & White and the Fuller Company, and McKim, Mead & White and the Denivelle Company (which at one time was Hammerstein & Denivelle), all dated in 1908 and the early part of 1909 (Q 40-41, pp. 174-5).

Mr. Fenner testified that Daniel T. Webster was in the employ of McKim, Mead & White and was general superintendent representing the architects in the construction of the Pennsylvania Station (Q 42-4, pp. 175-6).

Concerning the installation of samples by the bidders, he said he had no personal knowledge, but that certain correspondence in the files of McKim, Mead & White indicates that samples were furnished, and he identifies letters from McNulty Bros., H. W. Miller, George A. Fuller Co., and the architects, comprising 15 sheets in all, held together by a paper clip and introduced in evidence as "Defendants' Exhibit 6" (Q 47-9, pp. 176-7).

Mr. Fenner also identified the Denivelle release introduced in evidence as "Defendants' Exhibit 7" (Q 54-6, p. 178).

Mr. Fenner was with the architects McKim, Mead & White, when the Pennsylvania Station was under construction, and of his own knowledge, knew that Mr. Denivelle and his company installed imitation travertine in that building (Q 59-60, p. 179).

He testified that the policy of McKim, Mead & White
in certifying payments on account of work under construction was to cause an examination of the work to
determine its stage of completion and whether or not
the work was in accordance with the contract; and that
*a payment would indicate that the work had been done
to a certain point and was entirely satisfactory and in
accordance with the specifications* (Q 65-6, p. 180).

Mr. Fenner was advised that Mr. Denivelle, in a suit
in California, had testified that the work he did in the
Pennsylvania Station was an experiment, and he was
asked whether McKim, Mead & White would cause an
experiment to be installed in a building designed and
constructed under their direction. His answer was:

> "Why, the question is just what 'experiment'
> means. Certainly the preparation of samples was
> an experiment, for to the best of my knowledge
> nothing of the sort had ever been attempted
> before. As a result of the samples, McKim,
> Mead & White, and the officers representing the
> Railroad Company felt sufficient confidence in the
> result to warrant McKim, Mead & White in
> recommending its use to the Railroad Company
> and the Railroad Company in agreeing to its use
> and making the contract. It is obvious that both
> the Railroad Company and McKim, Mead &
> White felt pretty certain that they were going to
> get a successful result, and they wouldn't have
> been justified in trying what I understand as an
> experiment on so large a scale, and yet until the
> work was completed, and had stood certain tests
> of time and use, no one could be certain that the
> results indicated from the samples would actually
> be brought about in reality" (Q 69, p. 181).

When asked whether that was not also true of almost
every building construction, his answer was:

> "It's true of every new material, I should say,
> but not of every building construction. We know

perfectly well what the result of laying up a brick wall is going to be, or putting in an ordinary plastered ceiling, but here is a new material with no data, no precedent to enable anybody to determine with any accuracy, certainty or finality what the result would be. *The evidence produced by the samples convinced us all that we should get a satisfactory result''* (Q 71, p. 181).

He testified further that samples were furnished by other bidders.

He further testified that, assuming that the final payment to Mr. Denivelle had been in 1910, it would be proof that McKim, Mead & White had satisfied themselves that the job was all right and was in accordance with the specifications and a complete job at that time (record, pp. 181-2).

On cross-examination by counsel for plaintiff, when it was insinuated that the matter of vibration was a factor, Mr. Fenner said in his opinion ''there would be no more reason to anticipate difficulty due to vibration with that material (imitation travertine) than with any other similar applied material, like slabs of marble or slabs of stone'' (xQ 4, p. 183).

Mr. Fenner further testified that it was not unusual in work of this kind to require a maintenance bond, in fact it was quite usual to require a contractor to take care of defects that might arise within a certain period after a job was completed, and further that *it must be* assumed that *McKim, Mead & White in drawing up the specifications for the Pennsylvania Station, took into consideration the conditions which would arise owing to the use of that station by trains, etc.* (RDQ 1-4, pp. 185-6).

Frank A. Whipple

Frank A. Whipple, a witness subpoenaed by the defendants, had known Mr. Denivelle for about 24 years and worked for him on the Pennsylvania Station job. He said he worked on that job 6 or 7 months, starting in the Spring; that it was 1909 or 1910 (not remembering just which year it was) (Q 9-11, pp. 194-5).

He remembers that Mr. Denivelle submitted and installed a sample "just one piece of stone" (Q 17, p. 195).

He remembers seeing a sample that had been installed by McNulty before the job was started, and he tells where that McNulty sample was installed (Q 19-20, p. 196).

He also tells where the Denivelle sample was installed (Q 30, p. 197).

He says that he went to Canada in the *Spring of* 1911 and worked on the *Union Station at Ottawa,* for Mr. Denivelle, *installing imitation travertine,* and that the imitation travertine installed in the Union Station in Ottawa, was *pretty nearly the same as that in the Pennsylvania Station;* that he had charge of the applied work there, the same as at the Pennsylvania Station; that in both jobs there was applied work and cast work. He thinks this Ottawa Station job was in April, 1911 (Q 35-45, pp. 198-9).

Whipple also worked for Mr. Denivelle, installing some artificial travertine in a building at 23rd Street just east of Broadway in New York City, which he says was done in 1912 (Q 55-7, pp. 200-1).

Whipple went out to California with Denivelle, leaving New York on the 10th day of April, 1913 (Q 59-62, p. 201).

As to the activities of Whipple and Denivelle in California, see record p. 202.

Regarding the Union Station job at Ottawa, Canada, Whipple testifies that it was "virtually a duplicate of the Pennsylvania" and that the imitation travertine was in appearance like that which had been done in the Pennsylvania Station (Qs. 81-3, pp. 203-4).

On cross-examination the witness was coaxed along by Mr. Loftus plaintiff's attorney (who knew perfectly well that he was friendly with Denivelle, and would like to help him with his testimony if he could), and he had Whipple testify that vibration would cause trouble; that the only way to find out whether the work would stand up would be to put it up and try it out; and that he had heard that Denivelle had a gang of men there making repairs (xQ 18-24, pp. 206-7). None of this is important as we shall show.

He testified that when he first became acquainted with MacGruer & Simpson in 1913, "they were doing Machinery Hall when we got there," and that this was done in artificial travertine (xQ 29-32, p. 208).

The attention of the court is called to the fact that when Denivelle and Whipple reached California in 1913, the defendants here were *at that time doing Machinery Hall in artificial travertine.* Whipple testified that he and Denivelle taught the defendants how to apply travertine, and that they had another man who taught the defendants how to cast it (xQ 35-6, p. 208).

Mr. Whipple would not agree with Mr. Loftus that the 23rd Street job was a different method from that used in the Pennsylvania Station (xQ 47, p. 210).

On Re-direct Mr. Whipple testified that the Pennsylvania Station job, the 23rd Street job, the Ottawa Station job, were all done in the same manner, the only difference being that a different brush was used in the applied work to make the holes in the surface (R.D.Qs. 1-10, pp. 211-12).

Whipple further testified that the applied and imitation travertine work on the Exposition Buildings in California was of the same character as that done at the

Ottawa Station, and in the Pennsylvania Station, except that it was coarser and that the holes were made deeper (RDQ 19-20, p. 213); *that he went to California, representing Denivelle, to instruct MacGruer & Simpson and the other contractors on the Exposition buildings, how to make imitation travertine, and to get good material to stand on the outside of the buildings; that he did instruct the contractors how to make imitation travertine; that he saw that they made it according to his instructions; and that he instructed them according to Denivelle's instructions to him* (RDQ 23-9, p. 214).

He says that the work done on the exposition buildings, aside from using a different brush on the applied work, was the same as that done in the Pennsylvania Station.

Whipple did not go back to the Pennsylvania Station to do any repair work, and when he left it was all right. Before going to California, he went back to the Pennsylvania Station to put up some extension of imitation travertine (RDQ 42-4, pp. 216-7).

The court should understand that when "cast" work is referred to it is intended to describe imitation stone made in blocks or pieces, and then put in position on the wall, and that when applied work is referred to it means imitation travertine produced on the surface, somewhat as a room or building is plastered. Both forms are, and have been commonly employed.

On re-cross-examination, Mr. Loftus again tried to coax this witness to say that the work done in the Pennsylvania Station was an experiment; to show that changes had been made as the work progressed; and that there was no way other than putting it in place, to determine whether or not it would be a good job.

But on Re-direct, Whipple had to admit that as a representative of Denivelle on the Pennsylvania Station job, he inspected and passed upon each piece

of cast imitation travertine that was put on the wall; that he did not knowingly put into that wall a defective slab of imitation travertine; and that when he passed it it was in his judgment fit to go on the wall (record, p. 219).

Daniel T. Webster

Daniel T. Webster testified that he was associated with McKim, Mead & White from 1893 until 1911 (Q 7, p. 238); that he was delegated by McKim, Mead & White as general superintendent in the construction of the Pennsylvania Railroad Station (Q 9, 298).

He first met Denivelle in 1909, and according to his recollection Denivelle was requested by McKim, Mead & White to make some samples of imitation travertine and to get in touch with him to see the original stone (Q 14, p. 239).

He testified that Denivelle's first sample was a small piece which Webster thinks was made by Denivelle at the request of Mr. Mead, one of the members of the firm (Q 17, p. 239).

He describes his duties as a representative of McKim, Mead & White, and states that he had as assistant, among others, Clay M. McClure (pp. 240-1).

Webster identified "Defendants' Exhibit 1" as a copy of the specifications for the artificial stone work on the Pennsylvania Station, such specifications being prepared in the office of McKim, Mead & White (Q 33, p. 242).

Webster, after identifying a lot of documentary exhibits—letters passing from and to McNulty Bros., George A. Fuller Co., Deneville, McKim, Mead & White and others (Q 37-62, pp. 242-7), testified that *there were four bidders for the imitation travertine work on the Pennsylvania Station, all of whom submitted bids to the George A. Fuller Co.* (Q 63, p. 247).

He remembers that McNulty Bros. submitted samples of imitation travertine (Q 73, p. 249).

Beginning with Q 74, p. 249 and including Q 92, p. 253, Mr. Webster examined and identified certain documentary exhibits introduced as Defendants' Exhibits 9, 10, 11, 12, 13, 14, 15, 16, 17 and 18. He says that in March, 1910, both Miller and Denivelle submitted a bid for the six map spaces in the Pennsylvania Station (Q 94-5, p. 253). (Note that this was for additional work of the same kind that Denivelle had already done.

Webster testified that at that time (March, 1910) the Denivelle Company had installed quite a lot of imitation travertine (Q. 98, p. 253).

Webster identified other documentary exhibits shown him and introduced as Defendants' Exhibits 19, 20 and 21 (pp. 254-5).

Webster was asked to read "Defendants' Exhibit 20" (carbon copy of a letter from McKim, Mead & White to George A. Fuller Co.), and to state whether the statements therein set forth, as to the condition of the work to be performed by the Denivelle Company was in accordance with his recollection, and he stated that to the best of his knowledge it was (Q 100-1, p. 254).

Webster remembered that a release was procured from the Denivelle Company by the Fuller Co., and he identified "Defendants' Exhibit 7" as that release, stating that he was familiar with Denivelle's signature, and that the signature on that exhibit was that of Denivelle (Q 105-110, pp. 255-6).

Webster identified other exhibits offered in evidence as Defendants' Exhibit 22, 23, 24, 25, 26, 27, 28, 29, 30, 31, 32, 33 and 34, consisting of correspondence between the architects, McKim, Mead & White, and the builders, George A. Fuller Company, and Denivelle in 1910 (record pp. 256-261).

Webster also identified certain bills from the Deni-velle Company and certain other letters introduced as Defendants' Exhibits 36 to 39 inclusive (pp. 262-3).

It will be noted that the bill dated January 7, 1911—Defendants' Exhibit 37—is characterized by Mr. Webster as one for "a minor repair."

Webster also identified "Defendants' Exhibit 4—Bond and Contract"—for the Pennsylvania Station job (Q 150-1, pp. 263-4).

He says that the work done under such bond and contract was under his supervision, representing the architects, McKim, Mead & White (Q 152, p. 264).

Webster testified that it was his duty to see that the work on the Pennsylvania Station job was done in accordance with Denivelle's contract and specifications; that he passed upon the work and approved it; and that it was done in a manner satisfactory to him and his firm as representing the owners of the property (Qs. 160-3, pp. 265-6).

Webster was friendly with Denivelle, and so Mr. Loftus on cross-examination took up the question of experiment. Webster was willing to help Denivelle if he could, but he parried the question, as to whether McKim, Mead & White would undertake "experimental" work in the building of the Pennsylvania Station (xQ 1, p. 266).

But using a little more persuasion, Mr. Loftus got Mr. Webster to state some things were done which suggested "experiment" to him (xQ 3-4, p. 267).

He had Mr. Webster testify that the use of white portland cement was relatively new in 1908, and on cross-examination Mr. Loftus suggested many things to Mr. Webster which might induce Webster to agree with Mr. Loftus that the Pennsylvania job was an experiment. But Mr. Loftus pressed him a little too far when he asked him whether he regarded the travertine work as an experiment, for Webster answerd:

> "That's not for me to say; the question of policy of using materials was determined by the firm, and any architect who does not occasionally experiment with new materials would lead a pretty monotonous existence" (xQ 18, p. 271).

Mr. Loftus was not satisfied, but still wanted this man Webster to characterize this work as an experiment, so he went at him again with the inquiry as to whether or not the firm of McKim, Mead & White had a reputation for introducing novelties in building construction, and Webster's answer was:

> "It did; it was progressive. But it never did so without a trial of the material or getting opinions from experts or others, as to the advisability of using this material. Architecture in general is more or less experimenting with different kinds of materials and models to get the effects the architects wish to obtain." (xQ. 19, p. 271.)

Mr. Loftus was persistent, and in answer to xQ. 21, he got Mr. Webster to tell about some changes and experimentations which Mr. Denivelle carried out and which, this court will note, *related mainly to the apparatus employed, and not to the composition or process embodied in making the imitation travertine* (xQ 21, p. 272).

In answer to xQ 22 (pp. 272-3), Mr. Webster told how Denivelle got the contract instead of McNulty or some of the other bidders, even though the Fuller Company had recommended that the contract be awarded to McNulty Bros.

On re-direct examination Webster testified that the contract for artificial travertine was awarded to Deni-

velle *after he had furnished a satisfactory sample;* that
McNulty Brothers submitted a sample, and Miller submitted a sample; that they all put in bids, but that the
Denivelle Company's bid was the lowest; that the
architects required the use of white *portland cement;
that the sample submitted by Denivelle was sufficient in
color and structure to satisfy the architects that they
could use imitation travertine in the Pennsylvania Station; that if the sample submitted by Denivelle had not
been satisfactory they would not have used imitation
travertine; that the Pennsylvania Station in any part
was no more of an experiment than any other building
designed and constructed by McKim, Mead & White;*
that in all such buildings architects have to experiment
as they go along, to determine different materials, ornamentation and models, etc.; *that there are genuine rules
to follow; that where a new material comes up for consideration you have to be pretty careful;* and that when
the Pennsylvania Station was finally finished and paid
for, and particularly Denivelle's work, *the architects
did not regard it as an experiment; "they were quite
satisfied and so stated to Mr. Denivelle."* It was in
*every way according to the specifications a complete and
satisfactory job, and an architect would not approve a
bill for work done unless he was satisfied that it was a
complete and efficient job.* (RDQs. 1-18, pp. 275-9.)

On re-cross examination Mr. Loftus had Webster
testify as to the novelty of white portland cement and
why it was difficult to use white portland cement as
compared with other cements, and also that Denivelle
had made some repairs or replacements after the contract was concluded. He does not recollect the year, but
he thinks it was about 1912. Afterwards, in answer to
interrogatories by defendants' counsel, *Mr. Webster admitted that such repairs would have to be made in almost
any building where you have expansion cracks* (p. 281).

Mr. Webster, being recalled, testified that the various documentary exhibits which he had identified were written on or about the dates which appear thereon (p. 282).

WILLIAM COOK.

William Cook, was another one of Denivelle's employes who not only worked on the imitation travertine job in the Pennsylvania Station but also went out to California with Denivelle and worked on the Exposition Buildings. He testified that he personally did a piece of the work in the Pennsylvania Station, filling in a section about 12 ft. high and 10 ft. wide, in which is known as applied work (Q 10, p. 285).

He says that when he did this piece of work in the Pennsylvania Station, the rest of the wall—the upper portion of it—had been completed with imitation travertine (Qs. 12-13, p. 285).

He says he went to California in 1913 and was employed on the Exposition Buildings from September 1913 to May 1915.

Cook's testimony is interesting because he worked on an imitation. travertine job for Denivelle in connection with the Robert Goelet house. He also worked on an imitation travertine job for Mr. Denivelle in 1915—the Astor Market at 95th Street and Broadway, New York City (Qs. 15-17, p. 286, Qs. 30-32, p. 287).

He testified that the imitation travertine work done by Mr. Denivelle and upon which he was employed in the Pennsylvania Station and in the Goelet House and the Astor Market, was all of the same character, varying only in the texture of the so-called "stippling" to produce the holes or vermiculations. He says he worked on the Goelet House in 1912 (Qs. 35-37, p. 238; Qs. 41-46, p. 289).

On cross-examination, Cook was asked to describe the conditions under which the work was done in the Pennsylvania Station, to show that it was not open to the public while the work was going on, which of course is immaterial on the question of public use and sale. He was also taken in cross-examination over the alleged difficulties had with the contractors, including MacGruer & Simpson of San Francisco. *He reiterated that the travertine work on Machinery Hall was done under the instructions of Denivelle, and that part of his duty was to show MacGruer & Simpson's workmen how to do this imitation travertine work.* And Mr. Loftus had him say that they had considerable difficulty with the workmen on the Exposition Buildings, as they were opposed to it; that he had never seen any imitation travertine before the Pennsylvania Station job; and that he thought Denivelle, in taking the Pennsylvania Station job, was taking an awful chance. He says he never made any repairs on the travertine work in the Pennsylvania Station but that he believed Denivelle had men working there at different times—he couldn't tell just what dates.

We submit that none of the testimony on cross-examination is sufficient to warrant a conclusion that Denivelle was engaged in an experiment, but on the contrary, as we shall at large discuss later in this brief, the fact that Denivelle did the Ottawa Station, the Vanderbilt Hotel Bar, the Goelet House, the Astor Market, the 23rd Street job, the Evans Museum at Philadelphia, and the Exposition Buildings shortly after finishing the Pennsylvania Station job, shows that if that job was ever an experiment, it had ceased to be an experiment when he took these other jobs.

WALTER H. CLOUGH.

Mr. Clough at the time the Pennsylvania Station work was done, was connected with the George A. Fuller Company, having been with that company from 1900 until the Fall of 1916, and was superintendent of construction and manager of the Philadelphia office, and assistant general manager in charge of the New York construction, and later became vice-president of that company (Qs. 1-6, p. 416).

He was chief executive in charge of the Pennsylvania Station work for the George A. Fuller Company, and had supervision of that construction (Qs. 9-12, p. 417).

Concerning the work done by Denivelle or his company in the Pennsylvania Station, Mr. Clough identified "Defendants' Exhibit 40," comprising 53 sheets of paper, all secured by four large paper fasteners, included in which was a letter from the Denivelle Hydraulic Composite Stone Co. dated *March 9, 1909*, to George A. Fuller Company, and a copy of the contract between the Denivelle Company and the George A. Fuller Company dated the *5th day of March, 1909*. Mr. Clough identified these papers, stating that he executed the contract on behalf of the Fuller Company (Qs. 14-17, pp. 417-8).

He said those papers constituted a part of the archives of the George A. Fuller Company (Q 23, p. 419).

Referring to the letter from the Denivelle Hydraulic Composite Stone Company dated *March 9, 1909*, Mr. Clough said that that letter was the basis of the negotiations for the Denivelle contract (Q 25, p. 419).

He said that it was the custom of the Fuller Company to collect all papers bearing on a particular contract, and attach them to the contract (Q 26, p. 420). (These papers are introduced as "Defendants' Exhibit 40—Fuller file.")

Mr. Clough further testified that in addition to the bid received from the Denivelle Company, the Fuller Company received bids from other concerns. He was

shown "Defendants' Exhibit 7—Denivelle Release"—
and stated the effect of such release to be *"that the
work was completed in accordance with the contract and
to the satisfaction of the builders and the architects"*
(Q 35, p. 421, italics ours).

He explains that the giving of the maintenance bond
would not indicate that the work was incomplete, but
only required that defects occurring within a limited
time be repaired without cost to the owners or contractors, and that excepting for such repairs the job was
complete (Qs. 37-40, p. 422).

On cross-examination, Mr. Clough was asked to name
others who had submitted samples of artificial travertine, and he named Miller and McNulty (xQ 44, p. 423).

Clay M. McClure.

Mr. McClure was also an employe of McKim, Mead &
White on the Pennsylvania Station job, being superintendent in charge of erection of the building, working
with Mr. Webster.

He recalls the imitation travertine work done by the
Denivelle Company, and that as a preliminary to that
work specifications were submitted by the office of Mc-
Kim, Mead & White and several were invited to prepare
and submit samples, those submitting samples being
Denivelle, Miller and McNulty (Q 17, p. 427).

He indicated the place where the samples were to be
installed and tells where they were installed. He said
that after they were installed they were inspected by
the office of McKim, Mead & White (Qs. 21-3, p. 428).

Asked as to whether or not that imitation travertine
work would be characterized as an "experiment," his
answer was:

> "I think to refer to it as experimental work is
> very foolish; very sad. It was the beginning, so

far as I know, of the imitation work, and in a
sense might be referred to as such. We now make
it much better but it would never have been allowed to be put in there if we didn't think it was
something more—more definite—more than an
experiment. It was intended to be a fair and
square proposition, and we were satisfied that it
was such or it would have never gone in, I am
confident. We believed then, as we still believe,
that it was a fair representation of the stuff—the
real travertine stone from Italy. I don't think
that McKim, Mead & White could be induced to
place that, or any other product, in a building of
such magnitude and monumental nature, on a
purely experimental basis; they might try it on a
small insignificant house where the display (out-
lay?), etc., is of small moment, but on the
other hand, on a building of this character, I
think it was out of the question'' (Q 24, p. 428).

On this point, the answer of Mr. McClure to Q 27 is
illuminating. (See also Qs. 28-29, p. 432.)

On cross-examination, Mr. McClure was taken over
the question as to who had charge of the work, and
whether Mr. Webster was his superior, and what materials were employed in making the imitation travertine, by Denivelle. He was asked whether or not white
portland cement in 1909 was a new product, and he
stated that it was not very old but had been used many
years before (xQs. 16-19, p. 434).

He was asked on cross-examination to tell why he did
not regard the use of artificial travertine in the Pennsylvania Station as an experiment, and he explains fully in
answer to xQ 23 and xQ 24 why that was so. He says
architects and builders do not regard white portland
cement as being any different from ordinary portland
cement. He admitted that there were unusual conditions in the Pennsylvania Station, too numerous to men-

tion, but he says *they were all taken into consideration when the plans were drawn* (xQs. 45-8, pp. 439-40).

He saw Denivelle making imitation travertine stone in the Pennsylvania Station (xQ 55, p. 440).

JACOB N. KRAFFT.

Jacob N. Krafft was connected with McNulty Bros. from 1902-1918 (Q 10, p. 87).

McNulty Brothers went into bankruptcy in 1918. P. H. McNulty, head of that concern at one time, died in 1916. Mr. Krafft remembers that McNulty Brothers made a sample of imitation travertine and installed it in the Pennsylvania Station in 1909 (Qs. 23-6, p. 89).

His recollection is that four concerns were invited to experiment in the production of an imitation of travertine for the Pennsylvania Station on condition that a bid for the work be submitted simultaneously with the sample, and that the successful bidder, or the one who got the contract, would pay to each of the others who submitted samples, the sum of $200 (Q 29, p. 90).

He says that H. W. Miller and Denivelle and Mc-Nulty Brothers and one other, submitted samples and bids to the George A. Fuller Company (Qs, 30-2, pp. 90-1).

He is acquainted with Denivelle and knows that Denivelle got the contract and paid McNulty Brothers the sum of $200 (Q 42, p. 92).

McNulty Brothers had a contract with the George A. Fuller Company in 1912 for the Widener Building in Philadelphia, that work being in charge of Mr. Massimo employed by McNulty Brothers, and required the use of imitation travertine.

Certain information upon which Mr. Krafft based his deposition was obtained by him from P. G. Moore, Jr., who had formerly been the bookkeeper for McNulty

Bros., and who is now employed by the estate of P. H.
McNulty, having charge of the books at 549 West 52nd
Street, New York City (Q 73, p. 100).

Mr. Krafft on cross-examination, testified that it was
his impression that the sample of imitation travertine
submitted by McNulty Bros. for the Pennsylvania Station *was left in place, for there was no reason why it
should not have been, as it was in proper position and
a good imitation* (xQs. 44-5, p. 108).

He says that the sample was made in accordance with
the plans and specifications, and he describes accurately
where it was placed in the Pennsylvania Station (Qs.
55-69, pp. 108-110).

Mr. Krafft also testifies concerning the payment of
$200 by Denivelle to the McNulty Company in accord-
ance with the terms of the bidding (xQs. 75-9, pp. 110-1).

Mr. Krafft also testifies concerning the difficulty with
Denivelle, who charged that the imitation travertine
which was incorporated by McNulty Bros. in the Widener Building in Philadelphia, was an infringement of the
Denivelle patent (xQs. 80-8, pp. 111-2).

(NOTE: At the time Denivelle made this charge of infringement he *had no patent,* but had filed an application for a patent on the apparatus, which application
became abandoned and never matured into a patent.)

CARL HENRY MEYN.

Carl Henry Meyn was formerly employed by H. W.
Miller, Inc. He testified that the Miller Company had
a contract for all the plastering in the Pennsylvania
Station (Q 16, p. 122).

He further testified that the Miller Company installed
a sample of imitation travertine in the Pennsylvania
Station and that he was in charge of the making of this
sample and its installation; and that it was installed in

the rotunda of the arcade leading to the main waiting room from the Seventh Avenue entrance; and that it was in the form of a section of the entablature (Qs. 18-28, pp. 122-3).

He says that it was placed in position alongside of samples submitted by other firms—the Denivelle Hydraulic Composite Stone Company and McNulty Bros. (Qs. 30-1, p. 123); that the Miller Company received its instructions regarding the installation of this sample from McKim, Mead & White, the architects; and that in its construction the Miller Company had a sample of natural travertine stone which had been given to them by the architects; and that the samples were made with the idea of getting a large contract for such imitation travertine stone; that the Miller Company submitted a bid for that work on estimates made up by the witness, the bid being submitted to the George A. Fuller Company (Qs. 34-7, p. 124); that the Miller Company failed to get the contract which was given to the Denivelle Company; and that the George A. Fuller Company paid the Miller Company $200. Mr. Meyn testified that he had known Denivelle for about 20 years; that he was present in the Pennsylvania Station when the Denivelle Company was installing its imitation travertine; and that to the best of his recollection it was in the early part of 1909 (Qs. 47-8, p. 125).

According to Mr. Meyn, the bidders, other than the Miller Co., on the imitation travertine work in the Pennsylvania Station, were McNulty Bros. and the Denivelle Company.

In the preparation of the Miller bid he worked from specifications and plans secured from the George A. Fuller Company, and he remembers Daniel T. Webster as being the superintendent on the job for the architects, McKim, Mead & White (Qs. 52-5, p. 126).

It is interesting to note Mr. Meyn's description of how the Miller specimen of imitation travertine was made. From this it appears that they tried salt to obtain the holes or vermiculations, casting the plastic material over grains of salt which were subsequently washed out of the completed cast. They also used crumbs of semi-dry material spread on a slab, over which was poured the veins and the body color. He says that the specimen installed by the Miller Co. was made by the latter method (Qs. 56-7, pp. 126-7).

He says that the McNulty sample, the Denivelle sample and the Miller sample were all located in the same arcade; they were all under installation at the same time (Qs. 58-9, p. 127). (See also Qs. 92-105, pp. 131-3 for a full description of how the Miller specimen of imitation travertine for the Pennsylvania Station was made.)

Another method of making imitation travertine is set forth in answer to xQs. 46-47, p. 140, wherein particles of paraffin were used for making the holes.

On cross-examination Mr. Meyn states that the Miller sample was made of white portland cement, and that it was made in three pieces, the total dimensions being 6 ft. square (xQs. 48-51, p. 140).

He reiterates his testimony that all the samples— Miller, Denivelle and McNulty—were being installed at the same time (xQ 72, pp. 142-3).

He identifies Defendants' Exhibit 1 as the specifications upon which the Miller bids were based (RDQs. 3-4, p. 147).

Louis S. Massimo.

Mr. Massimo, at the time he testified, was employed by the Miller Company. He had formerly worked for McNulty Bros. for a period of 15 years extending from 1903-1918 (Qs. 8-12, p. 298).

He is acquainted with Mr. Denivelle, he and Denivelle having been employed by H. Berger & Sons many years ago. While with McNulty Bros. he had to do with the imitation travertine specimen installed by that company in the Pennsylvania Station in 1909 (Qs. 20-2, p. 299).

He says that specimen was put in the arcade leading in from Seventh Avenue, and describes it as a part of the cornice—an angle piece—and he remembers that at the time that was installed by McNulty Bros. he saw Miller's sample and Denivelle's sample (Qs. 26-34, p. 300).

He describes the Denivelle and Miller samples as being the same form of mitered or angled piece as the McNulty sample. He states that the object of McNulty Bros. submitting the sample was for getting the contract for the entire work of imitation travertine; and that McNulty Bros. submitted a bid for that work (Qs. 43-44, p. 302).

He says that the McNulty sample was made by Giobbe, from a mixture of Keene's cement and coloring, and *embodied crumbly material pressed or cast on a glue mold of a "creamish" color—the color of real travertine—with veinings of lighter material than the body and some darker, and having holes in the strata* (Qs. 47-9, p. 302).

McNulty did not get the contract but was paid by the Denivelle Company the sum of $200 (Qs. 53-5, p. 303).

While with McNulty Bros. he furnished imitation travertine and installed it in the Widener Building in Philadelphia. The material comprised blocks approximately 16 inches high, 2 feet wide, and 1¼ inches thick, which blocks were made on the premises. In answer to Q. 76, p. 366, he tells how the Widener imitation travertine blocks were made.

There is a still further description of how the Widener blocks were made, at pp. 307-8 of the record.

Mr. Massimo tells about the letter from Denivelle, in which it was charged that the work on the Widener Building, constituted an infringement of the Denivelle patent; and how he invited Denivelle to go to Philadelphia and witness just how the Widener imitation travertine blocks were being made; and he states that this was between April 1915 and September 1915, at which time the Widener Building was finished (Qs. 97-106, pp. 309-312).

Mr. Massimo saw the main waiting room of the Pennsylvania Station when Denivelle was installing the imitation travertine therein.

On cross-examination, Mr. Massimo details the circumstances surrounding the conversation with Denivelle on the question of infringement, and identifies a letter dated June 14, 1915, introduced in evidence as ''Plaintiff's Exhibit B,'' said letter being the one sent by Denivelle to McNulty (xQs. 124-6; p. 314).

PETER G. MOORE.

Mr. Peter G. Moore was examined and produced books in his charge belonging to McNulty Bros., in which were found items showing that the McNulty sample for the Pennsylvania Station was made in the latter part of 1908 (Q. 34, p. 409); and that Denivelle paid the sum of $200 to McNulty Bros. in June, 1909 (Q. 40, p. 42).

The books also showed entries in connection with the Widener Building in Philadelphia, showing that the contract for that building was made in April 1914.

SAMUEL L. KRINEY.

Mr. Kriney was employed by McNulty Bros. from 1902 until 1917, and he remembers the sample of artificial travertine installed by McNulty in the Pennsylvania Station. He describes it as a mitered sample, and tells where it was placed in the Pennsylvania Station (Qs. 10-19, pp. 450-1).

He also remembers that considerable imitation travertine was installed in the Widener Building by McNulty Bros. (Q 24, p. 452).

The court will have noticed frequent references to other imitation travertine work done by Denivelle about the time he finished the Pennsylvania Station. This work may be enumerated as follows:

Railroad Station, Ottawa, Canada.......... 1911
Barroom, Vanderbilt Hotel, N. Y............ 1911
Robert Goelet House, Goshen, N. Y......... 1912
Job at 23rd St. near Broadway, N. Y........ 1912
Evans Museum, Philadelphia, Pa............ 1914
Astor Market, Broadway near 96th St., N. Y.. 1915

Reference has been made in some of the depositions which have been considered concerning the Goelet house, but we will now briefly refer to the deposition of Mr. Shreve.

RICHMOND H. SHREVE.

Mr. Shreve is an architect, a member of the firm of Carrere & Hastings, and was in the employ of that firm at the time the Goelet house was under construction. Briefly, his testimony is that *the installation of artificial travertine in the Goelet house was done by Denivelle under contract dated April 4, 1912,* and he identified various exhibits, consisting of letters from the Denivelle Company and copies of letters from Carrere & Hastings, all introduced in evidence as "Defendants' Exhibit 2" (Qs. 15-22, pp. 151-3).

Mr. Shreve says concerning the Goelet house, that he dealt with the contract, gave orders for the work, recalled all the rules of its being executed, and saw it in place; that that contract was executed by the Denivelle Company and Denivelle was paid for it; and that the work was *complete in 1913* (Qs. 23-5, pp. 153-4).

He says that his firm of Carrere & Hastings was represented on that job by J. F. Gaylor and Vance Torbert.

Referring to a memorandum which had been taken from the books of Carrere & Hastings, payments were made on the Goelet house to the Denivelle Company over a period extending from *August 1912* to June 1914 (see record, p. 167); and he states that the contract for the imitation travertine in the Goelet house was given to Denivelle by the owner on the advice of Carrere & Hastings *because of the imitation travertine work which Denivelle had done in the Pennsylvania Station* (RDQ 66, pp. 164-5).

Julius F. Gaylor.

Mr. Julius F. Gaylor, as an employe of Carrere & Hastings, was in charge of the work on the Goelet house, and Denivelle had the contract for the stucco and imitation travertine work (Qs. 17-20, p. 222).

He identified "Defendants' Exhibit 2"—correspondence between the Denivelle Company and Carrere & Hastings—(Q 24, p. 223) and pointed out his initials "J. F. G." on several of those documents.

Referring to the memorandum which had been produced by Mr. Gaylor, showing the dates of payments to Denivelle, Mr. Gaylor testified that on the respective dates such payments had been made to the Denivelle Company (Q 41, p. 227).

Mr. Gaylor said he negotiated the contract for the Goelet house with Denivelle, and that in such negotiations *Denivelle called his attention to the imitation travertine work which Denivelle had done in the Pennsylvania Station, and that he went to the station to inspect that work before the contract was given to Denivelle, and at that time the station job was completed* (Qs. 42-7, p. 228).

It will be noted that Denivelle's contract for the Goelet House was made in April, 1912, so it was prior to that date that Mr. Gaylor saw the finished product installed by Denivelle in the Pennsylvania Station. But more important is the fact that Denivelle used this Pennsylvania Station job as a reference or specimen of his work to induce the granting of the Goelet contract to him.

Mr. Gaylor testified to installing imitation travertine in the Goelet house in the hall *by using the workmen of the general contractor* (Qs. 55-60, pp. 229-30).

The Court will note that at the time Denivelle was carrying out his Goelet House contract, Mr. Gaylor and the general contractor were also installing imitation travertine in another part of the Goelet House. This will have an important bearing on the question of abandonment which will be discussed hereinaftter.

Mr. Gaylor states that the Denivelle job on the Goelet house was completed to his satisfaction, and to that of Carrere & Hastings (Q 70, p. 232).

Vance W. Torbert.

Mr. Torbert was also called as a witness, and he corroborated Mr. Shreve and Mr. Gaylor concerning Denivelle's imitation travertine work on the Goelet house (p. 187).

Concerning the work on the Ottawa Railroad Station, both Mr. Webster and Mr. Whipple testified, as has been shown. Mr. Whipple also testified concerning Denivelle's imitation travertine work on the 23rd Street job in New York, and Mr. Cook testified concerning the Denivelle imitation travertine job in the Astor market. The barroom in the Vanderbilt Hotel was done by Deniville in imitation travertine, as shown by the depositions of Davis Brown and Walter L. Hopkins.

DAVIS BROWN.

Referring to Mr. Brown's testimony, we find that Denivelle and Brown were apprentice boys with Morrison, 29 or 30 years ago. Mr. Brown had the plastering contract for the Vanderbilt Hotel. He knew that in addition to Denivelle, McNulty Bros. and Miller had bid on the Pennsylvania Station job (Qs. 17-18, p. 500).

His testimony concerning the Denivelle imitation travertine in the barroom of the Vanderbilt Hotel can be found in Q 25, p. 502; and *he says the hotel was opened in December* 1911, *so that the barroom with its imitation travertine finish was completed before that* (Q 33, p. 503).

In passing it will be noted that Davis Brown did the *Lord & Taylor Building in New York in imitation travertine in* 1913. He says that was a monumental job. As a matter of fact, the entire store covering nearly a block of ground, has an interior finish on the first floor anyway, of imitation travertine.

PATRICK J. DURKIN.

In the deposition of Mr. Durkin we will find testimony concerning *Denivelle's imitation travertine work in the Evans Museum in Philadelphia, which was done in* 1914 by a contract dated July 9, 1914 (Q 22, p. 489).

Mr. Durkin permitted certain pages to be removed from his books showing the entries relating to this work done by Denivelle or his company, and they were introduced as "Defendants' Exhibits 42 and 43." There can be no possible mistake in this matter.

Argument.

All this work done by Denivelle at or about the time he finished the Pennsylvania Station job, shows conclusively that if that imitation travertine work in the Pennsylvania Station could ever have been regarded as an experiment, as that term is used in the patent law, it must have ceased to be an experiment the very first time that Denivelle made reference to it for the purpose of getting other imitation travertine work to do. He must have been satisfied as early as April 1912 or earlier, that it was no longer an experiment. He calls it an experiment, but of course such a designation is but a self-serving declaration, which is of no avail when his conduct in connection with the taking of other work is taken into consideration. Not only that, but it is *because of this Pennsylvania Station work that Denivelle was invited by the Exposition authorities to go to California in 1913 under contract, to show the contractors and workmen engaged in putting up the Exposition buildings how to make imitation travertine, and he got paid for it.* He held himself out as one who knew how to make imitation travertine because he had done it in the Pennsylvania Station, and they employed him for that reason.

Our contention is that the only experiment that took place in connection with this whole business was when McKim, Mead & White were seeking specimens from almost every plasterer in the City of New York, so that they might convince themselves that the real travertine could be successfully imitated, and that the imitation could be employed in the Pennsylvania Station. By the specimens submitted they were satisfied that this could be done, and accordingly they prepared the specifications calling for imitation travertine.

Now when Denivelle, Miller, McNulty and others, following those specifications, prepared and erected a specimen in this Pennsylvania Station, they were engaged in a contest to get a contract, and it was a contest which did not call for any experiment but simply the taking into consideraton of the conditions set forth in the specifications and the magnitude of the job; and each of them submitted a sample embodying what they regarded as a compliance with the conditions of the specifications, and they bid as low as they could for the work involved.

HENRY A. COUSINS.

One of those to whom McKim, Mead & White resorted in their quest for imitation travertine, was Henry A. Cousins, and his testimony is very interesting and will be briefly referred to.

Mr. Cousins has been in the business of manufacturing artificial stone for 49 years. *He made samples of imitation travertine in* 1908 at the request of the Fuller Company, the builders of the Pennsylvania Station, following a specimen of the genuine travertine which he procured from the Mycenian Marble Company (Qs. 19-21, p. 329). The samples made by Mr. Cousins at the request of the Fuller Company, *were to show how closely an imitation of the genuine could be made,* and they were made in connection with the proposed wall treatment of the Pennsylvania Station (Qs. 23-9, p. 330).

At page 331, Mr. Cousins tells how he made these samples, and the court will note that *they were made in exactly the same manner as set out in the Denivelle patent* (Qs. 30-3, pp. 330-2).

The Cousins samples were delivered to the Fuller Company and apparently the Fuller Company displayed them to other plasterers who were likewise engaged at that time—1908—in producing samples to satisfy the Fuller Company and the architects that a satisfactory imitation travertine could be made and used.

The court will note that these samples were made about *a year preceding the preparation of the specifications* which were submitted to Denivelle, Miller, McNulty and other contractors who bid on the job.

In other words, the Fuller Company and McKim, Mead & White, as early as 1908, were endeavoring to satisfy themselves that they could employ imitation travertine in the Pennsylvania Station, and when they were satisfied that this was so they then prepared—in 1909—the specifications calling for imitation travertine made of white portland cement, and obtained bids for the installation thereof.

Cousins states that his concern figured on the work and made a bid (Qs. 47-8, p. 334).

Since that time, Mr. Cousins has made and installed imitation travertine in 1915 and 1918 in the Dental Dispensary at Rochester, N. Y., and in other buildings (Qs. 56-7, p. 335).

He states that before making these samples for the Fuller Company he made other imitations of stone of the same materials and that travertine was not made by one formula but by many formulae (Qs. 70-1, p. 337).

Counsel for the plaintiff in the court below, in answer to an inquiry from Judge Bourquin as to whether or not it was the contention of plaintiff that claims 9 and 10 would prevent the defendant from making an imitation of travertine, advised the court that those claims did cover broadly the making of imitation travertine, regardless of the method employed—in other words, that no one could produce a sample of travertine stone without infringing the Denivelle patent.

Mr. Cousins describes another method employed by him in making imitation travertine, which he installed in the Cunard Building, New York, and in the Knickerbocker Building, New York (Q 101, p. 341).

Mr. Cousins had given a careful study as an expert, to the Denivelle patent, and (in answer to Q 144, p. 351) he states his understanding of that patent. That the Denivelle patent sets forth only the usual and well-known method of using plaster and cementitious materials in the manufacture of imitation of stone is clearly apparent from Mr. Cousins' deposition, beginning at page 353 to and including page 361 of the record.

It will be particularly noted that Mr. Cousins is of the opinion that the Denivelle patent is mainly devoted to the manufacture of pre-cast blocks of imitation travertine although he says that claim 9 might be interpreted to cover either pre-cast or applied work, but that claim 10 is for applied work. On cross-examination he says that *in 1908 travertine was regarded as a marble and that the imitations thereof were made in the same way that they made artificial marble* (xQ 192, p. 362).

In answer to xQ 215, page 365, Mr. Cousins describes how artificial marble is made.

Tommaso V. Coronato.

The witness, Coronato, was formerly employed by Mr. Cousins when the business was known as the Mycenian Marble Company. He left the employ of Mr. Cousins in 1907 and was away 22 months before he went back again. While he was in the employ of Nickman & Noscenti, he, with his employer Noscenti, went to the Fuller Company's office to see the specimens of imitation travertine, and he was there told that they were made by Mr. Cousins. *He said they went there to see this sample of artificial travertine so that he could make a copy and give it to McNulty as McNulty was figuring on the job* (Q 223, p. 373).

He made a specimen of imitation travertine and it was taken by his employers to McNulty Bros. (Q 228, p. 374), after which he went back to work for Mr. Cousins or the Mycenian Marble Company, in March 1908 (Q 230, p. 374).

Mr. Coronato tells, in answer to Q 243, p. 375, how he made this sample of imitation travertine. (See also Q 254, p. 377.)

Frank J. Morkel.

Mr. Frank J. Morkel has been in the plastering business for 33 years. He testified concerning the use of imitation travertine in the Widener Memorial Library at Cambridge, Mass., in 1914—mostly cast work—and he tells how the castings were made (Qs. 8-11, pp. 388-9).

There was also applied work in the Cambridge Library, and Mr. Morkel tells how that was made (Q 16, p. 389).

In 1913 his employer did a job at the St. Elmo Club at New Haven, of San Quentin stone, which he says has a similar texture and color to travertine, but without the colored veins. (Qs. 17-20, pp. 390-1.)

Mr. Morkel describes what is known as semi-dry material as that term is used in the Denivelle patent (Qs. 34-6, p. 393).

At pages 395 to 397 inclusive, in answer to Q 41, Mr. Morkel describes the manufacture of imitation marble by a method which he says has been used for over 33 years. Compare this method with that of the Denivelle patent.

PHILIP LIVA.

The witness, Liva, at the time he testified, was in the employ of the witness Durkin. He had previously been in the employ of Hammerstein & Denivelle and McNulty Bros. (Q 8, p. 460).

He worked for Hammerstein & Denivelle in 1907 and 1909, and was engaged in making molds for the travertine job of Denivelle in the Pennsylvania Station (Qs. 11-4, pp. 460-1).

Evidently this was before Denivelle obtained the contract and while he was engaged in the manufacture of the specimen which was submitted with his bid, because the witness Liva, says Denivelle tried to have a good system put out for the Pennsylvania Station (Q 31, p. 463).

He left Denivelle's employ because he assumed he was going to get the job of sperintendent, but when it was given to another man he was dissatisfied and left, but he went back to work for Denivelle in 1913 (Q 38, p. 464; also Q 56, p. 466).

After leaving Denivelle he went to work for McNulty Bros. (Qs. 60-2, p. 466).

Mr. Liva testified that McNulty Bros. installed artificial travertine in the Orpheum Theatre in Boston, in 1914 or 1915 (Q 63, p. 466).

Liva also knew of the McNulty work on the Widener Building in Philadelphia (xQ 68-9, p. 467).

WALTER L. HOPKINS

Mr. Hopkins, an architect in the employ of Warren & Wetmore, corroborated the testimony of Davis Brown, as to the work done by Denivelle in the barroom of the Vanderbilt Hotel. Mr. Hopkins was in charge, on behalf of the architects, of the construction of the Vanderbilt Hotel. He says the imitation travertine in the bar-room of the Vanderbilt Hotel was done by Denivelle, and was in no sense regarded as an experiment (Q 27, p. 477).

Mr. Hopkins testified that when a contractor demands and receives payment in full for a job, and the architects authorize payment of his bill, that is an indication that the work has been finished according to the plans and specifications, and to the satisfaction of the architects (Q 28, p. 477).

He says the Vanderbilt Hotel was opened to the public on the 31st day of December, 1911 (Q. 19, p. 476).

Hopkins says that before putting the imitation travertine in the barroom of the Vanderbilt Hotel, he had seen the imitation travertine which had been installed by Denivelle in the Pennsylvania Railroad Station (RDQ 55, p. 484).

John Fincke

Mr. John Fincke testified concerning the installation of imitation travertine in the Campbell Funeral Chapel on Broadway, New York City. This work was done in 1911 or 1912, according to Fincke (Q 8-12, p. 318). Fincke was the builder and Almiroty the architect.

Incidentally, it will be noted that Mr. Fincke states that when the Pennsylvania Station job *"was put on the market for estimating, all the firms in New York City were interested in figuring it and making samples for it* (xQ 75, p. 325).

Randolph H. Almiroty

Mr. Almiroty, the architect for the Campbell Funeral Chapel, fixes the date when that job was done, as between 1915 and 1916, about August 1916 (Q 9-10, p. 455).

He was acquainted with Denivelle, as was also Fincke, and he remembers Denivelle's Pennsylvania Station job. *He says that Denivelle told him all about that contract and took him through the building and showed him the working and process of construction, etc.* (Q 19, p. 455).

The court will particularly note that Mr. Almiroty was shown by Denivelle how the work was being done, and how he was making imitation travertine, while the Pennsylvania Station job was in course of construction (Q 20-5, p. 456).

We refer to this because counsel for the plaintiff sought to bring out on the cross-examination of nearly all the witnesses who knew about the Pennsylvania Station job, that Denivelle's work was carried on in secret, and that the building was not open to the public until 1910 or 1911. We assume this was done with the idea of fixing as late a date as possible when the *use* of imitation travertine installed by Denivelle *became a public use.* All of this seems immaterial to us, and we submit that it is immaterial, for whether or not Denivelle did his work in secret, and whether or not public use of the Station began in 1909, 1910, 1911 or 1912, is immaterial, *our contention being that at the time Denivelle, in competition with others working from plans and specifications submitted by the architects, bid on that work, submitting a sample of it, and at the time he took the contract to do that work—which was in 1909—that then and there he made a public use and sale of a specimen of his invention,* if he ever made an invention. If that is not sufficient, certainly when Denivelle first made a piece of imitation travertine which passed the inspection of Mr. Webster and the architects, and installed it on the wall of that waiting room in the Pennsylvania Station, and was paid for it, that was a sale of his invention. And the documentary evidence showing Denivelle's demands for payments on account of the job, and his receipt of payments thereon, and finally his demand for and receipt of the *final* payment, and the giving of a release, certainly shows a complete use and sale of his invention. ALL OF THESE THINGS TOOK PLACE MORE THAN TWO YEARS BEFORE HE FILED HIS APPLICATION FOR PATENT.

Recapitulation.

As early as 1908, Denivelle and others engaged in the work of ornamental plastering, made samples of artificial travertine at the request of the architects and builders, in order that it might be determined whether such material could be employed in connection with genuine travertine in the Pennsylvania Station. Afterward, in 1909, the architects prepared specifications for this imitation travertine and sought and received bids, the bidders being required to submit a specimen with their bids, prepared and erected in accordance with the plans and specifications. There were four contestants, each of whom submitted and installed a specimen and submitted a bid. These contestants were, besides Denivelle, Miller, McNulty and Mycenian Marble Company. Denivelle was the lowest bidder, and notwithstanding that the general contractors, Fuller & Company, recommended that the contract be awarded to McNulty Bros. *as having submitted the best samples,* even though their bid was higher, Denivelle finally got the contract in March, 1909.

In taking the contract, Denivelle obligated himself to pay to the unsuccessful bidders the sum of $200 each, and this was paid. By the terms of Denivelle's contract, he had to do the work in accordance with the specifications and drawings, and furnish a bond that the work would be so done and *to the satisfaction of the builders and architects,* and *within a certain period.* This will be discussed further in connection with a review of the documentary exhibits—Denivelle's contract, bond, specifications, etc.

After Denivelle had completed his Pennsylvania job he was the successful bidder for work on the Goelet house, and through Mr. Webster he did similar work in the Railroad Station at Ottawa, Canada. Also before going to California in 1913, Denivelle did some imitation travertine work on 23rd Street, New York City; and later in the Astor Market, New York City; the Evans Museum, Philadelphia; and the barroom of the Vanderbilt Hotel in New York. The Goelet house and the barroom of the Vanderbilt Hotel were given to Denivelle to do because of the work which he had done in the Pennsylvania Station.

It seems also that after Denivelle had carried out his contract in the Pennsylvania Station, there was some imitation travertine work to be done around the map spaces in the waiting room, and here again Denivelle was a competing bidder with the Miller Company.

In 1912 Denivelle went out to California under contract with the Exposition authorities, to instruct the various contractors how to make and install imitation travertine, and his testimony is that he did instruct them how to do it; that he got paid for that work, and in his own affidavit we find him stating as follows:

> "Said defendants acting under the directions of affiant became thoroughly familiar with affiant's patented process and product aforesaid during the building of the Panama-Pacific International Exposition, particularly during the years 1913 and 1914, when the said defendants, under the direction of affiant, applied affiant's patented process and product as an exterior covering for

the walls of the Machinery Hall at the Panama-Pacific International Exposition; that said artificial travertine so used on said Machinery Hall was applied by the workmen employed by the said George Smith MacGruer and Robert Morton Simpson, and was done under the supervision and instruction of affiant and assistants'' (record p. 31).

All of this, we contend, shows that Denivelle had put his alleged invention, whatever it was, into public use, and had taken numerous contracts therefor, for which he was paid and by which he profited, long prior—and certainly more than two years prior—to the filing of the application on which his patent issued. And in view of this evidence, this Honorable Court, notwithstanding its previous decision in connection with this patent, should not only affirm the decree of the District Court concerning *the specific claims* mentioned in that decree, but in order to insure that no further suit will be brought on this patent and that no use of it shall be made to intimidate those engaged in the plastering art, it should declare the *entire patent* to be invalid and void *ab initio*. It certainly shows that the Pennsylvania Station job was in no sense an experiment by Denivelle.

In this connection we believe that we are entirely justified in charging Denivelle with perjury when he made the affidavit accompanying his application for patent, and swore that the subject matter had not been in public use or on sale more than two years, and thereby deceived the Patent Office; and that when he testified in the previous suit which was before this Honorable Court on appeal, he did not tell the entire truth, all with the sole purpose of deceiving the trial court.

Denivelle's Contract.

We ask the Court to carefully consider the contract for this Pennsylvania Station work done by Denivelle. It will be noted that this contract was dated March 5, 1909, and was between the Denivelle Hydraulic Composite Stone Company and the George A. Fuller Company.

In the first paragraph it is specified that the work shall be done under the direction of the Fuller Company and McKim, Mead & White, and in accordance with the specifications. It is further provided that the work shall be subject at all times to the inspection and acceptance of the architects, and "at completion, shall be made entirely satisfactory."

The contractor, the Fuller Company, or its agents, shall at all times have free access to the plant of the sub-contractor, the Denivelle Company; and the sub-contractor, the Denivelle Company, shall furnish a bond to the contractor in the sum of $50,000.00.

Under paragraph 3 of this agreement, the Denivelle Company was required to remove all materials condemned by the contractor and to take down all portions of the work which the architects or contractor shall condemn as unsound or improper.

Under paragraph 4 it is provided that the contractor might, under certain contingencies, take possession of the sub-contractor's plant and materials and complete the job.

Under paragraph 8 it is provided that "no certificate given or payment made under this contract, except the final certificate or final payment, shall be conclusive evidence of the performance of this contract either wholly or in part, and that *no payment shall be construed to be in acceptance of defective work or improper materials.*

Under paragraph 9 it is provided that the sub-contractor, the Denivelle Company, "shall repair and make good any damage or fault in the building that may appear within one year *after its completion,* as the result of imperfect or defective work done or materials furnished."

Paragraph 11 provides that the sub-contractor, the Denivelle Company, shall assume and defend against *any patent suits* which might be brought in connection with the installation of the work. (Note that at this time, March, 1909, the subject of patents was called to Denivelle's attention.)

Paragraph 13 provides that "no alterations shall be made in the work shown or described by the drawings and specifications" excepting they be duly authorized.

Paragraph 15 provides that the sub-contractor, the Denivelle Company, shall receive $109,378.00 for this work, and that while the work is progressing, installments of this sum might be paid "upon presentation to the contractor of a written certificate giving quantity of work done and value of the same;" but that 15% shall be withheld until the time of final payment; and that "final payment shall be made within 30 days after this contract is fulfilled."

The agreement then sets forth a schedule of prices on which to base payments as the work progresses.

There is a provision also in the 16th paragraph showing when the various parts of the work shall be completed. The *arcade must be completed by March* 25, 1909, and the *main waiting room by May* 15, 1909; and *"this contract shall be entirely completed within 8 months from the date hereof."*

The faithful performance of this contract was guaranteed by a bond for $50,000 dated the 19th day of April, 1909.

Specifications for Pennsylvania Station Work.

Having seen from the foregoing reference to the
Denivelle agreement or contract and bond, that Denivelle was required to do the work in accordance with
the specifications submitted by the architects, and under
the supervision of the architects and builders, it will
now be of interest to examine those specifications.

At page 5 of the copy of the specifications (introduced as Defendants' Exhibit 1), concerning the materials to be employed, it is to be noted that "all artificial stone, either granite or *travertine,* shall be composed of a high grade white portland cement, pure
white quartz, iron oxide, "Vulcanite" or an equally
good portland cement and clean, sharp sand with iron
reinforcements where necessary. And, further, "all
artificial stone shall be of a hard material to match in
color and texture the real stone, and the color in every
case shall be a body color and not a wash."

Under the heading "Samples" at page 6 of the specification, it is required that "the contractor shall submit
to the architects with his estimate, samples at least
4 feet by 4 feet in area, of the artificial granite and
Roman travertine he proposes to furnish. These samples shall be left with the architects until the completion
of the building. *All artificial granite and travertine furnished by the contractor for the building, shall equal
the approved samples.*

It will be further noted under the heading, "Models—
Ornaments, Etc.," that full plaster models must be
provided by the contractor and set in place.

Under the heading of "Repairs" at page 7, it is
provided—"the contractor to make all repairs to the
work of this contract and turn same over to the owners
in perfect condition." And on the same page, under the

heading "Guaranty," the contractor is held responsible for any must make good any defects arising within one year after completion and acceptance of the work.

The remainder of the specification is devoted to specifying the extent of real and artificial travertine which is to be employed, and describing certain drawings, and specifying where the real and artificial travertine is to be located. Obviously, Denivelle's bid, based on these specifications, was for only the imitation travertine.

Comparison of This Case With Prior Case.

This Court will probably be told by counsel for the plaintiff that this case is based upon the same defenses that were involved in the prior case, so far as public use and sale is concerned, but we do not believe that we shall have to dwell at great length to show this Court that even if that were so, it is a very different case from the prior case.

In the present case there appears the testimony of witnesses of unimpeachable character, who have no interest in this litigation whatsoever, comprising the architects and the builders and workmen under whose direction and supervision the Denivelle imitation travertine was installed in the Pennsylvania Station. And we we have in this case, what was not in the prior case at all—a great mass of documentary evidence, including the specifications for the Pennsylvania Station work, the contract and bond under which that work was done, and memoranda showing payments to Denivelle upon the builder's certificates that certain of the work had been done; and finally, the last and final payment and release executed by Denivelle; all of which, we contend, shows beyond any question of a doubt that Denivelle had completed this work and made a sale of it as early as 1909, certainly as early as 1910, which was more than two years before he filed his application for patent.

In this case, as in the former case, Denivelle alone testified for the plaintiff. It was his testimony in the former case which influenced this court to hold that his work in the Pennsylvania Station was an experiment and not a public use or a public sale.

In addition, we have shown that about the time Denivelle finished his Pennsylvania Station job, and before he went to California in 1912, he made quite an extensive use of his invention, having done the Goelet house; the Station at Ottawa, Canada; the building on 23d Street, New York; the Astor market; the barroom of the Vanderbilt Hotel; and the Evans Museum at Philadelphia; and that in 1913, still looking for business, and because of the reputation which he had acquired for making a satisfactory imitation of travertine, he was employed by the Panama-Pacific Exposition authorities under salary to proceed to California and teach the various contractors how to produce imitation travertine; and this he says he did.

In his testimony in the prior case and in the affidavit introduced in evidence in this case, he shows clearly that *it was imitation travertine embodying his alleged invention*—if invention there be in this patent—*in the Pennsylvania Station and also in the buildings of the Panama-Pacific Exposition.*

We shall reserve for a later portion of this brief, a discussion of the law on this question, and while of course we take no exception to the law as laid down by the Supreme Court of the United States in the *Elizabeht Pavement* case, upon which this Honorable Court based its decision in the prior suit, yet whether or not a thing actually used in public is a public use, or whether a device which has been sold more than two years before

an application was filed can be regarded as a sale and
a public use of a complete invention, does not and obviously cannot rest solely upon whether the use took
place in public and by the public; the question is
whether it was complete at the time it was put into
use, and whether it was complete at the time the sale
or offer for sale was made, and not an experiment. An
offer to sell is just as effective as an actual sale to
invalidate the patent.

Denivelle Abandoned His Invention.

Here is a defense which was not discussed at all in
the prior suit. The law provides, as has been pointed
out, that the patentee may obtain a patent under certain conditions *providing he has not abandoned it to the
public.* Now, abandonment is something that may be
proven by the acts of the individual in and about the
same, and on this point we call attention to the fact that
*Denivelle stood by without protest and permitted other
plasterers to compete with him to get the Pennsylvania
Station job, on the identical specifications under which
he made his installation, and made no claim at any time
that such specifications covered an invention to which
he asserted exclusive right.* Further than this, after
Denivelle had practically completed the work in the Pennsylvania Station, he and Miller were again competitive
bidders for finishing the wall about the map spaces in
the Pennsylvania Station with artificial travertine.
*Still no protest from Denivelle that he was the inven-
tor of the subject matter of this patent.*

He must have known of Davis Brown's installation
of imitation travertine in the Lord & Taylor Building,
for this was a monumental department store building on
Fifth Avenue in the City of New York, covering the entire block from 38th to 39th Streets.

He must have known of the Fincke work in Campbell's
Undertaking rooms; and he must have known that these

people who were competing with him for the Pennsylvania Station work would naturally bid on and install artificial travertine wherever it was required for others.

The only protest that Denivelle ever made until he brought the suit against Ceriat and others, was when he protested to McNulty Bros. in 1915, in connection with the work which they were doing on the Widener Building, and *at that time he had no patent* but merely a pending application which has since become abandoned, covering mainly the multiple spouted container with which Denville formed the colored lines or striae and the method of forming such lines by the use of the same container. He was promptly challenged on this complaint and sent a representative down to Philadelphia, to see how the Widener work was being done. It appears, from Mr. Massimo's testimony, that it was being done *in exactly the manner in which the travertine is made in accordance with Denivelle's later patent, the one here in suit;* and yet Denivelle had not as yet applied for that patent.

Because of Denivelle's inactivity and his failure to assert his rights to this alleged invention, he permitted others to engage in the manufacture of travertine and did not claim the alleged invention or seek a patent therefor, until after he had ascertained what McNulty was doing in Philadelphia.

All of this, we submit, is sufficient to show that Denivelle abandoned his invention *long before* he applied for the patent here in suit, assuming for the sake of argument that he had in fact made an invention.

Incidentally, the attention of the court is called to the fact that the Lord & Taylor building, in which imitation travertine was installed by Davis Brown, was done early in 1913, more than two years before the application for the patent here in suit was filed.

If a device is in an experimental state it makes no difference how long it may be in public use or used by the public before application for patent be made, but *it must clearly appear*, as in the *Elizabeth Pavement* case, that *it is in an experimental state*. If in an experimental state, it is immaterial when it was introduced into public use.

There was considerable evidence brought out by the plaintiff on cross-examination of defendants' witnesses, directed to showing that the work in the Pennsylvania Station was done behind closed doors, and that the public was not admitted until the building was finished and opened to the public; and to fix the date when the Goelet house was finished and occupied; and concerning the completion of the Exposition Buildings and the Widener Memorial Library at Cambridge, which was done by the Klee-Thompson Company; and when the Vanderbilt Hotel in which Denivelle finished the barroom, was opened to the public—all that is immaterial to the issues here raised. If it can be found that Denivelle, in all the work which he did, including the Pennsylvania Station work; the Railroad Station at Ottawa; the Goelet house; the Astor market; the Evans Museum at Philadelphia; the building on 23rd Street, New York; and finally the Exposition Buildings was merely experimenting,—which seems inconceivable to us in view of the evidence—it is absolutely immaterial when that work was completed; when the buildings were finished and occupied or opened to the public, or to what extent they were used by the public.

We have Mr. Townsend's statement in his opening in the court below, that the Pennsylvania Station "was completed and first opened to the public in *the early part of* 1910" (record, p. 533).

Another significant statement of Mr. Townsend in his opening in the court below, is as follows:

"So that in the end of 1912, in December, Mr. Denivelle came to the Coast, at the invitation of the Exposition authorities, told them what he believed he could produce, and that he had put this work in the Pennsylvania Station, and that as an architecturally enduring matter it was a question of time as to how it was going to come out. However, it so impressed the authorities that they agreed to adopt the Denivelle method of surfacing the Exposition buildings with artificial travertine, as it early became known by that name" (record, p. 534).

The only doubt was *whether it was architecturally enduring?* Now that same doubt as to architectural endurance may be said to apply to any structure. No man could have foretold that the Pyramids of Egypt would have shown the architectural endurance which has kept them practically intact for centuries. It is well-known, and no doubt this court will take judicial notice of the fact, that all plastering and stucco jobs will in time develop cracks and need repairs. Sometimes this occurs sooner than expected, in fact brick and stone structures, because of a faulty foundation perhaps, develop similar cracks and imperfections. Indeed, we urge that Denivelle, when he took the job to finish the Station at Ottawa, Canada, in the same manner in which he had finished the Pennsylvania Station, was satisfied that the thing was complete, although there as in any other case, its architectural endurance was uncertain. This job at Ottawa, was done by Denivelle in 1911, and the Goelet house followed shortly after.

But as before stated, the date when any of these jobs was finished is immaterial, it being conceded by all parties that the Pennsylvania Station job and many

other jobs done by Denivelle, occurred more than two
years before the filing of the application for the patent
here at issue.

It is to Denivelle's interest of course, for him to contend that all of this work which preceded the filing of
his application for patent, was experimental work, but
can this court agree with that contention in view of the
evidence submitted by the defendants, and in view of
the law as it is found in the decisions of the Supreme
Court of the United States and other Federal Courts?

This Honorable Court in its previous decision on this
patent, quotes at large from the case of *Elizabeth* v.
Pavement Co. (97 U. S. 126, 24 L. Ed. 1000). In that
quotation we call attention to the following:

> "Any attempt to use it (his invention) for
> profit, and not by way of experiment, for a longer
> period than two years before the application,
> would deprive the inventor of his right to a
> patent."

Other Cases Relied on By Defendants.

We think that it might be of assistance to this Honorable Court at this time to discuss the cases relied on
by the defendants here in the court below, and to
compare some of those cases with the *Elizabeth Pavement* case, and we feel convinced that this court will
agree with us and the court below that *Denivelle had
completed his invention at the time he installed the first
piece of artificial travertine in the Pennsylvania Station,
and that he made a sale or an offer to sell a specimen
of that invention at the time he put in his bid accompanied by a sample made in accordance with the specifications prepared by the architect.*

It is not open to Denivelle to contend that this Pennsylvania Station work does not embody the invention

set forth in his patent, for he has maintained from the very beginning that such was the fact. His contract with the builders of the Pennsylvania Station, as we have shown, was awarded early in 1909—in March of that year—and he was required to complete that job within eight months, and some portions of it within a lesser time. He did not file his application for the patent here at issue until October 20, 1915, although he had filed an application on the 2nd of August, 1913, which application was abandoned. (This latter application is Defendants' Exhibit 25, record p. 594.)

The Supreme Court of the United States in *Root* v. *Third Avenue Rwy.* (146 U. S. 221, 36 L. E. 946), clearly distinguishes that case from the *Elizabeth Pavement* case. In the *Elizabeth Pavement* case *the inventor conducted his experiment at his own expense,* and while it was conducted in public over a period of years—as it must have been in order to determine whether or not it was a satisfactory thing—it was nevertheless during all that period an experiment. In the *Root* case, as here, those engaged in the construction of a public utility sought the services of one skilled in the art, and that person claims to have solved the problem. On his plans and specifications he was given a contract to construct a cable railway in San Francisco. It was constructed and he was paid for it.

Denivelle or his Company, on plans and specifications, offered to furnish imitation travertine. It was furnished, and he or his Company was paid for it. Unlike the *Root* case, in the present case there were three other competitive bidders with Denivelle, each of whom submitted a specimen prepared in accordance with the specifications and offered to do the work.

The Supreme Court in the *Root* case, very properly held that the patent was invalid because of a public use

and sale more than two years before the application was
filed, and on this case alone we venture to believe that
this court will come to a different conclusion from that
which it expressed in its previous decision. This case
was not before this court in the *Ceriat* case.

There is another decision of the Supreme Court of
the United States which we believe will be of interest to
this Honorable Court, and that is *International Tooth
Crown Co.* v. *Gaylord* (140 U. S. 55, 35 L. E. 347). In
that case the inventor of a tooth crown, a practicing
dentist, having successfully used the device in his own
practice, *went about the country, and for a consideration
taught other dentists how to make tooth crowns in accordance with his invention, and received pay for such
instruction.* He did this more than two years before
he applied for his patent, and when he tried to enforce
his patent against alleged infringers, they raised this
defense of two years' public use and sale.

Here, again, there is a marked similarity between the
case at bar and the *Tooth Crown* case. Denivelle made
quite a reputation with his imitation travertine in the
Pennsylvania Station. It led directly to his obtaining
other work, for instance, the Ottawa Station, the Goelet
house, the barroom in the Vanderbilt Hotel, and the
Evans Museum in Philadelphia. It induced the Exposition authorities to send for Denivelle, and they employed him to teach various contractors who were at
work making the imitation stucco finish for the walls
of the Exposition buildings, how to make imitation travertine; and this took place in the latter part of 1912
and early in 1913. And Denivelle did teach them how
to make imitation travertine (so he says), and he got
paid for it as in the *Tooth Crown* case. It comes with
bad grace from Denivelle, to characterize his work as
an experiment.

We also call attention to the decisions of the Supreme Court of the United States in *Consolidated Fruit Jar* v. *Wright,* 94 U. S. 92, 24 L. Ed. 68, and in *Egbert* v. *Lipman,* 104 U. S. 333, 26 L. Ed. 755.

It is immaterial that Denivelle claims he made changes in the work as he went along. The fact is he was required to do that work *in accordance with his contract* and *to the satisfaction of the architects and builders,* and it was required that *it should be in accordance with the sample which Denivelle had submitted with his bid.* It nowhere appears that he changed the method of putting the ingredients together, or the ingredients. His experiments mainly were directed *to devising means or apparatus* for producing the blocks of imitation travertine, and he later applied for a patent on the device for forming the colored lines and the method of forming such lines by the use of that apparatus. But assuming that there were changes, such changes do not convert a completed invention into an experimental device.

In *Jenner* v. *Borven,* 139 F. R. 556, the original machine, during the two years preceding the filing of the application, was altered and improved perhaps, by the introduction of additional pressure rollers, such rollers being necessary to render the machine effective.

Similar cases where changes made within the two-year period were offered to show that the original device was an experiment, but in which the court held otherwise, are to be found in:

> *Star Mfg. Co.* v. *Crescent Forge & Shovel Co.,*
> 179 F. R. 856;
> *Williamson* v. *Electric Service Supplies Co.,*
> 238 F. R. 353;
> *Griggs Mfg. Co.* v. *Sprague,* 123 U. S. 249,
> 31 L. Ed. 141.

The decision in *Williamson* v. *Electric Service Supplies Co.* will also be interesting on another point, which is that *the sale and use having been established more than two years before the filing of the application, the burden of proof that such sale and use was experimental, is on the plaintiff.*

On this point also see *Westinghouse* v. *Saranac,* 108 F. 230.

Denivelle offered no proof at the trial in the court below to rebut the testimony offered by the defendants, showing that the Pennsylvania Station work and other work by Denivelle constituted a public use and sale or offer to sell a complete thing, and not an experimental use.

The sale of a single specimen made more than two years before the filing of the application, is quite sufficient. (*Swain* v. *Holyoke,* 111 F. 408.) In this case, as in the case at bar, the contention was made that the device which was sold was an experimental device.

It cannot be doubted that Denivelle made and sold a specimen of his device when he installed on the wall of the Pennsylvania Station, a single pre-cast block of imitation travertine made in that manner in which he was required to make it, and which had passed the inspection of his own employe, Whipple, who testified that when he permitted a block to be put on the wall of that Station it was in his judgment fit to go thereon, and such block was passed and approved by Webster, representing the architects, and was finally approved by the builders and the architects, and Denivelle was paid for it. That was a sale even though Denivelle's entire job was not completed.

A conditional sale, under the terms of which the device could be returned if found unsatisfactory by the purchaser, if such a sale was made more than two years before the filing of the application, is sufficient. (*Craig* v. *Michigan,* 72 F. R. 173.)

It is immaterial that the maker and his workmen within the two years make frequent visits to see the machine, to make repairs, and to see if improvements would suggest themselves. Under those conditions such a machine does not become experimental. (*Delemater* v. *Heath,* 58 F. R. 414.)

It makes no difference that the alleged novelty or inventive subject matter in the thing which is sold is hidden and covered up, and that its presence cannot be discovered without dismantling the machine, such a sale, if made more than two years before the application, is sufficient to invalidate the patent (*Hall* v. *McNeale,* 107 U. S. 190, 27 L. Ed. 369).

Our adversaries may direct the attention of this Honorable Court to *Harmon* v. *Struthers,* 57 F. R. 637, but in that case the use was by the patentee's employers, who, with his consent, embodied his invention in certain machines for the purpose of testing out the practicability of the invention, and was without profit to the patentee—clearly an experimental use.

They may also cite *Penn Electrical Co.* v. *Conroy,* 159 F. R. 943, but in that case there was no sale of the machine forming the subject of the patent but only of *the product of the machine,* and the machine itself was kept locked up and operated in secrecy during the period of testing.

Or our adversaries may refer to *Campbell* v. *New York,* 47 F. R. 515. But here the use for more than two years was an unauthorized use by one who had surreptitiously obtained knowledge of what the inventor was trying to accomplish, and without his consent embodied his invention in the construction which was sold.

Doubt As to Durability Not Sufficient to Sustain the Finding of Experiment.

As the basis of characterizing the Pennsylvania Station work as an "experiment," Denivelle alleges that there was considerable doubt in his own mind and in that of the architects and builders, as to whether or not the imitation travertine would prove to be durable. Counsel for the plaintiff also in his cross-examination of the defendants' witnesses, sought to obtain from them some expression of opinion upon which this doubt as to durability might be predicated, but in *Root* v. *Third Avenue Railway,* 146 U. S. 221, 36 L. Ed. 946, the Supreme Court has distinctly held that such a doubt and the delay in filing an application for patent based thereon, was not sufficient to show that the thing constituted an experiment, or a sufficient cause for delaying the filing of the application. We quote as follows from that decision:

"In explanation of his delay in applying for the patent, he testifies that before he began the construction of the road, one of the projectors expressed a doubt in regard to the durability of such a structure, and a fear that the jar of street traffic, as well as that of the cars, would in time loosen the ribs and separate them from the surrounding concrete, and the structure would thus fail; that doubts were expressed also by others; that, while the plaintiff believed that there was more than an even chance of its proving a durable and desirable structure, he still had some doubt in his own mind, which was somewhat increased by the doubts expressed to him by others, in whom he had confidence; that as causes which would contribute to the destruction of the road, there were (1) the moving of cars over a rail connected to iron work without the intervention of any wood; (2) the street traffic of trucks and teams, to which such a structure would necessarily be exposed; (3) the changes of temperature; and (4) the effect of time, and the danger of water following down the different members of the iron work, and the rust separating them from the concrete; and that there was no way of determining these matters but by a trial in a public street through a long period of time."

But commenting on this testimony of the patentee for the purpose of saving his patent, which, like the Denivelle patent, was applied for more than four years after the road was constructed and put in use, the Supreme Court used the following language which is quite as applicable to the case here at bar as to the one which was before it:

"But it does not appear that he (the inventor) expressed his doubts to the projectors of the road, either before its construction was commenced, or during its construction, or while he remained its superintendent after it was completed; or that he communicated to anyone what he noticed during the Spring of 1879, or that he entertained any fear arising therefrom."

Denivelle says he expressed a doubt to Mr. McKim at the time McKim asked him to produce imitation travertine, as to his ability to do it, that is to say to produce a specimen which would satisfy the architect, but this took place long before the competitive bidding and the submission of samples accompanying the bids. And it is to be observed further that Denivelle, in competition with others, agreed to do the work in accordance with certain specifications for a certain sum and within a certain period, at least his contract required him to do the work within a certain period of time.

We feel quite sure that this court will be interested in reading the Supreme Court's decision in *Root* v.

Third Avenue Railway Co., and particularly that portion wherein the court distinguishes that case from the *Elizabeth Pavement* case, in fact we think the whole law of this case, insofar as it involves the question as to whether or not Denivelle abandoned his alleged invention and whether or not the patent is void *ab initio* is to be found in this one decision, the Supreme Court referring to and quoting from *Smith & Griggs Mfg. Co.* v. *Sprague,* 123 U. S. 249; *Hall* v. *Macneale,* 107 U. S. 90; *Egbert* v. *Lipmann,* 104 U. S. 333.

The other decision of the Supreme Court upon which the defendants rely—that of *International Tooth Crown Co.* v. *Gaylord,* 140 U. S. 55—supports our defense of abandonment based on Denivelle offering for pay, to instruct, and instructing others how to manufacture imitation travertine in accordance with his alleged inventon, *long before he applied for his patent.* In that respect his actions were the same as the alleged inventor of the tooth crown n the *Tooth Crown* case.

Denivelle's Abandoned Application.

There was some intimation or insinuation that the application for the patent here at issue, filed in October 1915, should receive some revivifying effect from Denivelle's abandoned application which was filed August 2, 1913, as such abandoned application was pending at the time this application was filed, on the theory that the application for the patent in the suit was a continuing application of the one filed in 1913. Sometimes a continuing application is filed and a prior application abandoned. *But it cannot be regarded as a continuing application unless it is for the same invention as the prior application.*

The defendants here have introduced in evidence a certified copy of the file wrapper and contents of Denivelle's abandoned application (Defendants' Exhibit 25, record p. 594). This was not before the court in the previous case, and the court will notice that it is not now offered as an exhibit by plaintiff.

The plaintiff introduced in evidence a certified copy of the file wrapper and contents of the patent in suit (Plaintiff's Exhibit 4, record p. 544).

A comparison of these two exhibits will show conclusively that the prior application *made no disclosure whatsoever* of the alleged invention covered by the second application. There was, it is true, a method claim in the prior application, but it was directed to *a method of forming the colored lines* in a piece of artificial stone. There was nothing in that application looking to the production of the vermiculated surface of imitation travertine by the employment of loose lumpy semi-dry material.

In addition to the single method claim in that application, there were a number of claims for the multiple spouted apparatus by which the colored lines were produced.

That application cannot possibly carry back Denivelle's date of filing for the alleged invention of the patent here at issue. The application on which that patent issued is in no sense a continuing application. Even if the date were early enough—*and it is not, because Denivelle made a sale of his invention four years before that application was filed*—he can derive no benefit from that earlier filing date.

But that application has a significant bearing on Denivelle's *claim* to be the inventor of the subject matter of the patent here at issue. It is a solemn declaration that as late as the 2nd day of August, 1913, when Denivelle filed that first application, *he did not then assert* that he was the inventor of *this method of making imi-*

*tation travertine by the use of colored lines loose lumpy
semi-dry material, and the body fill, etc., as set forth
in his later application.* Denivelle knew better than to
claim to have invented that process. He knew—and
every other plasterer knew—that that was the common
process employed for years in the manufacture of many
forms of artificial stone, as testified to by many of the
witnesses in this case.

Another significant thing is that *while this first application of Denivelle was pending in the Patent Office,*
he apparently discovered that other people were making
imitation travertine in the way in which he had made
it in his Pennsylvania Station job and other jobs, and
he charged the McNulty Company, who were using that
identical process which Denivelle had used in the Pennsylvania Station, with infringing his rights, based on
his earlier application. Presumably that was because
McNulty Bros. *were using a teapot to make the lines.*
However, it was shortly after this controversy with
McNulty over the Widener Building in Philadelphia,
that Denivelle filed his application for the patent here
in suit, which for the *first time* put him in a position
of claiming to have invented this, what we believe to be
an old, well-known way of producing imitation stone.

We again urge upon this Honorable Court that Denivelle's inactivity when he knew that others were prepared
to construct imitation travertine in accordance with the
builder's specifications, when considered in connection
with the subject matter of his abandoned application,
is conclusive proof either that he did not produce the
alleged invention of the patent here at issue, or that
having produced it he abandoned it, *claiming only to be
the inventor of the method of forming the lines by
means of a multiple spouted apparatus.*

"He who is silent when he should speak will
not be heard when he would speak."

It occurs to us that not only is this evidence of abandonment, but when Denivelle paid to his unsuccessful competitive bidders the sum of $200 each, *for the specimens* which they had installed at the time they submitted their bids—all of which took place either late in 1908 or early in 1909—he thereby himself made a purchase of a specimen of the thing covered by his patent more than two years before his application was filed.

Denivelle's Application for Patent in Suit Not a Continuing Application.

Plaintiff's counsel in the *Ceriat* suit argued that the Denivelle invention of the patent in suit should have the benefit of the filing date of Denivelle's abandoned application, which application was filed August 2, 1913, on the theory that the application upon which the patent in suit issued was a "continuing applicaton, and he did this without even properly proving, as he might have done, the filng of the aforesaid abandoned application. The only proof that the plaintiff introduced n the *Ceriat* case of the filing of this abandoned application was what purported to be an official letter from the Patent Office taken from the office file of the attorney. No proof was offered to show that that was in fact an official communication from the Patent Office, and even if that had been proven, it would not have been proof of the filing of the Denivelle abandoned application in August 1913.

At the trial of the present case in the District Court, it was evidently the intenton of counsel for plantiff to again omit adequate and proper proof of the filing of this prior Denivelle application and *the contents thereof*, and this court would not now be advised of what that application really disclosed but for the fact that de-

fendants' counsel offered in evidence a certified copy of
the file wrapper and contents of that application. Under
the statute, such a certified copy is *prima facie* proof
of the fact that such a document is in the archives of
the United States Patent Office, and of the contents
of that document.

If the application upon which the patent here at issue
was granted, could lawfully be regarded as a continuation of Denivelle's prior application, that would of
course take Denivelle's date of filing back to the date
of that prior application, and it would materially reduce
the period within which Denivelle had put his alleged
invention on sale and in public use prior to the filing of
the application here in suit. This would not help the
plaintiff because, even assuming for the sake of argument that his abandoned application can lawfully take
his date back to August 1913, this court will remember
that the Pennsylvania Station work was done in 1909-10,
and the Railroad Station at Ottawa, Canada, was done
early in 1911. Both Denivelle and his counsel admit
that the Pennsylvania Station was completed and
opened to the public "in the early part of 1910" (Record
p. 533).

It will be remembered that Denivelle's contract with
the builders of the Pennsylvania Station required him
to complete the arcade by the 25th day of March, 1909,
and the main waiting room by the 15th day of May,
1909, and that Denivelle submitted samples and sold
his work to the Pennsylvania Station on the 5th day of
March, 1909, the date of his contract. So that even
though the application on which the patent here in suit
issued could be regarded as a continuing application of
Denivelle's abandoned application, there would still be
a public use and offer for sale and a sale of a specimen
of Denivelle's invention more than two years before the
filing of that abandoned application.

Whether or not a second application can be regarded as a continuing application depends upon whether or not they are for *the same invention,* and whether they are for the same invention depends upon the subject matter of the *claims* of the respective applications.

An inspection of this abandoned application of Denivelle will show that it was directed to a particular apparatus whereby a series of jets or sprays of cementitious material could be simultaneously laid upon the surface of a mold to form colored lines in artificial stone surfaces. There was one claim, as the application was originally filed, for a method, but *not the method* subsequently covered by the application for the patent in suit. The method of claim 1 of the abandoned application is as follows:

> "1. The method of producing artificial stone surfaces which comprises the application of a series of jets or sprays of a mobile substance upon a surface by the movement of a vessel containing the substance and having discharge mouths, and moving said vessel along the surface upon which the substance is to be deposited, thereby forming substantially parallel lines or veins of the substance, and then filling in the plastic body over said veins to incorporate said veins into and upon the surface of the body."

The remaining claims of the abandoned application related to the multiple spouted apparatus therein shown and described.

This court will observe that in the method of the abandoned application there is nothing said about building up the cast block by the use of "semi-dry loose lumpy material," or the formation of pockets, and so far as this abandoned application is concerned, the product may well be a piece of artificial stone having an absolutely smooth surface divided by colored striations.

An examination of the patent in suit and of the file
wrapper and contents upon which that patent issued,
will show that Denivelle *for the first time* described the
employment of "semi-dry loose lumpy material" for the
purpose of producing the pockets, voids or vermiculations. It is obvious therefore that the alleged inventions
of the respective applications were not the same, and
that they are in no sense continuing applications.

The court will observe that this abandoned application
of Denivelle was rejected time and time again, and by
the very first amendment which was filed in that application Denivelle eliminated claim 1, the method claim,
and continued the prosecution of that application for the
apparatus alone. Furthermore, on the 30th day of
October 1915, the Patent Office finally rejected all of the
claims of this prior application of Denivelle, and as
Denivelle took no appeal from that decision, as he might
have done, he must be regarded as acquiescing therein.
And, as stated in the official letter of November 2, 1916,
that application became abandoned through failure of
the applicant to take an appeal to the Examiners-in-
Chief.

Defenses of Lack of Novelty and Invention—Non-Infringement—and Invalidity of Claims 9 and 10 Because of Absence of Oath.

Of the foregoing defenses, only one was used by the
court below as a basis for the decree, and that was that
claims 9 and 10—the so-called "product claims" of the
Denivelle patent—are invalid because not supported by
the oath of the patentee. That of lack of novelty and invention was briefly referred to by the court below, the
learned judge's remarks concerning old practises in
the manufacture of imitation stone being based upon
the *testimony* of the defendants' witnesses, and not

specifically directed to any of the patents of the prior art introduced' as exhibits by the defendant. The defense of non-infringement was not referred to at all by the District Court.

It may be that this court will have already concluded by what has been hereinbefore set forth, that the Denivelle patent is clearly void and invalid because of Denivelle's use and sale in the Pennsylvania Station job and other jobs more than two years before he filed his application, and will therefore regard it as unnecessary to consider any of the other defenses, but in order that this court may have before it a complete discussion of *all* the defenses we shall now take them up in order and discuss those above enumerated.

As to whether or not there is any novelty in the process and the alleged product of that process of the Denivelle patent, it must be first determined just what the alleged invention is that is supposed to be disclosed by the Denivelle patent, and more particularly by claims 1, 2, 5, 9 and 10 of that patent, which are specifically the claims which the defendants are charged with infringing.

The first three claims—1, 2 and 5—are for an alleged new process, and claims 9 and 10 are for the alleged new product. Claim 1 of the Denivelle patent may be analyzed as follows:

> (a) Depositing upon a prepared surface of desired form, a series of narrow layers of plastic material;

> (b) Depositing upon said layers and upon the exposed surfaces there between, a suitable material of such texture and consistency as will leave numerous small portions of said exposed surfaces out of contact with said material;

(c) Binding together said layers and said material with a fluid cement, and allowing the mass to set.

Considering this claim in connection with the specification, it will be found that step (a) is that which is described under the heading "Veining" in lines 75 to 92 of page 1 of the specification.

Step (b) is that which is described under the heading "Forming Pockets" in lines 100 to 112, page 1 of the specification, and in lines 1 to 9, page 2 of the specification.

Step (c) is that described under the heading "Bonding," found in lines 11 to 25 of page 2 of the specification.

Claim 2 is exactly the same as claim 1, the only difference being that it requires that the material employed in step (a) shall be "of a certain color" and the material employed in step (c) "of a different color."

At this point the court's attention is directed to the fact that the process described in claim 1, assuming that the materials are of the *same* color, would not produce any contrasting colored striations in the surface, but would only produce the pocket-like or vermiculated formation. Therefore, inasmuch as travertine stone not only has striations of contrasting shades as well as the pocket-like holes in the surface, the process of claim 1, if the materials employed were of the same shade, *would not produce imitation travertine.* The process of claim 2, however, would produce not only stria of different shades but the vermiculated surface as well, such as found in travertine stone.

Claim 5 describes a process which consists:

(a) Preparing a mold of suitable outline with an isolator;

(b) Forming veins of plastic material over this prepared surface;

(c) Depositing loose lumpy material over the veining to provide pockets;

(d) Binding the pocket-forming material with the veining material and leaving certain pockets exposed on the surface adjacent to the mold surface.

The isolating of the mold is that step described under the heading "Isolating" in lines 68 to 72 inclusive, page 1 of the specification.

The step of isolating or greasing the mold is necessary, according to all of the witnesses, in connection with all molds excepting those made of glass or other similar hard smooth material, in order that the cast cementitious block may be stripped or removed from the mold surface after it has set or hardened. It cannot be said to constitute any part of the process of manufacturing the cementitious block of imitation stone, but only in preparing the molds in which it is cast.

Claim 5, therefore, except for a change in language, covers identically the same process as that covered by claim 1. It is somewhat broader than claim 1, in that claim 1 requires that the veins be formed by depositing a series of narrow lines of plastic material on the mold surface, whereas claim 5 simply requires the *formation* of veins of plastic material. Under claim 1 these veins are formed of a series of narrow lines of cementitious material, whereas under claim 5 the whole

surface of the mold may be covered and then the veins
formed by combing through this plastic cementitious
covering with a suitable rake or comb, thus dividing the
material into lines and exposing the mold surface between the lines. The semi-dry, loose, lumpy material
which is then deposited under provisions of claim 5, is
the same as that described in the specification under the
heading "Forming Pockets." This manner of forming
the lines by using a comb was old long before Denivelle.

Claim 9 is for a cementitious structure. It comprises:

  1. A mass of cementitious material;

  2. One surface of which is shaped and striated
  and formed with small irregularly spaced depressions;

  3. The stria constituting the exposed portions
  of shallow inlays of uniformly colored cement.

Obviously this claim covers a pre-cast block of cementitious material. It does not relate to what has been
referred to as "applied work." Obviously it cannot
relate to such because the reference to "one surface"
of the mass presupposes that there is another surface,
and applied work has only one surface. It includes in
addition to the striations, the pockets or depressions.
The shallow inlays which constitute the stria are the
colored lines first laid upon the surface of the mold,
and when imbedded in the finished mass may be described as shallow inlays.

Claim 10 is hard to understand. Apparently it was
intended to cover what is known as applied work, and
yet it is hard to imagine applied work which can be
described as "formed of differently toned thin layers

or strata, the said layers only partly connected one to the other in such manner as to leave serrated voids in stratafied formation between said layers, said layers and voids existing only adjacent to the surface.'' That claims 9 and 10 are not intended to cover what has been referred to as applied work but, on the contrary, a precast block, would seem to be clearly indicated by the 'fact that Denivelle divided the application upon which the patent in suit issued, filing application No. 56879 upon which his patent No. 1,233,265 subsequently issued, which is specifically for the process of producing the so-called applied work.

It would seem to us that a proper interpretation of claim 10 would include only a pre-cast cementitious mass. In the specification there is a description of a process of making the so-called ''applied work,'' beginning with line 66, page 2, and ending with line 53 page 3, but that process produces the pockets not by the use of the so-called ''semi-dry'' or loose, lumpy material but by a stippling tool or brush.

Claims 9 and 10 are so indefinite and so comprehensive, that counsel for plaintiff at the trial in the court below, took the position that they were sufficient to prevent anyone reproducing in a cementitious mass, the stone known as travertine, or making an imitation of travertine. In other words, it was contended by counsel for plaintiff that under claims 9 and 10 this patentee could prevent anyone from making a cementitious imitation of this natural stone travertine in any manner whatsoever.

So far as the novelty of anything covered by the Denivelle patent is concerned, and so far as the alleged invention may be regarded as being the product of inventive skill rather than the product of mere mechanical skill, this court should consider the testimony of

Mr. Morkel and Mr. Cousins. They seem to make it clear that in this art in the manufacture of all kinds of artificial stone, what is set forth in the Denivelle patent was, and has been for a long time, common practice. This was recognized by the Learned Judge in the court below when he states:

> "The state of the art rendered its production a matter of craftsmanship more than of invention, and architects desiring any new imitation, commonly referred to makers of artificial stone to produce it" (record p. 675).

We will not analyze all of the patents introduced by the defendants, but a brief reference to a few of them will show that each and every one of the steps employed by Denivelle were but common well-known expedients employed by makers of artificial stone of every kind and character. The witnesses Cousins, Massimo and Morkel, long engaged in the production of artificial stone, make it clear that the materials employed by Denivelle were those which had been so employed almost from the beginning of the art. They testified that in the production of certain characters of stone imitations, colored cementitious material was applied to the greased or isolated mold surfaces in such manner as to produce colored lines and veins, and that loose, lumpy, cementitious material was also employed in the spaces between the lines backed up by a relatively fluid body fill, and that the blotting processes by the use of dry cement, were steps long known and commonly used in this art. It appears that with the utmost care the veins of the cast cementitious block would present blow holes or pockets, and that as they were undesired it was customary to fill them up on the surface during the polishing process. It further ap-

peared that another way of forming colored lines was
to cover the surface of the mold with a cementitious
mixture, and then run a comb through this soft material which divided it and exposed the surface of the
mold, permitting the next layer of material to come in
contact with the mold surface between the colored
lines.

A reading of the depositions of Mr. Cousins, Mr.
Massimo and Mr. Morkel cannot fail but impress this
court that all of the steps and all of the materials used
by Denivelle were such as had been commonly employed
in this art for many years.

As to the prior patents, it is only necessary to refer
to a few of them. The patent to Henderson No. 886124
dated April 28, 1908, introduced in evidence as Defendants' Exhibit 32 (record page 602), was directed to
producing artificial stone without the porous surface
which the patentee states was present in artificial stone
produced by prior processes. The significant part of
this patent to Henderson is found in lines 40 to 59
inclusive, page 2 of the specification, which for the
convenience of the court is here quoted:

> "If it be desired to vein the face of the stone
> in any manner to produce ornamental effects, or
> an imitation of marble, for example, I proceed
> as follows:—I first make a veining material from
> Portland cement and color and water, making
> said material of a little thicker consistency than
> that of the fluid mass heretofore described. This
> veining material I then spread in a thin layer
> in the previously lubricated mold, forming in it
> veins or cloud effects seen in natural marble.
> Then I gently pour the fluid aqueous mass of
> Portland cement, either neat or mixed, as stated,
> with marble dust, into the mold, without disturb-
> ing the tracings or veins of the material used for
> the veining effects, and I then apply the sprink-

ling of dry Portland cement, as before. The
stone, when removed from the mold, will present
on its face the veinings and cloud effects of the
natural marble.''

The patent to Bellamy No. 982029 dated January 17,
1911, Defendants' Exhibit 31 (record p. 602), in lines
5 to 25, page 2 of the specification, describes a process
of making a cementitious block of stone which undoubtedly produces upon the surface colored inlays.
We here quote the portion of the specification referred
to:

"In Fig. 7, a tile is represented such as would
be produced,—entirely consistent with this invention,—by depositing pieces a^2, a^2, of comminuted
plastic material of one color (for instance, red)
in the bottom of the press mold, commingled
with comminuted plastic material b^2 of another
color, for instance, blue,—these commingled separated portions of the plastic material being
superimposed by the sheet or layer c^2 of the
still different color,—it being understood that the
compression to which the materials are subjected as before described cause a flattening and
plane facing of the interspersed plastic portions
a^2 and b^2, and a displacement in all spaces between the portions a^2 and b^2 of so much of the
layer c^2 as to make the face stratum of the tile
solid, and with its continuous surfaced face a
mottling or variegation of the colors, for instance,
red, white and blue, of the portions a^2, b^2 and c^2.''

The patent to McKnight No. 247262 of September
20, 1881, introduced as Defendants' Exhibit 30 (record
p. 602), describes a method of producing a cementitious artificial stone having colored inlays produced
in that manner employed by Denivelle.
The British patent No. 12468 of 1893, introduced in
evidence as Defendants' Exhibit 37 (record p. 603),

describes the manufacture of a block of imitation stone
having colored lines manufactured in substantially the
same manner as that described in the Denivelle patent,
whereby colored inlays are produced on the surface of
the stone. We do not contend of course, that this patent
discloses the intentional production of pockets on the
surface.

The British patent No. 2011 of 1903, Defendants' Exhibit 38, introduced at page 603 of the record, is extremely interesting as it shows the employment of
what the patent describes as "small flakes or portions
of a pulpy mass of soft, but slightly dried plaster of
Paris or cement." This of course, is the semi-dry,
loose, lumpy cementitious material employed by Denivelle.

In view of the disclosures of these patents, we seriously doubt whether there was any invention whatsoever in the Denivelle patent.

The Defense of Non-Infringement.

**A process claim is infringed only when the series
of steps described and claimed are employed, or if
not exactly that series of steps, the equivalent thereof.**

An inspection of the Denivelle patent will show that
he produces the so-called "pockets" by employing a
mixture of colored cement with or without sand, or
other aggregates, and enough water or other liquid to
reduce the mixture to "a semi-dry and lumpy consistency." This semi-dry or lumpy material is distributed over the exposed surface of the mold between the
colored lines, or more or less evenly over the whole
form of the mold, and over the lines constituting the
veining. This is the second step of the *process* of the
Denivelle patent. By using this lumpy, semi-dry, plastic material, the patentee explains, he prevents the

next coating or body filling and forming material from entirely covering the surface of the mold exposed between the lines of colored plastic material forming the veins, thus producing the "pockets" or vemiculated surface. The patent states, "Coating 4 is so applied, and is of such loose, lumpy consistency as to provide in the finished surface of the cast a porous, pocket-like appearance between the straited poured lines or veins 3," described as operation (2). (Specification, page 2, lines 4 to 9 inclusive.)

There is another way described of forming these pockets in the so-called "applied" work, wherein a stiff wire brush is punched in to the surface after it has set, but before hardening. This step, that is to say, the employment of a semi-dry, loose, lumpy cementitious material is found in each of claims 1, 2 and 5.

The process of forming the pockets by the stippling method by punching the surface of the plastered wall with a stiff wire brush, and also forming the colored stria or lines by shallow inlays, is covered by another Denivelle patent No. 1,233,265 dated July 10, 1917, granted on an application constituting a division of the application on which the patent in suit was issued. A consideration of this Denivelle patent shows that claims 9 and 10 of Denivelle patent No. 1,212,331 here in suit, *must be construed to cover a pre-cast block and a pre-cast block made in that manner described in the specification.* There is no claim found in the Denivelle patent in suit for that process referred to as process "B," and described at length in line 67, page 2 of the specification, to and including line 54, page 3, of the specification.

In view of the state of the art therefore, and in view of the testimony of Mr. Cousins, Mr. Morkel, Mr. Meyn and other witnesses for the defendant, the

Denivelle patent in suit and the claims here at issue must be interpreted to include the employment of "semi-dry, loose, lumpy" cementitious material for the purpose of the formation of the pockets or vermiculations.

Several of the witnesses testified to using various methods for forming these pockets, including the employment of semi-dry, loose, lumpy, cementitious material. Rock salt was employed which, sprinkled upon the surface of the mold, was imbedded in and exposed on the surface of the cast, and later washed out, leaving the pockets or voids. Loose sand was employed sprinkled upon the surface of the mold, and later washed out of the surface of the cast. Wax in the form of lumps was employed. These were laid on the surface of the mold and became imbedded in the cast, and were subsequently melted and washed out.

Defendant's Process a Chemical Process and not an Infringement.

At the time the contract for the Los Angeles Biltmore job was under consideration, Denivelle was one of the competitive bidders with these defendants. The contract was awarded to these defendants. Denivelle assumed that it was the intention of these defendants, in carrying out this contract, to make their imitation travertine in the way he says it was made by them under his direction on the Exposition Buildings, and which he contends is the method of his patent. He notified these defendants that they must not infringe his patent. He was told by them that they had no intention of infringing his patent, but that they were going to get around it in some way. This they had a right to do if they could. They had in their employ as foreman, a man by the name of Delaney, and Delaney and these defendants working together experimented in their own shop to devise a method of producing the pockets or vermiculations *without employing the layer of semi-dry, loose, lumpy, cementitious material,* and they hit upon the employment of *calcium carbide.*

The defendants' method may be described as follows: The mold surface is prepared as all mold surfaces are prepared, by applying thereto a coating of grease. This for the purpose of assuring that the casting, when hardened and set, may be readily removed from the surface of the mold. On this greased mold surface the defendants lay a series of lines of colored cementitious material to form the colored lines or stria in the cast. Between these lines on the greased surface of the mold, the defendants sprinkle calcium carbide crystals in such quantity and of such a size as will produce the desired effect. They then pour into the mold the body layer of cementitious material of sufficient fluidity so that it will entirely cover the colored lines and the crystals of calcium carbide. The water in this body fill, acting upon the calcium carbide crystals, sets up a chemical action producing a gas, which gas, expanding and flowing along the surface of the mold, and in the surface of the body fill adjacent the surface of the mold, produces the pockets. After setting for a sufficient length of time to harden, the cast is removed, and the surface next to the mold and between the colored lines, is found to be honeycombed with openings or pockets which are filled with a white ash caused by the disintegration or consumption of the calcium carbide under the action of the water contained in the body fill. This ash is washed out by a stream of water, leaving the pockets or vermiculations, and producing such pockets with a very natural undercut appearance.

It will be noted that there is but one form of cementitious material employed by these defendants: the plastic material forming the lines, and the plastic material poured in over the lines and the calcium carbide being of the same kind. No "semi-dry, loose, lumpy, cementitious material" is employed by these defendants. The defendants' process, as before stated, was produced by their foreman, Delaney, and at the defendants' request, Delaney applied for and secured Letters Patent of the United States No. 1,468,343 dated September 18, 1923, for his new process. (See Defendants' Exhibit 29.)

Denivelle's theory, as expressed by him on the witness stand, is that the calcium carbide which, by means of the chemical reaction and the generation of gas, forms the pockets in the defendants' process, because they can be described as "loose, lumpy material," renders the defendants' process an infringement of his patent. On cross-examination, he was compelled to admit that ordinary gravel could be described as loose, lumpy material in the same manner that calcium carbide could be thus described, but he had the effrontery to contend that if one used gravel in the same manner that the defendants used calcium carbide, a cast would be produced with pockets.

Now, this court will certainly take judicial notice of the fact that if a plastic cementitious body fill is poured in over a layer of gravel or lines of gravel, sprinkled between the colored lines, the gravel would become a permanent part of the cast when set, and that no pockets at all would result.

We do not believe that this court will, for one moment, hold that the chemical process employed by these defendants, whereby the pockets are formed by the generation of gas, can be held to be an infringement of the Denivelle patent. The Denivelle patent here in

suit, must be limited to the formation of pockets by
the employment of "semi-dry, loose, lumpy, cementitious material." That is true of claims 9 and 10 as
well as claims 1, 2 and 5, because if those claims are
to be sustained at all, they must be interpreted to cover
the method of making the product or its substantial
equivalent, which has been so fully described in the
Denivelle patent. Claims 9 and 10 cannot possibly be
interpreted to cover broadly the making of an imitation of travertine stone in *any* manner, because *no-
body would be entitled to a patent for merely producing an imitation of any natural product*. Furthermore,
as herein pointed out, claims 9 and 10 must be interpreted as covering a *pre-cast* block and not for an imitation travertine produced by the so-called "applied"
process, because that process was divided out of the
Denivelle patent and now constitutes the subject matter of his patent No. 1,233,265.

**Even though this court should adhere to its pre-
vious decision as to the validity of this Denivelle
patent, which seems impossible to us in view of the
new evidence found in this case, we submit that the
defendants' process and product, as made under the
Delaney patent, is an entirely different thing and cannot possibly be regarded as an infringement of the
Denivelle patent.**

Claims 9 and 10 Invalid Because Unsupported By Oath of the Patentee.

This is a defense which for the first time was raised
in this case. It was not involved in the prior *Ceriat*
case. The statute requires that every applicant for
a patent "shall make oath that he does verily believe
himself to be the original and first inventor or discoverer of the article, machine, manufacture, composi-

tion or improvement for which he solicits a patent; that he does not know and does not believe that the same was ever before known or used; and shall state of what country he is a citizen." (Revised Statutes, Sec. 4892.)

The file wrapper and contents of the Denivelle patent here in suit, shows that as filed it purported to disclose and claim as the subject matter, a *process* for manufacturing artificial stone, and that it was not for some time after the application was filed, and some time after one or more actions had been had thereon, both by the Patent Office and the attorney representing the applicant, that claims 9 and 10, purporting to be for a *product,* were introduced into the application. They were in fact, so far as the record of that file wrapper and contents shows, prepared and introduced by an associate attorney residing in Washington, D. C., without consultation with the applicant.

A product is one thing; a process is another. It is perhaps permissible to include them both in one patent, but Denivelle's application *as filed,* in fact the patent *as issued,* excepting for claims 9 and 10, contain no suggestion that this applicant or patentee asserted that he had invented a *product* as well as a process. No product was described in the application as filed, and if there had been, and the applicant had clearly represented that he had invented a product as well as a process, *he might have been lawfully permitted to introduce the product claims by amendment.* But in that case the law and the rules of practice in the Patent Office require that the applicant shall file a supplemental oath identifying his application and setting forth specifically that the subject matter of the proposed amendment—in this case the product claims—was of his invention; and that he had invented it before he filed his application; and that the same had not been in public use and on sale in the United States for more than two years before the application was filed; and that he had not abandoned it. We find no such oath in this application. The only oath found in the application is that which was filed with the application when it was originally filed, and *covered only the subject matter as it then stood, namely, a specification describing a process and claims covering a process.* Under the decisions therefore, of the Supreme Court of the United States in *Steward* v. *American Lava Co.,* 215 U. S. 168; and of the subordinate Federal Courts in *Westinghouse Mfg. Co.* v. *Metropolitan Electric Mfg. Co.,* 290 F. R. 664; *Cutter Co.* v. *Metropolitan Electric Mfg. Co.,* 275 F. R. 158; *American Lava Co.* v. *Steward,* 155 F. R. 731; *Beachy, et al.* v. *McWilliams,* 224 F. R. .717, claims 9 and 10 should be held to be invalid because not supported by the oath of the applicant or patentee.

While we have hereinbefore discussed all the defenses raised by the defendants' pleadings and proofs, and rely upon all of them, yet we feel that this Honorable Court will come to the conclusion that the new evidence submitted by the defendants is sufficient to conclusively show that Denivelle made a commercial use of his alleged invention over a period much in excess of two years prior to the filing of his application; and that the patent is absolutely void and invalid *in its entirety.* And we again suggest to this court the advisability of declaring the whole patent to be void and invalid notwithstanding that only a portion of the claims are directly involved herein, in order that it may not again be used to intimidate those who may be engaged in the manufacture of cementitious artificial travertine, even though made in accordance with the information contained in this patent, or be subjected to expensive law suits because of the alleged infringement of this patent.

The defense of non-infringement is one upon which alone this case could be disposed of, so far as these defendants are concerned, as is also that of abandonment. Of course abandonment is closely related to the defense of public use and sale. It arises here because the public use, and sale mainly relied on is that by the alleged inventor and patentee himself. There could of course be public use and sale by others than the patentee and alleged inventor without involving the question of abandonment.

In the present case the public use and sale by Denivelle is not alone a sufficient defense to invalidate the patent, but it is sufficient to warrant this court in holding that if Denivelle ever made an invention he abandoned it to the public by his failure and neglect to file his application within a reasonable time after he began work on the Pennsylvania Station.

It is again pointed out in closing, that both Denivelle and his counsel admit that the Pennsylvania Station contract was completed "early in 1910." Therefore, even if his abandoned application which was filed in August, 1913, could be held to be an application disclosing the same invention as that upon which the patent here at issue was granted, and the latter a continuing application, that would not help Denivelle, because more than two years elapsed from the completion of the contract in 1910 until the filing of this first application of Denivelle in August, 1913, which later became an abandoned application.

Plaintiff's counsel bases one of the assignments of error on the admission of certain testimony for alleged lack of notice, pleading, etc. Without admitting that such evidence was offered without notice, in support of our contention that evidence of the prior state of the art is admissible without notice, we call the attention of this court to the decision of the Supreme Court in *Brown* v. *Piper,* 37 U. S. 200, 23 L. Ed. 200.

Conclusion.

In conclusion we submit that the decree of the District Court should be affirmed, not only on the grounds embodied therein, but on the further grounds that Denivelle abandoned his alleged invention before applying for a patent therefor, and that the defendants have not infringed that patent even if it may be assumed that the patent is a valid patent.

Respectfully submitted,

T. HART ANDERSON,
Attorney for Defendants-Appellees.

MUNN, ANDERSON & MUNN, of New York, N. Y.,
Of Counsel for Defendants-Appellees.

APPENDIX.

The foregoing portion of our brief was completed and printed before we had seen the brief of our adversaries, which is of such a character that we feel it necessary to make a brief reference thereto. Incidentally, we ask this court to note that our brief is being prepared under the disadvantage of being 3,000 miles away from the documentary exhibits which, while of the utmost importance in this cause, were omitted from the printed record at the request of counsel for plaintiff. Our adversaries' brief came to us on the 27th inst. and we have only had time to give it a hasty examination, and as Mr. Anderson, who will argue this case, must leave here on the 4th of November, there remains but little time to prepare and print this supplementary addition to our brief, so that it must be considerably shorter than perhaps it should be in order to cover all of the inaccuracies which are to be found in our adversaries' brief.

We shall not have time to dwell at large upon the unfair attempt on the part of plaintiff, to make it appear that these defendants, their counsel and those who testified for them, have conspired to defeat the Denivelle patent by fair means and foul. This charge is based upon the testimony of Mr. MacGruer to the effect that by letters and by personal visitation in December, 1923, to various parties in and about Chicago, New York and Washington, he sought to obtain evidence as to Denivelle's activities in and around New York, and more particularly concerning his work in the Pennsylvania Station. And they would have it appear that because those witnesses have testified—some of them very reluctantly, we submit—that is evidence of a conspiracy to defeat this patent; plaintiff's theory being that they are all infringers and all are afraid of what might happen to them should this court adhere to its previous decision.

But while plaintiff's counsel dwells at length on this effort of Mr. MacGruer and his counsel to obtain from these parties evidence concerning the actual facts in connection with Denivelle's activities, to disprove his contention that the Pennsylvania Station job was but an experiment, he is entirely silent on what we regard as a very questionable proceeding on the part of Denivelle.

As required by statute and the rules of the Supreme Court in equity, notice was served upon counsel for plaintiff of the intention of the defendants to take the depositions of certain named witnesses in New York and Washington. Now, what happens? Before the date set for beginning the taking of the depositions, we received a telephone call from Mr. Loftus in Washington, who advised us that he was there in attendance upon the Supreme Court of the United States, and inquiring whether or not it would be possible for us to arrange to take the deposition of the witness Krafft while he (Loftus) was detained in Washington, before proceeding in New York, as it was our intention to do and as it was so stated in the notice. This was several days before the date named in the notice of our intention to proceed in New York.

To accommodate Mr. Loftus, we did arrange to take the deposition of the witness Krafft in Washington, and when we reached there we found Mr. Denivelle present. That did not surprise us, but what did surprise us was to find that Denivelle had caused someone to interview Krafft.

Upon our return to New York, on the day of the taking of the Krafft deposition, Denivelle was on the same train, and thereafter it developed that he had been to see almost every witness we called—from eminent architects down to the journeymen plasterers, Cook and Whipple, who were former employes of Denivelle. On some of them, because of their previous relations, his visit had the effect of making them reluctant to testify as to the true conditions. At least, we submit, it made some of them willing to acquiesce in Denivelle's persuasive suggestions that he was constantly experimenting with all the imitation travertine jobs with which he and they had been associated.

As has been pointed out in the foregoing brief, they were not willing to characterize these jobs, including the Pennsylvania Station job, as experiments, but many of them were willing to help Denivelle, if they could, to sustain this proposition.

The attack on the witness Brown, which is found in our adversaries' brief, we submit comes with poor grace when we note Mr. Brown's refusal to testify concerning what took place when Mr. Denivelle visited him at his home just before Brown was called as a witness, on the ground that he did not believe it right or proper to disclose what took place when Denivelle, an old friend, made a social call. It is perfectly obvious that this call of Denivelle on Brown was not a social call. It was no more a social call on Brown than it was on the witness Cook, whom Denivelle visited while Cook was at work on a plastering job. Nor was it a social call when Denivelle, a cross between an artist and a plasterer, invited the journeyman plasterer Whipple, to come in to New York and have lunch with him. That it was not a social call that Denivelle made on Brown is shown by the fact that Denivelle left with Brown "a part of his printed matter—he showed me, I believe—the Appellate Court out in San Francisco; he asked me to read it over carefully to see what interesting reading matter it was."

We submit that it is an entirely different proposition for a defendant to seek evidence by correspondence and personal visitation from those whom he believes may know the facts he desires to prove than for a party to call upon noticed witnesses before they can reach the witness stand, as Denivelle has done in this case.

The foregoing is of course a side issue, the main question in this case being whether the Denivelle patent is a valid patent, and whether, if valid, these defendants have infringed that patent.

Plaintiff's Brief Concerning the Ceriat Suit and the Preliminary Injunction in the Present Suit.

It is pointed out at page 6 of plaintiff's brief, that the affidavits filed by the defendants in opposition to the motion for preliminary injunction are reproduced in this record. We call attention to the fact that of those affidavits only one—that of Denivelle—was introduced as an exhibit in this case; and we submit that the plaintiff has no right in his brief to refer to any other of the affidavits or any of the documents connected with the motion for preliminary injunction, which were not exhibits in this case.

The affidavit of Twaits, part of which is quoted at page 19 of plaintiff's brief, was not offered in evidence in this case. The affidavit of John H. Delaney, referred to at page 79 of the plaintiff's brief, was not offered as an exhibit in this case. And plaintiff's counsel has reproduced in this case and printed at pages 56-57-58-59 of his brief, matter that was excluded by the trial court in the *Ceriat* case.

Then, again, he makes a point that most of the witnesses whose depositions were first taken and introduced by these defendants, were named in an alleged notice of taking testimony by the defendant Ceriat. But this court will understand that of all the witnesses who have testified in this case, none of them were heard in the *Ceriat* case, with the exception of Denivelle and Morkel.

Plaintiff's Patent—Plaintiff's Exhibit 3.

At page 24 of plaintiff's brief, we find an admission that the so-called "applied" method is covered by a separate patent, so that the patent here in suit is, as we have heretofore pointed out, for the so-called "process of producing a casting" and the product of that process. That product, in order to be an imitation of travertine, must have in addition to the honey-combed or vermiculated surface formation, lines or striations of a different color tone. Our adversaries say in their brief:

> "Manifestly, without striations, *i. e.*, veins, it is not imitation travertine by whatever process produced." (Plaintiff's brief, p. 131.)

We have heretofore called attention to the fact that certain of the claims upon which these defendants are sued, would not produce such an imitation of travertine.

Claim 1 is silent as to the color of any of the ingredients and does not require that the series of narrow layers of plastic material shall be of a different color from the rest of the material. So far as claim 1 is concerned, all of the material employed may be white or black. Obviously, the use of that process of claim 1 with all white or all black material, would not produce imitation travertine.

Claim 2, on the other hand, requires that the narrow layers of plastic material shall be of "a certain color," and that the material which is deposited between these narrow layers of plastic material shall be "of a different color." Now, if the colors selected were of what has been described by one of the witnesses—"a creamish color"—that process of claim 2 would produce an imitation of travertine.

Claim 5 also is silent as to the color of the materials employed. If the process set forth in that claim were carried out by the use of all white or all black material, obviously an imitation of travertine would not be produced.

Claim 9, a product claim, requires that one surface shall be shaped and striated, but there is nothing in that claim to indicate that the stria are of a different color from the rest of the surface.

Claim 10 speaks of the layers being of different tones, but if one layer is laid over the other, as it would be if this claim were interpreted to cover what has been referred to as "applied" work, obviously only one color tone would be exposed on the surface of the finished product.

Claims 9 and 10 are silent as to the employment of loose, lumpy, cementitious material, such as is fully described in the specification. This form of pocket-forming material is specifically mentioned in claim 5, and while not so specifically mentioned in claims 1 and 2, yet as therein described:

> "a suitable material of such texture and consistency as will leave numerous small portions of said exposed surfaces out of contact with said material necessarily includes such loose, lumpy, cementitious material and only that kind of material."

That is the only method of producing the "pockets" in employing the so-called "cast" process described in the Denivelle patent, and if claims 9 and 10 for the product, which our adversaries contend cover an imitation of travertine stone regardless of the manner in which it be made, can be sustained at all, they must be limited to such an artificial travertine produced by the use of the loose, lumpy, cementitious material described in the paent. We do not believe that this court will hold that it is a patentable invention to produce an imitation of any natural stone regardless of the specific manner in which that imitation can be produced.

As before pointed out, we are laboring under a disadvantage in that none of the very important documentary exhibits have been reproduced in the record before this Honorable Court. There is only one copy of each of those documentary exhibits.

But assuming that the copy of the file wrapper and contents of the Denivelle patent here at issue has been correctly reproduced in the Ceriat record (a copy of which we have before us), it will be pointed out that this Denivelle application was filed on the 20th of October, 1915. The invention was entitled, "Manufacture of Artificial Stone," and it was a process which was illustrated in the drawings and described in the specification, and which formed the subject matter of the original claims. No claim was made for the product of the process, nor did the applicant advise the Patent Office that he claimed to be the inventor of a product until the amendment of September 2, 1916, presented almost a year after the filing of the application. This amendment was presented by an associate attorney residing in Washington, and was accompanied by no explanation whatsoever as to why these claims were not earlier presented; nor was it accompanied by a supplemental oath.

In each of the original claims covering the so-called "casting" process, as distinguished from the "applied" process, which latter process was at that time also included in this application, there is a step defined as "depositing a loose, lumpy material over the veining material." We have previously called attention to the fact that this so-called "applied" work or process was divided out of this application and constitutes the subject matter of another Denivelle patent, and in this statement, we are happy to say, counsel for plaintiff agrees with us, for we find in his brief the following statement:

> "The so-called 'applied method,' not here involved (method B), being covered by a separate patent not here in issue." (Plaintiff's brief page 24.)

So far as these process claims are concerned, not only did Denivelle wait until October, 1915, to file his application for patent, when it is admitted by him and his counsel that his contract in the Pennsylvania Station was completed, final payment demanded, and release executed as early as November 19, 1910 (Defendant's Exhibit 7—Book of Exhibits, page 137; see Plaintiff's brief page 97), but it was not until September, 1916, that, by the insertion of the product claims (claims 9 and 10), he set up the claim that he had invented a product as well as a process. In other words, before he sought these product claims, a sample of travertine alleged to have been made in accordance with Denivelle's process, had been sold by him and was in public use in the Pennsylvania Station for six years.

We think it advisable at this point to take up and discuss the defense of public use, sale and abandonment by Denivelle, as those defenses are treated in the plaintiff's brief, leaving for the moment the defense that the product claims are invalid because not supported by the oath of the applicant, and the defense of noninfringement, both of which are important, to be considered by this Court only in the event that it should be disinclined to reverse its prior decision.

Public Use, Sale and Abandonment by Denivelle.

Throughout the plaintiff's brief there appears to be a deliberate attempt to confuse the issue which is raised by these defenses. So far as Denivelle's acts are concerned, in connection with the Pennsylvania Station and other jobs, it is not a prior use or a public use and sale by others before his invention which it is attempted to prove. In a sense it may show, so far as the others are concerned, a public use of Denivelle's alleged invention. He sold something to the Pennsylvania Station which was made in accordance with plans and specifications of the architects. Obviously, that was not a prior use, that is to say, a use prior to Denivelle's alleged invention. But when Denivelle offered to sell this thing to the Pennsylvania Station, that is to say, an imitation of travertine, and effected a sale of it, he thereby and by that act created the statutory defense of a public use and sale of a specimen of imitation travertine made in accordance with the process of his patent. It is absolutely immaterial when this Station was completed and opened to the public. It is absolutely immaterial when the Goelet house was completed and occupied. It would be ridiculous to argue that the sale of a heating plant for a building, or of a system of ventilation and water supply, which might have been installed months before the building was completed and occupied, was not sold or put into public use until the building was entirely completed and occupied or used.

If it may be assumed that Denivelle, after he got this Pennsylvania Station contract, was conducting experiments as the work went on, and finally evolved the process set forth in his patent, it cannot be denied by him that his contract was completed, and he demanded payment, therefor, and executed the required release in connection therewith, as early as November 19, 1910.

This means that if that were the earliest date which the defendants might insist upon as the date when Denivelle completed, delivered, and received payment for, a specimen of his invention, that will be quite sufficient, considering that he waited until October, 1915, to file his application. It is conceded by everybody—admitted by Denivelle and his counsel—that this Pennsylvania Station job was the first "practical" embodiment of his alleged invention.

It is to be noted that Denivelle points with pride to this Pennsylvania Station job, and it is important to note that he charcaterizes it as "practical," stating that:

> "The intrinsic merit of the invention has found expression in a large practical way in its extensive use by affiant in the monumental structure of the Pennsylvania Railroad Station in New York City. * * *" (Record, p. 28, Denivelle's affidavit on Motion for Preliminary Injunction.)

When did Denivelle first come to the conclusion that this Pennsylvania Station installation constituted a "practical" use of his alleged invention? Was it after he had gotten the contract in competition with others, based upon the submission of a specimen which he was required to duplicate as to composition and finish? Was it after he had covered a portion of the wall with pre-cast blocks of imitation travertine, which in construction and finish, complied with the specimen which he submitted with his bid, and which was approved by Mr. Webster representing the architects, and for which Denivelle demanded and received proper payment for work completed? Was it in 1910, when Denivelle had completed his contract and demanded and received payment therefor? Or did he have to wait until August,

1915, to come to the conclusion that its installation was a practical illustration of his invention?

The architects were satisfied long before this competitive bidding and the submission and installation of samples, that they could obtain and employ a satisfactory imitation of travertine, and Denivelle was one of four who offered to supply imitation travertine in accordance with the specimen and the architect's specifications. It wasn't Denivelle who had to be satisfied that he had made a satisfactory imitation of travertine. He had to satisfy the architects and builders. It is immaterial what Denivelle actually did in the production of this artificial travertine, so long as he followed the requirements of the contract, and his payment depended upon his satisfying the architects and builders that he was giving them what they had purchased from him.

It is again pointed out that so far as materials are concerned, Denivelle was required by the specifications to employ certain materials; he made no selection of these materials as being best adapted for his work and based upon his experiments. There was nothing of an experimental nature for Denivelle to do after he had accepted that contract, excepting perhaps to improve instrumentalities employed in the making of the precast blocks. It will be noted that it was long prior to the date of the contract that the architects began their investigation to determine whether or not these plasterers in New York, like Denivelle, could furnish them with a satisfactory imitation of travertine stone. (See Denivelle's alleged conversation with Mead quoted in this Court's previous decision.)

We have not before us as we write this brief, all of the documentary exhibits to which we shall refer in our arguments of this case, but we find quoted in plaintiff's brief, some rather significant extracts from these documentary exhibits.

It appears from Exhibit 5 (evidently found at page 2, of the Book of Documentary Exhibits), a letter dated July 20, 1908, signed by Denivelle as president of his then company, Hammerstein & Denivelle Company, addressed to the George A. Fuller Company (a portion of which is quoted at page 87 of plaintiff's brief). From that quotation it will be noted by this court that Denivelle offered to do certain "work to be made in *our* composite granite and Roman travertine in cast, individual slabs and blocks * * * by an *accurate* method and process that *guarantees* uniform results; producing not an imitation, but an *exceedingly durable* and *true substitute* for the real *travertine* and granite *without the slightest danger of flaking or disintegration.*" (Italics ours.)

Does this indicate any doubt of Denivelle as to the "archictectural endurance" of his imitation travertine?

In this case "common sense" should have as much bearing as the law. Now, what would the common sense of an individual gather from this letter of Denivelle, dated in July, 1908? Is it not fair to assume that by that date Denivelle had completed all his experiments, and had decided that he could furnish *"our* composite granite and Roman travertine" produced by "an *accurate* method and process," of such a character that he could not only say it was not an imitation, but "an *exceedingly durable* and true substitute for the real travertine," and that he *"guarantees* uniform results" of such a character that there will not be "the slightest danger of flaking or disintegration?" This was before the contract was awarded.

On page 88 of plaintiff's brief, we find another letter from the Hammerstein & Denivelle Company, signed by Denivelle, dated the 31st day of August, 1908, in which he offers "to furnish and erect complete" in the Pennsylvania Station "according to revised plans and specifications, the entire artificial travertine made on the same basis as our sample and later samples to be submitted." Does this indicate a doubt?

Now, what was "our sample" referred to in Denivelle's letter of August 31st, 1908? It was, as common sense seems to dictate, that true substitute for real travertine, which Denivelle, in his letter of July 20, 1908, refers to as "our composite granite and Roman travertine," and which he says was produced by "an accurate method and process," and was "exceedingly durable," and one which he could guarantee to be free from "the slightest danger of flaking or disintegration." Remember that Denivelle claims to have made a sample and submitted it to Mead long prior to getting his contract.

Does not common sense compel us to come to the conclusion that it was this perfected imitation of travertine which Denivelle with such assurance guaranteed to the builders of the Pennsylvania Station? And does it not show that prior to getting the contract, he had experimented sufficiently to know that this thing he represented as "our" travertine imitation or substitute, was a perfected thing?

His bid was accepted. He entered into the contract to furnish this *guaranteed true substitute for travertine.* He got paid for it. And now he asks this Court to believe and reiterate its former decision, based on an insufficient record, that he was still experimenting all during the Pennsylvania Station work, and all during the Goelet house work, and other jobs, and all during the work on the Exposition Buildings in San Francisco.

He offered to sell a specimen of his invention as early as 1908, as shown by these two letters from which we have quoted, and under the law an offer to sell is just as much of a bar as an actual sale, because the words of the statute require that a patentable invention shall not have been in public use or "on sale" in the United States for more than two years before the filing of the application. If, when Denivelle signed his contract, he did not then make a technical sale or public use, he certainly did at the time when, having installed a certain portion of the work required by his contract, he demanded and received pay therefor; and if he did not do it at that time, he certainly did it in 1910 when he completed his contract and demanded and received payment therefor, and executed a release.

As hereinbefore pointed out, in the *Ceriat* case, there was no testimony at all which characterized the Pennsylvania Station job as an experiment, excepting that of Denivelle, and of course, that can only be regarded as a self-serving declaration.

We have heretofore quoted a portion of the decision of the Supreme Court in the *Elizabeth Pavement* case, taken from that portion of the decision in that case which is quoted by this Honorable Court in its previous and published decision. That quotation is to the effect that "any attempt to use it (his invention) for profit, and not by way of experiment, for a longer period than two years before the application, would deprive the inventor of his right to a patent." (*Elizabeth v. Pavement Co.*, 97 U. S. 126, 24 L. Ed. 1,000.)

DENIVELLE USED HIS ALLEGED INVENTION FOR PROFIT FOR APPROXIMATELY FIVE YEARS BEFORE HE APPLIED FOR HIS PATENT.

Repairs and Alterations Do No Make Experiment

We have, in the main section of this brief, pointed out that it is immaterial that a thing that is sold or put into public use may require alteration or repair.

Even that fact does not change a completed thing into an experiment. It would be surprising if a plastering or cement contract of the character executed by Denivelle, in a new and massive building, would not develop imperfections in course of time. It is quite customary that such contracts require the repairing of such defects and imperfections as may develop during a certain period after completion. It is not surprising that they called upon Denivelle, even as late as 1912, to make some minor repairs; and the fact that Denivelle begged of these people to give him what might be called a "bonus" or adjusted compensation to the extent of $3,500 on his plea that he had lost money on the contract, and that in consideration for this gratuity Denivelle promised to give the matter his personal attention, so far as repairs of defects and imperfections were concerned, could not possibly turn this *"practical"* installation of Denivelle's alleged invention into an experiment, or show that he was still experimenting as late as 1912.

Even Denivelle's friend Webster testified:

"RDQ. 15. But when that building was finally finished and Mr. Denivelle was paid for it, was that regarded as an experiment by McKim, Mead & White?

A. I don't think so; they were quite satisfied and so stated to Mr. Denivelle.

"RDQ. 16. It was in every way according to specifications a complete and satisfactory job?

A. Complete up to that time, yes."

"RDQ. 18. He (an architect) wouldn't approve a bill unless he was satisfied that so far as that particular building was concerned, it was a complete and efficient job?

A. No." (Record, pp. 278-9.)

This is a very different case from the *Elizabeth Pavement* case. There the actions of the inventor were such as to clearly indicate an experiment, and the experiment was carried on at his own expense. He didn't sell something guaranteeing it, receiving payment for it, and then characterize it as an experiment, as Denivelle has done. We again assert, notwithstanding the criticisms of our adversaries, that the case of *Root* v. *Third Avenue Railroad* is "on all fours" with the present case, and is the last word of the Supreme Court on the law where the circumstances are as they appear in this case.

Application for Patent in Suit Not a Continuaton of the 1913 Application.

In order that this Court may not be confused by the misleading argument of the plaintiff in his effort to show that Denivelle's application which he filed in 1913, was in effect an application covering the present invention, we again point out that in that application Denivelle, so far as any process is concerned, held himself out to be the inventor of a process of forming colored lines in artificial stone, and an apparatus for doing that. Nothing was said in that application concerning a process for producing a honey-combed or vermiculated surface or "pockets" by the employment of loose, lumpy, cementitious material. The subject matter of that application was entirely rejected by the Patent Office, and it was finally rejected, and the further prosecution of it would have required an appeal to the Examiners-in-Chief, which appeal was never taken, and accordingly the application became abandoned. It was abandoned not because of the filing of the present application; and in order to hold that the present application is a continuation of that application and thereby give Denivelle the benefit of the earlier filing date, it must be found that Denivelle had two applications pending at the same time covering the same invention. This is a ridiculous proposition.

At the time of filing that earlier application Denivelle's sole contention was that he had devised a new process of forming colored lines in artificial stone, and an apparatus therefor. So far as artificial travertine is concerned, there was nothing claimed in that application by means of which "pockets" would be produced.

We again urge that Denivelle's inaction in and about this alleged invention, and his free employment of it in the Goelet house and other jobs, knowing as he did that others were not only prepared to produce cementitious imitation travertine, and in fact had offered, in competition with him, to do it,—in fact permitting the builders of the Goelet house to apply cementitious imitation travertine to the hall of that house, coincident with his cementitious imitation travertine work on that house himself,—as we submit, shows abandonment.

As to Claims 9 and 10.

We have heretofore in the preceding section of this brief, treated of the defense based upon lack of the patentee's oath. We do not believe it is necessary to further comment on that defense. We note that our adversaries have tried to confuse the question as to whether or not this applicant has received a patent for something which was not originally disclosed or claimed in his application, and not covered by the oath accompanying the application as originally filed, or by a supplemental oath, with the question as to whether or not a reissue patent covers an invention different from that of the original patent.

It is not material whether these claims 9 and 10 are in fact of such a character that they could rightly appear in this patent. It may have been entirely proper for this patentee to have introduced those claims into this patent. They are for a product, it is true, and a product has long been regarded as a different invention from a process. It has long been customary for the Patent Office to grant, and the courts to uphold, patents covering both a process and a product. But there was no product such as now covered by claims 9 and 10, described in this application or shown in the drawing at the time it was filed, and even if it had been, the rules of practice require that where something that might have been claimed in the application as filed, was not claimed therein, if it be subsequently claimed, as by amendment, the applicant must file a supplemental oath that he was the inventor of it; that he invented it before the application was filed; and that it has never been in public use or on sale, etc., covering the statutory requirements.

How can it be possible for the plaintiff's attorney to argue that the presumption is that such a supplemental oath was taken by the applicant, in view of what the Supreme Court has said in the *Stewart* v. *Lava Company* case, and the decisions of the subordinate courts holding that the lack of such an oath is fatal to claims introduced by amendment? Counsel knows that this presumption does not apply in such a case.

The Court will note that claims 9 and 10 do not include in words, the employment of loose, lumpy, cementitious material, so that an imitation of travertine stone such as Denivelle admits was made by the other contestants with him for the Pennsylvania Station job, would appear to have all the characteristics of the subject matter of these claims; for Denivelle says:

"Witness saw the samples that these other firms submitted, and each sample was a cementitious structure in imitation of veining, and each of them had pockets.'' (Plaintiff's Brief, p. 72.)

This has reference to the samples submitted by Mc-Nulty Brothers, Miller, and the other competitor with Denivelle.

Now, unless claims 9 and 10 are held to be for imitation travertine in which the pockets are formed by the employment of loose, lumpy, cementitious material, obviously the samples which these bidders practically sold in 1909 for $200.00 each, to Denivelle, would constitute a sale more than two years before application for patent and complete anticipation for these claims. This brings us to the question of infringement, and we shall in the following section of our brief discuss the absolutely unfair and deceptive manner in which counsel for plaintiff has treated this question in their brief.

Non Infringement.

Like Denivelle when he testified in court, counsel for the plaintiff does not fully describe the process as used by these defendants. They content themselves with a statement that the defendants form colored lines of cementitious material on a greased mold surface, and that they then deposit loose, lumpy material—calcium carbide—in the spaces between the colored lines, and that they then fill in the mold, or spread over the lines and the calcium carbide, a relatively fluid, cementitious material. They do not point out that the moisture in this filling material, when it comes in contact with the calcium carbide, sets up a chemical action, producing a gas, which is the well-known acetyline gas. This gas, acting upon the semi-plastic filling material in the surface adjacent to the mold surface, expands and causes the formation of the pockets, or the honey-combed effect. This is an entirely different operation from that described in the Denivelle patent wherein loose, lumpy, semi-dry, cementitious material prevents the ready flow of the fluid filling material, and for that reason and because the loose, lumpy, cementitious material becomes a permanent part of the structure, forms the pockets.

It would have been entirely fair, we submit, for the plaintiff's counsel to have admitted what we can demonstrate to the satisfaction of this court if permitted to do so, that the calcium carbide employed by the defendants operates in a chemical manner, and that no part of it becomes a part of the finished structure. It can be carelessly referred to, as both Denivelle and his counsel have referred to it, as "loose, lumpy material," but that does not make it the equivalent of the *loose, lumpy, cementitious, semi-dry material employed by Denivelle.*

We again submit, therefore, with the utmost confidence, our defense that even if this Denivelle patent could, by any possibility, be held to be a good and valid patent, these defendants have done what they had a right to do—devised a process which does not infringe the process claims of this patent, because it is an entirely different process from anything described in the patent—and unless claims 9 and 10 receive an interpretation which will put within their language all forms of an imitation of travertine stone, regardless of how such imitations are made, then those claims must be limited to the production of imitation travertine by the employment of loose, lumpy, semi-dry, cementitious material, and when so interpreted they are not infringed.

We shall not take the time to discuss the many cases cited by our adversaries in the plaintiff's brief, particularly those cases relating to public use and sale, for we believe that the law as decided by the Supreme

Court is well understood by all of us, and that it will be conceded to be as follows: That the offer for sale, or sale, or the operation for profit, or the offer to operate for profit, of a specimen of the invention in the United States more than two years before the filing of the application for patent, renders the patent absolutely invalid. As to whether or not a thing so offered for sale, or sold, or used, is a completed invention or merely an experiment, must be decided by the circumstances in each case.

It is true that a use for any length of time, whether in secret or in public, for experimental purposes, no matter how long continued, will not invalidate the patent. Our adversaries call attention to the fact that some of the uses proven by the defendants were not old enough, that is to say, they did not occur two years before the filing of the Denivelle application; and they take objection to the evidence relating to Denivelle's Ottawa Station job on the ground that that was a use in a foreign country, and is ineffective to support the defense of public use and sale. But this court, we feel sure, will observe that these instances where Denivelle sold and installed specimens of his imitation travertine manufactured by his process, have a double significance in this case: Where they occurred more than two years before the application was filed in this country they are of course relevant to prove public use or sale by Denivelle. They are also relevant as an indication that Denivelle, when he completed his Pennsylvania Station job, had perfected his invention, and was no longer experimenting. And they are also relevant to prove abandonment by Denivelle, and this is true whether Denivelle's sale and installation and practise of his process occurred in the United States or elsewhere.

We submit that an inventor must be diligent to protect his rights, and the fact that Denivelle, after completing the Pennsylvania Station job, installed these numerous specimens of imitation travertine in the Goelet house, in the Ottawa Station, and elsewhere, shows that he had no intention of taking out a patent, and that he abandoned whatever he may be found to have created, to the public.

Incidentally, we again call attention to the fact that if Denivelle's alleged conversation with Mr. Mead (which is quoted in the previous decision of this Honorable Court), actually took place, Denivelle had satisfied Mead long before he took the contract for the Pennsylvania Station, that he could produce a specimen of imitation travertine which could be used on that job. This conversation alone, if it actually took place, shows the utmost confidence of Denivelle, not only that he could produce a satisfactory imitation of travertine in a small piece, but that he could teach workmen how to do it when engaged in the construction of a large job.

Respectfully submitted,

T. HART ANDERSON,
Of Counsel for Defendants-Appellants.

Lightning Source UK Ltd.
Milton Keynes UK
UKHW010340120219
337137UK00004B/206/P